W9-AOZ-835

COLLECTED WORKS OF JOHN STUART MILL

VOLUME XIX

Essays on
Politics and Society

by JOHN STUART MILL

Editor of the Text

J. M. ROBSON

Professor of English
Victoria College, University of Toronto

Introduction by

ALEXANDER BRADY

Professor Emeritus of Political Economy
University of Toronto

UNIVERSITY OF TORONTO PRESS

ROUTLEDGE & KEGAN PAUL

LIBRARY
COLBY-SAWYER COLLEGE
NEW LONDON, NH 03257

B
1602
.A2
1963
c.1

#2887215

© *University of Toronto Press 1977*
Toronto and Buffalo
Printed in Canada

ISBN 0-8020-5345-9
LC 76-57079
London: Routledge & Kegan Paul
ISBN 0-7100-8643-1

This volume has been published
with the assistance of a
grant from the Canada Council

This book has been published during the
Sesquicentennial year of the University of Toronto

LIBRARY
COLBY-SAWYER COLLEGE
NEW LONDON, NH 03257

Contents

* *

CONTENTS

ESSAYS ON POLITICS AND SOCIETY

THOUGHTS ON PARLIAMENTARY REFORM

1859

EDITOR'S NOTE

Dissertations and Discussions, III (1867), 1–46, where the title is footnoted, "Pamphlet, February 1859." Reprinted from the 2nd ed., "with additions," of the pamphlet version with the same title (London: Parker and Son, 1859); the first ed. also was published in 1859 by Parker. Identified in JSM's bibliography as "A pamphlet entitled 'Thoughts on Parliamentary Reform' published in the spring of 1859" (MacMinn, 92). There are no corrections or emendations in the copy of the 1st ed. of the pamphlet version in the Somerville College Library.

For a discussion of the composition of this work, see the Textual Introduction, lxxxiii–lxxxv above.

The text below is that of *D&D,* III (1867), the only edition of that volume to appear in JSM's lifetime. It is collated with the two pamphlet versions of 1859.

In the footnoted variants, "67" indicates *D&D,* III; "59²" indicates the 2nd ed. of the pamphlet; "59¹" indicates the 1st ed. of the pamphlet. JSM quotes a passage from his "Recent Writers on Reform" (which appeared after the 1st ed. of *Thoughts on Parliamentary Reform*) in the 2nd ed. of the pamphlet, but not in the *D&D* version (presumably because "Recent Writers on Reform" appears immediately following this essay in *D&D*). The changes in that passage are therefore given as variants only to "Recent Writers on Reform" (see 339ᵏ and 358–70 below).

Mill also quotes from *Thoughts on Parliamentary Reform* in *Considerations on Representative Government*; see 491–5, 495n–496n, 496–7, and 498–9 below, where the variants are given.

Thoughts on Parliamentary Reform

*a*AT THE INTERVAL of about a generation from the passing of the first Reform Act, by a sort of universal consent the Legislature is about to employ itself in enacting a second.[*] This determination has been adopted in circumstances strikingly contrasted with those by which it is usual for constitutional changes to be ushered in, and, at least immediately, brought about. The change to which all are looking forward, has not been pressed upon the ruling powers by impetuous and formidable demonstrations of public sentiment, nor preceded by signs of wide-spread discontent with the working of the existing political institutions. It was thought a great thing that the Reform Bill of 1832 could be passed without an armed insurrection: to all appearance, that of 1859 will become law without having required, or occasioned, any unusual amount even of peaceful agitation. And this is the more noticeable, because there has been, at various times since 1832, much greater dissatisfaction than at present with public affairs; a much stronger sense of practical grievances, combined with a far greater amount of physical suffering which could, with more or less truth or plausibility, be traced to defects in institutions or in the social system. Yet at none of these times had any proposal of a further Parliamentary Reform the smallest chance of success; while now, every party in the State, and almost every individual politician of mark, is pledged to the support of some such measure. An alteration is to be made in the constitution of Parliament, rather because everybody sees such alteration to be right in itself, than because anybody either vehemently desires it, or is expecting from it any great or conspicuous practical result.

[*See "A Bill to Amend the Laws relating to the Representation of the People in England and Wales, and to facilitate the Registration and Voting of Electors," 22 Victoria (28 February, 1859), *Parliamentary Papers*, 1859 (Session 1), II, 649–715.]

*a*591, 592 Nearly the whole of this pamphlet, including the argument on the Ballot, was written five years ago, in anticipation of the Reform Bill of Lord Aberdeen's Government. [*See* 318n *below.*] The causes which at that period kept back the question itself prevented the publication of these remarks upon it. Subsequent reflection has only strengthened the opinions then expressed. They are now published, because it is at the present time, if ever, that their publication can have any chance of being useful. [*This comment appears on a page preceding the text.*]

This state of things, so apparently anomalous, is one of the most satis-factory signs of the times, and a significant exemplification of the new character which has been permanently impressed upon the politics of this empire by the great popular triumph twenty-six years ago. The Reform Act, and the mustering and trial of strength between the Progressive and the Stationary forces which filled the fifteen years from 1832 to 1846, have inaugurated Improvement as the general law of public affairs: Improvement in itself, Improvement for its own sake, not such particular improvements only as any section of the public deems called for by its own immediate interest. And the result has confirmed the assertion always made by enlightened Radicals—that a government really inspired by a spirit of Improvement, a government under which there is a fair assurance that what-ever in the laws or in their administration comes to be widely recognised as an evil, will be *b*(by however gradual and cautious a process)*b* corrected, satisfies the political cravings of the British people; and that they are not inclined to push for constitutional changes, further than as these may flow, by natural sequence, from the workings of a progressive government. Such reasonable assurance the British people now have: and the effect is, that while the love of improvement for itself, apart from its connexion with special or personal interests, has a much more positive existence in their minds than it ever had before, they have so full a reliance that anything which they recognise as an improvement will in time be obtained, that they seldom feel stirred up to demand it with loudness and importunity. This is the only explanation why Parliamentary Reform, though there seldom has been a time when there was less of clamorous demonstration in its behalf, is felt by the leaders of all parties, and all sections of opinion, to be a political necessity.

A constitutional reform brought forward in such circumstances; wel-comed by a sort of unanimous concurrence of all parties, but not called for ardently, nor likely to be supported vehemently or enthusiastically, by any; cannot be expected to make more than a very moderate change in the exist-ing distribution of political power. No considerable section of existing political men desire more; and the active force out of doors is wanting to enable them to carry it if they did. Whatever is proposed, either by the present Administration, or by any who are likely to succeed them, will be a half-measure; will be of the nature of a compromise; and will appear to many, probably to the whole body of Democratic Reformers, to be far short of their just claims. A reconstitution of the representative system on fixed and definite principles, is not at present to be looked for. It is not what is promised; and the state of opinion, and of European politics, is not favourable to its being carried. It is, however, indispensable that the Re-

*b-b*591, 592   , by . . . process,

form should not be merely nominal; that it should be a real change, a substantial improvement, which may be accepted as a step by those whom it will by no means permanently satisfy, and may hold out sufficient promise of good to be really valued. The point for consideration, therefore, is, what are the qualities most valuable in a half-measure: for with less than these, no Reformer ought to be even temporarily satisfied. Now, in a good half-measure of Reform, there are at least two essential requisites. In the first place, it should be aimed at the really worst features of the existing system. Since it does not profess to do everything, it should do what is most required: it should apply a corrective where one is the most urgently needed. Secondly, it should be conceived with an eye to the further changes which may be expected hereafter. This does not mean that it should necessarily be framed with a view to accelerate further changes, but rather to guide and regulate them when they arrive. A legislator is bound not to think solely of the present effects of his measures; he must consider what influence the acts he does now, may have over those of his successors. Whatever change he introduces, should be a step in the direction in which a further advance is, or will hereafter be, desirable. His half-measure should be so constructed as to recognise and embody the principles which, if no hindrance existed, would form the best foundation of a complete measure.

The first condition, that of breaking in upon the existing system at its worst point, will be in a considerable degree fulfilled by any measure which clears away the small constituencies.

The most peccant element in the present state of the representation is not the small number of the electors, taken in the aggregate. They are too few, doubtless, and they will always be too few while any are excluded whose admission would not deteriorate the quality of the mass. At present, too, admission and exclusion are capricious; the same description of persons are admitted in cities and parliamentary boroughs, who are excluded in all other towns and in the rural districts. Whatever qualification, or variety of qualifications, may be fixed upon, it is reasonable that they should be the same in one place as in another. But these are not the crying evils. They might be removed without making any very material difference, either in the composition of the House of Commons, or in the inducements acting on its members. The most serious mischief is, not that only a fraction of the community have the right to vote, but that the majority of the House is returned by a very small fraction of that fraction. The small boroughs, those which number from 200 to 400 electors, are the seat of all the evils which the Reform Act of 1832 intended, and was believed, to annihilate. Many of them are still pocket boroughs; the members they return are almost as much the nominees of some great family in the neighbourhood, as were the members for Gatton and Old Sarum. The others are mostly the prize of the highest bidder. If recent legislation[*] has rendered direct bribery a more hazardous experiment than the candidates like to venture on, success belongs to him who expends most money in opening the public-houses, or in hiring agents, canvassers, printers, and committee-rooms. Local interests being divided, the worst portion of the electors, those who are corrupted by money or by drunkenness, turn the scale. Between the nomination boroughs and the corrupt boroughs, a large portion of the House are still what they were before 1832, either the delegates of individuals, or the representatives of their own purses. Wherever these petty constituencies are not under the thraldom of some one individual, every fresh contested election becomes more and more an affair of mere money. This is a growing mischief, even in the large constituencies; from the very small ones it is almost inseparable: nor is anything else to be expected from them, than that they should become demoralized more and more. The theory professed by anti-reformers is, that political rights should be reserved for property and intelligence. By upholding the small boroughs, they dedicate a large and almost predominant portion of the representation to the needy, the dependent, and the uneducated.

To correct this evil, without throwing down the barrier between the borough and the county constituencies, a change which, even if desirable, is not at present attainable, there is an obvious expedient; to unite the small towns into districts of boroughs, as is already the case in Wales and in Scotland. The "Parliamentary Representation Bill" introduced by Lord John Russell in 1852,[†] adopted this expedient; but unfortunately in so perverted a shape, as to satisfy nobody, and to create greater anomalies than it cured.

One of the declared principles of Lord John Russell's Bill was, that there should be no disfranchisement; and in this perhaps he may have been in the right; since few, if any, of the small boroughs are so absolutely insignificant as to require their entire exclusion from the representation. But Lord John Russell thought it necessary that every existing small borough should become the nucleus of a separate aggregation of townships. He eked out the constituencies by annexing insignificant places close by, instead of going a little farther off for considerable unrepresented towns; while in no case did he think it admissible to include two places which already returned members to Parliament, in one and the same district. Thus, to take the very first entry in the schedule, Berkshire possesses two small boroughs, only a few miles apart: Abingdon, with 312 electors; Wallingford, with 428. In-

[*See 17 & 18 Victoria, c. 102 (1854).]

[†"A Bill to Extend the Right of voting for Members of Parliament, and to amend the Laws relating to the Representation of the People in Parliament," 15 Victoria (12 February, 1852), *Parliamentary Papers*, 1852, III, 353–96.]

stead of throwing these places and half a dozen others into one district, Lord John Russell looked out for two still smaller places at double the distance, and added Farringdon to one borough and Wantage to the other; making, instead of one good constituency, two bad ones—as bad as, or very little better than, the present. The next county, Buckinghamshire, contains two boroughs still nearer together, each returning two members, though the one (Marlow) has only 354, the other (Wycombe) but 346 electors. In forming a district it would be natural to throw these two into one; and one member is as much as even then their joint importance would entitle them to. Lord John Russell left to each of the boroughs its two members, reinforcing them by four small places, every one more distant from the present boroughs than these are from one another.

While the representation of the small boroughs was thus patched up, a host of towns, dispersed all over the country, far exceeding them in population and importance, were left, as at present, unrepresented. The new places taken in to form a district, never exceeded the smallest scantling which, it was supposed, would afford the minimum of a presentable constituency. Thus Reigate, at that time a nomination borough, requiring to be extended, the town of Dorking was added to it, and nothing more; while Croydon, Kingston, and Epsom, towns in the immediate neighbourhood, all of them with equal or greater claims to be represented, were put aside.

Had this schedule been adopted, it would have spotted the map of England with groups of small places so capriciously distributed as to bring the very idea of districts of boroughs into contempt, and without mitigating, but rather in some respects increasing, the present causes of complaint. The small constituencies would still have remained small, while, instead of being what they professed to be, they would have been more than ever rural constituencies, in subjection, under any ordinary circumstances, to the neighbouring landed proprietors. The villages of 1000 and towns of 2000 and 3000 inhabitants, which were taken to make up a number, would have been a clear addition to the agricultural influence in the House. It is just possible, though scarcely probable, that bribery might have been diminished; but the local influences would have gained whatever the direct money-power lost, and the members for the districts would have been merely an inferior sort of county members.

Yet, if the principle of combining several boroughs was once admitted, what course could be more obvious than to take all the present boroughs, and all unrepresented towns of more than a certain amount of population (say, for example, 5000), and leaving out all those, whether existing as boroughs or still to be created, whose importance entitles them to one member, or more than one, of their own, to arrange the others in groups according to geographical convenience, care being taken to give to each group something like the same number of electors. No reason is apparent why this plan was not adopted, except the misplaced scruple against merging two existing boroughs into one. If what is now a borough, is to become one of a group, what difference can it make to the electors whether they are bound up with existing, or only with newly enfranchised co-electors? What could be more absurd than that Calne and Chippenham, both nomination boroughs, and actually conterminous, should (as in Lord John Russell's scheme) subsist as a sort of double star, with each its separate system of planets; or that Amesbury and Downton should be recalled from Schedule A to furnish a supplementary constituency to the little borough of Wilton, instead of adding it to the adjacent city of Salisbury? The proper aggregate number of members for small towns being first, after due consideration, determined, all places of such size as to be politically entitled to the designation of towns should be admitted to share in it. The greater the number of places included in each district, the better prospect of a creditable choice. The local influences of families and corporations would then have more chance of neutralizing one another; and with the aid of stringent measures against all forms of corruption, there would be some prospect that the choice of representatives might occasionally be made on public rather than on private grounds.

Subsequently to Lord John Russell's abortive attempt, another Reform Bill, to which he was also a party, was brought into Parliament, by Lord Aberdeen's Government.[*] In this second Bill, the principle of grouping boroughs, which had been introduced in so awkward a manner in the former Bill, was dropped altogether; and the older plan, a complete disfranchisement of some boroughs, and a reduction of others from two members to one, was reverted to; the representation, withdrawn from them, being transferred to single towns not at present represented, or added to the representation of those constituencies which were thought entitled to a greater number of members than they possess. Most of the private projects of Reform hitherto promulgated, proceed on the same idea, involving a large amount of disfranchisement. All such schemes are good and commendable, in so far as they get rid of the small and dependent constituencies; but they do so, as it seems to me, in a manner far more objectionable than that of merging those small constituencies in districts of boroughs. For, in the first place, many electors would be entirely disfranchised who are as well entitled as other people to vote for representatives, though not to have representatives to themselves; and, in the next place, this method falls greatly short of the other in extent of enfranchisement. For the improved

[*"A Bill further to amend the Laws relating to the Representation of the People in England and Wales," 17 Victoria (16 February, 1854), in *Parliamentary Papers*, 1854, V, 375–418.]

repartition of the suffrage by grouping of boroughs provides also for a considerable extension. Even the ten-pound householders of all the unenfranchised towns with more than 5000 inhabitants, would be a large addition to the numerical amount of the constituency, obtained without lowering the qualification, or introducing any change which could alarm timidity in the conditions for the exercise of the suffrage.

If, indeed, every elector in the disfranchised boroughs, and every ten-pound householder in the unrepresented towns, obtains a vote for the county, by the adoption, in the new Reform Bill, of Mr. Locke King's proposal (already once affirmed by the House of Commons),[*] the two objections just mentioned will cease to exist. But in that case those objections will give place to a still more fatal one; for such a measure would be little less than the complete political extinction of the rural districts. Except in the few places where there is still a yeomanry, as in Cumberland, Westmoreland, and in some degree North Yorkshire and Kent, there exists in the agricultural population no class but the farmers, intermediate between the landlords and the labourers. A ten-pound franchise will admit no agricultural labourer; and the farmers and landlords would collectively be far outnumbered by the ten-pound householders of all the small towns in England. To enable the agricultural population to hold its fair share of the representation under any uniform and extensive suffrage short of universal, it seems absolutely necessary that the town electors should, as a rule, be kept out of the county constituencies. And the sole alternative is to form them, or the great bulk of them, into constituencies by themselves.

It has been stated as an objection to the formation of districts of boroughs, that elections would be rendered more expensive. The candidates, it has been said, would require as many committees as there are boroughs, and other things in proportion. The objection cannot weigh much with reference to the particular question, since every other mode of forming district constituencies would be liable to it in an equal, if not a greater degree. No elections are free from it, except those for single, and even for small towns: for if the town is of any size, the candidates have almost always a plurality of committees for the different quarters or divisions. But the remark points to one of the most conspicuous vices of the existing electoral system; the only one which can dispute pre-eminence with the multitude of small constituencies; and one against which the new Reform Bill, if it is to deserve support, should contain some decided and effectual provision. In a good representative system there would be no election expenses, to be borne by the candidate. Their effect is wholly pernicious. Politically, they constitute

[*See "A Bill to Extend the franchise in Counties in England and Wales, and to improve the Representation of the People in Respect of such franchise," 21 Victoria (27 April, 1858), *Parliamentary Papers*, 1857–58, I, 561–4.]

a property qualification of the worst kind. The old property qualification, given up by everybody, and at length abolished, only required that a member of Parliament should possess a fortune; this requires that he should have spent one. Morally, it is still worse; not only by the profligate and demoralizing character of much of the expenditure, but by the corrupting effect of the notion inculcated on the voter, that the person he votes for should pay a large sum of money for permission to serve the public. Does any one expect his attorney to pay for liberty to conduct his lawsuit? or his physician to pay for leave to cure him of a disease? On the contrary, he pays them at a high price for undertaking his business. If the office of a member of Parliament were felt to be a public trust, which no one has a moral right to take upon himself for any purpose but that of fulfilling its duties, would it be endured for an instant that, in addition to performing those duties without salary, he should make a large payment besides for the privilege of performing them? Such a practice is the surest proof that to vote for a candidate is regarded either as help given him towards attaining private ends, or at least as a compliment to his vanity, for which he should be willing to pay an equivalent. They must be poor politicians who do not know the vast efficacy of such indirect moral influences; though there is hardly anything which, in this country, is so little considered by statesmen and public functionaries. The incidental circumstances which surround a public act, and betoken the expectation entertained by society in regard to it, irrevocably determine the moral sentiment which adheres to the act in the mind of an average individual. So long as the candidate himself, and the customs of the world, seem to regard the function of a member of Parliament less as a duty to be discharged, than as a personal favour to be solicited, no effort will avail to implant in an ordinary voter the feeling that the election of a member of Parliament is also a matter of duty, and that he is not at liberty to bestow his vote on any other consideration than that of personal fitness. The necessary expenses of an election, those which concern all the candidates equally, should, it has often been urged, be defrayed either by the municipal body or by the State. With regard to the sources of expense which are personal to the individual candidate, committees, canvassing, even printing and public meetings, it is in every way better that these things should not be done at all, unless done by the gratuitous zeal, or paid for by the contributions, of his supporters. Even now there are several members of Parliament whose elections cost them nothing, the whole expense being defrayed by their constituents. Of these members we may be completely assured that they are elected from public motives; that they are the men whom the voters really wish to see elected, in preference to all others, either on account of the principles they represent, or the services they are thought qualified to render. Every other member, even on the supposition of an honest choice, may, for aught it is possible to know, be elected, not as the best man, but as the best rich man, who can be had.

If it be asked, in what manner the object here pointed out is to be realized, I believe that there is one, and but one, means which would probably be effectual. No mere prohibitory law would accomplish the purpose, but it would probably be effected if every member of Parliament, previously to taking his seat, were required to make a declaration on honour that he had not paid, and a solemn engagement not to pay, money or money's worth, directly or indirectly, on account of his election. A declaration on honour is still not thought lightly of, by any who, unless by a rare exception, are likely to be returned to Parliament. I am quite alive to the fact that the veracity even of an affirmation thus sanctioned could not be depended on if opinion ceased to enforce it; and that the declaration might, like political oaths, come to be considered a mere form. The great reluctance, however, invariably manifested to require such a disclaimer, even in the case of bribery, shows that it is considered likely to have some efficacy. And I believe that the laxity which prevails on the subject of many of the public declarations required by law, arises from their being exacted for purposes which the public do not, and in most cases ought not, to approve. Opinion tolerates a false disclaimer, only when it already tolerates the thing disclaimed. And I am not aware that the toleration extends to any case in which the obligation is further enforced, as it ought to be in this case, by the penalties of perjury. Let law and opinion conspire to the end that election expenses be suppressed, and a denial on honour will be considered binding.

It has already been remarked, that a Bill such as we may expect, a measure of compromise, which does not profess to make any alteration in fundamentals, but only to introduce such amendments as are consistent with the general outline of the existing arrangements; a Bill, therefore, which cannot satisfy the wishes of those who think the present system radically defective—ought to fulfil two conditions: it should remove or alleviate the most peccant parts of the existing system; and, as far as it goes, it should be a recognition and embodiment of the principles which are fittest to preside over an entire renovation; so that it may not be an impediment to further improvement, but, on the contrary, a step towards the quarter in which, if anywhere, further improvement is to be looked for. The former of these topics having been considered, the latter, and more difficult, remains. In order to judge how this partial reform may be made conformable to the principles of a thorough reform, it is necessary to consider what these principles are: a subject which for a century past has been often enough discussed, but on which, as on all great subjects, there still remain many things to be said. We should endeavour to set before ourselves the ideal conception of a perfect representative government, however distant, not to say doubtful, may be the hope of actually obtaining it: to the intent that whatever is now done may if possible be in the direction of what is best, and may bring the actual fact nearer, and not further off from the standard of right, at however great a distance it may still remain from that standard. Though we may be only sailing from the port of London to that of Hull, let us still guide our navigation by the North Star.

First, then, in every system of representation which can be conceived as perfect, every adult human being,* it appears to me, would have the means of exercising, through the electoral suffrage, a portion of influence on the management of public affairs. It may be said, that the largest, or a very large portion of the people, in this and other countries, are not fit for political influence; that they would make a bad use of it; that it is impossible to foresee a time when they could safely be trusted with it. I am not prepared to contest all this; but I cannot look upon the necessity of withholding this function from any portion of the community otherwise than as a very great evil; against which it is the bounden duty of governments, of teachers, and of individuals, each in his sphere, to struggle, and never to be contented unless they are making sensible progress towards getting rid of it. It is important that every one of the governed should have a voice in the government, because it can hardly be expected that those who have no voice will not be unjustly postponed to those who have. It is still more important as one of the means of national education. A person who is excluded from all participation in political business is not a citizen. He has not the feelings of a citizen. To take an active interest in politics is, in modern times, the first thing which elevates the mind to large interests and contemplations; the first step out of the narrow bounds of individual and family selfishness, the first opening in the contracted round of daily occupations. The person who in any free country takes no interest in politics, unless from having been taught that he ought not to do so, must be too ill-informed, too stupid, or too selfish, to be interested in them; and we may rely on it that he cares as little for anything else, which does not directly concern himself or his personal connexions. Whoever is capable of feeling any common interest with his kind, or with his country, or with his city, is interested in politics; and to be interested in them, and not wish for a voice in them, is an impossibility. The possession and the exercise of political, and among others of electoral,

*I pass over the question whether insane persons, or persons convicted of crime, should be exceptions to this general provision. As far as the direct influence of their votes went, it would scarcely be worth while to exclude them. But, as an aid to the great object of giving a moral character to the exercise of the suffrage, it might be expedient that in case of crimes evincing a high degree of insensibility to social obligation, the deprivation of this and other civic rights should form part of the sentence.

rights, is one of the chief instruments both of moral and of intellectual training for the popular mind; and all governments must be regarded as extremely imperfect, until every one who is required to obey the laws, has a voice, or the prospect of a voice, in their enactment and administration.

But ought every one to have an *equal* voice? This is a totally different proposition; and in my judgment as palpably false, as the other is true and important. Here it is that I part company, on the question of principle, with the democratic reformers. Agreeing with them in looking forward to universal suffrage as an ultimate aim, I altogether dissent from their advocacy of electoral districts, understood as a means of giving equal weight to the vote of every individual. They say, that every one has an equal interest in being well governed, and that every one, therefore, has an equal claim to control over his own government. I might agree to this, if control over his own government were really the thing in question; but what I am asked to assent to is, that every individual has an equal claim to control over the government of other people. The power which the suffrage gives is not over himself alone; it is power over others also: whatever control the voter is enabled to exercise over his own concerns, he exercises the same degree of it over those of every one else. Now, it can in no sort be admitted that all persons have an equal claim to power over others. The claims of different people to such power differ as much, as their qualifications for exercising it beneficially.

If it is asserted that all persons ought to be equal in every description of right recognised by society, I answer, not until all are equal in worth as human beings. It is the fact, that one person is *not* as good as another; and it is reversing all the rules of rational conduct, to attempt to raise a political fabric on a supposition which is at variance with fact. Putting aside for the present the consideration of moral worth, of which, though more important even than intellectual, it is not so easy to find an available test; a person who cannot read, is not as good, for the ᶜpurposeᶜ of human life, as one who can. A person who can read, but cannot write or calculate, is not as good as a person who can do both. A person who can read, write and calculate, but who knows nothing of the properties of natural objects, or of other places and countries, or of the human beings who have lived before him, or of the ideas, opinions, and practices of his fellow-creatures generally, is not so good as a person who knows these things. A person who has not, either by reading or conversation, made himself acquainted with the wisest thoughts of the wisest men, and with the great examples of a beneficent and virtuous life, is not so good as one who is familiar with these. A person who has even filled himself with this various knowledge, but has not digested it—who could give no clear and coherent account of it, and has never

ᶜ⁻ᶜ591, 592 purposes

exercised his own mind, or derived an original thought from his own observation, experience, or reasoning, is not so good, for any human purpose, as one who has. There is no one who, in any matter which concerns himself, would not rather have his affairs managed by a person of greater knowledge and intelligence, than by one of less. There is no one who, if he was obliged to confide his interest jointly to both, would not desire to give a more potential voice to the more educated and more cultivated of the two.

This is no justification for making the less educated the slave, or serf, or mere dependent of the other. The subjection of any one individual or class to another, is always and necessarily disastrous in its effects on both. That power should be exercised over any portion of mankind without any obligation of consulting them, is only tolerable while they are in an infantine, or a semi-barbarous state. In any civilized condition, power ought never to be exempt from the necessity of appealing to the reason, and recommending itself by motives which justify it to the conscience and feelings, of the governed. In the present state of society, and under representative institutions, there is no mode of imposing this necessity on the ruling classes, as towards all other persons in the community, except by giving to every one a vote. But there is a wide interval between refusing votes to the great majority, and acknowledging in each individual among them a right to have his vote counted for exactly as much as the vote of the most highly educated person in the community; with the further addition that, under the name of equality, it would in reality count for vastly more, as long as the uneducated so greatly outnumber the educated. There is no such thing in morals as a *right* to power over others; and the electoral suffrage is that power. When all have votes, it will be both just in principle and necessary in fact, that some mode be adopted of giving greater weight to the suffrage of the more educated voter; some means by which the more intrinsically valuable member of society, the one who is more capable, more competent for the general affairs of life, and possesses more of the knowledge applicable to the management of the affairs of the community, should, as far as practicable, be singled out, and allowed a superiority of influence proportioned to his higher qualifications.

The most direct mode of effecting this, would be to establish plurality of votes, in favour of those who could afford a reasonable presumption of superior knowledge and cultivation. If every ordinary unskilled labourer had one vote, a skilled labourer, whose occupation requires an exercised mind and a knowledge of some of the laws of external nature, ought to have two. A foreman, or superintendent of labour, whose occupation requires something more of general culture, and some moral as well as intellectual qualities, should perhaps have three. A farmer, manufacturer, or trader, who requires a still larger range of ideas and knowledge, and the power of guiding and attending to a great number of various operations at once, should have three or four. A member of any profession requiring a long, accurate, and systematic mental cultivation,—a lawyer, a physician or surgeon, a clergyman of any denomination, a literary man, an artist, a public functionary (or, at all events, a member of every intellectual profession at the threshold of which there is a satisfactory examination test) ought to have five or six. A graduate of any university, or a person freely elected a member of any learned society, is entitled to at least as many. A certificate of having passed through a complete course of instruction at any place of education publicly recognised as one where the higher branches of knowledge are taught, should confer a plurality of votes; and there ought to be an organization of voluntary examinations throughout the country (agreeably to the precedent set by the middle-class examinations so wisely and virtuously instituted by the University of Oxford) at which any person whatever might present himself, and obtain, from impartial examiners, a certificate of his possessing the acquirements which would entitle him to any number of votes, up to the largest allowed to one individual. The presumption of superior instruction derived from mere pecuniary qualification is, in the system of arrangements we are now considering, inadmissible. It is a presumption which often fails, and to those against whom it operates, it is always invidious. What it is important to ascertain is education; and education can be tested directly, or by much stronger presumptive evidence than is afforded by income, or payment of taxes, or the quality of the house which a person inhabits.

The perfection, then, of an electoral system would be, that every person should have one vote, but that every well-educated person in the community should have more than one, on a scale corresponding as far as practicable to their amount of education. And neither of these constituents of a perfect representative system is admissible without the other. While the suffrage is confined altogether to a limited class, that class has no occasion for plural voting; which would probably, in those circumstances, only create an oligarchy within an oligarchy. On the other hand, if the most numerous class, which (saving honourable exceptions on one side, or disgraceful ones on the other) is the lowest in the educational scale, refuses to recognise a right in the better educated, in virtue of their superior qualifications, to such plurality of votes as may prevent them from being always and hopelessly outvoted by the comparatively incapable, the numerical majority must submit to have the suffrage limited to such portion of their numbers, or to have such a distribution made of the constituencies, as may effect the necessary balance between numbers and education in another manner.*

*One mode of effecting this has been urged, with considerable emphasis, in a

Since the time is not come for obtaining, or even asking for, a representative system founded on the preceding principles, the point for practical consideration is, what measure it is possible to adopt now, which may in any degree conform to and recognise these principles, and facilitate instead of impeding a further application of them when circumstances may require or admit of it.

One means for this purpose very obviously presents itself. It is universally agreed that the expected measure, whatever else it may contain, shall include a considerable extension of the suffrage: the desirable object will be realized if this extension be made subordinate to an Educational Qualification. Even in the most democratic system of representative government, some sort of educational qualification is required by principle. We must never lose sight of the truth, that the suffrage for a member of Parliament is power over others, and that to power over others no *right* can possibly exist. Whoever wishes to exercise it, is bound to acquire the necessary quali-

---

memorial addressed to Lord Palmerston, and bearing the signatures of many persons distinguished in literature and science. [See "The Educational Franchise," *The Times,* 19 Dec., 1857, p. 8.] It consists in giving to certain classes and professions, considered as of an intellectual character, a representation apart; the persons composing them throughout the country being registered as a separate constituency, and having a large number of representatives separately allotted to them, to be elected by them in local divisions. The object aimed at by this scheme is the same which I have in view; but, with sincere deference to some of those whose names are appended to it, I cannot think that they have chosen an eligible mode of encountering the difficulty. Nothing could be invented more calculated to make the privilege assigned to education, and the educated class itself, unpopular, and to create a permanent opposition and rivalry between the representatives of the educated and those of the presumed uneducated. Neither should I expect that the specially and professionally educated classes would be by any means so certain to return good representatives of their own, as they would be to form a valuable element in a miscellaneous constituency. It is a melancholy truth, but it is one which the experience of all academies and learned or scientific bodies establishes, that the suffrages of a select class of intellectual men are rarely given to the most really intellectual of their own number. Not the men of genius who are in advance of the body, and who compel it to advance, but the well-tutored and inoffensive mediocrities who best represent its average composition, are those whom it delights to honour. The man of real eminence, on the contrary, is the candidate whom it could with most effect present to a mixed constituency. In this as in every other case, it is not separating classes of persons and organizing them apart, but fusing them with other classes very different from themselves, which eliminates class interests and class feelings. One who desires to be a legislator should rest on recommendations not addressing themselves to a class, but to feelings and interests common to all classes: the simple as well as the learned should feel him to be their representative; otherwise his words and thoughts will do worse than even fall dead on their minds; will be apt to rouse in them a sentiment of opposition.

fications, as far as their acquisition is practicable to him. I have expressed my conviction that in the best possible system of representation, every person without exception would have a vote; but this does not imply that any one should have it unconditionally; only that the conditions should be such as all could fulfil. The greatest amount of education which can be fairly regarded as within the reach of every one, should be exacted as a peremptory condition from all claimants of the franchise.

Society is at present as backward in providing education, as in recognising its claims; and the general standard of instruction in England is so low, that if anything more than the merest elements were required, the number of voters would be even smaller than at present. But reading, writing, and the simple rules of arithmetic, can now be acquired, it may be fairly said, by any person who desires them; and there is surely no reason why every one who applies to be registered as an elector, should not be required to copy a sentence of English in the presence of the registering officer, and to perform a common sum in the rule of three. The principle of an educational qualification being thus established, more might hereafter be required when more had been given; but household, or even universal suffrage, with this small amount of educational requirement, would probably be safer than a much more restricted suffrage without it. Reading, writing, and arithmetic are but a low standard of educational qualification; yet even this would probably have sufficed to save France from her present degradation. The millions of voters who, in opposition to nearly every educated person in the country, made Louis Napoleon President, were chiefly peasants who could neither read nor write, and whose knowledge of public men, even by name, was limited to oral tradition.

If there ever was a political principle at once liberal and conservative, it is that of an educational qualification. None are so illiberal, none so bigoted in their hostility to improvement, none so superstitiously attached to the stupidest and worst of old forms and usages, as the uneducated. None are so unscrupulous, none so eager to clutch at whatever they have not and others have, as the uneducated in possession of power. An uneducated mind is almost incapable of clearly conceiving the rights of others. There is a great abatement in the dread which people of property once entertained of universal suffrage. Recent example has shown that, if it subverts a constitution, it is as likely to do so in favour of despotism as of democracy. But, whatever be the most probable complexion of the evil to be feared, no lover of improvement can desire that the *predominant* power should be turned over to persons in the mental and moral condition of the English working classes; and no Conservative needs object to making the franchise accessible to those classes at the price of a moderate degree of useful and honourable exertion. To make a participation in political rights the reward of mental improvement, would have many inestimable effects besides the obvious one. It would do more than merely admit the best and exclude the worst of the working classes; it would do more than make an honourable distinction in favour of the educated, and create an additional motive for seeking education. It would cause the electoral suffrage to be in time regarded in a totally different light. It would make it be thought of, not as now, in the light of a possession to be used by the voter for his own interest or pleasure, but as a trust for the public good. It would stamp the exercise of the suffrage as a matter of judgment, not of inclination; as a public function, the right to which is conferred by fitness for the intelligent performance of it.

Nobody will pretend that these effects would be completely produced by so low an educational qualification as reading, writing, and arithmetic; but it would be a considerable step towards them. The very novelty of the requirement—the excitement and discussion which it would produce in the class chiefly affected by it—would be the best sort of education; would make an opening in their minds that would let in light—would set them thinking in a perfectly new manner respecting political rights and responsibilities. That all should be admitted to the franchise who can fulfil these simple requirements, is not to be expected, nor even desired, unless means were also taken to give to the higher grades of instruction additional or more influential votes. Without such a provision, the educational test adapted for permanency would require to be much more stringent. What should now be pressed on the consideration of practical statesmen is, that any lowering of the pecuniary qualification for the purpose of giving the franchise to a greater number of the working classes, should be combined with the further condition of an educational test. It would not be indispensable to disfranchise, on this ground, any electors already registered; but upon all new applicants the test should be imperative. It would be a most substantial improvement in the existing representative system, if all householders, or even all five-pound householders, without distinction of sex— for why should the vote-collector make a distinction where the tax-gatherer makes none?—were admitted as electors, on condition of proving to the registering officer that they could read, write, and calculate.

This, then, is one important principle which the expected Reform Bill, without going to any length in innovation which need alarm anybody, may inaugurate. Another principle, only second to this in value, which might also on the present occasion be admitted into the Constitution, is the representation of minorities.

I am inclined to think that the prejudice which undoubtedly exists in the minds of democrats against this principle, arises only from their not having sufficiently considered its mode of operation. It is an eminently democratic principle. The elementary propositions of the democratic creed imply it as an inevitable corollary. Even the government of mere numbers requires that every number should tell in proportion to its amount. What is anti-democratic is, that the minority should be allowed to outweigh the majority; but the principle of universal suffrage requires that, as far as is consistent with practicability, every minority in the constituency should be represented by a minority in the representative body; and a mode of voting which does not keep this object in view, is contrary to popular government; it does not sum up the opinion of the community correctly. There is no true popular representation if three-fifths of the people return the whole House of Commons, and the remaining two-fifths have no representatives. Not only is this not government by the people, it is not even government by a majority of the people: since the government will be practically in the hands of a majority of the majority. A Parliament may be obtained by universal suffrage, which may represent the opinions of a bare majority of the people; and again, when this Parliament proceeds to legislate, it may pass laws by a bare majority of itself. The governing body, reduced by this double process of elimination, may represent the opinions or wishes of little more than a fourth of the population. If numbers are to be the rule, a third of the people ought not indeed to have two-thirds of the representation, but every third of the people is entitled to a third of the representation; and though there is no possibility of securing this with any degree of precision, it is better to make some approach to it than to ignore minorities altogether.

If the House of Commons were elected by the entire population in a single list, every one would see that the mode of voting would entirely disfranchise the minority. The party which was numerically strongest would rule without opposition, until by its abuse of power it had provoked a change of public sentiment; and then the whole party would be turned out at once, and the same unrestrained rule would pass into the hands of its opponents. People do not fear any similar inconvenience in the present case, because they reckon that the party which is in the minority in some places will have the majority in others, and that the local minorities will be virtually represented by the nominees of majorities of their own way of thinking elsewhere. And doubtless this is to a considerable extent the fact; and it generally will be so in the case of those great sections of opinion which pervade all classes, and divide society nearly equally. But it will not be so with others. In France, for example, it is probable that the Protestants do not form the numerical majority of any constituency. If the politics, therefore, of the moment were to turn on any question specially interesting them as Protestants, they would be entirely unrepresented. *d*Under universal suffrage, the*d* class of mere manual labourers would everywhere form a large majority in any electoral

*d–d*591, 592 The

district grounded solely on a local division of the country. It might happen, therefore, that every single member of the Legislature would represent the opinions and feelings of manual labourers alone.

To enable minorities to be represented without placing them on an equality with majorities, it would be necessary that every constituency should return at least three members; and I venture to suggest that this is a sufficient number, and that no electoral body ought to return more. When men vote for a long list, they usually adopt entire that which is presented to them by some knot of politicians who assume the management of elections. They have no personal knowledge or preference in the case of so large a number, and they consequently elect, as a matter of course, whoever are held forth to them as the candidates of their party. Assuming, then, that each constituency elects three representatives, two modes have been proposed, in either of which a minority, amounting to a third of the constituency, may, by acting in concert, and determining to aim at no more, return one of the members. One plan is that each elector should only be allowed to vote for two, or even for one, although three are to be elected. The other leaves to the elector his three votes, but allows him to give all of them to one candidate. The first of these plans was adopted in the Reform Bill of Lord Aberdeen's Government; but I do not hesitate most decidedly to prefer the second, which has been advocated in an able and conclusive pamphlet by Mr. James Garth Marshall.[*] The former plan must be always and inevitably unpopular, because it cuts down the privileges of the voter, while the latter, on the contrary, extends them. And I am prepared to maintain that the permission of cumulative votes, that is, of giving either one, two, or three votes to a single candidate, is in itself, even independently of its effect in giving a representation to minorities, the mode of voting which gives the most faithful expression of the wishes of the elector. On the existing plan, an elector who votes for three, can give his vote for the three candidates whom he prefers to their competitors; but among those three he may desire the success of one, immeasurably more than that of the other two, and may be willing to relinquish them entirely for an increased chance of attaining the greater object. This portion of his wishes he has now no means of expressing by his vote. He may sacrifice two of his votes altogether, but in no case can he give more than a single vote to the object of his preference. Why should the mere fact of preference be alone considered, and no account whatever be taken of the degree of it? The power to give several votes to a single candidate would be eminently favourable to those whose claims to be chosen are derived from personal qualities, and not from their being the mere symbols of an opinion. For if the voter gives his suffrage to a candidate

[*Minorities and Majorities; their relative rights. A letter to the Lord John Russell, M.P. on Parliamentary Reform (London: Ridgway, 1853).]

in consideration of pledges, or because the candidate is of the same party with himself, he will not desire the success of that individual more than of any other who will take the same pledges, or ᵉwhoᵉ belongs to the same party. When he is especially concerned for the election of some one candidate, it is on account of something which personally distinguishes that candidate from others on the same side. Where there is no overruling local influence in favour of an individual, those who would be benefited as candidates by the cumulative vote, would generally be the persons of greatest real or reputed virtue or talents.

In the preceding review of the essentials of a new Parliamentary Reform, no mention has been made of the Ballot. I hope to show sufficient reasons why this should be included, not among the things which ought, but among those which ought not, to form part of a measure for reforming the representation. It appears to me that secret suffrage, a very right and justifiable demand when originally made, would at present, and still more in time to come, produce far greater evil than good.

The operation of the Ballot is, that it enables the voter to give full effect to his own private preferences, whether selfish or disinterested, under no inducement to defer to the opinions or wishes of others, except as these may influence his own. It follows, and the friends of the ballot have always said, that secrecy is desirable, in cases in which the motives acting on the voter through the will of others are likely to mislead him, while, if left to his own preferences, he would vote as he ought. It equally follows, and is also the doctrine of the friends of the ballot, that when the voter's own preferences are apt to lead him wrong, but the feeling of responsibility to others may keep him right, not secrecy, but publicity, should be the rule.*

*This is the criterion distinctly laid down by a philosopher who did more than any other man of his generation towards making Ballot the creed of Parliamentary Reformers:

"There are occasions on which the use of the ballot is advantageous: there are occasions on which it is hurtful. If we look steadily to the end, to which all institutions profess to be directed, we shall not find it very difficult to draw the line of demarcation.

A voter may be considered as subject to the operation of two sets of interests: the one, interests arising out of the good or evil for which he is dependent upon the will of other men; the other, interests in respect to which he cannot be considered as dependent upon any determinate man or men.

There are cases in which the interests for which he is not dependent upon other men impel him in the right direction. If not acted on by other interests, he will, in such cases, vote in that direction. If, however, he is acted upon by interests dependent upon other men, interests more powerful than the former, and impelling in the opposite direction, he will vote in the opposite direction.

ᵉ–ᵉ+67

It is for this reason that no one, either Conservative or Reformer, approves of vote by ballot in Parliament itself. A member of Parliament, however ^gsecure^g against misleading influences from without, would often promote his private interest by voting wrong; and the chief security against this violation of his trust, is the publicity of his vote, and the effect on his mind of the opinion which will be formed of his conduct by other people.

Thirty years ago it was still true that in the election of members of Parliament, the main evil to be guarded against was that which the ballot would exclude—coercion by landlords, employers, and customers. At present, I conceive, a much greater source of evil is the selfishness, or the selfish partialities, of the voter himself. A "base and mischievous vote" is now, I am convinced, much oftener given from the voter's personal interest, or class interest, or some mean feeling in his own mind, than from any fear of consequences at the hands of others: and to these evil influences the ballot would enable him to yield himself up, free from all sense of shame or responsibility.

In times not long gone by, the higher and richer classes were in complete possession of the government. Their power was the master grievance of the country. The habit of voting at the bidding of an employer, or of a landlord, was so firmly established, that hardly anything was capable of shaking it but a strong popular enthusiasm, seldom known to exist but in a good cause. A vote given in opposition to these influences was therefore, in general, an honest, a public-spirited vote: but in any case, and by whatever motive

---

What is necessary, therefore, is to save him from the operation of those interests. This is accomplished by enabling him to vote in secret; for, in that case, the man who could otherwise compel his vote, is ignorant in what direction it has been given. In all cases, therefore, in which the independent interests of the voter, those which, in propriety of language, may be called his *own* interests, would dictate the good and useful vote; but in which cases, at the same time, he is liable to be acted upon in the way either of good or of evil, by men whose interests would dictate a base and mischievous vote, the ballot is a great and invaluable security. . . .

There is, however, another set of cases, in which those interests of the voter, which have their origin primarily in himself, and not in other men, draw in the hurtful direction, and in which he is not liable to be operated upon by any other interests of other men, than those which each possesses in common with the rest of the community. If allowed, in this set of cases, to vote in secret, he will be sure to vote as the sinister interest impels. If forced to vote in public, he will be subject to all the restraint which the eye of the community, fixed upon his virtue or knavery, is calculated to produce; and, in such cases, the ballot is only an encouragement to evil." ^f[James] Mill's *History of British India*. [3rd ed., 6 vols. (London: Baldwin, Cradock, and Joy, 1826), Vol. III, pp. 451–2.]^f

^f–f+67
^g–g591, 592   secured

dictated, it was almost sure to be a good vote, for it was a vote against the monster evil—the overruling influence of oligarchy. Could the voter at that time have been enabled, with safety to himself, to exercise his privilege freely, even though neither honestly nor intelligently, it would have been a great gain to reform; for it would have broken the yoke of the then ruling power in the country—the power which had created and which maintained all that was bad in the institutions and the administration of the State—the power of landlords and boroughmongers.

The ballot was not adopted; but the progress of circumstances has done and is doing more and more, in this respect, the work of the ballot. Both the political and the social state of the country, as they affect this question, have greatly changed, and are changing every day. The higher classes are not now masters of the country. A person must be blind to all the signs of the times, who could think that the middle classes are as subservient to the higher, or the working classes as dependent on the higher and middle, as they were a quarter of a century ago. The events of that quarter of a century have not only taught each class to know its own collective strength, but have put the individuals of a lower class in a condition to show a much bolder front to those of a higher. In a majority of cases, the vote of the electors, whether in opposition to or in accordance with the wishes of their superiors, is now not the effect of coercion, which there are no longer the same means of applying, but the expression of their own personal or political partialities. The very vices of the present electoral system are a proof of this. The growth of bribery, so loudly complained of previous to the late Act, and the spread of the contagion to places formerly free from it, are evidence that the local influences are no longer paramount; that the electors now vote to please themselves, and not other people. There is, no doubt, in counties and in the smaller boroughs, a large amount of servile dependence still remaining; but the temper of the times is adverse to it, and the force of events is constantly tending to diminish it. A good tenant can now feel that he is as valuable to his landlord as his landlord is to him; a prosperous tradesman can afford to feel independent of any particular customer. At every election the votes are more and more the voters' own. It is their minds, far more than their personal circumstances, that now require to be emancipated. They are no longer passive instruments of other men's will—mere organs for putting power into the hands of a controlling oligarchy. The electors themselves are becoming the oligarchy.

Exactly in proportion as the vote of the elector is determined by his own will, and not by that of somebody who is his master, his position is similar to that of a member of Parliament, and publicity is indispensable. So long as any portion of the community are unrepresented, the argument of the Chartists against ballot in conjunction with a restricted suffrage, is unassail-

LIBRARY
COLBY-SAWYER COLLEGE
NEW LONDON, NH 03257

able. The present electors, and the bulk of those whom any probable Reform Bill would add to the number, are the middle class; and have as much a class interest, distinct from the working classes, as landlords or great manufacturers. Were the suffrage extended to all skilled labourers, even these would, or might, still have a class interest distinct from the unskilled. Suppose it extended to all men—suppose that what was formerly called by the misapplied name of universal suffrage, and now by the silly and insulting title of manhood suffrage, became the law—the voters would still have a class interest, as distinguished from women. Suppose that there were a question before the Legislature specially affecting women; as whether women should be allowed to graduate at Universities; whether the mild penalties inflicted on ruffians who beat their wives daily almost to death's door, should be exchanged for something more effectual; or suppose that any one should propose in the British Parliament, what one State after another in America is enacting not by a mere law, but by a provision of their revised Constitutions—that married women should have a right to their own property. Are not a man's wife and daughters entitled to know whether he votes for or against a candidate who will support these propositions?

It will of course be objected, that these arguments derive all their weight from the supposition of an unjust state of the *h*suffrage: That*h* if the opinion of the non-electors is likely to make the elector vote more honestly, or more beneficially, than he would vote if left to himself, they are more fit to be electors than he is, and ought to have the *i*franchise: That*i* whoever is fit to influence electors, is fit to be an *j*elector: That*j* those to whom voters ought to be responsible, should be themselves voters; and, being such, should have the safeguard of the ballot, to shield them from the undue influence of powerful individuals or classes to whom they ought *not* to be responsible.

This argument is specious, and I once thought it conclusive. It now appears to me fallacious. All who are fit to influence electors are not, for that reason, fit to be themselves electors. This last is a much greater power than the former, and those may be ripe for the minor political function who could not as yet be safely trusted with the superior. The opinions and wishes of the poorest and rudest class of labourers may be very useful as one influence among others on the minds of the voters, as well as on those of the Legislature; and yet it might be highly mischievous to give them the preponderant influence, by admitting them, in their present state of morals and intelligence, to the full exercise of the suffrage. It is precisely this indirect influence of those who have not the suffrage over those who have, which, by its progressive growth, softens the transition to every fresh extension of the fran-

*h-h*591, 592   suffrage. That
*i-i*591, 592   franchise. That
*j-j*591, 592   elector. That

LIBRARY
COLBY-SAWYER COLLEGE
NEW LONDON, NH 03257

chise, and is the means by which, when the time is ripe, the extension is peacefully brought about. But there is also another and a still deeper consideration, which should never be left out of the account in political speculations. The notion is itself unfounded, that publicity, and the sense of being answerable to the public, are of no use unless the public are qualified to form a sound judgment. It is a very superficial view of the utility of public opinion, to suppose that it does good, only when it succeeds in enforcing a servile conformity to itself. To be under the eyes of others—to have to defend oneself to others—is never more important than to those who act in opposition to the opinion of others, for it obliges them to have sure ground of their own. Nothing has so steadying an influence, as working against pressure. Unless when under the temporary sway of passionate excitement, no one will do that which he expects to be greatly blamed for, unless from a preconceived and fixed purpose of his own; which is always evidence of a thoughtful and deliberate character, and, except in radically bad men, generally proceeds from sincere and strong personal convictions. Even the bare fact of having to give an account of their conduct, is a powerful inducement to adhere to conduct of which, at least, some decent account can be given. If any one thinks that the mere obligation of preserving decency is not a very considerable check on the abuse of power, he has never had his attention called to the conduct of those who do not feel under the necessity of observing that restraint. Publicity is inappreciable, even when it does no more than prevent that which can by no possibility be plausibly defended—than compel deliberation, and force every one to determine, before he acts, what he shall say if called to account for his actions.

But if not now (it may be said), at least hereafter, when all are fit to have votes, and when all men and women are admitted to vote, in virtue of their fitness,—*then* there can no longer be danger of class legislation; then the electors, being the nation, can have no interest apart from the general interest: even if individuals still vote according to private or class inducements, the majority will have no such inducement; and as there will then be no non-electors to whom they ought to be responsible, the effect of the ballot, excluding none but the sinister influences, will be wholly beneficial.

Even in this I do not agree. I cannot think that even if the people were fit for, and had obtained, universal suffrage, the ballot would be desirable. First, because it could not, in such circumstances, be supposed to be needful. Let us only conceive the state of things which the hypothesis implies: a people universally educated, and every grown-up human being possessed of a vote. If, even when only a small proportion are electors, and the majority of the population almost uneducated, public opinion is already, as every one now sees that it is, the ruling power in the last resort; it is a chimera to suppose that over a community who all read, and who all have votes, any power could be exercised by landlords and rich people against their own inclination, which it would be at all difficult for them to throw off. But though the protection of secrecy would then be needless, the control of publicity would be as needful as ever. The universal observation of mankind has been very fallacious, if the mere fact of being one of the community, and not being in a position of pronounced contrariety of interest to the public at large, is enough to ensure the performance of a public duty, without either the stimulus or the restraint derived from the opinion of our fellow-creatures. A man's own particular share of the public interest, even though he may have no private interest drawing him in the opposite direction, is not, as a general rule, found sufficient to make him do his duty to the public without other external inducements. Neither can it be admitted that even if all had votes, they would give their votes as honestly in secret as in public. The proposition that the electors, when they compose the whole of the community, cannot have an interest in voting against the interest of the community, will be found on examination to have more sound than meaning in it. Though the community as a whole can have (as the terms imply) no other interest than its collective interest, any or every individual in it may. A man's interest consists of whatever he takes interest *in*. Everybody has as many different interests as he has feelings; likings or dislikings, either of a selfish or of a better kind. It cannot be said that any of these, taken by itself constitutes "his interest": he is a good man or a bad, according as he prefers one class of his interests or another. A man who is a tyrant at home will be apt to sympathize with tyranny (when not exercised over himself): he will be almost certain not to sympathize with resistance to tyranny. An envious man will vote against Aristides because he is called the Just. A selfish man will prefer even a trifling individual benefit, above his share of the advantage which his country would derive from a good law; because interests peculiar to himself are those which the habits of his mind both dispose him to dwell on, and make him best able to estimate. A great number of the electors will have two sets of preferences, those on private, and those on public grounds. The last are the only ones which the elector would like to avow. The best side of their character is that which people are anxious to show, even to those who are no better than themselves. People will give dishonest or mean votes from lucre, from malice, from pique, from personal rivalry, from the interests or prejudices of class or sect, far more readily in secret than in public. And cases exist—they may come to be very frequent—in which almost the only restraint upon a majority of knaves, consists in their involuntary respect for the opinion of an honest minority. In such a case as that of the repudiating States of North America, is there not some check to the unprincipled voter in the shame of looking an honest man in the face? Since all this good would be sacrificed by the ballot, even in the circumstances most favourable to it—

circumstances not likely to be seen realized by any one now alive—a much stronger case is requisite than can now be made out for its necessity (and the case is continually becoming still weaker), to make its adoption desirable, or even tolerable.

For it must be borne in mind that the ballot cannot be, and has not been, defended otherwise than as a necessary evil. Necessary it might have been, but an evil it could never fail to be. The moral sentiment of mankind, in all periods of tolerably enlightened morality, has condemned concealment, unless when required by some overpowering motive; and if it be one of the paramount objects of national education to foster courage and public spirit, it is high time now that people should be taught the duty of asserting and acting openly on their opinions. Disguise in all its forms is a badge of slavery. No one will require from slaves the virtues of freemen, nor will scan nicely the means by which slaves effect their emancipation. They begin by resisting covertly; but when the time is come for rebelling openly, a man must have the soul of a slave who prefers the slave's weapon for himself, however his distrust of the courage of others may lead him to sanction its employment. And there is truth in what has always been urged by the enemies of the ballot—that, even supposing it necessary, it could only produce its effect at the price of much lying. The friends of the ballot have indulged a faint hope that it would put an end to canvassing. If it really held out this prospect, the force of the objection to it would be considerably weakened; but such a result is not in the nature of man and of things. As long as human beings exist, the most direct mode of obtaining a person's vote will be to ask him for it. People will solicit a promise, even when they can have no positive assurance that the promise is kept; and a man who thinks that he has power over another, and who is disposed to make a tyrannical use of it, will question him about his vote, even when he has no guarantee for obtaining a true answer but the man's veracity, or his awkwardness. The voter might, on the plea of public principle, refuse to give any answer; but, unless he was otherwise known to be a man of unusually high principle, the refusal would justly be considered a sufficient proof that a true answer would disclose what it is his interest to conceal. Supporters of the ballot have argued that the voter might resort to those evasive answers which integrity permits in the case of an impertinent question; but an evasive answer to a first question only succeeds when made to an equal, who does not consider himself at liberty to ask a second: and besides, the majority of electors have neither address nor readiness for such evasions; and when they really feel themselves in the power of the questioner, a downright lie, enforced by asseveration if doubted, would be their only resource. Reformers may once have been disposed to wink at this evil, in order to prevent the still greater one of bad government; but it is in itself no small item in the account. It would perhaps be a greater evil in this country than in any other. There are but few points in which the English, as a people, are entitled to the moral pre-eminence with which they are accustomed to compliment themselves at the expense of other nations: but, of these points, perhaps the one of greatest importance is, that the higher classes do not lie, and the lower, though mostly habitual liars, are ashamed of lying. To run any risk of weakening this feeling, a difficult one to create, or, when once gone, to restore, would be a permanent evil too great to be incurred for so very temporary a benefit as the ballot would confer, even on the most exaggerated estimate of its necessity.

There is a suggestion of another kind, respecting the mode of voting, which has found a favourable reception from some of the supporters and from some of the opponents of the ballot. It is that of collecting the votes of the electors at their own homes, a voting paper being left at the door, like the memorandum of a tax-collector, and filled up by the voter without the trouble of going to the poll. This expedient has been recommended, both on the score of saving expense, and on that of obtaining the votes of many electors who otherwise would not vote, and who are regarded by the advocates of the plan as a particularly desirable class of voters. The scheme has been carried into practice in the election of poor-law guardians, and its success in that instance is appealed to in favour of adopting it in the more important case of voting for a member of the Legislature. But the two cases appear to me to differ in the point on which the benefits of the expedient depend. In a local election for a special kind of administrative business, which consists mainly in the dispensation of a public fund, it is an object to prevent the choice from being exclusively in the hands of those who actively concern themselves about it; for the public interest which attaches to the election being of a limited kind, and in most cases not very great in degree, the disposition to make themselves busy in the matter is apt to be in a great measure confined to persons who hope to turn their activity to their own private advantage; and it may be very desirable to render the intervention of other people as little onerous to them as possible, if only for the purpose of swamping these private interests. But when the matter in hand is the great business of national government, in which every one must take an interest who cares for anything out of himself, or who cares even for himself intelligently, it is much rather an object to prevent those from voting who are indifferent to the subject, than to induce them to vote by any other means than that of awakening their dormant minds. The voter who does not care enough about the election to go to the poll, is the very man who, if he can vote without that small trouble, will give his vote to the first person who asks for it, or on the most trifling or frivolous inducement. A man who does not care whether he votes, is not likely to care much which way he votes; and he who is in that state of mind has no moral right to vote at all; since if he does so, a vote which is not the expression of a conviction, counts for as much, and goes as far in determining the result, as one which perhaps represents the thoughts and purposes of a life. These reasons appear to me decisive against the change proposed, and in favour of the present plan of delivering the vote at a public polling-place: but the places of voting should be sufficiently numerous and convenient to enable the poorest elector to vote without losing his day's wages; and, as already intimated, the expense of the poll should not be a charge upon the candidates, but upon the county or borough, or upon the State.*k*

*k*592 SUPPLEMENT./This pamphlet was written and published before I had seen or heard of Mr. [Thomas] Hare's important Treatise on Representation [London: Longman, 1859]; which, had I been acquainted with it, would have enabled me greatly to improve those parts of my own performance, which go over the same ground with Mr. Hare. It would have been impossible to reprint this tract without making any reference to the great enlargement which my opinions on the subject have received from Mr. Hare's speculations; and a new edition having been called for, the easiest, if not the best, mode in which I can perform this duty, is by subjoining, from an article contributed by me to *Fraser's Magazine* for April last, a somewhat full exposition of the great idea by which that sagacious thinker has (it is no exaggeration to say) given a new aspect to the principle of popular representation. [*Here follows, in 592, a section of "Recent Writers on Reform," Fraser's Magazine, LIX (April, 1859), 500–8. This section will be found at 358–70 below, as part of that article; the variants between the original article and the pamphlet's quotation from it are given there.*]

RECENT WRITERS ON REFORM

1859

Dissertations and Discussions, III (1867), 47–96, where the title is footnoted, *"Fraser's Magazine*, April 1859.—1. 'A Plea for the Constitution.' / By John Austin, Esq., formerly Professor of Jurisprudence at the/London University, and Reader on the same subject at the Inner/Temple. [London: Murray,] 1859./ 2. 'Political Progress not necessarily Democratic; or, Relative/Equality the true Foundation of Liberty.' By James Lorimer, Esq.,/Advocate. [London and Edinburgh: Williams and Norgate,] 1857./ 3. 'A Treatise on the Election of Representatives, Parliamentary/and Municipal.' By Thomas Hare, Esq., Barrister-at-Law. [London: Longman, Brown, Green, Longmans, & Roberts,] 1859." /Reprinted from *Fraser's Magazine*, LIX (Apr., 1859), 489–508, signed "J.S.M.", where a footnote to the title gives the same list of works. Identified in JSM's bibliography as "An article entitled 'Recent Writers on Reform' being a review of writings by Austin, Lorimer and Hare; in Fraser's Magazine for April 1859" (MacMinn, 92). An offprint from *Fraser's* (paged 1–20) in the Somerville College Library has no corrections or emendations.

For comments on the composition of the work, see the Textual Introduction, lxxxiv–lxxxv above.

The text below is that in *D&D*, III (1867), the only edition of that volume in JSM's lifetime. In the footnoted variants, "67" indicates *D&D*, III; "59[1]" indicates *Fraser's Magazine*. JSM quotes passages from this essay in *Thoughts on Parliamentary Reform*, 2nd pamphlet edition (see 358–70), and *Considerations on Representative Government* (see 368); changes in the quotations are indicated as variants, in which "59[2]" indicates *Thoughts on Parliamentary Reform*, and "61[1]", "61[2]", and "65" indicate the editions of *Considerations on Representative Government*.

Recent Writers on Reform

THE PRESENT Reform movement, which differs from other similar movements in not having been immediately preceded by any strong manifestation of popular discontent, seems likely to be still further distinguished by the quality of the contributions made by individual thinkers towards the better understanding of the philosophical elements of the subject. There is a natural connexion between the two characteristics. During the storm which preceded and accompanied the Reform discussions of 1831 and 1832, no voice was raised, because none would have been audible, save those which shouted for or against the one thing which the public so loudly cried for. But the present demand for Parliamentary Reform, being in an unusual degree the product of calm reason, leaves room to hope that any appeal to reason may be listened to, and encourages the superior intellects to bring forward any thoughts they possess which seem to them to have a useful bearing upon the questions at issue.

From the publications of more or less mark which have been called forth by the prospect of another Parliamentary reform, we select three, among the most distinguished by their thoughtful character, and by the mental qualities of the writers. Their objects, their doctrines, their practical conclusions, are widely different, but they are the productions of highly-instructed and disciplined minds; they all deserve and will repay meditation, and one of them we hold to be the most important work ever written on the practical part of the subject. Before attempting an analysis of Mr. Hare's admirable treatise, we shall endeavour to give some notion of the merits, as well as of what we deem the errors, of the other productions on our list.

Of the three writers, Mr. Austin alone is opposed to any further Parliamentary reform; the two others are strong reformers, each according to his particular mode of thought. Mr. Austin has claims to an attentive hearing which cannot be lightly estimated. His book on the "Province of Jurisprudence"[*] stepped at once into the very highest authority on what may be termed the metaphysics of law; though it was only the introduction to a course of lectures, delivered but not printed, every part of which was at least equal in merit to the preliminary portion. Whoever is acquainted either with

[*_The Province of Jurisprudence Determined_ (London: Murray, 1832).]

these or with the writings attributed to Mr. Austin which have been published anonymously, regrets that a mind so fitted by capacity and acquirements for untying the hard knots which the philosophy of law is full of, and which are the great impediment to simplicity and intelligibility in its practice, should have accomplished only a small part of the work to which his peculiar combination of endowments especially called him. We shall rejoice that he has resumed the pen, even on a question on which we differ with him, if it authorizes us to hope that we may yet see the completion of his great book. The worth, to us, of his present performance, does not lie in his conclusions, but in some of his premises. We receive it as an exposition of what, in the opinion of probably the most intellectual man who is an enemy to further reform, are the specific evils to be apprehended from it. Whoever points out the rocks and shoals with which our course is beset, does us a service which may be all the greater because we are not terrified thereby into renouncing the voyage. Mr. Austin is perhaps no unlikely person to over-estimate some dangers, but he is not a man to conjure up any which are entirely chimerical; and it may readily be admitted that every plan of reform ought to stand his test; ought to show, either that it does not tend to produce the evils dreaded by him, or that its tendency to do so can be counteracted.

The first half of Mr. Austin's pamphlet is occupied by an analytical examination of the actual constitution of this country, and a display of what he deems its characteristic advantages. In his estimate of these, few Englishmen will disagree with him: but when he connects them pre-eminently with those elements in the distribution of political power which further reform may be expected to weaken, several of his observations seem questionable. Thus he enlarges, with reason, on the necessity to the successful working of a free, or even of any constitution, of a spirit of compromise. "All successful government, and all prosperous society, is carried on and maintained by a mutual give and take."[*] As little can he be gainsaid when he affirms that this spirit is remarkably an attribute of English politics. If any one of the three powers in the British constitution exerted the whole of its legal rights, and pressed every difference of opinion to the utmost, the action of the government would be paralyzed, and its energies absorbed, by internal contests, which would induce an ultimate disruption of the whole fabric. It is equally true that this habitual willingness on the part of every constituted authority to acquiesce cheerfully in the necessary conditions of stable government, has been found very difficult to introduce where it did not previously exist: and eminent political thinkers have founded their systems on the belief that this conscientious or prudent self-restraint was too difficult to be ever really practised, and that the co-ordinate powers in a balanced constitution will always struggle with each other, until one of them has completely subordi-

[*Austin, *A Plea for the Constitution*, p. 6.]

nated the others to itself. On all this we entirely agree with Mr. Austin; but not in the passage which follows:

But though this talent for compromise is one of the conditions of happy political society, few nations have possessed it in a high degree; and none but the people of England have ever possessed the degree of it which is one of the principal conditions of enduring free government. . . . The long duration of a system so difficult to work . . . has doubtless arisen to a great extent from the habitual reverence of the several members of the Parliament for their respective constitutional rights, and from the habitual moderation (if not the habitual courtesy) which tempers and sets a measure to their hottest contentions. This habitual reverence for the constitutional rights of others, and this habitual moderation in Parliamentary battle and victory, have mainly arisen from the breeding of the men who have formed the great majority of the Lower House. If the composition of the House should in this respect deteriorate, the spirit of compromise will be enfeebled, and the difficulty of working the system will be vastly aggravated. [Pp. 6–7.]

With submission, we think there is a mistake here. The English are not the only people who have shown an eminent degree of what Mr. Austin calls a "talent for compromise." The Americans possess it largely, and have proved it super-abundantly in the course of their history, short as that history is. The only questions on which the Union has been agitated by important differences of opinion are the tariff and the slavery questions; and whenever either of these quarrels has reached a height which threatened seriously to interfere with the working of the national institutions, it has been closed up for the moment by a legislative compromise. The whole history of each is a series of such compromises: and if none of these have been of long duration, it is because, as most Englishmen will now admit, the questions are such as in their nature cannot and ought not to be the subjects of permanent compromise. These facts indicate that Mr. Austin cannot be right in ascribing the temperate and conciliatory spirit of English contests mainly to "the breeding of the men who have formed the great majority of the Lower House," a cause which was not found to produce any similar effect on the royalist and aristocratic party in France; though doubtless it has contributed much to the calmness and amenity with which the debates of the British Parliament have usually been conducted, and which deserve to be placed in the number of the safeguards against precipitate and passionate action on the part of the assembly itself. The compromising temper which English and American politicians have in common, and the want of which is one cause of the repeated failures of liberal institutions elsewhere, is sometimes ascribed to the less inflammable character of their northern blood; but may more rationally be attributed to their greater political experience, and longer possession of free government. They are content to exercise a limited power, because they have never felt or been subject to any power which was not obviously limited. We think Mr. Austin would have been nearer the truth, while even his own argument would not have suffered, if he had attributed this quality in the English and Americans to the complicated and balanced character of their political institutions. Democratic as the American government is, the powers of every magistrate and of every assembly composing it, are narrowly hemmed in by those of other functionaries and public bodies. No American assembly is encouraged by the constitution to believe that its will is law. We agree with those who think that the spirit of conciliation and compromise could with difficulty establish itself in any government which consisted of one sovereign assembly, whether accompanied or not by an hereditary president under a royal title.

Mr. Austin considers the British Government to be not only the most free, but also the most democratical government which has "governed a great nation through a long and eventful period." [P. 9.] This may be admitted, so long as the solidity of the Federal and State Governments of America "has not been tried by time." But Mr. Austin is unfortunate in the argument he uses to prove that, "in spirit and effect," apart from the form of the constitution, the English Government is "the most democratical of all governments, past and present."

The interests and opinions, [he says,] of the entire population of the country (and not only those of the sovereign body), are habitually consulted by the Legislature and by the executive Government. In the United States, the large slave population are excluded from political power, and almost from legal rights; whilst their interests and feelings are set at naught by the Governments, and are scorned or slighted by the great majority of the public. (P. 10.)

The American Government is here stated to be practically less democratic than the English, because it disregards the interests and feelings of a portion of the people *quoad* whom the American Government is not a democracy at all, but the closest, hardest, and most exclusive of aristocracies. To have any bearing on the merits of democratic institutions, the comparison should not have been made with the American Federation, but with the free Northern States, which alone have any pretension to be democracies. As well might any one tell us that Europe is a great slave country, meaning by Europe, Russia.

Mr. Austin expatiates on the advantage we derive from the fact that, while the electors are a democratic body, the elected are mostly, in the personal and social meaning of the term, aristocratic. He says:

The art of statesmanship, like other high and difficult arts, can only be acquired by those who make it their principal business. The aristocracy in question, being men of independent means, can afford to devote themselves to public life; whilst men whose time and thoughts are absorbed by their private affairs, cannot give themselves thoroughly to the concerns of the nation. From the possession of an aristocratical body specially affected to practical politics, the nation derives the well-known advantages which arise from the division of labour. A larger proportion of competent statesmen will naturally be furnished by a body comparatively skilled, than by the bodies (far more numerous) whose attention to public business is necessarily intermittent, and whose knowledge of those interests is therefore necessarily superficial. To this it must be added that, in consequence of the high and undisputed positions occupied socially by the aristocracy in question, they naturally acquire a cool self-possession, a quick insight into men, and a skill in dealing with men, which are specially necessary to statesmen in a free and *parliamentary* country. From their high social positions, and the peculiar influences acting upon them from the cradle, they are naturally restrained in a more than common degree by the sentiment of gentlemanly honour. As filling those high positions, and as being permanently occupied with public life, they are more obvious to the public eye, and are more restrained by public opinion, than men whose social positions are comparatively humble, and whose public lives are comparatively intermittent and obscure. On account of their independence in respect of pecuniary means . . . they are under smaller temptations than political adventurers to succumb to a ministry of which they conscientiously disapprove, or to flatter their constituencies at the expense of the public interests, in prejudices and illusions which in their hearts they despise. (Pp. 13–14.)

Surely this is a large superstructure on a small basis of reality. Whatever may be the advantages of pecuniary independence in Members of Parliament, and whatever superiority in point of "gentlemanly honour" may accrue to them from the class to which they principally belong, the advantage of having a body of instructed and trained statesmen and legislators is, we should have thought, almost the last which any one could possibly represent us as deriving from them. The classes spoken of have it in their power to be all that Mr. Austin has described, but how many of them actually are so? Since public opinion began to require some amount of appropriate knowledge and training in the members of an Administration, it has never been possible to find a sufficient number of such men to form a Cabinet, much less a Legislature. Is it not a speaking fact that, at this critical moment, not a man can be thought of as fit to lead the great Liberal party, except one or the other of two noblemen advanced in years?[*] And even they are not thought to be fit absolutely, but only fitter than any one else. We have no desire to see a Parliament of rich elderly manufacturers, but we certainly prefer them to the young fribbles of family who formerly did us the honour to legislate for us. We, too, maintain that statesmanship of any high quality can only be looked for in persons who devote themselves to it as an art. There have been aristocratic governments which were carried on by such persons—the open aristocracy of Rome for example, and the close aristocracy of Venice; and we acknowledge that the influences of unbalanced

[*Lord Palmerston and Lord John Russell.]

*a–a*Source,591 Parliamentary

democracy have a tendency to prevent the formation of such a class. But it answers no good purpose to argue as if we at present enjoyed a benefit which we neither have nor ever had, and are as little likely to have under the existing mixed government as under a republic.

The objections to Parliamentary reform which compose the latter half of Mr. Austin's performance, consist of presumptive objections to any change, and positive ones to the particular changes most widely advocated. Of those which bear against reform in general, the principal one is this: that all practical evils which admit of legislative correction are as likely to be remedied under the present constitution of the Legislature as under any other: that the undiscerning conservatism called into existence by the French Revolution has disappeared, and all parties in Parliament are well disposed towards legal and administrative reforms, which are now impeded by no serious difficulties but those inherent in their subjects, and (we must add) by the private interests, not indeed of the rulers, but of those whom the rulers trust, and by the spirit of routine and obstruction, which is not peculiar to any set of institutions, but common to all established systems. With this modification, we agree to some extent with Mr. Austin. There *is* a spirit of improvement, common to all parties, in many of the details of government; and it may perhaps be true that there is hardly any beneficial change, demanded by a mature public opinion, which, after a moderate interval, would not have a good chance of being carried, under our present political institutions. For what practical end, then, do we desire a more popular basis for those institutions? Mainly for that of maturing and enlightening public opinion itself. Parliament has another function besides that of making laws. The House of Commons is not only the most powerful branch of the Legislature; it is also the great council of the nation; the place where the opinions which divide the public on great subjects of national interest, meet in a common arena, do battle, and are victorious or vanquished. This latter function the House of Commons does not fulfil, if the most numerous class, and that which is least favoured by fortune, after it has once begun to have and to express opinions, remains without direct representation there. Besides being an instrument of government, Parliament is a grand institution of national education, having for one of its valuable offices to create and correct that public opinion whose mandates it is required to obey. That which Acts of Parliament and votes of money can do for the political instruction of the people, falls short of what might be done by the discussions in Parliament itself, if those who most need instruction were there in the persons of their representatives, saying their best for their opinions; counted among those whose reason a minister or an orator must appeal to; when they were wrong, some one taking pains to answer them, and to make the answer understood by them: not left, as now, under the gloomy persuasion that their interests are dealt with in their absence, and unheard—that Parliament occupies itself with everything rather than with the burthen which is weighing on their hearts, and even when it busies itself about the same questions, never for an instant looks at them from their point of view. Is it wonderful if they should think that "les absents ont toujours tort,"[*] and should persist in errors when their errors are ignored by their superiors, and are never met and encountered in equal conflict, with opportunity of explanation and rejoinder?

There is a further practical consideration appropriate to the present time. The non-represented classes, as a body, are just now, to all appearance, peaceful and acquiescent. But they were not always so; we are not far from the days of Chartist insurrections, and monster petitions signed by millions of men. If the existing tranquillity is caused by the people's having grown wiser—expecting more from themselves, and less from what the Government can do in any direct way to improve their condition, the main argument for excluding them from the suffrage is very much abated. But if the cause be lassitude, or despair of success, or that they are at present tolerably prosperous, such times as we have seen not many years ago we shall see again; and concessions which, made at the present calm season, can be accompanied by proper safeguards, may then be wrung from Parliament without any safeguards at all, under the same imminent dangers which prevailed in 1832. Prudence and foresight, therefore, combine with principle in recommending that the present favourable opportunity be made use of for placing our representative system on a footing which can be defended on intelligible principles of justice, and such that the greatest number of persons, consistent with safety, shall have evident cause to be well affected towards it.

Mr. Austin proceeds to set forth the evils which he would anticipate, either from universal suffrage, or from any such reform as would vest the predominant power in the lower portion of the middle class. A House of Commons returned by universal suffrage (which he always supposes unguarded by provisions that would give a share of influence to any but the numerical majority), though it would not, he says, attempt to carry out Socialist theories—

Would ruin our finances, and destroy our economical prosperity, by insensate interferences with the natural arrangements of society, which would not be the less pernicious for not being inspired by theory. No man, looking attentively at the realities around him, can doubt that a great majority of the working classes are imbued with principles essentially socialist; that their very natural opinions on political and commercial subjects are partial applications of the premises which are the groundwork of the socialist theories. They believe, for example, very generally, that the rate of wages depends upon the will of the employers; that the prices of provisions and other articles of general consumption, depend

[*Cf. Jean Baptiste Gresset, *Le Méchant*, Act II, Scene vii.]

upon the will of the sellers; that the wealth of the richer classes is somehow sub-
tracted from their own; and that capital is not an adminicle, but an antagonist of
labour. We might, therefore, expect from a House of Commons representing the
prejudices of the non-proprietary class, a minimum rate of wages, a maximum
price of provisions and other necessaries of life, with numberless other restric-
tions on the actual freedom of contracting. We might also expect from such an
assembly that they would saddle the richer classes, and especially the owners of
so-called "realized" property, with the entire burthen of taxation; destroying or
diminishing thereby the motives to accumulation, together with the efficient demand for the labour of their own constituents. (P. 19.)

Mr. Austin has put his estimate of what might be the practical result of a
Parliament elected by equal and universal suffrage, at the very worst possible;
far worse than we consider at all probable. But *might*, in a case of this importance, is as conclusive as *would*; and those who look the most hopefully
to universal suffrage, seldom propose to introduce it otherwise than gradually
and tentatively, with the power of stopping short wherever a tendency begins
to manifest itself towards making legislation subservient to the misunderstood class interests of labourers and artisans. But while no rational person
would entrust the preponderant power in the State to persons aiming at the
objects which Mr. Austin describes, there is no reason why even these
should not be represented as one class among others—why they, like so many
other classes having sinister interests or absurd opinions, should not have
their spokesmen in Parliament, to ventilate their nonsense, and secure attention to their sense and to the facts of their position. Until this is the case, the
working classes, with however good intentions on the part of the Legislature,
will never obtain complete justice (though they may receive mischievous
courtship), and if they did, would never believe that they had obtained it.
We will go a step further. We are completely at issue with those who are
unable to see that there is a true side to many of the crudest notions of the
working classes, and that there is something, and even much, which can be
rationally done for them in the direction of what seem their wildest aberrations. From the cast of his mind, we should have thought Mr. Austin
one of the likeliest of all men to recognise this; and we would gladly believe
that, when he appears to see in the great fact of Socialism only simple
"insanity," as when he calls the revolutionary movements of 1848 an "atrocious outbreak," [p. 18,] he rather gives way to an impulse of passion than
expresses a deliberate judgment.

To any system which should "give to the lower classes of the vast middle
class an unchecked ascendancy in the House of Commons," [p. 22,] Mr.
Austin is no less opposed; partly because, as he thinks, any such measure
would be a step to universal suffrage, and partly for the following reasons:

From what is known of the constituencies in which these classes actually predominate, we may infer that the majority of the reformed assembly would probably be composed in no small measure of men endowed with no higher faculties

than glibness of tongue and adroitness in managing elections; and ready, moreover, to court their constituents at the cost of the public interests, by bowing to their prejudices and even to their momentary caprices. The aristocracies of birth and social position, and still more the aristocracy of mind, would be generally distasteful to the constituencies. On finance and political economy, on law and the administration of justice, on the education of the lower and superior classes, on the relations of the country to other independent states, and on almost all the subjects of our domestic and foreign policy, the constituencies would think like men who have not considered such subjects, or have considered them slightly, and through the medium of popular prejudices. Sound financiers and political economists, profound theoretical and practical lawyers, men eminent in science and letters, distinguished journalists and philosophical statesmen (such, for example, as Mr. Burke), would not be appreciated by the reformed constituencies, or would even be objects of their positive dislike. . . . According to the true theory of the British constitution, the powers residing in the electoral body of the Commons are completely delegated to the Commons House, insomuch that the members of that assembly are not severally representatives of their respective constituencies, but are representatives of the entire kingdom. If this theory were generally disregarded in practice . . . the House of Commons would become a congress of ambassadors deputed by communities substantially independent states; and as being provided with several, and often conflicting instructions, they would form a body of representatives incapable of united action. . . . Now it has been shown by frequent experience that the conceptions of Parliamentary Government commonly entertained by the lower middle classes are inconsistent with this necessary theory. In the event of a reform giving to those classes an unchecked ascendancy in the House of Commons, the constituencies would dictate to their representatives their votes on particular questions, and owing to their servile deference to the prejudices and caprices of their constituents, the representatives would pledge themselves very generally to follow their imperative instructions. There is a mischievous and growing tendency in the House of Commons to encroach upon the functions of the Executive Government. . . . The functions thus usurped by the House of Commons are transferred from experienced and responsible to inexperienced and irresponsible hands, while the House, by attending to business for which its constitution unfits it, performs its legislative functions with diminished care, and neglects its important office of supervising and checking the Executive. In the event of a reform such as we are now contemplating, this mischievous and growing tendency would be greatly strengthened. Many of the representatives would be notable vestrymen, or men of the like character—men of limited views, of considerable capacity for details, of untiring activity and of restless and intrusive ambition. Meddling with administrative details would suit their capacity and taste; and by wrenching the business of the Executive from the ministers of the Crown, they would exalt themselves in the eyes of the country, or at least in those of their several localities. The respective functions of the several branches of the Parliament would be imperfectly apprehended by the reformed constituencies, and as they would naturally sympathize with the aggressive ambition of their representatives, they would back their encroachments on the province of the Crown. (Pp. 23–5.)

Could we be disposed to give "unchecked ascendancy" in Parliament to a single type of any description, the small tradesman is scarcely the one we should select. Yet it is important that real evils should not be exaggerated.

The shopocracy, like other powers of darkness, is not so black as it is painted. If the metropolitan districts, to which mainly it owes its bad reputation, do not return many distinguished men, let it be remembered that distinguished men seldom offer themselves for those districts. Men who wish to give their time to other matters than local business, do not like to live in the midst of a numerous and *exigeant* constituency. When candidates of any eminence have presented themselves, they have generally been elected. Lord John Russell never lost an election for the City, nor Sir William Molesworth for Southwark. In the second rank of politicians, Sir Benjamin Hawes, Sir William Clay, and others, who sat many years for metropolitan districts, are surely much superior to average members for small boroughs; nor is it any ordinary member of the House of Commons that is entitled to look down on Mr. Ayrton, who often says a useful word in Parliament when there is no one else to say it. We think it a mistake also to suppose that middle class constituencies prefer to be represented by persons like themselves. A lord or a baronet, who speaks them fair, and will swallow pledges on all the questions of the day, is the man for them. They do not elect "vestrymen." It would be more true to say that they allow vestrymen to elect for them. Still, there is a foundation of truth for many of Mr. Austin's apprehensions. He has marked some of the dangers to be avoided.

We shall touch only on one more point in Mr. Austin's discourse, and it is one on which we thoroughly agree with him: the importance of adapting our improvements, whenever it is possible, to the framework of the existing Constitution. This is one of the subjects on which knowledge of mankind teaches the most important lessons—on which inexperienced political theorists are most apt to differ from experienced. Until mankind are much more improved than there is any present hope of, even good political institutions cannot dispense with the support afforded by traditional sentiment. "The principle of public utility, applied to so vast a subject as the constitution of a Sovereign Government, leads generally to an invincible diversity of views." [P. 37.] An attachment resting on authority and habit to the existing Constitution "in and for itself," is, as Mr. Austin remarks [p. 37], in the existing state of the human mind, an almost indispensable condition of the stability of free government; which has the greatest difficulty in taking firm root among any people whose misfortune it is, never to have had institutions capable of inspiring such an attachment. Such a people, when they break entirely with their past, are apt to fall by degrees into a condition of passive indifference, and what Mr. Austin calls political scepticism.

The second work on our list, that of Mr. Lorimer, is not a dissertation on the question of the day, but an elaborate though concise treatise on the philosophy of government; of which we must of necessity confine ourselves to the parts which have a direct bearing on immediate practice. Mr. Lorimer is as much an enemy as Mr. Austin to the absolute dominion of the numerical majority; perhaps even more so: for Mr. Austin's quarrel with the multitude turns chiefly, it would seem, on their existing errors and prejudices, which may admit of removal; but Mr. Lorimer deems their autocracy to be unjust in itself, as well as destructive in its consequences. With Aristotle, Polybius, and others of the ancients, he regards the democracy of numbers as the "final form of degeneracy of all governments;"[*] inasmuch as, to the evils of every other government, the natural progress of democracy is a spontaneous corrective; but when democracy has itself become predominant, there is no other growing influence by which *its* characteristic evils can be kept under; society has then reached the last step of the ladder, and the next move can only carry it over the top, to begin again at the bottom with the despotism of one. But Mr. Lorimer is no preacher of despair; nor is the course he recommends that of a sullen opposition to the claims of the numerical majority. His hope is, by "removing the sources of theoretical conflict between political doctrines which have hitherto been supposed to be irreconcileable, and showing the possibility of their simultaneous recognition," to "pave the way for a safer progress on a road which not Englishmen only, but every civilized people, must inevitably tread." [P. vii.] It is useless to resist a natural law face to face; we should endeavour, by availing ourselves of other natural laws, to convert it from a peril into a blessing. Mr. Lorimer thinks it neither just nor practicable, finally to exclude any one from a vote;* and he would apparently have little objection even to immediate universal suffrage. But it must not be *equal* suffrage. Mr. Lorimer would give a voice to every one, but a more potential voice, by means of plurality of voting, to those classes who, either because they are presumably more enlightened than the majority, or merely because their biasses are different, form the natural counterpoise.

This is the chief practical idea of Mr. Lorimer's work; and there must be something in it apparently well adapted to the needs of the present time, since, new as it is in speculation, it has occurred almost simultaneously to three writers of very different schools, each of them probably—the last certainly—without any knowledge of the other two: Mr. Lorimer, Lord Robert Cecil (in the *Oxford Essays*),[†] and the author of the present article, in a pamphlet entitled *Thoughts on Parliamentary Reform*.[‡] It is a suggestion

[*Lorimer, *Political Progress not Necessarily Democratic*, pp. 130–1.]

*He seems disposed to exclude women (see note to p. 213), not because he wishes them to have no influence, but because he thinks their indirect influence sufficient. We shall see that if he applied this standard of judgment in all cases, it would upset his whole theory.

[†"The Theories of Parliamentary Reform," in *Oxford Essays*, 4 vols. (London: Parker, 1855–58), Vol. IV, pp. 51–79.]

[‡See above, pp. 311–39.]

which deserves, as well as requires, unprejudiced consideration. Its merit is, that it affords a basis of settlement which can be, with their eyes open, accepted by both parties. All arguments grounded on probable dangers fall dead and meaningless on the minds of those who have the physical force. Very few individuals, and no classes, ever were withheld from seeking power for themselves, by predictions of the bad use they would make of it. It is their sense of justice that must be appealed to, and to do that with effect, what is proposed must be visibly just. No one who has begun to concern himself about politics will think it just that his opinions and wishes should be counted for nothing at all, in matters in which his greatest interests are involved. Such a political arrangement, considered as final, is revolting both to the universal conscience, and to the sense of dignity which it is desirable to encourage in every human being. But it is a very different thing when the question is between, not some influence and none, but a greater influence and a less. Between something and nothing, the ratio, morally and mathematically, is infinite; between less and more, it is finite and appreciable. No one feels insulted and injured by the admission that those who are jointly interested with himself, and more capable, ought to have greater individual weight in the common deliberations.

But, proportional to the value of the principle, would be the mischief of applying it, misunderstood and perverted from its purpose. Its excellence is, that while it fulfils the demands of expediency, it approves itself to the natural sense of justice. If plural voting were made to depend on conditions which cannot possibly commend themselves to the conscience of the majority; if, as Lord Robert Cecil proposes, the additional votes were given, not to the educated as such, but to mere riches, as measured by taxation;[*] the whole scheme would be looked upon as nothing but a trick for rendering the concession of the suffrage nugatory: it would be for ever, or for a long period, discredited and depopularized, and would lose all its chances of serving as a permanent barrier against the class-legislation of manual labourers. What justice can any one be expected to see in his having only one vote, while others have more than one, not because he has less knowledge and ability, but because he is less fortunate? Lord R. Cecil, and those who agree with him, lay great stress upon the analogy of a joint-stock company, in which every shareholder has a number of votes bearing some proportion to the number of shares belonging to him.[†] As if the business of government, like that of a mercantile association, were concerned only with property! The directors of a company exist as such, solely to administer its capital, and have no power of causing to the subscribers either good or harm, except through the interest they possess in that. But the stake which an individual

[*See "Theories of Parliamentary Reform," pp. 61ff.]
[†See *ibid*., p. 63.]

has in good government is far other than his κτησίδιον*—nothing less than his entire earthly welfare, in soul, body, and mind. The government to which he is subject has power over all his sources of happiness, and can inflict on him a thousand forms of intolerable misery. Even as regards property, the stake of the day labourer is not measured by the little he calls his own, but by the bond that unites his interest, no less than that of the rich, with the general security of property; which could not be impaired without rendering his means of employment and subsistence more scanty and precarious.

Our objections to Lord Robert Cecil apply in some degree to Mr. Lorimer, though the latter considers riches not as a title to power in themselves, but as an evidence of education; and would give plurality of votes not to property alone, but to all reasonable presumptions of superior intelligence. Mr. Lorimer has, however, a general theory of government, from which this and most of his other practical recommendations are presented as corollaries. He thinks that the constitution of the Legislature should be an exact mirror of the existing constitution of society. He would have the national polity recognise, on the one hand, the just claims, together with the intrinsic powers, of man as man; but also, on the other, all *de facto* social inequalities. He is of opinion that each person should have an amount of power assigned to him by political institutions, as nearly identical as the imperfection of human arrangements will admit, with the influence he actually exercises:

The sum of *influences* should stand over against the sum of *individual senti-ments*, and the institutions of the State should be the expression of the former, not of the latter. As regards the individual, whatever may be the amount of in-fluence which belongs to his character in society generally, whether it be greater or less than that of a simple human unit, to the benefit of that influence in regu-lating the public and private laws of the country, and to nothing more, is he en-titled. If the voice of one man be ten times as powerful as that of another, then he contributes ten times as much to swell that general voice, of which voice the laws are the articulate utterance. But as the State can never take cognizance of individual importance directly, the principle of classification becomes indispens-able, [&c.] (Pp. 17–18.)

The perfection of social organization in all its forms, from the simplest to the most complex, will be in direct proportion to the completeness with which it recognises the inequalities which exist among the members of the society with which it deals. (P. 49.)

The office of the suffrage is to give political expression to the social powers actually existing in the community. (P. 226.)

And more fully as follows:

*Epictetus. [See *Discourses*, trans. W. A. Oldfather, 2 vols. (London: Heine-mann; New York: Putnam's Sons, 1926, 1928), Vol. I, p. 8 (I.i.10), and Vol. II, p. 180 (III.xxiii.32).]

The partial character of the representation which is secured by the universal equal suffrage, and its consequent inadequacy to satisfy the conditions of the suffrage as we have defined them, comes out perhaps most clearly of all when we consider that, in addition to depriving some classes of the political influence corresponding to their social position, and thus to a certain extent disfranchising them, it deprives every individual, to whatever class he may belong, of the whole direct political influence which corresponds to the social influence which he has acquired. A and B, at the age of twenty-one we shall say, are both fairly represented by the manhood suffrage. At the age of forty, by a life of virtuous effort, A has merited and obtained the consideration of his fellow citizens; and his case will be no unusual one if his influence, whether for good or evil, has increased tenfold. In his person, consequently, now centre the *pouvoirs de fait* to ten times the extent to which they belonged to him at the former period of his life. B, on the contrary, differs from what he was, only in having lost the *potentiality* of influence, which renders every man important at the commencement of his career. He has done and suffered nothing to forfeit his public rights. He is neither a criminal, a lunatic, nor a pauper; and the influences of a human unit still are his. This, however, is but one-tenth of that which now belongs to A, and a suffrage which establishes an equality between these two individuals consequently leaves nine-tenths of A's actual social influence unrepresented. Can it be said of such a suffrage that it actually translates social into political power? (P. 227.)

Now this theory, as it seems to us, is not only erroneous, but involves some confusion of ideas. If by the social influence of A we are to understand (as is the most obvious interpretation) the power he exercises over the convictions and inclinations of others through the affection with which he inspires them, or the high opinion they entertain of him, all this influence he will possess under equal and universal suffrage. Indeed, under no suffrage *but* that which is equal and universal, *can* his political influence be exactly co-extensive with his moral influence, measured by the number of persons who look up to his judgment, and are willing to accept him as their leader. If besides this influence, supposed to be ten times that of B, he has also ten votes of his own to B's one, the effect is not, as Mr. Lorimer professes, to recognise, but to double, A's superiority of importance. It is for the very opposite reason to Mr. Lorimer's, that the third writer to whom we have referred[*] made the suggestion of giving a number of votes proportional to degree of education, as indicated by whatever tests, other than that of wealth, may be the most truly discriminative. He proposed it, not because educated persons have already a greater influence, but because, though they *b*ought*b* to have that influence, yet without some such provision they possibly might *not*.

In so far, on the other hand, as the existing social influences contemplated by Mr. Lorimer include the power which one person exercises over others, not through his personal superiority, but his social status, and above all, that

[*I.e., Mill himself; see pp. 353 and 324–8 above.]
*b-b*591   *ought*

which is exercised not through their spontaneous feelings, but their personal interests, the doctrine is liable to still graver objections. These influences are of society's own making, and it cannot be necessary that society should bend to forces created by itself, as it does to laws of nature over which it has no control. If a peer, simply by being a peer, exercises social influence, it is a vicious circle to maintain that the Constitution ought for that reason to give him additional political influence, when the peerage and its influences only exist at all because the Constitution wills it. Before recognising and doubling this influence, there is a preliminary question to be settled—whether the influence is beneficial. Even in the case of influences not wholly the creation of law, but which can be increased or diminished by it, such as those of wealth, it is indispensable to consider whether they are salutary influences; and if so, to what degree; since if they exist beyond the degree which is salutary, it may be a merit and not a fault in the system of suffrage that by taking no notice of these influences, it not only avoids strengthening, but does something towards weakening them. For though we concede to Mr. Lorimer that a Government cannot for long together be better than the collective mind of the community, it can do a great deal to uphold or to undermine the social influences which either pervert or improve the collective mind.

We have spoken of Mr. Lorimer's theory as he himself enunciates it; not precisely as he applies it, for he is often willing that in apportioning political influences according to social influence, the indirect political influence already possessed should be counted as part. We wonder he does not see, that for the purposes of the present question it is the whole. Under a limited suffrage, indeed, it is within possibility that persons or classes may possess a social influence not represented by any corresponding political one: but under equal and universal suffrage this is impossible; all social influences tell politically at their full value, except indeed those with which the ballot would interfere; and if Mr. Lorimer thinks that these ought not to be interfered with, he should be an enemy to the ballot, but not to equal and universal suffrage. We assume in this argument, that the suffrage is accompanied with such auxiliary arrangements as may prevent the virtual disfranchisement of minorities; for while this disfranchisement continues to exist as at present, the suffrage would not be really equal and universal, whatever it might be called.

There is much more that we would gladly notice in Mr. Lorimer's book, which contains many shrewd remarks, and some noble thoughts and aspirations, in the chapters entitled "By what means may the public spirit be influenced and directed?" "Of the leaders of thought, scientific and popular;" "Of the universal duty of active-mindedness," and elsewhere. He has also a negative merit, in our eyes not inconsiderable: he does not give in to the sophistical doctrine of a representation of interests. This theory owes all its plausibility to being mistaken for a principle from which it is totally distinct. As regards interests in themselves, whenever not identical with the general interest, the less they are represented the better. What is wanted is a representation, not of men's differences of interest, but of the differences in their intellectual points of view. Shipowners are to be desired in Parliament, because they can instruct us about ships, not because they are interested in having protecting duties. We want from a lawyer in Parliament his legal knowledge, not his professional interest in the expensiveness and unintelligibility of the law.

Commending Mr. Lorimer's treatise to the attention of students in politics, we pass to a book[*] in our opinion of far superior value: in which, for the first time, a way is really shown to that reconciliation and simultaneous recognition of the best principles and ends of rival theories, which the generality of political writers have despaired of, which Mr. Lorimer aims at, but which Mr. Hare actually realizes, and has not only illuminated it with the light of an advanced political philosophy, but embodied it in a draft of an Act of Parliament, prepared with the hand of a master in the difficult art of practical legislation.

ᶜThough Mr. Hare has delivered an opinion—and generally, in our judgment, a wise one—on nearly all the questions at present in issue connected with representative government; the originality of his plan, as well as most of the effects to be expected from it, turn on the development which he has given to what is commonly called the Representation of Minorities. He has raised this principle to an importance and dignity which no previous thinker had ascribed to it. As conceived by him, it should be called the real, instead of nominal, representation of every individual elector.

That minorities in the nation *ought* in principle, if it be possible, to be represented by corresponding minorities in the legislative assembly, is a necessary consequence from all premises on which any representation at all can be defended. In a deliberative assembly the minority must perforce give way, because the decision must be either aye or no; but it is not so in choosing those who are to form the deliberative body: *that* ought to be the express image of the wishes of the nation, whether divided or unanimous, in the designation of those by whose united councils it will be ruled; and any section of opinion which is unanimous within itself, ought to be able, in due proportion to the rest, to contribute its elements towards the collective deliberation. At present, if three-fifths of the electors vote for one person

[*Thomas Hare, *A Treatise on the Election of Representatives.*]

ᶜ⁻ᶜ370   [*printed as a supplement to the 2nd pamphlet edition of* Thoughts on Parliamentary Reform; *cf.* 339ᵏ above]

and two-fifths for another, every individual of the two-fifths is, for the purposes of that election, as if he did not exist: his intelligence, his preference,
have gone for nothing in the composition of the Parliament. Whatever was
the object designed by the Constitution in giving him a vote, that object, at
least on the present occasion, has not been fulfilled: and if he can be reconciled to his position, it must be by the consideration that some other time
he may be one of a majority, and another set of persons instead of himself
may be reduced to ciphers: just as, before a regular government had been
established, a man might have consoled himself for being robbed, by the
hope that another time he might be able to rob some one else. But this compensation, however gratifying, will be of no avail to him if he is everywhere
overmatched; and the same may be said of the elector who is habitually
outvoted.

Of late years several modes have been suggested of giving an effective
voice to a minority; by limiting each elector to fewer votes than the number
of members to be elected, or allowing him to concentrate all his votes on
the same candidate. These various schemes are praiseworthy so far as they
go, but they attain the object very imperfectly. All plans for dividing a merely
local representation in unequal ratios, are limited by the small number of
members which can be, and the still smaller which ought to be, assigned to
any one constituency. There are considerable objections to the election even
of so many as three by every constituent body. This, however, under present
arrangements, is the smallest number which would admit of any representation of a minority; and in this case the minority must amount to at least a
third of the whole. All smaller minorities would continue, as at present, to
be disfranchised; and in a minority of a third, the whole number must unite
in voting for the same candidate. There may therefore be a minority within
the minority who have sacrificed their individual preference, and from
whose vote nothing can with certainty be concluded but that they dislike
less the candidate they voted for, than they do the rival candidate.*

Mr. Hare offers an outlet from this difficulty. The object being that the
suffrages of those who are in a minority locally, should tell in proportion to
their number on the composition of the Parliament; since this is *all* that is
required, why should it be imperative that their votes should be received
only for some one who is a *local* candidate? Why might they not give their
suffrage to any one who is a candidate anywhere, their number of votes
being added to those which he may obtain elsewhere? Suppose that a com-

*These semi-dissentients might even amount to a majority of the minority;
for (as Mr. Hare remarks) if fifty persons agree to combine their strength, who,
left to themselves, would have divided their votes among ten candidates, six of
the fifty may impose their candidate on all the rest, though perhaps only relatively
preferred by them.

parison between the number of members of the House and of registered electors in the kingdom, gives a quotient of 2000 as the number of electors per member, on an average of the whole country (which, according to Mr. Hare's calculation, ^{d}would be^d not far from the fact, if the existing electoral body ^{e}were^e augmented by 200,000): why should not any candidate, who can obtain 2000 suffrages in the whole kingdom, be returned to Parliament? By the supposition, 2000 persons are sufficient to return a member; and there are 2000 who unanimously desire to have him for their representative. Their claim to be represented surely does not depend on their all residing in the same place. Since one member can be given to every 2000, the most just mode of arrangement and distribution must evidently be, to give the member to 2000 electors who have voted for him, rather than to 2000 some of whom have voted against him. We should then be assured that every member of the House has been wished for by 2000 of the electoral body; while in the other case, even if all the electors have voted, he may possibly have been wished for by no more than a thousand and one.

This arrangement provides for all the difficulties involved in representation of minorities. The smallest minority obtains an influence proportioned to its numbers; the largest obtains no more. The representation becomes, what under no other system it can be, really equal. Every member of ^{f}parliament^f is the representative of an unanimous constituency. No one is represented, or rather misrepresented, by a member whom he has voted against. Every elector in the kingdom is represented by the candidate he most prefers, if as many persons in the whole extent of the country are found to agree with him, as come up to the number entitled to a representive.

To enable the scheme to work in the manner intended, a second and subsidiary expedient is necessary. A candidate who enjoys a wide-spread popularity, if votes are received for him everywhere, will often be voted for by many times the number of persons forming the quota entitled to a member. If this multitude of votes were all counted for his return, the number of members required to constitute the House would not be obtained; while the many thousand votes given for these favourite characters, will have had no more influence than the simple 2000 given for the least popular candidate who is returned at all. To obviate this, Mr. Hare proposes that no more than 2000 votes be counted for any one; that whoever has obtained that number be declared duly elected, and the remainder of his votes be set free to be given to another. For this purpose (while no one's vote would be counted for more than one candidate) voters should make a practice of putting into their voting papers a second name, and as many other names

d–d591,592   is
e–e591,592   is supposed to be
f–f591,592   Parliament

as they like, in the order of their preference, of persons for whom they are willing to vote in case their vote is not needed for the one who stands first in their list. Suppose that 8000 electors give their first vote to the same candidate. Only 2000 of these (that being the supposed amount of the electoral quota) will be counted for his return. We will not discuss *which* 2000 should be chosen out of the 8000, as this is the solitary point we have yet discovered, in which Mr. Hare's arrangements appear to us susceptible of improvement. The 2000, on whatever principle selected, form the constituency whom this candidate will represent. His name will then be cancelled in the remaining 6000 papers, each of which will be counted as a vote for the person next in order who is named in them, unless he also shall have been already returned by other votes—and so on. In this manner the 8000 electors who prefer A. B. will obtain from among the list of persons by whom they have declared their willingness to be represented, the full complement of four members due to them, A. B. being one; or will have exerted an amount of influence equal to the return of four members, in the election of some greater number.

Of this breadth, clearness, and simplicity are the principles of the plan. Indeed, if Mr. Hare had stopped here, the chief difficulty he would have had to encounter would have been the doubt whether a scheme so theoretically perfect could be brought into practical operation. But since he has taken the trouble to point out, even to the minutest detail, the mode in which the plan can be executed, and has drawn up in all legal form the statute necessary to give it effect, the danger now is lest the inevitable prominence of the mechanical arrangements should confuse the mind of a mere cursory reader, and enable the scheme to be represented as too complex and subtle to be workable. Such a notion would be extremely erroneous. Mr. Hare's draft of a Bill is ten times more simple and intelligible than the Reform Act, or almost any other Act of Parliament which deals with a great subject. Its details are worked out with infinite care and sagacity, and accompanied with an explanatory comment which must satisfy any one not only of the possibility, but the facility of carrying them into effect. Seldom has it happened that a great political idea could be realized by such easy and simple machinery; and there is not a serious objection, nor a genuine difficulty, of however slight a nature, which will not, we think, be found to have been foreseen and met.

That these arrangements are just and reasonable, and afford a complete remedy for an evil for which none but very imperfect palliatives were supposed to be attainable, is obvious almost at first sight. But it was not till after mature reflection, and diligent study of Mr. Hare's admirable exposition, that we fully realized the greatness of the incidental benefits, not at first apparent, which would result from the substitution of personal instead of exclusively local representation.

In the first place, it would prodigiously improve the *personnel* of the national representation. At present, were they ever so desirous, a great majority of the most distinguished men in the country have little or no chance of being elected anywhere as members of the House of Commons. The admirers, and those who would be the supporters, of a person whose claims rest on acknowledged personal merit, are generally dispersed throughout the country, while there is no one place in which his influence would not be far outweighed by that of some local grandee, or *notabilité de clocher*, who neither has, nor deserves to have, the smallest influence anywhere else. If a man of talents and virtue could count as votes for his return all electors in any part of the kingdom who would like to be represented by him, every such person who is well known to the public would have a probable chance; and under this encouragement nearly all of them, whose position and circumstances were compatible with Parliamentary duties, might be willing to offer themselves to the electors. Those voters who did not like either of the local candidates, or who believed that one whom they did not like was sure to prevail against them, would have all the available intellectual strength of the country from whom to select the recipient of their otherwise wasted vote. An assembly thus chosen would contain the *élite* of the nation.

Nor must it be supposed that only the minorities, or weaker parties in the localities, would give themselves a wider range of choice, to acquire, by combining with one another, their just share in the representation. The majorities also would be brought under inducements to make a more careful choice. There are few things more discreditable to the country than the mode in which the member for a borough, when not the mere creature of the local influences, is generally selected. What do the body of those who give him their suffrages usually know of him? Unless in the case of those who live among them, and are known to them privately, nothing at all, except that he is of the right political party; that he calls himself the Liberal or the Conservative candidate. But there are Liberal and Conservative candidates of all qualities; and what are the qualifications looked for by the attorney, the ᵍparliamentaryᵍ agent, or the half-dozen local leaders, who bring down the candidate from London? What they seek for is a man with money, and willing to spend it—if of any social rank, so much the better—and who will make professions on some subjects, and be silent on others, according to what they tell him is required by the local opinion. Whatever may be his worth, or want of worth, in other respects, the voters who are on the same side in politics vote for him *en masse*: whether he is to their taste or not, they cannot, by proposing another candidate, divide the party; they must either bring him in, or lose their votes, and give a victory to the other side. Under Mr. Hare's plan things would be far otherwise. The candidate of the party

ᵍ⁻ᵍ59¹,592   Parliamentary

which is strong enough to carry its nominee would still, no doubt, be generally selected by the local leaders; when many persons are to be brought to act together, some must take the initiative. But the position and interest of the leaders would be much changed. They could no longer count upon bringing up the whole strength of the party, to return any professed Liberal or Conservative who would make it worth their while. An elector even of their own party, who was dissatisfied with the candidate offered him, would not then be obliged to vote for that candidate or remain unrepresented. He would have the option of contributing to give his country, or his party, the benefit of a better representative elsewhere; and his leaders would be under the necessity of offering him some one whom he would consider creditable, to be secure of his vote. It is probable that a competition would spring up among constituencies for the most creditable candidates, and that the stronger party in every locality (local influences apart) would be anxious to bring forward the ablest and most distinguished men on their own side, that they might be sure of uniting the whole of their local strength, and have a chance of being reinforced by stray votes from other parts of the country.

A member who had already served in Parliament with any distinction, would under this system be almost sure of his re-election. At present the first man in the *h*house*h* may be thrown out of Parliament precisely when most wanted, and may be kept out for several years, from no fault of his own, but because a change has taken place in the local balance of parties, or because he has voted against the prejudices or local interests of some influential portion of his constituents. Under Mr. Hare's system, if he has not deserved to be thrown out, he will be nearly certain to obtain votes from other places, sufficient, with his local strength, to make up the quota of 2000 (or whatever the number may be) necessary for his return to Parliament.

The considerations on which we have hitherto dwelt are independent of any possible changes in the composition of the electoral body. But the bearing of Mr. Hare's proposals on the question of extending the suffrage, is of the very greatest importance. Why is nearly the whole educated class united in uncompromising hostility to a purely democratic suffrage? Not so much because it would make the most numerous class, that of manual labourers, the *strongest* power; *that* many of the educated class would think only just. It is because it would make them the *sole* power; because in every constituency the votes of that class would swamp and politically annihilate all other members of the community taken together; would put them in the same position, as regards Parliament, in which the labouring classes are now, without the same imposing physical strength out of doors; and would produce (or would be in danger of producing) a Legislature reflecting exclusively the opinions and preferences of the most ignorant class, with no member

*h–h*591 House

of any higher standard to compare and confront themselves with, except such as may have stripped themselves of their superiority by conforming to the prejudices of their supporters. But if the greater number could obtain their share of political power without silencing the smaller number; if the educated and the propertied classes could still be represented, though by a minority, in the House; there would not, in the minds of many of those classes, be the same insuperable objection to the political preponderance of the majority. Represented as *that* minority would be likely then to be, by the ablest heads and noblest hearts in the nation, their representatives would probably acquire considerable personal ascendancy over the other section of the House; especially as the majorities would have been under the inducements already spoken of to get themselves represented by the most intelligent and morally recommendable persons they could find. The cause of the minority would be likely to be supported with such consummate skill, and such a weight of moral authority, as might prove a sufficient balance to the superiority of numbers on the other side, and enable the opinions of the higher and middle classes to prevail when they were right, even in an assembly of which the majority had been chosen by the poor. We have not the smallest wish that they should prevail when they were wrong, as no doubt they often would be. So much confidence, indeed, have we in the *moral* efficacy of such a representation of minorities as Mr. Hare's scheme would give, that we should not despair of its rendering ultimately unnecessary the system, which in principle we have advocated, of plural voting, an expedient not included in Mr. Hare's plan, though perfectly compatible with it.

Meanwhile, however, and so long as the working classes are not admitted to the suffrage so indiscriminately as to outnumber the other electors, those classes have a most direct interest in the due representation of minorities, since in numerous cases they would themselves be in a position to benefit by it. There is great difficulty, under the present machinery, in measuring out influence to the working classes, so as to be just to them without being unjust to every one else. They are not represented even as a class, unless they are the majority of the constituency, and if they are, nobody else is represented. A strong sense of the importance of their obtaining, by whatever means, a certain number of members who actually represent *them*, has led an intelligent writer, Mr. Bagehot, to propose so violent a remedy as that of giving up the representation of the large towns to day-labourers, by establishing, in them, equal and universal suffrage, thereby disfranchising the higher and middle classes of those places, who comprise the majority of the most intellectual persons in the kingdom.[*] All this Mr. Hare's plan

[*See Walter Bagehot, *Parliamentary Reform* (London: Chapman and Hall, [1859]), pp. 34ff.]

*i-i*591,592   the

would supersede. By admitting the working classes into the constituencies generally, in such numbers as to constitute a large minority therein, they would be enabled to return all their leaders, and a considerable number of other members, without swamping, or even outnumbering, the rest of the electors. They would be relieved from the mischievous alternative of all or none. They would have the exact amount of influence in the composition of Parliament which it was the intention of the Legislature to give them; whereas on the present system the effects of any extension of the suffrage would be so entirely uncertain, that to be sure of not giving them more than Parliament is willing to allow, it would be thought necessary to give much less than is fairly allowable.

Consider next the check which would be given to bribery and intimidation in the return of members to Parliament. Who, by bribery and intimidation, could get together 2000 electors from a hundred different parts of the country? Intimidation would have no means of acting over so large a surface; and bribery requires secresy, and an organized machinery, which can only be brought into play within narrow local limits. Where would then be the advantage of bribing or coercing the 200 or 300 electors of a small borough? They could not of themselves make up the quota, and nobody could know what part of the country the remaining 1700 or 1800 suffrages might come from. In places so large as to afford the number of 2000 electors, bribery or intimidation would have the same chances as at present. But it is not in such places that, even now, these malpractices are successful. As regards bribery (Mr. Hare truly remarks), the chief cause of it is, that in a closely contested election certain votes are indispensable: the side which cannot secure those particular votes is sure to be defeated. But under Mr. Hare's plan no vote would be indispensable. A vote from any other part of the country would serve the purpose as well; and a candidate might be in a minority at the particular place, and yet be returned.

Those who demand equal electoral districts should strenuously support Mr. Hare's plan; for it fulfils, in a far preferable manner, their professed purposes. In his system all the constituencies are equal, and all unanimous. Disfranchisement becomes unnecessary, for every place is represented in the ratio, and no place in more than the ratio, due to its number of electors. The endless disputations, the artful manipulation and elaborate ponderation of interests, to endeavour to make sure (which can never really be done) that there shall always be places enough returning persons of certain descriptions, may all now be dispensed with. Every description of persons, every class, every so-called interest, will be sure of exactly the amount of representation it is entitled to. The system, moreover, is self-adjusting: there would not be need of an Act of Parliament once in every quarter of a century to readjust the representation. Every year the whole number of registered electors would be ascertained, and the quota necessary for returning a member declared: this done, the rest of the machinery would work of itself. There need be no grouping of boroughs; the boroughs and the electors inhabiting them would spontaneously group themselves. Nor need there be any limit to the number of places returning members. Mr. Hare would have any town or district, or any corporate body (an inn of court, for example), permitted to call itself a Parliamentary constituency, if it chose. This would excite, he thinks, a salutary emulation to elect the best men; and small bodies are the most likely to bring forward, from personal knowledge, men of merit not yet generally known. Of course, no constituency would have a member to itself, unless it contained the quota of electors. If it were a small body, the member who might be returned for it would be the representative of many other electors, and perhaps of other places or bodies; but he would not be called the member for any place or body in which he had not the local majority. Nor need it be apprehended that by the greater play given to influences of a wider and more national character, local influences would be deprived of any weight which justly belongs to them. Local influences would be safe in the hands of the local majority, through whom alone those influences are effective at present. The power which would be called into action for national purposes, under motives of a national character, is a power now wasted and thrown away. The instrument by which larger and higher elements would be brought into the arena of public affairs, would be mainly the votes which are now virtual nonentities.

But in no way would the effects of this masterly contrivance be more unspeakably beneficial, than in raising the tone of the whole political morality of the country. A representative would be under nothing like the same temptation to gain or keep his seat by time-serving arts, and sacrifices of his convictions to the local or class prejudices and interests of any given set of electors. Unless the prejudice was universal in the nation, a spirited resistance would cause his name to be inscribed in the voting-papers of some electors in almost every place in which it was heard of. The elevating effect on the minds of the electors themselves would be still more valuable. Hardly anything within the scope of possible attainment would do so much to make the voting for a member of Parliament be felt as a moral act, involving a real responsibility. Every elector's interest in his representative would be at the highest pitch. The member would be the elector's own representative, not chosen for him, but by him. Instead of having been chosen, perhaps *against* him, by electors of sentiments the remotest possible from his, he will not even have been accepted by him as a compromise; he is the man whom the elector has really preferred. No longer required to choose between two or some small number of candidates, much alike probably in all respects except the party banner they carry, and seldom having any strong public recommendation *but* that, to the suffrage of any one who votes for them; the elector would have the opportunity, if he chose, of tendering his vote for the ablest and best man in the Empire who is willing to serve. Is not this a situation to rouse a moral feeling in any one, who has sufficient conscience belonging to him to have any of it to bestow on the performance of a public duty? It is the seeming insignificance of men's individual acts that deadens their consciences respecting them. The self-deluding sophistry of indolence or indifference operates by "What does it matter?" Place before any one a high object; show him that he can individually do something to promote that object; and if there is a spark of virtue in the man, it will be kindled into a glow. To the new feeling of duty would be added a pride in making a good choice—a desire to connect himself as a constituent with some one who is an honour to the nation—to be known to him and to the world as one who has voluntarily sought him out to give him his vote. Mr. Hare, when he reaches this part of his subject, rises into a noble enthusiasm, which is irresistibly attractive when combined, as it is in him, with a sober and sagacious perception of the relation between means and ends, and a far-sighted circumspection in guarding his arrangements against all possibilities of miscarriage and abuse.

   With this exalted sense of the moral responsibility of an elector, Mr. Hare is, as might be expected, an enemy to the ballot.* His plan requires voting papers, but he would have them signed by the elector, and delivered personally "by every voter at his proper polling-place" [pp. 144–5]; saving the case of necessary absence, when arrangements are suggested (p. 318) for transmitting his voting paper, with proper evidence of his identity, to a central office. There are serious objections to voting papers under the existing system, of which the strongest is the facilities and efficacy they would give to undue influences; since the act of subservience would be done in the privacy of home, where the eye of the public would be absent, but the hand of the briber, or the *vultus instantis tyranni*, might and would be present. The system of personal representation does so much in other respects to weaken the inducements to the exercise of the undue influences, that it can afford to leave them such advantages as voting papers would give. But the evil is a real, and, in any system but Mr. Hare's, a conclusive objection.
   On many other points in the theory and practice of representation Mr. Hare's opinions are valuable, but not in the same degree original. On some minor questions he has not, perhaps, bestowed the same maturity of meditation as on the one which is peculiarly his own. He would remove all disqualifications for membership (pp. 136ff.). Neither clergymen, nor judicial officers, nor persons in official employment, should in his opinion be excluded

   *Pp. 168ff.

from Parliament. If attendance in the House is inconsistent with a function-ary's official duties, it should be left (he thinks) to the functionary's superiors to remove him. In some of these cases Mr. Hare may be in the right, but he takes no notice of the reasons which are commonly considered to justify the exclusion: in the case of clergymen and of judges, the importance of their not being thought to be political partisans; in that of subordinates in Government offices, a more cogent reason. These officers are kept out of Parliament, that their appointments may not be the wages of Parliamentary support. Not so much for fear of corrupting Parliament, though that also deserves to be considered; but as the sole means of keeping up a high stan-dard of qualifications in the officers themselves. The whole efficiency of the public service depends on the personal qualities of a few individuals, whom the public never see, and hardly ever hear of. Their places, if allowed to be held by members of Parliament, would often be given to political tools, who would not then have capable prompters under them on whom to rely; and by the time they had learnt their business, if they ever did learn it, they would be changed, to give their places to others, as officials who can sit in Parliament now are, at every change of ministry.

We heartily join in Mr. Hare's condemnation of the proposal for payment of members of Parliament. "The constant meddling of a body of men, paid for making laws, and acting under the notion that they are bound to do some-thing for their salaries, would in this country be intolerable" (p. 122). [ik]Moreover, as Mr. Lorimer remarks (p. 169)[k], by creating a pecuniary [l]"inducement to persons of the lowest class to devote themselves to public affairs, the calling of the demagogue would be formally inaugurated."[l] Noth-ing is more to be deprecated than making it the private interest of a number of active persons to urge the form of government in the direction of its natural perversion. The indications which either a multitude or an individual can give, when merely left to their own weaknesses, afford but a faint idea of what those weaknesses would become when played upon by a thousand flat-terers. If there were six hundred and fifty-eight places, of certain, however moderate, emolument, to be gained by persuading the multitude that igno-rance is as good as knowledge, and better, it is terrible odds that they would believe and act upon the lesson.[j] The objection, however, to the payment of members, as Mr. Hare remarks, is chiefly applicable to payment from the public purse. If a person who cannot give his time to Parliament without losing his means of subsistence, is thought so highly qualified for it by his supporters as to be provided by them with the necessary income at their own

[j-j] *[quoted in* Considerations on Representative Government; *cf.* 499n *below]*
[k-k]611,612,65   As Mr. Lorimer remarks
[l-l]611,612,65   *[not in quotation marks]*

expense,—this sort of *ᵐ*payment*ᵐ* of a member of Parliament may be equally useful and honourable; and of this resource it is open even to the working classes to avail themselves. They are perfectly capable of supporting their Parliamentary representatives, as they already do the managers of their trade societies.

Though Mr. Hare is strongly averse to this "point of the Charter," he would relieve candidates from the heavy burthen of election expenses, except a payment of fifty pounds, which he would require from each on declaring himself a candidate, "to prevent any trifling or idle experiment, whereby the lists of candidates might be encumbered with the names of persons who can have no rational expectation of being usefully placed in nomination." [P. 126.]

This preliminary payment should

*ⁿ*Exonerate*ⁿ* the candidate from all liability in respect of any further expenses, except such as he may voluntarily incur. Such voluntary expenses will of course, as now, vary according to the peculiar circumstances of every candidate. They will probably be in the inverse ratio of his political eminence and distinction. Men of high character and reputation, and those whose political conduct and discretion have been tested and proved by experience, would stand in need of no more than that announcement of their names which the gazetted list would publish. A man of less distinction might require something more; possibly the charges of a public meeting, and of an advertisement or printed address, declaring his general views on political questions. This, perhaps, would be less necessary if the candidate were a person of any mark in literature or science, and had in his previous career become known to the public. Those who would probably be compelled to spend most, would be the persons who have the least to recommend them besides their money. (Pp. 126–7.)

With regard to the suffrage, Mr. Hare does not deliver a decided opinion as to the most proper test of capacity, but lays down the broad principle, that it should be

*ᵒ*One*ᵒ* which will exclude no man of ordinary industry and skill in his calling, and ordinary prudence and self-denial in his conduct. It cannot be necessary that the suffrage should be given to every youth as soon as he is out of his apprenticeship: it is not necessary that it should be given without regard to property, or to position, as the head of a family, or to participation in the burdens of citizenship, at least to one in early manhood, whilst the character is in process of formation, and the pleasures and anticipations of life exercise a strong influence on his conduct, and divert him from more serious thought on subjects not directly affecting his own career. . . . The qualification, however, should be accessible to every man when he acquires a home, and settles to the line of occupation for which the preparatory course of his earlier years has fitted him. (P. 309.)

*m–m*591,592 'payment'
*n–n*Source,591,592 exonerate
*o–o*Source,591,592 one

This general doctrine is sufficiently liberal to satisfy any one; but when Mr. Hare (p. 313) considers the present 10*l.* qualification in the large towns, and one varying from that to 6*l.* in the smaller towns and in the counties, to be a standard "so low that it is within the reach of every well-conducted man who is not a victim of some extraordinary misfortune, forming an exception to the general lot" [p. 313], we fear statistics will not bear him out. An educational test he deems inapplicable (p. 310), because "it would be next to impossible to apply" such a test "to every individual of a multitude" (not true of the simple test of writing and arithmetic, which might with ease be applied to every elector at the registry); because "it may exclude men of much practical knowledge and good sense" (we greatly question the knowledge and good sense, as applicable to politics, of any one who has not the power and habit of reading); and finally, because "it would operate severely on those who were more advanced in life, and to whom elementary tests are less suitable." [Pp. 310–11.] The rights of *existing* electors should certainly be reserved; but in the case of any others, the supposed hardship, being merely that of not being entrusted with duties they are not fit for, is no subject for complaint.

Mr. Hare passes an unqualified and most just condemnation on the exclusion of women from the suffrage:

In all cases where a woman is *sui juris*, occupying a house or tenement, or possessed of a freehold, or is otherwise in a position which, in the case of a male, would amount to a qualification, there is no sound reason for excluding her from the parliamentary franchise. The exclusion is probably a remnant of the feudal law, and is not in harmony with the other civil institutions of the country. There would be great propriety in celebrating a reign which has been productive of so much moral benefit, by the abolition of an anomaly which is so entirely without any justifiable foundation. (P. 320.)

Such is this remarkable book: of the contents of which we have been compelled to leave a great portion unnoticed, including the simple arrangements by which the system of voting is adapted to the case of single elections, and of municipalities. In our brief exposition we have given a much more adequate idea of Mr. Hare's specific proposals, than of the instructive and impressive discussions by which he introduces them. Yet if the book made no practical suggestions whatever, and had no value but that of the principles it enforces, it would still deserve a high rank among manuals of political thought. We trust it will be widely read, and we are convinced that, by competent thinkers, the system it embodies will be recognised as alone just in principle, as one of the greatest of all practical improvements, and as the most efficient possible safeguard of further Parliamentary Reform.[c]

CONSIDERATIONS ON REPRESENTATIVE GOVERNMENT

1861

EDITOR'S NOTE

3rd ed. London: Longman, Green, Longman, Roberts & Green, 1865. Reprinted from the 2nd ed. (London: Parker, Son, and Bourn, 1861), and 1st ed. (London: Parker, Son, and Bourn, 1861). Identified in JSM's bibliography as "'Considerations on Representative Government' an 8vo Volume, published in April 1861" (MacMinn, 93). There are no corrections or emendations in the Somerville College Library copies of the 1st, 2nd, and People's Editions.

For a discussion of the composition of the work, see the Textual Introduction, lxxxv–lxxxvii above.

The text below, that of the 3rd edition (the last in JSM's lifetime), has been collated with those of the 2nd, 1st, and People's editions. In the footnoted variants, the 3rd edition is indicated by "65", the 2nd by "61²", and the 1st by "61¹". JSM quotes from his "Recent Writers on Reform" (see 499n) and *Thoughts on Parliamentary Reform* (see 491–5, 495n–496n, 496–7, and 498–9); the changes are indicated as variants, in which "59¹" indicates "Recent Writers on Reform," and "59²" indicates *Thoughts on Parliamentary Reform*, 2nd pamphlet ed. Substantive variants between the People's Edition and the Library Edition of 1865 are given in Appendix E.

Preface

THOSE WHO HAVE DONE ME the honour of reading my previous writings, will probably receive no strong impression of novelty from the present volume; for the principles are those to which I have been working up during the greater part of my life, and most of the practical suggestions have been anticipated by others or by myself. There is novelty, however, in the fact of bringing them together, and exhibiting them in their connexion; and also, I believe, in much that is brought forward in their support. Several of the opinions at all events, if not new, are for the present as little likely to meet with general acceptance as if they were.

It seems to me, however, from various indications, and from none more than the recent debates on Reform of Parliament, that both Conservatives and Liberals (if I may continue to call them what they still call themselves) have lost confidence in the political creeds which they nominally profess, while neither side appears to have made any progress in providing itself with a better. Yet such a better doctrine must be possible; not a mere compromise, by splitting the difference between the two, but something wider than either, which, in virtue of its superior comprehensiveness, might be adopted by either Liberal or Conservative without renouncing anything which he really feels to be valuable in his own creed. When so many feel obscurely the want of such a doctrine, and so few even flatter themselves that they have attained it, any one may without presumption offer what his own thoughts, and the best that he knows of those of others, are able to contribute towards its formation. *a*

*a*61² [*rule, and paragraph*] The only change, not purely verbal, in the present edition, (except a short note inserted at p. 264 [528 *of the present edition*],) consists of the addition of a few pages to the Seventh Chapter, written to clear up some of the difficulties expressed by objectors to the plan, there advocated, for the representation of minorities.

CHAPTER I

To What Extent Forms of Government are a Matter of Choice

ALL SPECULATIONS concerning forms of government bear the impress, more or less exclusive, of two conflicting theories respecting political institutions; or, to speak more properly, conflicting conceptions of what political institutions are.

By some minds, government is conceived as strictly a practical art, giving rise to no questions but those of means and an end. Forms of government are assimilated to any other expedients for the attainment of human objects. They are regarded as wholly an affair of invention and contrivance. Being made by man, it is assumed that man has the choice either to make them or not, and how or on what pattern they shall be made. Government, according to this conception, is a problem, to be worked like any other question of business. The first step is to define the purposes which governments are required to promote. The next, is to inquire what form of government is best fitted to fulfil those purposes. Having satisfied ourselves on these two points, and ascertained the form of government which combines the greatest amount of good with the least of evil, what further remains is to obtain the concurrence of our countrymen, or those for whom the institutions are intended, in the opinion which we have privately arrived at. To find the best form of government; to persuade others that it is the best; and having done so, to stir them up to insist on having it, is the order of ideas in the minds of those who adopt this view of political philosophy. They look upon a constitution in the same light (difference of scale being allowed for) as they would upon a steam plough, or a threshing machine.

To these stand opposed another kind of political reasoners, who are so far from assimilating a form of government to a machine, that they regard it as a sort of spontaneous product, and the science of government as a branch (so to speak) of natural history. According to them, forms of government are not a matter of choice. We must take them, in the main, as we find them. Governments cannot be constructed by premeditated design. They "are not made, but grow."[*] Our business with them, as with the other facts of the universe, is to acquaint ourselves with their natural properties, and adapt ourselves to them. The fundamental political institutions of a people are

[*See Mackintosh, *The History of England*, Vol. I, p. 72.]

considered by this school as a sort of organic growth from the nature and life of that people: a product of their habits, instincts, and unconscious wants and desires, scarcely at all of their deliberate purposes. Their will has had no part in the matter but that of meeting the necessities of the moment by the contrivances of the moment, which contrivances, if in sufficient conformity to the national feelings and character, commonly last, and by successive aggregation constitute a polity, suited to the people who possess it, but which it would be vain to attempt to superinduce upon any people whose nature and circumstances had not spontaneously evolved it.

It is difficult to decide which of these doctrines would be the most absurd, if we could suppose either of them held as an exclusive theory. But the principles which men profess, on any controverted subject, are usually a very *incomplete* exponent of the opinions they really hold. No one believes that every people is capable of working every sort of institutions. Carry the analogy of mechanical contrivances as far as we will, a man does not choose even an instrument of timber and iron on the sole ground that it is in itself the best. He considers whether he possesses the other requisites which must be combined with it to render its employment advantageous, and in particular whether those by whom it will have to be worked, possess the knowledge and skill necessary for its management. On the other hand, neither are those who speak of institutions as if they were a kind of living organisms, really the political fatalists they give themselves out to be. They do not pretend that mankind have absolutely no range of choice as to the government they will live under, or that a consideration of the consequences which flow from different forms of polity is no element at all in deciding which of them should be preferred. But though each side greatly exaggerates its own theory, out of opposition to the other, and no one holds without modification to either, the two doctrines correspond to a deep-seated difference between two modes of thought; and though it is evident that neither of these is entirely in the right, yet it being equally evident that neither is wholly in the wrong, we must endeavour to get down to what is at the root of each, and avail ourselves of the amount of truth which exists in either.

Let us remember, then, in the first place, that political institutions (however the proposition may be at times ignored) are the work of men; owe their origin and their whole existence to human will. Men did not wake on a summer morning and find them sprung up. Neither do they resemble trees, which, once planted, "are aye growing" while men "are sleeping."[*]

[*Walter Scott, *The Heart of Midlothian*, in *Tales of My Landlord, 2nd series, collected and arranged by Jedediah Cleishbotham*, 4 vols. (Edinburgh: Constable, 1818), Vol. I, p. 194.]

*a-a*611 imperfect

In every stage of their existence they are made what they are by human voluntary agency. Like all things, therefore, which are made by men, they may be either well or ill made; judgment and skill may have been exercised in their production, or the reverse of these. And again, if a people have omitted, or from outward pressure have not had it in their power, to give themselves a constitution by the tentative process of applying a corrective to each evil as it arose, or as the sufferers gained strength to resist it, this retardation of political progress is no doubt a great disadvantage to them, but it does not prove that what has been found good for others would not have been good also for them, and will not be so still when they think fit to adopt it.

On the other hand, it is also to be borne in mind that political machinery does not act of itself. As it is first made, so it has to be worked, by men, and even by ordinary men. It needs, not their simple acquiescence, but their active participation; and must be adjusted to the capacities and qualities of such men as are available. This implies three conditions. The people for whom the form of government is intended must be willing to accept it; or at least not so unwilling, as to oppose an insurmountable obstacle to its establishment. They must be willing and able to do what is necessary to keep it standing. And they must be willing and able to do what it requires of them to enable it to fulfil its purposes. The word "do" *bis to*b be understood as including forbearances as well as acts. They must be capable of fulfilling the conditions of action, and the conditions of self-restraint, which are necessary either for keeping the established polity in existence, or for enabling it to achieve the ends, its conduciveness to which forms its recommendation.

The failure of any of these conditions renders a form of government, whatever favourable promise it may otherwise hold out, unsuitable to the particular case.

The first obstacle, the repugnance of the people to the particular form of government, needs little illustration, because it never can in theory have been overlooked. The case is of perpetual occurrence. Nothing but foreign force would induce a tribe of North American Indians to submit to the restraints of a regular and civilized government. The same might have been said, though somewhat less absolutely, of the barbarians who overran the Roman Empire. It required centuries of time, and an entire change of circumstances, to discipline them into regular obedience even to their own leaders, when not actually serving under their banner. There are nations who will not voluntarily submit to any government but that of certain families, which have from time immemorial had the privilege of supplying them with chiefs. Some nations could not, except by foreign conquest, be

*b–b*611, 612   must

made to endure a monarchy; others are equally averse to a republic. The hindrance often amounts, for the time being, to impracticability.

But there are also cases in which, though not averse to a form of government—possibly even desiring it—a people may be unwilling or unable to fulfil its conditions. They may be incapable of fulfilling such of them as are necessary to keep the government even in nominal existence. Thus a people may prefer a free government, but if, from indolence, or carelessness, or cowardice, or want of public spirit, they are unequal to the exertions necessary for preserving it; if they will not fight for it when it is directly attacked; if they can be deluded by the artifices used to cheat them out of it; if by momentary discouragement, or temporary panic, or a fit of enthusiasm for an individual, they can be induced to lay their liberties at the feet even of a great man, or trust him with powers which enable him to subvert their institutions; in all these cases they are more or less unfit for liberty: and though it may be for their good to have had it even for a short time, they are unlikely long to enjoy it. Again, a people may be unwilling or unable to fulfil the duties which a particular form of government requires of them. A rude people, though in some degree alive to the benefits of civilized society, may be unable to practise the forbearances which it demands: their passions may be too violent, or their personal pride too exacting, to forego private conflict, and leave to the laws the avenging of their real or supposed wrongs. In such a case, a civilized government, to be really advantageous to them, will require to be in a considerable degree despotic: ᶜto bᶜ one over which they do not themselves exercise control, and which imposes a great amount of forcible restraint upon their actions. Again, a people must be considered unfit for more than a limited and qualified freedom, who will not co-operate actively with the law and the public authorities, in the repression of evil-doers. A people who are more disposed to shelter a criminal than to apprehend him; who, like the Hindoos, will perjure themselves to screen the man who has robbed them, rather than take trouble or expose themselves to vindictiveness by giving evidence against him; who, like some nations of Europe down to a recent date, if a man poniards another in the public street, pass by on the other side, because it is the business of the police to look to the matter, and it is safer not to interfere in what does not concern them; a people who are revolted by an execution, but not shocked at an assassination—require that the public authorities should be armed with much sterner powers of repression than elsewhere, since the first indispensable requisites of civilized life have nothing else to rest on. These deplorable states of feeling, in any people who have emerged from savage life, are, no doubt, usually the consequence of previous bad government, which has taught them to regard the law as

ᶜ⁻ᶜ+65

made for other ends than their good, and its administrators as worse enemies than those who openly violate it. But however little blame may be due to those in whom these mental habits have grown up, and however the habits may be ultimately conquerable by better government, yet while they exist, a people so disposed cannot be governed with as little power exercised over them, as a people whose sympathies are on the side of the law, and who are willing to give active assistance in its enforcement. Again, representative institutions are of little value, and may be a mere instrument of tyranny or intrigue, when the generality of electors are not sufficiently interested in their own government to give their vote, or, if they vote at all, do not bestow their suffrages on public grounds, but sell them for money, or vote at the beck of some one who has control over them, or whom for private reasons they desire to propitiate. Popular election thus practised, instead of a security against misgovernment, is but an additional wheel in its machinery. Besides these moral hindrances, mechanical difficulties are often an insuperable impediment to forms of government. In the ancient world, though there might be, and often was, great individual ^{d}or local^d independence, there could be nothing like a regulated popular government, beyond the bounds of a single city-community; because there did not exist the physical conditions for the formation and propagation of a public opinion, except among those who could be brought together to discuss public matters in the same agora. This obstacle is generally thought to have ceased by the adoption of the representative system. But to surmount it completely, required the press, and even the newspaper press, the real equivalent, though not in all respects an adequate one, of the Pnyx and the Forum. There have been states of society in which even a monarchy of any great territorial extent could not subsist, but unavoidably broke up into petty principalities, either mutually independent, or held together by a loose tie like the feudal: because the machinery of authority was not perfect enough to carry orders into effect at a great distance from the person of the ruler. He depended mainly upon voluntary fidelity for the obedience even of his army, nor did there exist the means of making the people pay an amount of taxes sufficient for keeping up the force necessary to compel obedience throughout a large territory. In these and all similar cases, it must be understood that the amount of the hindrance may be either greater or less. It may be so great as to make the form of government work very ill, without absolutely precluding its existence, or hindering it from being practically preferable to any other which can be had. This last question mainly depends upon a consideration which we have not yet arrived at—the tendencies of different forms of government to promote Progress.

We have now examined the three fundamental conditions of the adapta-

$^{d-d}$+65

tion of forms of government to the people who are to be governed by them. If the supporters of what may be termed the naturalistic theory of politics, mean but to insist on the necessity of these three conditions; if they only mean that no government can permanently exist, which does not fulfil the first and second conditions, and, in some considerable measure, the third; their doctrine, thus limited, is incontestable. Whatever they mean more than this, appears to me *e* untenable. All that we are told about the necessity of an historical basis for institutions, of their being in harmony with the national usages and character, and the like, means either this, or nothing to the purpose. There is a great quantity of mere sentimentality connected with these and similar phrases, over and above the amount of rational meaning contained in them. But, considered practically, these alleged requisites of political institutions are merely so many facilities for realizing the three conditions. When an institution, or a set of institutions, has the way prepared for it by the opinions, tastes, and habits of the people, they are not only more easily induced to accept it, but will more easily learn, and will be, from the beginning, better disposed, to do what is required of them both for the preservation of the institutions, and for bringing them into such action as enables them to produce their best results. It would be a great mistake in any legislator not to shape his measures so as to take advantage of such pre-existing habits and feelings, when available. On the other hand, it is an exaggeration to elevate these mere aids and facilities into necessary conditions. People are more easily induced to do, and do more easily, what they are already used to; but people also learn to do things new to them. Familiarity is a great help; but much dwelling on an idea will make it familiar, even when strange at first. There are abundant instances in which a whole people have been eager for untried things. The amount of capacity which a people possess for doing new things, and adapting themselves to new circumstances, is itself one of the elements of the question. It is a quality in which different nations, and different stages of civilization, differ much from one another. The capability of any given people for fulfilling the conditions of a given form of government, cannot be pronounced on by any sweeping rule. Knowledge of the particular people, and general practical judgment and sagacity, must be the guides. There is also another consideration not to be lost sight of. A people may be unprepared for good institutions; but to kindle a desire for them is a necessary part of the preparation. To recommend and advocate a particular institution or form of government, and set its advantages in the strongest light, is one of the modes, often the only mode within reach, of educating the mind of the nation not only for accepting or claiming, but also for working, the institution. What means had Italian patriots, during the last and present generation, of pre-

*e*61[1], 61[2]   altogether

paring the Italian people for freedom in unity, but by inciting them to demand it? Those, however, who undertake such a task, need to be duly impressed, not solely with the benefits of the institution or polity which they recommend, but also with the capacities, moral, intellectual, and active, required for working it; that they may avoid, if possible, stirring up a desire too much in advance of the capacity.

The result of what has been said is, that, within the limits set by the three conditions so often adverted to, institutions and forms of government *are* a matter of choice. To inquire into the best form of government in the abstract (as it is called) is not a chimerical, but a highly practical employment of scientific intellect; and to introduce into any country the best institutions which, in the existing state of that country, are capable of, in any tolerable degree, fulfilling the conditions, is one of the most rational objects to which practical effort can address itself. Everything which can be said by way of disparaging the efficacy of human will and purpose in matters of government, might be said of it in every other of its applications. In all things there are very strict limits to human power. It can only act by wielding some one or more of the forces of nature. Forces, therefore, that can be applied to the desired use, must exist; and will only act according to their own laws. We cannot make the river run backwards;[*] but we do not therefore say that watermills "are not made, but grow." In politics as in mechanics, the power which is to keep the engine going must be sought for *outside* the machinery; and if it is not forthcoming, or is insufficient to surmount the obstacles which may reasonably be expected, the contrivance will fail. This is no peculiarity of the political art; and amounts only to saying that it is subject to the same limitations and conditions as all other arts.

At this point we are met by another objection, or the same objection in a different form. The forces, it is contended, on which the greater political phenomena depend, are not amenable to the direction of politicians or philosophers. The government of a country, it is affirmed, is, in all substantial respects, fixed and determined beforehand by the state of the country in regard to the distribution of the elements of social power. Whatever is the strongest power in society will obtain the governing authority; and a change in the political constitution cannot be durable unless preceded or accompanied by an altered distribution of power in society itself. A nation, therefore, cannot choose its form of government. The mere details, and practical organization, it may choose; but the essence of the whole, the seat of the supreme power, is determined for it by social circumstances.

That there is a portion of truth in this doctrine, I at once admit; but to make it of any use, it must be reduced to a distinct expression and proper limits. When it is said that the strongest power in society will make itself

[*Cf. "De Tocqueville on Democracy in America [II]," p. 158 above.]

strongest in the government, what is meant by power? Not thews and sinews; otherwise pure democracy would be the only form of polity that could exist. To mere muscular strength, add two other elements, property and intelligence, and we are nearer the truth, but far from having yet reached it. Not only is a greater number often kept down by a less, but the greater number may have a preponderance in property, and individually in intelligence, and may yet be held in subjection, forcibly or otherwise, by a minority in both respects inferior to it. To make these various elements of power politically influential, they must be organized; and the advantage in organization is necessarily with those who are in possession of the government. A much weaker party in all other elements of power, may greatly preponderate when the powers of government are thrown into the scale; and may long retain its predominance through this alone: though, no doubt, a government so situated is in the condition called in mechanics unstable equilibrium, like a thing balanced on its smaller end, which, if once disturbed, tends more and more to depart from, instead of reverting to, its previous state.

But there are still stronger objections to this theory of government in the terms in which it is usually stated. The power in society which has any tendency to convert itself into political power, is not power quiescent, power merely passive, but active power; in other words, power actually exerted; that is to say, a very small portion of all the power in existence. Politically speaking, a great part of all power consists in will. How is it possible, then, to compute the elements of political power, while we omit from the computation anything which acts on the will? To think that, because those who wield the power in society wield in the end that of government, therefore it is of no use to attempt to influence the constitution of the government by acting on opinion, is to forget that opinion is itself one of the greatest active social forces. One person with a belief, is a social power equal to ninety-nine who have only interests. They who can succeed in creating a general persuasion that a certain form of government, or social fact of any kind, deserves to be preferred, have made nearly the most important step which can possibly be taken towards ranging the powers of society on its side. On the day when the proto-martyr was stoned to death at Jerusalem, while he who was to be the Apostle of the Gentiles stood by "consenting unto his death,"[*] would any one have supposed that the party of that stoned man were then and there the strongest power in society? And has not the event proved that they were so? Because theirs was the most powerful of then existing beliefs. The same element made a monk of Wittenberg, at the meeting of the Diet of Worms, a more powerful social force than the Emperor Charles the Fifth, and all the princes there assembled. But these, it may be said, are cases in which religion was concerned, and religious convictions

[*See Acts, 8:1.]

are something peculiar in their strength. Then let us take a case purely political, where religion, *so far as* concerned at all, was chiefly on the losing side. If any one requires to be convinced that speculative thought is one of the chief elements of social power, let him bethink himself of the age in which there was scarcely a throne in Europe which was not filled by a liberal and reforming king, a liberal and reforming emperor, or, strangest of all, a liberal and reforming pope; the age of Frederic the Great, of Catherine the Second, of Joseph the Second, of Peter Leopold, of Benedict XIV, of Ganganelli, of Pompal, of *Aranda*; when the very Bourbons of Naples were liberals and reformers, and all the active minds among the noblesse of France were filled with the ideas which were soon after to cost them so dear. Surely a conclusive example how far mere physical and economic power is from being the whole of social power. It was not by any change in the distribution of material interests, but by the spread of moral convictions, that negro slavery has been put an end to in the British Empire and elsewhere. The serfs in Russia *h* owe their emancipation, if not to a sentiment of duty, at least to the growth of a more enlightened opinion respecting the true interest of the State. It is what men think, that determines how they act; and though the persuasions and convictions of average men are in a much greater degree determined by their personal position than by reason, no little power is exercised over them by the persuasions and convictions of those whose personal position is different, and by the united authority of the instructed. When, therefore, the instructed in general can be brought to recognise one social arrangement, or political or other institution, as good, and another as bad, one as desirable, another as condemnable, very much has been done towards giving to the one, or withdrawing from the other, that preponderance of social force which enables it to subsist. And the maxim, that the government of a country is what the social forces in existence compel it to be, is true only in the sense in which it favours, instead of discouraging, the attempt to exercise, among all forms of government practicable in the existing condition of society, a rational choice.

*f–f*611, 612   if
*g–g*611   D'Aranda
*h*611, 612   will

CHAPTER II

The Criterion of a Good Form
of Government

THE FORM OF GOVERNMENT for any given country being (within certain definite conditions) amenable to choice, it is now to be considered by what test the choice should be directed; what are the distinctive characteristics of the form of government best fitted to promote the interests of any given society.

Before entering into this inquiry, it may seem necessary to decide what are the proper functions of government: for, government altogether being only a means, the eligibility of the means must depend on their adaptation to the end. But this mode of stating the problem gives less aid to its investigation than might be supposed, and does not even bring the whole of the question into view. For, in the first place, the proper functions of a government are not a fixed thing, but different in different states of society; much more extensive in a backward than in an advanced state. And, secondly, the character of a government or set of political institutions cannot be sufficiently estimated while we confine our attention to the legitimate sphere of governmental functions. For though the goodness of a government is necessarily circumscribed within that sphere, its badness unhappily is not. Every kind and degree of evil of which mankind are susceptible, may be inflicted on them by their government; and none of the good which social existence is capable of, can be any further realized than as the constitution of the government is compatible with, and allows scope for, its attainment. Not to speak of indirect effects, the direct meddling of the public authorities has no necessary limits but those of human ᵃexistenceᵃ; and the influence of government on the well-being of society can be considered or estimated in reference to nothing less than the whole of the interests of humanity.

Being thus obliged to place before ourselves, as the test of good and bad government, so complex an object as the aggregate interests of society, we would willingly attempt some kind of classification of those interests, which, bringing them before the mind in definite groups, might give indication of the qualities by which a form of government is fitted to promote those various interests respectively. It would be a great facility if we could say, the good of society consists of such and such elements; one of these elements

ᵃ⁻ᵃ611   life

requires such conditions, another such others; the government, then, which unites in the greatest degree all these conditions, must be the best. The theory of government would thus be built up from the separate theorems of the elements which compose a good state of society.

Unfortunately, to enumerate and classify the constituents of social well-being, so as to admit of the formation of such theorems, is no easy task. Most of those who, in the last or present generation, have applied themselves to the philosophy of politics in any comprehensive spirit, have felt the importance of such a classification; but the attempts which have been made towards it are as yet limited, so far as I am aware, to a single step. The classification begins and ends with a partition of the exigencies of society between the two heads of Order and Progress (in the phraseology of French thinkers); Permanence and Progression, in the words of Coleridge.[*] This division is plausible and seductive, from the apparently cleancut opposition between its two members, and the remarkable difference between the sentiments to which they appeal. But I apprehend that (however admissible for purposes of popular discourse), the distinction between Order, or Permanence, and Progress, employed to define the qualities necessary in a government, is unscientific and incorrect.

For, first, what are Order and Progress? Concerning Progress there is no difficulty, or none which is apparent at first sight. When Progress is spoken of as one of the wants of human society, it may be supposed to mean Improvement. That is a tolerably distinct idea. But what is Order? Sometimes it means more, sometimes less, but hardly ever the whole of what human society needs except improvement.

In its narrowest acceptation, Order means Obedience. A government is said to preserve order, if it succeeds in getting itself obeyed. But there are different degrees of obedience, and it is not every degree that is commendable. Only an unmitigated despotism demands that the individual citizen shall obey unconditionally every mandate of persons in authority. We must at least limit the definition to such mandates as are general, and issued in the deliberate form of laws. Order, thus understood, expresses, doubtless, an indispensable attribute of government. Those who are unable to make their ordinances obeyed, cannot be said to govern. But though a necessary condition, this is not the object of government. That it should make itself obeyed is requisite, in order that it may accomplish some other purpose. We are still to seek what is this other purpose, which government ought to fulfil, abstractedly from the idea of improvement, and which has to be fulfilled in every society, whether stationary or progressive.

[*On the Constitution of Church and State, in On the Constitution of Church and State, and Lay Sermons, ed. Henry Nelson Coleridge (London: Pickering, 1839), p. 24.]

In a sense somewhat more enlarged, Order means the preservation of peace, by the cessation of private violence. Order is said to exist, where the people of the country have, as a general rule, ceased to prosecute their quarrels by private force, and acquired the habit of referring the decision of their disputes and the redress of their injuries to the public authorities. But in this larger use of the term, as well as in the former narrow one, Order expresses rather one of the conditions of government, than either its purpose or the criterion of its excellence. For the habit may be well established of submitting to the government, and referring all disputed matters to its authority, and yet the manner in which the government deals with those disputed matters, and with the other things about which it concerns itself, may differ by the whole interval which divides the best from the worst possible.

If we intend to comprise in the idea of Order, all that society requires from its government, which is not included in the idea of Progress, we must define Order as the preservation of all kinds and amounts of good which already exist, and Progress as consisting in the increase of them. This distinction does comprehend in one or the other section everything which a government can be required to promote. But, thus understood, it affords no basis for a philosophy of government. We cannot say that, in constituting a polity, certain provisions ought to be made for Order and certain others for Progress; since the conditions of Order, in the sense now indicated, and those of Progress, are not opposite, but the same. The agencies which tend to preserve the social good which already exists, are the very same which promote the increase of it, and *vice versâ*: the sole difference being, that a greater degree of those agencies is required for the latter purpose than for the former.

What, for example, are the qualities in the citizens individually, which conduce most to keep up the amount of good conduct, of good management, of success and prosperity, which already exist in society? Everybody will agree that those qualities are, industry, integrity, justice, and prudence. But are not these, of all qualities, the most conducive to improvement? and is not any growth of these virtues in the community, in itself the greatest of improvements? If so, whatever qualities in the government are promotive of industry, integrity, justice, and prudence, conduce alike to permanence and to progression; only there is needed more of those qualities to make the society decidedly progressive, than merely to keep it permanent.

What, again, are the particular attributes in human beings, which seem to have a more especial reference to Progress, and do not so directly suggest the ideas of Order and Preservation? They are chiefly the qualities of mental activity, enterprise, and courage. But are not all these qualities fully as much required for preserving the good we have, as for adding to it? If there is anything certain in human affairs, it is that valuable acquisitions are only to be retained by the continuation of the same energies which gained them. Things left to take care of themselves inevitably decay. Those whom success induces to relax their habits of care and thoughtfulness, and their willingness to encounter disagreeables, seldom long retain their good fortune at its height. The mental attribute which seems exclusively dedicated to Progress, and is the culmination of the tendencies to it, is Originality, or Invention. Yet this is no less necessary for Permanence; since, in the inevitable changes of human affairs, new inconveniences and dangers continually grow up, which must be encountered by new resources and contrivances, in order to keep things going on even only as well as they did before. Whatever qualities, therefore, in a government, tend to encourage activity, energy, courage, originality, are requisites of Permanence as well as of Progress; only a somewhat less degree of them will on the average suffice for the former purpose than for the latter.

To pass now from the mental to the outward and objective requisites of society; it is impossible to point out any contrivance in politics, or arrangement of social affairs, which conduces to Order only, or to Progress only; whatever tends to either promotes both. Take, for instance, the common institution of a police. Order is the object which seems most immediately interested in the efficiency of this part of the social organization. Yet if it is effectual to promote Order, that is, if it represses crime, and enables every one to feel his person and property secure, can any state of things be more conducive to Progress? The greater security of property is one of the main conditions and causes of greater production, which is Progress in its most familiar and vulgarest aspect. The better repression of crime represses the dispositions which tend to crime, and this is Progress in a somewhat higher sense. The release of the individual from the cares and anxieties of a state of imperfect protection, sets his faculties free to be employed in any new effort for improving his own state and that of others: while the same cause, by attaching him to social existence, and making him no longer see present or prospective enemies in his fellow-creatures, fosters all those feelings of kindness and fellowship towards others, and interest in the general well-being of the community, which are such important parts of social improvement.

Take, again, such a familiar case as that of a good system of taxation and finance. This would generally be classed as belonging to the province of Order. Yet what can be more conducive to Progress? A financial system which promotes the one, conduces, by the very same excellences, to the other. Economy, for example, equally preserves the existing stock of national wealth, and favours the creation of more. A just distribution of burthens, by holding up to every citizen an example of morality and good conscience applied to difficult adjustments, and an evidence of the value which the highest authorities attach to them, tends in an eminent degree to educate the moral sentiments of the community, both in respect of strength and of discrimination. Such a mode of levying the taxes as does not impede the industry, or unnecessarily interfere with the liberty, of the citizen, promotes, not the preservation only, but the increase of the national wealth, and encourages a more active use of the individual faculties. And *vice versâ*, all errors in finance and taxation which obstruct the improvement of the people in wealth and morals, tend also, if of sufficiently serious amount, positively to impoverish and demoralize them. It holds, in short, universally, that when Order and Permanence are taken in their widest sense, for the stability of existing advantages, the requisites of Progress are but the requisites of Order in a greater degree; those of Permanence merely those of Progress, in a somewhat smaller measure.

In support of the position that Order is intrinsically different from Progress, and that preservation of existing and acquisition of additional good are sufficiently distinct to afford the basis of a fundamental classification, we shall perhaps be reminded that Progress may be at the expense of Order; that while we are acquiring, or striving to acquire, good of one kind, we may be losing ground in respect to others; thus there may be progress in wealth, while there is deterioration in virtue. Granting this, what it proves is, not that Progress is generically a different thing from Permanence, but that wealth is a different thing from virtue. Progress is Permanence and something more; and it is no answer to this, to say that Progress in one thing does not imply Permanence in everything. No more does Progress in one thing imply Progress in everything. Progress of any kind includes Permanence in that same kind: whenever Permanence is sacrificed to some particular kind of Progress, other Progress is still more sacrificed to it; and if it be not worth the sacrifice, not the interest of Permanence alone has been disregarded, but the general interest of Progress has been mistaken.

If these improperly contrasted ideas are to be used at all in the attempt to give a first commencement of scientific precision to the notion of good government, it would be more philosophically correct to leave out of the definition the word Order, and to say that the best government is that which is most conducive to Progress. For Progress includes Order, but Order does not include Progress. Progress is a greater degree of that of which Order is a less. Order, in any other sense, stands only for a part of the prerequisites of good government, not for its idea and essence. Order would find a more suitable place among the conditions of Progress; since, if we would increase our sum of good, nothing is more indispensable than to take due care of what we already have. If we are endeavouring after more riches, our very first rule should be, not to squander uselessly our existing means. Order, thus considered, is not an additional end to be reconciled with Progress, but a part and means of Progress itself. If a gain in one respect is purchased by a more than equivalent loss in the same or in any other, there is not Progress. Conduciveness to Progress, thus understood, includes the whole excellence of a government.

But, though metaphysically defensible, this definition of the criterion of good government is not appropriate, because, though it contains the whole of the truth, it recals only a part. What is suggested by the term Progress is the idea of moving onward, whereas the meaning of it here is quite as much the prevention of falling back. The very same social causes—the same beliefs, feelings, institutions, and practices—are as much required to prevent society from retrograding, as to produce a further advance. Were there no improvement to be hoped for, life would be not the less an unceasing struggle against causes of deterioration; as it even now is. Politics, as conceived by the ancients, consisted wholly in this. The natural tendency of men and their works was to degenerate, which tendency, however, by good institutions virtuously administered, it might be possible for an indefinite length of time to counteract. Though we no longer hold this opinion; though most men in the present age profess the contrary creed, believing that the tendency of things, on the whole, is towards improvement; we ought not to forget, that there is an incessant and ever-flowing current of human affairs towards the worse, consisting of all the follies, all the vices, all the negligences, indolences, and supinenesses of mankind; which is only controlled, and kept from sweeping all before it, by the exertions which some persons constantly, and others by fits, put forth in the direction of good and worthy objects. It gives a very insufficient idea of the importance of the strivings which take place to improve and elevate human nature and life, to suppose that their chief value consists in the amount of actual improvement realized by their means, and that the consequence of their cessation would merely be that we should remain as we are. A very small diminution of those exertions would not only put a stop to improvement, but would turn the general tendency of things towards deterioration; which, once begun, would proceed with increasing rapidity, and become more and more difficult to check, until it reached a state often seen in history, and in which many large portions of mankind even now grovel; when hardly anything short of superhuman power seems sufficient to turn the tide, and give a fresh commencement to the upward movement.

These reasons make the word Progress as unapt as the terms Order and Permanence, to become the basis for a classification of the requisites of a form of government. The fundamental antithesis which these words express does not lie in the things themselves, so much as in the types of human character which answer to them. There are, we know, some minds in which caution, and others in which boldness, predominates: in some, the desire to avoid imperilling what is already possessed is a stronger sentiment than that which prompts to improve the old and acquire new advantages; while there are others who lean the contrary way, and are more eager for future than careful of present good. The road to the ends of both is the same; but they are liable to wander from it in opposite directions. This consideration is of importance in composing the *personnel* of any political body: persons of both types ought to be included in it, that the tendencies of each may be tempered, in so far as they are excessive, by a due proportion of the other. There needs no express provision to ensure this object, provided care is taken to admit nothing inconsistent with it. The natural and spontaneous admixture of the old and the young, of those whose position and reputation are made, and those who have them still to make, will in general sufficiently answer the purpose, if only this natural balance is not disturbed by artificial regulation.

Since the distinction most commonly adopted for the classification of social exigencies does not possess the properties needful for that use, we have to seek for some other leading distinction better adapted to the purpose. Such a distinction would seem to be indicated by the considerations to which I now proceed.

If we ask ourselves on what causes and conditions good government in all its senses, from the humblest to the most exalted, depends, we find that the principal of them, the one which transcends all others, is the qualities of the human beings composing the society over which the government is exercised.

We may take, as a first instance, the administration of justice; with the more propriety, since there is no part of public business in which the mere machinery, the rules and contrivances for conducting the details of the operation, are of such vital consequence. Yet even these yield in importance to the qualities of the human agents employed. Of what efficacy are rules of procedure in securing the ends of justice, if the moral condition of the people is such that the witnesses generally lie, and the judges and their subordinates take bribes? Again, how can institutions provide a good municipal administration, if there exists such indifference to the subject, that those who would administer honestly and capably cannot be induced to serve, and the duties are left to those who undertake them because they have some private interest to be promoted? Of what avail is the most broadly popular representative system, if the electors do not care to choose the best member of parliament, but choose him who will spend most money to be elected? How can a representative assembly work for good, if its members can be bought, or if their excitability of temperament, uncorrected by public discipline or private self-control, makes them incapable of calm deliberation, and they resort to manual violence on the floor of the House, or shoot at one another with rifles? How, again, can government, or any joint concern, be carried on in a tolerable manner by a people so envious, that if one among them seems likely to succeed in anything, those who ought to co-operate with him form a tacit combination to make him fail? Whenever the general disposition of the people is such, that each individual regards those only of his interests which are selfish, and does not dwell on, or concern himself for, his share of the general interest, in such a state of things good government is impossible. The influence of defects of intelligence in obstructing all the elements of good government requires no illustration. Government consists of acts done by human beings; and if the agents, or those who choose the agents, or those to whom the agents are responsible, or the lookers-on whose opinion ought to influence and check all these, are mere masses of ignorance, stupidity, and baleful prejudice, every operation of government will go wrong: while, in proportion as the men rise above this standard, so will the government improve in quality; up to the point of excellence, attainable but nowhere attained, where the officers of government, themselves persons of superior virtue and intellect, are surrounded by the atmosphere of a virtuous and enlightened public opinion.

The first element of good government, therefore, being the virtue and intelligence of the human beings composing the community, the most important point of excellence which any form of government can possess is to promote the virtue and intelligence of the people themselves. The first question in respect to any political institutions is, how far they tend to foster in the members of the community the various desirable qualities, moral *b*and*b* intellectual; or rather (following Bentham's more complete classification) moral, intellectual, and active.[*] The government which does this the best, has every likelihood of being the best in all other respects, since it is on these qualities, so far as they exist in the people, that all possibility of goodness in the practical operations of the government depends.

We may consider, then, as one criterion of the goodness of a government, the degree in which it tends to increase the sum of good qualities in the governed, collectively and individually; since, besides that their well-being is the sole object of government, their good qualities supply the moving force which works the machinery. This leaves, as the other constituent element of the merit of a government, the quality of the machinery itself; that is, the degree in which it is adapted to take advantage of the amount of

[*See, e.g., *Leading Principles of the Constitutional Code*, in *Works*, Vol. II, p. 272.]

*b-b*611   or

good qualities which may at any time exist, and make them instrumental to the right purposes. Let us again take the subject of judicature as an example and illustration. The judicial system being given, the goodness of the administration of justice is in the compound ratio of the worth of the men composing the tribunals, and the worth of the public opinion which influences or controls them. But all the difference between a good and a bad system of judicature lies in the contrivances adopted for bringing whatever moral and intellectual worth exists in the community to bear upon the administration of justice, and making it duly operative on the result. The arrangements for rendering the choice of the judges such as to obtain the highest average of virtue and intelligence; the salutary forms of procedure; the publicity which allows observation and criticism of whatever is amiss; the liberty of discussion and censure through the press; the mode of taking evidence, according as it is well or ill adapted to elicit truth; the facilities, whatever be their amount, for obtaining access to the tribunals; the arrangements for detecting crimes and apprehending offenders;—all these things are not the power, but the machinery for bringing the power into contact with the obstacle: and the machinery has no action of itself, but without it the power, let it be ever so ample, would be wasted and of no effect. A similar distinction exists in regard to the constitution of the executive departments of administration. Their machinery is good, when the proper tests are prescribed for the qualifications of officers, the proper rules for their promotion; when the business is conveniently distributed among those who are to transact it, a convenient and methodical order established for its transaction, a correct and intelligible record kept of it after being transacted; when each individual knows for what he is responsible, and is known to others as responsible for it; when the best-contrived checks are provided against negligence, favoritism, or jobbery in any of the acts of the department. But political checks will no more act of themselves, than a bridle will direct a horse without a rider. If the checking functionaries are as corrupt or as negligent as those whom they ought to check, and if the public, the mainspring of the whole checking machinery, are too ignorant, too passive, or too careless and inattentive, to do their part, little benefit will be derived from the best administrative apparatus. Yet a good apparatus is always preferable to a bad. It enables such insufficient moving or checking power as exists, to act at the greatest advantage; and without it, no amount of moving or checking power would be sufficient. Publicity, for instance, is no impediment to evil nor stimulus to good if the public will not look at what is done; but without publicity, how could they either check or encourage what they were not permitted to see? The ideally perfect constitution of a public office is that in which the interest of the functionary is entirely coincident with his duty. No mere system will make it so, but still less can it be made so without a system, aptly devised for the purpose.

What we have said of the arrangements for the detailed administration of the government, is still more evidently true of its general constitution. All government which aims at being good, is an organization of some part of the good qualities existing in the individual members of the community, for the conduct of its collective affairs. A representative constitution is a means of bringing the general standard of intelligence and honesty existing in the community, and the individual intellect and virtue of its wisest members, more directly to bear upon the government, and investing them with greater influence in it, than they would ᶜin generalᶜ have under any other mode of organization; though, under any, such influence as they do have is the source of all good that there is in the government, and the hindrance of every evil that there is not. The greater the amount of these good qualities which the institutions of a country succeed in organizing, and the better the mode of organization, the better will be the government.

We have now, therefore, obtained a foundation for a twofold division of the merit which any set of political institutions can possess. It consists partly of the degree in which they promote the general mental advancement of the community, including under that phrase advancement in intellect, in virtue, and in practical activity and efficiency; and partly of the degree of perfection with which they organize the moral, intellectual, and active worth already existing, so as to operate with the greatest effect on public affairs. A government is to be judged by its action upon men, and by its action upon things; by what it makes of the citizens, and what it does with them; its tendency to improve or deteriorate the people themselves, and the goodness or badness of the work it performs for them, and by means of them. Government is at once a great influence acting on the human mind, and a set of organized arrangements for public business: in the first capacity its beneficial action is chiefly indirect, but not therefore less vital, while its mischievous action may be direct.

The difference between these two functions of a government is not, like that between Order and Progress, a difference merely in degree, but in kind. We must not, however, suppose that they have no intimate connexion with one another. The institutions which ensure the best management of public affairs practicable in the existing state of cultivation, tend by this alone to the further improvement of that state. A people which had the most just laws, the purest and most efficient judicature, the most enlightened administration, the most equitable and least onerous system of finance, compatible with the stage it had attained in moral and intellectual advancement, would be in a fair way to pass rapidly into a higher stage. Nor is there any mode in which political institutions can contribute more effectually to the im-

ᶜ–ᶜ+61², 65

provement of the people, than by doing their more direct work well. And, reversely, if their machinery is so badly constructed that they do their own particular business ill, the effect is felt in a thousand ways in lowering the morality and deadening the intelligence and activity of the people. But the distinction is nevertheless real, because this is only one of the means by which political institutions improve or deteriorate the human mind, and the causes and modes of that beneficial or injurious influence remain a distinct and much wider subject of study.

Of the two modes of operation by which a form of government or set of political institutions affects the welfare of the community—its operation as an agency of national education, and its arrangements for conducting the collective affairs of the community in the state of education in which they already are; the last evidently varies much less, from difference of country and state of civilization, than the first. It has also much less to do with the fundamental constitution of the government. The mode of conducting the practical business of government, which is best under a free constitution, would generally be best also in an absolute monarchy: only, an absolute monarchy is not so likely to practise it. The laws of property, for example; the principles of evidence and judicial procedure; the system of taxation and of financial administration, need not necessarily be different in different forms of government. Each of these matters has principles and rules of its own, which are a subject of separate study. General jurisprudence, civil and penal legislation, financial and commercial policy, are sciences in themselves, or rather, separate members of the comprehensive science or art of government: and the most enlightened doctrines on all these subjects, though not equally likely to be understood ^{d}or^d acted on under all forms of government, yet, if understood and acted on, would in general be equally beneficial under them all. It is true that these doctrines could not be applied without some modifications to all states of society and of the human mind: nevertheless, by far the greater number of them would require modifications solely of detail, to adapt them to any state of society sufficiently advanced to possess rulers capable of understanding them. A government to which they would be wholly unsuitable, must be one so bad in itself, or so opposed to public feeling, as to be unable to maintain itself in existence by honest means.

It is otherwise with that portion of the interests of the community which relate to the better or worse training of the people themselves. Considered as instrumental to this, institutions need to be radically different, according to the stage of advancement already reached. The recognition of this truth, though for the most part empirically rather than philosophically, may be regarded as the main point of superiority in the political theories of the present above those of the last age; in which it was customary to claim

$^{d-d}$611, 612   and

representative democracy for England or France by arguments which would equally have proved it the only fit form of government for Bedouins or Malays. The state of different communities, in point of culture and development, ranges downwards to a condition very little above the highest of the beasts. The upward range, too, is considerable, and the future possible extension vastly greater. A community can only be developed out of one of these states into a higher, by a concourse of influences, among the principal of which is the government to which they are subject. In all states of human improvement ever yet attained, the nature and degree of authority exercised over individuals, the distribution of power, and the conditions of command and obedience, are the most powerful of the influences, except their religious belief, which make them what they are, and enable them to become what they can be. They may be stopped short at any point in their progress, by defective adaptation of their government to ᵉthatᵉ particular stage of advancement. And the one indispensable merit of a government, in favour of which it may be forgiven almost any amount of other demerit compatible with progress, is that its operation on the people is favourable, or not unfavourable, to the next step which it is necessary for them to take, in order to raise themselves to a higher level.

Thus (to repeat a former example), a people in a state of savage independence, in which every one lives for himself, exempt, unless by fits, from any external control, is practically incapable of making any progress in civilization until it has learnt to obey. The indispensable virtue, therefore, in a government which establishes itself over a people of this sort is, that it make itself obeyed. To enable it to do this, the constitution of the government must be nearly, or quite, despotic. A constitution in any degree popular, dependent on the voluntary surrender by the different members of the community of their individual freedom of action, would fail to enforce the first lesson which the pupils, in this stage of their progress, require. Accordingly, the civilization of such tribes, when not the result of juxtaposition with others already civilized, is almost always the work of an absolute ruler, deriving his power either from religion or military prowess; very often from foreign arms.

Again, uncivilized races, and the bravest and most energetic still more than the rest, are averse to continuous labour of an unexciting kind. Yet all real civilization is at this price; without such labour, neither can the mind be disciplined into the habits required by civilized society, nor the material world prepared to receive it. There needs a rare concurrence of circumstances, and for that reason often a vast length of time, to reconcile such a people to industry, unless they are for a while compelled to it. Hence even personal slavery, by giving a commencement to industrial life, and enforcing

ᵉ⁻ᵉ61¹   their

it as the exclusive occupation of the most numerous portion of the community, may accelerate the transition to a better freedom than that of fighting and rapine. It is almost needless to say that this excuse for slavery is only available in a very early state of society. A civilized people have far other means of imparting civilization to those under their influence; and slavery is, in all its details, so repugnant to that government of law, which is the foundation of all modern life, and so corrupting to the master-class when they have once come under civilized influences, that its adoption under any circumstances whatever in modern society is a relapse into worse than barbarism.

At some period, however, of their history, almost every people, now civilized, have consisted, in majority, of slaves. A people in that condition require to raise them out of it a very different polity from a nation of savages. If they are energetic by nature, and especially if there be associated with them in the same community an industrious class who are neither slaves nor slave-owners (as was the case in Greece), they need, probably, no more to ensure their improvement than to make them free: when freed, they may often be fit, like Roman freedmen, to be admitted at once *to* the full rights of citizenship. This, however, is not the normal condition of slavery, and is generally a sign that it is becoming obsolete. A slave, properly so called, is a being who has not learnt to help himself. He is, no doubt, one step in advance of a savage. He has not the first lesson of political society still to acquire. He has learnt to obey. But what he obeys is only a direct command. It is the characteristic of *born* slaves to be incapable of conforming their conduct to a rule, or law. They can only do what they are ordered, and only when they are ordered to do it. If a man whom they fear is standing over them and threatening them with punishment, they obey; but when his back is turned, the work remains undone. The motive determining them must appeal not to their interests, but to their instincts; immediate hope or immediate terror. A despotism, which may tame the savage, will, in so far as it is a despotism, only confirm the slaves in their incapacities. Yet a government under their own control would be entirely unmanageable by them. Their improvement cannot come from themselves, but must be superinduced from without. The step which they have to take, and their only path to improvement, is to be raised from a government of will to one of law. They have to be taught self-government, and this, in its initial stage, means the capacity to act on general instructions. What they require is not a government of force, but one of guidance. Being, however, in too low a state to yield to the guidance of any but those to whom they look up as the possessors of force, the sort of government fittest for them is one which possesses force, but seldom uses it: a parental despotism or aristocracy, re-

*–*611   into

sembling the St. Simonian form of socialism; maintaining a general superintendence over all the operations of society, so as to keep before each the sense of a present force sufficient to compel his obedience to the rule laid down, but which, owing to the impossibility of descending to regulate all the minutiæ of industry and life, necessarily leaves and induces individuals to do much of themselves. This, which may be termed the government of leading-strings, seems to be the one required to carry such a people the most rapidly through the next necessary step in social progress. Such appears to have been the idea of the government of the Incas of Peru; and such was that of the Jesuits ᵍofᵍ Paraguay. I need scarcely remark that leading-strings are only admissible as a means of gradually training the people to walk alone.

It would be out of place to carry the illustration further. To attempt to investigate what kind of government is suited to every known state of society, would be to compose a treatise, not on representative government, but on political science at large. For our more limited purpose we borrow from political philosophy only its general principles. To determine the form of government most suited to any particular people, we must be able, among the defects and shortcomings which belong to that people, to distinguish those that are the immediate impediment to progress; to discover what it is which (as it were) stops the way. The best government for them is the one which tends most to give them that for want of which they cannot advance, or advance only in a lame and lopsided manner. We must not, however, forget the reservation necessary in all things which have for their object improvement, or Progress; namely, that in seeking the good which is needed, no damage, or as little as possible, be done to that already possessed. A people of savages should be taught obedience, but not in such a manner as to convert them into a people of slaves. And (to give the observation a higher generality) the form of government which is most effectual for carrying a people through the next stage of progress, will still be very improper for them if it does this in such a manner as to obstruct, or positively unfit them for, the step next beyond. Such cases are frequent, and are among the most melancholy facts in history. The Egyptian hierarchy, the paternal despotism of China, were very fit instruments for carrying those nations up to the point of civilization which they attained. But having reached that point, they were brought to a permanent halt, for want of mental liberty and individuality; requisites of improvement which the institutions that had carried them thus far, entirely incapacitated them from acquiring; and as the institutions did not break down and give place to others, further improvement stopped. In contrast with these nations, let us consider the example of an opposite character afforded by another and a comparatively insignificant Oriental

ᵍ–ᵍ61¹, 61² in

people—the Jews. They, too, had an absolute monarchy and a hierarchy, and their organized institutions were as obviously of sacerdotal origin as those of the Hindoos. These did for them what was done for other Oriental races by their institutions—subdued them to industry and order, and gave them a national life. But neither their kings nor their priests ever obtained, as in those other countries, the exclusive moulding of their character. Their religion, which enabled persons of genius and a high religious tone to be regarded and to regard themselves as inspired from heaven, gave existence to an inestimably precious unorganized institution—the Order (if it may be so termed) of Prophets. Under the protection, generally though not always effectual, of their sacred character, the Prophets were a power in the nation, often more than a match for kings and priests, and kept up, in that little corner of the earth, the antagonism of influences which is the only real security for continued progress. Religion consequently was not there, what it has been in so many other places—a consecration of all that was once established, and a barrier against further improvement. The remark of a distinguished Hebrew, M. Salvador, that the Prophets were, in Church and State, the equivalent of the modern liberty of the press,[*] gives a just but not an adequate conception of the part fulfilled in national and universal history by this great element of Jewish life; by means of which, the canon of inspiration never being complete, the persons most eminent in genius and moral feeling could not only denounce and reprobate, with the direct author- ity of the Almighty, whatever appeared to them deserving of such treatment, but could give forth better and higher interpretations of the national religion, which thenceforth became part of the religion. Accordingly, whoever can divest himself of the habit of reading the Bible as if it was one book, which until lately was equally inveterate in Christians and in unbelievers, sees with admiration the vast interval between the morality and religion of the Penta- teuch, or even of the historical books (the unmistakeable work of Hebrew Conservatives of the sacerdotal order), and the morality and religion of the Prophecies: a distance as wide as between these last and the Gospels. Condi- tions more favourable to Progress could not easily exist: accordingly, the Jews, instead of being stationary like other Asiatics, were, next to the Greeks, the most progressive people of antiquity, and, jointly with them, have been the starting-point and main propelling agency of modern cultivation.

It is, then, impossible to understand the question of the adaptation of forms of government to states of society, without taking into account not only the next step, but all the steps which society has yet to make; both those which can be foreseen, and the far wider indefinite range which is at present out of sight. It follows, that to judge of the merits of forms of govern-

[*Joseph Salvador, *Histoire des institutions de Moïse et du peuple Hébreu,* 3 vols. (Paris: Ponthieu, 1828), Vol. I, Bk. II, Chap. iii, *passim.*]

ment, an ideal must be constructed of the form of government most eligible in itself, that is, which, if the necessary conditions existed for giving effect to its beneficial tendencies, would, more than all others, favour and promote not some one improvement, but all forms and degrees of it. This having been done, we must consider what are the mental conditions of all sorts, necessary to enable this government to realize its tendencies, and what, therefore, are the various defects by which a people is made incapable of reaping its benefits. It would then be possible to construct a theorem of the circumstances in which that form of government may wisely be introduced; and also to judge, in cases in which it had better not be introduced, what inferior forms of polity will best carry those communities through the intermediate stages which they must traverse before they can become fit for the best form of government.

Of these inquiries, the last does not concern us here; but the first is an essential part of our subject: for we may, without rashness, at once enunciate a proposition, the proofs and illustrations of which will present themselves in the ensuing pages; that this ideally best form of government will be found in some one or other variety of the Representative System.

CHAPTER III

That the Ideally Best Form of Government is Representative Government

IT HAS LONG (perhaps throughout the entire duration of British freedom) been a common ᵃsayingᵃ, that if a good despot could be ensured, despotic monarchy would be the best form of government. I look upon this as a radical and most pernicious misconception of what good government is; which, until it can be got rid of, will fatally vitiate all our speculations on government.

The supposition is, that absolute power, in the hands of an eminent individual, would ensure a virtuous and intelligent performance of all the duties of government. Good laws would be established and enforced, bad laws would be reformed; the best men would be placed in all situations of trust; justice would be as well administered, the public burthens would be as light and as judiciously imposed, every branch of administration would be as purely and as intelligently conducted, as the circumstances of the country and its degree of intellectual and moral cultivation would admit. I am willing, for the sake of the argument, to concede all this; but I must point out how great the concession is; how much more is needed to produce even an approximation to these results, than is conveyed in the simple expression, a good despot. Their realization would in fact imply, not merely a good monarch, but an all-seeing one. He must be at all times informed correctly, in considerable detail, of the conduct and working of every branch of administration, in every district of the country, and must be able, in the twenty-four hours per day which are all that is granted to a king as to the humblest labourer, to give an effective share of attention and superintendence to all parts of this vast field; or he must at least be capable of discerning and choosing out, from among the mass of his subjects, not only a large abundance of honest and able men, fit to conduct every branch of public administration under supervision and control, but also the small number of men of eminent virtues and talents who can be trusted not only to do without that supervision, but to exercise it themselves over others. So extraordinary are

ᵃ⁻ᵃ61¹, 61² form of speech

the faculties and energies required for performing this task in any support-able manner, that the good despot whom we are supposing can hardly be imagined as consenting to undertake it, unless as a refuge from intolerable evils, and a transitional preparation for something beyond. But the argument can do without even this immense item in the account. Suppose the difficulty vanquished. What should we then have? One man of superhuman mental activity managing the entire affairs of a mentally passive people. Their pas-sivity is implied in the very idea of absolute power. The nation as a whole, and every individual composing it, are without any potential voice in their own destiny. They exercise no will in respect to their collective interests. All is decided for them by a will not their own, which it is legally a crime for them to disobey. What sort of human beings can be formed under such a regimen? What development can either their thinking or their active faculties attain under it? On matters of pure theory they might perhaps be allowed to speculate, so long as their speculations either did not approach politics, or had not the remotest connexion with its practice. On practical affairs they could at most be only suffered to suggest; and even under the most moderate of despots, none but persons of already admitted or reputed superiority could hope that their suggestions would be known to, much less regarded by, those who had the management of affairs. A person must have a very un-usual taste for intellectual exercise in and for itself, who will put himself to the trouble of thought when it is to have no outward effect, or qualify him-self for functions which he has no chance of being allowed to exercise. The only sufficient incitement to mental exertion, in any but a few minds in a generation, is the prospect of some practical use to be made of its results. It does not follow that the nation will be wholly destitute of intellectual power. The common business of life, which must necessarily be performed by each individual or family for themselves, will call forth some amount of intelli-gence and practical ability, within a certain narrow range of ideas. There may be a select class of *savants*, who cultivate science with a view to its physical uses, or for the pleasure of the pursuit. There will be a bureaucracy, and persons in training for the bureaucracy, who will be taught at least some empirical maxims of government and public administration. There may be, and often has been, a systematic organization of the best mental power in the country in some special direction (commonly military) to promote the grandeur of the despot. But the public at large remain without information and without interest on all the greater matters of practice; or, if they have any knowledge of them, it is but a *dilettante* knowledge, like that which people have of the mechanical arts who have never handled a tool. Nor is it only in their intelligence that they suffer. Their moral capacities are equally stunted. Wherever the sphere of action of human beings is artificially cir-cumscribed, their sentiments are narrowed and dwarfed in the same proportion. The food of feeling is action: even domestic affection lives upon voluntary good offices. Let a person have nothing to do for his country, and he will not care for it. It has been said of old, that in a despotism there is at most but one patriot, the despot himself; and the saying rests on a just appreciation of the effects of absolute subjection, even to a good and wise master. Religion remains: and here at least, it may be thought, is an agency that may be relied on for lifting men's eyes and minds above the dust at their feet. But religion, even supposing it to escape perversion for the purposes of despotism, ceases in these circumstances to be a social concern, and narrows into a personal affair between an individual and his Maker, in which the issue at stake is but his private salvation. Religion in this shape is quite consistent with the most selfish and contracted egoism, and identifies the votary as little in feeling with the rest of his kind as sensuality itself.

A good despotism means a government in which, so far as depends on the despot, there is no positive oppression by officers of state, but in which all the collective interests of the people are managed for them, all the thinking that has relation to collective interests done for them, and in which their minds are formed by, and consenting to, this abdication of their own energies. Leaving things to the Government, like leaving them to Providence, is synonymous with caring nothing about them, and accepting their results, when disagreeable, as visitations of Nature. With the exception, therefore, of a few studious men who take an intellectual interest in speculation for its own sake, the intelligence and sentiments of the whole people are given up to the material interests, and when these are provided for, to the amusement and ornamentation, of private life. But to say this is to say, if the whole testimony of history is worth anything, that the era of national decline has arrived: that is, if the nation had ever attained anything to decline from. If it has never risen above the condition of an Oriental people, in that condition it continues to stagnate. But if, like Greece or Rome, it had realized anything higher, through the energy, patriotism, and enlargement of mind, which as national qualities are the fruits solely of freedom, it relapses in a few generations into the Oriental state. And that state does not mean stupid tranquillity, with security against change for the worse; it often means being overrun, conquered, and reduced to domestic slavery, either by a stronger despot, or by the nearest barbarous people who retain along with their savage rudeness the energies of freedom.

Such are not merely the natural tendencies, but the inherent necessities of despotic government; from which there is no outlet, unless in so far as the despotism consents not to be despotism; in so far as the supposed good despot abstains from exercising his power, and, though holding it in reserve, allows the general business of government to go on as if the people really governed themselves. However little probable it may be, we may imagine a despot observing many of the rules and restraints of constitutional government. He might allow such freedom of the press and of discussion as would enable a public opinion to form and express itself on national affairs. He might suffer local interests to be managed, without the interference of authority, by the people themselves. He might even surround himself with a council or councils of government, freely chosen by the whole or some portion of the nation; retaining in his own hands the power of taxation, and the supreme legislative as well as executive authority. Were he to act thus, and so far abdicate as a despot, he would do away with a considerable part of the evils characteristic of despotism. Political activity and capacity for public affairs would no longer be prevented from growing up in the body of the nation; and a public opinion would form itself, not the mere echo of the government. But such improvement would be the beginning of new difficulties. This public opinion, independent of the monarch's dictation, must be either with him or against him; if not the one, it will be the other. All governments must displease many persons, and these having now regular organs, and being able to express their sentiments, opinions adverse to the measures of government would often be expressed. What is the monarch to do when these unfavourable opinions happen to be in the majority? Is he to alter his course? Is he to defer to the nation? If so, he is no longer a despot, but a constitutional king; an organ or first minister of the people, distinguished only by being irremovable. If not, he must either put down opposition by his despotic power, or there will arise a permanent antagonism between the people and one man, which can have but one possible ending. Not even a religious principle of passive obedience and "right divine" would long ward off the natural consequences of such a position. The monarch would have to succumb, and conform to the conditions of constitutional royalty, or give place to some one who would. The despotism, being thus chiefly nominal, would possess few of the advantages supposed to belong to absolute monarchy; while it would realize in a very imperfect degree those of a free government; since however great an amount of liberty the citizens might practically enjoy, they could never forget that they held it on sufferance, and by a concession which under the existing constitution of the state might at any moment be resumed; that they were legally slaves, though of a prudent, or indulgent, master.

It is not much to be wondered at, if impatient or disappointed reformers, groaning under the impediments opposed to the most salutary public improvements by the ignorance, the indifference, the intractableness, the perverse obstinacy of a people, and the corrupt combinations of selfish private interests armed with the powerful weapons afforded by free institutions, should at times sigh for a strong hand to bear down all these obstacles, and compel a recalcitrant people to be better governed. But (setting aside the fact, that for one despot who now and then reforms an abuse, there are ninety-nine who do nothing but create them) those who look in any such direction for the realization of their hopes leave out of the idea of good government its principal element, the improvement of the people themselves. One of the benefits of freedom is that under it the ruler cannot pass by the people's minds, and amend their affairs for them without amending *them*[b]. If it were possible for [c]the[c] people to be well governed in spite of themselves, their good government would last no longer than the freedom of a people usually lasts who have been liberated by foreign arms without their own co-operation. It is true, a despot may educate the people; and to do so really, would be the best apology for his despotism. But any education which aims at making human beings other than machines, in the long run makes them claim to have the control of their own actions. The leaders of French philosophy in the eighteenth century had been educated by the Jesuits. Even Jesuit education, it seems, was sufficiently real to call forth the appetite for freedom. Whatever invigorates the faculties, in however small a measure, creates an increased desire for their more unimpeded exercise: and a popular education is a failure, if it educates the people for any state but that which it will certainly induce them to desire, and most probably to demand.

I am far from condemning, in cases of extreme exigency, the assumption of absolute power in the form of a temporary dictatorship. Free nations have, in times of old, conferred such power by their own choice, as a necessary medicine for diseases of the body politic which could not be got rid of by less violent means. But its acceptance, even for a time strictly limited, can only be excused, if, like Solon or Pittacus, the dictator employs the whole power he assumes in removing the obstacles which debar the nation from the enjoyment of freedom. A good despotism is an altogether false ideal, which practically (except as a means to some temporary purpose) becomes the most senseless and dangerous of chimeras. Evil for evil, a good despotism, in a country at all advanced in civilization, is more noxious than a bad one; for it is far more relaxing and enervating to the thoughts, feelings, and energies of the people. The despotism of Augustus prepared the Romans for Tiberius. If the whole tone of their character had not first been prostrated by nearly two generations of that mild slavery, they would probably have had spirit enough left to rebel against the more odious one.

There is no difficulty in showing that the ideally best form of government is that in which the sovereignty, or supreme controlling power in the last resort, is vested in the entire aggregate of the community; every citizen not only having a voice in the exercise of that ultimate sovereignty, but being,

*b–b*61[1], 61[2]   *them*
*c–c*61[1], 61[2]   a

at least occasionally, called on to take an actual part in the government, by the personal discharge of some public function, local or general.

To test this proposition, it has to be examined in reference to the two branches into which, as pointed out in the last chapter, the inquiry into the goodness of a government conveniently divides itself, namely, how far it promotes the good management of the affairs of society by means of the existing faculties, moral, intellectual, and active, of its various members, and what is its effect in improving or deteriorating those faculties.

The ideally best form of government, it is scarcely necessary to say, does not mean one which is practicable or eligible in all states of civilization, but the one which, in the circumstances in which it is practicable and eligible, is attended with the greatest amount of beneficial consequences, immediate and prospective. A completely popular government is the only polity which can make out any claim to this character. It is pre-eminent in both the departments between which the excellence of a political ^{d}constitution^d is divided. It is both more favourable to present good government, and promotes a better and higher form of national character, than any other polity whatsoever.

Its superiority in reference to present well-being rests upon two principles, of as universal truth and applicability as any general propositions which can be laid down respecting human affairs. The first is, that the rights and interests of every or any person are only secure from being disregarded, when the person interested is himself able, and habitually disposed, to stand up for them. The second is, that the general prosperity attains a greater height, and is more widely diffused, in proportion to the amount and variety of the personal energies enlisted in promoting it.

Putting these two propositions into a shape more special to their present application; human beings are only secure from evil at the hands of others, in proportion as they have the power of being, and are, self-*protecting*; and they only achieve a high degree of success in their struggle with Nature, in proportion as they are self-*dependent*, relying on what they themselves can do, either separately or in concert, rather than on what others do for them.

The former proposition—that each is the only safe guardian of his own rights and interests—is one of those elementary maxims of prudence, which every person, capable of conducting his own affairs, implicitly acts upon, wherever he himself is interested. Many, indeed, have a great dislike to it as a political doctrine, and are fond of holding it up to obloquy, as a doctrine of universal selfishness. To which we may answer, that whenever it ceases to be true that mankind, as a rule, prefer themselves to others, and those nearest to them to those more remote, from that moment Communism is not only practicable, but the only defensible form of society; and will, when that

$^{d-d}$61^1, 61^2 Constitution

time arrives, be assuredly carried into effect. For my own part, not believing in universal selfishness, I have no difficulty in admitting that Communism would even now be practicable among the *élite* of mankind, and may become so among the rest. But as this opinion is anything but popular with those defenders of existing institutions who find fault with the doctrine of the general predominance of self-interest, I am inclined to think they do in reality believe, that most men consider themselves before other people. It is not, however, necessary to affirm even thus much, in order to support the claim of all to participate in the sovereign power. We need not suppose that when power resides in an exclusive class, that class will knowingly and deliberately sacrifice the other classes to themselves: it suffices that, in the absence of its natural defenders, the interest of the excluded is always in danger of being overlooked; and, when looked at, is seen with very different eyes from those of the persons whom it directly concerns. In this country, for example, what are called the working classes may be considered as excluded from all direct participation in the government. I do not believe that the classes who do participate in it, have in general any intention of sacrificing the working classes to themselves. They once had that intention; witness the persevering attempts so long made to keep down wages by law. But in the present day, their ordinary disposition is the very opposite: they willingly make considerable sacrifices, especially of their pecuniary interest, for the benefit of the working classes, and err rather by too lavish and indiscriminating beneficence; nor do I believe that any rulers in history have been actuated by a more sincere desire to do their duty towards the poorer portion of their countrymen. Yet does Parliament, or almost any of the members composing it, ever for an instant look at any question with the eyes of a working man? When a subject arises in which the labourers as such have an interest, is it regarded from any point of view but that of the employers of labour? I do not say that the working men's view of these questions is in general nearer to truth than the other: but it is sometimes quite as near; and in any case it ought to be respectfully listened to, instead of being, as it is, not merely turned away from, but ignored. On the question of strikes, for instance, it is doubtful if there is so much as one among the leading members of either House, who is not firmly convinced that the reason of the matter is unqualifiedly on the side of the masters, and that the men's view of it is simply absurd. Those who have studied the question, know well how far this is from being the case; and in how different, and how infinitely less superficial a manner the point would have to be argued, if the classes who strike were able to make themselves heard in Parliament.

It is an inherent condition of human affairs, that no intention, however sincere, of protecting the interests of others, can make it safe or salutary to tie up their own hands. Still more obviously true is it, that by their own

hands only can any positive and durable improvement of their circumstances in life be worked out. Through the joint influence of these two principles, all free communities have both been more exempt from social injustice and crime, and have attained more brilliant prosperity, than any
others, or than they themselves after they lost their freedom. Contrast the
free states of the world, while their freedom lasted, with the cotemporary
subjects of monarchical or oligarchical despotism: the Greek cities with the
Persian satrapies; the Italian republics, and the free towns of Flanders and
Germany, with the feudal monarchies of Europe; Switzerland, Holland,
and England, with Austria or ante-revolutionary France. Their superior
prosperity was too obvious ever to have been gainsayed: while their superiority in good government and social relations, is proved by the prosperity,
and is manifest besides in every page of history. If we compare, not one age
with another, but the different governments which coexisted in the same
age, no amount of disorder which exaggeration itself can pretend to have
existed amidst the publicity of the free states, can be compared for a moment with the contemptuous trampling upon the mass of the people which
pervaded the whole life of the monarchical countries, or the disgusting individual tyranny which was of more than daily occurrence under the systems
of plunder which they called fiscal arrangements, and in the secrecy of their
frightful courts of justice.

It must be acknowledged that the benefits of freedom, so far as they have
hitherto been enjoyed, were obtained by the extension of its privileges to a
part only of the community; and that a government in which they are extended impartially to all is a desideratum still unrealized. But though every
approach to this has an independent value, and in many cases more than
an approach could not, in the existing state of general improvement, be
made, the participation of all in these benefits is the ideally perfect conception of free government. In proportion as any, no matter who, are excluded
from it, the interests of the excluded are left without the guarantee accorded
to the rest, and they themselves have less scope and encouragement than
they might otherwise have to that exertion of their energies for the good of
themselves and of the community, to which the general prosperity is always
proportioned.

Thus stands the case as regards present well-being; the good management of the affairs of the existing generation. If we now pass to the influence
of the form of government upon character, we shall find the superiority of
popular government over every other to be, if possible, still more decided
and indisputable.

This question really depends upon a still more fundamental one—viz.
which of two common types of character, for the general good of humanity,
it is most desirable should predominate—the active, or the passive type;

that which struggles against evils, or that which endures them; that which bends to circumstances, or that which endeavours to *make circumstances bend* to itself.

The commonplaces of moralists, and the general sympathies of mankind, are in favour of the passive type. Energetic characters may be admired, but the acquiescent and submissive are those which most men personally prefer. The passiveness of our neighbours increases our *f* sense of security, and plays into the hands of our wilfulness. Passive characters, if we do not happen to need their activity, seem an obstruction the less in our own path. A contented character is not a dangerous rival. Yet nothing is more certain, than that improvement in human affairs is wholly the work of the uncontented characters; and, moreover, that it is much easier for an active mind to acquire the virtues of patience, than for a passive one to assume those of energy.

Of the three varieties of mental excellence, intellectual, practical, and moral, there never could be any doubt in regard to the first two, which side had the advantage. All intellectual superiority is the fruit of active effort. Enterprise, the desire to keep moving, to be trying and accomplishing new things for our own benefit or that of others, is the parent even of speculative, and much more of practical, talent. The intellectual culture compatible with the other type is of that feeble and vague description, which belongs to a mind that stops at amusement, or at simple contemplation. The test of real and vigorous thinking, the thinking which ascertains truths instead of dreaming dreams, is successful application to practice. Where that purpose does not exist, to give definiteness, precision, and an intelligible meaning to thought, it generates nothing better than the mystical metaphysics of the Pythagoreans or the Vedas. With respect to practical improvement, the case is still more evident. The character which improves human life is that which struggles with natural powers and tendencies, not that which gives way to them. The self-benefiting qualities are all on the side of the active and energetic character: and the habits and conduct which promote the advantage of each individual member of the community, must be at least a part of those which conduce most in the end to the advancement of the community as a whole.

But on the point of moral preferability, there seems at first sight to be room for doubt. I am not referring to the religious feeling which has so generally existed in favour of the inactive character, as being more in harmony with the submission due to the divine will. Christianity as well as other religions has fostered this sentiment; but it is the prerogative of Christianity, as regards this and many other perversions, that it is able to throw them off.

e-e611, 612   bend circumstances
f611, 612   own

Abstractedly from religious considerations, a passive character, which yields to obstacles instead of striving to overcome them, may not indeed be very useful to others, no more than to itself, but it might be expected to be at least inoffensive. Contentment is always counted among the moral virtues. But it is a complete error to suppose that contentment is necessarily or naturally attendant on passivity of character; and unless it is, the moral consequences are mischievous. Where there exists a desire for advantages not possessed, the mind which does not potentially possess them by means of its own energies, is apt to look with hatred and malice on those who do. The person bestirring himself with hopeful prospects to improve his circumstances, is the one who feels goodwill towards others engaged in, or who have succeeded in, the same pursuit. And where the majority are so engaged, those who do not attain the object have had the tone given to their feelings by the general habit of the country, and ascribe their failure to want of effort or opportunity, or to their personal ill luck. But those who, while desiring what others possess, put no energy into striving for it, are either incessantly grumbling that fortune does not do for them what they do not attempt to do for themselves, or overflowing with envy and ill-will towards those who possess what they would like to have.

In proportion as success in life is seen or believed to be the fruit of fatality or accident and not of exertion, in that same ratio does envy develope itself as a point of national character. The most envious of all mankind are the Orientals. In Oriental moralists, in Oriental tales, the envious man is markedly prominent. In real life, he is the terror of all who possess anything desirable, be it a palace, a handsome child, or even good health and spirits: the supposed effect of his mere look constitutes the all-pervading superstition of the evil eye. Next to Orientals in envy, as in ᵍactivityᵍ, are some of the Southern Europeans. The Spaniards pursued all their great men with it, embittered their lives, and generally succeeded in putting an early stop to their successes.* With the French, who are essentially a southern people, the double education of despotism and Catholicism has, in spite of their impulsive temperament, made submission and endurance the common character of the people, and their most received notion of wisdom and excellence: and if envy of one another, and of all superiority, is not more rife among them than it is, the circumstance must be ascribed to the many

*I limit the expression to past time, because I would say nothing derogatory of a great, and now at last a free, people, who are entering into the general movement of European progress with a vigour which bids fair to make up rapidly the ground they have lost. No one can doubt what Spanish intellect and energy are capable of; and their faults as a people are chiefly those for which freedom and industrial ardour are a real specific.

ᵍ⁻ᵍ611   inactivity [*printer's error?*]

valuable counteracting elements in the French character, and most of all to the great individual energy which, though less persistent and more intermittent than in the self-helping and struggling Anglo-Saxons, has nevertheless manifested itself among the French in nearly every direction in which the operation of their institutions has been favourable to it.

There are, no doubt, in all countries, really contented characters, who not merely do not seek, but do not desire, what they do not already possess, and these naturally bear no ill-will towards such as have apparently a more favoured lot. But the great mass of seeming contentment is real discontent, combined with indolence or self-indulgence, which, while taking no legitimate means of raising itself, delights in bringing others down to its own level. And if we look narrowly even at the cases of innocent contentment, we perceive that they only win our admiration, when the indifference is solely to improvement in outward circumstances, and there is a striving for perpetual advancement in spiritual worth, or at least a disinterested zeal to benefit others. The contented man, or the contented family, who have no ambition to make any one else happier, to promote the good of their country or their neighbourhood, or to improve themselves in moral excellence, excite in us neither admiration nor approval. We rightly ascribe this sort of contentment to mere unmanliness and want of spirit. The content which we approve, is an ability to do cheerfully without what cannot be had, a just appreciation of the comparative value of different objects of desire, and a willing renunciation of the less when incompatible with the greater. These, however, are excellences more natural to the character, in proportion as it is actively engaged in the attempt to improve its own or some other lot. He who is continually measuring his energy against difficulties, learns what are the difficulties insuperable to him, and what are those which though he might overcome, the success is not worth the cost. He whose thoughts and activities are all needed for, and habitually employed in, practicable and useful enterprises, is the person of all others least likely to let his mind dwell with brooding discontent upon things either not worth attaining, or which are not so to him. Thus the active, self-helping character is not only intrinsically the best, but is the likeliest to acquire all that is really excellent or desirable in the opposite type.

The striving, go-ahead character of England and the United States is only a fit subject of disapproving criticism, on account of the very secondary objects on which it commonly expends its strength. In itself it is the foundation of the best hopes for the general improvement of mankind. It has been acutely remarked, that whenever anything goes amiss, the habitual impulse of French people is to say, "Il faut de la patience;" and of English people, "What a shame." The people who think it a shame when anything goes wrong—who rush to the conclusion that the evil could and ought to have been prevented, are those who, in the long run, do most to make the world better. If the desires are low placed, if they extend to little beyond physical comfort and the show of riches, the immediate results of the energy will not be much more than the continual extension of man's power over material objects; but even this makes room, and prepares the mechanical appliances, for the greatest intellectual and social achievements; and while the energy is there, some persons will apply it, and it will be applied more and more, to the perfecting not of outward circumstances alone, but of man's inward nature. Inactivity, unaspiringness, absence of desire, *h*are a more fatal hindrance to improvement than any misdirection of energy; and are*h* that through which alone, when existing in the mass, any very formidable misdirection by an energetic few becomes possible. It is this, mainly, which retains in a savage or semi-savage state the great majority of the human race.

Now there can be no kind of doubt that the passive type of character is favoured by the government of one or a few, and the active self-helping type by that of the Many. Irresponsible rulers need the quiescence of the ruled, more than they need any activity but that which they can compel. Submissiveness to the prescriptions of men as necessities of nature, is the lesson inculcated by all governments upon those who are wholly without participation in them. The will of superiors, and the law as the will of superiors, must be passively yielded to. But no men are mere instruments or materials in the hands of their rulers, who have will or spirit or a spring of internal activity in the rest of their proceedings: and any manifestation of these qualities, instead of receiving encouragement from despots, has to get itself forgiven by them. Even when irresponsible rulers are not sufficiently conscious of danger from the mental activity of their subjects to be desirous of repressing it, the position itself is a repression. Endeavour is even more effectually restrained by the certainty of its impotence, than by any positive discouragement. Between subjection to the will of others, and the virtues of self-help and self-government, there is a natural incompatibility. This is more or less complete, according as the bondage is strained or relaxed. Rulers differ very much in the length to which they carry the control of the free agency of their subjects, or the supersession of it by managing their business for them. But the difference is in degree, not in principle; and the best despots often go the greatest lengths in chaining up the free agency of their subjects. A bad despot, when his own personal indulgences have been provided for, may sometimes be willing to let the people alone; but a good despot insists on doing them good, by making them do their own business in a better way than they themselves know of. The regulations which restricted to fixed processes all the leading branches of French manufactures, were the work of the great Colbert.

*h-h*61¹, 61² is a . . . and is

Very different is the state of the human faculties where a human being feels himself under no other external restraint than the necessities of nature, or mandates of society which he has his share in imposing, and which it is open to him, if he thinks them wrong, publicly to dissent from, and exert himself actively to get altered. No doubt, under a government partially popular, this freedom may be exercised even by those who are not partakers in the full privileges of citizenship. But it is a great additional stimulus to any one's self-help and self-reliance when he starts from *i* even ground, and has not to feel that his success depends on the impression he can make upon the sentiments and dispositions of a body of whom he is not one. It is a great discouragement to an individual, and a still greater one to a class, to be left out of the constitution; to be reduced to plead from outside the door to the arbiters of their destiny, not taken into the consultation within. The maximum of the invigorating effect of freedom upon the character is only obtained, when the person acted on either is, or is looking forward to *i*becoming*i*, a citizen as fully privileged as any other. What is still more important than even this matter of feeling, is the practical discipline which the character obtains, from the occasional demand made upon the citizens to exercise, for a time and in their turn, some social function. It is not sufficiently considered how little there is in most men's ordinary life to give any largeness either to their conceptions or to their sentiments. Their work is a routine; not a labour of love, but of self-interest in the most elementary form, the satisfaction of daily wants; neither the thing done, nor the process of doing it, introduces the mind to thoughts or feelings extending beyond individuals; if instructive books are within their reach, there is no stimulus to read them; and in most cases the individual has no access to any person of cultivation much superior to his own. Giving him something to do for the public, supplies, in a measure, all these deficiencies. If circumstances allow the amount of public duty assigned him to be considerable, it makes him an educated man. Notwithstanding the defects of the social system and moral ideas of antiquity, the practice of the dicastery and the ecclesia raised the intellectual standard of an average Athenian citizen far beyond anything of which there is yet an example in any other mass of men, ancient or modern. The proofs of this are apparent in every page of our great historian of Greece;[*] but we need scarcely look further than to the high quality of the addresses which their great orators deemed best calculated to act with effect on their understanding and will. A benefit of the same kind, though far less in degree, is produced on Englishmen of the lower middle class by their liability to be placed on juries and to serve parish offices; which, though it does not occur to so many, nor is so continuous, nor introduces them to so

[*George Grote, *A History of Greece*, 12 vols. (London: Murray, 1846–56).]
*i*61¹, 61² an   *i-i*61¹ become

great a variety of elevated considerations, as to admit of comparison with the public education which every citizen of Athens obtained from her democratic institutions, ^kmust make^k them nevertheless very different beings, in range of ideas and development of faculties, from those who have done nothing in their lives but drive a quill, or sell goods over a counter. Still more salutary is the moral part of the instruction afforded by the participation of the private citizen, if even rarely, in public functions. He is called upon, while so engaged, to weigh interests not his own; to be guided, in case of conflicting claims, by another rule than his private partialities; to apply, at every turn, principles and maxims which have for their reason of existence the ^lcommon^l good: and he usually finds associated with him in the same work minds more familiarized than his own with these ideas and operations, whose study it will be to supply reasons to his understanding, and stimulation to his feeling for the general ^minterest^m. He is made to feel himself one of the public, and whatever is ⁿfor their benefit to be for his benefitⁿ. Where this school of public spirit does not exist, scarcely any sense is entertained that private persons, in no eminent social situation, owe any duties to society, except to obey the laws and submit to the government. There is no unselfish sentiment of identification with the public. Every thought ^oor^o feeling, either of interest or of duty, is absorbed in the individual and in the family. The man never thinks of any collective interest, of any objects to be pursued jointly with others, but only in competition with them, and in some measure at their expense. A neighbour, not being an ally or an associate, since he is never engaged in any common undertaking for ^p joint benefit, is therefore only a rival. Thus even private morality suffers, while public is actually extinct. Were this the universal and only possible state of things, the utmost aspirations of the lawgiver or the moralist could only stretch to making the bulk of the community a flock of sheep innocently nibbling the grass side by side.

From these accumulated considerations it is evident, that the only government which can fully satisfy all the exigencies of the social state, is one in which the whole people participate; that any participation, even in the smallest public function, is useful; that the participation should everywhere be as great as the general degree of improvement of the community will allow; and that nothing less can be ultimately desirable, than the admission of all to a share in the sovereign power of the state. But since all cannot, in a community exceeding a single small town, participate personally in any but some very minor portions of the public business, it follows that the ideal type of a perfect government must be representative.

^{k-k}61[1]   makes
^{m-m}61[1]   good
^{o-o}61[1], 61[2]   and

^{l-l}61[1]   general
ⁿ⁻ⁿ61[1]   their interest to be his interest
^p61[1]   the

CHAPTER IV

Under What Social Conditions
Representative Government
is Inapplicable

WE HAVE RECOGNISED in representative government the ideal type of the most perfect polity, for which, in consequence, any portion of mankind are better adapted in proportion to their degree of general improvement. As they range lower and lower in development, that form of government will be, generally speaking, less suitable to them; though this is not true universally: for the adaptation of a people to representative government does not depend so much upon the place they occupy in the general scale of humanity, as upon the degree in which they possess certain special requisites; requisites, however, so closely connected with their degree of general advancement, that any variation between the two is rather the exception than the rule. Let us examine at what point in the descending series representative government ceases altogether to be admissible, either through its own unfitness, or the superior fitness of some other regimen.

First, then, representative, like any other government, must be unsuitable in any case in which it cannot permanently subsist—*i.e.* in which it does not fulfil the three fundamental conditions enumerated in the first chapter. These were—1. That the people should be willing to receive it. 2. That they should be willing and able to do what is necessary for its preservation. 3. That they should be willing and able to fulfil the duties and discharge the functions which it imposes on them.

The willingness of the people to accept representative government, only becomes a practical question, when an enlightened ruler, or a foreign nation or nations who have gained power over the country, are disposed to offer it the boon. To individual reformers the question is almost irrelevant, since, if no other objection can be made to their enterprise than that the opinion of the nation is not yet on their side, they have the ready and proper answer, that to bring it over to their side is the very end they aim at. When opinion is really adverse, its hostility is usually to the fact of change, rather than to representative government in itself. The contrary case is not indeed unexampled; there has sometimes been a religious repugnance to any limitation of the power of a particular line of rulers; but in general, the doctrine of passive obedience meant only submission to the will of the powers that be, whether monarchical or popular. In any case in which the attempt to introduce representative government is at all likely to be made, indifference to it, and inability to understand its processes and requirements, rather than positive opposition, are the obstacles to be expected. These, however, are as fatal, and may be as hard to be got rid of as actual aversion; it being easier, in most cases, to change the direction of an active feeling, than to create one in a state previously passive. When a people have no sufficient value for, and attachment to, a representative constitution, they have next to no chance of retaining it. In every country, the executive is the branch of the government which wields the immediate power, and is in direct contact with the public; to it, principally, the hopes and fears of individuals are directed, and by it both the benefits, and the terrors and *prestige*, of government, are mainly represented to the public eye. Unless, therefore, the authorities whose office it is to check the executive are backed by an effective opinion and feeling in the country, the executive has always the means of setting them aside, or compelling them to subservience, and is sure to be well supported in doing so. Representative institutions necessarily depend for permanence upon the readiness of the people to fight for them in case of their being endangered. If too little valued for this, they seldom obtain a footing at all, and if they do, are almost sure to be overthrown, as soon as the head of the government, or any party leader who can muster force for a *coup de main*, is willing to run some small risk for absolute power.

These considerations relate to the *a*first two*a* causes of failure in a representative government. The third is, when the people want either the will or the capacity to fulfil the part which belongs to them in a representative constitution. When nobody, or only some small fraction, feels the degree of interest in the general affairs of the State necessary to the formation of a public opinion, the electors will seldom make any use of the right of *b* suffrage but to serve their private interest, or the interest of their locality, or of some one with whom they are connected as adherents or dependents. The small class who, in this state of public feeling, gain the command of the representative body, for the most part use it solely as a means of seeking their fortune. If the executive is weak, the country is distracted by mere struggles for place; if strong, it makes itself despotic, at the cheap price of appeasing the representatives, or such of them as are capable of giving trouble, by a share of the spoil; and the only fruit produced by national representation is, that in addition to those who really govern, there is an

*a–a*611   two first
*b*611   the

assembly quartered on the public, and no abuse in which a portion of the assembly are interested is at all likely to be removed. When, however, the evil stops here, the price may be worth paying, for the publicity and discussion which, though not an invariable, are a natural accompaniment of any, even nominal, representation. In the modern kingdom of Greece, for example,* it can hardly be doubted, that the place-hunters who chiefly compose the representative assembly, though they contribute little or nothing directly to good government, nor even much temper the arbitrary power of the executive, yet keep up the idea of popular rights, and conduce greatly to the real liberty of the press which exists in that country. This benefit, however, is entirely dependent on the co-existence with the popular body of an hereditary king. If, instead of struggling for the favours of the chief ruler, these selfish and sordid factions struggled for the chief place itself, they would certainly, as in Spanish America, keep the country in a state of chronic revolution and civil war. A despotism, not even legal, but of illegal violence, would be alternately exercised by a succession of political adventurers, and the name and forms of representation would have no effect but to prevent despotism from attaining the stability and security by which alone its evils can be mitigated, or its few advantages realized.

The preceding are the cases in which representative government cannot permanently exist. There are others in which it possibly might exist, but in which some other form of government would be preferable. These are principally when the people, in order to advance in civilization, have some lesson to learn, some habit not yet acquired, to the acquisition of which representative government is likely to be an impediment.

The most obvious of these cases is the one already considered, in which the people have still to learn the first lesson of civilization, that of obedience. A race who have been trained in energy and courage by struggles with Nature and their neighbours, but who have not yet settled down into permanent obedience to any common superior, would be little likely to acquire this habit under the collective government of their own body. A representative assembly drawn from among themselves would simply reflect their own turbulent insubordination. It would refuse its authority to all proceedings which would impose, on their savage independence, any improving restraint. The mode in which such tribes are usually brought to submit to the primary conditions of civilized society, is through the necessities of warfare, and the despotic authority indispensable to military command. A military leader is the only superior to whom they will submit, except occasion-

*[65] Written before the salutary revolution of 1862, which, provoked by popular disgust at the system of governing by corruption, and the general demoralization of political men, has opened to that rapidly improving people a new and hopeful chance of real constitutional government.

ally some prophet supposed to be inspired from above, or conjurer regarded as possessing miraculous power. These may exercise a temporary
ascendancy, but as it is merely personal, it rarely effects any change in the
general habits of the people, unless the prophet, like Mahomet, is also a
military chief, and goes forth the armed apostle of a new religion; or unless
the military chiefs ally themselves with his influence, and turn it into a prop
for their own government.

A people are no less unfitted for representative government by the contrary fault to that last specified; by extreme passiveness, and ready submission to tyranny. If a people thus prostrated by character and circumstances could obtain representative institutions, they would inevitably
choose their tyrants as their representatives, and the yoke would be made
heavier on them by the contrivance which *primâ facie* might be expected
to lighten it. On the contrary, many a people has gradually emerged from
this condition by the aid of a central authority, whose position has made it
the rival, and has ended by making it the master, of the local despots, and
which, above all, has been single. French history, from Hugh Capet to
Richelieu and Louis XIV, is a continued example of this course of things.
Even when the King was scarcely so powerful as many of his chief feuda-
tories, the great advantage which he derived from being but one, has been
recognised by French historians. To him the eyes of *all* the locally oppressed were turned; he was the object of hope and reliance throughout the
kingdom; while each local potentate was only powerful within a more or
less confined space. At his hands, refuge and protection were sought from
every part of the country, against first one, then another, of the immediate
oppressors. His progress to ascendancy was slow; but it resulted from suc-
cessively taking advantage of opportunities which offered themselves only
to him. It was therefore, sure; and, in proportion as it was accomplished, it
abated, in the oppressed portion of the community, the habit of submitting
to oppression. The King's interest lay in encouraging all partial attempts
on the part of the serfs to emancipate themselves from their masters, and
place themselves in immediate subordination to himself. Under his protection numerous communities were formed which knew no one above them
but the King. Obedience to a distant monarch is liberty itself compared with
the dominion of the lord of the neighbouring castle: and the monarch was
long compelled by necessities of position to exert his authority as the ally,
rather than the master, of the classes whom he had aided in effecting their
liberation. In this manner a central power, despotic in principle though
generally much restricted in practice, was mainly instrumental in carrying
the people through a necessary stage of improvement, which representative
government, if real, would most likely have prevented them from entering

upon. *c* Nothing short of despotic rule, or a general massacre, could *d*have effected*d* the emancipation of the serfs in the Russian Empire.

The same passages of history forcibly illustrate another mode in which unlimited monarchy overcomes obstacles to the progress of civilization which representative government would have had a decided tendency to aggravate. One of the strongest hindrances to improvement, up to a rather advanced stage, is an inveterate spirit of locality. Portions of mankind, in many other respects capable of, and prepared for, freedom, may be un- qualified for amalgamating into even the smallest nation. Not only may jealousies and antipathies repel them from one another, and bar all possi- bility of voluntary union, but they may not yet have acquired any of the feelings or habits which would make the union real, supposing it to be nomi- nally accomplished. They may, like the citizens of an ancient community, or those of an Asiatic village, have had considerable practice in exercising their faculties on village or town interests, and have even realized a toler- ably effective popular government on that restricted scale, and may yet have but slender sympathies with anything beyond, and no habit or capacity of dealing with interests common to many such communities. I am not aware that history furnishes any example in which a number of these political atoms or corpuscles have coalesced into a body, and learnt to feel them- selves one people, except through previous subjection to a central authority common to all.* It is through the habit of deferring to that authority, enter- ing into its plans and subserving its purposes, that a people such as we have supposed, receive into their minds the conception of large interests, com- mon to a considerable geographical extent. Such interests, on the contrary, are necessarily the predominant consideration in the mind of the central ruler; and through the relations, more or less intimate, which he progres- sively establishes with the localities, they become familiar to the general mind. The most favourable concurrence of circumstances under which this step in improvement could be made, would be one which should raise up representative institutions without representative government; a represent- ative body, or bodies, drawn from the localities, making itself the auxiliary and instrument of the central power, but seldom attempting to thwart or control it. The people being thus taken, as it were, into council, though not sharing the supreme power, the political education given by the central

---

*Italy, which alone can be quoted as an exception, is only so in regard to the final stage of its transformation. The more difficult previous advance from the city isolation of Florence, Pisa, or Milan, to the provincial unity of Tuscany or Lombardy, took place in the usual manner.

*c*61¹, 61² There are parts of Europe where the same work is still to be done, and no prospect of its being done by any other means.
*d–d*61¹, 61²   effect

authority is carried home, much more effectually than it could otherwise be, to the local chiefs and to the population generally; while, at the same time, a tradition is kept up of government by general consent, or at least, the sanction of tradition is not given to government without it, which, when consecrated by custom, has so often put a bad end to a good beginning, and is one of the most frequent *causes* of the sad fatality which in most countries has stopped improvement in so early a stage, because the work of some one period has been so done as to bar the needful work of the ages following. Meanwhile, it may be laid down as a political truth, that by irresponsible monarchy rather than by representative government can a multitude of insignificant political units be welded into a people, with common feelings of cohesion, power enough to protect itself against conquest or foreign aggression, and affairs sufficiently various and considerable of its own to occupy worthily and expand to fit proportions the social and political intelligence of the population.

For these several reasons, kingly government, free from the control (though perhaps strengthened by the support) of representative institutions, is the most suitable form of polity for the earliest stages of any community, not excepting a city-community like those of ancient Greece: where, accordingly, the government of kings, under some real but no ostensible or constitutional control by public opinion, did historically precede by an unknown and probably great duration all free institutions, and gave place at last, during a considerable lapse of time, to oligarchies of a few families.

A hundred other infirmities or short-comings in a people might be pointed out, which *pro tanto* disqualify them from making the best use of representative government; but in regard to these it is not equally obvious that the government of One or a Few would have any tendency to cure or alleviate the evil. Strong prejudices of any kind; obstinate adherence to old habits; positive defects of national character, or mere ignorance, and deficiency of mental cultivation, if prevalent in a people, will be in general faithfully reflected in their representative assemblies: and should it happen that the executive administration, the direct management of public affairs, is in the hands of persons comparatively free from these defects, more good would frequently be done by them when not hampered by the necessity of carrying with them the voluntary assent of such bodies. But the mere position of the rulers does not in these, as it does in the other cases which we have examined, of itself invest them with interests and tendencies operating in the beneficial direction. From the general weaknesses of the people or of the state of civilization, the One and his counsellors, or the Few, are not likely to be habitually exempt; except in the case of their being foreigners, belonging to a superior people or a more advanced state of society.

*e–e*611, 612   cases [*printer's error?*]

Then, indeed, the rulers may be, to almost any extent, superior in civilization to those over whom they rule; and subjection to a foreign government of this description, notwithstanding its inevitable evils, is often of the greatest advantage to a people, carrying them rapidly through several stages of progress, and clearing away obstacles to improvement which might have lasted indefinitely if the subject population had been left unassisted to its native tendencies and chances. In a country not under the dominion of foreigners, the only cause adequate to producing similar benefits is the rare accident of a monarch of extraordinary genius. There have been in history a few of these who, happily for humanity, have reigned long enough to render some of their improvements permanent, by leaving them under the guardianship of a generation which had grown up under their influence. Charlemagne may be cited as one instance; Peter the Great is another. Such examples however are so unfrequent that they can only be classed with the happy accidents, which have so often decided at a critical moment whether some leading portion of humanity should make a sudden start, or sink back towards barbarism: chances like the existence of Themistocles at the time of the Persian invasion, or of the first or third William of Orange. It would be absurd to construct institutions for the mere purpose of taking advantage of such possibilities; especially as men of this calibre, in any distinguished position, do not require despotic power to enable them to exert great influence, as is evidenced by the three last mentioned. The case most requiring consideration in reference to institutions, is the not very uncommon one, in which a small but leading portion of the population, from difference of race, more civilized origin, or other peculiarities of circumstance, are markedly superior in civilization and general character to the remainder. Under these conditions, government by the representatives of the mass would stand a chance of depriving them of much of the benefit they might derive from the greater civilization of the superior ranks; while government by the representatives of those ranks would probably rivet the degradation of the multitude, and leave them no hope of decent treatment except by ridding themselves of one of the most valuable elements of future advancement. The best prospect of improvement for a people thus composed, lies in the existence of a constitutionally unlimited, or at least a practically preponderant, authority in the chief ruler of the dominant class. He alone has by his position an interest in raising and improving the mass, of whom he is not jealous, as a counterpoise to his associates, of whom he is. And if fortunate circumstances place beside him, not as controllers but as subordinates, a body representative of the superior caste, which by its objections and questionings, and its occasional outbreaks of spirit, keeps alive habits of collective resistance, and may admit of being, in time and by degrees, expanded into a really national representation (which is in substance the history of the English Parliament), the nation has then the most favourable prospects of improvement, which can well occur to a community thus circumstanced and constituted.

Among the tendencies which, without absolutely rendering a people unfit for representative government, seriously incapacitate them from reaping the full benefit of it, one deserves particular notice. There are two states of the inclinations, intrinsically very different, but which have something in common, by virtue of which they often coincide in the direction they give to the efforts of individuals and of nations: one is, the desire to exercise power over others; the other is disinclination to have power exercised over themselves. The difference between different portions of mankind in the relative strength of these two dispositions, is one of the most important elements in their history. There are nations in whom the passion for governing others is so much stronger than the desire of personal independence, that for the mere shadow of the one they are found ready to sacrifice the whole of the other. Each one of their number is willing, like the private soldier in an army, to abdicate his personal freedom of action into the hands of his general, provided the army is triumphant and victorious, and he is able to flatter himself that he is one of a conquering host, though the notion that he has himself any share in the domination exercised over the conquered is an illusion. A government strictly limited in its powers and attributions, required to hold its hands from overmeddling, and to let most things go on without its assuming the part of guardian or director, is not to the taste of such a /people. In/ their eyes the possessors of authority can hardly take too much upon themselves, provided the authority itself is open to general competition. An average individual among them prefers the chance, however distant or improbable, of wielding some share of power over his fellow-citizens, above the certainty, to himself and others, of having no unnecessary power exercised over them. These are the elements of a people of place-hunters; in whom the course of politics is mainly determined by place-hunting; where equality alone is cared for, but not liberty; where the contests of political parties are but struggles to decide whether the power of meddling in everything shall belong to one class or another, perhaps merely to one knot of public men or another; where the idea entertained of democracy is merely that of opening offices to the competition of all instead of a few; where, the more popular the institutions, the more innumerable are the places created, and the more monstrous the over-government exercised by all over each, and by the executive over all. It would be as unjust as it would be ungenerous to offer this, or anything approaching to it, as an unexaggerated picture of the French people; yet the degree in which they do participate in this type of character, has caused representative government by a limited

/-/611   people; in

class to break down by excess of corruption, and the attempt at representative government by the whole male population to end in giving one man the power of consigning any number of the rest, without trial, to Lambessa or Cayenne, provided he allows all of them to think themselves not excluded from the possibility of sharing his favours. The point of character which, beyond any other, fits the people of this country for representative government, is, that they have almost universally the contrary characteristic. They are very jealous of any attempt to exercise power over them, not sanctioned by long usage and by their own opinion of right; but they in general care very little for the exercise of power over others. Not having the smallest sympathy with the passion for governing, while they are but too well acquainted with the motives of private interest from which that office is sought, they prefer that it should be performed by those to whom it comes without seeking, as a consequence of social position. If foreigners understood this, it would account to them for some of the apparent contradictions in the political feelings of Englishmen; their unhesitating readiness to let themselves be governed by the higher classes, coupled with so little personal subservience to them, that no people are so fond of resisting authority when it oversteps certain prescribed limits, or so determined to make their rulers always remember that they will only be governed in the way they themselves like best. Place-hunting, accordingly, is a form of ambition to which the English, considered nationally, are almost strangers. If we except the few families or connexions of whom official employment lies directly in the way, Englishmen's views of advancement in life take an altogether different direction—that of success in business, or in a profession. They have the strongest distaste for any mere struggle for office by political parties or individuals: and there are few things to which they have a greater aversion than to the multiplication of public employments: a thing, on the contrary, always popular with the bureaucracy-ridden nations of the Continent, who would rather pay higher taxes, than diminish by the smallest fraction their individual chances of a place for themselves or their relatives, and among whom a cry for retrenchment never means abolition of offices, but the reduction of the salaries of those which are too considerable for the ordinary citizen to have any chance of being appointed to them.

CHAPTER V

Of the Proper Functions of Representative Bodies

IN TREATING of representative government, it is above all necessary to keep in view the distinction between its idea or essence, and the particular forms in which the idea has been clothed by accidental historical developments, or by the notions current at some particular period.

The meaning of representative government is, that the whole people, or some numerous portion of them, exercise through deputies periodically elected by themselves, the ultimate controlling power, which, in every constitution, must reside somewhere. This ultimate power they must possess in all its completeness. They must be masters, whenever they please, of all the operations of government. There is no need that the constitutional law should itself give them this mastery. It does not, in the British Constitution. But what it does give, practically amounts to this. The power of final control is as essentially single, in a mixed and balanced government, as in a pure monarchy or democracy. This is the portion of truth in the opinion of the ancients, revived by great authorities in our own time, that a balanced constitution is impossible. There is almost always a balance, but the scales never hang exactly even. Which of them preponderates, is not always apparent on the face of the political institutions. In the British Constitution, each of the three co-ordinate members of the sovereignty is invested with powers which, if fully exercised, would enable it to stop all the machinery of government. Nominally, therefore, each is invested with equal power of thwarting and obstructing the others: and if, by exerting that power, any of the three could hope to better its position, the ordinary course of human affairs forbids us to doubt that the power would be exercised. There can be no question that the full powers of each would be employed defensively, if it found itself assailed by one or both of the others. What then prevents the same powers from being exerted aggressively? The unwritten maxims of the Constitution —in other words, the positive political morality of the country: and this positive political morality is what we must look to, if we would know in whom the really supreme power in the Constitution resides.

By constitutional law, the Crown can refuse its assent to any Act of Parliament, and can appoint to office and maintain in it any Minister, in opposition to the remonstrances of Parliament. But the constitutional morality of the country nullifies these powers, preventing them from being ever used; and, by requiring that the head of the Administration should always be virtually appointed by the House of Commons, makes that body the real sovereign of the State. These unwritten rules, which limit the use of lawful powers, are, however, only effectual, and maintain themselves in existence, on condition of harmonizing with the actual distribution of real political strength. There is in every constitution a strongest power—one which would gain the victory, if the compromises by which the Constitution habitually works were suspended, and there came a trial of strength. Constitutional maxims are adhered to, and are practically operative, so long as they give the predominance in the Constitution to that one of the powers which has the preponderence of active power out of doors. This, in England, is the popular power. If, therefore, the legal provisions of the British Constitution, together with the unwritten maxims by which the conduct of the different political authorities is in fact regulated, did not give to the popular element in the Constitution that substantial supremacy over every department of the government, which corresponds to its real power in the country, the Constitution would not possess the stability which characterizes it; either the laws or the unwritten maxims would soon have to be changed. The British *government* is thus a representative government in the correct sense of the term: and the powers which it leaves in hands not directly accountable to the people, can only be considered as precautions which the ruling power is willing should be taken against its own errors. Such precautions have existed in all well-constructed democracies. The Athenian Constitution had many such provisions; and so has that of the United States.

But while it is essential to representative government that the practical supremacy in the state should reside in the representatives of the people, it is an open question what actual functions, what precise part in the machinery of government, shall be directly and personally discharged by the representative body. Great varieties in this respect are compatible with the essence of representative government, provided the functions are such as secure to the representative body the control of everything in the last resort.

There is a radical distinction between controlling the business of government, and actually doing it. The same person or body may be able to control everything, but cannot possibly do everything; and in many cases its control over everything will be more perfect, the less it personally attempts to do. The commander of an army could not direct its movements *b* effectually if he himself fought in the ranks, or led an assault. It is the same with bodies of men. Some things cannot be done except by bodies; other things cannot be well done by them. It is one question, therefore, what a popular assembly

*a–a*611 Government
*b*611, 612   so

should control, another what it should itself do. It should, as we have already seen, control all the operations of government. But in order to determine through what channel this general control may most expediently be exercised, and what portion of the business of government the representative assembly should hold in its own hands, it is necessary to consider what kinds of business a numerous body is competent to perform properly. That alone which it can do well, it ought to take personally upon itself. With regard to the rest, its proper province is not to do it, but to take means for having it well done by others.

For example, the duty which is considered as belonging more peculiarly than any other to an assembly representative of the people, is that of voting the taxes. Nevertheless, in no country does the representative body undertake, by itself or its delegated officers, to prepare the estimates. Though the supplies can only be voted by the House of Commons, and though the sanction of the House is also required for the appropriation of the revenues to the different items of the public expenditure, it is the maxim and the uniform practice of the Constitution that money can be granted only on the proposition of the Crown. It has, no doubt, been felt, that moderation as to the amount, and care and judgment in the detail of its application, can only be expected when the ᶜexecutiveᶜ government, through whose hands it is to pass, is made responsible for the plans and calculations on which the disbursements are grounded. Parliament, accordingly, is not expected, nor even permitted, to originate directly either taxation or expenditure. All it is asked for is its consent, and the sole power it possesses is that of refusal.

The principles which are involved and recognised in this constitutional doctrine, if followed as far as they will go, are a guide to the limitation and definition of the general functions of representative assemblies. In the first place, it is admitted in all countries in which the representative system is practically understood, that numerous representative bodies ought not to administer. The maxim is grounded not only on the most essential principles of good government, but on those of the successful conduct of business of any description. No body of men, unless organized and under command, is fit for action, in the proper sense. Even a select board, composed of few members, and these specially conversant with the business to be done, is always an inferior instrument to some one individual who could be found among them, and would be improved in character if that one person were made the chief, and all the others reduced to subordinates. What can be done better by a body than by any individual, is deliberation. When it is necessary, or important, to secure hearing and consideration to many conflicting opinions, a deliberative body is indispensable. Those bodies, therefore, are frequently useful, even for administrative business, but in general only as ad-

ᶜ⁻ᶜ61¹, 61² Executive

visers; such business being, as a rule, better conducted under the responsibility of one. Even a joint-stock company has always in practice, if not in theory, a managing director; its good or bad management depends essentially on some one person's qualifications, and the remaining directors, when of any use, are so by their suggestions to him, or by the power they possess of watching him, and restraining or removing him in case of misconduct. That they are ostensibly equal sharers with him in the management is no advantage, but a considerable set-off against any good which they are capable of doing: it weakens greatly the sense in his own mind, and in those of other people, of that individual responsibility in which he should stand forth personally and undividedly.

But a popular assembly is still less fitted to administer, or to dictate in detail to those who have the charge of administration. Even when honestly meant, the interference is almost always injurious. Every branch of public administration is a skilled business, which has its own peculiar principles and traditional rules, many of them not even known, in any effectual way, except to those who have at some time had a hand in carrying on the business, and none of them likely to be duly appreciated by persons not practically acquainted with the department. I do not mean that the transaction of public business has esoteric mysteries, only to be understood by the initiated. Its principles are all intelligible to any person of good sense, who has in his mind a true picture of the circumstances and conditions to be dealt with: but to have this he must know those circumstances and conditions; and the knowledge does not come by intuition. There are many rules of the greatest importance in every branch of public business (as there are in every private occupation), of which a person fresh to the subject neither knows the reason or even suspects the existence, because they are intended to meet dangers or provide against inconveniences which never entered into his thoughts. I have known public men, ministers, of more than ordinary natural capacity, who on their first introduction to a department of business new to them, have excited the mirth of their inferiors by the air with which they announced as a truth hitherto set at nought, and brought to light by themselves, something which was probably the first thought of everybody who ever looked at the subject, given up as soon as he had got on to a second. It is true that a great statesman is he who knows when to depart from traditions, as well as when to adhere to them. But it is a great mistake to suppose that he will do this better for being ignorant of the traditions. No one who does not thoroughly know the modes of action which common experience has sanctioned, is capable of judging of the circumstances which require a departure from those ordinary modes of action. The interests dependent on the acts done by a public department, the consequences liable to follow from any particular mode of conducting it, require for weighing and estimating them a kind of knowledge, and of specially exercised judgment, almost as rarely found in those not bred to it, as the capacity to reform the law in those who have not professionally studied it. All these difficulties are sure to be ignored by a representative assembly which attempts to decide on special acts of administration. At its best, it is inexperience sitting in judgment on experience, ignorance on knowledge: ignorance which never suspecting the existence of what it does not know, is equally careless and supercilious, making light of, if not resenting, all pretensions to have a judgment better worth attending to than its own. Thus it is when no interested motives intervene: but when they do, the result is jobbery more unblushing and audacious than the worst corruption which can well take place in a public office under a government of publicity. It is not necessary that the interested bias should extend to the majority of the assembly. In any particular case it is often enough that it affects two or three of their number. Those two or three will have a greater interest in misleading the body, than any other of its members are likely to have in putting it right. The bulk of the assembly may keep their hands clean, but they cannot keep their minds vigilant or their judgments discerning in matters they know nothing about: and an indolent majority, like an indolent individual, belongs to the person who takes most pains with it. The bad measures or bad appointments of a minister may be checked by Parliament; and the interest of ministers in defending, and of rival partisans in attacking, *d*secures*d* a tolerably equal discussion: but *quis custodiet custodes?*[*] who shall check the Parliament? A minister, a head of an office, feels himself under some responsibility. An assembly in such cases feels under no responsibility at all: for when did any member of Parliament lose his seat for the vote he gave on any detail of administration? To a minister, or the head of an office, it is of more importance what will be thought of his proceedings some time hence, than what is thought of them at the instant: but an assembly, if the cry of the moment goes with it, however hastily raised or artificially stirred up, thinks itself and is thought by everybody to be completely exculpated however disastrous may be the consequences. Besides, an assembly never personally experiences the inconveniences of its bad measures, until they have reached the dimensions of national evils. Ministers and administrators see them approaching, and have to bear all the annoyance and trouble of attempting to ward them off.

The proper duty of a representative assembly in regard to matters of administration, is not to decide them by its own vote, but to take care that the persons who have to decide them shall be the proper persons. Even this

[*Juvenal, *Satires*, in *Juvenal and Persius* (Latin and English), trans. G. G. Ramsay (London: Heinemann; New York: Putnam's Sons, 1918), p. 110 (VI. 347–8).]

*d-d*611   secure

they cannot advantageously do by nominating the individuals. There is no act which more imperatively requires to be performed under a strong sense of individual responsibility than the nomination to employments. The experience of every person conversant with public affairs bears out the assertion, that there is scarcely any act respecting which the conscience of an average man is less sensitive; scarcely any case in which less consideration is paid to qualifications, partly because men do not know, and partly because they do not care for, the difference in qualifications between one person and another. When a minister makes what is meant to be an honest appointment, that is when he does not actually job it for his personal connexions or his party, an ignorant person might suppose that he would try to give it to the person best qualified. No such thing. An ordinary minister thinks himself a miracle of virtue if he gives it to a person of merit, or who has a claim on the public on any account, though the claim or the merit may be of the most opposite description to that required. *Il fallait un calculateur, ce fut un danseur qui l'obtint,*[*] is hardly more of a caricature than in the days of Figaro; and the minister doubtless thinks himself not only blameless but meritorious if the man dances well. Besides, the qualifications which fit special individuals for special duties can only be recognised by those who know the individuals, or who make it their business to examine and judge of persons from what they have done, or from the evidence of those who are in a position to judge. When these conscientious obligations are so little regarded by great public officers who can be made responsible for their appointments, how must it be with assemblies who cannot? Even now, the worst appointments are those which are made for the sake of gaining support or disarming opposition in the representative body: what might we expect if they were made by the body itself? Numerous bodies never regard special qualifications at all. Unless a man is fit for the gallows, he is thought to be about as fit as other people for almost anything for which he can offer himself as a candidate. When appointments made by a ᵉpublicᵉ body are not decided as they almost always are, by party connexion or private jobbing, a man is appointed either because he has a reputation, often quite undeserved, for *general* ability, or ᶠfrequentlyᶠ for no better reason than that he is personally popular.

It has never been thought desirable that Parliament should itself nominate even the members of a Cabinet. It is enough that it virtually decides who shall be prime minister, or who shall be the two or three individuals from

[*Pierre-Augustin Caron de Beaumarchais, *La Folle Journée, ou Le Mariage de Figaro*, in *Oeuvres complètes*, 7 vols. (Paris: Collin, 1809), Vol. II, pp. 276–7 (Act V, Scene iii).]

ᵉ–ᵉ61¹, 61² popular
ᶠ–ᶠ61¹ oftener

whom the prime minister shall be chosen. In doing this it merely recognises the fact that a certain person is the candidate of the party whose general policy commands its support. In reality, the only thing which Parliament decides is, which of two, or at most three, parties or bodies of men, shall furnish the executive government: the opinion of the party itself decides which of its members is fittest to be placed at the head. According to the existing practice of the British Constitution, these things seem to be on as good a footing as they can be. Parliament does not nominate any minister, but the Crown appoints the head of the administration in conformity to the general wishes and inclinations manifested by Parliament, and the other ministers on the recommendation of the chief; while every minister has the undivided moral responsibility of appointing fit persons to the other offices of administration which are not permanent. In a republic, some other *garrangement* would be necessary: but the nearer it approached in practice to that which has long existed in England, the more likely it would be to work well. Either, as in the American republic, the head of the Executive must be elected by some agency entirely independent of the representative body; or the body must content itself with naming the prime minister, and making him responsible for the choice of his associates and subordinates. *hToh* all these considerations, at least theoretically, I fully anticipate a general assent: though, practically, the tendency is strong in representative bodies to interfere more and more in the details of administration, by virtue of the general law, that whoever has the strongest power is more and more tempted to make an excessive use of it; and this is one of the practical dangers to which the futurity of representative governments will be exposed.

But it is equally true, though only of late and slowly beginning to be acknowledged, that a numerous assembly is as little fitted for the direct business of legislation as for that of administration. There is hardly any kind of intellectual work which so much needs to be done not only by experienced and exercised minds, but by minds trained to the task through long and laborious study, as the business of making laws. This is a sufficient reason, were there no other, why they can never be well made but by a committee of very few persons. A reason no less conclusive is, that every provision of a law requires to be framed with the most accurate and long-sighted perception of its effect on all the other provisions; and the law when made should be capable of fitting into a consistent whole with the previously existing laws. It is impossible that these conditions should be in any degree fulfilled when laws are voted clause by clause in a miscellaneous assembly. The incongruity of such a mode of legislating would strike all minds, were it not that our laws are already, as to form and construction,

*g–g*611   management [*printer's error?*]
*h–h*611   In

such a chaos, that the confusion and contradiction seem incapable of being made greater by any addition to the mass. Yet even now, the utter unfitness of our legislative machinery for its purpose is making itself practically felt every year more and more. The mere time necessarily occupied in getting through Bills, renders Parliament more and more incapable of passing any, except on detached and narrow points. If a Bill is prepared which even attempts to deal with the whole of any subject (and it is impossible to legislate properly on any part without having the whole present to the mind), it hangs over from session to session through sheer impossibility of finding time to dispose of it. It matters not though the Bill may have been deliberately drawn up by the authority deemed the best qualified, with all appliances and means to boot; or by a select commission, chosen for their conversancy with the subject, and having employed years in considering and digesting the particular measure: it cannot be passed, because the House of Commons will not forego the precious privilege of tinkering it with their clumsy hands. The custom has of late been to some extent introduced, when the principle of a Bill has been affirmed on the second reading, of referring it for consideration in detail to a Select Committee: but it has not been found that this practice causes much less time to be lost afterwards in carrying it through the Committee of the whole House: the opinions or private crotchets which have been overruled by knowledge, always insist on giving themselves a second chance before the tribunal of ignorance. Indeed, the practice itself has been adopted principally by the House of Lords, the members of which are less busy and fond of meddling, and less jealous of the importance of their individual voices, than those of the elective House. And when a Bill of many clauses does succeed in getting itself discussed in detail, what can depict the state in which it comes out of Committee! Clauses omitted, which are essential to the working of the rest; incongruous ones inserted to conciliate some private interest, or some crotchety member who threatens to delay the Bill; articles foisted in on the motion of some sciolist with a mere smattering of the subject, leading to consequences which the member who introduced or those who supported the Bill did not at the moment foresee, and which need an amending Act in the next session to correct their mischiefs. It is *one of the evils of* the present mode of managing these things, that the explaining and defending of a Bill, and of its various provisions, is scarcely ever performed by the person from whose mind they emanated, who probably has not a seat in the House. Their defence rests upon some minister or member of Parliament who did not frame them, who is dependent on cramming for all his arguments but those which are perfectly obvious, who does not know the full strength of his case, nor the best reasons by which to support it, and is wholly incapable of meeting unforeseen objections. This

*i-i*611   an evil inherent in

evil, as far as Government Bills are concerned, admits of remedy, and has been remedied in some representative constitutions, by allowing the Government to be represented in either House by persons in its confidence, having a right to speak, though not to vote.

If that, as yet considerable, majority of the House of Commons who never desire to move an amendment or make a speech, would no longer leave the whole regulation of business to those who do; if they would bethink themselves that better qualifications for legislation exist, and may be found if sought for, than a fluent tongue, and the faculty of getting elected by a constituency; it would soon be recognised, that in legislation as well as administration, the only task to which a representative assembly can possibly be competent, is not that of doing the work, but of causing it to be done; of determining to whom or to what sort of people it shall be confided, and giving or withholding the national sanction to it when performed. Any government fit for a high state of civilization, would have as one of its fundamental elements a small body, not exceeding in number the members of a Cabinet, who should act as a Commission of Legislation, having for its appointed office to make the laws. If the laws of this country were, as surely they will soon be, revised and put into a connected form, the Commission of Codification by which this is effected should remain as a permanent institution, to watch over the work, protect it from deterioration, and make further improvements as often as required. No one would wish that this body should of itself have any power of *enacting* laws: the Commission would only embody the element of intelligence in their construction; Parliament would represent that of will. No measure would become a law until expressly sanctioned by Parliament; and Parliament, or either House, would have the power not only of rejecting but of sending back a Bill to the Commission for reconsideration *jor* improvement. Either House might also exercise its initiative, by referring any subject to the Commission, with directions to prepare a law. The Commission, of course, would have no power of refusing its instrumentality to any legislation which the country desired. Instructions, concurred in by both Houses, to draw up a Bill which should effect a particular purpose, would be imperative on the Commissioners, unless they preferred to resign their office. Once framed, however, Parliament should have no power to alter the measure, but solely to pass or reject it; or, if partially disapproved of, remit it to the Commission for reconsideration. The Commissioners should be appointed by the Crown, but should hold their offices for a time certain, say five years, unless removed on an address from the two Houses of Parliament, grounded either on personal misconduct (as in the case of judges), or on refusal to draw up a Bill in obedience to the demands of Parliament. At the expiration of the five years a member should

*j-j*611, 612   and

cease to hold office unless reappointed, in order to provide a convenient mode of getting rid of those who had not been found equal to their duties, and of infusing new and younger blood into the body.

The necessity of some provision corresponding to this was felt even in the Athenian Democracy, where, in the time of its most complete ascendancy, the popular Ecclesia could pass Psephisms (mostly decrees on single matters of policy), but laws, so called, could only be made or altered by a different and less numerous body, renewed annually, called the Nomothetæ, whose duty it also was to revise the whole of the laws, and keep them consistent with one another. In the English Constitution there is great difficulty in introducing any arrangement which is new both in form and in substance, but comparatively little repugnance is felt to the attainment of new purposes by an adaptation of existing forms and traditions. It appears to me that the means might be devised of enriching the Constitution with this great improvement through the machinery of the House of Lords. A Commission for preparing Bills would in itself be no more an innovation on the Constitution than the Board for the administration of the Poor Laws, or the Inclosure Commission. If, in consideration of the great importance and dignity of the trust, it were made a rule that every person appointed a member of the Legislative Commission, unless removed from office on an address from Parliament, should be a Peer for life, it is probable that the same good sense and taste which leave the judicial functions of the Peerage practically to the exclusive care of the ^{k}law lords^k, would leave the business of legislation, except on questions involving political principles and interests, to the professional legislators; that Bills originating in the Upper House would always be drawn up by them; that the Government would devolve on them the framing of all its Bills; and that private members of the House of Commons would gradually find it convenient, and likely to facilitate the passing of their measures through the two Houses, if instead of bringing in a Bill and submitting it directly to the House, they obtained leave to introduce it and have it referred to the Legislative Commission. For it would, of course, be open to the House to refer for the consideration of that body not a subject merely, but any specific proposal, or a Draft of a Bill *in extenso*, when any member thought himself capable of preparing one such as ought to pass; and the House would doubtless refer every such draft to the Commission, if only as materials, and for the benefit of the suggestions it might contain: as they would, in like manner, refer every amendment or objection, which might be proposed in writing by any member of the House after a measure had left the Commissioners' hands. The alteration of ^{l}Bills^l by a Committee of the whole House would cease, not by formal abolition, but by desuetude; the

$^{k-k}$611, 612   Law Lords
$^{l-l}$611, 612   bills

right not being abandoned, but laid up in the same armoury with the royal veto, the right of withholding the supplies, and other ancient instruments of political warfare, which no one desires to see used, but no one likes to part with, lest they should at any time be found to be still needed in an extra-ordinary emergency. By such arrangements as these, legislation would assume its proper place as a work of skilled labour and special study and experience; while the most important liberty of the nation, that of being governed only by laws assented to by its elected representatives, would be fully preserved, and made more valuable by being detached from the serious, but by no means unavoidable, drawbacks which now accompany it in the form of ignorant and ill-considered legislation.

Instead of the function of governing, for which it is radically unfit, the proper office of a representative assembly is to watch and control the government: to throw the light of publicity on its acts; to compel a full exposition and justification of all of them which any one considers questionable; to censure them if found condemnable, and, if the men who compose the government abuse their trust, or fulfil it in a manner which conflicts with the deliberate sense of the nation, to expel them from office, and either expressly or virtually appoint their successors. This is surely ample power, and security enough for the liberty of the nation. In addition to this, the Parliament has an office, not inferior even to this in importance; to be at once the nation's Committee of Grievances, and its Congress of Opinions; an arena in which not only the general opinion of the nation, but that of every section of it, and as far as possible of every eminent individual whom it contains, can produce itself in full light and challenge discussion; where every person in the country may count upon finding somebody who speaks his mind, as well or better than he could speak it himself—not to friends and partisans exclusively, but in the face of opponents, to be tested by adverse controversy; where those whose opinion is overruled, feel satisfied that it is heard, and set aside not by a mere act of will, but for what are thought superior reasons, and commend themselves as such to the representatives of the majority of the nation; where every party or opinion in the country can muster its strength, and be cured of any illusion concerning the number or power of its adherents; where the opinion which prevails in the nation makes itself manifest as prevailing, and marshals its hosts in the presence of the government, which is thus enabled and compelled to give way to it on the mere manifestation, without the actual employment, of its strength; where statesmen can assure themselves, far more certainly than by any other signs, what elements of opinion and power are growing, and what declining, and are enabled to shape their measures with some regard not solely to present exigencies, but to tendencies in progress. Representative assemblies are often taunted by their enemies with being places of mere talk and *bavardage*. There has seldom been more misplaced derision. I know not how a representative assembly can more usefully employ itself than in talk, when the subject of talk is the great public interests of the country, and every sentence of it represents the opinion either of some important body of persons in the nation, or of an individual in whom some such body have reposed their confidence. A place where every interest and shade of opinion in the country can have its cause even passionately pleaded, in the face of the government and of all other interests and opinions, can compel them to listen, and either comply, or state clearly why they do not, is in itself, if it answered no other purpose, one of the most important political institutions that can exist anywhere, and one of the foremost benefits of free government. Such "talking" would never be looked upon with disparagement if it were not allowed to stop "doing;" which it never would, if assemblies knew and acknowledged that talking and discussion are their proper business, while *doing*, as the result of discussion, is the task not of a miscellaneous body, but of individuals specially trained to it; that the fit office of an assembly is to see that those individuals are honestly and intelligently chosen, and to interfere no further with them, except by unlimited latitude of suggestion and criticism, and by applying or withholding the final seal of national assent. It is for want of this judicious reserve, that popular assemblies attempt to do what they cannot do well—to govern and legislate—and provide no machinery but their own for much of it, when of course every hour spent in talk is an hour withdrawn from actual business. But the very fact which most unfits such bodies for a Council of Legislation, qualifies them the more for their other office—namely, that they are not a selection of the greatest political minds in the country, from whose opinions little could with certainty be inferred concerning those of the nation, but are, when properly constituted, a fair sample of every grade of intellect among the people which is at all entitled to a voice in public affairs. Their part is to indicate wants, to be an organ for popular demands, and a place of adverse discussion for all opinions relating to public matters, both great and small; and, along with this, to check by criticism, and eventually by withdrawing their support, those high public officers who really conduct the public business, or who appoint those by whom it is conducted. Nothing but the restriction of the function of representative bodies within these rational limits, will enable the benefits of popular control to be enjoyed in conjunction with the no less important requisites (growing ever more important as human affairs increase in scale and in complexity) of skilled legislation and administration. There are no means of combining these benefits, except by separating the functions which guarantee the one from those which essentially require the other; by disjoining the office of control and criticism from the actual conduct of affairs, and devolving the former on the representatives of the Many, while securing for the latter, under strict responsibility to the nation, the acquired knowledge and practised intelligence of a specially trained and experienced Few.

The preceding discussion of the functions which ought to devolve on the sovereign representative assembly of the nation, would require to be followed by an inquiry into those properly vested in the minor representative bodies, which ought to exist for purposes that regard only localities. And such an inquiry forms an essential part of the present treatise; but many reasons require its postponement, until we have considered the most proper composition of the great representative body, destined to control as sovereign the enactment of laws and the administration of the general affairs of the nation.

CHAPTER VI

Of the Infirmities and Dangers to which Representative Government is Liable

THE DEFECTS of any form of government may be either negative or positive. It is negatively defective if it does not concentrate in the hands of the authorities, power sufficient to fulfil the necessary offices of a government; or if it does not sufficiently develope by exercise the active capacities and social feelings of the individual citizens. On neither of these points is it necessary that much should be said at this stage of our inquiry.

The want of an amount of power in the government, adequate to preserve order and allow of progress in the people, is incident rather to a wild and rude state of society generally, than to any particular form of political union. When the people are too much attached to savage independence, to be tolerant of the amount of power to which it is for their good that they should be subject, the state of society (as already observed) is not yet ripe for representative government. When the time for that government has arrived, sufficient power for all needful purposes is sure to reside in the sovereign assembly; and if enough of it is not entrusted to the executive, this can only arise from a jealous feeling on the part of the assembly towards the administration, never likely to exist but where the constitutional power of the assembly to turn them out of office has not yet sufficiently established itself. Wherever that constitutional right is admitted in principle and fully operative in practice, there is no fear that the assembly will not be willing to trust its own ministers with any amount of power really desirable; the danger is, on the contrary, lest they should grant it too ungrudgingly, and too indefinite in extent, since the power of the minister is the power of the body who make and who keep him so. It is, however, very likely, and is one of the dangers of a controlling assembly, that it may be lavish of powers, but afterwards interfere with their exercise; may give power by wholesale and take it back in detail, by multiplied single acts of interference in the business of administration. The evils arising from this assumption of the actual function of governing, in lieu of that of criticising and checking those who govern, have been sufficiently dwelt upon in the preceding chapter. No safeguard can in the nature of things be provided against this improper meddling, except a strong and general conviction of its injurious character.

The other negative defect which may reside in a government, that of not bringing into sufficient exercise the individual faculties, moral, intellectual, and active, of the people, has been exhibited generally in setting forth the distinctive mischiefs of despotism. As between one form of popular government and another, the advantage in this respect lies with that which most widely diffuses the exercise of public functions; on the one hand, by excluding fewest from the suffrage; on the other, by opening to all classes of private citizens, so far as is consistent with other equally important objects, the widest participation in the details of judicial and administrative business; as by jury trial, admission to municipal offices, and above all by the utmost possible publicity and liberty of discussion, whereby not merely a few individuals in succession, but the whole public, are made, to a certain extent, participants in the government, and sharers in the instruction and mental exercise *derivable* from it. The further illustration of these benefits, as well as of the limitations under which they must be *aimed at*, will be better deferred until we come to speak of the details of administration.

The *positive* evils and dangers of the representative, as of every other form of government, may be reduced to two heads: first, general ignorance and incapacity, or, to speak more moderately, insufficient mental qualifications, in the controlling body; secondly, the danger of its being under the influence of interests not identical with the general welfare of the community.

The former of these evils, deficiency in high mental qualifications, is one to which it is generally supposed that popular government is liable in a greater degree than any other. The energy of a monarch, the steadiness and prudence of an aristocracy, are thought to contrast most favourably with the vacillation and shortsightedness of even *a* qualified democracy. These propositions, however, are not by any means so well founded as they at first sight appear.

Compared with simple monarchy, representative government is in these respects at no disadvantage. Except in a rude age, hereditary monarchy, when it is really such, and not aristocracy in disguise, *far* surpasses democracy in all the forms of incapacity supposed to be characteristic of the last. I say, except in a rude age, because in a really rude state of society there is a considerable guarantee for the intellectual and active capacities of the sovereign. His personal will is constantly encountering obstacles from the wilfulness of his subjects, and of powerful individuals among their number. The circumstances of society do not afford him much temptation

---

a-a611, 612   derived   b-b611   pursued
c-c611, 612   the most   d-d611, 612   much

to mere luxurious self-indulgence; mental and bodily activity, especially political and military, are his principal excitements; and among turbulent chiefs and lawless followers he has little authority, and is seldom long secure *even* of his throne, unless he possesses a considerable amount of personal daring, dexterity, and energy. The reason why the average of talent is so high among the Henries and Edwards of our history, may be read in the tragical fate of the second Edward and the second Richard, and the civil wars and disturbances of the reigns of John and his incapable successor. The troubled period of the Reformation also produced several eminent hereditary monarchs, Elizabeth, Henri Quatre, Gustavus Adolphus; but they were mostly bred up in adversity, succeeded to the throne by the unexpected failure of nearer heirs, or had to contend with great difficulties in the commencement of their reign. Since European life assumed a settled aspect, anything above mediocrity in a hereditary king has become extremely rare, while the general average has been even below mediocrity, both in talent and in vigour of character. A monarchy constitutionally absolute now only maintains itself in existence (except temporarily in the hands of some active-minded usurper) through the mental qualifications of a permanent bureaucracy. The Russian and Austrian Governments, and even the French Government in its normal condition, are oligarchies of officials, of whom the head of the State does little more than select the chiefs. I am speaking of the regular course of their administration; for the will of the master of course determines many of their particular acts.

The governments which have been remarkable in history for sustained mental ability and vigour in the conduct of affairs, have generally been aristocracies. But they have been, without any exception, aristocracies of public functionaries. The ruling bodies have been so narrow, that each member, or at least each influential member, of the body, was able to make, and did make, public business an active profession, and the principal occupation of his life. The only aristocracies which have manifested high governing capacities, and acted on steady maxims of policy, through many generations, are those of Rome and Venice. But, at Venice, though the privileged order was numerous, the actual management of affairs was rigidly concentrated in a small oligarchy within the oligarchy, whose whole lives were devoted to the study and conduct of the affairs of the state. The Roman government partook more of the character of an open aristocracy like our own. But the really governing body, the Senate, was *in general* exclusively composed of persons who had exercised public functions, and had either already filled or were looking forward to fill the *higher* offices of the state, at the peril of a severe responsibility in case of incapacity and

e–e+61², 65   *f–f*+61², 65
*g–g*61¹   highest

failure. When once members of the Senate, their lives were pledged to the conduct of public affairs; they were not permitted even to leave Italy except in the discharge of some public trust; and unless turned out of the Senate by the censors for character or conduct deemed disgraceful, they retained their powers and responsibilities to the end of life. In an aristocracy thus constituted, every member felt his personal importance entirely bound up with the dignity and estimation of the commonwealth which he administered, and with the part he was able to play in its councils. This dignity and estimation were quite different things from the prosperity *h*or*h* happiness of the general body of the citizens, and were often wholly incompatible with it. But they were closely linked with the external success and aggrandize-ment of the State: and it was, consequently, in the pursuit of that object almost exclusively, that either the Roman or the Venetian aristocracies manifested the systematically wise collective policy, and the great individual capacities for government, for which history has deservedly given them credit.

It thus appears that the only governments, not representative, in which high political skill and ability have been other than exceptional, whether under monarchical or aristocratic forms, have been essentially bureaucracies. The work of government has been in the hands of governors by profession; which is the essence and meaning of bureaucracy. Whether the work is done by them because they have been trained to it, or they are trained to it because it is to be done by them, makes a great difference in many respects, but none at all as to the essential character of the rule. Aristocracies, on the other hand, like that of England, in which the class who possessed the power derived it merely from their social position, without being specially trained or devoting themselves exclusively to it (and in which, therefore, the power was not exercised directly, but through representative institutions oligarchi-cally constituted) have been, in respect to intellectual endowments, much on a par with democracies; that is, they have manifested such qualities in any considerable degree, only during the temporary ascendancy which great and popular talents, united with a distinguished position, have given to some one man. Themistocles and Pericles, Washington and Jefferson, were not more completely exceptions in their several democracies, and were assuredly much more *i*splendid*i* exceptions, than the Chathams and Peels of the representative aristocracy of Great Britain, or even the Sullys and Colberts of the aristocratic monarchy of France. A great minister, in the aristocratic governments of modern Europe, is almost as rare a phenomenon as a great king.

The comparison, therefore, as to the intellectual attributes of a govern-

*h–h*611   and
*i–i*611   brilliant

ment, has to be made between a representative democracy and a bureaucracy: all other governments may be left out of the account. And here it must be acknowledged that a bureaucratic government has, in some important respects, greatly the advantage. It accumulates experience, acquires well-tried and well-considered traditional maxims, and makes provision for appropriate practical knowledge in those who have the actual conduct of affairs. But it is not equally favourable to individual energy of mind. The disease which afflicts bureaucratic governments, and which they usually die of, is routine. They perish by the immutability of their maxims; and, still more, by the universal law that whatever becomes a routine loses its vital principle, and having no longer a mind acting within it, goes on revolving mechanically though the work it is intended to do remains undone. A bureaucracy always tends to become a pedantocracy. When the bureaucracy is the real government, the spirit of the corps (as with the Jesuits) bears down the individuality of its more distinguished members. In the profession of government, as in other professions, the sole idea of the majority is to do what they have been taught; and it requires a popular government to enable the conceptions of the man of original genius among them, to prevail over the obstructive spirit of trained mediocrity. Only in a popular government (setting apart the accident of a highly intelligent despot) could Sir Rowland Hill have been victorious over the Post Office. A popular government installed him *in* the Post Office, and made the body, in spite of itself, obey the impulse given by the man who united special knowledge with individual vigour and originality. That the Roman aristocracy escaped this characteristic disease of a bureaucracy, was evidently owing to its popular element. All special offices, both those which gave a seat in the Senate and those which were sought by senators, were conferred by popular election. The Russian government is a characteristic exemplification of both the good and bad side of bureaucracy: its fixed maxims, directed with Roman perseverance to the same unflinchingly-pursued ends from age to age; the remarkable skill with which those ends are generally pursued; the frightful internal corruption, and the permanent organized hostility to improvements from without, which even the autocratic power of a vigorous-minded Emperor is seldom or never sufficient to overcome; the patient obstructiveness of the body being in the long run more than a match for the fitful energy of one man. The Chinese Government, a bureaucracy of Mandarins, is, as far as known to us, another apparent example of the same qualities and defects.

In all human affairs, conflicting influences are required, to keep one another alive and efficient even for their own proper uses; and the exclusive pursuit of one good object, apart from some other which should accompany it, ends not in excess of one and defect of the other, but in the decay and loss even of that which has been exclusively cared for. Government by trained officials cannot do, for a country, the things which can be done by a free government; but it might be supposed capable of doing some things which free government, of itself, cannot do. We find, however, that an outside element of freedom is necessary to enable it to do effectually or permanently even its own business. And so, also, freedom cannot produce its best effects, and often breaks down altogether, unless means can be found of combining it with trained and skilled administration. There could not be a moment's hesitation between representative government, among a people in any degree ripe for it, and the most perfect imaginable bureaucracy. But it is, at the same time, one of the most important ends of political institutions, to attain as many of the qualities of the one as are consistent with the other; to secure, as far as they can be made compatible, the great advantage of the conduct of affairs by skilled persons, bred to it as an intellectual profession, along with that of a general control vested in, and seriously exercised by, bodies representative of the entire people. Much would be done towards this end by recognising the line of separation, discussed in the preceding chapter, between the work of government properly so called, which can only be well performed after special cultivation, and that of selecting, watching, and, when needful, controlling the governors, which in this case, as in *j* others, properly devolves, not on those who do the work, but on those for whose benefit it ought to be done. No progress at all can be made towards obtaining a skilled democracy, unless the democracy are willing that the work which requires skill should be done by those who possess it. A democracy has enough to do in providing itself with an amount of mental competency sufficient for its own proper work, that of superintendence and check.

How to obtain and secure this amount, is one of the questions to be taken into consideration in judging of the proper constitution of a representative body. In proportion as its composition fails to secure this amount, the assembly will encroach, by special acts, on the province of the executive; it will expel a good, or elevate and uphold a bad, ministry; it will connive at, or overlook, in them, abuses of trust, will be deluded by their false pretences, or will withhold support from those who endeavour to fulfil their trust conscientiously; it will countenance, or impose, a selfish, a capricious and impulsive, a short-sighted, ignorant, and prejudiced general policy, foreign and domestic; it will abrogate good laws, or enact bad ones, let in new evils, or cling with perverse obstinacy to old; it will even, perhaps, under misleading impulses, momentary or permanent, emanating from itself or from its constituents, tolerate or connive at proceedings which set law aside altogether, in cases where equal justice would not be agreeable to

*j*611   all

popular feeling. Such are among the dangers of representative government, arising from a constitution of the representation which does not secure an adequate amount of intelligence and knowledge in the representative assembly.

We next proceed to the evils arising from the prevalence of modes of action in the representative body, dictated by sinister interests (to employ the useful phrase introduced by Bentham),[*] that is, interests conflicting more or less with the general good of the community.

It is universally admitted, that, of the evils incident to monarchical and aristocratic governments, a large proportion arise from this cause. The interest of the monarch, or the interest of the aristocracy, either collective or that of its individual members, is promoted, or they themselves think that it will be promoted, by conduct opposed to that which the general interest of the community requires. The interest, for example, of the government is to tax heavily: that of the community is, to be as little taxed as the necessary expenses of good government permit. The interest of the king, and of the governing aristocracy, is to possess, and exercise, unlimited power over the people; to enforce, on their part, complete conformity to the will and preferences of the rulers. The interest of the people is, to have as little control exercised over them in any respect, as is consistent with attaining the legitimate ends of government. The interest, or apparent and supposed interest, of the king or aristocracy, is to permit no censure of themselves, at least in any form which they may consider either to threaten their power, or seriously to interfere with their free agency. The interest of the people is that there should be full liberty of censure on every public officer, and on every public act or measure. The interest of a ruling class, whether in an aristocracy or an aristocratic monarchy, is to assume to themselves an endless variety of unjust privileges, sometimes benefiting their pockets at the expense of the people, sometimes merely tending to exalt them above others, or, what is the same thing in different words, to degrade others below themselves. If the people are disaffected, which under such a government they are very likely to be, it is the interest of the king or aristocracy to keep them at a low level of intelligence and education, foment dissensions among them, and even prevent them from being too well off, lest they should "wax fat, and kick;" agreeably to the maxim of Cardinal Richelieu in his celebrated *Testament Politique*.[†] All these things are for the interest of a king or aristocracy, in a purely selfish point of view, unless a sufficiently strong

[*See, e.g., *Rationale of Judical Evidence, Works*, Vol. VII, p. 385.]

[†Cf. Armand du Plessis, Cardinal Duc de Richelieu, *Maximes d'état ou Testament politique*, 2 vols. (Paris: Le Breton, 1764), Vol. I, p. 225. The quotation actually derives from Deuteronomy, 32:15.]

counter-interest is created by the fear of provoking resistance. All these evils have been, and many of them still are, produced by the sinister interests of kings and aristocracies, where their power is sufficient to raise them above the opinion of the rest of the community; nor is it rational to expect, as the consequence of such a position, any other conduct.

These things are superabundantly evident in the case of a monarchy or an aristocracy; but it is sometimes rather gratuitously assumed, that the same kind of injurious influences do not operate in a democracy. Looking at democracy in the way in which it is commonly conceived, as the rule of the numerical majority, it is surely possible that the ruling power may be under the dominion of sectional or class interests, pointing to conduct different from that which would be dictated by impartial regard for the interest of all. Suppose the majority to be whites, the minority negroes, or *vice versâ*: is it likely that the majority would allow equal justice to the minority? Suppose the majority Catholics, the minority Protestants, or the reverse; will there not be the same danger? Or let the majority be English, the minority Irish, or the contrary: is there not a great probability of similar evil? In all countries there is a majority of poor, a minority who, in con-tradistinction, may be called rich. Between these two classes, on many questions, there is complete opposition of apparent interest. We will suppose the majority sufficiently intelligent to be aware that it is not for their advantage to weaken the security of property, and that it would be weakened by any act of arbitrary spoliation. But is there not a considerable danger lest they should throw upon the possessors of what is called realized property, and upon the larger incomes, an unfair share, or even the whole, of the burden of taxation, and having done so, add to the amount without scruple, expending the proceeds in modes supposed to conduce to the profit and advantage of the labouring class? Suppose, again, a minority of skilled labourers, a majority of unskilled: the experience of many Trade Unions, unless they are greatly calumniated, justifies the apprehension that equality of earnings might be imposed as an obligation, and that piecework ^{k}, pay-ment by the hour,^{k} and all practices which enable superior industry or abil-ities to gain a superior reward, might be put down. Legislative attempts to raise wages, limitation of competition in the labour market, taxes or restric-tions on machinery, and on improvements of all kinds tending to dispense with any of the existing labour—even, perhaps, protection of the home pro-ducer against foreign industry—are very natural (I do not venture to say whether probable) results of a feeling of class interest in a governing major-ity of manual labourers.

It will be said that none of these things are for the *real* interest of the

$^{k-k}$+61^2, 65

most numerous class: to which I answer, that if the conduct of human beings was determined by no other interested considerations than those which constitute their "real" interest, neither monarchy nor oligarchy would be such bad governments as they are; for assuredly very strong arguments may be, and often have been, adduced to show that either a king or a governing senate are in much the most enviable position when ruling justly and vigilantly over an active, wealthy, enlightened, and high-minded people. But a king only now and then, and an oligarchy in no known instance, have taken this exalted view of their self-interest: and why should we expect a loftier mode of thinking from the labouring classes? It is not what their interest is, but what they suppose it to be, that is the important consideration with respect to their conduct: and it is quite conclusive against any theory of government, that it assumes the numerical majority to do habitually what is never done, nor expected to be done, save in very exceptional cases, by any other depositaries of power—namely, to direct their conduct by their real ultimate interest, in opposition to their immediate and apparent interest. No one, surely, can doubt that *many of* the pernicious measures above enumerated, and many others as bad, would be for the immediate interest of the general body of unskilled labourers. It is quite possible that they would be for the selfish interest of the whole existing generation of the class. The relaxation of industry and activity, and diminished encouragement to saving, which would be their ultimate consequence, might perhaps be little felt by the class of unskilled labourers in the space of a single life-time. Some of the most fatal changes in human affairs have been, as to their more manifest immediate effects, beneficial. The establishment of the despotism of the Cæsars was a great benefit to the entire generation in which it took place. It put a stop to civil war, abated a vast amount of malversation and tyranny by prætors and proconsuls; it fostered many of the graces of life, and intellectual cultivation in all departments not political; it produced monuments of literary genius dazzling to the imaginations of shallow readers of history, who do not reflect that the men to whom the despotism of Augustus (as well as of Lorenzo de' Medici and of Louis XIV) owes its brilliancy, were all formed in the generation preceding. The accumulated riches, and the mental energy and activity, produced by centuries of freedom, remained for the benefit of the first generation of slaves. Yet this was the commencement of a *régime* by whose gradual operation all the civilization which had been gained, insensibly faded away, until the Empire which had conquered and embraced the world in its grasp, so completely lost even its military efficiency, that invaders whom three or four legions had always sufficed to coerce, were able to overrun and occupy

*l-l+*65

nearly the whole of its vast territory. The fresh impulse given by Christianity came but just in time to save arts and letters from perishing, and the human race from sinking back into perhaps endless night.

When we talk of the interest of a body of men, or even of an individual man, as a principle determining their actions, the question what would be considered their interest by an unprejudiced observer, is one of the least important parts of the whole matter. As Coleridge observes, the man makes the motive, not the motive the man.[*] What it is the man's interest to do or refrain from, depends less on any outward circumstances, than upon what sort of man he is. If you wish to know what is practically a man's interest, you must know the cast of his habitual feelings and thoughts. Everybody has two kinds of interests, interests which he cares for, and interests which he does not care for. Everybody has selfish and unselfish interests, and a selfish man has cultivated the habit of caring for the former, and not caring for the latter. Every one has present and distant interests, and the improvident man is he who cares for the present interests and does not care for the distant. It matters little that on any correct calculation the latter may be the more considerable, if the habits of his mind lead him to fix his thoughts and wishes solely on the former. It would be vain to attempt to persuade a man who beats his wife and illtreats his children, that he would be happier if he lived in love and kindness with them. He would be happier if he were the kind of person who *could* so live; but he is not, and it is probably too late for him to become, that kind of person. Being *ᵐwhatᵐ* he is, the gratification of his love of domineering, and the indulgence of his ferocious temper, are to his perceptions a greater good to himself, than he would be capable of deriving from the pleasure and affection of those dependent on him. He has no pleasure in their pleasure, and does not care for their affection. His neighbour, who does, is probably a happier man than he; but could he be persuaded of this, the persuasion would, most likely, only still further exasperate his malignity or his irritability. On the average, a person who cares for other people, for his country, or for mankind, is a happier man than one who does not; but of what use is it to preach this doctrine to a man who cares for nothing but his own ease, or his own pocket? He cannot care for other people if he would. It is like preaching to the worm who crawls on the ground, how much better it would be for him if he were an eagle.

Now it is an universally observed fact, that the two evil dispositions in question, the disposition to prefer a man's selfish interests to those which he shares with other people, and his immediate and direct interests to

[*Samuel Taylor Coleridge, "The Statesman's Manual," in *On the Constitution of Church and State, and Lay Sermons* (London: Pickering, 1839), p. 220.]

*ᵐ⁻ᵐ*611, 612   as

those which are indirect and remote, are characteristics most especially called forth and fostered by the possession of power. The moment a man, or a class of men, find themselves with power in their hands, the man's individual interest, or the class's separate interest, acquires an entirely new degree of importance in their eyes. Finding themselves worshipped by others, they become worshippers of themselves, and think themselves entitled to be counted at a hundred times the value of other people; while the facility they acquire of doing as they like without regard to consequences, insensibly weakens the habits which make men look forward even to such consequences as affect themselves. This is the meaning of the universal tradition, grounded on universal experience, of men's being corrupted by power. Every one knows how absurd it would be to infer from what a man is or does when in a private station, that he will be and do exactly the like when a despot on a throne; where the bad parts of his human nature, instead of being restrained and kept in subordination by every circumstance of his life and by every person surrounding him, are courted by all persons, and ministered to by all circumstances. It would be quite as absurd to entertain a similar expectation in regard to a class of men; the Demos, or any other. Let them be ever so modest and amenable to reason while there is a power over them stronger than they, we ought to expect a total change in this respect when they themselves become the strongest power.

Governments must be made for human beings as they are, or as they are capable of speedily becoming: and in any state of cultivation which mankind, or any class among them, have yet attained, or are likely soon to attain, the interests by which they will be led, when they are thinking only of self-interest, will be almost exclusively those which are obvious at first sight, and which operate on their present condition. It is only a disinterested regard for others, and especially for what comes after them, for the idea of posterity, of their country, or of mankind, whether grounded on sympathy or on a conscientious feeling, which ever directs the minds and purposes of classes or bodies of men towards distant or unobvious interests. And it cannot be maintained that any form of government would be rational, which required as a condition that these exalted principles of action should be the guiding and master motives in the conduct of average human beings. A certain amount of conscience, and of disinterested public spirit, may fairly be calculated on in the citizens of any community ripe for representative government. But it would be ridiculous to expect such a degree of it, combined with such intellectual discernment, as would be proof against any plausible fallacy tending to make that which was for their class interest appear the dictate of justice and of the general good. We all know what specious fallacies may be urged in defence of every act of injustice yet proposed for the imaginary benefit of the mass. We know how many, not otherwise fools or bad men, have thought it justifiable to repudiate the national debt. We know how many, not destitute of ability, and of considerable popular influence, think it fair to throw the whole burthen of taxation upon savings, under the name of realized property, allowing those whose progenitors and themselves have always spent all they received, to remain, as a reward for such exemplary conduct, wholly untaxed. We know what powerful arguments, the more dangerous because there is a portion of truth in them, may be brought against all inheritance, against the power of bequest, against every advantage which one person seems to have over another. We know how easily the uselessness of almost every branch of knowledge may be proved, to the complete satisfaction of those who do not possess it. How many, not altogether stupid men, think the scientific study of languages useless, think ancient literature useless, all erudition useless, logic and metaphysics useless, poetry and the fine arts idle and frivolous, political economy purely mischievous? Even history has been pronounced useless and mischievous by able men. Nothing but that acquaintance with external nature, empirically acquired, which serves directly for the production of objects necessary to existence or agreeable to the senses, would get its utility recognised if people had the least encouragement to disbelieve it. Is it reasonable to think that even much more cultivated minds than those of the numerical majority can be expected to be, will have so delicate a conscience, and so just an appreciation of what is against their own apparent interest, that they will reject these and the innumerable other fallacies which will press in upon them from all quarters as soon as they come into power, to induce them to follow their own selfish inclinations and short-sighted notions of their own good, in opposition to justice, at the expense of all other classes and of posterity?

One of the greatest dangers, therefore, of democracy, as of all other forms of government, lies in the sinister interest of the holders of power: it is the danger of class legislation; of government intended for (whether really effecting it or not) the immediate benefit of the dominant class, to the lasting detriment of the whole. And one of the most important questions demanding consideration, in determining the best constitution of a representative government, is how to provide efficacious securities against this evil.

If we consider as a class, politically speaking, any number of persons who have the same sinister interest,—that is, whose direct and apparent interest points towards the same description of bad measures; the desirable object would be that no class, and no combination of classes likely to combine, *should* be able to exercise a preponderant influence in the government. A modern community, not divided within itself by strong antipathies

*n-n*611   shall

of race, language, or nationality, may be considered as in the main divisible into two sections, which, in spite of partial variations, correspond on the whole with two divergent directions of apparent interest. Let us call them (in brief general terms) labourers on the one hand, employers of labour on the other: including however along with employers of labour, not only retired capitalists, and the possessors of inherited wealth, but all that highly paid description of labourers (such as the professions) whose education and way of life assimilate them with the rich, and whose prospect and ambition it is to raise themselves into that class. With the labourers, on the other hand, may be ranked those smaller employers of labour, who by interests, habits, and educational impressions, are assimilated in wishes, tastes, and objects to the labouring classes; comprehending a large proportion of petty tradesmen. In a state of society thus composed, if the representative system could be made ideally perfect, and if it were possible to maintain it in that state, its organization must be such, that these two classes, manual labourers and their affinities on one side, employers of labour and their affinities on the other, should be, in the arrangement of the representative system, equally balanced, each influencing about an equal number of votes in Parliament: since, assuming that the majority of each class, in any difference between them, would be mainly governed by their class interests, there would be a minority of each in whom that consideration would be subordinate to reason, justice, and the good of the whole; and this minority of either, joining with the whole of the other, would turn the scale against any demands of their own majority which were not such as ought to prevail. The reason why, in any tolerably constituted society, justice and the general interest mostly in the end carry their point, is that the separate and selfish interests of mankind are almost always divided; some are interested in what is wrong, but some, also, have their private interest on the side of what is right: and those who are governed by higher considerations, though too few and weak to prevail ^{o}against the whole of the others^o, usually after sufficient discussion and agitation become strong enough to turn the balance in favour of the body of private interests which is on the same side with them. The representative system ought to be so constituted as to maintain this state of things: it ought not to allow any of the various sectional interests to be so powerful as to be capable of prevailing against truth and justice and the other sectional interests combined. There ought always to be such a balance preserved among personal interests, as may render any one of them dependent for its successes, on carrying with it at least a large proportion of those who act on higher motives, and more comprehensive and distant views.

$^{o-o}$611   alone

CHAPTER VII

Of True and False Democracy;
Representation of All, and
Representation of the Majority Only

IT HAS BEEN SEEN, that the dangers incident to a representative democracy are of two kinds: danger of a low grade of intelligence in the representative body, and in the popular opinion which controls it; and danger of class legislation on the part of the numerical majority, these being all composed of the same class. We have next to consider, how far it is possible so to organize the democracy, as, without interfering materially with the characteristic benefits of democratic government, to do away with these two great evils, or at least to abate them, in the utmost degree attainable by human contrivance.

The common mode of attempting this is by limiting the democratic character of the representation, through a more or less restricted suffrage. But there is a previous consideration which, duly kept in view, considerably modifies the circumstances which are supposed to render such a restriction necessary. A completely equal democracy, in a nation in which a single class composes the numerical majority, cannot be divested of certain evils; but those evils are greatly aggravated by the fact, that the democracies which at present exist are not equal, but systematically unequal in favour of the predominant class. Two very different ideas are usually confounded under the name democracy. The pure idea of democracy, according to its definition, is the government of the whole people by the whole people, equally represented. Democracy as commonly conceived and hitherto practised, is the government of the whole people by a mere majority of the people, exclusively represented. The former is synonymous with the equality of all citizens; the latter, strangely confounded with it, is a government of privilege, in favour of the numerical majority, who alone possess practically any voice in the State. This is the inevitable consequence of the manner in which the votes are now taken, to the complete disfranchisement of minorities.

The confusion of ideas here is great, but it is so easily cleared up, that one would suppose the slightest indication would be sufficient to place the matter in its true light before any mind of average intelligence. It would be so, but for the power of habit; owing to which the simplest idea, if unfamiliar, has as great difficulty in making its way to the mind as a far more complicated one. That the minority must yield to the majority, the smaller number to the greater, is a familiar idea; and accordingly men think there is no necessity for using their minds any further, and it does not occur to them that there is any medium between allowing the smaller number to be equally powerful with the greater, and blotting out the smaller number altogether. In a representative body actually deliberating, the minority must of course be overruled; and in an equal democracy (since the opinions of the constituents, when they insist on them, determine those of the representative body) the majority of the people, through their representatives, will outvote and prevail over the minority and their representatives. But does it follow that the minority should have no representatives at all? Because the majority ought to prevail over the minority, must the majority have all the votes, the minority none? Is it necessary that the minority should not even be heard? Nothing but habit and old association can reconcile any reasonable being to the needless injustice. In a really equal democracy, every or any section would be represented, not disproportionately, but proportionately. A majority of the electors would always have a majority of the representatives; but a minority of the electors would always have a minority of the representatives. Man for man, they would be as fully represented as the majority. Unless they are, there is not equal government, but a government of inequality and privilege: one part of the people rule over the rest: there is a part whose fair and equal share of influence in the representation is withheld from them; contrary to all just government, but above all, contrary to the principle of democracy, which professes equality as its very root and foundation.

The injustice and violation of principle are not less flagrant because those who suffer by them are a minority; for there is not equal suffrage where every single individual does not count for as much as any other single individual in the community. But it is not only ᵃaᵃ minority who suffer. Democracy, thus constituted, does not even attain its ostensible object, that of giving the powers of government in all cases to the numerical majority. It does something very different: it gives them to a majority of the majority; who may be, and often are, but a minority of the whole. All principles are most effectually tested by extreme cases. Suppose then, that, in a country governed by equal and universal suffrage, there is a contested election in every constituency, and every election is carried by a small majority. The Parliament thus brought together represents little more than a bare majority of the people. This Parliament proceeds to legislate, and

ᵃ⁻ᵃ61¹ the

adopts important measures by a bare majority of itself. What guarantee is there that these measures accord with the wishes of a majority of the people? Nearly half the electors, having been outvoted at the hustings, have had no influence at all in the decision; and the whole of these may be, a majority of them probably are, hostile to the measures, having voted against those by whom they have been carried. Of the remaining electors, nearly half have chosen representatives who, by supposition, have voted against the measures. It is possible, therefore, and *b*not at all improbable*b*, that the opinion which has prevailed was agreeable only to a minority of the nation, though a majority of that portion of it, whom the institutions of the country have erected into a ruling class. If democracy means the certain ascendancy of the majority, there are no means of insuring that, but by allowing every individual figure to tell equally in the summing up. Any minority left out, either purposely or by the play of the machinery, gives the power not to a majority, but to a minority in some other part of the scale.

The only answer which can possibly be made to this reasoning is, that as different opinions predominate in different localities, the opinion which is in a minority in some places has a majority in others, and on the whole every opinion which exists in the constituencies obtains its fair share of voices in the representation. And this is roughly true in the present state of the constituency; if it were not, the discordance of the House with the general sentiment of the country would soon become evident. But it would be no longer true if the present constituency were much enlarged; still less, if made co-extensive with the whole population; for in that case the majority in every locality would consist of manual labourers; and when there was any question pending, on which these classes were at issue with the rest of the community, no other class could succeed in getting represented anywhere. Even now, is it not a great grievance, that in every Parliament a very numerous portion of the electors, willing and anxious to be represented, have no member in the House for whom they have voted? Is it just that every elector of Marylebone is obliged to be represented by two nominees of the vestries, every elector of Finsbury or Lambeth by those (as is generally believed) of the publicans? The constituencies to which most of the highly educated and public spirited persons in the country belong, those of the large towns, are now, in great part, either unrepresented or misrepresented. The electors who are on a different side in party politics from the local majority, are unrepresented. Of those who are on the same side, a large proportion are misrepresented; having been obliged to accept the man who had the greatest number of supporters in their political party, though his opinions may differ from theirs on every other point. The state of things is, in some respects, even worse than if the minority were not allowed

*b–b*611   even probable

to vote at all; for then, at least the majority might have a member who would represent their own best mind: while now, the necessity of not dividing the party, for fear of letting in its opponents, induces all to vote either for the *first person who* presents himself wearing their colours, or for the one brought forward by their local leaders; and these, if we pay them the compliment, which they very seldom deserve, of supposing their choice to be unbiassed by their personal interests, are compelled, that they may be sure of mustering their whole strength, to bring forward a candidate whom none of the party will strongly object to—that is, a man without any distinctive peculiarity, any known opinions except the shibboleth of the party. This is strikingly exemplified in the United States; where, at the election of President, the strongest party never dares put forward any of its strongest men, because every one of these, from the mere fact that he has been long in the public eye, has made himself objectionable to some portion or other of the party, and is therefore not so sure a card for rallying all their votes, as a person who has never been heard of by the public at all until he is produced as the candidate. Thus, the man who is chosen, even by the strongest party, represents perhaps the real wishes only of the narrow margin by which that party outnumbers the other. Any section whose support is necessary to success, possesses a veto on the candidate. Any section which holds out more obstinately than the rest, can compel all the others to adopt its nominee; and this superior pertinacity is unhappily more likely to be found among those who are holding out for their own interest, than for that of the public. *The choice of the majority is therefore very likely to be* determined by that portion of the body who are the most timid, the most narrow-minded and prejudiced, or who cling most tenaciously to the exclusive class-interest; *in which case* the electoral rights of the minority, while useless for the purposes for which votes are given, serve only for compelling the majority to accept the candidate of the weakest or worst portion of themselves.

That, while recognising these evils, many should consider them as the necessary price paid for a free government, is in no way surprising: it was the opinion of all the friends of freedom, up to a recent period. But the habit of passing them over as irremediable has become so inveterate, that many persons seem to have lost the capacity of looking at them as things which they would be glad to remedy if they could. From despairing of a cure, there is too often but one step to denying the disease; and from this follows dislike to having a remedy proposed, as if the proposer were creating a mischief instead of offering relief from one. People are so inured to

c–c611, 612   person who first
d–d611   Speaking generally, the choice of the majority is
e–e611   and

the evils, that they feel as if it were unreasonable, if not wrong, to complain of them. Yet, avoidable or not, he must be a purblind lover of liberty on whose mind they do not weigh; who would not rejoice at the discovery that they could be dispensed with. Now, nothing is more certain, than that the virtual blotting-out of the minority is no necessary or natural consequence of freedom; that, far from having any connexion with democracy, it is diametrically opposed to the first principle of democracy, representation in proportion to numbers. It is an essential part of democracy that minorities should be adequately represented. No real democracy, nothing but a false show of democracy, is possible without it.

Those who have seen and felt, in some degree, the force of these considerations, have proposed various expedients by which the evil may be, in a greater or less degree, mitigated. Lord John Russell, in one of his Reform Bills, introduced a provision, that certain constituencies should return three members, and that in these each elector should be allowed to vote only for two;[*] and Mr. Disraeli, in the recent debates, revived the memory of the fact by reproaching him for it;[†] being of opinion, apparently, that it befits a Conservative statesman to regard only means, and to disown scornfully all fellow-feeling with any one who is betrayed, even once, into thinking of ends.* Others have proposed that each elector should be allowed to vote only for one. By either of these plans, a minority equalling or exceeding a third of the local constituency, would be able, if it attempted no more, to return one out of three members. The same result might be attained in a still better way, if, as proposed in an able pamphlet by Mr. James Garth Marshall,[‡] the elector retained his three votes, but was at liberty to be-

[*See *Parliamentary Papers*, 1854, Vol. V, p. 377.]

[†See *Parliamentary Debates*, 3rd ser., Vol. 157, col. 854 (19 March, 1860).]

*This blunder of Mr. Disraeli (from which, greatly to his credit, Sir John Pakington took an opportunity, soon after, of separating himself [see *Parliamentary Debates*, 3rd ser., Vol. 157, col. 1043 (22 March, 1860)]) is a speaking instance, among many, how little the Conservative leaders understand Conservative principles. Without presuming to require from political parties such an amount of virtue and discernment as that they should comprehend, and know when to apply, the principles of their opponents, we may yet say that it would be a great improvement if each party understood and acted upon its own. Well would it be for England if Conservatives voted consistently for everything conservative, and Liberals for everything liberal. We should not then have to wait long for things which, like the present and many other great measures, are eminently both the one and the other. The Conservatives, as being by the law of their existence the stupidest party, have much the greatest sins of this description to answer for: and it is a melancholy truth, that if any measure were proposed, on any subject, truly, largely, and far-sightedly conservative, even if Liberals were willing to vote for it, the great bulk of the Conservative party would rush blindly in and prevent it from being carried.

[‡*Minorities and Majorities.*]

stow them all upon the same candidate. These schemes, though infinitely better than none at all, are yet but makeshifts, and attain the end in a very imperfect manner; since all local minorities of less than a third, and all minorities, however numerous, which are made up from several constituencies, would remain unrepresented. It is much to be lamented, however, that none of these plans have been carried into effect, as any of them would have recognised the right principle, and prepared the way for its more complete application. But real equality of representation is not obtained, unless any set of electors amounting to the average number of a constituency, wherever in the country they happen to reside, have the power of combining with one another to return a representative. This degree of perfection in representation appeared impracticable, until a man of great capacity, fitted alike for large general views and for the contrivance of practical details—Mr. Thomas Hare—had proved its possibility by drawing up a scheme for its accomplishment, embodied in a Draft of an Act of Parliament:[*] a scheme which has the almost unparalleled merit, of carrying out a great principle of government in a manner approaching to ideal perfection as regards the special object in view, while it attains incidentally several other ends, of scarcely inferior importance.

According to this plan, the unit of representation, the quota of electors who would be entitled to have a member to themselves, would be ascertained by the ordinary process of taking averages, the number of voters being divided by the number of seats in the House: and every candidate who obtained that quota would be returned, from however great a number of local constituencies it might be gathered. The votes would, as at present, be given locally; but any elector would be at liberty to vote for any candidate, in whatever part of the country he might offer himself. Those electors, therefore, who did not wish to be represented by any of the local candidates, might aid by their vote in the return of the person they liked best among all those throughout the country, who had expressed a willingness to be chosen. This would, so far, give reality to the electoral rights of the otherwise virtually disfranchised minority. But it is important that not those alone who refuse to vote for any of the local candidates, but those also who vote for one of them and are defeated, should be enabled to find elsewhere the representation which they have not succeeded in obtaining in their own district. It is therefore provided that an elector may deliver a voting paper, containing other names in addition to the one which stands foremost in his preference. His vote would only be counted for one candidate; but if the object of his first choice failed to be returned, from not having obtained the quota, his second perhaps might be more fortunate. He may extend his list to a greater number, in the order of his preference, so that if the names

[*In his *Treatise on the Election of Representatives*.]

which stand near the top of the list either cannot make up the quota, or are able to make it up without his vote, the vote may still be used for some one whom it may assist in returning. To obtain the full number of members required to complete the House, as well as to prevent very popular candidates from engrossing nearly all the suffrages, it is necessary, however many votes a candidate may obtain, that no more of them than the quota should be counted for his return: the remainder of those who voted for him would have their votes counted for the next person on their respective lists who needed them, and could by their aid complete the quota. To determine which of a candidate's votes should be used for his return, and which set free for others, several methods are proposed, into which we shall not here enter. He would of course retain the votes of all those who would not otherwise be represented; and for the remainder, drawing lots, in default of better, would be an unobjectionable expedient. The voting papers would be conveyed to a central office, where the votes would be counted, the number of first, second, third, and other votes given for each candidate ascertained, and the quota would be allotted to every one who could make it up, until the number of the House was complete; first votes being preferred to second, second to third, and so forth. The voting papers, and all the elements of the calculation, would be placed in public repositories, accessible to all whom they concerned; and if any one who had obtained the quota was not duly returned, it would be in his power easily to prove it.

These are the main provisions of the scheme. For a more minute knowledge of its very simple machinery, I must refer to Mr. Hare's *Treatise on the Election of Representatives* (a small volume published in 1859),* and to a pamphlet by Mr. Henry Fawcett *f*(now Professor of Political Economy in the University of Cambridge)*f*, published in 1860, and entitled *Mr. Hare's Reform Bill simplified and explained.*[*] This last is a very clear and concise exposition of the plan, reduced to its simplest elements, by the omission of some of Mr. Hare's original provisions, which, though in themselves beneficial, were thought to take more from the simplicity of the scheme than they added to its practical *g*usefulness*g*. The more these works are studied, the stronger, I venture to predict, will be the impression of the perfect feasibility of the scheme, and its transcendent advantages. Such and so numerous are these, that, in my conviction, they place Mr. Hare's plan among the very greatest improvements yet made in the theory and practice of government.

---

*[61²] In a second edition, published recently [1861], Mr. Hare has made important improvements in some of the detailed provisions.

[*Westminster: Brettnell, 1860.]

f-f+65
*g-g*61¹, 61²   advantages

In the first place, it secures a representation, in proportion to numbers, of every division of the electoral body: not two great parties alone, with perhaps a few large sectional minorities in particular places, but every minority in the whole nation, consisting of a sufficiently large number to be, on principles of equal justice, entitled to a representative. Secondly, no elector would, as at present, be nominally represented by some one whom he had not chosen. Every member of the House would be the representative of an unanimous constituency. He would represent a thousand electors, or two thousand, or five thousand, or ten thousand, as the quota might be, every one of whom would have not only voted for him, but selected him from the whole country; not merely from the assortment of two or three perhaps rotten oranges, which may be the only choice offered to him in his local market. Under this relation the tie between the elector and the representative would be of a strength, and a value, of which at present we have no experience. Every one of the electors would be personally identified with his representative, and the representative with his constituents. Every elector who voted for him, would have done so either because [h], among all the candidates for Parliament who are favourably known to a certain number of electors, he is the one[h] who best expresses the voter's own opinions, or because he is one of those whose abilities and character the voter most respects, and whom he most willingly trusts to think for him. The member would represent persons, not the mere bricks and mortar of the town—the voters themselves, not a few vestrymen or parish notabilities merely. All, however, that is worth preserving in the representation of places would be preserved. Though the Parliament of the nation ought to have as little as possible to do with purely local affairs, yet, while it has to do with them, there ought to be members specially commissioned to look after the interests of every important locality: and these there would still be. In every locality which [i]could make up the quota within itself,[i] the majority would generally prefer to be represented by one of themselves; by a person of local knowledge, and residing in the locality, if there is any such person to be found among the candidates, who is otherwise [j]well qualified to be[j] their representative. It would be the minorities chiefly, who being unable to return the local member, would look out elsewhere for a candidate likely to obtain other votes in addition to their own.

Of all modes in which a national representation can possibly be constituted, this one affords the best security for the intellectual qualifications desirable in the representatives. At present, by universal admission, it is

[h–h]61[1], 61[2]   he is the person, in the whole list of candidates for Parliament,
[i–i]61[1]   contained many more voters than the quota (and there probably ought to be o local constituency which does not)
[j–j]61[1]   eligible as

becoming more and more difficult for any one, who has only talents and character, to gain admission into the House of Commons. The only persons who can get elected are those who possess local influence, or make their way by lavish expenditure, or who, on the invitation of three or four tradesmen or attorneys, are sent down by one of the two great parties from their London clubs, as men whose votes the party can depend on under all circumstances. On Mr. Hare's system, those who did not like the local candidates, *k*or who could not succeed in carrying the local candidate they preferred, would have the power to*k* fill up their voting papers by a selection from all the persons of national reputation, on the list of candidates, with whose general political principles they were in sympathy. Almost every person, therefore, who had made himself in any way honourably distinguished, though devoid of local influence, and having sworn allegiance to no political party, would have a fair chance of making up the quota; and with this encouragement such persons might be expected to offer themselves, in numbers hitherto undreamt of. Hundreds of able men of independent thought, who would have no chance whatever of being chosen by the majority of any existing constituency, have by their writings, or their exertions in some field of public usefulness, made themselves known and approved by a few persons in almost every district of the kingdom; and if every vote that would be given for them in every place could be counted for their election, they might be able to complete the number of the quota. In no other way which it seems possible to suggest, would Parliament be so certain of containing the very *élite* of the country.

And it is not solely through the votes of minorities that this system of election would raise the intellectual standard of the House of Commons. Majorities would be compelled to look out for members of a much higher calibre. When the individuals composing the majority would no longer be reduced to Hobson's choice, of either voting for the person brought forward by their local leaders, or not voting at all; when the nominee of the leaders would have to encounter the competition not solely of the candidate of the minority, but of all the men of established reputation in the country who were willing to serve; it would be impossible any longer to foist upon the electors the first person who presents himself with the catchwords of the party in his mouth, and three or four thousand pounds in his pocket. The majority would insist on having a candidate worthy of their choice, or they would carry their votes somewhere else, and the minority would prevail. The slavery of the majority to the least estimable portion of their *l*number*l* would be at an end: the very best and most capable of the local notabilities would be put forward by preference; if possible, such as were known in

*k–k*61¹   would]   61²   would have the power to
*l–l*61¹   numbers [*printer's error?*]

some advantageous way beyond the locality, that their local strength might have a chance of being fortified by stray votes from elsewhere. Constituencies would become competitors for the best candidates, and would vie with one another in selecting from among the men of local knowledge and connexions those who were most distinguished in every other respect.

The natural tendency of representative government, as of modern civilization, is towards collective mediocrity: and this tendency is increased by all reductions and extensions of the franchise, their effect being to place the principal power in the hands of classes more and more below the highest level of instruction in the community. But though the superior intellects and characters will necessarily be outnumbered, it makes a great difference whether or not they are heard. In the false democracy which, instead of giving representation to all, gives it only to the local majorities, the voice of the instructed minority may have no organs at all in the representative body. It is an admitted fact that in the American democracy, which is constructed on this faulty model, the highly-cultivated members of the community, except such of them as are willing to sacrifice their own opinions and modes of judgment, and become the servile mouthpieces of their inferiors in knowledge, *m*seldom*m* even offer themselves for Congress or the State Legislatures, so *n*little likelihood have they*n* of being returned. Had a plan like Mr. Hare's by good fortune suggested itself to the enlightened and *o*patriotic*o* founders of the American Republic, the Federal and State Assemblies would have contained many of these distinguished men, and democracy would have been spared its greatest reproach and one of its most formidable evils. Against this evil the system of personal representation, proposed by Mr. Hare, is almost a specific. The minority of instructed minds scattered through the local constituencies, would unite to return a number, proportioned to their own numbers, of the very ablest men the country contains. They would be under the strongest inducement to choose such men, since in no other mode could they make their small numerical strength tell for anything considerable. The representatives of the majority, besides that they would themselves be improved in quality by the operation of the system, would no longer have the whole field to themselves. They would indeed outnumber the others, as much as the one class of electors outnumbers the other in the country: they could always outvote them, but they would speak and vote in their presence, and subject to their criticism. When any difference arose, they would have to meet the arguments of the instructed few, by reasons, at least apparently, as cogent; and since they could not, as those do who are speaking to persons already unanimous, simply assume

*m-m*61[1], 61[2]   do not
*n-n*61[1], 61[2]   certain is it that they would have no chance
*o-o*61[1]   disinterested

that they are in the right, it would occasionally happen to them to become convinced that they were in the wrong. As they would in general be well-meaning (for thus much may reasonably be expected from a fairly-chosen national representation), their own minds would be insensibly raised by the influence of the minds with which they were in contact, or even in conflict. The champions of unpopular doctrines would not put forth their arguments merely in books and periodicals, read only by their own side; the opposing ranks would meet face to face and hand to hand, and there would be a fair comparison of their intellectual strength, in the presence of the country. It would then be found out whether the opinion which prevailed by counting votes, would also prevail if the votes were weighed as well as counted.[*] The multitude have often a true instinct for distinguishing an able man, when he has the means of displaying his ability in a fair field before them. If such a man fails to obtain *P*at least some portion*P* of his just weight, it is through institutions or usages which keep him out of sight. In the old democracies there were no means of keeping out of sight any able man: the bema was open to him; he needed nobody's consent to become a public adviser. It is not so in a representative government; and the best friends of representative democracy can hardly be without misgivings, that the Themistocles or Demosthenes whose counsels would have saved the nation, might be unable during his whole life ever to obtain a seat. But if the presence in the representative assembly can be insured, of even a few of the first minds in the country, though the remainder consist only of average minds, the influence of these leading spirits is sure to make itself sensibly felt in the general deliberations, even though they be known to be, in many respects, opposed to the tone of popular opinion and feeling. I am unable to conceive any mode by which the presence of such minds can be so positively insured, as by that proposed by Mr. Hare.

This portion of the Assembly would also be the appropriate organ of a great social function, for which there is no provision in any existing democracy, but which in no government can remain permanently unfulfilled without condemning that government to infallible degeneracy and decay. This may be called the function of Antagonism. In every government there is some power stronger than all the rest; and the power which is strongest tends perpetually to become the sole power. Partly by intention, and partly unconsciously, it is ever striving to make all other things bend to itself; and is not content while there is anything which makes permanent head against it, any influence not in agreement with its spirit. Yet if it succeeds in sup-

[*Cf. Samuel Taylor Coleridge, " 'Blessed are ye that sow beside all waters' " (Lay Sermon II), in *On the Constitution of Church and State, and Lay Sermons* (London: Pickering, 1839), p. 409.]

*P-P*611, 612   any portion whatever

pressing all rival influences, and moulding everything after its own model, improvement, in that country, is at an end, and decline commences. Human improvement is a product of many factors, and no power ever yet constituted among mankind includes them all: even the most beneficent power only contains in itself some of the requisites of good, and the remainder, if progress is to continue, must be derived from some other source. No community has ever long continued progressive, but while a conflict was going on between the strongest power in the community and some rival power; between the spiritual and temporal authorities; the military or territorial and the industrious classes; the king and the people; the orthodox, and religious reformers. When the victory on either side was so complete as to put an end to the strife, and no other conflict took its place, first stagnation followed, and then decay. The ascendancy of the numerical majority is less unjust, and on the whole less mischievous, than many others, but it is attended with the very same kind of dangers, and even more certainly; for when the government is in the hands of One or a Few, the Many are always existent as a rival power, which may not be strong enough ever to control the other, but whose opinion and sentiment are a moral, and even a social, support to all who, either from conviction or contrariety of interest, are opposed to any of the tendencies of the ruling authority. But when the Democracy is supreme, there is no One or Few strong enough for dissentient opinions and injured or menaced interests to lean upon. The great difficulty of democratic government has hitherto seemed to be, how to provide, in a democratic society, what circumstances have provided hitherto in all the societies which have maintained themselves ahead of others— a social support, a *point d'appui*, for individual resistance to the tendencies of the ruling power; a protection, a rallying point, for opinions and interests which the ascendant public opinion views with disfavour. For want of such a *point d'appui*, the older societies, and all but a few modern ones, either fell into dissolution or became stationary (which means slow deterioration) through the exclusive predominance of a part only of the conditions of social and mental well-being.

Now, this great want the system of Personal Representation is fitted to supply, in the most perfect manner which the circumstances of modern society admit of. The only quarter in which to look for a supplement, or completing corrective, to the instincts of a democratic majority, is the instructed minority: but, in the ordinary mode of constituting democracy, this minority has no organ: Mr. Hare's system provides one. The representatives who would be returned to Parliament by the aggregate of minorities, would afford that organ in its greatest perfection. A separate organization of the instructed classes, even if practicable, would be invidious, and could only escape from being offensive by being totally without influence. But if the *élite* of these classes formed part of the Parliament, by the same title as any other of its members—by representing the same number of citizens, the same numerical fraction of the national will—their presence could give umbrage to nobody, while they would be in the position of highest vantage, both for making their opinions and counsels heard on all important subjects, and for taking an active part in public business. Their abilities would probably draw to them more than their numerical share of the actual administration of government; as the Athenians did not confide responsible public functions to Cleon or Hyperbolus (the employment of Cleon at Pylos and Amphipolis was purely exceptional), but Nicias, and Theramenes, and Alcibiades, were in constant employment both at home and abroad, though known to sympathize more with oligarchy than with democracy. The instructed minority would, in the actual voting, count only for their numbers, but as a moral power they would count for much more, in virtue of their knowledge, and of the influence it would give them over the rest. An arrangement better adapted to keep popular opinion within reason and justice, and to guard it from the various deteriorating influences which assail the weak side of democracy, could scarcely by human ingenuity be devised. A democratic people would in this way be provided with what in any other way it would almost certainly miss—leaders of a higher grade of intellect and character than itself. Modern democracy would have its occasional Pericles, and its habitual group of superior and guiding minds.

With all this array of reasons, of the most fundamental character, on the affirmative side of the question, what is there on the negative? Nothing that will sustain examination, when people can once be induced to bestow any real examination upon a new thing. Those indeed, if any such there be, who under pretence of equal justice, aim only at substituting the class ascendancy of the poor for that of the rich, will of course be unfavourable to a scheme which places both on a level. But I do not believe that any such wish exists at present among the working classes of this country, though I would not answer for the effect which opportunity and demagogic artifices may hereafter have in exciting it. In the United States, where the numerical majority have long been in full possession of collective despotism, they would probably be as unwilling to part with it as a single despot, or an aristocracy. But I believe that the English democracy would as yet be content with protection against the class legislation of others, without claiming the power to exercise it in their turn.

Among the ostensible objectors to Mr. Hare's scheme, some profess to think the plan unworkable; but these, it will be found, are generally people who have barely heard of it, or have given it a very slight and cursory examination. Others are unable to reconcile themselves to the loss of what they term the local character of the representation. A nation does not seem to them to consist of persons, but of artificial units, the creation of geography and statistics. Parliament must represent towns and counties, not human beings. But no one seeks to annihilate towns and counties. Towns and counties, it may be presumed, are represented, when the human beings who inhabit them are represented. Local feelings cannot exist without somebody who feels them; nor local interests without somebody interested in them. If the human beings whose feelings and interests these are, have their proper share of representation, these feelings and interests are represented, in common with all other feelings and interests of those persons. But I cannot see why the feelings and interests which arrange mankind according to localities, should be the only ones thought worthy of being represented; or why people who have other feelings and interests, which they value more than they do their geographical ones, should be restricted to these as the sole principle of their political classification. The notion that Yorkshire and Middlesex have rights apart from those of their inhabitants, or that Liverpool and Exeter are the proper objects of the legislator's care, in contradistinction to the population of those places, is a curious specimen of delusion produced by words.

In general, however, objectors cut the matter short by affirming that the people of England will never consent to such a system. What the people of England are likely to think of those who pass such a summary sentence on their capacity of understanding and judgment, deeming it superfluous to consider whether a thing is right or wrong before affirming that they are certain to reject it, I will not undertake to say. For my own part, I do not think that the people of England have deserved to be, without trial, stigmatized as insurmountably prejudiced against anything which can be proved to be good either for themselves or for others. It also appears to me that when prejudices persist obstinately, it is the fault of nobody so much as of those who make a point of proclaiming them insuperable, as an excuse to themselves for never joining in an attempt to remove them. Any prejudice whatever will be insurmountable, if those who do not share it themselves, truckle to it, and flatter it, and accept it as a law of nature. I believe, however, that *q*in this case*q* there is in general, among those who have yet heard of the proposition, no other hostility to it, than the natural and healthy distrust attaching to all novelties which have not been sufficiently canvassed to make generally manifest all the pros and cons of the question. The only serious obstacle is the unfamiliarity: this indeed is a formidable one, for the imagination much more easily reconciles itself to a great alteration in substance, than to a very small one in names and forms. But unfamiliarity is a disadvantage which, when there is any real value in an idea, it only requires time to remove. And in these days of discussion, and generally awakened interest

*q-q*61¹   of prejudice, properly speaking, there is in this case none except on the lips of those who talk about it; and that in improvement, what formerly was the work of centuries, often requires only years.

*Since the first publication of this Treatise, several adverse criticisms have been made on Mr. Hare's plan, which indicate at least a careful examination of it, and a more intelligent consideration than had previously been given to its pretensions. This is the natural progress of the discussion of great improvements. They are at first met by a blind prejudice, and by arguments to which only blind prejudice could attach any value. As the prejudice weakens, the arguments it employs for some time increase in strength; since, the plan being better understood, its inevitable inconveniences, and the circumstances which militate against its at once producing all the benefits it is intrinsically capable of, come to light along with its merits. But, of all the objections, having any semblance of reason, which have come under my notice, there is not one which had not been foreseen; considered and canvassed by the supporters of the plan, and found either unreal or easily surmountable.

The most serious, in appearance, of the objections, may be the most briefly answered; the assumed impossibility of guarding against fraud, or suspicion of fraud, in the operations of the Central Office. Publicity, and complete liberty of inspecting the voting papers after the election, were the securities provided; but these, it is maintained, would be unavailing; because, to check the returns, a voter would have to go over all the work that had been done by the staff of clerks. This would be a very weighty objection, if there were any necessity that the returns should be verified individually by every voter. All that a simple voter could be expected to do in the way of verification, would be to check the use made of his own voting paper; for which purpose every paper would be returned, after a proper interval, to the place from whence it came. But what he could not do, would be done for him by the unsuccessful candidates and their agents. Those among the defeated, who thought that they ought to have been returned, would, singly or a number together, employ an agency for verifying the entire process of the election; and if they detected *material* error, the documents would be referred to a Committee of the House of Commons, by whom the entire electoral operations of the nation would be examined and verified, *at a tenth part the expense of time and money* necessary for the scrutiny of a single return before an Election Committee under the system now in force.

Assuming the plan to be workable, two modes have been alleged, in which its benefits might be frustrated, and injurious consequences "produced"

---

r–r465+61², 65
s–s61²   an
t–t61²   with a tenth part the time and expense
u–u61²   superinduced

in lieu of them. First, it is said that undue power would be given to knots or cliques; sectarian combinations; associations for special objects, such as the Maine Law League, the Ballot or Liberation Society; or bodies united by class interests or community of religious persuasion. It is in the second place objected, that the system would admit of being worked for party purposes. A central organ of each political party would send its list of 658 candidates all through the country, to be voted for by the whole of its supporters in every constituency. Their votes would far outnumber those which could ever be obtained by any independent candidate. The "ticket" system, it is contended, would, as it does in America, operate solely in favour of the great organized parties, whose tickets would be accepted blindly, and voted for in their integrity; and would hardly ever be outvoted, except occasionally by the sectarian groups, or knots of men bound together by a common crotchet, who have been already spoken of.

The answer to this appears to ^{v}be^v conclusive. No one pretends that under Mr. Hare's or any other plan, organization would cease to be an advantage. Scattered elements are always at a disadvantage, compared with organized bodies. As Mr. Hare's plan cannot alter the nature of things, we must expect that all parties or sections, great or small, which possess organization, would avail themselves of it to the utmost to strengthen their influence. But under the existing system those influences are everything. The scattered elements are absolutely nothing. The voters who are neither bound to the great political nor to any of the little sectarian divisions, have no means of making their votes available. Mr. Hare's plan gives them the means. They might be more, or less, dexterous in using it. They might obtain their share of influence, or much less than their share. But whatever they did acquire would be clear gain. And when it is assumed that every petty interest, or combination for a petty object, would give itself an organization, why should we suppose that the great interest of national intellect and character would alone remain unorganized? If there would be Temperance tickets, and Ragged School tickets, and the like, would not one public-spirited person in a constituency be sufficient to put forth a "personal merit" ticket, and circulate it through a whole neighbourhood? And might not a few such persons, meeting in London, select from the list of candidates the most distinguished names, without regard to technical divisions of opinion, and publish them at a trifling expense through all the constituencies? It must be remembered that the influence of the two great parties, under the present mode of election, is unlimited: in Mr. Hare's scheme it would be great, but confined within bounds. Neither they, nor any of the smaller knots, would be able to elect more members than in proportion to the relative number of their adherents. The ticket system in America operates under conditions the reverse of this.

$^{v-v}61^2$ me

In America electors vote for the party ticket, because the election goes by a mere majority, and a vote for any one who is certain not to obtain the majority, is thrown away. But, on Mr. Hare's system, a vote given to a person of known worth has almost as much chance of obtaining its object, as one given to a party candidate. It might be hoped, therefore, that every Liberal or Conservative, who was anything besides a Liberal or a Conservative—who had any preferences of his own in addition to those of his party— would scratch through the names of the more obscure and insignificant party candidates, and inscribe in their stead some of the men who are an honour to the nation. And the probability of this fact would operate as a strong inducement with those who drew up the party lists, not to confine themselves to pledged party men, but to include along with these, in their respective tickets, such of the national notabilities as were more in sympathy with their side than with the opposite.

The real difficulty, for it is not to be dissembled that there is a difficulty, is that the independent voters, those who are desirous of voting for unpatronized persons of merit, would be apt to put down the names of a few such persons, and to fill up the remainder of their list with mere party candidates, thus helping to swell the numbers against those by whom they would prefer to be represented. There would be an easy remedy for this, should it be necessary to resort to it, namely, to impose a limit to the number of secondary or contingent votes. No voter is likely to have an independent preference, grounded on knowledge, for 658, or even for 100 candidates. There would be little objection to his being limited to twenty, fifty, or whatever might be the number in the selection of whom there was some probability that his own choice would be exercised—that he would vote as an individual, and not as one of the mere rank and file of a party. But even without this restriction, the evil would be likely to cure itself as soon as the system came to be well understood. To counteract it would become a paramount object with all the knots and cliques whose influence is so much deprecated. From these, each in itself a small minority, the word would go forth, "Vote for your *special* candidates only; or at least put their names foremost, so as to give them the full chance which your numerical strength warrants, of obtaining the quota by means of first votes, or without descending low in the scale." And those voters who did not belong to any clique, would profit by the lesson.

The minor groups would have precisely the amount of power which they ought to have. The influence they could exercise would be exactly that which their number of voters entitled them to; not a particle more; while, to ensure even that, they would have a motive to put up, as representatives of their special objects, candidates whose other recommendations would enable them to obtain the suffrages of voters not of the sect or clique. It is curious to observe how the popular line of argument in defence of existing systems veers round, according to the nature of the attack made upon them. Not many years ago it was the favourite argument in support of the then existing system of representation, that under it all "interests" or "classes" were represented. And certainly, all interests or classes of any importance ought to be represented, that is, ought to have spokesmen, or advocates, in Parliament. But from thence it was argued that a system ought to be supported, which gave to the partial interests not advocates merely, but the tribunal itself. Now behold the change. Mr. Hare's system makes it impossible for partial interests to have the command of the tribunal, but it ensures them advocates, and for doing even this it is reproached. Because it unites the good points of class representation and the good points of numerical representation, it is attacked from both sides at once.

But it is not such objections as these that are the real difficulty in getting the system accepted; it is the exaggerated notion entertained of its complexity, and the consequent doubt whether it is capable of being carried into effect. The only complete answer to this objection would be actual trial. When the merits of the plan shall have become more generally known, and shall have gained for it a wider support among impartial thinkers, an effort should be made to obtain its introduction experimentally in some limited field, such as the municipal election of some great town. An opportunity was lost, when the decision was taken to divide the West Riding of Yorkshire for the purpose of giving it four members; instead of trying the new principle, by leaving the constituency undivided, and allowing a candidate to be returned on obtaining either in first or secondary votes, a fourth part of the whole number of votes given. Such experiments would be a very imperfect test of the worth of the plan: but they would be an exemplification of its mode of working; they would enable people to convince themselves that it is not impracticable; would familiarize them with its machinery, and afford some materials for judging whether the difficulties which are thought to be so formidable, are real or only imaginary. The day when such a partial trial shall be sanctioned by Parliament, will, I believe, inaugurate a new era of Parliamentary Reform; destined to give to Representative Government a shape fitted to its mature and triumphant period, when it shall have passed through the militant stage in which alone the world has yet seen it.[r]*

*[65] In the interval between the last and present editions of this treatise, it has become known that the experiment here suggested has actually been made on a larger than any municipal or provincial scale, and has been in course of trial for several years. In the Danish Constitution (not that of Denmark proper, but the Constitution framed for the entire Danish kingdom) the equal representation of minorities was provided for on a plan so nearly identical with Mr. Hare's, as to add another to the many examples how the ideas which resolve difficulties arising out of a general situation of the human mind or of society,

present themselves, without communication, to several superior minds at once. This feature of the Danish electoral law has been brought fully and clearly before the British public in an able paper by Mr. Robert Lytton, forming one of the valuable reports by Secretaries of Legation, printed by order of the House of Commons in 1864. ["Report by Mr. Lytton, Her Majesty's Secretary of Legation, on the Election of Representatives for the Rigsraad," *Parliamentary Papers*, 1864, LXI, 578–99.] Mr. Hare's plan, which may now be also called M. Andræ's, has thus advanced from the position of a simple project to that of a realized political fact.

Though Denmark is as yet the only country in which Personal Representation has become an institution, the progress of the idea among thinking minds has been very rapid. In almost all the countries in which universal suffrage is now regarded as a necessity, the scheme is rapidly making its way: with the friends of democracy, as a logical consequence of their principle; with those who rather accept than prefer democratic government, as an indispensable corrective of its inconveniences. The political thinkers of Switzerland led the way. Those of France followed. To mention no others, within a very recent period two of the most influential and authoritative political writers in France, one [Edouard de Laboulaye] belonging to the moderate liberal and the other [Louis Blanc] to the extreme democratic school, have given in a public adhesion to the plan. Among its German supporters is numbered one of the most eminent political thinkers in Germany [Robert Mohl], who is also a distinguished member of the liberal Cabinet of the Grand Duke of Baden. This subject, among others, has its share in the important awakening of thought in the American republic, which is already one of the fruits of the great pending contest for human freedom. In the two principal of our Australian colonies Mr. Hare's plan has been brought under the consideration of their respective legislatures, and though not yet adopted, has already a strong party in its favour; while the clear and complete understanding of its principles, shown by the majority of the speakers both on the Conservative and on the Radical side of general politics, shows how unfounded is the notion of its being too complicated to be capable of being generally comprehended and acted on. Nothing is required to make both the plan and its advantages perfectly intelligible to all, except that the time should have come when they will think it worth their while to take the trouble of really attending to it.

CHAPTER VIII

Of the Extension of the Suffrage

SUCH A REPRESENTATIVE DEMOCRACY as has now been sketched, representative of all, and not solely of the majority—in which the interests, the opinions, the grades of intellect which are outnumbered would nevertheless be heard, and would have a chance of obtaining by weight of character and strength of argument, an influence which would not belong to their numerical force—this democracy, which is alone equal, alone impartial, alone the government of all by all, the only true type of democracy—would be free from the greatest evils of the falsely-called democracies which now prevail, and from which the current idea of democracy is exclusively derived. But even in this democracy, absolute power, if they chose to exercise it, would rest with the numerical majority; and these would be composed exclusively of a single class, alike in biasses, prepossessions, and general modes of thinking, and a class, to say no more, not the most highly cultivated. The constitution would therefore still be liable to the characteristic evils of class government: in a far less degree, assuredly, than that exclusive government by a class, which now usurps the name of democracy; but still, under no effective restraint, except what might be found in the good sense, moderation, and forbearance, of the class itself. If checks of this description are sufficient, the philosophy of constitutional government is but solemn trifling. All trust in constitutions is grounded on the assurance they may afford, not that the depositaries of power will not, but that they cannot, misemploy it. Democracy is not the ideally best form of government unless this weak side of it can be strengthened; unless it can be so organized that no class, not even the most numerous, shall be able to reduce all but itself to political insignificance, and direct the course of legislation and administration by its exclusive class interest. The problem is, to find the means of preventing this abuse, without sacrificing the characteristic advantages of popular government.

These twofold requisites are not fulfilled by the expedient of a limitation of the suffrage, involving the compulsory exclusion of any portion of the citizens from a voice in the representation. Among the foremost benefits of free government is that education of the intelligence and of the sentiments, which is carried down to the very lowest ranks of the people when they are called to take a part in acts which directly affect the great interests of their country. On this topic I have already dwelt so emphatically, that I only return to it, because there are few who seem to attach to this effect of popular institutions all the importance to which it is entitled. People think it fanciful to expect so much from what seems so slight a cause—to recognise a potent instrument of mental improvement in the exercise of political franchises by manual labourers. Yet unless substantial mental cultivation in the mass of mankind is to be a mere vision, this is the road by which it must come. If any one supposes that this road will not bring it, I call to witness the entire contents of M. de Tocqueville's great work;[*] and especially his estimate of the Americans. Almost all travellers are struck by the fact that every American is in some sense both a patriot, and a person of cultivated intelligence; and M. de Tocqueville has shown how close the connexion is between these qualities and their democratic institutions. No such wide diffusion of the ideas, tastes, and sentiments of educated minds, has ever been seen elsewhere, or even conceived *a* as attainable.* Yet this is nothing to what we might look for in a government equally democratic in its unexclusiveness, but better organized in other important points. For political life is indeed in America a most valuable school, but it is a school from which the ablest teachers are excluded; the first minds in the country being as effectually shut out from the national representation, and from public functions generally, as if they were under a formal disqualification. The Demos, too, being in America the one source of power, all the selfish ambition of the country gravitates towards it, as it does in despotic countries towards the monarch: the people, like the despot, is pursued with adulation and

[*De la Démocratie en Amérique, 4 vols. (Paris: Gosselin, 1835, 1840).]

*[65] The following "extract from the Report of the English Commissioner to the New York Exhibition," which I quote from Mr. Carey's Principles of Social Science [3 vols. (London: Trübner, 1858)], bears striking testimony to one part, at least, of the assertion in the text:

"We have a few great engineers and mechanics, and a large body of clever workmen; but the Americans seem likely to become a whole nation of such people. Already, their rivers swarm with steamboats; their valleys are becoming crowded with factories; their towns, surpassing those of every state of Europe, except Belgium, Holland, and England, are the abodes of all the skill which now distinguishes a town population; and there is scarcely an art in Europe not carried on in America with equal or greater skill than in Europe, though it has been here cultivated and improved through ages. A whole nation of Franklins, Stephensons, and Watts in prospect, is something wonderful for other nations to contemplate. In contrast with the comparative inertness and ignorance of the bulk of the people of Europe, whatever may be the superiority of a few well-instructed and gifted persons, the great intelligence of the whole people of America is the circumstance most worthy of public attention."

*a*611, 612 of

sycophancy, and the corrupting effects of power fully keep pace with its improving and ennobling influences. If, even with this alloy, democratic institutions produce so marked a superiority of mental development in the lowest class of Americans, compared with the corresponding classes in England and elsewhere, what would it be if the good portion of the influence could be retained without the bad? And this, to a certain extent, may be done; but not by excluding that portion of the people, who have fewest intellectual stimuli of other kinds, from so inestimable an introduction to large, distant, and complicated interests as is afforded by the attention they may be induced to bestow on political affairs. It is by political discussion that the manual labourer, whose employment is a routine, and whose way of life brings him in contact with no variety of impressions, circumstances, or ideas, is taught that remote causes, and events which take place far off, have a most sensible effect even on his personal interests; and it is from political discussion, and collective political action, that one whose daily occupations concentrate his interests in a small circle round himself, learns to feel for and with his fellow-citizens, and becomes consciously a member of a great community. But political discussions fly over the heads of those who have no votes, and are not endeavouring to acquire them. Their position, in comparison with the electors, is that of the audience in a court of justice, compared with the twelve men in the jury-box. It is not *their* suffrages that are asked, it is not their opinion that is sought to be influenced; the appeals are made, the arguments addressed, to others than them; nothing depends on the decision *b*they*b* may arrive at, and there is no necessity and very little inducement to them to come to any. Whoever, in an otherwise popular government, has no vote, and no prospect of obtaining it, will either be a permanent malcontent, or will feel as one whom the general affairs of society do not concern; for whom they are to be managed by others; who "has no business with the laws except to obey them,"[*] nor with public interests and concerns except as a looker-on. What he will know or care about them from this position, may partly be measured by what an average woman of the middle class knows and cares about politics, compared with her husband or brothers.

Independently of all these considerations, it is a personal injustice to withhold from any one, unless for the prevention of greater evils, the ordinary privilege of having his voice reckoned in the disposal of affairs in which he has the same interest as other people. If he is compelled to pay, if he may be compelled to fight, if he is required implicitly to obey, he should be legally entitled to be told what for; to have his consent asked, and his

[*See Samuel Horsley, *The Speeches in Parliament of Samuel Horsley*, ed. H. Horsley (Dundee: Chalmers, 1813), pp. 167–8.]

*b-b*611   *they*

opinion counted at its worth, though not at more than its worth. There ought to be no pariahs in a full-grown and civilized nation; no persons disqualified, except through their own default. Every one is degraded, whether aware of it or not, when other people, without consulting him, take upon themselves unlimited power to regulate his destiny. And even in a much more improved state than the human mind has ever yet reached, it is not in nature that they who are thus disposed of should meet with as fair play as those who have a voice. Rulers and ruling classes are under a necessity of considering the interests and wishes of those who have the suffrage; but of those who are excluded, it is in their option whether they will do so or not; and however honestly disposed, they are in general too fully occupied with things which they *must* attend to, to have much room in their thoughts for anything which they can with impunity disregard. No arrangement of the suffrage, therefore, can be permanently satisfactory, in which any person or class is peremptorily excluded; in which the electoral privilege is not open to all persons of full age who desire to obtain it.

There are, however, certain exclusions, required by positive reasons, which do not conflict with this principle, and which, though an evil in themselves, are only to be got rid of by the cessation of the state of things which requires them. I regard it as wholly inadmissible that any person should participate in the suffrage, without being able to read, write, and, I will add, perform the common operations of arithmetic. Justice demands, even when the suffrage does not depend on it, that the means of attaining these elementary acquirements should be within the reach of every person, either gratuitously, or at an expense not exceeding what the poorest, who *c* earn their own living, can afford. If this were really the case, people would no more think of giving the suffrage to a man who could not read, than of giving it to a child who could not speak; and it would not be society that would exclude him, but his own laziness. When society has not performed its duty, by rendering this amount of instruction accessible to all, there is some hardship in the case, but it is a hardship that ought to be borne. If society has neglected to discharge two solemn obligations, the more important and more fundamental of the two must be fulfilled first: universal teaching must precede universal enfranchisement. No one but those in whom an *à priori* theory has silenced common sense, will maintain, that power over others, over the whole community, should be imparted to people who have not acquired the commonest and most essential requisites for taking care of themselves; for pursuing intelligently their own interests, and those of the persons most nearly allied to them. This argument, doubtless, might be pressed further, and made to prove much more. It would be eminently desirable that other things besides reading, writing, and arithmetic,

*c*611 can

could be made necessary to the suffrage; that some knowledge of the con-
formation of the earth, its natural and political divisions, the elements of
general history, and of the history and institutions of their own country,
could be required from all electors. But these kinds of knowledge, however
indispensable to an intelligent use of the suffrage, are not, in this country,
nor probably anywhere save in the Northern United States, accessible to the
whole people; nor does there exist any trustworthy machinery for ascertaining whether they have been acquired or not. The attempt, at present, would
lead to partiality, chicanery, and every kind of fraud. It is better that the
suffrage should be conferred indiscriminately, or even withheld indiscriminately, than that it should be given to one and withheld from another
at the discretion of a public officer. In regard, however, to reading, writing,
and calculating, there need be no difficulty. It would be easy to require
from every one who presented himself for registry, that he should, in the
presence of the registrar, copy a sentence from an English book, and perform a sum in the rule of three; and to secure, by fixed rules and complete
publicity, the honest application of so very simple a test. This condition,
therefore, should in all cases accompany universal suffrage; and it would,
after a few years, exclude none but those who cared so little for the privilege,
that their vote, if given, would not *d*in general*d* be an indication of any real
political opinion.

It is also important, that the assembly which votes the taxes, either
general or local, should be elected exclusively by those who pay something
towards the taxes imposed. Those who pay no taxes, disposing by their
votes of other people's money, have every motive to be lavish, and none to
economize. As far as money matters are concerned, any power of voting
possessed by them is a violation of the fundamental principle of free government; a severance of the power of control, from the interest in its beneficial
exercise. It amounts to allowing them to put their hands into other people's
pockets, for any purpose which they think fit to call a public one; which in
*e*some of*e* the great towns of the United States is known to have produced a
scale of local taxation onerous beyond example, and wholly borne by the
wealthier classes. That representation should be coextensive with taxation,
not stopping short of it, but also not going beyond it, is in accordance with
the theory of British institutions. But to reconcile this, as a condition
annexed to the representation, with universality, it is essential, as it is on
many other accounts desirable, that taxation, in a visible shape, should
descend to the poorest class. In this country, and in most others, there is
probably no labouring family which does not contribute to the indirect
taxes, by the purchase of tea, coffee, sugar, not to mention narcotics or

d–d+612, 65
e–e+612, 65

stimulants. But this mode of defraying a share of the public expenses is hardly felt: the payer, unless a person of education and reflection, does not identify his interest with a low scale of public expenditure, as closely as when money for its support is demanded directly from himself; and even supposing him to do so, he would doubtless take care that, however lavish an expenditure he might, by his vote, assist in imposing upon the government, it should not be defrayed by any additional taxes on the articles which he himself consumes. It would be better that a direct tax, in the simple form of a capitation, should be levied on every grown person in the community; or that every such person should be admitted an elector, on allowing himself to be rated *extra ordinem* to the assessed taxes; or that a small annual payment, rising and falling with the gross expenditure of the country, should be required from every registered elector; that so every one might feel that the money which he assisted in voting was partly his own, and that he was interested in keeping down its amount.

However this may be, I regard it as required by first principles, that the receipt of parish relief should be a peremptory disqualification for the franchise. He who cannot by his labour suffice for his own support, has no claim to the privilege of helping himself to the money of others. By becoming dependent on the remaining members of the community for actual subsistence, he abdicates his claim to equal rights with them in other respects. Those to whom he is indebted for the continuance of his very existence, may justly claim the exclusive management of those common concerns, to which he now brings nothing, or less than he takes away. As a condition of the franchise, a term should be fixed, say five years previous to the registry, during which the applicant's name has not been on the parish books as a recipient of relief. To be an uncertificated bankrupt, or to have taken the benefit of the Insolvent Act, should disqualify for the franchise until the person has paid his debts, or at least proved that he is not now, and has not for some long period been, dependent on eleemosynary support. Nonpayment of taxes, when so long persisted in that it cannot have arisen from inadvertence, should disqualify while it lasts. These exclusions are not in their nature permanent. They exact such conditions only as all are able, or ought to be able, to fulfil if they choose. They leave the suffrage accessible to all who are in the normal condition of a human being: and if any one has to forego it, he either does not care sufficiently for it, to do for its sake what he is already bound to do, or he is in a general condition of depression and degradation in which this slight addition, necessary for the security of others, would be unfelt, and on emerging from which, this mark of inferiority would disappear with the rest.

In the long run, therefore (supposing no restrictions to exist but those of which we have now treated), we might expect that all, except that (it is to be hoped) progressively diminishing class, the recipients of parish relief, would be in possession of votes, so that the suffrage would be, with that slight abatement, universal. That it should be thus widely expanded, is, as we have seen, absolutely necessary to an enlarged and elevated conception of good government. Yet in this state of things, the great majority of voters, in most countries, and emphatically in this, would be manual labourers; and the twofold danger, that of too low a standard of political intelligence, and that of class legislation, would still exist, in a very perilous degree. It remains to be seen whether any means exist by which these evils can be obviated.

They are capable of being obviated, if men sincerely wish it; not by any artificial contrivance, but by carrying out the natural order of human life, which recommends itself to every one in things in which he has no interest or traditional opinion running counter to it. In all human affairs, every person directly interested, and not under positive tutelage, has an admitted claim to a voice, and when his exercise of it is not inconsistent with the safety of the whole, cannot justly be excluded from it. But *f*though every one ought to have a voice—*f* that every one should have an equal voice is a totally different proposition. When two persons who have a joint interest in any business, differ in opinion, does justice require that both opinions should be held of exactly equal value? If with equal virtue, one is superior to the other in knowledge and intelligence—or if with equal intelligence, one excels the other in virtue—the opinion, the judgment, of the higher moral or intellectual being, is worth more than that of the inferior: and if the institutions of the country virtually assert that they are of the same value, they assert *g*a*g* thing which is not.[*] One of the two, as the wiser or better man, has a claim to superior weight: the difficulty is in ascertaining which of the two it is; a thing impossible as between individuals, but, taking men in bodies and in numbers, it can be done with a *h*certain*h* approach to accuracy. There would be no pretence for applying this doctrine to any case which *i*could*i* with reason be considered as one of individual and private right. In an affair which concerns only one of two persons, that one is entitled to follow his own opinion, however much wiser the other may be than himself. But we are speaking of things which equally concern them both; where, if the more ignorant does not yield his share of the matter to the guidance of the wiser man, the wiser man must resign his to that of the more ignorant. Which of these modes of getting over the difficulty is most for the interest of both, and most conformable to the general fitness of

[*Cf. Jonathan Swift, *Gulliver's Travels*, Voyage IV, Chap. iii, in *Works*, Vol. XII, ed. Walter Scott (Edinburgh: Constable, 1814).]

*f-f*611, 612   (though . . . voice)   *g-g*611   the
*h-h*611   sufficient   *i-i*611   can

things? If it be deemed unjust that either should have to give way, which injustice is greatest? that the better judgment should give way to the worse, or the worse to the better?

Now, national affairs are exactly such a joint concern, with the difference, that no one needs ever be called upon for a complete sacrifice of his own opinion. It can always be taken into the calculation, and counted at a certain figure, a higher figure being assigned to the suffrages of those whose opinion is entitled to greater weight. There is not, in this arrangement, anything necessarily invidious to those to whom it assigns the lower degrees of influence. Entire exclusion from a voice in the common concerns, is one thing: the concession to others of a more potential voice, on the ground of greater capacity for the management of the joint interests, is another. The two things are not merely different, they are incommensurable. Every one has a right to feel insulted by being made a nobody, and stamped as of no account at all. No one but a fool, and only a fool of a peculiar description, feels offended by the acknowledgment that there are others whose opinion, and even whose wish, is entitled to a greater amount of consideration than his. To have no voice in what are partly his own concerns, is a thing which nobody willingly submits to; but when what is partly his concern is also partly another's, and he feels the other to understand the subject better than himself, that the other's opinion should be counted for more than his own, accords with his expectations, and with the course of things which in all other affairs of life he is accustomed to acquiesce in. It is only necessary that this superior influence should be assigned on grounds which he can comprehend, and of which he is able to perceive the justice.

I hasten to say, that I consider it entirely inadmissible, unless as a temporary makeshift, that the superiority of influence should be conferred in consideration of property. I do not deny that property is a kind of test; education in most countries, though anything but proportional to riches, is on the average better in the richer half of society than in the poorer. But the criterion is so imperfect; accident has so much more to do than merit with enabling men to rise in the world; and it is so impossible for any one, by acquiring any amount of instruction, to make sure of the corresponding rise in station, that this foundation of electoral privilege is always, and will continue to be, supremely odious. To connect plurality of votes with any pecuniary qualification would be not only objectionable in itself, but a sure mode of *discrediting* the principle, and making its permanent maintenance impracticable. The Democracy, at least of this country, are not at present jealous of personal superiority, but they are naturally and most justly so of that which is grounded on mere pecuniary circumstances. The only thing which can justify reckoning one person's opinion as equivalent to more

*j-j*611 compromising

than one, is individual mental superiority; and what is wanted is some approximate means of ascertaining that. If there existed such a thing as a really national education, or a trustworthy system of general examination, education might be tested directly. In the absence of these, the nature of a person's occupation is some test. An employer of labour is on the average more intelligent than a labourer; for he must labour with his head, and not solely with his hands. A foreman is generally more intelligent than an ordinary labourer, and a labourer in the skilled trades than in the unskilled. A banker, merchant, or manufacturer, is likely to be more intelligent than a tradesman, because he has larger and more complicated interests to manage. In all these cases it is not the having merely undertaken the superior function, but the successful performance of it, that tests the qualifications; for which reason, as well as to prevent persons from engaging nominally in an occupation for the sake of the vote, it would be proper to require that the occupation should have been persevered in for some length of time (say three years). Subject to some such condition, two or more votes might be allowed to every person who exercises any of these superior functions. The liberal professions, when really and not nominally practised, imply, of course, a still higher degree of instruction; and *wherever* a sufficient examination, or any serious conditions of education, are required before entering on a profession, its members could be admitted at once to a plurality of votes. The same rule might be applied to graduates of universities; and even to those who bring satisfactory certificates of having passed through the course of study required by any school at which the higher branches of knowledge are taught, under proper securities that the teaching is real, and not a mere pretence. The "local" or "middle class" examinations for the degree of Associate, so laudably and public-spiritedly established by the *Universities of Oxford and Cambridge*, and any similar ones which may be instituted by other competent bodies (provided they are fairly open to all comers), afford a ground on which plurality of votes might with great advantage be accorded to those who have passed the test. All these suggestions are open to much discussion in the detail, and to objections which it is of no use to anticipate. The time is not come for giving to such plans a practical shape, nor should I wish to be bound by the particular proposals which I have made. But it is to me evident, that in this direction lies the true ideal of representative government; and that to work towards it, by the best practical contrivances which can be found, is the path of real political improvement.

If it be asked, to what length the principle admits of being carried, or how many votes might be accorded to an individual on the ground of superior

*k–k*611   whenever
*l–l*611, 612   University of Oxford

qualifications, I answer, that this is not in itself very material, provided the distinctions and gradations are not made arbitrarily, but are such as can be understood and accepted by the general conscience and understanding. But it is an absolute condition, not to overpass the limit prescribed by the fundamental principle laid down in a former chapter as the condition of excellence in the constitution of a representative system. The plurality of votes must on no account be carried so far, that those who are privileged by it, or the class (if any) to which they mainly belong, shall outweigh by means of it all the rest of the community. The distinction in favour of education, right in itself, is further and strongly recommended by its preserving the educated from the class legislation of the uneducated; but it must stop short of enabling them to practise class legislation on their own account. Let me add, that I consider it an absolutely necessary part of the plurality scheme, that it be open to the poorest individual in the community to claim its privileges, if he can prove that, in spite of all difficulties and obstacles, he is, in point of intelligence, entitled to them. There ought to be voluntary examinations at which any person whatever might present himself, might prove that he came up to the standard of knowledge and ability laid down as sufficient, and be admitted, in consequence, to the plurality of votes. A privilege which is not refused to any one who can show that he has realized the conditions on which in theory and principle it is dependent, would not ^{m}necessarily^m be repugnant to any one's sentiment of justice: but it would certainly be so, if, while conferred on general presumptions not always infallible, it were denied to direct proof.

Plural voting, though practised in vestry elections and those of poor-law guardians, is so unfamiliar in elections to parliament, that it is not likely to be soon or willingly adopted: but as the time will certainly arrive when the only choice will be between this and equal universal suffrage, whoever does not desire the last, cannot too soon begin to reconcile himself to the former. In the meantime, though the suggestion, for the present, may not be a practical one, it will serve to mark what is best in principle, and enable us to judge of the eligibility of any indirect means, either existing or capable of being adopted, which may promote in a less perfect manner the same end. A person may have a double vote by other means than that of tendering two votes at the same hustings; he may have a vote in each of two different constituencies: and though this exceptional privilege at present belongs rather to superiority of means than of intelligence, I would not abolish it where it exists, since until a truer test of education is adopted, it would be unwise to dispense with even so imperfect a one as is afforded by pecuniary circumstances. Means might be found of giving a further extension to the privilege, which would connect it in a more direct manner with

$^{m-m}$+61^2, 65

superior education. In any future Reform Bill which lowers greatly the pecuniary conditions of the suffrage, it might be a wise provision to allow all graduates of universities, all persons who *have* passed creditably through the higher schools, all members of the liberal professions, and perhaps some others, to be registered specifically in those characters, and to give their votes as such in any constituency in which they *choose* to register: retaining, in addition, their votes as simple citizens in the localities in which they reside.

Until there shall have been devised, and until opinion is willing to accept, some mode of plural voting which may assign to education, as such, the degree of superior influence due to it, and sufficient as a counterpoise to the numerical weight of the least educated class; for so long, the benefits of completely universal suffrage cannot be obtained without bringing with them, as it appears to me, more than equivalent evils. It is possible, indeed (and this is perhaps one of the transitions through which we may have to pass in our progress to a really good representative system), that the barriers which restrict the suffrage might be entirely levelled in some particular constituencies, whose members, consequently, would be returned principally by manual labourers; the existing electoral qualification being maintained elsewhere, or any alteration in it being accompanied by such a grouping of the constituencies as to prevent the labouring class from becoming preponderant in Parliament. By such a compromise, the anomalies in the representation would not only be retained, but augmented: this how-ever is not a conclusive objection; for if the country does not choose to pursue the right ends by a regular system directly leading to them, it must be content with an irregular makeshift, as being greatly preferable to a system free from irregularities, but regularly adapted to wrong ends, or in which some ends equally necessary with the others have been left out. It is a far graver objection, that this adjustment is incompatible with the inter-community of local constituencies which Mr. Hare's plan requires; that under it every voter would remain imprisoned within the one or more constituencies in which his name is registered, and unless willing to be represented by one of the candidates for those localities, would not be represented at all.

So much importance do I attach to the emancipation of those who already have votes, but whose votes are useless, because always outnumbered; so much should I hope from the natural influence of truth and reason, if only secured a hearing and a competent advocacy—that I should not despair of the operation even of equal and universal suffrage, if made real by the proportional representation of all minorities, on Mr. Hare's principle. But

n–n611, 612   had
o–o611, 612   chose

if the best hopes which can be formed on this subject were certainties, I should still contend for the principle of plural voting. I do not propose the plurality as a thing in itself undesirable, which, like the exclusion of part of the community from the suffrage, may be temporarily tolerated while necessary to prevent greater evils. I do not look upon equal voting as among the things which are good in themselves, provided they can be guarded against inconveniences. I look upon it as only relatively good; less objectionable than inequality of privilege grounded on irrelevant or adventitious circumstances, but in principle wrong, because recognising a wrong standard, and exercising a bad influence on the voter's mind. It is not useful, but hurtful, that the constitution of the country should declare ignorance to be entitled to as much political power as knowledge. The national institutions should place all things that they are concerned with, before the mind of the citizen in the light in which it is for his good that he should regard them: and as it is for his good that he should think that every one is entitled to some influence, but the better and wiser to more than others, it is important that this conviction should be professed by the State, and embodied in the national institutions. Such things constitute the *spirit* of the institutions of a country: that portion of their influence which is least regarded by common, and especially by English, thinkers; though the institutions of every country, not under great positive oppression, produce more effect by their spirit than by any of their direct provisions, since by it they shape the national character. The American institutions have imprinted strongly on the American mind, that any one man (with a white skin) is as good as any other; and it is felt that this false creed is nearly connected with some of the more unfavourable points in American character. It is not a small mischief that the constitution of any country should sanction this creed; for the belief in it, whether express or tacit, is almost as detrimental to moral and intellectual excellence, as any effect which most forms of government can produce.

It may, perhaps, be said, that a constitution which gives equal influence, man for man, to the most and to the least instructed, is nevertheless conducive to progress, because the appeals constantly made to the less instructed classes, the exercise given to their mental powers, and the exertions which the more instructed are obliged to make for enlightening their judgment and ridding them of errors and prejudices, are powerful stimulants to their advance in intelligence. That this most desirable effect really attends the admission of the less educated classes to some, and even to a large share of power, I admit, and have already strenuously maintained. But theory and experience alike prove that a counter current sets in when they are made the possessors of all power. Those who are supreme over everything, whether they be One, or Few, or Many, have no longer need of the arms of reason: they can make their mere will prevail; and those who cannot be resisted are usually far too well satisfied with their own opinions to be willing to change them, or listen without impatience to any one who tells them that they are in the wrong. The position which gives the strongest stimulus to the growth of intelligence, is that of rising into power, not that of having achieved it; and of all resting-points, temporary or permanent, in the way to ascendancy, the one which developes the best and highest qualities is the position of those who are strong enough to make reason prevail, but not strong enough to prevail against reason. This is the position in which, according to the principles we have laid down, the rich and the poor, the much and the little educated, and all the other classes and denominations which divide society between them, ought as far as practicable to be placed. And by combining this principle with the otherwise just one of allowing superiority of weight to superiority of mental qualities, a political constitution would realize that kind of relative perfection, which is alone compatible with the complicated nature of human affairs.

In the preceding argument for universal, but graduated suffrage, I have taken no account of difference of sex. I consider it to be as entirely irrelevant to political rights, as difference in height, or in the colour of the hair. All human beings have the same interest in good government; the welfare of all is alike affected by it, and they have equal need of a voice in it to secure their share of its benefits. If there be any difference, women require it more than men, since, being physically weaker, they are more dependent on law and society for protection. Mankind have long since abandoned the only premises which will support the conclusion that women ought not to have votes. No one now holds that women should be in personal servitude; that they should have no thought, wish, or occupation, but to be the domestic drudges of husbands, fathers, or brothers. It is allowed to unmarried, and wants but little of being conceded to married women, to hold property, and have pecuniary and business interests, in the same manner as men. It is considered suitable and proper that women should think, and write, and be teachers. As soon as these things are admitted, the political disqualification has no principle to rest on. The whole mode of thought of the modern world is, with increasing emphasis, pronouncing against the claim of society to decide for individuals what they are and are not fit for, and what they shall and shall not be allowed to attempt. If the principles of modern politics and political economy are good for anything, it is for proving that these points can only be rightly judged of by the individuals themselves: and that, under complete freedom of choice, wherever there are real diversities of aptitude, the great number will apply themselves to the things for which they are on the average fittest, and the exceptional course will only be taken by the exceptions. Either the whole tendency of modern social improvements has been wrong, or it ought to be carried out to the total abolition of all exclusions and disabilities which close any honest employment to a human being.

But it is not even necessary to maintain so much, in order to prove that women should have the suffrage. Were it as right, as it is wrong, that they should be a subordinate class, confined to domestic occupations and subject to domestic authority, they would not the less require the protection of the suffrage to secure them from the abuse of that authority. Men, as well as women, do not need political rights in order that they may govern, but in order that they may not be misgoverned. The majority of the male sex are, and will be all their lives, nothing else than labourers in corn-fields or manufactories; but this does not render the suffrage less desirable for them, nor their claim to it less irresistible, when not likely to make a bad use of it. Nobody pretends to think that women would make a bad use of the suffrage. The worst that is said is, that they would vote as mere dependents, at the bidding of their male relations. If it be so, so let it be. If they think for themselves, great good will be done, and if they do not, no harm. It is a benefit to human beings to take off their fetters, even if they do not desire to walk. It would already be a great improvement in the moral position of women, to be no longer declared by law incapable of an opinion, and not entitled to a preference, respecting the most important concerns of humanity. There would be some benefit to them individually in having something to bestow which their male relatives cannot exact, and are yet desirous to have. It would also be no small ᵖbenefitᵖ that the husband would necessarily discuss the matter with his wife, and that the vote would not be his exclusive affair, but a joint concern. People do not sufficiently consider how markedly the fact, that she is able to have some action on the outward world independently of him, raises her dignity and value in a vulgar man's eyes, and makes her the object of a respect which no personal qualities would ever obtain for one whose social existence he can entirely appropriate. The vote itself, too, would be improved in quality. The man would often be obliged to find honest reasons for his vote, such as might induce a more upright and impartial character to serve with him under the same banner. The wife's influence would often keep him true to his own sincere opinion. Often, indeed, it would be used, not on the side of public principle, but of the personal interest or worldly vanity of the family. But wherever this would be the tendency of the wife's influence, it is exerted to the full already, in that bad direction; and with the more certainty, since under the present law and custom she is generally too utter a stranger to politics in any sense in which they involve principle, to be able to realize to herself that there is a point of honour in them; and most people have as little

ᵖ–ᵖ61¹, 61² matter

sympathy in the point of honour of others, when their own is not placed in the same thing, as they have in the religious feelings of those whose religion differs from theirs. Give the woman a vote, and she comes under the operation of the political point of honour. She learns to look on politics as a thing on which she is allowed to have an opinion, and in which if one has an opinion it ought to be acted upon; she acquires a sense of personal accountability in the matter, and will no longer feel, as she does at present, that whatever amount of bad influence she may exercise, if the man can but be persuaded, all is right, and his responsibility covers all. It is only by being herself encouraged to form an opinion, and obtain an intelligent comprehension of the reasons which ought to prevail with the conscience against the temptations of personal or family interest, that she can ever cease to act as a disturbing force on the political conscience of the man. Her indirect agency can only be prevented from being politically mischievous, by being exchanged for direct.

I have supposed the right of suffrage to depend, as in a good state of things it would, on personal conditions. Where it depends, as in this and most other countries, on conditions of property, the contradiction is even more flagrant. There is something more than ordinarily irrational in the fact, that when a woman can give all the guarantees required from a male elector, independent circumstances, the position of a householder and head of a family, payment of taxes, or whatever may be the conditions imposed, the very principle and system of a representation based on property is set aside, and an exceptionally personal disqualification is created for the mere purpose of excluding her. When it is added that in the country where this is done, a woman now reigns, and that the most glorious ruler whom that country ever had was a woman, the picture of unreason, and scarcely disguised injustice, is complete. Let us hope that as the work proceeds of pulling down, one after another, the remains of the mouldering fabric of monopoly and tyranny, this one will not be the last to disappear; that the opinion of Bentham, of Mr. Samuel Bailey, of Mr. Hare, and many other of the most powerful political thinkers of this age and country (not to speak of others), will make its way to all minds not rendered obdurate by selfishness or inveterate prejudice; and that, before the lapse of another generation, the accident of sex, no more than the accident of skin, will be deemed a sufficient justification for depriving its possessor of the equal protection and just privileges of a citizen.

CHAPTER IX

Should there be Two Stages of Election?

IN SOME REPRESENTATIVE CONSTITUTIONS, the plan has been adopted of choosing the members of the representative body by a double process, the primary electors only choosing other electors, and these electing the member of parliament. This contrivance was probably intended as a slight impediment to the full sweep of popular feeling; giving the suffrage, and with it the complete ultimate power, to the Many, but compelling them to exercise it through the agency of a comparatively few, who, it was supposed, would be less moved than the Demos by the gusts of popular passion; and as the electors, being already a select body, might be expected to exceed in intellect and character the common level of their constituents, the choice made by them was thought likely to be more careful and enlightened, and would in any case be made under a greater feeling of responsibility, than election by the masses themselves. This plan of filtering, as it were, the popular suffrage through an intermediate body, admits of a very plausible defence; since it may be said, with great appearance of reason, that less intellect and instruction are required for judging who among our neighbours can be most safely trusted to choose a member of parliament, than who is himself fittest to be one.

In the first place, however, if the dangers incident to popular power may be thought to be in some degree lessened by this indirect arrangement, so also are its benefits; and the latter effect is much more certain than the former. To enable the system to work as desired, it must be carried into effect in the spirit in which it is planned; the electors must use the suffrage in the manner supposed by the theory, that is, each of them must not ask himself who the member of parliament should be, but only whom he would best like to choose one for him. It is evident, that the advantages which indirect is supposed to have over direct election, require this disposition of mind in the voter; and will only be realized by his taking the doctrine *au sérieux*, that his sole business is to choose the choosers, not the member himself. The supposition must be, that he will not occupy his thoughts with political opinions and measures, or political men, but will be guided by his personal respect for some private individual, to whom he will give a general power of attorney to act for him. Now if the primary electors adopt this view of their position, one of the principal uses of giving them a vote at all is defeated: the political function to which they are called fails of developing public spirit and political intelligence; of making public affairs an object of interest to their feelings and of exercise to their faculties. The supposition, moreover, involves inconsistent conditions; for if the voter feels no interest in the final result, how or why can he be expected to feel any in the process which leads to it? To wish to have a particular individual for his representative in parliament, is possible to a person of a very moderate degree of virtue and intelligence; and to wish to choose an elector who will elect that individual, is a natural consequence: but for a person who does not care who is elected, or feels bound to put that consideration in abeyance, to take any interest whatever in merely naming the worthiest person to elect another according to his own judgment, implies a zeal for what is right in the abstract, an habitual principle of duty for the sake of duty, which is possible only to persons of a rather high grade of cultivation, who, by the very possession of it, show that they may be, and deserve to be, trusted with political power in a more direct shape. Of all public functions which it is possible to confer on the poorer members of the community, this surely is the least calculated to kindle their feelings, and holds out least natural inducement to care for it, other than a virtuous determination to discharge conscientiously whatever duty one has to perform: and if the mass of electors cared enough about political affairs to set any value on so limited a participation in them, they would not be likely to be satisfied without one much more extensive.

In the next place, admitting that a person who, from his narrow range of cultivation, cannot judge well of the qualifications of a candidate for parliament, may be a sufficient judge of the honesty and general capacity of somebody whom he may depute to choose a member of parliament for him; I may remark, that if the voter acquiesces in this estimate of his capabilities, and really wishes to have the choice made for him by a person in whom he places reliance, there is no need of any constitutional provision for the purpose; he has only to ask this confidential person privately what candidate he had better vote for. In that case the two modes of election coincide in their result, and every advantage of indirect election is obtained under direct. The systems only diverge in their operation, if we suppose that the voter would prefer to use his own judgment in the choice of a representative, and only lets another choose for him because the law does not allow him a more direct mode of action. But if this be his state of mind; if his will does not go along with the limitation which the law imposes, and he desires to make a direct choice, he can do so notwithstanding the law. He has only to choose as elector a known partisan of the candidate he prefers, or some one who will pledge himself to vote for that candidate. And this is so much the natural working of election by two stages, that, except in a condition of complete political indifference, it can scarcely be expected to act otherwise. It is in this way that the election of the President of the United States practically *takes place*. Nominally, the election is indirect: the population at large does not vote for the President; it votes for electors who choose the President. But the electors are always chosen under an express engagement to vote for a particular candidate: nor does a citizen ever vote for an elector because of any preference for the man; he votes for the *Lincoln ticket, or the Breckenridge* ticket. It must be remembered, that the electors are not chosen in order that they may search the country and find the fittest person in it to be President, or to be a member of parliament. There would be something to be said for the practice if this were so: but it is not so; nor ever will be, until mankind in general are of opinion, with Plato, that the proper person to be entrusted with power is the person most unwilling to accept it.[*] The electors are to make choice of one of those who have offered themselves as candidates: and those who choose the electors, already know who these are. If there is any political activity in the country, all electors, who care to vote at all, have made up their minds which of these candidates they would like to have; and will make that the sole consideration in giving their vote. The partisans of each candidate will have their list of electors ready, all pledged to vote for that individual; and the only question practically asked of the primary elector will be, which of these lists he will support.

The case in which election by two stages answers well in practice, is when the electors are not chosen solely as electors, but have other important functions to discharge, which precludes their being selected solely as delegates to give a particular vote. This combination of circumstances exemplifies itself in another American institution, the Senate of the United States. That assembly, the Upper House, as it were, of Congress, is considered to represent not the people directly, but the States as such, and to be the guardian of that portion of their sovereign rights which they have not alienated. As the internal sovereignty of each State is, by the nature of an equal federation, equally sacred whatever be the size or importance of the State, each returns to the Senate the same number of members (two), whether it be little Delaware, or the "Empire State" of New York. These members are not chosen by the population, but by the State Legislatures,

[*See *Republic* (Greek and English), trans. Paul Shorey, 2 vols. (London: Heinemann; New York: Putnam's Sons, 1930, 1935), Vol. I, pp. 74 (346a), 80 (347c-d), Vol. II, pp. 142 (520d), 144 (521a). Cf. p. 498 below.]

*a-a*611   operates
*b-b*611   Breckenridge ticket, or the Lincoln

themselves elected by the people of each State; but as the whole ordinary business of a legislative assembly, internal legislation and the control of the executive, devolves upon these bodies, they are elected with a view to those objects more than to the other; and in naming two persons to represent the State in the Federal Senate, they for the most part exercise their own judgment, with only that general reference to public opinion necessary in all acts of the government of a democracy. The elections, thus made, have proved eminently successful, and are conspicuously the best of all the elections in the United States, the Senate invariably consisting of the most distinguished men among those who have made themselves sufficiently known in public life. After such an example, it cannot be said that indirect popular election is never advantageous. Under certain conditions, it is the very best system that can be adopted. But those conditions are hardly to be obtained in practice, except in a federal government like that of the United States, where the election can be entrusted to local bodies whose other functions extend to the most important concerns of the nation. The only bodies in any analogous position which exist, or are likely to exist, in this country, are the municipalities, or any other boards which have been or may be created for similar local purposes. Few persons, however, would think it any improvement in our ^cparliamentary^c constitution, if the members for the City of London were chosen by the Aldermen and Common Council, and those for the borough of Marylebone avowedly, as they already are virtually, by the vestries of the component parishes. Even if those bodies, considered merely as local boards, were far less objectionable than they are, the qualities that would fit them for the limited and peculiar duties of municipal or parochial ædileship, are no guarantee of any special fitness to judge of the comparative qualifications of candidates for a seat in Parliament. They probably would not fulfil this duty any better than it is fulfilled by the inhabitants voting directly; while, on the other hand, if fitness for electing members of ^dParliament^d had to be taken into consideration in selecting persons for the office of vestrymen or town councillors, many of those who are fittest for that more limited duty would inevitably be excluded from it, if only by the necessity there would be of choosing persons whose sentiments in general politics agreed with those of the voters who elected them. The mere indirect political influence of town-councils, has already led to a considerable perversion of municipal elections from their intended purpose, by making them a matter of party politics. If it were part of the duty of a man's book-keeper or steward to choose his physician, he would not be likely to have a better medical attendant than

c–c611, 612   Parliamentary
d–d611, 612   parliament

if he chose one for himself, while he would be restricted in his choice of a steward or book-keeper to such as might without too great danger to his health be entrusted with the other office.

It appears, therefore, that every benefit of indirect election which is attainable at all, is attainable under direct; that such of the benefits expected from it, as would not be obtained under direct election, will just as much fail to be obtained under indirect; while the latter has considerable disadvantages peculiar to itself. The mere fact that it is an additional and superfluous wheel in the machinery, is no trifling objection. Its decided inferiority as a means of cultivating public spirit and political intelligence, has already been dwelt upon: and if it had any effective operation at all—that is, if the primary electors did to any extent leave to their nominees the selection of their *parliamentary* representative,—the voter would be prevented from identifying himself with his member of Parliament, and the member would feel a much less active sense of responsibility to his constituents. In addition to all this, the comparatively small number of persons in whose hands, at last, the election of a member of Parliament would reside, could not but afford great additional facilities to intrigue, and to every form of corruption compatible with the station in life of the electors. The constituencies would universally be reduced, in point of conveniences for bribery, to the condition of the small boroughs at present. It would be sufficient to gain over a small number of persons, to be certain of being returned. If it be said that the electors would be responsible to those who elected them, the answer is obvious, that, holding no permanent office, or position in the public eye, they would risk nothing by a corrupt vote except what they would care little for, not to be appointed electors again: and the main reliance must still be on the penalties for bribery, the insufficiency of which reliance, in small constituencies, experience has made notorious to all the world. The evil would be exactly proportional to the amount of discretion left to the chosen electors. The only case in which they would probably be afraid to employ their vote for the promotion of their personal interest, would be when they were elected under an express pledge, as mere delegates, to carry, as it were, the votes of their constituents to the hustings. The moment the double stage of election began to have any effect, it would begin to have a bad effect. And this we shall find true of the principle of indirect election however applied, except in circumstances similar to those of the election of Senators in the United States.

*The best which could be said for this political contrivance is, that in

*e-e*61[1], 61[2] Parliamentary
*f-f*61[1], 61[2] It is unnecessary, as far as England is concerned, to say more in opposition to a scheme which has no foundation in any of the national traditions. An apology may even be expected for saying so much, against a political expedient which perhaps

some states of opinion it might be a more practicable expedient than that of plural voting for giving to every member of the community a vote of some sort, without rendering the mere numerical majority predominant in Parliament: as, for instance, if the present constituency of this country were increased by the addition of a numerous and select portion of the labouring classes, elected by the remainder. Circumstances might render such a scheme a convenient mode of temporary compromise, but it does not carry out any principle sufficiently thoroughly to be likely to recommend itself to any class of thinkers as a permanent arrangement.*

---

could not, in this country, muster a single adherent. But a conception so plausible at the first glance, and for which there are so many precedents in history, might perhaps, in the general chaos of political opinions, rise again to the surface, and be brought forward on occasions when it might be seductive to some minds; and it could not, therefore, even if English readers were alone to be considered, be passed altogether in silence.

CHAPTER X

Of the Mode of Voting

THE QUESTION OF GREATEST MOMENT in regard to modes of voting, is that of secrecy or publicity; and to this we will at once address ourselves.

It would be a great mistake to make the discussion turn on sentimentalities about skulking or cowardice. Secrecy is justifiable in many cases, imperative in some, and it is not cowardice to seek protection against evils which are honestly avoidable. Nor can it be reasonably maintained that no cases are conceivable, in which secret voting is preferable to public. But I must contend that these cases, in affairs of a political character, are the exception, not the rule.

The present is one of the many instances in which, as I have already had occasion to remark, the *spirit* of an institution, the impression it makes on the mind of the citizen, is one of the most important parts of its operation. The spirit of vote by ballot—the interpretation likely to be put on it in the mind of an elector—is that the suffrage is given to him for himself; for his particular use and benefit, and not as a trust for the public. For if it is indeed a trust, if the public are entitled to his vote, are not they entitled to know his vote? This false and pernicious impression may well be made on the generality, since it has been made on most of those who of late years have been conspicuous advocates of the ballot. The doctrine was not so understood by its earlier promoters; but the effect of a doctrine on the mind is best shown, not in those who form it, but in those who are formed by it. Mr. Bright and his school of democrats think themselves greatly concerned in maintaining that the franchise is what they term a right, not a trust. Now this one idea, taking root in the general mind, does a moral mischief outweighing all the good that the ballot could do, at the highest possible estimate of it. In whatever way we define or understand the idea of a right, no person can have a right (except in the *purely* legal sense) to power over others: every such power, which he is allowed to possess, is morally, in the fullest force of the term, a trust. But the exercise of any political function, either as an elector or as a representative, is power over others. Those who say that the suffrage is not a trust but a right, *will scarcely accept the con-

a–a+61², 65
*b–b*61¹, 61² can scarcely have considered the consequences

clusions[b] to which their doctrine leads. If it is a right, if it belongs to the voter for his own sake, on what ground can we blame him for selling it, or using it to recommend himself to any one whom it is his interest to please? A person is not expected to consult exclusively the public benefit in the use he makes of his house, or his three per cent. stock, or anything [c]else[c] to which he really has a right. The suffrage is indeed due to him, among other reasons, as a means to his own protection, but only against treatment from which he is equally bound, so far as depends on his vote, to protect every one of his fellow-citizens. His vote is not a thing in which he has an option; it has no more to do with his personal wishes than the verdict of a juryman. It is strictly a matter of duty; he is bound to give it according to his best and most conscientious opinion of the public good. Whoever has any other idea of it is unfit to have the suffrage; its effect on him is to pervert, not to elevate his mind. Instead of opening his heart to an exalted patriotism and the obligation of public duty, it awakens and nourishes in him the disposition to use a public function for his own interest, pleasure, or caprice; the same feelings and purposes, on a humbler scale, which actuate a despot and [d] oppressor. Now, an ordinary citizen in any public position, or on whom there devolves any social function, is certain to think and feel, respecting the obligations it imposes on him, exactly what society appears to think and feel in conferring it. What seems to be expected from him by society forms a standard which he may fall below, but which he [e]will seldom[e] rise above. And the interpretation which he is almost sure to put upon secret voting, is that he is not bound to give his vote with any reference to those who are not allowed to know how he gives it; but may bestow it simply as he feels inclined.

This is the decisive reason why the argument does not hold, from the use of the ballot in clubs and private societies, to its adoption in parliamentary elections. A member of a club is really, what the elector falsely believes himself to be, under no obligation to consider the wishes or interests of any one else. He declares nothing by his vote, but that he is or is not willing to associate, in a manner more or less close, with a particular person. This is a matter on which, by universal admission, his own pleasure or inclination is entitled to decide: and that he should be able so to decide it without risking a quarrel, is best for everybody, the rejected person included. An additional reason rendering the ballot unobjectionable in these cases, is that it does not necessarily or naturally lead to lying. The persons concerned are of the same class or rank, and it would be considered improper in one of them to press [f]another[f] with questions as to how he had voted. It is far otherwise in parliamentary elections, and is likely to remain so, as long as the social relations exist which produce the demand for the ballot; as long as one person is sufficiently the superior of another, to think himself entitled to dictate his vote. And while this is the case, silence or an evasive answer is certain to be construed as proof that the vote given has not been that which was desired.

In any political election, even by universal suffrage (and still more obviously in the case of a restricted suffrage), the voter is under an absolute moral obligation to consider the interest of the public, not his private advantage, and give his vote to the best of his judgment, exactly as he would be bound to do if he were the sole voter, and the election depended upon him alone. This being admitted, it is at least a *primâ facie* consequence, that the duty of voting, like any other public duty, should be performed under the eye and criticism of the public; every one of whom has not only an interest in its performance, but a good title to consider himself wronged if it is performed otherwise than honestly and carefully. Undoubtedly neither this nor any other maxim of political morality is absolutely inviolable; it may be overruled by still more cogent considerations. But its weight is such that the cases which admit of a departure from it must be of a strikingly exceptional character.

It may, unquestionably, be the fact, that if we attempt, by publicity, to make the voter responsible to the public for his vote, he will practically be made responsible for it to some powerful individual, whose interest is more opposed to the general interest of the community, than that of the voter himself would be, if, by the shield of secrecy, he were released from responsibility altogether. When this is the condition, in a high degree, of a large proportion of the voters, the ballot may be the smaller evil. When the voters are slaves, anything may be tolerated which enables them to throw off the yoke. The strongest case for the ballot is when the mischievous power of the Few over the Many is increasing. In the decline of the Roman republic, the reasons for the ballot were irresistible. The oligarchy was yearly becoming richer and more tyrannical, the people poorer and more dependent, and it was necessary to erect stronger and stronger barriers against such abuse of the franchise as rendered it but an instrument the more in the hands of unprincipled persons of consequence. As little can it be doubted that the ballot, so far as it existed, had a beneficial operation in the Athenian constitution. Even in the least unstable of the Grecian commonwealths, freedom might be for the time destroyed by a single unfairly obtained popular vote: and though the Athenian voter was not sufficiently dependent to be habitually coerced, he might have been bribed, or intimidated by the lawless outrages of some knot of individuals, such as were not uncommon even at Athens among the youth of rank and fortune. The ballot was in these cases a valuable instrument of order, and conduced to the Eunomia by which Athens was distinguished among the ancient commonwealths.

But in the more advanced states of modern Europe, and especially in this country, the power of coercing voters has declined and is declining; and bad voting is now less to be apprehended from the influences to which the voter is subject at the hands of others, than from the sinister interests and discreditable feelings which belong to himself, either individually or as a member of a class. To secure him against the first, at the cost of removing all restraint from the last, would be to exchange a smaller and a diminishing evil for a greater and increasing one. On this topic, and on the question generally, as applicable to England at the present date, I have, in a pamphlet on Parliamentary Reform, expressed myself in terms which as I do not feel that I can improve upon, I will venture here to transcribe.

Thirty years ago, it was still true that in the election of members of Parliament, the main evil to be guarded against was that which the ballot would exclude—coercion by landlords, employers, and customers. At present, I conceive, a much greater source of evil is the selfishness, or the selfish partialities, of the voter himself. A ᵍbase and mischievous voteᵍ is now, I am convinced, much oftener given from the voter's personal interest, or class interest, or some mean feeling in his own mind, than from any fear of consequences at the hands of others: and to these ʰ influences the ballot would enable him to yield himself up, free from all sense of shame or responsibility.

In times not long gone by, the higher and richer classes were in complete possession of the government. Their power was the master grievance of the country. The habit of voting at the bidding of an employer, or of a landlord, was so firmly established, that hardly anything was capable of shaking it but a strong popular enthusiasm, seldom known to exist but in a good cause. A vote given in opposition to these influences was therefore, in general, an honest, a public-spirited vote; but in any case, and by whatever motive dictated, it was almost sure to be a good vote, for it was a vote against the monster evil, the over-ruling influence of oligarchy. Could the voter at that time have been enabled, with safety to himself, to exercise his privilege freely, even though neither honestly nor intelligently, it would have been a great gain to reform; for it would have broken the yoke of the then ruling power in the country—the power which had created and which maintained all that was bad in the institutions and the administration of the State—the power of landlords and boroughmongers.

The ballot was not adopted; but the progress of circumstances has done and is doing more and more, in this respect, the work of the ballot. Both the political and the social state of the country, as they affect this question, have greatly changed, and are changing every day. The higher classes are not now masters of the country. A person must be blind to all the signs of the times, who could think that the middle classes are as subservient to the higher, or the working classes as dependent on the higher and middle, as they were a quarter of a

ᵍ⁻ᵍ592   'base and mischievous vote'
ʰ592   evil

century ago. The events of that quarter of a century have not only taught each class to know its own collective strength, but have put the individuals of a lower class in a condition to show a much bolder front to those of a higher. In a majority of cases, the vote of the electors, whether in opposition to or in accordance with the wishes of their superiors, is not now the effect of coercion, which there are no longer the same means of applying, but the expression of their own personal or political partialities. The very vices of the present electoral system are a proof of this. The growth of bribery, so loudly complained of *i* , and the spread of the contagion to places formerly free from it, are evidence that the local influences are no longer paramount; that the electors now vote to please themselves, and not other people. There is, no doubt, in counties and in the smaller boroughs, a large amount of servile dependence still remaining; but the temper of the times is adverse to it, and the force of events is constantly tending to diminish it. A good tenant can now feel that he is as valuable to his landlord as his landlord is to him; a prosperous tradesman can afford to feel independent of any particular customer. At every election the votes are more and more the voters' own. It is their minds, far more than their personal circumstances, that now require to be emancipated. They are no longer passive instruments of other men's will—mere organs for putting power into the hands of a controlling oligarchy. The electors themselves are becoming the oligarchy.

Exactly in proportion as the vote of the elector is determined by his own will, and not by that of somebody who is his master, his position is similar to that of a member of Parliament, and publicity is indispensable. So long as any portion of the community are unrepresented, the argument of the Chartists, against ballot in conjunction with a restricted suffrage, is unassailable. The present electors, and the bulk of those whom any probable Reform Bill would add to the number, are the middle class; and have as much a class interest, distinct from the working classes, as landlords or great manufacturers. Were the suffrage extended to all skilled labourers, even these would, or might, still have a class interest distinct from the unskilled. Suppose it extended to all men—suppose that what was formerly called by the misapplied name of universal suffrage, and now by the silly *i* title of manhood suffrage, became the law; the voters would still have a class interest, as distinguished from women. Suppose that there were a question before the Legislature specially affecting women; as whether women should be allowed to graduate at Universities; whether the mild penalties inflicted on ruffians who beat their wives daily almost to death's door, should be exchanged for something more effectual; or suppose that any one should propose in the British Parliament, what one State after another in America is enacting not by a mere law, but by a provision of their revised Constitutions—that married women should have a right to their own property. Are not a man's wife and daughters entitled to know whether he votes for or against a candidate who will support these propositions?

It will of course be objected, that these arguments derive all their weight from the supposition of an unjust state of the suffrage: That if the opinion of the non-electors is likely to make the elector vote more honestly, or more beneficially, than he would vote if left to himself, they are more fit to be electors than he is, and ought to have the franchise: That whoever is fit to influence electors, is fit to be an elector: That those to whom voters ought to be responsible, should be

*i*592   previous to the late Act
*j*592   and insulting

themselves voters; and being such, should have the safeguard of the ballot, to shield them from the undue influence of powerful individuals or classes to whom they ought *k*not*k* to be responsible.

This argument is specious, and I once thought it conclusive. It now appears to me fallacious. All who are fit to influence electors are not, for that reason, fit to be themselves electors. This last is a much greater power than the former, and those may be ripe for the minor political function, who could not as yet be safely trusted with the superior. The opinions and wishes of the poorest and rudest class of labourers may be very useful as one influence among others on the minds of the voters, as well as on those of the Legislature; and yet it might be highly mischievous to give them the preponderant influence, by admitting them, in their present state of morals and intelligence, to the full exercise of the suffrage. It is precisely this indirect influence of those who have not the suffrage over those who have, which, by its progressive growth, softens the transition to every fresh extension of the franchise, and is the means by which, when the time is ripe, the extension is peacefully brought about. But there is *l* another and a still deeper consideration, which should never be left out of the account in political speculations. The notion is itself unfounded, that publicity, and the sense of being answerable to the public, are of no use unless the public are qualified to form a sound judgment. It is a very superficial view of the utility of public opinion, to suppose that it does good, only when it succeeds in enforcing a servile conformity to itself. To be under the eyes of others—to have to defend oneself to others—is never more important than to those who act in opposition to the opinion of others, for it obliges them to have sure ground of their own. Nothing has so steadying an influence as working against pressure. Unless when under the temporary sway of passionate excitement, no one will do that which he expects to be greatly blamed for, unless from a preconceived and fixed purpose of his own; which is always evidence of a thoughtful and deliberate character, and, except in radically bad men, generally proceeds from sincere and strong personal convictions. Even the bare fact of having to give an account of their conduct, is a powerful inducement to adhere to conduct of which at least some decent account can be given. If any one thinks that the mere obligation of preserving decency is not a very considerable check on the abuse of power, he has never had his attention called to the conduct of those who do not feel under the necessity of observing that restraint. Publicity is inappreciable, even when it does no more than prevent that which can by no possibility be plausibly defended—than compel deliberation, and force every one to determine, before he acts, what he shall say if called to account for his actions.

But, if not now (it may be said), at least hereafter, when all are fit to have votes, and when all men and women are admitted to vote in virtue of their fitness; *then* there can no longer be danger of class legislation; then the electors, being the nation, can have no interest apart from the general interest: even if individuals still vote according to private or class inducements, the majority will have no such inducement; and as there will then be no non-electors to whom they ought to be responsible, the effect of the ballot, excluding none but the sinister influences, will be wholly beneficial.

Even in this I do not agree. I cannot think that even if the people were fit for, and had obtained, universal suffrage, the ballot would be desirable. First, be-

*k–k*592   *not*
*l*592   also

cause it could not, in such circumstances, be supposed to be needful. Let us only conceive the state of things which the hypothesis implies; a people universally educated, and every grown-up human being possessed of a vote. If, even when only a small proportion are electors, and the majority of the population almost uneducated, public opinion is already, as every one now sees that it is, the ruling power in the last resort; it is a chimera to suppose that over a community who all read, and who all have votes, any power could be exercised by landlords and rich people against their own inclination, which it would be at all difficult for them to throw off. But though the protection of secrecy would then be needless, the control of publicity would be as needful as ever. The universal observation of mankind has been very fallacious, if the mere fact of being one of the community, and not being in a position of pronounced contrariety of interest to the public at large, is enough to ensure the performance of a public duty, without either the stimulus or the restraint derived from the opinion of our fellow-creatures. A man's own particular share of the public interest, even though he may have no private interest drawing him in the opposite direction, is not, as a general rule, found sufficient to make him do his duty to the public without other external inducements. Neither can it be admitted that even if all had votes, they would give their votes as honestly in secret as in public. The proposition that the electors, when they compose the whole of the community, cannot have an interest in voting against the interest of the community, will be found on examination to have more sound than meaning in it. Though the community as a whole can have (as the terms imply) no other interest than its collective interest, any or every individual in it may. A man's interest consists of whatever he takes interest *in*. Everybody has as many different interests as he has feelings; likings or dislikings, either of a selfish or of a better kind. It cannot be said that any of these, taken by itself, constitutes "his interest:" he is a good man or a bad, according as he prefers one class of his interests or another. A man who is a tyrant at home will be apt to sympathize with tyranny (when not exercised over himself): he will be almost certain not to sympathize with resistance to tyranny. An envious man will vote against Aristides because he is called the Just. A selfish man will prefer even a trifling individual benefit, ^{m}to^m his share of the advantage which his country would derive from a good law; because interests peculiar to himself are those which the habits of his mind both dispose him to dwell on, and make him best able to estimate. A great number of the electors will have two sets of preferences—those on private, and those on public grounds. The last are the only ones which the elector would like to avow. The best side of their character is that which people are anxious to show, even to those who are no better than themselves. People will give dishonest or mean votes from lucre, from malice, from pique, from personal rivalry, ^{n}even^n from the interests or prejudices of class or sect, ^{o} more readily in secret than in public. And cases exist—they may come to be ^{p}more^p frequent—in which almost the only restraint upon a majority of knaves consists in their involuntary respect for the opinion of an honest minority. In such a case as that of the repudiating States of North America, is there not some check to the unprincipled voter in the shame of looking an honest man in the face? Since all this good would be sacrificed by the ballot, even in the circumstances most favourable to it, ^{q} a much stronger case is requisite

$^{m-m}$592   above $^{n-n}$+611, 612, 65
^{o}592   far $^{p-p}$592   very
^{q}592   —circumstances not likely to be seen realized by any one now alive—

than can now be made out for its necessity (and the case is continually becoming still weaker) to make its adoption desirable *r* . *

On the other debateable points connected with the mode of voting, it is not necessary to expend so many words. The system of personal representation, as organized by Mr. Hare, renders necessary the employment of voting papers. But it appears to me indispensable that the signature of the elector should be affixed to the paper at a public polling place, or if there be no such place conveniently accessible, at some office open to all the world, and in the presence of a responsible public officer. The proposal which has been thrown out of allowing the voting papers to be filled up at the voter's own residence, and sent by the post, or called for by a public officer, I should regard as fatal. The act would be done in the absence of the salutary and the presence of all the pernicious influences. The briber might, in the shelter of privacy, behold with his own eyes his bargain fulfilled, and the intimidator could see the extorted obedience rendered irrevocably on the spot; while the beneficent counter-influence of the presence of those who knew the voter's real sentiments, and the inspiring effect of the sympathy of those of his own party or opinion, would be shut out.†

*_Thoughts on Parliamentary Reform_, 2nd ed., pp. 31–7. [See pp. 332–7 above.]

†"This expedient has been recommended, both on the score of saving expense, and on that of obtaining the votes of many electors who otherwise would not vote, and who are regarded by the advocates of the plan as a particularly desirable class of voters. The scheme has been carried into practice in the election of poor-law guardians, and its success in that instance is appealed to in favour of adopting it in the more important case of voting for a member of the Legislature. But the two cases appear to me to differ in the point on which the benefits of the expedient depend. In a local election for a special kind of administrative business, which consists mainly in the dispensation of a public fund, it is an object to prevent the choice from being exclusively in the hands of those who actively concern themselves about it; for the public interest which attaches to the election being of a limited kind, and in most cases not very great in degree, the disposition to make themselves busy in the matter is apt to be in a great measure confined to persons who hope to turn their activity to their own private advantage; and it may be very desirable to render the intervention of other people as little onerous to them as possible, if only for the purpose of swamping these private interests. But when the matter in hand is the great business of national government, in which every one must take an interest who cares for anything out of himself, or who cares even for himself intelligently, it is much rather an object to prevent those from voting who are indifferent to the subject, than to induce them to vote by any other means than that of awakening their dormant minds. The voter who does not care enough about the election to go to the poll, is the very man who, if he can vote without that small trouble, will give his vote to the first person who asks for it, or on the most trifling or frivolous inducement. A man who does not care whether he votes, is not likely to care much which way he votes; and he who is in that state of mind has no moral right to vote at all;

*r*592 , or even tolerable

The polling places should be so numerous as to be within easy reach of every voter; and no expenses of conveyance, at the cost of the candidate, should be tolerated under any pretext. The infirm, and they only on medical certificate, should have the right of claiming suitable carriage conveyance, at the cost of the State, or of the locality. Hustings, poll-clerks, and all the necessary machinery of elections, should be at the public charge. Not only the candidate should not be required, he should not be permitted, to incur any but a limited and trifling expense for his election. Mr. Hare thinks it desirable that a sum of 50*l.* should be required from every one who places his name on the list of candidates, to prevent persons who have no chance of success, and no real intention of attempting it, from becoming candidates in wantonness or from mere love of notoriety, and perhaps carrying off a few votes which are needed for the return of more serious aspirants. There is one expense which a candidate or his supporters cannot help incurring, and which it can hardly be expected that the public should defray for every one who may choose to demand it; that of making his claims known to the electors, by advertisements, placards, and circulars. For all necessary expenses of this kind the 50*l.* proposed by Mr. Hare, if allowed to be drawn upon for these purposes (it might be made 100*l.* if requisite), ought to be sufficient. If the friends of the candidate choose to go to expense 'for' committees and canvassing, there are no means of preventing them; but such expenses out of the candidate's own pocket, or any expenses whatever beyond the deposit of 50*l.* (or 100*l.*) should be illegal and punishable. If there appeared any likelihood that opinion would refuse to connive at falsehood, a declaration on oath or honour should be required from every member on taking his seat, that he had not expended, nor would expend, money or money's worth, beyond the 50*l.*, directly or indirectly, for the purposes of his election; and if the assertion were proved to be false or the pledge to have been broken, he should be liable to the penalties of perjury. It is probable that those penalties, by showing that the Legislature was in earnest, would turn the course of opinion in the same direction, and would hinder it from regarding, as it has hitherto done, this most serious crime against society as a venial peccadillo. When once this effect had been produced, there need be no doubt that the declaration on oath or honour would be considered binding.* "Opinion tolerates a false disclaimer, only when it

---

since, if he does so, a vote which is not the expression of a conviction, counts for as much, and goes as far in determining the result, as one which *s* represents the thoughts and purposes of a life." *Ibid.*, pp. 39–40. [See pp. 338–9 above.]

*Several of the witnesses before the Committee of the House of Commons in 1860, on the operation of the Corrupt Practices Prevention Act [17 & 18 Victoria, c. 102 (1854)], some of them of great practical experience in election matters,

already tolerates the thing disclaimed."[*] This is notoriously the case with regard to electoral corruption. There has never yet been, among political men, any real and serious attempt to prevent bribery, because there has been no real desire that elections should not be costly. Their costliness is an advantage to those who can afford the expense, by excluding a multitude of competitors; and anything, however noxious, is cherished as having a con-

---

were favourable (either absolutely or as a last resort) to the principle of requiring a declaration from members of Parliament; and were of opinion that, if supported by penalties, it would be, to a great degree, effectual. (*Evidence* ["Report from the Select Committee on the Corrupt Practices Prevention Act," *Parliamentary Papers*, 1860, X], pp. 46, 54–7, 67, 123, 198–202, 208.) The Chief Commissioner [Gillery Pigott] of the Wakefield Inquiry [see "Report of the Commissioners appointed to Inquire into the Existence of Corrupt Practices at Elections for the Borough of Wakefield," *Parliamentary Papers*, 1860, XXVIII] said (in reference certainly to a different proposal), "If they see that the Legislature is earnest upon the subject, the machinery will work. . . . I am quite sure that if some personal stigma were applied upon conviction of bribery, it would change the current of public opinion." ([*Parliamentary Papers*, 1860, X,] pp. 32 and 26.) A distinguished member of the Committee (and of the present Cabinet) [Sir George Cornewall Lewis; see *ibid*., p. 8] seemed to think it very objectionable to attach the penalties of perjury to a merely promissory as distinguished from an assertory oath: but he was reminded [by John Arthur Roebuck], that the oath taken by a witness in a court of justice is a promissory oath: and the rejoinder (that the witness's promise relates to an act to be done at once, while the member's would be a promise for all future time) would only be to the purpose, if it could be supposed that the swearer might forget the obligation he had entered into, or could possibly violate it unawares: contingencies which, in a case like the present, are out of the question.

A more substantial difficulty is, that one of the forms most frequently assumed by election expenditure, is that of subscriptions to local charities, or other local objects; and it would be a strong measure to enact that money should not be given in charity, within a place, by the member for it. When such subscriptions are *bonâ fide*, the popularity which may be derived from them is an advantage which it seems hardly possible to deny to superior riches. But the greatest part of the mischief consists in the fact that money so contributed is employed in bribery, under the *u*euphemistic*u* name of keeping up the member's interest. To guard against this, it should be part of the member's promissory declaration, that all sums expended by him in the place, or for any purpose connected with it or with any of its inhabitants, (with the exception perhaps of his own hotel expenses,) should pass through the hands of the election auditor, and be by him (and not by the member himself or his friends) applied to its declared purpose.

The principle of making all lawful expenses of elections a charge not upon the candidate, but upon the locality, was upheld by two of the best witnesses. (Pp. 20, 65–70, 277.) [For the identification of the witnesses, see Appendix F, under Parliamentary Papers, "Report from the Committee on the Corrupt Practices Prevention Act" (1860).]

[*Mill, *Thoughts on Parliamentary Reform*, 2nd ed., p. 16; see p. 321 above.]

*u-u*611, 612   euphonious

servative tendency, if it limits the access to Parliament to rich men. This is a rooted feeling among our legislators of both political parties, and is almost the only point on which I believe them to be really ill-intentioned. They care comparatively little who votes, as long as they feel assured that none but persons of their own class can be voted for. They know that they can rely on the fellow-feeling of one of their class with another, while the subservience of *nouveaux enrichis* who are knocking at the door of the class, is a still surer reliance; and that nothing very hostile to the class interests or feelings of the rich need be apprehended under the most democratic suffrage, as long as democratic persons can be prevented from being elected to Parliament. But, even from their own point of view, this balancing of evil by evil, instead of combining good with good, is a wretched policy. The object should be to bring together the best members of both classes, under such a tenure as shall induce them to lay aside their class preferences, and pursue jointly the path traced by the common interest; instead of allowing the class feelings of the Many to have full swing in the constituencies, subject to the impediment of having to act through persons imbued with the class feelings of the Few.

There is scarcely any mode in which political institutions are more morally mischievous—work greater evil through their spirit—than by representing political functions as a favour to be conferred, a thing which the depositary is to ask for as desiring it for himself, and even pay for as if it were designed for his pecuniary benefit. Men are not fond of paying large sums for leave to perform a laborious duty. Plato had a much juster view of the conditions of good government, when he asserted that the persons who should be sought out to be invested with political power are those who are personally most averse to it, and that the only motive which can be relied on for inducing the fittest men to take upon themselves the toils of government, is the fear of being governed by worse men.[*] What must an elector think, when he sees three or four gentlemen, none of them previously observed to be lavish of their money on projects of disinterested beneficence, vying with one another in the sums they expend to be enabled to write M.P. after their names? Is it likely he will suppose that it is for *his* interest they incur all this cost? And if he forms an uncomplimentary opinion of their part in the affair, what moral obligation is he likely to feel as to his own? Politicians are fond of treating it as the dream of enthusiasts, that the electoral body will ever be uncorrupt: truly enough, until they are willing to become so themselves: for the electors, assuredly, will take their moral tone from the candidates. So long as the elected member, in any shape or manner, pays for his seat, all endeavours will fail to make the business of election anything but a selfish bargain on all sides. "So long as the candidate himself, and the customs of the world, seem

[*See *Republic*, Vol. I, pp. 74 (346a), 80 (347c-d), Vol. II, pp. 142 (520d), 144 (521a). Cf. p. 484 above.]

to regard the function of a member of ^{v}parliament^v less as a duty to be discharged, than ^{w} a personal favour to be solicited, no effort will avail to implant in an ordinary voter the feeling that the election of a member of ^{x}parliament^x is also a matter of duty, and that he is not at liberty to bestow his vote on any other consideration than that of personal fitness."[*]

The same principle which demands that no payment of money, for election purposes, should be either required or tolerated on the part of the person elected, dictates another conclusion, apparently of contrary tendency, but really directed to the same object. It negatives what has often been proposed as a means of rendering Parliament accessible to persons of all ranks and circumstances; the payment of members of parliament. If, as in some of our colonies, there are scarcely any fit persons who can afford to attend to an unpaid occupation, the payment should be an indemnity for loss of time or money, not a salary. The greater latitude of choice which a salary would give, is an illusory advantage. No remuneration which any one would think of attaching to the post would attract to it those who were seriously engaged in other lucrative professions, with a prospect of succeeding in them. The ^{y}business^y of a member of parliament would therefore become an occupation in itself; carried on, like other professions, with a view chiefly to its pecuniary returns, and under the demoralizing influences of an occupation essentially precarious. It would become an object of desire to adventurers of a low class; and 658 persons in possession, with ten or twenty times as many in expectancy, would be incessantly bidding to attract or retain the suffrages of the electors, by promising all things, honest or dishonest, possible or impossible, and rivalling each other in pandering to the meanest feelings and most ignorant prejudices of the vulgarest part of the crowd. The auction between Cleon and the sausage-seller in Aristophanes[†] is a fair caricature of what would be always going on. Such an institution would be a perpetual blister applied to the most peccant parts of human nature. It amounts to offering 658 prizes for the most successful flatterer, the most adroit misleader of a body of his fellow-countrymen. Under no despotism has there been such an organized system of tillage for raising a rich crop of vicious courtiership.* When, by

[*Mill, *Thoughts on Parliamentary Reform*, 2nd ed., pp. 14–15; see p. 320 above.]

[†*The Knights*, in *Comediae cum commentariis et scholiis*, 9 vols. (Leipzig: Weidmann, 1794–1822).]

*"^{z}As Mr. Lorimer remarks^z, by creating a pecuniary ^{a}inducement to persons of the lowest class to devote themselves to public affairs, the calling of the demagogue would be formally inaugurated.^{a} Nothing is more to be deprecated than

$^{v-v}$592   Parliament ^{w}592   as
$^{x-x}$592, 61^1, 61^2 Parliament $^{y-y}$61^1 occupation
$^{z-z}$591   Moreover, as Mr. Lorimer remarks (p. 169)
$^{a-a}$591   'inducement . . . inaugurated'

reason of pre-eminent qualifications (as may at any time happen to be the case), it is desirable that a person entirely without independent means, either derived from property or from a trade or profession, should be brought into Parliament to render services which no other person accessible can render as well, there is the resource of a public subscription; he may be supported while in Parliament, like Andrew Marvel, by the contributions of his constituents. This mode is unobjectionable, for such an honour will never be paid to mere subserviency: bodies of men do not care so much for the difference between one sycophant and another, as to go to the expense of his maintenance in order to be flattered by that particular individual. Such a support will only be given in consideration of striking and impressive personal qualities, which though no absolute proof of fitness to be a national representative, are some presumption of it, and, at all events, some guarantee for the possession of an independent opinion and will.

---

making it the private interest of a number of active persons to urge the form of government in the direction of its natural perversion. The indications which either a multitude or an individual can give, when merely left to their own weaknesses, afford but a faint idea of what those weaknesses would become when played upon by a thousand flatterers. If there were 658 places of certain, however moderate, emolument, to be gained by persuading the multitude that ignorance is as good as knowledge, and better, it is terrible odds that they would believe and act upon the lesson." (Article in *Fraser's Magazine* for April 1859, headed "Recent Writers on Reform." [See p. 368 above.])

CHAPTER XI

Of the Duration of Parliaments

AFTER HOW LONG A TERM should members of parliament be subject to re-election? The principles involved are here very obvious; the difficulty lies in their application. On the one hand, the member ought not to have so long a tenure of his seat as to make him forget his responsibility, take his duties easily, conduct them with a view to his own personal advantage, or neglect those free and public conferences with his constituents, which, whether he agrees or differs with them, are one of the benefits of representative government. On the other hand, he should have such a term of office to look forward to, as will enable him to be judged not by a single act, but by his course of action. It is important that he should have the greatest latitude of individual opinion and discretion, compatible with the popular control essential to free government; and for this purpose it is necessary that the control should be exercised, as in any case it is best exercised, after sufficient time has been given him to show all the qualities he possesses, and to prove that there is some other way than that of a mere obedient voter and advocate of their opinions, by which he can render himself in the eyes of his constituents a desirable and creditable representative.

a It is impossible to fix, by any universal rule, the boundary between these principles. Where the democratic power in the constitution is weak or over-passive, and requires stimulation; where the representative, on leaving his constituents, enters at once into a courtly or aristocratic atmosphere, whose influences all tend to deflect his course into a different direction from the popular one, to tone down any democratic feelings which he may have brought with him, and make him forget the wishes and grow cool to the interests of those who chose him; the obligation of a frequent return to them for a renewal of his commission, is indispensable to keeping his temper and character up to the right mark. Even three years, in such circumstances, are almost too long a period; and any longer term is absolutely inadmissible. Where, on the contrary, democracy is the ascendant power, and still tends to increase, requiring rather to be moderated in its exercise than encouraged to any abnormal activity; where unbounded publicity, and an ever present

*a*611   [*no paragraph*]

newspaper press, give the representative assurance that his every act will be immediately known, discussed, and judged by his constituents, and that he is always either gaining or losing ground in their estimation—while by the same means, the influence of their sentiments, and all other democratic influences, are kept constantly alive and active in his own mind; less than five years would hardly be a sufficient period to prevent timid subserviency. The change which has taken place in English politics as to all these features, explains why annual parliaments, which forty years ago stood prominently in front of the creed of the more advanced reformers, are so little cared for and so seldom heard of at present. It deserves consideration, that, whether the term is short or long, during the last year of it the members are in the position in which they would always be if parliaments were annual: so that if the term were very brief, there would virtually be annual parliaments during a great proportion of all time. As things now are, the period of seven years, though of unnecessary length, is hardly worth altering for any benefit likely to be produced; especially since the possibility, always impending, of an earlier dissolution, keeps the motives for standing well with constituents always before the member's eyes.

Whatever may be the term most eligible for the duration of the mandate, it might seem natural that the individual member should vacate his seat at the expiration of that term from the day of his election, and that there should be no general renewal of the whole House. A great deal might be said for this system, if there were any practical object in recommending it. But it is condemned by much stronger reasons than can be alleged in its support. One is, that there would be no means of promptly getting rid of a majority which had pursued a course offensive to the nation. The certainty of a general election after a limited, which would often be a nearly expired, period, and the possibility of it at any time when the minister either desires it for his own sake, or thinks that it would make him popular with the country, tend to prevent that wide divergence between the feelings of the assembly and those of the constituency, which might subsist indefinitely if the majority of the House had always several years of their term still to run—if it received new infusions drop by drop, which would be more likely to assume than to modify the qualities of the mass they were joined to. It is as essential that the general sense of the House should accord in the main with that of the nation, as it is that distinguished individuals should be able, without forfeiting their seats, to give free utterance to the most unpopular sentiments. There is another reason, of much weight, against the gradual and partial renewal of a representative assembly. It is useful that there should be a periodical general muster of opposing forces, to gauge the state of the national mind, and ascertain, beyond dispute, the relative strength of different parties and opinions. This is not done conclusively by any partial renewal, even where, as in some of the French constitutions, a large fraction, a fifth or a third, go out at once.

The reasons for allowing to the executive the power of dissolution, will be considered in a subsequent chapter, relating to the constitution and functions of the Executive in a representative government.

CHAPTER XII

Ought Pledges to be Required from Members of Parliament?

SHOULD A MEMBER of the legislature be bound by the instructions of his constituents? Should he be the organ of their sentiments, or of his own? their ambassador to a congress, or their professional agent, empowered not only to act for them, but to judge for them what ought to be done? These two theories of the duty of a legislator in a representative government have each its supporters, and each is the recognised doctrine of some representative governments. In the Dutch United Provinces, the members of the States General were mere delegates; and to such a length was the doctrine carried, that when any important question arose which had not been provided for in their instructions, they had to refer back to their constituents, exactly as an ambassador does to the government from which he is accredited. In this and most other countries which possess representative constitutions, law and custom warrant a member of parliament in voting according to his opinion of right, however different from that of his constituents: but there is a floating notion of the opposite kind, which has considerable practical operation on many minds, even of members of parliament, and often makes them, independently of desire for popularity, or concern for their re-election, feel bound in conscience to *let* their conduct, on questions on which their constituents have a decided opinion, be the expression of that opinion rather than of their own. Abstractedly from positive law, and from the historical traditions of any particular people, which of these notions of the duty of a representative is the true one?

Unlike the questions which we have hitherto treated, this is not a question of constitutional legislation, but of what may more properly be called constitutional morality—the ethics of representative government. It does not so much concern institutions, as the temper of mind which the electors ought to bring to the discharge of their functions; the ideas which should prevail as to the moral duties of an elector. For, let the system of representation be what it may, it will be converted into one of mere delegation if the electors so choose. As long as they are free not to vote, and free to vote as they like, they cannot be prevented from making their vote depend on any condition they think fit to annex to it. By refusing to elect any one who will not pledge

*a-a*611 make

himself to all their opinions, and even, if they please, to consult with them before voting on any important subject not foreseen, they can reduce their representative to their mere mouthpiece, or compel him in honour, when no longer willing to act in that capacity, to resign his seat. And since they have the power of doing this, the theory of the Constitution ought to suppose that they will wish to do it; since the very principle of constitutional government requires it to be assumed, that political power will be abused to promote the particular purposes of the holder; not because it always is so, but because such is the natural tendency of things, to guard against which is the especial use of free institutions. However wrong, therefore, or however foolish, we may think it in the electors to convert their representative into a delegate, that stretch of the electoral privilege being a natural and not improbable one, the same precautions ought to be taken as if it were certain. We may hope that the electors will not act on this notion of the use of the suffrage; but a representative government needs to be so framed that even if they do, they shall not be able to effect what ought not to be in the power of any body of persons—class legislation for their own benefit.

When it is said that the question is only one of political morality, this does not extenuate its importance. Questions of constitutional morality are of no less practical moment than those relating to the constitution itself. The very existence of some governments, and all that renders others endurable, rests on the practical observance of doctrines of constitutional morality; traditional notions in the minds of the several constituted authorities, which modify the use that might otherwise be made of their powers. In unbalanced governments—pure monarchy, pure aristocracy, pure democracy—such maxims are the only barrier which restrains the government from the utmost excesses in the direction of its characteristic tendency. In imperfectly balanced governments, where some attempt is made to set constitutional limits to the impulses of the strongest power, but where that power is strong enough to overstep them with at least temporary impunity, it is only by doctrines of constitutional morality, recognised and sustained by opinion, that any regard at all is preserved for the checks and limitations of the constitution. In well balanced governments, in which the supreme power is divided, and each sharer is protected against the usurpations of the others in the only manner possible—namely, by being armed for defence with weapons as strong as the others can wield for attack—the government can only be carried on by forbearance on all sides to exercise those extreme powers, unless provoked by conduct equally extreme on the part of some other sharer of power: and in this case we may truly say, that only by the regard paid to maxims of constitutional morality is the constitution kept in existence. The question of pledges is not one of those which vitally concern the existence of representative governments; but it is very material to their beneficial operation. The laws cannot prescribe to the electors the principles by which they shall direct their choice; but it makes a great practical difference by what principles they think they ought to direct it. And the whole of that great question is involved in the inquiry, whether they should make it a condition that the representative shall adhere to certain opinions laid down for him by his constituents.

No reader of this treatise can doubt what conclusion, as to this matter, results from the general principles which it professes. We have from the first affirmed, and unvaryingly kept in view, the coequal importance of two great requisites of government: responsibility to those, for whose benefit political power ought to be, and always professes to be, employed; and jointly therewith, to obtain, in the greatest measure possible, for the function of government, the benefits of superior intellect, trained by long meditation and practical discipline to that special task. If this second purpose is worth attaining, it is worth the necessary price. Superior powers of mind and profound study are of no use, if they do not sometimes lead a person to different conclusions from those which are formed by ordinary powers of mind without study: and if it be an object to possess representatives in any intellectual respect superior to average electors, it must be counted upon that the representative will sometimes differ in opinion from the majority of his constituents, and that when he does, his opinion will be the oftenest right of the two. It follows, that the electors will not do wisely, if they insist on absolute conformity to their opinions, as the condition of his retaining his seat.

The principle is, thus far, obvious; but there are real difficulties in its application: and we will begin by stating them in their greatest force. If it is important that the electors should choose a representative more highly instructed than themselves, it is no less necessary that this wiser man should be responsible to them; in other words, they are the judges of the manner in which he fulfils his trust: and how are they to judge, except by the standard of their own opinions? How are they even to select him in the first instance, but by the same standard? It will not do to choose by mere brilliancy—by superiority of showy talent. The tests by which an ordinary man can judge *beforehand* of mere ability are very imperfect: such as they are, they have almost exclusive reference to the arts of expression, and little or none to the worth of what is expressed. The latter cannot be inferred from the former; and if the electors are to put their own opinions in abeyance, what criterion remains to them of the ability to govern well? Neither, if they could ascertain, even infallibly, the ablest man, ought they to allow him altogether to judge for them, without any reference to their own opinions. The ablest candidate may be a Tory, and the electors Liberals; or a Liberal, and they may be Tories. The political questions of the day may be Church questions, and

b–b+612, 65

he may be a High Churchman, or a Rationalist, while they may be Dissenters, or Evangelicals; and *vice versâ*. His abilities, in these cases, might only enable him to go greater lengths, and act with greater effect, in what they may conscientiously believe to be a wrong course; and they may be bound, by their sincere convictions, to think it more important that their representative should be kept, on these points, to what they deem the dictate of duty, than that they should be represented by a person of more than average abilities. They may also have to consider, not solely how they can be most ably represented, but how their particular moral position and mental point of view shall be represented at all. The influence of every mode of thinking which is shared by numbers, ought to be felt in the legislature: and the ᶜconstitutionᶜ being supposed to have made due provision that other and conflicting modes of thinking shall be represented likewise, to secure the proper representation for their own mode may be the most important matter which the electors on the particular occasion have to attend to. In some cases, too, it may be necessary that the representative should have his hands tied, to keep him true to their interest, or rather to the public interest as they conceive it. This would not be needful under a political system which assured them an indefinite choice of honest and unprejudiced candidates; but under the existing system, in which the electors are almost always obliged, by the expenses of election and the general circumstances of society, to select their representative from persons of a station in life widely different from theirs, and having a different class-interest, who will affirm that they ought to abandon themselves to his discretion? Can we blame an elector of the poorer classes, who has only the choice among two or three rich men, for requiring from the one he votes for, a pledge to those measures which he considers as a test of emancipation from the class-interests of the rich? It ᵈmoreover always happensᵈ to some members of the electoral body, to be obliged to accept the representative selected by a majority of their own side. But though a candidate of their own choosing would have no chance, their votes may be necessary to the success of the one chosen for them; and their only means of exerting their share of influence on his subsequent conduct, may be to make their support of him dependent on his pledging himself to certain conditions.

These considerations and counter-considerations are so intimately interwoven with one another; it is so important that the electors should choose as their representatives wiser men than themselves, and should consent to be governed according to that superior wisdom, while it is impossible that conformity to their own opinions, when they have opinions, should not enter largely into their judgment as to who possesses the wisdom, and how

ᶜ–ᶜ61¹ Constitution
ᵈ–ᵈ61¹, 61² will, moreover, always happen

far its presumed possessor has verified the presumption by his conduct; that it seems quite impracticable to lay down for the elector any positive rule of duty: and the result will depend, less on any exact prescription, or authoritative doctrine of political morality, than on the general tone of mind of the electoral body, in respect to the important requisite, of deference to mental superiority. Individuals, and peoples, who are acutely sensible of the value of superior wisdom, are likely to recognise it, where it exists, by other signs than thinking exactly as they do, and even in spite of considerable differences of opinion: and when they have recognised it they will be far too desirous to secure it, at any admissible cost, to be prone to impose their own opinion as a law upon persons whom they look up to as wiser than themselves. On the other hand, there is a character of mind which does not look up to any one; which thinks no other person's opinion much better than its own, or nearly so good as that of a hundred or a thousand persons like itself. Where this is the turn of mind of the electors, they will elect no one who is not, or at least who does not profess to be, the image of their own sentiments, and will continue him no longer than while he reflects those sentiments in his conduct: and all aspirants to political honours will endeavour, as Plato says in the *Gorgias*, to fashion themselves after the model of the Demos, and make themselves as like to it as possible.[*] It cannot be denied, that a complete democracy has a strong tendency to cast the sentiments of the electors in this mould. Democracy is not favourable to the reverential spirit. That it destroys reverence for mere social position must be counted among the good, not the bad part of its influences; though by doing this it closes the principal *school* of reverence (as to merely human relations) which exists in society. But also democracy, in its very essence, insists so much more forcibly on the things in which all are entitled to be considered equally, than on those in which one person is entitled to more consideration than another, that respect for even personal superiority is likely to be below the mark. It is for this, among other reasons, I hold it of so much importance, that the institutions of the country should stamp the opinions of persons of a more educated class as entitled to greater weight than those of the less educated: and I should still contend for assigning plurality of votes to authenticated superiority of education, were it only to give the tone to public feeling, irrespective of any direct political consequences.

When there does exist in the electoral body an adequate sense of the extraordinary difference in value between one person and another, they will not lack signs by which to distinguish the persons whose worth for their

[*See *Gorgias*, in *Lysis, Symposium, Gorgias* (Greek and English), trans. W. R. M. Lamb (London: Heinemann; New York: Putnam's Sons, 1925), pp. 484–6 (513^{a-c}).]

purposes is the greatest. Actual public services will naturally be the foremost indication: to have filled posts of magnitude, and done important things in them, of which the wisdom has been justified by the results; to have been the author of measures which appear from their effects to have been wisely planned; to have made predictions which have been often verified by the event, seldom or never falsified by it; to have given advice, which when taken has been followed by good consequences, when neglected, by bad. There is doubtless a large portion of uncertainty in these signs of wisdom; but we are seeking for such as can be applied by persons of ordinary discernment. They will do well not to rely much on any one indication, unless corroborated by the rest; and, in their estimation of the success or merit of any practical effort, to lay great stress on the general opinion of disinterested persons conversant with the subject matter. The tests which I have spoken of are only applicable to tried men; among whom must be reckoned those who, though untried practically, have been tried speculatively; who, in public speech or in print, have discussed public affairs in a manner which proves that they have given serious study to them. Such persons may, in the mere character of political thinkers, have exhibited a considerable amount of the same titles to confidence as those who have been proved in the position of practical statesmen. When it is necessary to choose persons wholly untried, the best criteria are, reputation for ability among those who personally know them, and the confidence placed and recommendations given by persons already looked up to. By tests like these, constituencies who sufficiently value mental ability, and eagerly seek for it, will generally succeed in obtaining men beyond mediocrity, and often men whom they can trust to carry on public affairs according to their unfettered judgment; to whom it would be an affront to require that they should give up that judgment at the behest of their inferiors in knowledge. If such persons, honestly sought, are not to be found, then indeed the electors are justified in taking other precautions; for they cannot be expected to postpone their particular opinions, unless in order that they may be served by a person of superior knowledge to their own. They would do well, indeed, even then, to remember, that when once chosen, the representative, if he devotes himself to his duty, has greater opportunities of correcting an original false judgment, than fall to the lot of most of his constituents; a consideration which generally ought to prevent them (unless compelled by necessity to choose some one whose impartiality they do not fully trust) from exacting a pledge not to change his opinion, or, if he does, to resign his seat. But when an unknown person, not certified in unmistakeable terms by some high authority, is elected for the first time, the elector cannot be expected not to make conformity to his own sentiments the primary requisite. It is enough if he does not regard a subsequent change of those sentiments, honestly avowed, with its grounds undisguisedly stated, as a peremptory reason for withdrawing his confidence.

Even supposing the most tried ability and acknowledged eminence of character in the representative, the private opinions of the electors are not to be placed entirely in abeyance. Deference to mental superiority is not to go the length of self-annihilation—abnegation of any personal opinion. But when the difference does not relate to the fundamentals of politics, however decided the elector may be in his own sentiments, he ought to consider that when an able man differs from him there is at least a considerable chance of his being in the wrong, and that even if otherwise, it is worth while to give up his opinion in things not absolutely essential, for the sake of the inestimable advantage of having an able man to act for him in the many matters in which he himself is not qualified to form a judgment. In such cases he often endeavours to reconcile both wishes, by inducing the able man to sacrifice his own opinion on the points of difference; but, for the able man to lend himself to this compromise, is treason against his especial office; abdication of the peculiar duties of mental superiority, of which it is one of the most sacred not to desert the cause which has the clamour against it, nor to deprive of his services those of his opinions which need them the most. A man of conscience and known ability should insist on full freedom to act as he in his own judgment deems best; and should not consent to serve on any other terms. But the electors are entitled to know how he means to act; what opinions, on all things which concern his public duty, he intends should guide his conduct. If some of these are unacceptable to them, it is for him to satisfy them that he nevertheless deserves to be their representative; and if they are wise, they will overlook, in favour of his general value, many and great differences between his opinions and their own. There are some differences, however, which they cannot be expected to overlook. Whoever feels the amount of interest in the government of his country which befits a freeman, has some convictions on national affairs which are like his life-blood; which the strength of his belief in their truth, together with the importance he attaches to them, forbid him to make a subject of compromise, or postpone to the judgment of any person, however greatly his superior. Such convictions, when they exist in a people, or in any appreciable portion of one, are entitled to influence in virtue of their mere existence, and not solely in that of the probability of their being grounded in truth. A people cannot be well governed in opposition to their primary notions of right, even though these may be in some points erroneous. A correct estimate of the relation which should subsist between governors and governed, does not require the electors to consent to be represented by one who intends to govern them in opposition to their fundamental convictions. If they avail themselves of his capacities of useful service in other respects, at a time when the points on which he is vitally at issue with them are not likely to be mooted, they are justified in dismissing him at the first moment when a question arises involving these, and on which there is not so assured a majority for what they deem right, as to make the dissenting voice of that particular individual unimportant. Thus (I mention names to illustrate my meaning, not for any personal application) the opinions supposed to be entertained by Mr. Cobden and Mr. Bright on resistance to foreign aggression, might be overlooked during the Crimean war, when there was an overwhelming national feeling on the contrary side, and might yet very properly lead to their rejection by the electors at the time of the Chinese quarrel (though in itself a more doubtful question), because it was then for some time a moot point whether their view of the case might not prevail.

As the general result of what precedes, we may affirm that actual pledges should not be required, unless, from unfavourable social circumstances or faulty institutions, the electors are so narrowed in their choice, as to be compelled to fix it on a person presumptively under the influence of partialities hostile to their interest: That they are entitled to a full knowledge of the political opinions and sentiments of the candidate; and not only entitled, but often bound, to reject one who differs from themselves on the few articles which are the foundation of their political belief: That in proportion to the opinion they entertain of the mental superiority of a candidate, they ought to put up with his expressing and acting on opinions different from theirs on any number of things not included in their fundamental articles of belief: That they ought to be unremitting in their search for a representative of such calibre as to be entrusted with full power of obeying the dictates of his own judgment: That they should consider it a duty which they owe to their fellow-countrymen, to do their utmost towards placing men of this quality in the legislature; and that it is of much greater importance to themselves to be represented by such a man, than by one who professes agreement in a greater number of their opinions: for the benefits of his ability are certain, while the hypothesis of his being wrong and their being right on the points of difference is a very doubtful one.

I have discussed this question on the assumption that the electoral system, in all that depends on positive institution, conforms to the principles laid down in the preceding chapters. Even on this hypothesis, the delegation theory of representation seems to me false, and its practical operation hurtful, though the mischief would in that case be confined within certain bounds. But if the securities by which I have endeavoured to guard the representative principle are not recognised by the Constitution; if provision is not made for the representation of minorities, nor any difference admitted in the numerical value of votes, according to some criterion of the amount of education possessed by the voters; in that case no words can exaggerate the importance in principle of leaving an unfettered discretion to the representative; for it would then be the only chance, under universal suffrage, for any other opinions than those of the majority to be heard in Parliament. In that falsely called democracy which is really the exclusive rule of the operative classes, all others being unrepresented and unheard, the only escape from class legislation in its narrowest, and political ignorance in its most dangerous, form, would lie in such disposition as the uneducated might have to choose educated representatives, and to defer to their opinions. Some willingness to do this might reasonably be expected, and everything would depend upon cultivating it to the highest point. But, once invested with political omnipotence, if the operative classes voluntarily concurred in imposing *e* in this or any other manner, any considerable limitation *f*upon*f* their self-opinion and self-will, they would prove themselves wiser than any class, possessed of absolute power, has shown itself, or, we may venture to say, is ever likely to show itself, under that corrupting influence.

*e*61[1], 61[2]   upon themselves
*f-f*61[1], 61[2]   to

CHAPTER XIII

Of a Second Chamber

OF ALL TOPICS relating to the theory of representative government, none have been the subject of more discussion, especially on the Continent, than what is known as the question of the Two Chambers. It has occupied a greater amount of the attention of thinkers than many questions of ten times its importance, and has been regarded as a sort of touchstone which distinguishes the partisans of limited from those of uncontrolled democracy. For my own part, I set little value on any check which a Second Chamber can apply to a democracy otherwise unchecked; and I am inclined to think that if all other constitutional questions are rightly decided, it is *but of secondary* importance whether the Parliament consists of two Chambers, or only of one.

If there are two Chambers, they may either be of similar, or of dissimilar composition. If of similar, both will obey the same influences, and whatever has a majority in one of the Houses will be likely to have it in the other. It is true that the necessity of obtaining the consent of both to the passing of any measure may at times be a material obstacle to improvement, since, assuming both the Houses to be representative, and equal in their numbers, a number slightly exceeding a fourth of the entire representation may prevent the passing of a Bill; while, if there is but one House, a Bill is secure of passing if it has a bare majority. But the case supposed is rather abstractedly possible than likely to occur in practice. It will not often happen that of two Houses similarly composed, one will be almost unanimous, and the other nearly equally divided: if a majority in one rejects a measure, there will generally have been a large minority unfavourable to it in the other; any improvement, therefore, which could be thus impeded, would in almost all cases be one which had not much more than a simple majority in the entire body, and the worst consequence that could ensue would be to delay for a short time the passing of the measure, or give rise to a fresh appeal to the electors to ascertain if the small majority in Parliament corresponded to an effective one in the country. The inconvenience of delay, and the advantage of the appeal to the nation, might be regarded in this case as about equally balanced.

*a–a*611, 612   of comparatively little

I attach little weight to the argument oftenest urged for having two Chambers—to prevent precipitancy, and compel a second deliberation; for it must be a very ill-constituted representative assembly in which the established forms of business do not require many more than two deliberations. The consideration which tells most, in my judgment, in favour of two Chambers (and this I do regard as of some moment) is the evil effect produced upon the mind of any holder of power, whether an individual or an assembly, by the consciousness of having only themselves to consult. It is important that no set of persons should *b*, in great affairs,*b* be able, even temporarily, to make their *sic volo* prevail, without asking any one else for his consent. A majority in a single assembly, when it has assumed a permanent character—when composed of the same persons habitually acting together, and always assured of victory in their own House—easily becomes despotic and overweening, if released from the necessity of considering whether its acts will be concurred in by another constituted authority. The same reason which induced the Romans to have two consuls, makes it desirable there should be two Chambers; that neither of them may be exposed to the corrupting influence of undivided power, even for the space of a single year. One of the most indispensable requisites in the practical conduct of politics, especially in the management of free institutions, is conciliation; a readiness to compromise; a willingness to concede something to opponents, and to shape good measures so as to be as little offensive as possible to persons of opposite views; and of this salutary habit, the mutual give and take (as it has been called) between two Houses is a perpetual school; useful as such even now, and its utility would probably be even more felt, in a more democratic constitution of the Legislature.

But the Houses need not both be of the same composition; they may be intended as a check on one another. One being supposed democratic, the other will naturally be constituted with a view to its being some restraint upon the democracy. But its efficacy in this respect, wholly depends on the social support which it can command outside the House. An assembly which does not rest on the basis of some great power in the country, is ineffectual against one which does. An aristocratic House is only powerful in an aristocratic state of society. The House of Lords was once the strongest power in our Constitution, and the Commons only a checking body: but this was when the Barons were almost the only power out of doors. I cannot believe that, in a really democratic state of society, the House of Lords would be of any practical value as a moderator of democracy. When the force on one side is feeble in comparison with that on the other, the way to give it effect is not to draw both out in line, and muster their strength in open field over against one another. Such tactics would ensure the utter defeat of the less

b-b+65

powerful. It can only act to advantage, by not holding itself apart, and compelling every one to declare himself either with or against it, but taking a position among ^{c}, rather than in opposition to, the crowd^c, and drawing to itself the elements most capable of allying themselves with it on any given point; not appearing at all as an antagonist body, to provoke a general rally against it, but working as one of the elements in a mixed mass, infusing its leaven, and often making what would be the weaker part the stronger, by the addition of its influence. The really moderating power in a democratic constitution, must act in and through the democratic House.

That there should be, in every polity, a centre of resistance to the predominant power in the Constitution—and in a democratic constitution, therefore, a nucleus of resistance to the democracy—I have already maintained; and I regard it as a fundamental maxim of government. If any people, who possess a democratic representation, are, from their historical antecedents, more willing to tolerate such a centre of resistance in the form of a Second Chamber or House of Lords than in any other shape, this constitutes a strong reason for having it in that shape. But it does not appear to me the best shape in itself, nor by any means the most efficacious for its object. If there are two Houses, one considered to represent the people, the other to represent only a class, or not to be representative at all, I cannot think that where democracy is the ruling power in society, the second House would have any real ability to resist even the aberrations of the first. It might be suffered to exist, in deference to habit and association, but not as an effective check. If it exercised an independent will, it would be required to do so in the same general spirit as the other House; to be equally democratic with it, and to content itself with correcting the accidental oversights of the more popular branch of the legislature, or competing with it in popular measures.

The practicability of any real check to the ascendancy of the majority, depends henceforth on the distribution of strength in the most popular branch of the governing body: and I have indicated the mode in which, to the best of my judgment, a balance of forces might most advantageously be established there. I have also pointed out, that even if the numerical majority were allowed to exercise complete predominance by means of a corresponding majority in ^{d}Parliament^d, yet if minorities also are permitted to enjoy the equal right due to them on strictly democratic principles, of being represented proportionally to their numbers, this provision will ensure the perpetual presence in the House, by the same popular title as its other members, of so many of the first intellects in the country, that without being in any way banded apart, or invested with any invidious prerogative, this

$^{c-c}$611   the crowd rather than one opposed to it
$^{d-d}$611   parliament

portion of the national representation will have a personal weight much more than in proportion to its numerical strength, and will afford, in a most effective form, the moral centre of resistance which is needed. A second Chamber, therefore, is not required for this purpose, and would not contribute to it, but might even, in some *conceivable modes, impede its attainment*. If, however, for the other reasons already mentioned, the decision were taken that there should be such a Chamber, it is desirable that it should be composed of elements which, without being open to the imputation of class interests adverse to the majority, would incline it to oppose itself to the class interests of the majority, and qualify it to raise its voice with authority against their errors and weaknesses. These conditions evidently are not found in a body constituted in the manner of our House of Lords. So soon as conventional rank and individual riches no longer overawe the democracy, a House of Lords becomes insignificant.

Of all principles on which a wisely conservative body, destined to moderate and regulate democratic ascendancy, could possibly be constructed, the best seems to be that exemplified in the Roman Senate, itself the most consistently prudent and sagacious body that ever administered public affairs. The deficiencies of a democratic assembly, which represents the general public, are the deficiencies of the public itself, want of special training and knowledge. The appropriate corrective is to associate with it a body of which special training and knowledge should be the characteristics. If one House represents popular feeling, the other should represent personal merit, tested and guaranteed by actual public service, and fortified by practical experience. If one is the People's Chamber, the other should be the Chamber of Statesmen; a council composed of all living public men who have passed through *important political offices or employments*. Such a chamber would be fitted for much more than to be a merely moderating body. It would not be exclusively a check, but also an impelling force. In its hands, the power of holding the people back would be vested in those most competent, and who would *generally* be most inclined, to lead them forward in any right course. The council to whom the task would be entrusted of rectifying the people's mistakes, would not represent a class believed to be opposed to their interest, but would consist of their own natural leaders in the path of progress. No mode of composition could approach to this in giving weight and efficacy to their function of moderators. It would be impossible to cry down a body always foremost in promoting improvements, as a mere obstructive body, whatever amount of mischief it might obstruct.

Were the place vacant in England for such a Senate (I need scarcely say

---

*e–e*611   degree tend to compromise it
*f–f*611   any important political office or employment
*g–g*611   then

that this is a mere hypothesis), it might be composed of some such elements as the following. All who were or had been members of the Legislative Commission described in a former chapter, and which I regard as an indispensable ingredient in a well constituted popular government. All who were or had been Chief Justices, or heads of any of the superior courts of law or equity. All who had for five years filled the office of puisne judge. All who had held for two years any Cabinet office: but these should also be eligible to the House of Commons, and if elected members of it, their peerage or senatorial office should be held in suspense. The condition of time is *h*needed*h* to prevent persons from being named Cabinet Ministers merely to give them a seat in the Senate; and the period of two years is suggested, that the same term which qualifies them for a pension might entitle them to a senatorship. All who had filled the office of Commander-in-Chief; and all who, having commanded an army or a fleet, had been thanked by Parliament for military or naval successes. *i*All who had held, during ten years, first-class diplomatic appointments.*i* All *j*who had been*j* Governors-General of India or British America, and all who had held for ten years any Colonial Governorships. The permanent civil service should also be represented; all should be senators who had filled, during ten years, the important offices of Under-Secretary to the Treasury, permanent Under-Secretary of State, or any others equally high and responsible. *k*If, along with the persons thus qualified by practical experience in the administration of public affairs, any representation of the speculative class were to be included—a thing in itself desirable—it would be worth consideration whether certain professorships, in certain national institutions, after a tenure of a few years, might confer a seat in the Senate. Mere scientific*k* and literary eminence are too indefinite and disputable: they imply a power of selection, whereas the other qualifications speak for themselves; if the writings by which reputation has been gained are unconnected with politics, they are no evidence of the special qualities required, while if political, they would enable successive Ministries to deluge the House with party tools.

The historical antecedents of England render it all but certain, that unless in the improbable case of a violent subversion of the existing Constitution, any second Chamber which could possibly exist would have to be built on the foundation of the House of Lords. It is out of the question to think practically of abolishing that assembly, to replace it by such a Senate as I have sketched, or by any other; but there might not be the same insuperable difficulty in aggregating the classes or categories just spoken of

*h–h*611 introduced

i–i+61², 65

j–j+61², 65

*k–k*611, 61² The functions conferring the senatorial dignity should be limited to those of a legal, political, or military or naval character. Scientific

to the existing body, in the character of Peers for life. An ulterior, and perhaps, on this supposition, a necessary step, might be, that the hereditary peerage should be present in the House by their representatives instead of personally: a practice already established in the case of the Scotch and Irish Peers, and which the mere multiplication of the order will probably at some time or other render inevitable. An easy adaptation of Mr. Hare's plan would prevent the representative Peers from representing exclusively the party which has the majority in the Peerage. If, for example, one representative were allowed for every ten peers, any ten might be admitted to choose a representative, and the peers might be free to group themselves for that purpose as they pleased. The election might be thus conducted: All peers who were candidates for the representation of their order should be required to declare themselves such, and enter their names in a list. A day and place should be appointed at which peers desirous of voting should be present, either in person, or, in the usual parliamentary manner, by their proxies. The votes should be taken, each peer voting for only one. Every candidate who had as many as ten votes should be declared elected. If any one had more, all but ten should be allowed to withdraw their votes, or ten of the number should be selected by lot. These ten would form his constituency, and the remainder of his voters would be set free to give their votes over again for some one else. This process should be repeated until (so far as possible) every peer present either personally or by proxy was represented. When a number less than ten remained over, if amounting to five they might still be allowed to agree on a representative; if fewer than five, their votes must be lost, or they might be permitted to record them in favour of somebody already elected. With this inconsiderable exception, every representative peer would represent ten members of the peerage, all of whom had not only voted for him, but selected him as the one, among all open to their choice, by whom they were most desirous to be represented. As a compensation to the Peers who were not chosen representatives of their order, they should be eligible to the House of Commons; a justice now refused to Scotch Peers, and to Irish Peers in their own part of the kingdom, while the representation in the House of Lords of any but the most numerous party in the Peerage is denied equally to both.

The mode of composing a Senate, which has been here advocated, not only seems the best in itself, but is that for which historical precedent, and actual brilliant success, can to the greatest extent be pleaded. It is not, however, the only feasible plan that might be proposed. Another possible mode of forming a Second Chamber, would be to have it elected by the First; subject to the restriction, that they should not nominate any of their own members. Such an assembly, emanating like the American Senate from popular choice, only once removed, would not be considered to clash with democratic institutions, and would probably acquire considerable popular influence. From the mode of its nomination it would be peculiarly unlikely to excite the jealousy of, or to come into any hostile collision with, the popular House. It would, moreover, (due provision being made for the representation of the minority,) be almost sure to be well composed, and to comprise many of that class of highly capable men, who, either from accident or for want of showy qualities, had been unwilling to seek, or unable to obtain, the suffrages of a popular constituency.

The best constitution of a Second Chamber, is that which embodies the greatest number of elements exempt from the class interests and prejudices of the majority, but having in themselves nothing offensive to democratic feeling. I repeat, however, that the main reliance for tempering the ascendancy of the majority cannot be placed in a Second Chamber of any kind. The character of a representative government is fixed by the constitution of the popular House. Compared with this, all other questions relating to the form of government are insignificant.

CHAPTER XIV

Of the Executive in a Representative Government

IT WOULD BE out of place, in this treatise, to discuss the question into what departments or branches the executive business of government may most conveniently be divided. In this respect the exigencies of different governments are different; and there is little probability that any great mistake will be made in the classification of the duties, when men are willing to begin at the beginning, and do not hold themselves bound by the series of accidents which, in an old government like ours, has produced the existing division of the public business. It may be sufficient to say, that the classification of functionaries should correspond to that of subjects, and that there should not be several departments independent of one another, to superintend different parts of the same natural whole; as in our own military administration down to a recent period, and in a less degree even at present. Where the object to be attained is single (such as that of having an efficient army), the authority commissioned to attend to it should be single likewise. The entire aggregate of means provided for one end, should be under one and the same control and responsibility. If they are divided among independent authorities, the means, with each of those authorities, become ends, and it is the business of nobody except the head of the Government, who is probably without the appropriate departmental experience, to take care of the real end. The different classes of means are not combined and adapted to one another under the guidance of any leading idea: and while every department pushes forward its own requirements, regardless of those of the rest, the purpose of the work is perpetually sacrificed to the work itself.

As a general rule, every executive function, whether superior or subordinate, should be the appointed duty of some given individual. It should be apparent to all the world, who did everything, and through whose default anything was left undone. Responsibility is null, when nobody knows who is responsible. Nor, even when real, can it be divided without being weakened. To maintain it at its highest, there must be one person who receives the whole praise of what is well done, the whole blame of what is ill. There are, however, two modes of sharing responsibility: by one it is only enfeebled, by the other, absolutely destroyed. It is enfeebled, when the concurrence of more than one functionary is required to the same act. Each one among them has still a real responsibility; if a wrong has been done, none of them can say he did not do it; he is as much a participant, as an accomplice is in an offence: if there has been legal criminality they may all be punished legally, and their punishment needs not be less severe than if there had been only one person concerned. But it is not so with the penalties, any more than with the rewards, of opinion: these are always diminished by being shared. Where there has been no definite legal offence, no corruption or malversation, only an error or an imprudence, or what may pass for such, every participator has an excuse to himself and to the world, in the fact that other persons are jointly involved with him. There is hardly anything, even to pecuniary dishonesty, for which men will not feel themselves almost absolved, if those whose duty it was to resist and remonstrate have failed to do it, still more if they have given a formal assent.

In this case, however, though responsibility is weakened, there still is responsibility: every one of those implicated has in his individual capacity assented to, and joined in, the act. Things are much worse when the act itself is only that of a majority—a Board, deliberating with closed doors, nobody knowing, or, except in some extreme case, being ever likely to know, whether an individual member voted for the act or against it. Responsibility, in this case, is a mere name. "Boards," it is happily said by Bentham, "are screens."[*] What "the Board" does is the act of nobody; and nobody can be made to answer for it. The Board suffers, even in reputation, only in its collective character; and no individual member feels this, further than his disposition leads him to identify his own estimation with that of the body—a feeling often very strong when the body is a permanent one, and he is wedded to it for better for worse; but the fluctuations of a modern official career give no time for the formation of such an *esprit de corps*; which, if it exists at all, exists only in the obscure ranks of the permanent subordinates. Boards, therefore, are not a fit instrument for executive business; and are only admissible in it, when, for other reasons, to give full discretionary power to a single minister would be worse.

On the other hand, it is also a maxim of experience, that in the multitude of counsellors there is wisdom; and that a man seldom judges right, even in his own concerns, still less in those of the public, when he makes habitual use of no knowledge but his own, or that of some single adviser. There is no necessary incompatibility between this principle and the other. It is easy to give the effective power, and the full responsibility, to one, providing him when necessary with advisers, each of whom is responsible only for the opinion he gives.

In general, the head of a department of the executive government is a

[*Letters to Lord Grenville on the Proposed Reform in the Administration of Civil Justice in Scotland, in Works, Vol. V, p. 17.]

mere politician. He may be a good politician, and a man of merit; and unless this is usually the case, the government is bad. But his general capacity, and the knowledge he ought to possess of the general interests of the country, will not, unless by occasional accident, be accompanied by adequate, and what may be called professional, knowledge of the department over which he is called to preside. Professional advisers must therefore be provided for him. Wherever mere experience and attainments are sufficient —wherever the qualities required in a professional adviser may possibly be united in a single well-selected individual (as in the case, for example, of a law officer), one such person for general purposes, and a staff of clerks to supply knowledge of details, meet the demands of the case. But, more frequently, it is not sufficient that the minister should consult some one competent person, and, when himself not conversant with the subject, act implicitly on that person's advice. It is often necessary that he should, not only occasionally but habitually, listen to a variety of opinions, and inform his judgment by the discussions among a body of advisers. This, for example, is emphatically necessary in military and naval affairs. The military and naval ministers, therefore, and probably several others, should be provided with a Council, composed, at least in those two departments, of able and experienced professional men. As a means of obtaining the best men for the purpose under every change of administration, they ought to be permanent: by which I mean, that they ought not, like the Lords of the Admiralty, to be expected to resign with the ministry by whom they were appointed: but it is a good rule that all who hold high appointments to which they have risen by selection, and not by the ordinary course of promotion, should retain their office only for a fixed term, unless reappointed; as is now the rule with Staff appointments in the British army. This rule renders appointments somewhat less likely to be jobbed, not being a provision for life, and at the same time affords a means, without affront to any one, of getting rid of those who are least worth keeping, and bringing in highly qualified persons of younger standing, for whom there might never be room if death vacancies, or voluntary resignations, were waited for.

The Councils should be consultative merely, in this sense, that the ultimate decision should rest undividedly with the minister himself: but neither ought they to be looked upon, or to look upon themselves, as ciphers, or as capable of being reduced to such at his pleasure. The advisers attached to a powerful and perhaps self-willed man, ought to be placed under conditions which make it impossible for them, without discredit, not to express an opinion, and impossible for him not to listen to and consider their recommendations, whether he adopts them or not. The relation which ought to exist between a chief and this description of advisers is very accurately hit by the constitution of the Council of the Governor-General and those of the different Presidencies in India. These Councils are composed of persons who have professional knowledge of Indian affairs, which the Governor-General and Governors usually lack, and which it would not be desirable to require of them. As a rule, every member of Council is expected to give an opinion, which is of course very often a simple acquiescence: but if there is a difference of sentiment, it is at the option of every member, and is the invariable practice, to record the reasons of his opinion: the Governor-General, or Governor, doing the same. In ordinary cases the decision is according to the sense of the majority; the Council, therefore, has a substantial part in the government: but if the Governor-General, or Governor, thinks fit, he may set aside even their unanimous opinion, recording his reasons. The result is, that the chief is individually and effectively responsible for every act of the Government. The members of Council have only the responsibility of advisers; but it is always known, from documents capable of being produced, and which if called for by Parliament or public opinion always are produced, what each has advised, and what reasons he gave for his advice: while, from their dignified position, and ostensible participation in all acts of government, they have nearly as strong motives to apply themselves to the public business, and to form and express a well-considered opinion on every part of it, as if the whole responsibility rested with themselves.

This mode of conducting the highest class of administrative business is one of the most successful instances of the adaptation of means to ends, which political history, not hitherto very prolific in works of skill and contrivance, has yet to show. It is one of the acquisitions with which the art of politics has been enriched by the experience of the East India Company's rule; and, like most of the other wise contrivances by which India has been preserved to this country, and an amount of good government produced which is truly wonderful considering the circumstances and the materials, it is probably destined to perish in the general holocaust which the traditions of Indian government seem fated to undergo, since they have been placed at the mercy of public ignorance, and the presumptuous vanity of political men. Already an outcry is raised for abolishing the Councils, as a superfluous and expensive clog on the wheels of government: while the clamour has long been urgent, and is daily obtaining more countenance in the highest quarters, for the abrogation of the professional civil service, which breeds the men that compose the Councils, and the existence of which is the sole guarantee for their being of any value.

A most important principle of good government in a popular constitution, is that no executive functionaries should be appointed by popular election: neither by the votes of the people themselves, nor by those of their representatives. The entire business of government is skilled employment; the qualifications for the discharge of it are of that special and professional kind, which cannot be properly judged of except by persons who have themselves some share of those qualifications, or some practical experience of them. The business of finding the fittest persons to fill public employments—not merely selecting the best who offer, but looking out for the absolutely best, and taking note of all fit persons who are met with, that they may be found when wanted—is very laborious, and requires a delicate as well as highly conscientious discernment; and as there is no public duty which is in general so badly performed, so there is none for which it is of greater importance to enforce the utmost practicable amount of personal responsibility, by imposing it as a special obligation on high functionaries in the several departments. All subordinate public officers who are not appointed by some mode of public competition, should be selected on the direct responsibility of the minister under whom they serve. The ministers, all but the chief, will naturally be selected by the chief; and the chief himself, though really designated by Parliament, should be, in a regal government, officially appointed by the Crown. The functionary who appoints should be the sole person empowered to remove any subordinate officer who is liable to removal; which the far greater number ought not to be, except for personal misconduct; since it would be *a* vain to expect that the body of persons by whom the whole detail of the public business is transacted, and whose qualifications are generally of much more importance to the public than those of the minister himself, will devote themselves to their profession, and acquire the knowledge and skill on which the minister must often place entire dependence, if they are liable at any moment to be turned adrift for no fault, that the minister may gratify himself, or promote his political interest, by appointing somebody else.

To the principle which condemns the appointment of executive officers by popular suffrage, ought the chief of the executive, in a republican government, to be an exception? Is it a good rule, which, in the American Constitution, provides for the election of the President once in every four years by the entire people? The question is not free from difficulty. There is unquestionably some advantage, in a country like America, where no apprehension needs be entertained of a *coup d'état*, in making the chief minister constitutionally independent of the legislative body, and rendering the two great branches of the government, while equally popular both in their origin and in their responsibility, an effective check on one another. The plan is in accordance with that sedulous avoidance of the concentration of great masses of power in the same hands, which is a marked characteristic of the American Federal Constitution. But the advantage, in this instance, is pur-

*a*61¹ in

chased at a price above all reasonable estimate of its value. It seems far better that the chief magistrate in a republic should be appointed avowedly, as the chief minister in a constitutional monarchy is virtually, by the representative body. In the first place, he is certain, when thus appointed, to be a more eminent man. The party which has the majority in Parliament would then, as a rule, appoint its own leader; who is always one of the foremost, and often the very foremost person in political life: while the President of the United States, since the last survivor of the founders of the republic disappeared from the scene, is almost always either an obscure man, or one who has gained any reputation he may possess in some other field than politics. And this, as I have before observed, is no accident, but the natural effect of the situation. The eminent men of a party, in an election extending to the whole country, are never its most available candidates. All eminent men have made personal enemies, or have done something, or at the lowest professed some opinion, obnoxious to some local or other considerable division of the community, and likely to tell with fatal effect upon the number of votes; whereas a man without antecedents, of whom nothing is known but that he professes the creed of the party, is readily voted for by its entire strength. Another important consideration is the great mischief of unintermitted electioneering. When the highest dignity in the State is to be conferred by popular election once in every few years, the whole intervening time is spent in what is virtually a canvass. President, ministers, chiefs of parties, and their followers, are all electioneerers: the whole community is kept intent on the mere personalities of politics, and every public question is discussed and decided with less reference to its merits than to its expected bearing on the presidential election. If a system had been devised to make party spirit the ruling principle of action in all public affairs, and create an inducement not only to make every question a party question, but to raise questions for the purpose of founding parties upon them, it would have been difficult to contrive any means better adapted to the purpose.

I will not affirm that it would at all times and places be desirable, that the head of the executive should be so completely dependent upon the votes of a representative assembly as the Prime Minister is in England, and is without inconvenience. If it were thought best to avoid this, he might, though appointed by Parliament, hold his office for a fixed period, independent of a parliamentary vote: which would be the American system, minus the popular election and its evils. There is another mode of giving the head of the administration as much independence of the legislature, as is at all compatible with the essentials of free government. He never could be unduly dependent on a vote of Parliament, if he had, as the British prime minister practically has, the power to dissolve the House and appeal to the people: if instead of being turned out of office by a hostile vote, he could only be reduced by it to the alternative of resignation or dissolution. The power of dissolving Parliament is one which I think it desirable he should possess, even under the system by which his own tenure of office is secured to him for a fixed period. There ought not to be any possibility of that deadlock in politics, which would ensue on a quarrel breaking out between a President and an Assembly, neither of whom, during an interval which might amount to years, would have any legal means of ridding itself of the other. To get through such a period without a *coup d'état* being attempted, on either side or on both, requires such a combination of the love of liberty and the habit of self-restraint, as very few nations have yet shown themselves capable of: and though this extremity were avoided, to expect that the two authorities would not paralyse each other's operations, is to suppose that the political life of the country will always be pervaded by a spirit of mutual forbearance and compromise, imperturbable by the passions and excitements of the keenest party struggles. Such a spirit may exist, but even where it does, there is imprudence in trying it too far.

Other reasons make it desirable that some power in the state (which can only be the executive) should have the liberty of at any time, and at discretion, calling a new parliament. When there is a real doubt which of two contending parties has the strongest following, it is important that there should exist a constitutional means of immediately testing the point, and setting it at rest. No other political topic has a chance of being properly attended to while this is undecided: and such an interval is mostly an interregnum for purposes of legislative or administrative improvement; neither party having sufficient confidence in its strength, to attempt things likely to provoke opposition in any quarter that has either direct or indirect influence in the pending struggle.

I have not taken account of the case in which the vast power centralized in the chief magistrate, and the insufficient attachment of the mass of the people to free institutions, give him a chance of success in an attempt to subvert the Constitution, and usurp sovereign power. Where such peril exists, no first magistrate is admissible whom the Parliament cannot, by a single vote, reduce to a private station. In a state of things holding out any encouragement to that most audacious and profligate of all breaches of trust, even this entireness of constitutional dependence is but a weak protection.

Of all officers of government, those in whose appointment any participation of popular suffrage is the most objectionable, are judicial officers. While there are no functionaries whose special and professional qualifications the popular judgment is less fitted to estimate, there are none in whose case absolute impartiality, and freedom from connexion with politicians or sections of politicians, are of anything like equal importance. Some thinkers, among others Mr. Bentham, have been of opinion that, although it is better that judges should not be appointed by popular election, the people of their district ought to have the power, after sufficient experience, of removing them from their trust. It cannot be denied that the irremovability of any public officer, to whom great interests are entrusted, is in itself an evil. It is far from desirable that there should be no means of getting rid of a bad or incompetent judge, unless for such misconduct as he can be made to answer for in a criminal court; and that a functionary on whom so much depends, should have the feeling of being free from responsibility except to opinion and his own conscience. The question however is, whether in the peculiar position of a judge, and supposing that all practicable securities have been taken for an honest appointment, irresponsibility, except to his own and the public conscience, has not on the whole, less tendency to pervert his conduct, than responsibility to the government, or to a popular vote. Experience has long decided this point in the affirmative, as regards responsibility to the executive; and the case is quite equally strong when the responsibility sought to be enforced is to the suffrages of electors. Among the good qualities of a popular constituency, those peculiarly incumbent upon a judge, calmness and impartiality, are not numbered. Happily, in that intervention of popular suffrage which is essential to freedom, they are not the qualities required. Even the quality of justice, though necessary to all human beings, and therefore to all electors, is not the inducement which decides any popular election. Justice and impartiality are as little wanted for electing a member of parliament, as they can be in any transaction of men. The electors have not to award something which either candidate has a right to, nor to pass judgment on the general merits of the competitors, but to declare which of them has most of their personal confidence, or best represents their political convictions. A judge is bound to treat his political friend, or the person best known to him, exactly as he treats other people; but it would be a breach of duty as well as an absurdity if an elector did so. No argument can be grounded on the beneficial effect produced on judges, as on all other functionaries, by the moral jurisdiction of opinion; for even in this respect, that which really exercises a useful control over the proceedings of a judge, when fit for the judicial office, is not (except sometimes in political cases) the opinion of the community generally, but that of the only public by whom his conduct or qualifications can be duly estimated, the bar of his own court. I must not be understood to say that the participation of the general public in the administration of justice is of no importance; it is of the greatest: but in what manner? By the actual discharge of a part of the judicial office, in the capacity of jurymen. This is one of the few cases in politics, in which it is better that the people should act directly and personally than through their representatives; being almost the only case in which the errors that a person exercising authority may commit, can be better borne than the consequences of making him responsible for them. If a judge could be removed from office by a popular vote, whoever was desirous of supplanting him would make capital for that purpose out of all his judicial decisions; would carry all of them, as far as he found practicable, by irregular appeal before a public opinion wholly incompetent, for want of having heard the case, or from having heard it without either the precautions or the impartiality belonging to a judicial hearing; would play upon popular passion and prejudice where they existed, and take pains to arouse them where they did not. And in this, if the case were interesting, and he took sufficient trouble, he would infallibly be successful, unless the judge or his friends descended into the arena, and made equally powerful appeals on the other side. Judges would end by feeling that they risked their office upon every decision they gave in a case susceptible of general interest, and that it was less essential for them to consider what decision was just, than what would be most applauded by the public, or would least admit of insidious misrepresentation. The practice introduced by some of the new or revised State Constitutions in America, of submitting judicial officers to periodical popular re-election, will be found, I apprehend, to be one of the most dangerous errors ever yet committed by democracy: and, were it not that the practical good sense which never totally deserts the people of the United States, is said to be producing a reaction, likely in no long time to lead to the retractation of the error, it might with reason be regarded as the first great downward step in the degeneration of modern democratic government.*

With regard to that large and important body which constitutes the permanent strength of the public service, those who do not change with changes of politics, but remain, to aid every minister by their experience and traditions, inform him by their knowledge of business, and conduct official details under his general control; those, in short, who form the class

---

*[61²] I have been informed, however, that in the States which have made their judges elective, the choice is not really made by the people, but by the leaders of parties; no elector ever thinking of voting for any one but the party candidate; and that, in consequence, the person elected is usually in effect the same who would have been appointed to the office by the President or by *b*the Governor of the State*b*. Thus one bad practice limits and corrects another: and *c*the*c* habit of voting *en masse* under a party banner, which is so full of evil in all cases in which the function of electing is rightly vested in the people, tends to alleviate a still greater mischief in a case where the officer to be elected is one who *ought* to be chosen not by the people but for them.

*b–b*612   a Minister of Justice
*c–c*612   that

of professional public servants, entering their profession as others do while young, in the hope of rising progressively to its higher grades as they advance in life; it is evidently inadmissible that these should be liable to be turned out, and deprived of the whole benefit of their previous service, except for positive, proved, and serious misconduct. Not, of course, such delinquency only as makes them amenable to the law; but voluntary neglect of duty, or conduct implying untrustworthiness for the purposes for which their trust is given them. Since, therefore, unless in case of personal culpability, there is no way of getting rid of them except by quartering them on the public as pensioners, it is of the greatest importance that the appointments should be well made in the first instance; and it remains to be considered, by what mode of appointment this purpose can best be attained.

In making first appointments, little danger is to be apprehended from want of special skill and knowledge in the choosers, but much from partiality, and private or political interest. Being *d*, as a rule,*d* appointed at the commencement of manhood, not as having learnt, but in order that they may learn, their profession, the only thing by which the best candidates can be discriminated, is proficiency in the ordinary branches of liberal education: and this can be ascertained without difficulty, provided there be the requisite pains and the requisite impartiality in those who are appointed to inquire into it. Neither the one nor the other can reasonably be expected from a minister; who must rely wholly on recommendations, and however disinterested as to his personal wishes, never will be proof against the solicitations of persons who have the power of influencing his *e*own*e* election, or whose political adherence is important to the ministry to which he belongs. These considerations have introduced the practice of submitting all candidates for first appointments to a public examination, conducted by persons not engaged in politics, and of the same class and quality with the examiners for honours at the Universities. This would probably be the best plan under any system; and under our parliamentary government it is the only one which affords a chance, I do not say of honest *f*appointment*f*, but even of abstinence from such as are manifestly and flagrantly profligate.

It is also absolutely necessary that the examinations should be competitive, and the appointments given to those who are most successful. A mere pass examination never, in the long run, does more than exclude absolute dunces. When the question, in the mind of the examiner, lies between blighting the prospects of an individual, and *g*neglecting*g* a duty to the public which, in the particular instance, seldom appears of first-rate importance; and when he is sure to be bitterly reproached for doing the first, while in general no one will either know or care whether he has done the latter; the balance, unless he is a man of very unusual stamp, inclines to the side of good-nature. A relaxation in one instance establishes a claim to it in others, which every repetition of indulgence makes it more difficult to resist; each of these in succession becomes a precedent for more, until the standard of proficiency sinks gradually to something almost contemptible. Examinations for degrees at the two great Universities have generally been as slender in their requirements, as those for honours are trying and serious. Where there is no inducement to exceed a certain minimum, the minimum comes to be the maximum: it becomes the general practice not to aim at more, and as in everything there are some who do not attain all they aim at, however low the standard may be pitched there are always several who fall short of it. When, on the contrary, the appointments are given to those, among a great number of candidates, who most distinguish themselves, and where the successful competitors are classed in order of merit, not only each is stimulated to do his very utmost, but the influence is felt in every place of liberal education throughout the country. It becomes with every schoolmaster an object of ambition, and an avenue to success, to have furnished pupils who have gained a high place in these competitions; and there is hardly any other mode in which the State can do so much to raise the quality of educational institutions throughout the country. Though the principle of competitive examinations for public employment is of such recent introduction in this country, and is still so imperfectly carried out, the Indian service being as yet nearly the only case in which it exists in its completeness, a sensible effect has already begun to be produced on the places of middle-class education; notwithstanding the difficulties which the principle has encountered from the disgracefully low existing state of education in the country, which these very examinations have brought into strong light. So contemptible has the standard of acquirement been found to be, among the youths who obtain the nomination from a minister, which entitles them to offer themselves as candidates, that the competition of such candidates produces almost a poorer result, than would be obtained from a mere pass examination; for no one would think of fixing the conditions of a pass examination so low, as is actually found sufficient to enable a young man to surpass his fellow-candidates. Accordingly, it is said that successive years show on the whole a decline of attainments, less effort being made, because the results of former examinations have proved that the exertions then used were greater than would have been sufficient to attain the object. Partly from this decrease of effort, and partly because, even at the examinations which do not require a previous nomination, conscious ignorance reduces the number of competitors to a mere handful, it has so happened that though there have always been a few instances of great proficiency, the lower part of the list of successful candidates represents but a very moderate amount of acquirement; and we have it on the word of the Commissioners that nearly all who have been unsuccessful have owed their failure to ignorance not of the higher branches of instruction, but of its very humblest elements—spelling and arithmetic.

The outcries which continue to be made against these examinations, by some of the organs of opinion, are often, I regret to say, as little creditable to the good faith as to the good sense of the assailants. They proceed partly by misrepresentation of the kind of ignorance, which, as a matter of fact, actually leads to failure in the examinations. They quote with emphasis the most recondite questions* which can be shown to have been ever asked, and make it appear as if unexceptionable answers to all these were made the *sine quâ non* of success. Yet it has been repeated to satiety, that such questions are not put because it is expected of every one that he should answer them, but in order that whoever is able to do so may have the means of proving and availing himself of that portion of his knowledge. It is not as a ground of rejection, but as an additional means of success, that this opportunity is given. We are then asked whether the kind of knowledge supposed in this, that, or the other question, is calculated to be of any use to the candidate after he has attained his object. People differ greatly in opinion as to what knowledge is useful. There are persons in existence, and a late Foreign Secretary of State[*] is one of them, who think English spelling a useless accomplishment in a diplomatic attaché, or a clerk in a Government office. About one thing the objectors seem to be unanimous, that general mental cultivation is not useful in these employments, whatever else may be so. If, however (as I presume to think), it is useful, or if any education at all is useful, it must be tested by the tests most likely to show whether the candidate possesses it or not. To ascertain whether he has been well educated, he must be interrogated in the things which he is likely to know if he has been well educated, even though not directly pertinent to the work to which he is to be appointed. Will those who object to his being questioned in classics and mathematics, in a country where the only things regularly taught are classics and mathematics, tell us what they would have

---

*Not always, however, the most recondite; for *h*a late denouncer*h* of competitive examination in the House of Commons had the *naïveté* to produce a set of almost elementary questions in algebra, history, and geography, as a proof of the exorbitant amount of high scientific attainment which the Commissioners were so wild as to exact. [See Baillie Cochrane, Speech on Civil Service Examinations, *Parliamentary Debates*, 3rd ser., Vol. 158, cols. 2063–5 (5 June, 1860).]

[*James Howard Harris, 3rd Earl of Malmesbury. See, e.g., his letter to the Civil Service Commissioners (22 Sept., 1858), in Appendix II of "Fourth Report of Her Majesty's Civil Service Commissioners," *Parliamentary Papers*, 1859, Vol. VIII, pp. 203–4.]

*h-h*611 one of the latest denouncers

him questioned in? There seems, however, to be equal objection to examining him in these, and to examining him in anything *but* these. If the Commissioners—anxious to open a door of admission to those who have not gone through the routine of a grammar-school, or who make up for the smallness of their knowledge of what is there taught, by greater knowledge of something else—allow marks to be gained by proficiency in any other subject of real utility, they are reproached for that too. Nothing will satisfy the objectors, but free admission of total ignorance.

We are triumphantly told, that neither Clive nor Wellington could have passed the test which is prescribed for an aspirant to an engineer cadetship. As if, because Clive and Wellington did not do what was not required of them, they could not have done it if it had been required. If it be only meant to inform us that it is possible to be a great general without these things, so it is without many other things which are very useful to great generals. Alexander the Great had never heard of Vauban's rules, nor could Julius Cæsar speak French. We are next informed that bookworms, a term which seems to be held applicable to whoever has the smallest tincture of book-knowledge, may not be good at bodily exercises, or have the habits of gentlemen. This is a very common line of remark with dunces of condition; but whatever the dunces may think, they have no monopoly of either gentlemanly habits or bodily activity. Wherever these are needed, let them be inquired into, and separately provided for, not to the exclusion of mental qualifications, but in addition. Meanwhile, I am credibly informed, that in the Military Academy at Woolwich, the competition cadets are as superior to those admitted on the old system of nomination, in these respects as in all others; that they learn even their drill more quickly; as indeed might be expected, for an intelligent person learns all things sooner than a stupid one: and that in general demeanour they contrast so favourably with their predecessors, that the authorities of the institution are impatient for the day to arrive when the last remains of the old leaven shall have disappeared from the place. If this be so, and it is easy to ascertain whether it is so, it is to be hoped we shall soon have heard for the last time that ignorance is a better qualification than knowledge, for the military, and *à fortiori* for every other, profession; or that any one good quality, however little apparently connected with liberal education, is at all likely to be promoted by going without it.

Though the first admission to government employment be decided by competitive examination, it would in most cases be impossible that subsequent promotion should be so decided: and it seems proper that this should take place, as it usually does at present, on a mixed system of seniority and selection. Those whose duties are of a routine character should rise by seniority to the highest point to which duties merely of that description can carry them; while those to whom functions of particular trust, and requiring special capacity, are confided, should be selected from the body on the discretion of the chief of the office. And this selection will generally be made honestly by him, if the original appointments take place by open competition: for under that system, his establishment will generally consist of individuals to whom, but for the official connexion, he would have been a stranger. If among them there be any in whom he, or his political friends, and supporters, take an interest, it will be but occasionally, and only when, to this advantage of connexion, is added, as far as the initiatory examination could test it, at least equality of real merit. And, except when there is a very strong motive to job these appointments, there is always a strong one to appoint the fittest person; being the one who gives to his chief the most useful assistance, saves him most trouble, and helps most to build up that reputation for good management of public business, which necessarily and properly redounds to the credit of the minister, however much the qualities to which it is immediately owing may be those of his subordinates.

CHAPTER XV

Of Local Representative Bodies

IT IS BUT A SMALL PORTION of the public business of a country, which can be well done, or safely attempted, by the central authorities; and even in our own government, the least centralized in Europe, the legislative portion at least of the governing body busies itself far too much with local affairs, employing the supreme power of the State in cutting small knots which there ought to be other and better means of untying. The enormous amount of private business which takes up the time of Parliament, and the thoughts of its individual members, distracting them from the proper occupations of the great council of the nation, is felt by all thinkers and observers as a serious evil, and what is worse, an increasing one.

It would not be appropriate to the limited design of this treatise, to discuss at large the great question, in no way peculiar to representative government, of the proper limits of governmental action. I have said elsewhere* what seemed to me most essential respecting the principles by which the extent of that action ought to be determined. But after subtracting from the functions performed by most European governments, those which ought not to be undertaken by public authorities at all, there still remains so great and various an aggregate of duties, that, if only on the principle of division of labour, it is indispensable to share them between central and local authorities. Not *only* are separate executive officers required for purely local duties (an amount of separation which exists under all governments), but the popular control over those officers can only be advantageously exerted through a separate organ. Their original appointment, the function of watching and checking them, the duty of providing, or the discretion of withholding, the supplies necessary for their operations, should rest, not with the national Parliament or the national executive, but with the people of the locality. *In some of the New England States these functions are still

On Liberty, concluding chapter [above, pp. 292 ff.]; and, at greater length, in the final chapter of *Principles of Political Economy* [*Collected Works*, Vol. III (Toronto: University of Toronto Press, 1965), pp. 936 ff.].

*a–a*611, 612   solely
*b–b*611, 612   That the people should exercise these functions directly and personally, is evidently inadmissible. Administration by the assembled people is a relic of barbarism, opposed to the whole spirit of modern life: yet so much has the course of

exercised directly by the assembled people; it is said, with better results than might be expected; and those highly educated communities are so well satisfied with this primitive mode of local government, that they have no desire to exchange it for the only representative system they are acquainted with, by which all minorities are disfranchised. Such very peculiar circumstances, however, are required to make this arrangement work tolerably in practice, that recourse must generally be had to the plan of representative sub-Parliaments for local affairs. These[b] exist in England, but very incompletely, and with great irregularity and want of system: in some other countries much less popularly governed, their constitution is far more rational. In England there has always been more liberty, but worse organization, while in other countries there is better organization, but less liberty. It is necessary, then, that in addition to the national representation, there should be municipal and provincial representations: and the two questions which remain to be resolved are, how the local representative bodies should be constituted, and what should be the extent of their functions.

In considering these questions, two points require an equal degree of our attention: how the local business itself can be best done; and how its transaction can be made most instrumental to the nourishment of public spirit and the development of intelligence. In an earlier part of this inquiry, I have dwelt in strong language—hardly any language is strong enough to express the strength of my conviction—on the importance of that portion of the operation of free institutions, which may be called the public education of the citizens. Now, of this operation the local administrative institutions are the chief instrument. Except by the part they may take as jurymen in the administration of justice, the mass of the population have very little opportunity of sharing personally in the conduct of the general affairs of the community. Reading newspapers, and perhaps writing to them, public meetings, and solicitations of different sorts addressed to the political authorities, are the extent of the participation of private citizens in general politics, during the interval between one parliamentary election and another. Though it is impossible to exaggerate the importance of these various liberties, both as securities for freedom and as means of general cultivation, the practice which they give is more in thinking than in action, and in thinking without the responsibilties of action; which with most people amounts to little more than passively receiving the thoughts of some one else. But in the case of local bodies, besides the function of electing, many

---

English institutions depended on accident, that this primitive mode of local government remained the general rule in parochial matters up to the present generation; and, having never been legally abolished, probably subsists unaltered in many rural parishes even now. There remains the plan of representative sub-Parliaments for local affairs: and these must henceforth be considered as one of the fundamental institutions of a free government. They

citizens in turn have the chance of being elected, and many, either by selection or by rotation, fill one or other of the numerous local executive offices. In these positions they have to act, for public interests, as well as to think and to speak, and the thinking cannot all be done by proxy. It may be added, that these local functions, not being in general sought by the higher ranks, carry down the important political education which they are the means of conferring, to a much lower grade in society. The mental discipline being thus a more important feature in local concerns than in the general affairs of the State, while there are not such vital interests dependent on the quality of the administration, a greater weight may be given to the former consideration, and the latter admits much more frequently of being postponed to it, than in matters of general legislation, and the conduct of imperial affairs.

The proper constitution of local representative bodies does not present much difficulty. The principles which apply to it do not differ in any respect from those applicable to the national representation. The same obligation exists, as in the case of the more important function, for making the bodies elective; and the same reasons operate as in that case, but with still greater force, for giving them a widely democratic basis: the dangers being less, and the advantages, in point of popular education and cultivation, in some respects even greater. As the principal duty of the local bodies consists of the imposition and expenditure of local taxation, the electoral franchise should vest in all who contribute to the local rates, to the exclusion of all who do not. I assume that there is no indirect taxation, no *octroi* duties, or that if there are, they are supplementary only; those on whom their burthen falls being also rated to a direct assessment. The representation of minorities should be provided for in the same manner as in the national Parliament, and there are the same strong reasons for plurality of votes. Only, there is not so decisive an objection, in the inferior as in the higher body, to making the plural voting depend (as in some of the local elections of our own country) on a mere money qualification: for the honest and frugal dispensation of money forms so much larger a part of the business of the local, than of the national body, that there is more justice as well as policy in allowing a greater proportional influence to those who have a larger money interest at stake.

In the most recently established of our local representative institutions, the Boards of Guardians, the justices of peace of the district sit *ex officio* along with the elected members, in number limited by law to a third of the whole. In the peculiar constitution of English society, I have no doubt of the beneficial effect of this provision. It secures the presence, in these bodies, of a more educated class than it would perhaps be practicable to attract thither on any other terms; and while the limitation in number of the *ex officio* members precludes them from acquiring predominance by mere numerical strength, they, as a virtual representation of another class, having sometimes a different interest from the rest, are a check upon the class interests of the farmers or petty shopkeepers who form the bulk of the elected Guardians. A similar commendation cannot be given to the constitution of the only provincial boards we possess, the Quarter Sessions, consisting of the justices of peace alone; on whom, over and above their judicial duties, some of the most important parts of the administrative business of the country depend for their performance. The mode of formation of these bodies is most anomalous, they being neither elected, nor, in any proper sense of the term, nominated, but holding their important functions, like the feudal lords to whom they succeeded, virtually by right of their acres: the appointment vested in the Crown (or, speaking practically, in one of themselves, the Lord Lieutenant) being made use of only as a means of excluding any one who it is thought would do discredit to the body, or, now and then, one who is on the wrong side in politics. The institution is the most aristocratic in principle which now remains in England; far more so than the House of Lords, for it grants public money and disposes of important public interests, not in conjunction with a popular assembly, but alone. It is clung to with proportionate tenacity by our aristocratic classes; but is obviously at variance with all the principles which are the foundation of representative government. In a County Board, there is not the same justification as in Boards of Guardians, for even an admixture of *ex officio* with elected members: since the business of a county being on a sufficiently large scale to be an object of interest and attraction to country gentlemen, they would have no more difficulty in getting themselves elected to the Board, than they have in being returned to Parliament as county members.

In regard to the proper circumscription of the constituencies which elect the local representative bodies; the principle which, when applied as an exclusive and unbending rule to Parliamentary representation, is inappropriate, namely community of local interests, is here the only just and applicable one. The very object of having a local representation, is in order that those who have any interest in common, which they do not share with the general body of their countrymen, may manage that joint interest by themselves: and the purpose is contradicted, if the distribution of the local representation follows any other rule than the grouping of those joint interests. There are local interests peculiar to every town, whether great or small, and common to all its inhabitants: every town, therefore, without distinction of size, ought to have its municipal council. It is equally obvious, that every town ought to have but one. The different quarters of the same town have seldom or never any material diversities of local interest; they all require to have the same things done, the same expenses incurred; and, except as to their churches, which it is probably desirable to leave under simply parochial management, the same arrangements may be made to serve for all. Paving, lighting, water supply, drainage, port and market regulations, cannot without great waste and inconvenience be different for different quarters of the same town. The subdivision of London into six or seven independent districts, each with its separate arrangements for local business (several of them without unity of administration even within themselves) prevents the possibility of consecutive or well regulated co-operation for common objects, precludes any uniform principle for the discharge of local duties, compels the general government to take things upon itself which would be best left to local authorities if there were any whose authority extended to the entire metropolis; and answers no purpose but to keep up the fantastical trappings of that union of modern jobbing and antiquated foppery, the Corporation of the City of London.

Another equally important principle is, that in each local circumscription there should be but one elected body for all local business, not different bodies for different parts of it. Division of labour does not mean, cutting up every business into minute fractions; it means the union of such operations as are fit to be performed by the same persons, and the separation of such as can be better performed by different persons. The executive duties of the locality do indeed require to be divided into departments, for the same reason as those of the state; because they are of diverse kinds, each requiring knowledge peculiar to itself, and needing, for its due performance, the undivided attention of a specially qualified functionary. But the reasons for subdivision which apply to the execution, do not apply to the control. The business of the elective body is not to do the work, but to see that it is properly done, and that nothing necessary is left undone. This function can be fulfilled for all departments by the same superintending body; and by a collective and comprehensive far better than by a minute and microscopic view. It is as absurd in public affairs as it would be in private, that every workman should be looked after by a superintendent to himself. The Government of the Crown consists of many departments, and there are many ministers to conduct them, but those ministers have not a Parliament apiece to keep them to their duty. The local like the national parliament, has for its proper business to consider the interest of the locality as a whole, composed of parts all of which must be adapted to one another, and attended to in the order and ratio of their importance. There is another very weighty reason for uniting the control of all the business of a locality under one body. The greatest imperfection of popular local institutions, and the chief cause of the failure which so often attends them, is the low calibre of the men by whom they are almost always carried on. That these should be of a very miscellaneous character is, indeed, part of the usefulness of the institution;

it is that circumstance chiefly which renders it a school of political capacity and general intelligence. But a school supposes teachers as well as scholars: the utility of the instruction greatly depends on its bringing inferior minds into contact with superior, a contact which in the ordinary course of life is altogether exceptional, and the want of which contributes more than anything else to keep the generality of mankind on one level of contented ignorance. The school, moreover, is worthless, and a school of evil instead of good, if through the want of due surveillance, and of the presence within itself of a higher order of characters, the action of the body is allowed, as it so often is, to degenerate into an equally unscrupulous and stupid pursuit of the self-interest of its members. Now it is quite hopeless to induce persons of a high class, either socially or intellectually, to take a share of local administration in a corner by piecemeal, as members of a Paving Board or a Drainage Commission. The entire local business of their town is not more than a sufficient object, to induce men whose tastes incline them and whose knowledge qualifies them for national affairs, to become members of a mere local body, and devote to it the time and study which are necessary to render their presence anything more than a screen for the jobbing of inferior persons under the shelter of their responsibility. A mere Board of Works, though it comprehend the entire metropolis, is sure to be composed of the same class of persons as the vestries of the London parishes; nor is it practicable, or even desirable, that such should not form the majority; but it is important for every purpose which local bodies are designed to serve, whether it be the enlightened and honest performance of their special duties, or the cultivation of the political intelligence of the nation, that every such body should contain a portion of the very best minds of the locality: who are thus brought into perpetual contact, of the most useful kind, with minds of a lower grade, receiving from them what local or professional knowledge they have to give, and in return inspiring them with a portion of their own more enlarged ideas, and higher and more enlightened purposes.

A mere village has no claim to a municipal representation. By a village I mean a place whose inhabitants are not markedly distinguished by occupation or social relations from those of the rural districts adjoining, and for whose local wants the arrangements made for the surrounding territory will suffice. Such small places have rarely a sufficient public to furnish a tolerable municipal council: if they contain any talent or knowledge applicable to public business, it is apt to be all concentrated in some one man, who thereby becomes the dominator of the place. It is better that such places should be merged in a larger circumscription. The local representation of rural districts will naturally be determined by geographical considerations; with due regard to those sympathies of feeling by which human beings are so much aided to act in concert, and which partly follow historical boundaries, such

as those of counties or provinces, and partly community of interest and occupation, as in agricultural, maritime, manufacturing, or mining districts.
Different kinds of local business may require different areas of representation.
The Unions of parishes have been fixed on as the most appropriate basis for
the representative bodies which superintend the relief of indigence; while,
for the proper regulation of highways, or prisons, or police, a larger extent,
like that of an average county, is not more than sufficient. In these large districts, therefore, the maxim, that an elective body constituted in any locality
should have authority over all the local concerns common to the locality,
requires modification from another principle; as well as from the competing
consideration, of the importance of obtaining for the discharge of the local
duties the highest qualifications possible. For example, if it be necessary (as
I believe it to be) for the proper administration of the Poor Laws, that the
area of rating should not be more extensive than most of the present Unions,
a principle which requires a Board of Guardians for each Union; yet, as a
much more highly qualified class of persons is likely to be obtainable for a
County Board, than those who compose an average Board of Guardians, it
may on that ground be expedient to reserve for the County Boards some
higher descriptions of local business, which might otherwise have been conveniently managed within itself by each separate Union.

Besides the controlling Council, or local sub-Parliament, local business
has its executive department. With respect to this, the same questions arise,
as with respect to the executive authorities in the State; and they may, for the
most part, be answered in the same manner. The principles applicable to all
public trusts are in substance the same. In the first place, each executive
officer should be single, and singly responsible for the whole of the duty
committed to his charge. In the next place, he should be nominated, not
elected. It is ridiculous that a surveyor, or a health officer, or even a collector
of rates, should be appointed by popular suffrage. The popular choice usually
depends on interest with a few local leaders, who, as they are not supposed
to make the appointment, are not responsible for it; or on an appeal to
sympathy, founded on having twelve children, and having been a rate-payer
in the parish for thirty years. If in cases of this description election by the
population is a farce, appointment by the local representative body is little
less objectionable. Such bodies have a perpetual tendency to become joint-
stock associations for carrying into effect the private jobs of their various
members. Appointments should be made on the individual responsibility of
the Chairman of the body, let him be called Mayor, Chairman of Quarter
Sessions, or by whatever other title. He occupies in the locality a position
analogous to that of the prime minister in the State, and under a well-organ-
ized system the appointment and watching of the local officers would be the
most important part of his duty: he himself being appointed by the Council

from its own number, subject either to annual re-election, or to removal by a vote of the body.

From the constitution of the local bodies, I now pass to the equally important and more difficult subject of their proper attributions. This question divides itself into two parts: what should be their duties, and whether they should have full authority within the sphere of those duties, or should be liable to any, and what, interference on the part of the central government.

It is obvious, to begin with, that all business purely local—all which concerns only a single locality—should devolve upon the local authorities. The paving, lighting, and cleansing of the streets of a town, and in ordinary circumstances the draining of its houses, are of little consequence to any but its inhabitants. The nation at large is interested in them in no other way, than that in which it is interested in the private well-being of ᶜallᶜ its individual citizens. But among the duties classed as local, or performed by local functionaries, there are many which might with equal propriety be termed national, being the share, belonging to the locality, of some branch of the public administration in the efficiency of which the whole nation is alike interested: the gaols, for instance, most of which in this country are under county management; the local police; the local administration of justice, much of which, especially in corporate towns, is performed by officers elected by the locality, and paid from local funds. None of these can be said to be matters of local, as distinguished from national, importance. It would not be a matter personally indifferent to the rest of the country, if any part of it became a nest of robbers or a focus of demoralization, owing to the maladministration of its police; or if, through the bad regulations of its gaol, the punishment which the courts of justice intended to inflict on the criminals confined therein (who might have come from, or committed their offences in, any other district), might be doubled in intensity, or lowered to practical impunity. The points, moreover, which constitute good management of these things, are the same everywhere; there is no good reason why police, or gaols, or the administration of justice, should be differently managed in one part of the kingdom and in another; while there is great peril that in things so important, and to which the most instructed minds available to the State are not more than adequate, the lower average of capacities which alone can be counted on for the service of the localities, might commit errors of such magnitude as to be a serious blot upon the general administration of the country. Security of person and property, and equal justice between individuals, are the first needs of society, and the primary ends of government: if these things can be left to any responsibility below the highest, there is nothing, except war and treaties, which requires a general government at all. Whatever are the best arrangements for securing these primary objects

ᶜ⁻ᶜ61¹   any of

should be made universally obligatory, and, to secure their enforcement, should be placed under central superintendence. It is often useful, and with the institutions of our own country even necessary, from the scarcity, in the localities, of officers representing the general government, that the execution of duties imposed by the central authority should be entrusted to function-aries appointed for local purposes by the locality. But experience is daily forcing upon the public a conviction of the necessity of having at least in-spectors appointed by the general government, to see that the local officers do their duty. If prisons are under local management, the central govern-ment appoints inspectors of prisons, to take care that the rules laid down by Parliament are observed, and to suggest others if the state of the gaols shows them to be requisite: as there are inspectors of factories, and inspec-tors of schools, to watch over the observance of the Acts of Parliament relat-ing to the first, and the fulfilment of the conditions on which State assistance is granted to the latter.

But, if the administration of justice, police and gaols included, is both so universal a concern, and so much a matter of general science independent of local peculiarities, that it may be, and ought to be, uniformly regulated throughout the country, and its regulation enforced by more trained and skilful hands than those of purely local authorities; there is also business, such as the administration of the poor laws, sanitary regulation, and others, which, while really interesting to the whole country, cannot consistently with the very purposes of local administration, be managed otherwise than by the localities. In regard to such duties, the question arises, how far the local authorities ought to be trusted with discretionary power, free from any superintendence or control of the State.

To decide this question, it is essential to consider what is the comparative position of the central and the local authorities, as to capacity for the work, and security against negligence or abuse. In the first place, the local rep-resentative bodies and their officers are almost certain to be of a much lower grade of intelligence and knowledge, than Parliament and the national executive. Secondly, besides being themselves of inferior qualifications, they are watched by, and accountable to, an inferior public opinion. The public under whose eyes they act, and by whom they are criticised, is both more limited in extent, and generally far less enlightened, than that which sur-rounds and admonishes the highest authorities at the capital; while the com-parative smallness of the interests involved, causes even that inferior public to direct its thoughts to the subject less intently, and with less solicitude. Far less interference is exercised by the press and by public discussion, and that which is exercised may with much more impunity be disregarded, in the proceedings of local, than in those of national authorities. Thus far, the advantage seems wholly on the side of management by the central government. But, when we look more closely, these motives of preference are found to be balanced by others fully as substantial. If the local authorities and public are inferior to the central ones in knowledge of the principles of administration, they have the ^{d}compensating^d advantage of a far more direct interest in the result. A man's neighbours or his landlord may be much cleverer than himself, and not without an indirect interest in his prosperity, but for all that, his interests will be better attended to in his own keeping than in theirs. It is further to be remembered, that even supposing the central government to administer through its own officers, its officers do not act at the centre, but in the locality; and however inferior the local public may be to the central, it is the local public alone which has any opportunity of watching them, and it is the local opinion alone which either acts directly upon their own conduct, or calls the attention of the government to the points in which they may require correction. It is but in extreme cases that the general opinion of the country is brought to bear at all upon details of local administration, and still more rarely has it the means of deciding upon them with any just appreciation of the case. Now, the local opinion necessarily acts far more forcibly upon purely local administrators. They, in the natural course of things, are permanent residents, not expecting to be withdrawn from the place when they cease to exercise authority in it; and their authority itself depends, by supposition, on the will of the local public. I need not dwell on the deficiencies of the central authority in detailed knowledge of local persons and things, and the too great engrossment of its time and thoughts by other concerns, to admit of its acquiring the quantity and quality of local knowledge necessary even for deciding on complaints, and enforcing responsibility from so great a number of local agents. In the details of management, therefore, the local bodies will generally have the advantage; but in comprehension of the principles even of purely local management, the superiority of the central government, when rightly constituted, ought to be prodigious: not only by reason of the probably great personal superiority of the individuals composing it, and the multitude of thinkers and writers who are at all times engaged in pressing useful ideas upon their notice, but also because the knowledge and experience of any local authority is but local knowledge and experience, confined to their own part of the country and its ^{e}modes^e of management, whereas the central government has the means of knowing all that is to be learnt from the united experience of the whole kingdom, with the addition of easy access to that of foreign countries.

The practical conclusion from these premises is not difficult to draw. The authority which is most conversant with principles should be supreme over

$^{d-d}$611   compensatory
$^{e-e}$611   mode

principles, while that which is most competent in details should have the details left to it. The principal business of the central authority should be to give instruction, of the local authority to apply it. Power may be localized, but knowledge, to be most useful, must be centralized; there must be somewhere a focus at which all its scattered rays are collected, that the broken and coloured lights which exist elsewhere may find there what is necessary to complete and purify them. To every branch of local administration which affects the general interest, there should be a corresponding central organ, either a minister, or some specially appointed functionary under him; even if that functionary does no more than collect information from all quarters, and bring the experience acquired in one locality to the knowledge of another where it is wanted. But there is also something more than this for the central authority to do. It ought to keep open a perpetual communication with the localities: informing itself by their experience, and them by its own; giving advice freely when asked, volunteering it when seen to be required; compelling publicity and recordation of proceedings, and enforcing obedience to every general law which the legislature has laid down on the subject of local management. That some such laws ought to be laid down few are likely to deny. The localities may be allowed to mismanage their own interests, but not to prejudice those of others, nor violate those principles of justice between one person and another, of which it is the duty of the State to maintain the rigid observance. If the local majority attempts to oppress the minority, or one class another, the State is bound to interpose. For example, all local rates ought to be voted exclusively by the local representative body; but that body, though elected solely by ratepayers, may raise its revenues by imposts of such a kind, or assess them in such a manner, as to throw an unjust share of the burthen on the poor, the rich, or some particular class of the population: it is the duty, therefore, of the legislature, while leaving the mere amount of the local taxes to the discretion of the local body, to lay down authoritatively the *modes* of taxation, and rules of assessment, which alone the localities shall be permitted to use. Again, in the administration of public charity, the industry and morality of the whole labouring population *depend*, to a most serious extent, upon adherence to certain fixed principles in awarding relief. Though it belongs essentially to the local functionaries to determine who, according to those principles, is entitled to be relieved, the national parliament is the proper authority to prescribe the principles themselves; and it would neglect a most important part of its duty if it did not, in a matter of such grave national concern, lay down imperative rules, and make effectual provision that those rules should not be departed from. What power of actual interference with the local administrators it may be necessary

*-*611 mode
*-*611, 612 depends

to retain, for the due enforcement of the laws, is a question of detail into which it would be useless to enter. The laws themselves will naturally define the penalties, and fix the mode of their enforcement. It may be requisite, to meet extreme cases, that the power of the central authority should extend to dissolving the local representative council, or dismissing the local executive: but not to making new appointments, or suspending the local institutions. Where Parliament has not interfered, neither ought any branch of the executive to interfere with authority; but as an adviser and critic, an enforcer of the laws, and a denouncer to Parliament or the local constituencies, of conduct which it deems condemnable, the functions of the executive are of the greatest possible value.

Some may think, that however much the central authority surpasses the local in knowledge of the principles of administration, the great object which has been so much insisted on, the social and political education of the citizens, requires that they should be left to manage these matters by their own, however imperfect, lights. To this it might be answered, that the education of the citizens is not the only thing to be considered; government and administration do not exist for that alone, great as its importance is. But the objection shows a very imperfect understanding of the function of popular institutions as a means of political instruction. It is but a poor education that associates ignorance with ignorance, and leaves them, if they care for knowledge, to grope their way to it without help, and to do without it if they do not. What is wanted is, the means of making ignorance aware of itself, and able to profit by knowledge; accustoming minds which know only routine, to act upon, and feel the value of, principles: teaching them to compare different modes of action, and learn, by the use of their reason, to distinguish the best. When we desire to have a good school, we do not eliminate the teacher. The old remark, "as the schoolmaster is, so will be the school," is as true of the indirect schooling of grown people by public business, as of the schooling of youth in academies and colleges. A government which attempts to do everything, is aptly compared by M. Charles de Rémusat to a schoolmaster who does all the pupils' tasks for them; he may be very popular with the pupils, but he will teach them little.[*] A government, on the other hand, which neither does anything itself that can possibly be done by any one else, nor shows any one else how to do anything, is like a school in which there is no schoolmaster, but only pupil-teachers who have never themselves been taught.

[*Cf. Charles François Marie de Rémusat, *Politique libérale* (Paris: Lévy frères, 1860), pp. 423–4.]

CHAPTER XVI

Of Nationality, as Connected with Representative Government

A PORTION OF MANKIND may be said to constitute a Nationality, if they are united among themselves by common sympathies, which do not exist between them and any others—which make them co-operate with each other more willingly than with other people, desire to be under the same government, and desire that it should be government by themselves or a portion of themselves, exclusively. This feeling of nationality may have been generated by various causes. Sometimes it is the effect of identity of race and descent. Community of language, and community of religion, greatly contribute to it. Geographical limits are one of its causes. But the strongest of all is identity of political antecedents; the possession of a national history, and consequent community of recollections; collective pride and humiliation, pleasure and regret, connected with the same incidents in the past. None of these circumstances however are either indispensable, or necessarily sufficient by themselves. Switzerland has a strong sentiment of nationality, though the cantons are of different races, different languages, and different religions. Sicily has *a*, throughout history,*a* felt itself quite distinct in nationality from Naples, notwithstanding identity of religion, almost identity of language, and a considerable amount of common historical antecedents. The Flemish and the Walloon provinces of Belgium, notwithstanding diversity of race and language, have a much greater feeling of common nationality, than the former have with Holland, or the latter with France. Yet in general the national feeling is proportionally weakened by the failure of any of the causes which contribute to it. Identity of language, literature, and, to some extent, of race and recollections, have maintained the feeling of nationality in considerable strength among the different portions of the German name, though they have at no time been really united under the same government; but the feeling has never reached to making the separate states desire to get rid of their autonomy. Among Italians an identity far from complete, of language and literature, combined with a geographical position which separates them by a distinct line from other countries, and, perhaps more than everything else, the possession of a common name, which makes them all glory in the past achievements in arts, arms, politics, religious primacy, science, and literature,

*a-a*611, 612 hitherto

of any who share the same designation, give rise to an amount of national feeling in the population, which, though still imperfect, has been sufficient to produce the great events now passing before us: notwithstanding a great mixture of races, and although they have never, in either ancient or modern history, been under the same government, except while that government extended or was extending itself over the greater part of the known world.

Where the sentiment of nationality exists in any force, there is a *primâ facie* case for uniting all the members of the nationality under the same government, and a government to themselves apart. This is merely saying that the question of government ought to be decided by the governed. One hardly knows what any division of the human race should be free to do, if not to determine, with which of the various collective bodies of human beings they choose to associate themselves. But, when a people are ripe for free institutions, there is a still more vital consideration. Free institutions are next to impossible in a country made up of different nationalities. Among a people without fellow-feeling, especially if they read and speak different languages, the united public opinion, necessary to the working of representative government, cannot exist. The influences which form opinions and decide political acts, are different in the different sections of the country. An altogether different set of leaders have the confidence of one part of the country and of another. The same books, newspapers, pamphlets, speeches, do not reach them. One section does not know what opinions, or what instigations, are circulating in another. The same incidents, the same acts, the same system of government, affect them in different ways; and each fears more injury to itself from the other nationalities, than from the common arbiter, the state. Their mutual antipathies are generally much stronger than *b*jealousy*b* of the government. That any one of them feels aggrieved by the policy of the common ruler, is sufficient to determine another to support that policy. Even if all are aggrieved, none feel that they can rely on the others for fidelity in a joint resistance; the strength of none is sufficient to resist alone, and each may reasonably think that it consults its own advantage most by bidding for the favour of the government against the rest. Above all, the grand and only *c*effectual*c* security in the last resort against the despotism of the government, is in that case wanting: the sympathy of the army with the people. The military are the part of every community in whom, from the nature of the case, the distinction between their fellow-countrymen and foreigners is the deepest and strongest. To the rest of the people, foreigners are merely strangers; to the soldier, they are men against whom he may be called, at a week's notice, to fight for life or death.

*b–b*611   dislike
*c–c*611, 612   reliable

The difference to him is that between friends and ^dfoes^d—we may almost say between fellow-men and another kind of animals: for as respects the enemy, the only law is that of force, and the only mitigation, the same as in the case of other animals—that of simple humanity. Soldiers to whose feelings half or three-fourths of the subjects of the same government are foreigners, will have no more scruple in mowing them down, and no more desire to ask the reason why, than they would have in doing the same thing against declared enemies. An army composed of various nationalities has no other patriotism than devotion to the flag. Such armies have been the executioners of liberty through the whole duration of modern history. The sole bond which holds them together is their officers, and the government which they serve; and their only idea, if they have any, of public duty, is obedience to orders. A government thus supported, by keeping its Hungarian regiments in Italy and its Italian in Hungary, can long continue to rule in both places with the iron rod of foreign conquerors.

If it be said that so broadly marked a distinction between what is due to a fellow-countryman and what is due merely to a human creature, is more worthy of savages than of civilized beings, and ought, with the utmost energy, to be contended against, no one holds that opinion more strongly than myself. But this object, one of the worthiest to which human endeavour can be directed, can never, in the present state of civilization, be promoted by keeping different nationalities of anything like equivalent strength, under the same government. In a barbarous state of society, the case is sometimes different. The government may then be interested in softening the antipathies of the races, that peace may be preserved, and the country more easily governed. But when there are either free institutions, or a desire for them, in any of the peoples artificially tied together, the interest of the government lies in an exactly opposite direction. It is then interested in keeping up and envenoming their antipathies; that they may be prevented from coalescing, and it may be enabled to use some of them as tools for the enslavement of others. The Austrian Court has now for a whole generation made these tactics its principal means of government; with what fatal success, at the time of the Vienna insurrection and the Hungarian contest, the world knows too well. Happily there are now signs that improvement is too far advanced, to permit this policy to be any longer successful.

For the preceding reasons, it is in general a necessary condition of free institutions, that the boundaries of governments should coincide in the main with those of nationalities. But several considerations are liable to conflict in practice with this general principle. In the first place, its application is often precluded by geographical hindrances. There are parts even of Europe, in which different nationalities are so locally intermingled, that it is

^{d–d}61¹ enemies

not practicable for them to be under separate governments. The population of Hungary is composed of Magyars, Slovacks, Croats, Serbs, Roumans, and in some districts, Germans, so mixed up as to be incapable of local separation; and there is no course open to them but to make a virtue of necessity, and reconcile themselves to living together under equal rights and laws. Their community of servitude, which dates only from the destruction of Hungarian independence in 1849, seems to be ripening and disposing them for such an equal union. The German colony of East Prussia is cut off from Germany by part of the ancient Poland, and being too weak to maintain separate independence, must, if geographical continuity is to be maintained, be either under a non-German government, or the intervening Polish territory must be under a German one. Another considerable region in which the dominant element of the population is German, the provinces of Courland, Esthonia, and Livonia, is condemned by its local situation to form part of a Slavonian state. In Eastern Germany itself there is a large Slavonic population: Bohemia is principally Slavonic, Silesia and other districts partially so. The most united country in Europe, France, is far from being homogeneous: independently of the fragments of foreign nationalities at its remote extremities, it consists, as language and history prove, of two portions, one occupied almost exclusively by a Gallo-Roman population, while in the other the Frankish, Burgundian, and other Teutonic races form a considerable ingredient.

When proper allowance has been made for geographical exigencies, another more purely moral and social consideration offers itself. Experience proves, that it is possible for one nationality to merge and be absorbed in another: and when it was originally an inferior and more backward portion of the human race, the absorption is greatly to its advantage. Nobody can suppose that it is not more beneficial to a Breton, or a Basque of French Navarre, to be brought into the current of the ideas and feelings of a highly civilized and cultivated people—to be a member of the French nationality, admitted on equal terms to all the privileges of French citizenship, sharing the advantages of French protection, and the dignity and *prestige* of French power—than to sulk on his own rocks, the half-savage relic of past times, revolving in his own little mental orbit, without participation or interest in the general movement of the world. The same remark applies to the Welshman or the Scottish Highlander, as members of the British nation.

Whatever really tends to the admixture of nationalities, and the blending of their attributes and peculiarities in a common union, is a benefit to the human race. Not by extinguishing types, of which, in these cases, sufficient examples are sure to remain, but by softening their extreme forms, and filling up the intervals between them. The united people, like a crossed breed of animals (but in a still greater degree, because the influences in

operation are moral as well as physical), inherits the special aptitudes and
excellences of all its progenitors, protected by the admixture from being
exaggerated into the neighbouring vices. But to render this admixture
possible, there must be peculiar conditions. The combinations of circumstances which occur, and which affect the result, are various.

The nationalities brought together under the same government, may be
about equal in numbers and strength, or they may be very unequal. If
unequal, the least numerous of the two may either be the superior in
civilization, or the inferior. Supposing it to be superior, it may either,
through that superiority, be able to acquire ascendancy over the other, or
it may be overcome by brute strength, and reduced to subjection. This last
is a sheer mischief to the human race, and one which civilized humanity
with one accord should rise in arms to prevent. The absorption of Greece
by Macedonia was one of the greatest misfortunes which ever happened to
the world: that of any of the principal countries of Europe by Russia would
be a similar one.

If the smaller nationality, supposed to be the more advanced in improvement, is able to overcome the greater, as the Macedonians, reinforced by
the Greeks, did Asia, and the English India, there is often a gain to
civilization; but the conquerors and the conquered cannot in this case live
together under the same free institutions. The absorption of the conquerors
in the less advanced people would be an evil: these must be governed as
subjects, and the state of things is either a benefit or a misfortune, according
as the subjugated people have or have not reached the state in which it is an
injury not to be under a free government, and according as the conquerors
do or do not use their superiority in a manner calculated to fit the conquered for a higher stage of improvement. This topic will be particularly
treated of in a subsequent chapter.

When the nationality which succeeds in overpowering the other, is both
the most numerous and the most improved; and especially if the subdued
nationality is small, and has no hope of reasserting its independence; then,
if it is governed with any tolerable justice, and if the members of the more
powerful nationality are not made odious by being invested with exclusive
privileges, the smaller nationality is gradually reconciled to its position, and
becomes amalgamated with the larger. No Bas-Breton, nor even any
Alsatian, has the smallest wish at the present day to be separated from
France. If all Irishmen have not yet arrived at the same disposition towards
England, it is partly because they are sufficiently numerous to be capable of
constituting a respectable nationality by themselves; but principally because,
until of late years, they had been so atrociously governed, that all their best
feelings combined with their bad ones in rousing bitter resentment against

*e-e*611   excellencies [*printer's error?*]

the Saxon rule. This disgrace to England, and calamity to the whole empire, has, it may be truly said, completely ceased for nearly a generation. No Irishman is now less free than an Anglo-Saxon, nor has a less share of every benefit either to his country or to his individual fortunes, than if he were sprung from any other portion of the British dominions. The only remaining real grievance of Ireland, that of the State Church, is one which half, or nearly half, the people of the larger island have in common with them. There is now next to nothing, except the memory of the past, and the difference in the predominant religion, to keep apart two races, perhaps the most fitted of any two in the world to be the completing counterpart of one another. The consciousness of being at last treated not only with equal justice but with equal consideration, is making such rapid way in the Irish nation, as to be wearing off all feelings that could make them insensible to the benefits which the less numerous and less wealthy people must necessarily derive, from being fellow-citizens instead of foreigners to those who are not only their nearest neighbours, but the wealthiest, and one of the freest, as well as most civilized and powerful, nations of the earth.

The cases in which the greatest practical obstacles exist to the blending of nationalities, are when the nationalities which have been bound together cases, each, confiding in its strength, and feeling itself capable of maintaining an equal struggle with any of the others, is unwilling to be merged in it: each cultivates with party obstinacy its distinctive peculiarities; obsolete customs, and even declining languages, are revived, to deepen the separation; each deems itself tyrannized over if any authority is exercised within itself by functionaries of a rival race; and whatever is given to one of the conflicting nationalities, is considered to be taken from all the rest. When nations, thus divided, are under a despotic government which is a stranger to all of them, or which though sprung from one, yet feeling greater interest in its own power than in any sympathies of nationality, assigns no privilege to either nation, and chooses its instruments indifferently from all; in the course of a few generations, identity of situation often produces harmony of feeling, and the different races come to feel towards each other as fellow-countrymen; particularly if they are dispersed over the same tract of country. But if the era of aspiration to free government arrives before this fusion has been effected, the opportunity has gone by for effecting it. From that time, if the unreconciled nationalities are geographically separate, and especially if their local position is such that there is no natural fitness or convenience in their being under the same government (as in the case of an Italian province under a French or German yoke), there is not only an obvious propriety, but, if either freedom or concord is cared for, a necessity, for breaking the connexion altogether. There may be cases in which the provinces, after separation, might usefully remain united by a federal tie: but it generally happens that if they are willing to forego complete independence, and become members of a federation, each of them has other neighbours with whom it would prefer to connect itself, having more sympathies in common, if not also greater community of interest.

CHAPTER XVII

Of Federal Representative
Governments

PORTIONS OF MANKIND who are not fitted, or not disposed, to live under the same internal government, may often with advantage be federally united, as to their relations with foreigners: both to prevent wars among themselves, and for the sake of more effectual protection against the aggression of powerful States.

To render a federation advisable, several conditions are necessary. The first is, that there should be a sufficient amount of mutual sympathy among the populations. The federation binds them always to fight on the same side; and if they have such feelings towards one another, or such diversity of feeling towards their neighbours, that they would generally prefer to fight on opposite sides, the federal tie is neither likely to be of long duration, nor to be well observed while it subsists. The sympathies available for the purpose are those of race, language, religion, and above all, of political institutions, as conducing most to a feeling of identity of political interest. When a few free states, separately insufficient for their own defence, are hemmed in on all sides by military or feudal monarchs, who hate and despise freedom even in a neighbour, those states have no chance for preserving liberty and its blessings, but by a federal union. The common interest arising from this cause has in Switzerland, for several centuries, been found adequate to maintain efficiently the federal bond, in spite not only of difference of religion when religion was the grand source of irreconcilable political enmity throughout Europe, but also in spite of great weakness in the constitution of the federation itself. In America, where all the conditions for the maintenance of union *existed* at the highest point, with the sole drawback of difference of institutions in the single but most important article of Slavery, this one difference *has gone* so far in alienating from each other's sympathies the two divisions of the Union, *that the maintenance or disruption of a tie of so much value to them both, depends on the issue of an obstinate civil war*.

*a–a*611   exist
*b–b*611   goes
*c–c*611, 612   as to be now actually effecting the disruption of a tie of so much value to them both

*d*A second condition of*d* the stability of a federal government, is that the separate states be not so powerful, as to be able to rely, for protection against foreign encroachment, on their individual strength. If they are, they will be apt to think that they do not gain, by union with others, the equivalent of what they sacrifice in their own liberty of action: and consequently, whenever the policy of the Confederation, in things reserved to its cognizance, is different from that which any one of its members would separately pursue, the internal and sectional breach will, through absence of sufficient anxiety to preserve the Union, be in danger of going so far as to dissolve it.

A third condition, not less important than the two others, is that there be not a very marked inequality of strength among the several contracting states. They cannot, indeed, be exactly equal in resources: in all federations there will be a gradation of power among the members; some will be more populous, rich, and civilized than others. There is a wide difference in wealth and population between New York and Rhode Island; between Berne, and Zug or Glaris. The essential is, that there should not be any one State so much more powerful than the rest, as to be capable of vying in strength with many of them combined. If there be such a one, and only one, it will insist on being master of the joint deliberations: if there be two, they will be irresistible when they agree; and whenever they differ, everything will be decided by a struggle for ascendancy between the rivals. This cause is alone enough to reduce the German Bund to almost a nullity, independently of its wretched internal constitution. It effects none of the real purposes of a confederation. It has never bestowed on Germany an uniform system of customs, nor so much as an uniform coinage; and has served only to give Austria and Prussia a legal right of pouring in their troops to assist the local sovereigns in keeping their subjects obedient to despotism: while in regard to external concerns, the Bund would make all Germany a dependency of Prussia, if there were no Austria, and of Austria if there were no Prussia: and in the meantime each petty prince has little choice but to be a partisan of one or the other, or to intrigue with foreign governments against both.

There are two different modes of organizing a Federal Union. The federal authorities may represent the Governments solely, and their acts may be obligatory only on the Governments as such, or they may have the power of enacting laws and issuing orders which are binding directly on individual citizens. The former is the plan of the German so-called Confederation, and of the Swiss Constitution previous to 1847. It was tried in America for a few years immediately following the War of Independence. The other principle is that of the existing Constitution of the United States,

*d–d*611, 612 The second condition for

and has been adopted within the last dozen years by the Swiss Confederacy. The Federal Congress of the American Union is a substantive part of the government of every individual State. Within the limits of its attributions, it makes laws which are obeyed by every citizen individually, executes them through its own officers, and enforces them by its own tribunals. This is the only principle which has been found, or which is ever likely, to produce an effective federal government. An union between the governments only, is a mere alliance, and subject to all the contingencies which render alliances precarious. If the acts of the President and of Congress were binding solely on the Governments of New York, Virginia, or Pennsylvania, and could only be carried into effect through orders issued by those Governments to officers appointed by them, under responsibility to their own courts of justice, no mandates of the Federal Government which were disagreeable to a local majority would ever be executed. Requisitions issued to a *government* have no other sanction, or means of enforcement, than war: and a federal army would have to be always in readiness, to enforce the decrees of the Federation against any recalcitrant State; subject to the probability that other States, sympathizing with the recusant, and perhaps sharing its sentiments on the particular point in dispute, would withhold their contingents, if not send them to fight in the ranks of the disobedient State. Such a federation is more likely to be a cause than a preventive of internal wars: and if such was not its effect in Switzerland until the events of the years immediately preceding 1847, it was only because the Federal Government felt its weakness so strongly, that it hardly ever attempted to exercise any real authority. In America, the experiment of a Federation on this principle broke down in the first few years of its existence; happily while the men of enlarged knowledge and acquired ascendancy, who founded the independence of the Republic, were still alive to guide it through the difficult transition. The *Federalist*, a collection of papers by three of these eminent men,[*] written in explanation and defence of the new Federal Constitution while still awaiting the national acceptance, is even now the most instructive treatise we possess on federal government.* In Germany, the more imperfect kind of federation, as all know, has not even answered the purpose of maintaining an alliance. It has never, in any European war, prevented single members of the Confederation from allying themselves with foreign powers against the rest. Yet this is the only federa-

[*Alexander Hamilton, John Jay, and James Madison, *The Federalist* (Philadelphia: Lippincott, 1864).]

*[65] Mr. [Edward Augustus] Freeman's *History of Federal Governments* [London and Cambridge: Macmillan, 1863], of which only the first volume has yet appeared, is already an accession to the literature of the subject, equally valuable by its enlightened principles and its mastery of historical details.

*e–e*611   Government

tion which seems possible among monarchical states. A king, who holds his power by inheritance, not by delegation, and who cannot be deprived of it, nor made responsible to any one for its use, is not likely to renounce having a separate army, or to brook the exercise of sovereign authority over his own subjects, not through him but directly, by another power. To enable two or more countries under kingly government to be joined together in an effectual confederation, it seems necessary that they should all be under the same king. England and Scotland were a federation of this description, during the interval of about a century between the union of the Crowns and that of the Parliaments. Even this was effective, not through federal institutions, for none existed, but because the regal power in both Constitutions was *during the greater part of that time* so nearly absolute, as to enable the foreign policy of both to be shaped according to a single will.

Under the more perfect mode of federation, where every citizen of each particular State owes obedience to two Governments, that of his own State, and that of the federation, it is evidently necessary not only that the constitutional limits of the authority of each should be precisely and clearly defined, but that the power to decide between them in any case of dispute should not reside in either of the Governments, or in any functionary subject to it, but in an umpire independent of both. There must be a Supreme Court of Justice, and a system of subordinate Courts in every State of the Union, before whom such questions shall be carried, and whose judgment on them, in the last stage of appeal, shall be final. Every State of the Union, and the Federal Government itself, as well as every functionary of each, must be liable to be sued in those Courts for exceeding their powers, or for non-performance of their federal duties, and must in general be obliged to employ those Courts as the instrument for enforcing their federal rights. This involves the remarkable consequence, actually realized in the United States, that a Court of Justice, the highest federal tribunal, is supreme over the various Governments, both State and Federal; having the right to declare that any law made, or act done by them, exceeds the powers assigned to them by the Federal Constitution, and, in consequence, has no legal validity. It was natural to feel strong doubts, before trial had been made, how such a provision would work; whether the tribunal would have the courage to exercise its constitutional power; if it did, whether it would exercise it wisely, and whether the Governments would consent to submit peaceably to its decision. The discussions on the American Constitution, before its final adoption, give evidence that these natural apprehensions were strongly felt; but they are now entirely quieted, since, during the two generations and more which have subsequently elapsed, nothing has occurred to verify them, though there have at times been disputes of con-

–+61², 65

siderable acrimony, and which became the badges of parties, respecting the limits of the authority of the Federal and State Governments. The eminently beneficial working of so singular a provision, is probably, as M. de Tocqueville remarks,[*] in a great measure attributable to the peculiarity inherent in a Court of Justice acting as such—namely, that it does not declare the law *eo nomine* and in the abstract, but waits until a case between man and man is brought before it judicially, involving the point in dispute: from which arises the happy effect, that its declarations are not made in a very early stage of the controversy; that much popular discussion usually precedes them; that the Court decides after hearing the point fully argued on both sides by lawyers of reputation; decides only as much of the question at a time as is required by the case before it, and its decision, instead of being volunteered for political purposes, is drawn from it by the duty which it cannot refuse to fulfil, of dispensing justice impartially between adverse litigants. Even these grounds of confidence would not have sufficed to produce the respectful submission with which all authorities have yielded to the decisions of the Supreme Court on the interpretation of the Constitution, were it not that complete reliance has been felt, not only on the intellectual pre-eminence of the judges composing that exalted tribunal, but on their entire superiority over either private or sectional partialities. This reliance has been in the main justified; but there is nothing which more vitally imports the American people, than to guard with the most watchful solicitude against everything which has the remotest tendency to produce deterioration in the quality of this great national institution. The confidence on which depends the stability of federal institutions *g*was*g* for the first time impaired, by the judgment declaring slavery to be of common right, and consequently lawful in the Territories while not yet constituted as States, even against the will of a majority of their inhabitants. *h*This memorable decision has probably done more than anything else to bring the sectional division to the crisis which *i*has issued in civil war*i.h* The main pillar of the American Constitution is scarcely strong enough, to bear many more such shocks.

The tribunals which act as umpires between the Federal and the State Governments, naturally also decide all disputes between two States, or between a citizen of one State and the government of another. The usual remedies between nations, war and diplomacy, being precluded by the federal union, it is necessary that a judicial remedy should supply their place. The Supreme Court of the Federation dispenses international law, and is

[*See *De la Démocratie en Amérique*, Vol. I, pp. 164–6 (Reeve translation, Vol. I, pp. 136–8).]

*g-g*61[1]   has been   *h-h*+61[2], 65
*i-i*61[2]   is now issuing in separation

the first great example of what is now one of the most prominent wants of civilized society, a real International Tribunal.

The powers of a Federal Government naturally extend not only to peace and war, and all questions which arise between the country and foreign governments, but to making any other arrangements which are, in the opinion of the States, necessary to their enjoyment of the full benefits of union. For example, it is a great advantage to them that their mutual commerce should be free, without the impediment of frontier duties and custom-houses. But this internal freedom cannot exist, if each State has the power of fixing the duties on interchange of commodities between itself and foreign countries; since every foreign product let in by one State, would be let into all the rest. And hence all custom duties and trade regulations, in the United States, are made or repealed by the Federal Government exclusively. Again, it is a great convenience to the States to have but one coinage, and but one system of weights and measures; which can only be ensured, if the regulation of these matters is entrusted to the Federal Government. The certainty and celerity of Post Office communication is impeded, and its expense increased, if a letter has to pass through half a dozen sets of public *offices*, subject to different supreme authorities: it is convenient, therefore, that all Post Offices should be under the Federal Government. But on such questions the feelings of different communities are liable to be different. One of the American States, under the guidance of a man who has displayed powers as a speculative political thinker superior to any who has appeared in American politics since the authors of the *Federalist*,* claimed a veto for each State on the custom laws of the Federal Congress: and that statesman, in a posthumous work of great ability, which has been printed and widely circulated by the legislature of South Carolina, vindicated this pretension on the general principle of limiting the tyranny of the majority, and protecting minorities by admitting them to a substantial participation in political power.[*] One of the most disputed topics in American politics, during the early part of this century, was whether the power of the Federal Government ought to extend, and whether by the Constitution it did extend, to making roads and canals at the cost of the Union. It is only in transactions with foreign powers that the authority of the Federal Government is of necessity complete. On every other subject, the question depends on how closely the people in general wish to draw the federal tie; what portion of their local freedom of action they are willing to surrender, in order to enjoy more fully the benefit of being one nation.

*Mr. Calhoun.

[*See John Caldwell Calhoun, "A Discourse on the Constitution and Government of the United States," in *Works*, 6 vols. (Columbia, S.C.: General Assembly of the State of South Carolina, 1851–56), Vol. I, pp. 331 ff.]

*j–j*611   officers [*printer's error?*]

Respecting the fitting constitution of a federal government within itself, much needs not be said. It of course consists of a legislative branch and an executive, and the constitution of each is amenable to the same principles as that of representative governments generally. As regards the mode of adapting these general principles to a federal government, the provision of the American Constitution seems exceedingly judicious, that Congress should consist of two Houses, and that while one of them is constituted according to population, each State being entitled to representatives in the ratio of the number of its inhabitants, the other should represent not the citizens, but the State Governments, and every State, whether large or small, should be represented in it by the same number of members. This provision precludes any undue power from being exercised by the more powerful States over the rest, and guarantees the reserved rights of the State Governments, by making it impossible, as far as the mode of representation can prevent, that any measure should pass Congress, unless approved not only by a majority of the citizens, but by a majority of the States. I have before adverted to the further incidental advantage obtained, of raising the standard of qualifications in one of the Houses. Being nominated by select bodies, the Legislatures of the various States, whose choice, for reasons already indicated, is more likely to fall on eminent men than any popular election—who have not only the power of electing such, but a strong motive to do so, because the influence of their State in the general deliberations must be materially affected by the personal weight and abilities of its representatives; the Senate of the United States, thus chosen, has always contained nearly all the political men of established and high reputation in the Union: while the Lower House of Congress has, in the opinion of competent observers, been generally as remarkable for the absence of conspicuous personal merit, as the Upper House for its presence.

When the conditions exist for the formation of efficient and durable Federal Unions, the multiplication of ^{k}them^k is always a benefit to the world. It has the same salutary effect as any other extension of the practice of co-operation, through which the weak, by uniting, can meet on equal terms with the strong. By diminishing the number of those petty states which are not equal to their own defence, it weakens the temptations to an aggressive policy, whether working directly by arms, or through the *prestige* of superior power. It of course puts an end to war and diplomatic quarrels, and usually also to restrictions on commerce, between the States composing the Union; while, in reference to neighbouring nations, the increased military strength conferred by it is of a kind to be almost exclusively available for defensive, scarcely at all for aggressive, purposes. A federal government has not a sufficiently concentrated authority, to conduct with much efficiency any war but one of self-defence, in which it can rely on the voluntary

$^{k-k}$611, 612   such

co-operation of every citizen: nor is there anything very flattering to national vanity or ambition in acquiring, by a successful war, not subjects, nor even fellow-citizens, but only new, and perhaps troublesome, independent members of the confederation. The warlike proceedings of the Americans in Mexico were purely exceptional, having been carried on principally by volunteers, under the influence of the migratory propensity which prompts individual Americans to possess themselves of unoccupied land; and stimulated, if by any public motive, not by that of national aggrandizement, but by the purely sectional purpose of extending slavery. There are few signs in the proceedings of Americans, nationally or individually, that the desire of territorial acquisition for their country as such, has any considerable power over them. Their hankering after Cuba is, in the same manner, merely sectional, and the northern States, those opposed to slavery, have never in any way favoured it.

The question may present itself (as in Italy at its present uprising) whether a country, which is determined to be united, should form a complete, or a merely federal union. The point is sometimes necessarily decided by the mere territorial magnitude of the united whole. There is a limit to the extent of country which can advantageously be governed, or even whose government can be conveniently superintended, from a single centre. There are vast countries so governed; but they, or at least their distant provinces, are in general deplorably ill administered, and it is only when the inhabitants are almost savages that they could not manage their affairs better separately. This obstacle does not exist in the case of Italy, the size of which does not come up to that of several very efficiently governed single states in past and present times. The question then is, whether the different parts of the nation require to be governed in a way so essentially different, that it is not probable the same Legislature, and the same ministry or administrative body, will give satisfaction to them all. Unless this be the case, which is a question of fact, it is better for them to be completely united. That a totally different system of laws, and very different administrative institutions, may exist in two portions of a country without being any obstacle to legislative unity, is proved by the case of England and Scotland. Perhaps, however, this undisturbed co-existence of two legal systems, under one united legislature, making different laws for the two sections of the country in adaptation to the previous differences, might not be so well preserved, or the same confidence might not be felt in its preservation, in a country whose legislators *were* more possessed (as is apt to be the case on the Continent) with the mania for uniformity. A people having that unbounded toleration which is characteristic of this country, for every description of anomaly, so long as those whose interests it concerns do not feel aggrieved by it, afforded an exceptionally advantageous field for trying this difficult experiment. In most

*l-l*611   are

countries, if it was an object to retain different systems of law, it might probably be necessary to retain distinct legislatures as guardians of them; which is perfectly compatible with a national Parliament and King, or a national Parliament without a King, supreme over the external relations of all the members of the body.

Whenever it is not deemed necessary to maintain permanently, in the different provinces, different systems of jurisprudence, and fundamental institutions grounded on different principles, it is always practicable to reconcile minor diversities with the maintenance of unity of government. All that is needful is to give a sufficiently large sphere of action to the local authorities. Under one and the same central government there may be local governors, and provincial assemblies for local purposes. It may happen, for instance, that the people of different provinces may have preferences in favour of different modes of taxation. If the general legislature could not be depended on for being guided by the members for each province in modifying the general system of taxation to suit that province, the Constitution might provide that as many of the expenses of government as could by any possibility be made local, should be defrayed by local rates imposed by the provincial assemblies, and that those which must of necessity be general, such as the support of an army and navy, should, in the estimates for the year, be apportioned among the different provinces according to some general estimate of their resources, the amount assigned to each being levied by the local assembly on the principles most acceptable to the locality, and paid *en bloc* into the national treasury. A practice approaching to this existed even in the old French monarchy, so far as regarded the *pays d'états*; each of which, having consented or been required to furnish a fixed sum, was left to assess it upon the inhabitants by its own officers, thus escaping the grinding despotism of the royal *intendants* and *subdélégués*; and this privilege is always mentioned as one of the advantages which mainly contributed to render them, as *ᵐ*some of them*ᵐ* were, the most flourishing provinces of France.

Identity of central government is compatible with many different degrees of centralization, not only administrative, but even legislative. A people may have the desire, and the capacity, for a closer union than one merely federal, while yet their local peculiarities and antecedents render considerable diversities desirable in the details of their government. But if there is a real desire on all hands to make the experiment successful, there needs seldom be any difficulty in not only preserving *ⁿ*these*ⁿ* diversities, but giving them the guarantee of a constitutional provision against any attempt at assimilation, except by the voluntary act of those who would be affected by the change.

*ᵐ⁻ᵐ*611   they
*ⁿ⁻ⁿ*611   those

CHAPTER XVIII

Of the Government of Dependencies by a Free State

FREE STATES, like all others, may possess dependencies, acquired either by conquest or by colonization; and our own is the greatest instance of the kind in modern history. It is a most important question, how such dependencies ought to be governed.

It is unnecessary to discuss the case of small posts, like Gibraltar, Aden, or Heligoland, which are held only as naval or military positions. The military or naval object is in this case paramount, and the inhabitants cannot, consistently with it, be admitted to the government of the place; though they ought to be allowed all liberties and privileges compatible with that restriction, including the free management of municipal affairs; and, as a compensation for being locally sacrificed to the convenience of the governing State, should be admitted to equal rights with its native subjects in all other parts of the empire.

Outlying territories of some size and population, which are held as dependencies, that is, which are subject, more or less, to acts of sovereign power on the part of the paramount country, without being equally represented (if represented at all) in its legislature, may be divided into two classes. Some are composed of people of similar civilization to the ruling country; capable of, and ripe for, representative government: such as the British possessions in America and Australia. Others, like India, are still at a great distance from that state.

In the case of dependencies of the former class, this country has at length realized, in rare completeness, the true principle of government. England has always felt under a certain degree of obligation to bestow on such of her outlying populations as were of her own blood and language, and on some who were not, representative institutions formed in imitation of her own: but until the present generation, she has been on the same bad level with other countries as to the amount of self-government which she allowed them to exercise through the representative institutions that she conceded to them. She claimed to be the supreme arbiter even of their purely internal concerns, according to her own, not their, ideas of how those concerns could be best regulated. This practice was a natural corollary from the vicious theory of colonial policy—once common to all Europe, and not yet completely relinquished by any other people—which regarded colonies as valuable by affording markets for our commodities, that could be kept entirely to ourselves: a privilege we valued so highly, that we thought it worth purchasing by allowing to the colonies the same monopoly of our market for their own productions, which we claimed for our commodities in theirs. This notable plan *for* enriching them and ourselves, by making each pay enormous sums to the other, dropping the greatest part by the way, has been for some time abandoned. But the bad habit of meddling in the internal government of the colonies, did not at once *terminate* when we relinquished the idea of making any profit by it. We continued to torment them, not for any benefit to ourselves, but for that of a section or faction among the colonists: and this persistence in domineering cost us a Canadian rebellion, before we had the happy thought of giving it up. England was like an ill brought-up elder brother, who persists in tyrannizing over the younger ones from mere habit, till one of them, by a spirited resistance, though with unequal strength, gives him notice to desist. We were wise enough not to require a second warning. A new era in the colonial policy of nations began with Lord Durham's Report;[*] the imperishable memorial of that nobleman's courage, patriotism, and enlightened liberality, and of the intellect and practical sagacity of its joint authors, Mr. Wakefield and the lamented Charles Buller.*

It is now a fixed principle of the policy of Great Britain, professed in theory and faithfully adhered to in practice, that her colonies of European race, equally with the parent country, possess the fullest measure of internal self-government. They have been allowed to make their own free representative constitutions, by altering in any manner they thought fit, the already very popular constitutions which we had given them. Each is governed by its own legislature and executive, constituted on highly democratic principles. The veto of the Crown and of Parliament, though nominally reserved, is only exercised (and that very rarely) on questions which concern the empire, and not solely the particular colony. How liberal a construction has been given to the distinction between imperial and colonial questions, is shown by the fact, that the whole of the unappropriated lands in the regions behind our American and Australian colonies, have been given up to the uncontrolled disposal of the colonial communities; though

[*"Report on the Affairs of British North America, from the Earl of Durham," *Parliamentary Papers*, 1839, Vol. XVII.]

*I am speaking here of the *adoption* of this improved policy, not, of course, of its original suggestion. The honour of having been its earliest champion belongs unquestionably to Mr. Roebuck.

a–a61¹   of
b–b61¹   die out

they might, without injustice, have been kept in the hands of the Imperial Government, to be administered for the greatest advantage of future emigrants from all parts of the empire. Every Colony has thus as full power over its own affairs, as it could have if it were a member of even the loosest federation; and much fuller than would belong to it under the Constitution of the United States, being free even to tax at its pleasure the commodities imported from the mother country. Their union with Great Britain is the slightest kind of federal union; but not a strictly equal federation, the mother country retaining to itself the powers of a Federal Government, though reduced in practice to their very narrowest limits. This inequality is, of course, as far as it goes, a disadvantage to the dependencies, which have no voice in foreign policy, but are bound by the decisions of the superior country. They are compelled to join England in war, without being in any way consulted previous to engaging in it.

Those (now happily not a few) who think that justice is as binding on communities as it is on individuals, and that men are not warranted in doing to other countries, for the supposed benefit of their own country, what they would not be justified in doing to other men for their own benefit—feel even this limited amount of constitutional subordination on the part of the colonies to be a violation of principle, and have often occupied themselves in looking out for means by which it may be avoided. With this view it has been proposed by some, that the colonies should return representatives to the British legislature; and by others, that the powers of our own, as well as of their Parliaments, should be confined to internal policy, and that there should be another representative body for foreign and imperial concerns, in which last the dependencies of Great Britain should be represented in the same manner, and with the same completeness, as Great Britain itself. On this system there would be a perfectly equal federation between the mother country and her colonies, then no longer dependencies.

The feelings of equity, and conceptions of public morality, from which these suggestions emanate, are worthy of all praise; but the suggestions themselves are so inconsistent with rational principles of government, that it is doubtful if they have been seriously accepted as a possibility by any reasonable thinker. Countries separated by half the globe do not present the natural conditions for being under one government, or even members of one federation. If they had sufficiently the same interests, they have not, and never can have, a sufficient habit of taking counsel together. They are not part of the same public; they do not discuss and deliberate in the same arena, but apart, and have only a most imperfect knowledge of what passes in the minds of one another. They neither know each other's objects, nor have confidence in each other's principles of conduct. Let any Englishman ask himself how he should like his destinies to depend on an assembly of which one-third was British American, and another third South African and Australian. Yet to this it must come, if there were anything like fair or equal representation; and would not every one feel that the representatives of Canada and Australia, even in matters of an imperial character, could not know, or feel any sufficient concern for, the interests, opinions, or wishes of English, Irish, and Scotch? Even for strictly federative purposes, the conditions do not exist, which we have seen to be essential to a federation. England is sufficient for her own protection without the colonies; and would be in a much stronger, as well as more dignified position, if separated from them, than when reduced to be a single member of an American, African, and Australian confederation. Over and above the commerce which she might equally enjoy after separation, England derives little advantage, except in *prestige*, from her dependencies; and the little she does derive is quite outweighed by the expense they cost her, and the dissemination they necessitate of her naval and military force, which in case of war, or any real apprehension of it, requires to be double or treble what would be needed for the defence of this country alone.

But though Great Britain could do perfectly well without her colonies, and though on every principle of morality and justice she ought to consent to their separation, should the time come when, after full trial of the best form of union, they deliberately desire to be dissevered; there are strong reasons for maintaining the present slight bond of connexion, so long as not disagreeable to the feelings of either party. It is a step, as far as it goes, towards universal peace, and general friendly co-operation among nations. It renders war impossible among a large number of otherwise independent communities; and moreover hinders any of them from being absorbed into a foreign state, and becoming a source of additional aggressive strength to some rival power, either more despotic or closer at hand, which ^cmight^c not always be so unambitious or so pacific as Great Britain. It at least keeps the markets of the different countries open to one another, and prevents that mutual exclusion by hostile tariffs, which none of the great communities of mankind, except England, have yet ^dcompletely^d outgrown. And in the case of the British possessions it has the advantage, specially valuable at the present time, of adding to the moral influence, and weight in the councils of the world, of the Power which, of all in existence, best understands liberty—and whatever may have been its errors in the past, has attained to more of conscience and moral principle in its dealings with foreigners, than any other great nation seems either to conceive as possible, or recognise as desirable. Since, then, the union can only continue, while it does continue, on the footing of an unequal federation, it is important

c–c611   may
d–d+612, 65

to consider by what means this small amount of inequality can be prevented from being either onerous or humiliating to the communities occupying the less exalted position.

The only inferiority necessarily inherent in the case is, that the mother country decides, both for the colonies and for herself, on questions of peace and war. They gain, in return, the obligation on the mother country to repel aggressions directed against them; but, except when the minor community is so weak that the protection of a stronger power is indispensable to it, reciprocity of obligation is not a full equivalent for non-admission to a voice in the deliberations. It is essential, therefore, that in all wars, save those which, like the Caffre or New Zealand wars, are incurred for the sake of the particular colony, the colonists should not (*ewithoute* their own voluntary request) be *fcalled onf* to contribute anything to the expense, except what may be required for the specific local defence of their own ports, shores, and frontiers against invasion. Moreover, as the mother country claims the privilege, at her sole discretion, of taking measures or pursuing a policy which may expose them to attack, it is just that she should undertake a considerable portion of the cost of their military defence even in time of peace; the whole of it, so far as it depends upon a standing army.

But there is a means, still more effectual than these, by which, and in general by which alone, a full equivalent can be given to a smaller community for sinking its individuality, as a substantive power among nations, in the greater individuality of a wide and powerful empire. This one indispensable, and at the same time sufficient, expedient, which meets at once the demands of justice and the growing exigencies of policy, is, to open the service of Government in all its departments, and in every part of the empire, on perfectly equal terms, to the inhabitants of the Colonies. Why does no one ever hear a breath of disloyalty from the *gIslandsg* in the British Channel? By race, religion, and geographical position they belong less to England than to France. But, while they enjoy, like Canada and New South Wales, complete control over their internal affairs and their taxation, every office or dignity in the gift of the Crown is freely open to the native of Guernsey or Jersey. Generals, admirals, peers of the United Kingdom, are made, and there is nothing which hinders prime ministers to be made, from those insignificant islands. The same system was commenced in reference to the Colonies generally, by an enlightened Colonial Secretary, too early lost, Sir William Molesworth, when he appointed Mr. Hinckes, a leading Canadian politician, to a West Indian government. It is a very shallow view of the springs of political action in a community, which thinks such things

e–e611   unless at
f–f611   made
g–g611, 612   islands

unimportant because the number of those in a position actually to profit by the concession might not be very considerable. That limited number would be composed precisely of those who have most moral power over the rest: and men are not so destitute of the sense of collective degradation, as not to feel the withholding of an advantage from even one person, because of a circumstance which they all have in common with him, an affront to all. If we prevent the leading men of a community from standing forth to the world as its chiefs and representatives in the general councils of mankind, we owe it both to their legitimate ambition, and to the just pride of the community, to give them in return an equal chance of occupying the same prominent position in a nation of greater power and importance. [h]

Thus far, of the dependencies whose population is in a sufficiently advanced state to be fitted for representative government. But there are others which have not attained that state, and which, if held at all, must be governed by the dominant country, or by persons delegated for that purpose by it. This mode of government is as legitimate as any other, if it is the one which in the existing state of civilization of the subject people, most facilitates their transition to a higher stage of improvement. There are, as we have already seen, conditions of society in which a vigorous despotism is in itself the best mode of government for training the people in what is specifically wanting to render them capable of a higher civilization. There are others, in which the mere fact of despotism has indeed no beneficial effect, the lessons which it teaches having already been only too completely learnt; but in which, there being no spring of spontaneous improvement in the people themselves, their almost only hope of making any steps in advance depends on the chances of a good despot. Under a native despotism, a good despot is a rare and transitory accident: but when the dominion they are under is that of a more civilized people, that people ought to be able to supply it constantly. The ruling country ought to be able to do for its subjects all that could be done by a succession of absolute monarchs, guaranteed by irresistible force against the precariousness of tenure attendant on barbarous despotisms, and qualified by their genius to anticipate all that experience has taught to the more advanced nation. Such is the ideal rule of a free people over a barbarous or semibarbarous one. We need not expect to see that ideal realized; but unless some approach to it is, the rulers are guilty of a

[h]611 Were the whole service of the British Crown opened to the natives of the Ionian Islands, we should hear no more of the desire for union with Greece. Such an union is not desirable for the people, to whom it would be a step backward in civilization; but it is no wonder if Corfu, which has given a Minister of European reputation [John Capodistrias] to the Russian Empire, and a President [Augustine Capodistrias] to Greece itself before the arrival of the Bavarians, should feel it a grievance that its people are not admissible to the highest posts in some government or other.] 612 *as* 611 . . . given a minister of . . . *as* 611

dereliction of the highest moral trust which can devolve upon a nation: and if they do not even aim at it, they are selfish usurpers, on a par in criminality with any of those whose ambition and rapacity have sported from age to age with the destiny of masses of mankind.

As it is already a common, and is rapidly tending to become the universal, condition of the more backward populations, to be either held in direct subjection by the more advanced, or to be under their complete political ascendancy; there are in this age of the world few more important problems, than how to organize this rule, so as to make it a good instead of an evil to the subject people, providing them with the best attainable present government, and with the conditions most favourable to future permanent improvement. But the mode of fitting the government for this purpose, is by no means so well understood as the conditions of good government in a people capable of governing themselves. We may even say, that it is not understood at all.

The thing appears perfectly easy to superficial observers. If India (for example) is not fit to govern itself, all that seems to them required is, that there should be a minister to govern it: and that this minister, like all other British ministers, should be responsible to the British Parliament. Unfortunately this, though the simplest mode of attempting to govern a dependency, is about the worst; and betrays in its advocates a total want of comprehension of the conditions of good government. To govern a country under responsibility to the people of that country, and to govern one country under responsibility to the people of another, are two very different things. What makes the excellence of the first, is that freedom is preferable to despotism: but the last *is* despotism. The only choice the case admits, is a choice of despotisms: and it is not certain that the despotism of twenty millions is necessarily better than that of a few, or of one. But it is quite certain, that the despotism of those who neither hear, nor see, nor know anything about their subjects, has many chances of being worse than that of those who do. It is not usually thought that the immediate agents of authority govern better because they govern in the name of an absent master, and of one who has a thousand more pressing interests to attend to. The master may hold them to a strict responsibility, enforced by heavy penalties; but it is very questionable if those penalties will often fall in the right place.

It is always under great difficulties, and very imperfectly, that a country can be governed by foreigners; even when there is no extreme disparity, in habits and ideas, between the rulers and the ruled. Foreigners do not feel with the people. They cannot judge, by the light in which a thing appears to their own minds, or the manner in which it affects their feelings, how it will affect the feelings or appear to the minds of the subject population.

What a native of the country, of average practical ability, knows as it were by instinct, they have to learn slowly, and after all imperfectly, by study and experience. The laws, the customs, the social relations, for which they have to legislate, instead of being familiar to them from childhood, are all strange to them. For most of their detailed knowledge they must depend on the information of natives; and it is difficult for them to know whom to trust. They are feared, suspected, probably disliked by the population; seldom sought by them except for interested purposes; and they are prone to think that the servilely submissive are the trustworthy. Their danger is of despising the natives; that of the natives is, of disbelieving that anything the strangers do can be intended for their good. These are but a part of the difficulties that any rulers have to struggle with, who honestly attempt to govern well a country in which they are foreigners. To overcome these difficulties in any degree, will always be a work of much labour, requiring a very superior degree of capacity in the chief administrators, and a high average among the subordinates: and the best organization of such a government is that which will best ensure the labour, develope the capacity, and place the highest specimens of it in the situations of greatest trust. Responsibility to an authority which has gone through none of the labour, acquired none of the capacity, and for the most part is not even aware that either, in any peculiar degree, is required, cannot be regarded as a very effectual expedient for accomplishing these ends.

The government of a people by itself has a meaning, and a reality; but such a thing as government of one people by another, does not and cannot exist. One people may keep another as a warren or preserve for its own use, a place to make money in, a human cattle farm to be worked for the profit of its own inhabitants. But if the good of the governed is the proper business of a government, it is utterly impossible that a people should directly attend to it. The utmost they can do is to give some of their best men a commission to look after it; to whom the opinion of their own country can neither be much of a guide in the performance of their duty, nor a competent judge of the mode in which it has been performed. Let any one consider how the English themselves would be governed, if they knew and cared no more about their own affairs, than they know and care about the affairs of the Hindoos. Even this comparison gives no adequate idea of the state of the case: for a people thus indifferent to politics altogether, would probably be simply acquiescent, and let the government alone: whereas in the case of India, a politically active people like the English, amidst habitual acquiescence, are every now and then interfering, and almost always in the wrong place. The real causes which determine the prosperity or wretchedness, the improvement or deterioration, of the Hindoos, are too far off to be within their ken. They have not the knowledge necessary for suspecting the existence of those causes, much less for judging of their operation. The most essential interests of the country may be well administered without obtaining any of their approbation, or mismanaged to almost any excess without attracting their notice. The purposes for which they are principally tempted to interfere, and control the proceedings of their delegates, are of two kinds. One is, to force English ideas down the throats of the natives; for instance, by measures of proselytism, or acts intentionally or unintentionally offensive to the religious feelings of the people. This misdirection of opinion in the ruling country is instructively exemplified (the more so, because nothing is meant but justice and fairness, and as much impartiality as can be expected from persons really convinced) by the demand now so general in England for having the Bible taught, at the option of pupils or of their parents, in the Government schools. From the European point of view nothing can wear a fairer aspect, or seem less open to objection on the score of religious freedom. To Asiatic eyes it is quite another thing. No Asiatic people ever believes that a government puts its paid officers and official machinery into motion unless it is bent upon an object; and when bent on an object, no Asiatic believes that any government, except a feeble and contemptible one, pursues it by halves. If Government schools and schoolmasters taught Christianity, whatever pledges might be given of teaching it only to those who spontaneously sought it, no amount of evidence would ever persuade the parents that improper means were not used to make their children Christians, or at all events, outcasts from Hindooism. If they could, in the end, be convinced of the contrary, it would only be by the entire failure of the schools, so conducted, to make any converts. If the teaching had the smallest effect in promoting its object, it would compromise not only the utility and even existence of the government education, but perhaps the safety of the government itself. An English Protestant would not be easily induced, by disclaimers of proselytism, to place his children in a Roman Catholic seminary: Irish Catholics will not send their children to schools in which they can be made Protestants: and we expect that Hindoos, who believe that the privileges of Hindooism can be forfeited by a merely physical act, will expose theirs to the danger of being made Christians!

Such is one of the modes in which the opinion of the dominant country tends to act more injuriously than beneficially on the conduct of its deputed governors. In other respects, its interference is likely to be oftenest exercised where it will be most pertinaciously demanded, and that is, on behalf of some interest of the English settlers. English settlers have friends at home, have organs, have access to the public; they have a common language, and common ideas with their countrymen: any complaint by an Englishman is more sympathetically heard, even if no unjust preference is intentionally accorded to it. Now, if there be a fact to which all experience testifies, it is that when a country holds another in subjection, the individuals of the ruling people who resort to the foreign country to make their fortunes, are of all others those who most need to be held under powerful restraint. They are always one of the chief difficulties of the government. Armed with the *prestige* and filled with the scornful overbearingness of the conquering nation, they have the feelings inspired by absolute power, without its sense of responsibility. Among a people like that of India, the utmost efforts of the public authorities are not enough for the effectual protection of the weak against the strong: and of all the strong, the European settlers are the strongest. Wherever the demoralizing effect of the situation is not in a most remarkable degree corrected by the personal character of the individual, they think the people of the country mere dirt under their feet: it seems to them monstrous that any rights of the natives should stand in the way of their smallest pretensions: the simplest act of protection to the inhabitants against any act of power on their part which they may consider useful to their commercial objects, they denounce, and sincerely regard, as an injury. So natural is this state of feeling in a situation like theirs, that even under the discouragement which it has hitherto met with from the ruling authorities it is impossible that more or less of the spirit should not perpetually break out. The Government, itself free from this spirit, is never able sufficiently to keep it down in the young and raw even of its own civil and military officers, over whom it has so much more control than over the independent residents. As it is with the English in India, so, according to trustworthy testimony, it is with the French in Algiers; so with the Americans, in the countries conquered from Mexico; so it seems to be with the Europeans in China, and already even in Japan: there is no necessity to recal how it was with the Spaniards in South America. In all these cases, the government to which these private adventurers are subject, is better than they, and does the most it can to protect the natives against them. Even the Spanish Government did this, sincerely and earnestly, though ineffectually, as is known to every reader of Mr. Helps' instructive history.[*] Had the Spanish Government been directly accountable to Spanish opinion, we may question if it would have made the attempt: for the Spaniards, doubtless, would have taken part with their Christian friends and relations rather than with Pagans. The settlers, not the natives, have the ear of the public at home; it is they whose representations are likely to pass for truth, because they alone have both the means and the motive to press them perseveringly upon the inattentive and uninterested public mind. The distrustful

[*Arthur Helps, *The Spanish Conquest in America, and its relation to the history of slavery and to the government of the Colonies*, 4 vols. (London: Parker, 1855–61).]

criticism with which Englishmen, more than any other people, are in the habit of scanning the conduct of their country towards foreigners, they usually reserve for the proceedings of the public authorities. In all questions between a government and an individual, the presumption in every Englishman's mind is, that the government is in the wrong. And when the resident English bring the batteries of English political action to bear upon any of the bulwarks erected to protect the natives against their encroachments, the executive, with their real but faint velleities of something better, generally find it safer to their parliamentary interest, and at any rate less troublesome, to give up the disputed position, than to defend it.

What makes matters worse is, that when the public mind is invoked (as, to its credit, the English mind is extremely open to be) in the name of justice and philanthropy, in behalf of the subject community or race, there is the same probability of its missing the mark. For in the subject community also there are oppressors and oppressed; powerful individuals or classes, and slaves prostrate before them; and it is the former, not the latter, who have the means of access to the English public. A tyrant or sensualist who has been deprived of the power he had abused, and instead of punishment, is supported in as great wealth and splendour as he ever enjoyed; a knot of privileged landholders, who demand that the State should relinquish to them its reserved right to a rent from their lands, or who resent as a wrong any attempt to protect the masses from their extortion; these have no difficulty in procuring interested or sentimental advocacy in the British Parliament and press. The silent myriads obtain none.

The preceding observations exemplify the operation of a principle—which might be called an obvious one, were it not that scarcely anybody seems to be aware of it—that, while responsibility to the governed is the greatest of all securities for good government, responsibility to somebody else not only has no such tendency, but is as likely to produce evil as good. The responsibility of the British rulers of India to the British nation is chiefly useful because, when any acts of the government are called in question, it ensures publicity and discussion; the utility of which does not require that the public at large should comprehend the point at issue, provided there are any individuals among them who do; for a merely moral responsibility not being responsibility to the collective people, but to every separate person among them who forms a judgment, opinions may be weighed as well as counted,[*] and the approbation or disapprobation of one person well versed in the subject, may outweigh that of thousands who know nothing about it at all. It is doubtless a useful restraint upon the immediate rulers that they can be put upon their defence, and that one or two of the jury will form an opinion worth having about their conduct, though that of the re-

[*Adapted from Coleridge; cf. p. 458n above.]

mainder will probably be several degrees worse than none. Such as it is, this is the amount of benefit to India, from the control exercised over the Indian government by the British Parliament and people.

It is not by attempting to rule directly a country like India, but by giving it good rulers, that the English people can do their duty to that country; and they can scarcely give it a worse one than an English Cabinet Minister, who is thinking of English, not Indian politics; who *seldom remains* long enough in office to acquire an intelligent interest in so complicated a subject; upon whom the factitious public opinion got up in Parliament, consisting of two or three fluent speakers, acts with as much force as if it were genuine; while he is under none of the influences of training and position which would lead or qualify him to form an honest opinion of his own. A free country which attempts to govern a distant dependency, inhabited by a dissimilar people, by means of a branch of its own executive, will almost inevitably fail. The only mode which has any chance of tolerable success, is to govern through a delegated body, of a comparatively permanent character; allowing only a right of inspection, and a negative voice, to the changeable Administration of the State. Such a body did exist in the case of India; and I fear that both India and England will pay a severe penalty for the shortsighted policy by which this intermediate instrument of government was done away with.

It is of no avail to say that such a delegated body cannot have all the requisites of good government; above all, cannot have that complete and ever-operative identity of interest with the governed, which it is so difficult to obtain even where the people to be ruled are in some degree qualified to look after their own affairs. Real good government is not compatible with the conditions of the case. There is but a choice of imperfections. The problem is, so to construct the governing body that, under the difficulties of the position, it shall have as much interest as possible in good government, and as little in bad. Now these conditions are best found in an intermediate body. A delegated administration has always this advantage over a direct one, that it has, at all events, no duties to perform except to the governed. It has no interests to consider except theirs. Its own power of deriving profit from misgovernment may be reduced—in the latest constitution of the East India Company it was reduced—to a singularly small amount: and it can be kept entirely clear of bias from the individual or class interests of any one else. When the home government and Parliament are swayed by *those* partial influences in the exercise of the power reserved to them in the last resort, the intermediate body is the certain advocate and champion of the dependency before the imperial tribunal. The intermediate body, moreover, is, in the

*ⁱ⁻ⁱ*611   does not remain
*ʲ⁻ʲ*611   such

natural course of things, chiefly composed of persons who have acquired professional knowledge of this part of their country's concerns; who have been trained to it in the place itself, and have made its administration the main occupation of their lives. Furnished with these qualifications, and not being liable to lose their office from the accidents of home politics, they identify their character and consideration with their special trust, and have a much more permanent interest in the success of their administration, and in the prosperity of the country which they administer, than a member of a Cabinet under a representative constitution can possibly have in the good government of any country except the one which he serves. So far as the choice of those who carry on the management on the spot devolves upon this body, *k*the appointments are*k* kept out of the vortex of party and parliamentary jobbing, and freed from the influence of those motives to the abuse of patronage, for the reward of adherents, or to buy off those who would otherwise be opponents, which are always stronger, with statesmen of average honesty, than a conscientious sense of the duty of appointing the fittest man. To put this one class of appointments as far as possible out of harm's way, is of more consequence than the worst which can happen to all other offices in the state; for, in every other department, if the officer is unqualified, the general opinion of the community directs him in a certain degree what to do; but in the position of the administrators of a dependency where the people are not fit to have the control in their own hands, the character of the government entirely depends on the qualifications, moral and intellectual, of the individual functionaries.

It cannot be too often repeated, that in a country like India everything depends on the personal qualities and capacities of the agents of government. This truth is the cardinal principle of Indian administration. The day when it comes to be thought that the appointment of persons to situations of trust from motives of convenience, already so criminal in England, can be practised with impunity in India, will be the beginning of the decline and fall of our empire there. Even with a sincere intention of preferring the best candidate, it will not do to rely on chance for supplying fit persons. The system must be calculated to form them. It has done this hitherto; and because it has done so, our rule in India has lasted, and been one of constant, if not very rapid, improvement in prosperity and good administration. As much bitterness is now manifested against this system, and as much eagerness displayed to overthrow it, as if educating and training the officers of government for their work were a thing utterly unreasonable and indefensible, an unjustifiable interference with the rights of ignorance and inexperience. There is a tacit conspiracy between those who would like to job in first-rate Indian offices for their connexions here, and those who, being

*k-k*611   their appointment is

already in India, claim to be promoted from the indigo factory or the attorney's office, to administer justice or fix the payments due to government from millions of people. The "monopoly" of the Civil Service, so much inveighed against, is like the monopoly of judicial offices by the bar; and its abolition would be like opening the bench in Westminster Hall to the first comer whose friends certify that he has now and then looked into Blackstone.[*] Were the course ever adopted of sending men from this country, or encouraging them in going out, to get themselves put into high appointments without having learnt their business by passing through the lower ones, the most important offices would be thrown to Scotch cousins and adventurers, connected by no professional feeling with the country or the work, held to no previous knowledge, and eager only to make money rapidly and return home. The safety of the country is, that those by whom it is administered *be* sent out in youth, as candidates only, to begin at the bottom of the ladder, and ascend higher or not, as, after a proper interval, they are proved qualified. The defect of the East India Company's system was, that though the best men were carefully sought out for the most important posts, yet if an officer remained in the service, promotion, though it might be delayed, came at last in some shape or other, to the least as well as to the most competent. Even the inferior in qualifications, among such a corps of functionaries, consisted, it must be remembered, of men who had been brought up to their duties, and had fulfilled them for many years, at lowest without disgrace, under the eye and authority of a superior. But though this diminished the evil, it was nevertheless considerable. A man who never becomes fit for more than an assistant's duty, should remain an assistant all his life, and his juniors should be promoted over him. With this exception, I am not aware of any real defect in the old system of Indian appointments. It had already received the greatest other improvement it was susceptible of, the choice of the original candidates by competitive examination: which, besides the advantage of recruiting from a higher grade of industry and capacity, has the recommendation, that under it, unless by accident, there are no personal ties between the candidates for offices and those who have a voice in conferring them.

It is in no way unjust, that public officers thus selected and trained should be exclusively eligible to offices which require specially Indian knowledge and experience. If any door to the higher appointments, without passing through the lower, be opened even for occasional use, there will be such incessant knocking at it by persons of influence, that it will be impossible ever to keep it closed. The only excepted appointment should be the high-

[*William Blackstone, *Commentaries on the Laws of England*, 4 vols. (Oxford: Clarendon Press, 1765–69).]

*l-l*611   are

est one of all. The Viceroy of British India should be a person selected from all Englishmen for his great general capacity for government. If he have this, he will be able to distinguish in others, and turn to his own use, that special knowledge and judgment in local affairs which he has not himself had the opportunity of acquiring. There are good reasons why *m*(saving exceptional cases)*m* the Viceroy should not be a member of the regular service. All services have, more or less, their class prejudices, from which the supreme ruler ought to be exempt. Neither are men, however able and experienced, who have passed their lives in Asia, so likely to possess the most advanced European ideas in general statesmanship; which the chief ruler should carry out with him, and blend with the results of Indian experience. Again, being of a different class, and especially if chosen by a different authority, he will seldom have any personal partialities to warp his appointments to office. This great security for honest bestowal of patronage existed in rare perfection, under the mixed government of the Crown and the East India Company. The supreme dispensers of office, the Governor-General and Governors, were appointed, in fact though not formally, by the Crown, that is, by the general Government, not by the intermediate body; and a great officer of the Crown probably had not a single personal or political connexion in the local service: while the delegated body, most of whom had themselves served in the country, had, and were likely to have, such connexions. This guarantee for impartiality would be much impaired, if the civil servants of Government, even though sent out in boyhood as mere candidates for employment, should come to be furnished, in any considerable proportion, by the class of society which supplies Viceroys and Governors. Even the initiatory competitive examination would then be an insufficient security. It would exclude mere ignorance and incapacity; it would compel youths of family to start in the race with the same amount of instruction and ability as other people; the stupidest son could not be put into the Indian service, as he can be into the Church; but there would be nothing to prevent undue preference afterwards. No longer all equally unknown and unheard of by the arbiter of their lot, a portion of the service would be personally, and a still greater number politically, in close relation with him. Members of certain families, and of the higher classes and influential connexions generally, would rise more rapidly than their competitors, and be often kept in situations for which they were unfit, or placed in those for which others were fitter. The same influences would be brought into play, which affect promotions in the army: and those alone, if such miracles of simplicity there be, who believe that these are impartial, would expect impartiality in those of India. This evil is, I fear, irremediable by any general measures which can be taken under the present system. No such

m-m+65

will afford a degree of security comparable to that which once flowed spontaneously from the so-called double government.

What is accounted so great an advantage in the case of the English system of government at home, has been its misfortune in India—that it grew up of itself, not from preconceived design, but by successive expedients, and by the adaptation of machinery originally created for a different purpose. As the country on which its maintenance depended, was not the one out of whose necessities it grew, its practical benefits did not come home to the mind of that country, and it would have required theoretic recommendations to render it acceptable. Unfortunately, these were exactly what it seemed to be destitute of: and undoubtedly the common theories of government did not furnish it with such, framed as those theories have been for states of circumstances differing in all the most important features from the case concerned. But in government, as in other departments of human agency, almost all principles which have been durable were first suggested by observation of some particular case, in which the general laws of nature acted in some new or previously unnoticed combination of circumstances. The institutions of Great Britain, and those of the United States, have had the distinction of suggesting most of the theories of government which, through good and evil fortune, are now, in the course of generations, re-awakening political life in the nations of Europe. It has been the destiny of the government of the East India Company, to suggest the true theory of the government of a semi-barbarous dependency by a civilized country, and after having done this, to perish. It would be a singular fortune if, at the end of two or three more generations, this speculative result should be the only remaining fruit of our ascendancy in India; if posterity should say of us, that having stumbled accidentally upon better arrangements than our wisdom would ever have devised, the first use we made of our awakened reason was to destroy them, and allow the good which had been in course of being realized to fall through and be lost, from ignorance of the principles on which it depended. *Dî meliora*:[*] but if a fate so disgraceful to England and to civilization can be averted, it must be through far wider political conceptions than merely English or European practice can supply, and through a much more profound study of Indian experience, and of the conditions of Indian government, than either English politicians, or those who supply the English public with opinions, have hitherto shown any willingness to undertake.

[*See, e.g., Cicero, *De Senectute* (Latin and English), trans. W. A. Falconer (London: Heinemann; New York: Putnam's Sons, 1922), p. 58 (xiv.47).]

CENTRALISATION

1862

EDITOR'S NOTE

Edinburgh Review, CXV (Apr., 1862), 323–58, where it is headed "Act. II—1. *L'Individu et L'État*. Par M. [Charles Brook] DUPONT-WHITE, / 2me ed. Paris: [Guillaumin,] 1858. / 2. *La Centralisation; suite à L'Individu et l'État*. Par M. / DUPONT-WHITE. Paris: [Guillaumin,] 1860. / 3. *De la Centralisation et de ses Effets*. Par M. [Camille Hyacinthe] ODILON-BARROT. Paris: [Dumineray,] 1861." Unsigned; not republished. Identified in JSM's bibliography as "A review of M. Dupont White and M. Odilon Barrot's writings on Centralization, in the Edinburgh Review for April 1862" (MacMinn, 94). There are no corrections or emendations in the two copies of the article in the Somerville College Library, though on one copy, having cancelled the heading, JSM inked an asterisk after the running title ("Centralisation") on p. 323, and added a note, which begins "*Edinburgh Review*, April 1862" and then lists the three titles as in the *Edinburgh* heading. This being the footnote form he uses in the articles reprinted in *Dissertations and Discussions*, it seems likely that he intended to reprint this article in Vol. III, but changed his mind for unknown reasons. (There are no other periodical articles of which two cut copies remain in JSM's library in Somerville College, and the copy mentioned above is in loose sheets, as though for the printer.)

For comments on the composition of the essay, and related matters, see the Textual Introduction, lxxxvii–lxxxviii above.

Centralisation

THESE WORKS EXPRESS the opinions of two able and accomplished writers, taken from opposite points of view, on that one among the political questions of the age which bears the strongest marks of being destined to remain a question for generations to come—Centralisation; or in other words, the limits which separate the province of government from that of individual and spontaneous agency, and of central from local government. The importance of this question is constantly tending to increase, by the perpetual growth of collective action among mankind, and the progress made in the settlement of other questions which stand before it in the natural order of discussion. The more noisy and exciting subject of Forms of Government, which has for so many ages occupied the front rank of political controversy, is likely, with all its difficulties, to be much sooner, at least theoretically, settled; both as being simpler in itself, and because it admits, in any given country, of a more definite answer; whereas the answer to the question between governmental or central, and private or local, action is perpetually varying; depending not on any single principle, but on a compromise between principles, the elements of which are not exactly the same in any two applications. The degree in which political authority can justly and expediently interfere, either to control individuals and voluntary associations, to supersede them by doing their work for them, to guide and assist, or to invoke and draw forth their agency, varies not only with the wants of every country and age, and the capabilities of every people, but with the special requirements of every kind of work to be done.

The most despotic government, indeed, must leave by far the greatest part of the world's business to be transacted by the individuals whom it directly concerns; while in the freest countries there is much which is and must be undertaken by governments, because it is indispensable that it should be done, and impossible that individuals should do it. But between these limits there is a vast extent of debateable ground, on which the question is merely one of degree, turning upon a comparison of advantages; and so great are the advantages of either mode of proceeding, where circumstances and habits have brought it into vigorous and well-directed action, that inexhaustible arguments may be found on each side of the question. Unfortunately it is not on the merits of either individual or government agency at its best, that the question depends, but on the imperfections and shortcomings of both in their average condition; by far the strongest arguments of each side being drawn, not from the excellence of the kind of agency it advocates, but from the infirmities of its rival.

There can, among English thinkers, be no doubt, and there is at present as little among the principal thinkers on the other side of the Channel, that in all the great civilised countries of the world, except England and the United States, the governmental and central element is the one in excess, and that in a prodigious degree. Englishmen are accustomed to think that the nations of the Continent—and France the most conspicuously, as being in all other respects the most advanced—have been kept in a state of political infancy by over-government: that the concentration of the entire direction of national affairs in a bureaucracy has been more crushing in its effects on the character and capabilities of the nation than tyranny itself, and the main instrument by which tyranny has been established and maintained: that the government, by doing everything through its own officers, which it can possibly contrive so to do—by regulating minutely whatever it allows to be done by others, and requiring, in all cases which involve the smallest collective action, its own previous assent formally obtained, not only to the thing to be done, but to every item of the means proposed for doing it—has dwarfed not only the political, but in a great measure the entire practical, capacity of the people, and even their intellectual activity and moral aspirations in every field of mental action except pure theory. This, which had long been an established opinion in England, has now (with some abatement for exaggeration) become also the opinion of France; or, at all events, of the great majority of French thinkers, who are likely in the long run to form and guide the national sentiment.

The reaction in France against governmentalism and centralism, and in favour of individual and local agency, is at present intense. There was an undercurrent in this direction, when the general stream of opinion was setting strongest towards the opposite side. In the first years of the Restoration, the best of the Liberals and the leaders of the Ultra-Royalists joined for a time in demanding local franchises and a limitation of the powers of government. As M. Odilon-Barrot truly says (p. 12), men of such opposite opinions as MM. de Villèle, de Corbière, Benjamin Constant, Fiévée, Châteaubriand, Royer-Collard, were in this one respect unanimous. Unfortunately the movement slackened when the two great parties, at that time equally in opposition against the *juste milieu* policy of Louis XVIII, conceived the hope of getting into their own hands the powers which they had been desirous of restraining. The renewed and more serious movement in this beneficent direction is usually dated from the publication of the great work of M. de Tocqueville.

That eminent and deeply to be lamented thinker, more than any other person, took the lead in the new tendency of opinion. It was promoted by the writings and exertions of that valuable body of men, the political economists of France; almost the only writers on political and social subjects who were able to continue their teaching without reserve during the first years of the present French Government; and to whose opinions their recent triumph on the comparatively limited subject of Free Trade, has given an importance which they had long merited, but had not previously attained. The spontaneity and unfettered action of the individual, and of voluntary association, are, as all know, the life of modern political economy. Of all persons, a political economist is the one to whose opinions and associations any avoidable intervention of government in the affairs of society is the most repugnant. Accordingly the non-intervention theory is, by some French political economists (men of great talents and virtues, such as M. Dunoyer), carried to a length which even in England would be accounted excessive. They allow no post-office, no government roads, no public provision for the poor, no aids to education. They rely solely on the voluntary principle for meeting requirements, which even in the countries where individual enterprise, public spirit, and capacity of voluntary co-operation are at the highest, it has been found or thought necessary that the government should take under its care.

But far beyond any writings, in producing the change now manifesting itself in French opinion, is the operation of political events. If anything could alleviate the painful regret with which we regard the despotic government of Napoleon the Third, it would be the mode in which that despotism is purging the vision and ripening the political judgment of the French mind. A few years have done the work of generations, in making the chief representatives of French intellect understand what it is in the social system and national habits of their country, which made it possible for them, in the sixty-second year of their struggle for freedom, to be thrown back for an indeterminate period into a political servitude no less complete than before its commencement. Since that time it has become the habitual theme of the principal leaders of opinion in France that liberty is a more precious thing than equality; that equality in slavery makes slavery still more slavish; and that a people are not and cannot be free, unless they have learnt to dare and do for themselves, not fitfully, at intervals of a generation, by turning out one set of masters and putting in another, but in the practice of daily life: that a government which is allowed to meddle in everything, let its forms be never so free, is at all times little different from a despotism, and a word of command to a file of soldiers may at any time convert it into an avowed one: and that a national character capable of maintaining the control of the nation over the great affairs of State, is not consistent with the habit of looking to rulers for authorisation and guidance at every step in the smaller concerns of life. This doctrine is now earnestly taught by almost every French writer who has either retained or acquired reputation as a political thinker during the ten years that have elapsed since the *coup d'état*. The great Review which numbers among its contributors, either habitual or occasional, nearly all the first minds in France, and which from the sustained ability as well as the quantity of its matter (a bulk equal to that of an English Review once a fortnight) takes rank as the most important organ of French intellect, is pervaded everywhere by anti-centralisation principles. Not content with this, the more ardent and energetic spirits determined to have a Review, of which anti-centralism and the principle of individual liberty should be the main and governing feature; and they founded, in November, 1860, the *Revue Nationale*, also published fortnightly, a work in general character inferior only to the *Revue des Deux Mondes*, and not surpassed even by that in the merit of its principal articles, and in its treatment of the greater questions of politics and society.* No reader of these Reviews can mistake for a moment either the direction or the intensity of the present movement in French public opinion. Those who still adhere to the banner of centralisation, "the most splendid conquest of our Revolution," as writers of M. Thiers' school delighted to call it, are as fully aware as others that the tide is against them. "We are saturated with government" was the expression, on a late occasion, of one of the most enlightened and intellectual of their number. "It requires," he added, "a great strength of conviction to enable me to write as I do," namely, in favour of centralisation and state interference.

The work of M. Odilon-Barrot of which we have transcribed the title, is one of the manifestations of the new tendency. It belongs to a series of publications which, under the title of *Études Contemporaines*, have been commenced by a body of known and distinguished lovers of liberty; two of which, M. de Haussonville's *Lettre au Sénat*,[*] and that entitled *Les Anciens Par-*

---

*It seems invidious to single out particular writers for commendation where the general level is so high; yet we may be permitted to name the two contributors, who, more even than the rest, have hitherto given to this Review the tone and character which distinguish it: M. Edouard Laboulaye, who of the rising celebrities of France is the most peculiarly identified with the philosophy of individual liberty; and M. Lanfrey, not only one of the most enlightened politicians, but one of the most powerful political writers in France. Among their auxiliaries may be numbered some of the principal representatives of French Protestantism, to which Europe already owes so much, and which is now zealously reasserting its place in the ranks both of speculative and of practical thought; in particular M. de Pressensé, the best known, out of France, of living French Protestant theologians, and the founder and leader of that portion of the French Protestant Church which rejects pecuniary assistance from the State.

[*Joseph Othenin Bernard de Cléron, Comte d'Haussonville, *Lettre au Sénat* (Paris: Dumineray, 1860).]

tis,[*] for which M. Prévost-Paradol was sentenced to fine and imprisonment, have, from their bearing on the affairs of the moment, attracted some attention from newspaper writers and readers in England. M. Odilon-Barrot's book is short, and aims at being popular rather than philosophical; but it puts forth clearly, with earnest conviction and strong feeling, the leading points of the case; the evils of over-government, both as a matter of theory and principle, and, in France, of sad practical experience.

M. Dupont-White's two treatises, or rather one treatise in two parts, are of higher pretensions, which their author is quite competent to support. With a wide range of knowledge, and great resources applicable to illustration, M. Dupont-White combines a force and liveliness of expression, which recall the manner of the best French writers; and, what is of still greater importance, he has that habit of seeking and power of perceiving general truths, which enables him to place the opinions he supports, whether right or wrong, on the truest and least exceptionable grounds which their nature admits of. In the present case, he has taken the side which we regard as, on the whole, wrong: he has placed himself in opposition to a movement which we hold to be, within its present limits, eminently wise and salutary. Nevertheless we consider his performance to be, both in a philosophical and a practical point of view, of real value. There is much that may be truly and reasonably said on his side of the question; and it is a service to truth, when the tendency of opinion is in one direction, to give a *résumé* of the real *other side* of the matter—the valid reasons which have a claim to be taken into consideration, and estimated at what they are worth, apart from the fallacies and nonsense of more vulgar advocates, which, when they have ceased to carry the general opinion with them, an opponent can afford to disregard. This we find in M. Dupont-White's work; and it is well that a book should exist, which supplies in some respects a needful limitation and correction to the ideas now prevalent, and tends to prevent the reaction against State and central agency from running into a contrary excess, not only in itself injurious, but naturally provocative of a counter-reaction.

To these merits of M. Dupont-White's book is to be added that of entire candour. He not only never misrepresents, but he never slurs over, or purposely understates, the arguments on the other side. In our opinion, he often—indeed generally—undervalues them; but he is scrupulous in bringing them forward, and stating them with as much force and plausibility as if they were his own. This candour in statement is naturally accompanied by similar candour in judgment. Doing careful justice to the reasons of his opponents, he is almost necessarily led to do a considerable measure of justice to their conclusions. His concessions, accordingly, are great and

[*Lucien Anatole Prévost-Paradol, *Les Anciens Partis* (Paris: Dumineray, 1860).]

numerous; and though his premises are mostly favourable to State interference, and those of M. Odilon-Barrot unfavourable, there is a much less
amount of divergence than would naturally be expected in their practical
conclusions. The following, for instance, is M. Odilon-Barrot's statement
of grievances,—of the principal evils which he denounces in the French
administrative system:

We do not seek to impair that splendid unity of France, which a powerfully
concentrated government may have helped to constitute, but which liberty alone
can cement and preserve. What we reject in centralisation is its excess. We regard
as excessive a centralisation, which by the confusion of spiritual and temporal
power, or by their alliance, infringes directly or indirectly, either for religious
or political purposes, upon freedom of conscience and worship. We object to a
centralisation which, sometimes on the plea of guardianship and sometimes of
police, subjects to its preventive control the collective and even the individual
rights of the citizens; which, for example, on the pretext that the communes are
incapable of managing their own affairs, manages them through its own agents,
appoints their mayors, their tax-collectors, their schoolmasters, their *curés*, and
almost their *gardes-champêtres*; will not suffer their councils to assemble without its permission; reserves to itself the framing of their annual estimates, and
even after an outlay has been voted and sanctioned, claims to govern its execution, by imposing on the unfortunate communes who pay the cost, its own plans,
its own engineers, its own architects. I hold as excessive a centralisation which so
ties up almost every act of a citizen by the necessity of a previous authorisation,
that he is not permitted to pray to God, nor to move from one place to another,
unless at its good pleasure. I denounce as an abuse, a centralisation which, while
giving to the agents of the Government all this power over private citizens,
refuses to them all judicial redress against those agents, who are declared
inviolable under the protection of a Council of State chosen by the Government;
a centralisation which, by means of conflicts which it raises and resolves at its
own option, supersedes the regular tribunals, and evokes to itself the decision
of every cause in which it declares itself to have an interest. I, lastly, reject a
centralisation of which the appetite, always excited and never satisfied, incessantly
menaces every thing resembling an independent existence which may still remain
in the country; extending its hand, now over the estates of hospitals, now over
those of communes, now over the great railway and insurance companies. A
centralisation such as this, which would end by reducing the individual to the
condition of an automaton, is what I attack, and I will attempt to portray its
fatal effects. (Pp. 63–6.)

Now, to almost every article of this programme M. Dupont-White has
given, in some part or other of his two volumes, either an express or an
implied adhesion. That worst tyranny of all, the emancipation of Government officers from responsibility to the courts of justice,—the impossibility
of suing or prosecuting a public functionary for any illegal act of power,
without the previous consent of the Government, through its organ, the
"Conseil d'État,"—M. Dupont-White calls an "enormity;" and says that its
continuance during thirty years of constitutional government is only intel-

ligible, because the publicity inherent in representative institutions was a sufficient practical guarantee against its mischiefs; thus showing with sufficient plainness what he thinks of the mode in which it must operate under the present French Government. We give M. Dupont-White credit for being kept right, by his feelings as a lover of liberty, on the principle of an institution which places the executive openly above the laws. But his notion that such an institution was or might be innocuous under a Parliamentary form of government, would almost lead us to think of him as one who only cares for protecting the collective body of the nation from great acts of high-handed oppression by the chiefs of the State, against which free discussion and representative institutions really are a considerable security; but thinks nothing of the universal habit of trembling before every petty public officer, which, beyond almost everything else that can be named, renders a people incapable of liberty. How should they not be slavish, when anyone wearing a Government uniform, so long as he takes care to be servile to all persons of station who are on good terms with the Government, can domineer at will over all the rest,—well knowing that instead of laying a complaint before the nearest magistrate, they have no refuge but an appeal to his own, perhaps distant, employer? What protection are a free press and Parliamentary government to them? Who will hear, or who will attend to, their complaints? It is a most significant fact, that, of this exclusive right to judge in its own cause, no French Government, however constitutional or liberal in its professions, has been able to make up its mind to divest itself. This alone, of the promises of the Charter of 1830, remained through the eighteen years of the reign of Louis Philippe unredeemed.

M. Odilon-Barrot's treatise falls in so thoroughly with the reigning tone of sentiment in this country, that we deem it needless to give any analysis of its contents; but we propose to do this rather fully in the case of M. Dupont-White. To understand a mode of thought different from our own, is always a valuable acquisition; and on a subject where everything depends on a correct balancing of opposite considerations, there is a peculiar propriety in studying the face of the question with which most of us are least familiar. It must be said, however, that the work of M. Dupont-White, though rich in matter, does not entirely satisfy us by the mode in which this matter is presented and disposed. There is true French point and felicity in the manner in which each thought is separately expressed. But we miss, in some degree, that well-marked separation of the various particulars of which the case is made up, ranging each idea or argument under the most appropriate head, which usually distinguishes the expositions and discussions of French thinkers,—that skilful marshalling of topics and arguments, which gives to their best works at once a scientific and an artistic character,— one thought never jostling or encumbering another, but appearing to occupy the position which is at once the most natural to it, and that in which it groups most impressively with, and lends the most effective support to, the rest. The titles of M. Dupont-White's chapters point to an arrangement of topics, but in the execution he almost loses sight of it; allowing a mind, full of the subject, to pour forth, in every one of the divisions, matter from all the rest, so profusely that though much of what he says is excellently well said, the general impression is almost one of confusion; and after a first reading, one rather feels that the writer has a great deal to say, and has brought forward many strong arguments, than knows exactly what these are, and to which of the difficulties of the subject they especially apply. We shall endeavour,—not adhering to the writer's own order, but taking his ideas where we find them, and his arguments and illustrative statements where he has expressed them best,—to give some conception of the general purport of his observations.

According to M. Dupont-White, the absorption of the last few generations in the work of establishing the control of nations over their rulers, together with the exaggerated claims made in behalf of governments by Socialists in theory, and by despotisms in practice, have engendered a prejudice in the contrary direction, which regards the intervention of the State in the affairs of society as inherently an evil and a danger. He looks upon the State as, in all stages of civilisation, the main instrument and organ of Progress; a strong and earnest faith in which is one of the most marked as well as the most honourable features of his treatise. Man (he says), as a being whose selfish are ordinarily stronger than his moral feelings, naturally requires to be governed.[*] He requires it more, not less, as society advances. For though, on the one hand, improvement, the result of experience, renders his selfishness in many respects more enlightened, yet, on the other, the advance of civilisation holds out to selfishness ever new opportunities and fields of action, to which the lessons of the past do not strictly apply, and in which the process of instructing and disciplining selfishness has to be continually renewed. Under these conditions, the conflicting self-interest of individuals, and, above all, of classes, requires an arbiter, deciding not on the impulses of the particular occasion, but on general rules and comprehensive views; and the Government, when properly constituted, and duly responsible to the nation, *is* that arbiter: being, by its position, more impartial than any separate section of society can possibly be, and therefore qualified to sit in judgment on the conflicting pretensions of each, and to make a fairer and better compromise between them than it is at all to be expected that they would be able to work out by a hostile struggle.

Against this doctrine, while confined to generals, there is nothing to be said. All theories permit the State to establish whatever laws are necessary

[*See *L'Individu et l'État*, pp. 217–18.]

to protect the legitimate rights of persons and classes against the selfishness of one another. But to prove that this is a growing exigency, that the demand for legal intervention is an increasing demand as society advances, which is the essential point of our author's case, his argument is as follows.

The first and greatest duty of the State, in all stages of society, is to protect the weak against the strong. Now, the operation of Progress is to give to the State ever new duties of this description to discharge. We can look back to a time when the State exerted very little power over the great majority of the community. But is it supposed that because the State did not, nobody else did? Quite the reverse. The State did not concern itself about the multitude, because they were under the absolute power of masters, who could be made responsible for them. Law and government recognised, as legally existing, only the few in authority: the slave-masters, the heads of families, the patriarchal chiefs of tribes or clans. Improving civilisation changes this state of things—relieves man from the power of man, and brings him under that of the law. Has not the State necessarily a wider range of action, when it is expected to protect the slave, the wife, the child, the debtor, instead of leaving them to the will and pleasure of masters, husbands, fathers, and creditors? These primitive superiors once had power of life and death over those who were subject to them. It was the State which freed the weaker party from this despotism. The State alone could have done it, and on the State rests the duty of doing it, wherever it still remains to be done.

All this is admitted, and forms no part of the debateable ground. The power here claimed for the State is within its acknowledged functions. As long as any wrongful authority is exercised by human beings over one another, the State has still the duty of abolishing it. As long as any, even necessary, authority can be tyrannically abused, it is incumbent on the State to repress and punish the tyranny. To protect all human beings against injury from those who are stronger than themselves, whether the superiority of strength is physical or the gift of the law, is a function conceded to governments by those who are most eager to restrict their action. But does it follow that by extending the protection of law to classes unjustly excluded from it, the business of protection is made more difficult or operose? It may require more tribunals, but why should it need more laws? What more need be done for the emancipated classes, than merely not to refuse to them the legal remedies which are open to all others?

M. Dupont-White answers: The State cannot leave the newly enfranchised classes to shift afterwards for themselves. Though enfranchised, they are still the weakest, unable to contend on equal terms with their former masters. These will be struggling to exert their old authority by new means, and take all advantage which the new social relations allow, of the superior strength which still remains to them. The State must be prepared to meet every such attempt at encroachment by fresh precautions and acts of guardianship.

Whenever (for example) the depressed classes of society are striving upwards, the constitution of property will infallibly require modification. The first use which the emancipated classes endeavour to make of their liberty, is to acquire property; but the organisation of society has previously been such as to make property inaccessible to them. Generations or even ages must pass, before the descendants of serfs are enabled to exert their labour and enterprise on terms of fair equality with their former masters. Nor has this ever been effected but through a succession of laws or edicts, and by holding out at every step the helping hand of the State. The history of modern Europe is a series of such legislative acts, of which the great changes made at the French Revolution were the culmination. The nations of our own day have experienced the same necessity when emancipating their colonial slaves. And we may remark in confirmation, that the question of property forms the principal difficulty in that great work of justice and civilisation now in progress, the enfranchisement of the Russian serfs. M. Dupont-White has an easy victory while he confines himself to barbarous or backward countries. The nominal emancipation of the peasants of Esthonia and Livonia left them nearly as much serfs as before. But he is mistaken in supposing that in the British West Indies it has been necessary to retain any State protectorship over the negroes. The measures of that character which he specifies were all antecedent to emancipation. They were the incidents and consequences of slavery, and ceased with it. The conclusion which they justify is directly opposite to that of M. Dupont-White. They illustrate a tendency, the reverse of that which he alleges; the diminished need of State action as institutions improve. They are an example, from how much minute supervision, from how many cares and labours for the protection and general benefit of the less favoured classes, the State can exempt itself by doing them complete justice once for all; how much of the energy and forethought of society in behalf of individuals, is only needed because it does not choose to set free their own.

When our author argues that many relations between man and man, which were once left to the arbitration of force or the authority of a master, become the subject of legal regulation in a more advanced state, he says what nobody denies; and it is only to make clear the general scope of his argument that we dwell on this portion of the subject. But we now come upon controverted ground. M. Dupont-White says:

When the State has put an end to the oppression of law, it has still to prevent *l'exploitation naturelle*, the unfair use of natural advantages. . . . Merely not to subordinate and sacrifice some to others as if they were an inferior species, cannot be the *dernier mot*, the last achievement of civilisation. Can we forget what an amount of difference exists between human beings, and think only of their general resemblance? Can it be overlooked, that these differences, left to themselves, would subject all weakness, bodily or intellectual, to the ascendancy of the strongest, the ablest, the most persevering; and that this domination by virtue of nature, would be as oppressive as that which was formerly exercised by virtue of the law? Nature itself requires to be rectified, as well as institutions. But who shall correct the abuse of natural superiorities except the State? And how can the State do so, unless by an accession of strength and of attributions? (*L'Individu et l'État*, pp. 54–5.)

Here commences the great divergence between our author's doctrine and that of nearly all English thinkers. These concede to the State the right and duty of regulating, and, when possible, abolishing, the artificial inequalities of which it is itself the author. But they do not admit that it should concern itself with natural inequalities. That "the abuse" of these should be corrected they willingly admit, for who will affirm that abuses of any kind ought not to be interfered with? But they consider nothing as an abuse of natural superiority, except force or fraud. Provided these are abstained from, they hold it good that the strong should be allowed to reap the full advantage of their strength. It is only thus, they think, that all the members of the community are incited to exert their strength, and to cultivate it. Those who take this ground have on their side much of the reason of the case; yet not all of it; for in racing for a prize, the stimulus to exertion on the part of the competitors is only at its highest when all start fair, that is, when natural inequalities are compensated by artificial weights; and the complaint is, that in the race of life all do not start fair; and that unless the State does something to strengthen the weaker side, the unfairness becomes utterly crushing and dispiriting.

According to M. Dupont-White, as productive industry advances, there is a natural and growing antagonism of conflicting interests—land, capital, and labour. Ought there, he asks, to be no moderator in these conflicts; no one to arbitrate between jarring self-interests, each equally inconsiderate of the reasonable claims of the others—and to prescribe, and if necessary enforce, some just rule, or to say the least, some admissible terms of compromise? To this question English thinkers almost unanimously answer— No. All that the State should do is to maintain the peace. Competition in a free market, can alone show what terms of accommodation are reasonable, and enforce those terms on the contending parties. If this were universally true, there would be an end to the question. That it is true for the most part, and that the onus of making out a case rests on those who contend for an exception, is indisputable. But M. Dupont-White easily proves, from the example of England itself, that exceptions in growing numbers do from time to time manifest themselves. From the period when England began to feel the effects of the astonishing growth of her manufacturing industry, new authoritative interferences with freedom of contract have been forced upon her every few years. Parliament has regulated the hours of labour. It has prohibited the employment of children under a certain age.[*] It has interdicted, in mines, the employment of women as well as children.[†] It has imposed upon manufacturers precautions against accident and unhealthiness, instead of depending on the operatives to enforce such precautions by refusal to work.[‡] It has insisted on a certain amount of professional competency in masters of merchantmen, lest people should voluntarily entrust themselves or their property to incapable seamanship.[§] It has made imperative on owners of emigrant ships to carry medical officers, and not to crowd their vessels beyond certain limits, that the greed of gain or the competition for cheapness may not avail itself of the opportunities which the poverty, ignorance, or recklessness of intending emigrants holds out.[‖] It has made unlawful the construction of houses which it deems unfit for the habitation of human beings; though the pure doctrine of competition would leave it to the poor to correct the evil by refusing to live in them.[§§]

M. Dupont-White argues, that it may be the duty of government to protect those who depend on labour for their subsistence, against excess of suffering from those industrial improvements, which in the first instance are only beneficial to employers and unproductive consumers. Again, he observes, every great industrial improvement is, or is thought to be, detrimental to some individual interests, which, left to the mere operation of the law, would have power to thwart the improvement, or to exact, as the price of acquiescence, terms extremely onerous to society. England has had cause to know this in the case of railways, docks, harbours, roads, town improvements. The intervention of the State is necessary, to quell the resistance of those private interests, and fix the compensation due to them. Such enterprises, also, often require pecuniary aid from the State. Even in England, ocean steam navigation and marine telegraphs are not able to dispense with it.

If it be said that civilisation, by diffusing knowledge and strengthening the moral sentiments, diminishes the necessity for government, inasmuch as it causes men to identify more and more their interest and feelings with the general good, M. Dupont-White, to a certain extent, admits the fact; but urges, that since the same progress makes society and its interests more complicated, greater compass and elevation of mind become necessary for

[*3 & 4 William IV, c. 103 (1833).]
[†5 & 6 Victoria, c. 99 (1842).]
[‡7 & 8 Victoria, c. 15 (1844).]
[§13 & 14 Victoria, c. 93 (1850).]
[‖5 & 6 William IV, c. 53 (1835).]
[§§11 & 12 Victoria, c. 63 (1848).]

comprehending them; while the amount of those qualities in society, instead of increasing with the need, rather tends to fall off, as the subdivision of labour, and increasing speciality of men's particular occupations, restrict the attention and accurate knowledge of each individual to a narrower circle of ideas. It is more necessary, therefore, in an advanced than even in a primitive state, that the more comprehensive interests should be taken charge of by persons who, being expressly dedicated to them, can make the study and understanding of them a speciality of their own (pp. 280–2). Besides, advancing civilisation constantly demands new public services, to which individuals and associations are not competent; and even in the case of those to which they are competent, government intervention is required to repress the abuses, negotiate the compromises, and decide the conflicts, to which that very fact gives rise. "Association easily passes into monopoly as regards the public, dictatorship as towards the shareholders" (p. 350). The State is essential as the protector of both against the recklessness or knavery of managers. Railways can be made and worked by private companies; but the State does not find it superfluous to limit the fares, and impose precautions for the safety of travellers, the commercial interests of the community, and in some respects (as by publicity and an audit) even that of the shareholders. Thus the increasing activity of the individual, in an improving society, does not take place at the expense of the activity of government. On the contrary, the more is done by the people themselves, the more there is for government to watch and superintend, and, if need be, to regulate.

If material progress thus tends to enlarge instead of narrowing the province of the State, this, in our author's opinion, is fully as true of moral progress. One of the surest results of improvement is to develope the conscience of society. The ethical requirements of mankind tend to increase. Acts which once seemed to them permissible or venial, they now feel prompted to repress; they are more sensitive to wrong, and require to extend the sphere, not only of social discountenance, but of prohibition and penalty. Judicial statistics show that while crimes of the old types tend to diminish, there is a steady increase of the general sum of offences, principally because legal punishment is from time to time extended to forms of fraud or injury which the previous laws did not reach. Not only does the general conscience become more delicately perceptive of wrongs, but of rights; as in the case of literary property, and property in designs or inventions. How much new action of governments has been rendered necessary by the determination of modern societies to suppress the slave-trade! What a world of labour and regulation has been imposed upon governments, since the conscience of nations became sensitive to the well-being and the reformation of criminals undergoing imprisonment! The laws against cruelty to animals bring an entire province of human conduct for the first time within the pale of law. Not content, too, with enforcing stricter justice, the requirements of the improved public conscience extend to increase of beneficence. Here, indeed, our author holds with all the world, that the proper sphere of coercive authority comes to an end. It is not for the State to enforce philanthropy by law. But what it cannot exact, improving morality demands that it shall itself practise. Not to speak of the obligation to supply the indigent with work or subsistence, a duty not universally admitted, though recognised by the English Poor Laws—

The State may make provision for certain of the wants of the individual; public worship, education, roads, administration of justice; erecting the services of the minister of religion, the schoolmaster, the judge, the engineer, into public functions. This is a bounty to the poor, who benefit by these public services in proportion to their need, but contribute to them only in proportion to their means. . . . The State also practises beneficence to the poor when it acts as their unpaid agent, receiving their small savings, paying them interest, and refunding the principal on demand. . . . Or its beneficence may take the form of direct charity; either permanent, such as assistance to hospitals, gratuitous schooling, &c. or by such occasional measures as are often required in civilised countries, in times of dearth, epidemics, inundations, or commercial crises. (*L'Individu et l'État*, p. 86.)

Our abstract of M. Dupont-White's case would be too much prolonged, were we to include the arguments which he draws from the particular circumstances and national character of France. We shall mention, one for which there is, at least, so much foundation as to make it plausible: that the love of distinction, in France, is a more powerful motive to action, and incentive to enterprise, than the desire of profit;—that to erect certain branches, even of private industry, into public services (as is the case in France with mining, civil engineering, and others), instead of being, as it would be in England, a sure way of perpetuating routine and stifling improvements, is in France the most effectual means of promoting them;— that persons are much more powerfully stimulated to bring to perfection industrial inventions and improvements, by the hope that decorations and honours will be conferred on them for it, than by what might seem the more natural prospect of enriching themselves and their families. However this may be, and even were it literally correct, the question remains whether this tendency of the national mind is not in great part created by the institutions and practices which it is invoked to defend.

Having stated his own side of the case, our author proceeds to the opposite side: the limitations which his theory requires, the objections to which it is liable, and the capacity and sufficiency of individual agency to carry on the progress of society, without the instrumentality of the State.

The limitations with which M. Dupont-White propounds his doctrine are great and important. His practical conclusions are not at all proportioned to the startling breadth and generality, and the occasionally paradoxical form, of his theoretical premises. He generally gives a full adhesion to the limiting principles, however he may or may not assign to them their just weight. Again and again he urges that there ought to be no State action which would really tend to impair the full development of the faculties of the individual.* The individual (he says) is the final object of all government; and *his* capacities and powers the fountain-head of all social good. What our author desires is not a government strong by the weakness and compression of individualities, but individuals active and strong in a strong State. The State must not interfere with thought, nor with its free expression. Some mere *modes* of expression, such as the theatre, clubs, public meetings, may require regulation; but such of them alone as Thought can afford to dispense with. The press must be free to do everything but defame character, or unnecessarily outrage feelings. In the matter of public instruction, the State may teach its own doctrines, but must allow full license of competition to those of others. In economical affairs, the State must not interfere with the right of the labourer to the free employment of his labour. Its regulative functions must be confined to those great aggregations of labour by the aid of large capitals, which are not a mere means of subsistence, but a power in society. In all things, the State is bound, no less than individuals, by the moral law. The rights of private property must be sacred to it. Confiscation, bankruptcy, alteration of the monetary standard, all modes of either open or disguised spoliation, are on its part a crime. But to define and limit the rights of property,—to decide what matters shall or shall not be allowed to become subjects of property, and under what limitations property may be transmitted,—all this is within State functions, and a most important part of them: a doctrine not likely to be questioned in England, though esteemed very heretical in France, where the foundation of the laws of property, and the answers to all disputed questions respecting it, are usually rested not on the obvious consideration of public good, but on a metaphysical abstraction called *le droit*.

The objections to his theory are discussed by M. Dupont-White at great length; especially if we count, in the reply to objections, his strictures on the efficacy of individual agency as an instrument of progress. The interest of the individual (he says) is an ample security for the interest of the individual. But it is scarcely a security at all for collective interests. To begin with one, the greatest of these, though not commonly classed under the head of interest—not *l'utile*, but *le vrai, le beau, et le bien*,—the pursuits, of which the reward is inward, not outward, and the external fruits only in

*See particularly *L'Individu et l'État*, pp. lxiii–lxiv; 53, 282, 283; 308–11; and *La Centralisation*, pp. 127–30.

a distant future. How can these prosper, without inducements held out, or, at the lowest, without means supplied, from other sources than the private interest of individuals? Private interest is not a sufficient stimulus in the sphere of the most ordinary utility, when that utility is collective, not individual. The strongest of all cases of coincidence between public and private interest, is that of protection against open violence. Is this, or can it be, anywhere left dependent on individual self-interest? The want in this case, it may indeed be said, is one which private individuals *cannot* provide for; but how many others are there which they can, but will not?

It is precisely the collective character of an interest which turns men back from the pursuit of it. Men do even that which concerns them most, only when it can be carried through by their own efforts, and when the benefit is for them-selves alone. Self-interest is an adequate motive to the cultivation of the earth, for success in this is the private concern of the individual; he and his take all the trouble, and reap the entire fruit. But the paving and lighting of a town, however important it may be to each, still, since he cannot accomplish it alone, and has no assurance that others will do the same as he—since his own effort avails nothing unless as a portion of the general effort—he remains inactive. Thus a collective interest is neglected by individuals, even though their own is included in it. The individual abstains from things the most advantageous to himself, when he is unable to execute them alone, and has no power of compelling others to do their part. (*L'Individu et l'État*, pp. 267–8.)

Besides, individuals may be too low placed to feel the stimulating influ-ence of self-interest. Inaction and torpidity as often result from the absence of aid and encouragement, as from their excess.

Love of personal comfort, and impatience of privations, are not an incentive capable of operating upon every one. These sentiments do not spring up in persons so steeped in misery that they care only to forget their condition, instead of improving it. The services which Necessity renders to Progress are limited; it can only develope what exists. Without it the qualities of the most privileged natures might never come to light; but it does not endow average human beings with courage and forethought; on the contrary, it plunges them and keeps them in a state of reckless self-abandonment. What is a stimulus to the strong, is to the ordinary man only a cause of despair. The education of necessity was never wanting to the Irish, or the North American Indians; to keep themselves alive was to them the business of life. Yet it did not teach either to the Irishman or the Iroquois the lesson of forethought. . . . Governments, wiser than sectarian theorists, have understood that it was their business, not indeed to take complete charge of the individual, but to offer him facilities, awaken his hopes, and lead him *towards* though not *to*, the end. . . . Do you dread the effect of such assistance in enervating those vigorous characters which can do without it? But a degree of tutelage may be imagined, beneficial to the greater number, yet not damaging to the more gifted natures. To find the limit and keep to it, may be a delicate point; but the path of all truth applicable to human uses, is one of compromise. Do you prefer to steer by only one principle, instead of combining several?

Conclude, then, if you are bold enough, for the suppression of hospitals—the ultimate and perfectly legitimate consequence of the individualist principle, and the doctrine of leaving people to necessity. (Pp. 298–9.)

One of the objections anticipated is, that the State is only the aggregate of individuals, and its rights their united rights; it can therefore have no right to employ force, but that which individuals have, namely, the right of self-defence. Repression of violence and fraud are hence the only rightful functions of the State. It is instituted for order only, not for progress.

Our author answers, that the State is more than a mere aggregation of individuals. "This is the definition of a caravanserai, of a place like Baden or Homburg, not of a society" (p. 168). The State is not the sum of the individuals comprising it, merely *as* individuals; each of them, in becoming a part of society, becomes something more than an individual. From the union of human beings in society, arise relations and necessities other than those of mere individuals; and it is not strange if there arise also rights which only the social state renders legitimate. Placing within the reach of man innumerable ends not else attainable, it warrants the use of additional means.

But (it may be said) since governments are composed of individuals, if individuals are not competent to carry on the great interests of the human race, why should better be expected from the individuals who compose the government? To this it is answered, first, that those individuals are, or ought to be, the *élite*; and, next, that they are, as a matter of course, more competent than others to what is made their especial business. In addition to this, the mere fact of their more elevated position (provided they are chosen indiscriminately, and not identified with castes or classes having separate interests,) tends of itself to give them a higher degree of impartiality,—an identity of interest with the community, as to all that concerns the relations of citizens among themselves, though not as to their relation with the government. In its position, what in individuals would require heroic virtue, demands no more than ordinary good sense and good intention. It costs but a small effort to a government to lay on a tax for supporting schools; while, for individuals to endow them from their own funds, requires real virtue. "For a master to set free his slaves, supposes a certain greatness of mind; but the commonest sense of morality in a State is enough to make it abolish slavery" (p. 346). It militates somewhat against this doctrine that slavery took so many ages to abolish. We must at least suppose that the government is not composed of slaveholders, nor under their influence; or that the ruler is a despot like Caracalla, to whose tyranny slave and citizen were much the same. Such (adds our author) is the effect of a commanding position, in elevating the ruler above the narrow interests which pervert mankind, that many of the worst sovereigns have made excellent laws, and enforced them between their subjects, while retaining for themselves the liberty of not obeying them. "Even Cæsar Borgia tolerated in his dominions no other poisoner than himself" (p. 308). With this remark, we close our summary of the first and most important of M. Dupont-White's two volumes.

Of the second, *La Centralisation*, it is not necessary to give so copious an abstract. It completes the theory of State influence, as contrasted with individual agency, by a corresponding theory of central, as preferable to local, government agency. The two questions, in truth, are fundamentally one. Whatever advantages, in promoting the general interest, governments have over individuals, the central government has over any local body; while local bodies stand nearer to the merits as well as the defects which belong to the spontaneous energies of the private citizen.

Of central contrasted with local authority, as of government contrasted with the individual, M. Dupont-White holds that it is more impartial. Local functionaries are too near to those over whom they administer; too much implicated in their interests and partialities; often identified, personally or by class, with a particular section among them. [Pp. 229 ff.] But to this idea M. Dupont-White adds another, different, but allied to it. The central government is naturally the organ of a more advanced portion of the nation. The public whose opinion acts upon governments, is principally that of the capital city. Local bodies are immediately amenable to an inferior, perhaps a very backward, part of the public. The ascendancy of central administration over local is, in our author's conception, that of the active and enlightened van of the community, over the more ignorant, more narrow-minded, and less public-spirited rearguard. The central power, of which he is anxious to maintain the predominance, is quite as much that of Paris as of the executive. Accordingly, he would assign to the capital a number of representatives, not smaller, as in England, but much larger than in the ratio of its population:

Suppose that, twelve or fifteen years ago, when there was a Chamber of 450 deputies, Paris had returned forty-five representatives instead of twelve; suppose (which is no strained hypothesis) that all these had voted and acted, as the twelve usually did, with the Opposition; a certain majority (there is every reason to think) would not have been formed, a certain Cabinet would not have lasted eight years, a certain Revolution, with all its consequences, would not have broken out. (*La Centralisation*, pp. 277–8.)

A suggestion curiously illustrative of one of the many political differences between England and France. It would occur to few persons in England that giving eighty or a hundred members to the metropolis would be the way to obtain a government of greater wisdom, and less exposed to revolution. But then, there is not that superiority of political capacity and intelligence in the middle and working classes of London over those of Warwickshire or Lancashire, which nearly all authorities concur in ascribing to those of Paris over every other part of France.

M. Dupont-White certainly mentions some astonishing exhibitions of folly and ignorance by mayors of great provincial towns. We wish he had told us whether these specimens of local functionaries were elected by their fellow-citizens, or actually nominated by the government. A government which has all the educated intelligence of the country against it, must often find itself under the necessity of appointing ignorant men. We cannot, without further information, accept these as examples of the working of free local institutions. It is more to the purpose, when our author states that neither elementary schools nor local roads (*chemins vicinaux*) could be got established in most of the localities, until the government of Louis Philippe enforced them by an act of authority.

Another of his arguments in recommendation of central control, is its necessity for the protection of minorities. In local as well as general affairs, the majority has a perpetual tendency to tyrannise over the rest. In justice to the minority, who may be taxed for purposes of which they very reasonably disapprove, an arbitrator is indispensable. Any arbitrator is preferable to the mere despotism of number; but the central government, from its distance and its elevated position, is in general an impartial umpire. Even in England, the chosen soil of freedom and individual spontaneity, there is a growing tendency to associate with local administration an organ of central control. Parochial or district management of the Poor Laws is now subordinated to a Poor Law Board. Charitable endowments, which formerly—as far as superintended at all—were under the superintendence of corporations and other local bodies, have been withdrawn from them, and placed under Charity Commissioners appointed by the State.[*]

M. Dupont-White does not seek to annihilate provincial and municipal institutions. He acknowledges their value for cultivating the intelligence of the citizens, and familiarising them with the management of interests not private and personal; but (he contends) it is not necessary for this purpose that the localities should have the complete control of their own affairs. It is not sovereignty they require, but a veto and an initiative; the power of rejecting, and that of proposing. That they should be at liberty to do anything of themselves, without leave from a superior, does not enter into his idea of their use. But he admits that the interference with them, at present, passes all reasonable bounds, and is not *de la tutelle*, but *de la pédagogie.** He declares for a great relaxation of this despotism, and is, upon occasion, as severe as any one upon the *manie réglementaire* of the French national mind [p. 71].

[*16 & 17 Victoria, c. 137 (1853).]
*La Centralisation, p. 86.

It is often objected that the State, by meddling in everything, takes on itself the blame of everything, and concentrates upon its own head all animosities (*toutes les haines*) [p. 117]. Our author treats this objection very lightly. He replies that there will always be *haine*, and that the State is the very properest quarter upon which it can discharge itself. It is far better that men whose interests are crossed should lay the blame on the Government, than on hostile classes, or on one another. Besides, hatred directed against a distant object is always less intense. In confirmation of which it might have been said, that the vengeance of a rude people falls less upon the original author of a supposed wrong, than upon the comparatively harmless subordinate instrument. A dispossessed Irish cottier did not shoot at his landlord, but at his landlord's agent, or the mere incoming tenant. Wherever there is not a strong central government, society, says our author, is all broken up by hatreds. Like the cities of Italy or Flanders in the Middle Ages, every town, family, or individual is the bitter enemy of its nearest neighbour (pp. 118–19). The perpetual causes of jarring which necessarily arise, are envenomed into animosity by the absence of an authorised arbitrator.

Our author, though a zealot for liberty, distinguishes between political and what he calls civil liberty [pp. 133 ff.]. Many writers have drawn this distinction, and have lavished their praises on civil, their suspicion and distrust on political, liberty. M. Dupont-White does the reverse. He is a vigorous partisan of political liberty—the control of the nation over the government. But he sets no value on civil liberty, which he considers to be synonymous with not being governed. By this paradoxical use of language he needlessly flies in the face of opinion, and renders his doctrines unpopular in a much greater degree than the practical use he makes of them will be found to warrant. For in reality he would release the private liberty of the citizen from most of the irksome restraints to which in Continental countries it is still subject: and his doctrine, in so far as different from that of moderate politicians in England, is chargeable not so much with repressing individual spontaneity, as with giving fatal facility and encouragement to its voluntary disuse.

Our author is weakest where he attempts to show that a people under a centralised government may be free; and that France, having always manifested a strong love of liberty, is no instance of the contrary. The security he relies on, to prevent a centralised government from overpowering political freedom, is that resistance is also centralised in the metropolis: a doctrine at which we may well wonder, in a book written subsequently to December 1851. It was then seen what this centralisation of resistance is good for, against a numerous and well disciplined army. Resistance is centralised, as Caligula wished his enemies to be centralised, that they might all be cut off at one blow. Uncentralised Spain is not a bright example of the influences of freedom; but her resistance to the first Napoleon when in full military possession of her capital, was a different thing, it must be confessed, from the resistance of France to his living imitator and representative.

Those who have accompanied us through our necessarily meagre abridgment of M. Dupont-White's pleading for State interference as an unavoidable consequence and indispensable instrument of progress, cannot have failed to observe one great deficiency, which cuts down his case to something far smaller in reality than in appearance. He does not distinguish, or distinguishes only casually and incidentally, between one mode of State interference and another. His main argument can at most only prove, that as society advances there is a frequent demand for new laws. This proposition most English opponents of centralisation would admit, without thinking that they made any great concession. When there were no railways, there needed no Railway Acts. When there were no joint-stock companies, no laws were needed for their formation, their winding up, or the responsibility of their shareholders or directors. When there was no insurance, no banks, no bills of exchange, there was no need of a great part of our mercantile law. But the new laws commonly require, to ensure their execution, only the ordinary tribunals. Extension of legislation in itself implies no fresh delegation of power to the executive; no discretionary authority, still less control, still less obligation to ask permission of the executive for every new undertaking. It does, at times, imply some increase of public functionaries and patronage. Many laws which protect collective against individual interests, would remain unexecuted if volunteer agency were solely relied on for carrying them into effect.* When Parliament made laws to be observed by schools, manufactories, or endowed charities, it had to create a staff of Inspectors or Commissioners to watch over the observance of those laws. But it is not necessary that these officers should have administrative control. Their business is to warn the chiefs of establishments when certain specified legal obligations are departed from, and to put the law in force against the offenders if the violations are persisted in. This is the kind of additional State interference, some amount of which is useful and inevitable as improvement proceeds. But this form of it does not, or at least need not, weaken the stimulus to individual effort. There may indeed

*This, M. Dupont-White says, is the case in France, with the laws for limiting the hours of children's labour in factories; even in a country which, unlike our own, attaches to every court of justice a public prosecutor. [See D.P. 41.3.116, *Loi relative au travail des enfants employés dans les manufactures, usines ou ateliers* (22 March, 1841).]

be over-legislation, as well as over-administration. A legislature, as well as an executive, may take upon itself to prescribe how individuals shall carry on their own business for their own profit. It may bind the operations of manufacture to an unchangeable routine, by all the *minutieux* regulations of Colbert. But when, instead of protecting individuals against themselves, it only protects them against others, from whom it would be either difficult or impossible for them to protect themselves, it is within its province. This is the principle which legitimates laws against false weights and measures, and the adoption of a common standard of them for the whole country;[*] which justifies the legal regulation of emigrant ships, and of the professional qualification of masters of merchant vessels; which requires that employers and parents shall not, by conspiring together, selfishly overwork children for their private gain, or work them at all, at times or in modes inconsistent with their proper education; which forbids that individuals should be allowed to build, and let out for dwelling in, places such as human beings cannot inhabit with decency or safety to their health. For though it may be alleged that, in this last case, acceptance of the conditions is voluntary, it is so only as regards the head of the family, who, being oftenest absent, suffers least from the evil; and it is not voluntary at all when better residences are not to be had; while, if bad ones are prohibited, the spontaneous provision of good ones follows as a matter of course.

It must, then, be granted that new legislation is often necessitated, by the progress of society, to protect from injury either individuals or the public: not only through the rising-up of new economical and social phenomena, each accompanied with its own public and private inconveniencies; but also because the more enlarged scale on which operations are carried on, involves evils and dangers which on a smaller scale it was allowable to overlook. One among a thousand illustrations which might be adduced of this incident of mere growth, is the vast trouble which society is now obliged to take in order to prevent its principal sources of water supply from being poisoned. As respects such new laws, and as much new agency as is needed to ensure their observance, the function of the State naturally does widen with the advance of civilisation. But this part of the case, though sometimes undervalued, is seldom, by English thinkers, denied: and to this extent only can English practice be cited in evidence that State intervention is, or ought to be, a growing fact.

Our author makes a stand on another doctrine, quite unassailable in principle—that the State may be required to render all such services as, being necessary or important to society, are not of a nature to remunerate any one for their performance. Thus, the State, or some public authority, must build and maintain light-houses and lay down buoys, it being impos-

[*See 5 George IV, c. 74 (1824); for the following laws, see p. 592 above.]

sible to make those who benefit by these essential requisites of navigation pay any compensation for their use. But though necessities of this description exist, it cannot be admitted that they tend, on the whole, to multiply as society advances. Though the progress of civilisation is constantly requiring new things to be done, it also multiplies the cases in which individuals or associations are able and willing to do them gratuitously. Our author, having pointed out many needful things which would never be done by the mere self-interest of individuals, does not seem to be aware that anything can be expected from their public spirit: apparently because public spirit in this form is almost entirely stifled in the countries with which he is most familiar, by the centralisation which he applauds. But in our uncentralised country, even such a public want as that of life-boats is supplied by private liberality, through the agency of a voluntary association. Societies are formed to watch even over the execution of laws, in the enforcement of which no individual is sufficiently interested; such as the laws against cruelty to animals. Naval expeditions for purposes of science or philanthropy have been fitted out by subscription; and private associations undertake on a large scale the education of the poor. For this, indeed, both here and in other countries, individual munificence had already made a large provision. For centuries past there have existed numerous endowments, by which not only the elements of letters, but the most complete intellectual education known when they were founded, was given without remuneration to a far larger class than has ever by any other means received it. M. Dupont-White fails to show that the province of government in works of public utility receives accessions at one end, greater than what private zeal and benevolence subtracts from it at the other; even though he swells his catalogue of things which can only be accomplished by the Government, with objects so exceptional as acquisition of territory for colonisation or commerce. And even as to these, his theory does not always hold. A company of merchant adventurers acquired India for Great Britain. France had the start of England in that part of the world; the empire which is now British was very near being French, and would have been so if the matter had not depended on the State but on individuals—if the central government would but have let Dupleix and Bussy alone. All the functions of Government which do not consist in affording legal protection, are in reality greatest when civilisation is at the lowest; when the poverty of individuals, their ignorance, and inaptness for combination, leaves society no resource but State action for anything requiring large means, co-operation of numbers, or elevated views. There was a time when neither roads, nor canals, nor drainage, nor irrigation, nor banks, nor schools, nor encouragement of arts, letters, or science, could possibly exist except as the work of the government. In an advanced stage of civilisation these things are better done by voluntary associations, or by the public indiscriminately; though we do not deny that, when so done, they create a necessity for new laws, inasmuch as all new good which arises in the world must be expected to bring new evil as its accompaniment.

A second oversight, which, as it seems to us, goes through the whole extent of M. Dupont-White's argument, is that he assumes the government, for whose prerogatives he is contending, to be an ideal government, bearing very little affinity to any actual one. He has a perfect right to exclude the despotism of one man, or the rule of a class or caste, which may have a positive interest in unjust laws and administration. He is entitled to stipulate for an elective government, with a free press, in which the opinion of the nation, collected in some fair manner, decides everything in the last resort. He is free to say, as he does*—If the government does not leave open to public discussion the whole range of politics, religion, and philosophy, it is not the kind of government which I contemplate. But after accepting these postulates, there is an additional assumption, which M. Dupont-White tacitly asks us to admit,—that the government is an embodiment of the *élite* of the nation. Now, exists there any such government? Can we at present foresee a time when there will be any such? Our author has not pointed out how it must be constituted to effect this object; and takes, indeed, anything but an enthusiastic view of the efficacy of forms of government, and of political contrivances generally. Yet he virtually assumes that under the government which his theory supposes, the persons at the head of affairs will be the choice spirits of the community. But this state of things is a mere ideal, to be unremittingly striven for, but seldom with any approach to attainment. The nearest approximation to it is usually found at those great national crises, which impose silence on petty jealousies, frighten away the herd of mediocrities from the arena, and call forth the great souls in all their strength. But the only permanent governments by men of capacity known to history, are some of the bad aristocracies, the Roman or Venetian, which our author, we presume, would sternly reprobate. That democracy is very far from realising this ideal, America is a sufficient example. If its conditions could be supposed present anywhere in our own age, it would probably be in England; yet does any Englishman believe that the members of the Cabinet are usually the ten or fifteen ablest and most enlightened members of the community, or that the Houses of Lords and Commons embody, or even reflect, the thoughts and opinions of the most eminent men in the country? Do we not think ourselves well off, if the majority of the Ministers are tolerable public speakers, and half of them or thereabouts moderately assiduous and competent men of business? Do we expect more from Parliament than that it should be a rather favourable representation of the average sentiments and opinions of the classes possess-

*L'Individu et l'État, p. xlix.

ing influence in the country? The moving power of Government and Parliament is the sentiment of the majority; not indeed hitherto in mere numbers, but in numbers and social importance combined. Sometimes the government is a little better, sometimes a little worse, than the general opinion of society; but in most cases, much the same. To suppose, therefore, that Government will do, better than individuals, anything which individuals are able and willing to do, is to suppose that the average of society is better than any individual in it, which is both a mathematical and a moral absurdity. Though the *élite* of society are not often found in the government, yet, when anything worthy of their efforts is open to fair competition, they will generally be competitors. The persons most capable of winning are among those who start in the race; and if society has any capacity of judging of work after it has been performed, these are more likely than others to be the successful competitors. Whatever is done by individuals, without a monopoly, has thus a considerable chance of being done by those who can do it best; and such will generally do it better than the government, which only represents the average.

A third defect in M. Dupont-White's argument is the very inadequate sense which he entertains of the manner in which individual capacity and efficiency are blunted, by being dependent, in nearly every effort they make, on leave from a superior. He asks, Have the French been, throughout their history, or are they now, a people devoid of energy, activity, and mental life? Yet we need quote no other opinion than his own, as to the *kind* of those qualities which generally characterises his countrymen. He has himself unconsciously pronounced the severest judgment upon them, as to this particular point. He says* that they are deficient in initiative; that they are energetic and active only in doing what is set down for them, and marked out by authority. He discusses this peculiarity, philosophises on it, makes theories about it, but steadily affirms it. The greatest enemies of centralisation have said nothing more stringent against the theory of national progress by government agency. To M. Dupont-White this deficiency proves that the French require to be much governed. Others see in it a proof and an effect of too much government. He asks, If a people will not make roads, or keep up schools, except on compulsion, is leaving them to themselves the way to make them do it? Certainly not. They are in a state of prostration from which they cannot rise without help. Let help be given to them. They require to be urged, not only by the government, but by everyone else to whom they look up. But urged to what? To let the government act for them? No; but to act for themselves. This is, at least, the ultimatum to which it should be endeavoured to bring them.

Turning now from the general question of government interference, to

*L'Individu et l'État, pp. 354, 355. La Centralisation, pp. 306 ff.

the comparative merits of central and of local government, we must admit that M. Dupont-White's doctrines on this subject are not only a legitimate corollary, but an indispensable corrective, of his opinions on the more fundamental point. Any despotism is preferable to local despotism. If we are to be ridden over by authority, if our affairs are to be managed for us at the pleasure of other people, heaven forefend that it should be at that of our nearest neighbours. To be under the control, or have to wait for the sanction, of a Minister or a Parliament, is bad enough; but defend us from the leading-strings of a Board of Guardians or a Common Council. In the former authorities there would be some knowledge, some general cultivation, some attention and habitual deference to the opinions of the more instructed minds. To be under the latter, would be in most localities, unless by the rarest accident, to be the slave of the vulgar prejudices, the cramped, distorted, and short-sighted views, of the public of a small town or a group of villages. It is only affairs of a simple character and on a humble scale, not exceeding the levying of a local rate, and the application of it to purposes strictly predetermined, that can with impunity be left to the unassisted and unchecked management of the representatives of a narrow locality. The most strenuous English champion of local liberties would probably admit, that the localities should do little more than execute, and provide the means for executing, laws and instructions laid down by the legislature of the empire. The parish, or the quarter-sessions, fix the local taxation; but they would not be permitted to levy it by an income-tax, or to assess it in any manner but the one authorised by Parliament, a percentage on the rent.

But it does not follow, because the local authority ought not to be supreme and absolute, that the central ought; or that the latter should be able, by an act of authority, to overrule the resistance, or dispense with the assent, of the former, in matters on which the legislature had not declared itself. Respecting the degree in which the central executive should co-operate with the localities in the control of local affairs, there are great differences of opinion amongst us. Our author is in the right in saying that our recent legislation has associated central with local authority in a far greater degree than before. The reason is, that the characteristic of the present age is the reform of abuses, and their reform could not be trusted to the persons and the institutions that had introduced them. But our author imagines the tendency, which really exists, to be much stronger than it is. He never wearies of repeating that England has found it necessary to centralise the relief of the poor. He is perhaps not aware that the relief of the poor in England is not central, but local, under central supervision; and that the Poor Law of 1834, which established the Central Board, also created the first tolerably-constituted Local Boards of Poor Law Administration which England has ever possessed.

Enlightened English opinion was never more hostile than now to the actual management of local affairs by central authority. The centralisation which it approves is that of knowledge and experience, rather than of power. It would not be content with what M. Dupont-White allows to local authorities, *le véto et l'initiative*.[*] The cases are few in which, by our recent legislation, the local authority has to ask permission of the central. Within the limits of its attributions, it generally has complete discretion, subject to central interference only when it infringes the distinctly expressed commands of Parliament.

It is further to be considered that if the authorities of a small rural district are unfit to be trusted with difficult public duties, it is not indispensable that local authorities should be on this contracted scale. There are provincial authorities as well as municipal. Our Quarter Sessions are such an authority. The Councils-General of French departments are another,—an institution which M. Dupont-White, M. Odilon-Barrot, and other writers of authority, represent as the only one of modern introduction which has struck root in the country, and under all political changes has continued to work wisely and beneficently. The French system errs, not solely in giving too little power to local bodies, but in having those bodies too numerous and too insignificant. It is not the law in England for every village to have its mayor and municipal council. Every parish, indeed, has its vestry, but the duties of this are now almost limited to the affairs of the parish church. Our *chemins vicinaux* are not made by parishes, but by the justices in sessions. The far greater number even of our towns are not corporate, and their local affairs are managed by the county magistrates, except when Parliament, by a Private Act, has provided a set of Commissioners or a Paving Board. A moderately sized town, or a Poor Law Union, is perhaps the smallest district which ought to have a local representation; and a great part of the business even of these would be better intrusted, if not to the Quarter Sessions, to a representative County Board, or some combination of both. Boards of this range of jurisdiction, composed as they would probably be, could be trusted to do whatever business was assigned to them, without subjection to the central executive; whose functions in regard to them might be limited to collecting and diffusing information, and calling the localities to account if they violated the rules laid down by Parliament for their observance, or usurped powers not confided to them by law.

Another point to which M. Dupont-White does not attach due importance, is the danger to liberty, from the increase of the power and patronage of government, inseparable from every extension of its superintendence over individuals and local bodies. One of the highest French authorities on constitutional government, M. Royer-Collard, long ago proclaimed that an

[*L'Individu et l'État, p. 81.]

administration strongly centralised is sure to be master of the assembly appointed to control it. In a speech delivered under the Villèle ministry, he asked —

Who votes at elections? The electors? No: very often it is only the ministry. The ministry votes by the whole mass of places and salaries in its gift, all or almost all, directly or indirectly, the reward of proved docility; by the whole mass of the business and interests which centralisation brings under its control; by all the establishments, religious, civil, military, scientific, which the localities fear to lose, or solicit to obtain; by roads, bridges, canals, town-halls, since the satisfaction of every public want is a favour of the administration, to attain which, the public, a courtier of a new description, must *please*. In a word, the ministry votes by all the weight of the Government, which is brought to bear with its whole force on every department, every commune, every profession, I might say every individual. And this Government, what is it? The Imperial Government, curtailed of no one of its hundred thousand arms; having, on the contrary, acquired new vigour from the struggle it has had to sustain against a few forms of freedom, and always recovering in case of need the instincts of its cradle, cunning and force. (Quoted by M. Léonce de Lavergne ["Royer-Collard, orateur et politique,"] in the *Revue des Deux Mondes* [XXXV,] for October 1, 1861, pp. 586–7.)

A government with all this mass of favours to give or to withhold, however free in name, wields a power of bribery scarcely surpassed by an avowed autocracy; rendering it master of the elections in almost any circumstances but those of rare and extraordinary public excitement. It is true that, even thus armed, it may break down; the Villèle and Polignac governments were defeated at two successive general elections. But this does not affect the practical truth of M. Royer-Collard's proposition. The Government remained master of the Chambers until the storm of public disapprobation had become equivalent to a revolution, and, when resisted, produced one. The public opinion which was strong enough to outvote the ministry, sufficed to turn out the king and the royal family in three days. The public opinion which eighteen years later was again able to expel a king and his dynasty, had failed six months before to carry a general election against a minister.[*] So completely does recent history bear out the assertion, that an over-centralised government is amenable to no check short of a revolution; and is lured to its ruin by an appearance of unlimited power, up to the very moment when it is abandoned by all mankind.

We have not yet noticed the great moral and political mischief of training a people to be one vast tribe of place-hunters. Yet if there be a fact respecting which all French thinkers—M. Dupont-White not excepted—are unanimous, it is that from the days of the First Empire this is the character which centralisation has impressed upon France. Our author, indeed, relies on the rewards of productive industry as a rival temptation to that of place. But

[*François Pierre Guizot.]

if all the higher and more dignified pursuits, even those of literature and science, are organised (which he seems to approve) as branches of the public service, what must be the consequence? That the ambitious and active part of the nation is divided into two classes, place-seekers and money-seekers.

It is from a sense of these evils, fully as much as from the fortunate national habit of distrusting the government, that nearly all English thinkers regard the presumption as always unfavourable to any extension of governmental functions, and hold as a rooted conviction that not only are there many of the greatest public concerns from which, as soon as the nation has emerged from the swathing bands of infancy, the State should hold its hand, but that even where no general principle forbids its interference, nothing should be done by it except what has been clearly proved to be incapable of being done by other means. Opinion in England only consented to national grants for education,[*] after private associations had tried their hand for many years, and had shown the limits of what they could be expected to do. The regulation of emigrant ships was only undertaken by government, after the horrors which arose from leaving them unregulated had become a scandal to the country, which there was no mode of stopping except by recourse to government. The creation of the Poor Law Board was only feasible, because the abuses of the Poor Laws[†] had reached a height of mischief which the country could no longer tolerate, while two centuries had proved that the qualities necessary for cleansing that Augean stable were only found in about one parish out of a thousand, and that even there the reform scarcely ever outlasted the life of its individual author. The general tone of English feeling on these subjects is on the whole, we think, very much what it ought to be. There is no blind prejudice against having recourse to the State, such as reaction against over-government seems to have raised up in some of the more thorough French reformers. But there is a strong persuasion that what can be tolerably done in any other way, had better be done in that way than by the government. State action is regarded as an extreme remedy, to be reserved, in general, for great purposes; for difficult and critical moments in the course of affairs, or concerns too vital to be trusted to less responsible hands. Few Englishmen, we believe, would grudge to the government, for a time, or permanently, the powers necessary to save from serious injury any great national interest; and equally few would claim for it the power of meddling with anything, which it could let alone without touching the public welfare in any vital part. And though the line thus indicated neither is, nor can be, very definitely drawn, a practical compromise of this sort between the State and the individual, and between

[*See 3 & 4 William IV, c. 96 (1833).]
[†See 43 Elizabeth, c. 2 (1601).]

central and local authority, is, we believe, the result which must issue from all prolonged and enlightened speculation and discussion on this great subject.

We should not be doing justice to M. Dupont-White, were we to dismiss his writings without giving a few specimens of the acute, and often finely expressed, incidental thoughts, in which his volumes abound beyond most of even the better class of contemporary works. Neither can we acquit our conscience without entering a protest against some opinions and sentiments, to which we regret that such a writer should have lent the authority of his talents. Of these, the following is the worst:

> Consider for an instant: if liberty is a principle of moral elevation, it is because it means power. A free man finds in the power which he enjoys over himself, the space necessary for his faculties, and a sentiment which exalts him in his own eyes. But, if so, how can the supreme power, with all the careers, all the horizons which it opens, all the sentiments which it awakens, fail to be a principle of exaltation analogous and even superior to liberty? (*L'Individu et l'État*, pp. xxi–xxii.)

We look upon this confounding of the love of liberty with the love of power, the desire not to be improperly controlled with the ambition of exercising control, to be both a psychological error, and the worst possible moral lesson. If there be an ethical doctrine which more than all others requires to be taught, and has been taught with deepest conviction by the great moral teachers, it is, that the love of power is the most evil passion of human nature; that power over others, power of coercion and compulsion, any power other than that of moral and intellectual influence, even in the cases where it is indispensable, is a snare, and in all others a curse, both to the possessor and to those over whom it is possessed; a burthen which no rightly constituted moral nature consents to take upon itself, but by one of the greatest sacrifices which inclination ever makes to duty. With the love of liberty it is wholly the reverse. The love of liberty, in the only proper sense of that word, is unselfish; it places no one in a position of hostility to the good of his fellow-creatures; all alike may be free, and the freedom of one has no solid security but in the equal freedom of the rest. The appetite for power is, on the contrary, essentially selfish; for all cannot have power; the power of one is power over others, who not only do not share in his elevation, but whose depression is the foundation on which it is raised. Accordingly the love of power is the passion of the τυραννικαὶ φυσεῖς[*]—of those, in all ages, who

[*See Plato, *Republic* (Greek and English), trans. Paul Shorey, 2 vols. (London: Heinemann; New York: Putnam's Sons, 1930, 1935), Vol. II, p. 352 (ix.2; 576a).]

have inflicted on the human race its greatest miseries: the love of liberty is usually that of its most illustrious benefactors.

The prosperity of England is greatly due to two institutions, the Navigation Laws and the Poor Laws; the former protecting British ships by excluding foreign vessels from British ports; to the latter . . . British industry owes the security it enjoys, and above all a rate of wages which allows it to produce and to sell at prices inaccessible to its competitors, and triumphant in almost all the markets of the world. (*L'Individu et l'État*, pp. 126, 129.)

We need not, at this time of day, say one word about the Navigation Laws, except that English commerce and navigation seem to have thriven wonderfully well since they were abolished.[*] But we have rarely seen a greater amount of error as to fact, compressed into a few words, than in the three statements, that wages are lower in England than on the Continent, that their lowness is owing to the Poor Laws, and that low wages are what enable her to sell her products at a lower price than other countries.

Why is the penal law applied without scruple to the most ignorant and stupid malefactor? Because he is reputed to know it. And how can he know it except by that divine ray [of conscience] which is the original patrimony of every intelligence? (*L'Individu et l'État*, p. 226.)

M. Dupont-White surely does not mistake a mere presumption of law for a fact, and believe that instinctive morality really reveals to the lowest of the low every important prohibition of the penal law! They neither know nor anticipate a particle more of it than what they have been taught. Conscience does not suggest to them what might seem its most obvious dictates, as that they should not wantonly ill-treat their wives (for example) or their animals.

M. Dupont-White approves and applauds religious liberty, and even equality carried to the length of providing churches, and state payment for all tolerably numerous communions. But he thinks it right that these favours should be conditional upon abstinence from doing anything to spread their opinions:

The laws of France require of them, in return for these bounties, that they should keep the peace, should not trouble one another, should abstain from propagandism, and not reawaken the passions of other times, in an age which has quite enough to do in managing its own. (*La Centralisation*, p. 291.)

When this is the price of state assistance to religion, assuredly M. de Pressensé and his friends have done well and wisely in repudiating it; though this refusal is about the greatest offence which as a body they could have given to the Imperial Government, insuring them its covert hostility, and as much quiet persecution as that Government or its functionaries think it prudent to venture on. For, in France, churches or communions not recog-

[*See 12 & 13 Victoria, c. 29 (1849).]

nised by the law, in other words not paid and controlled by the State, are not considered as having a right to the same religious freedom as other people.

We proceed to the pleasanter task of extracting a few of the valuable or striking thoughts which are scattered through M. Dupont-White's pages.

The nations which arrive earliest at a certain stage of human advancement are apt to stop short there:

> In general, the peoples which arrive the first at any kind of religious or political greatness, are liable to halt permanently at that point; whether it be that the influences of race, climate, and position which accelerated their development, have also the power to arrest it; or whether, being at first superior to those who surround them, they mistake their relative excellence for an absolute one, their superiority for perfection. (*L'Individu et l'État*, p. xxx.)

The separation between spiritual and temporal power a more important discovery than printing:

> The grand discovery of Western Europe is not the press, but the division of spiritual from temporal; printing, by itself, would only have served to multiply the Koran and the Vedas. (Pp. xxix–xxx.)

The things in which mankind chiefly improve, are those which admit of being, either literally or virtually, stored up:

> Whatever can be accumulated and capitalised, steadily increases: riches, science, and even morality. But poetry, eloquence, sculpture, are those of our own day superior to the *Iliad*, the Parthenon, the Athenian Bema? . . . The constituent elements of human nature, as of that of other animals, do not change. But certain human faculties yield products susceptible of being accumulated and transmitted: and from thence comes progress. (Pp. 360–1.)

Privileged classes the original source of elevated sentiments:

> The feudal lord, with his lofty idea of himself, rose to pride, which is the beginning of virtue. When such individuals are numerous, and compose a class, the class creates for the education of the country a grand type, capable of elevating all the rest. There is of course a great distance between sentiments and conduct, between the device and the exploit; but it is much to exalt the ideal standard of a society. No great soul is born into the world which does not become greater by striving after this model. From a heroic mask, something permanently remains, and passes into the features of a people. It is a great deficiency in the Russians, never to have had chivalry. The sentiment even of honour came to us from the feudal period. . . . Society cannot afford to part with anything which stiffens up to a greater stature the poverty of human nature—*qui peut guinder notre indigente espèce*. (*La Centralisation*, pp. 15–16 and 112.)

We cannot end more appropriately than with one other quotation, which gives an emphatic rebuke to a sentiment deeply engrafted on the French mind, and until lately predominant in nearly all its marked manifestations;

but of which we should have expected to find a denunciation anywhere rather than in a defence of centralisation. "Unity," says M. Dupont-White, "is but another word for intolerance" (p. 188). Unity, indeed, is a phrase, which, as it comes from the lips of a politician, either theoretical or practical, nurtured in the stifling governmentalism of the Imperial school, is one of the curses of Europe. It stands for the negation of the main determining principle of improvement, and even of the permanence of civilisation, which depends on diversity, not unity. "One God, one France, one King, one Chamber," was the exclamation of a member of the first Constituent Assembly. Sir Walter Scott appended to it as an appropriate commentary, "one mouth, one nose, one ear, and one eye."[*] And if the jest sets in a strong light the ridiculousness, it does nothing like justice to the mischievousness, of the wretched propensity, which, in order that all the affairs of mankind may be cut after a single pattern, tends irresistibly to subject all of them to a single will.

[*Walter Scott, *The Life of Napoleon Buonaparte* (Edinburgh: Cadell, 1827), Vol. I, p. 178. The member of the Constituent Assembly is identified by Scott as Rabaut St. Etienne.]

APPENDICES

Appendix A

Taylor's Statesman (1837)

London & Westminster Review, V & XXVII (Apr., 1837), 1–32, headed "ART. I. / THE STATESMAN. / *The Statesman*. By Henry Taylor, Esq., author of Philip van / Artevelde. Duodecimo, pp. 267. [London:] Longmans, 1836." Running head: "Taylor's Statesman." Signed "Φ"; not republished. JSM's bibliography identifies, as his, "Part of the article on Taylor's 'Statesman' in the same number of the same review." (I.e., as that containing his review of Fonblanque's *England Under Seven Administrations*.) (MacMinn, 48.) There is no copy in the Somerville College Library. In the library of the University of London (Senate House), there is a copy with George Grote's signature, identifying him as the co-author of this review.

THE STATESMAN is a short volume of essays, by the author of *Philip van Artevelde*:[*] and whoever has read with the same feelings as ourselves that very beautiful poem, alike distinguished for noble sentiment, beauty of expression, and interest in the story as well as in the characters, cannot have turned without elevated expectations to a fresh production of the same hand. Van Artevelde himself, the hero of that poem, as he appears both in the acquisition and in the exercise of supreme authority over his fellow-citizens of Ghent, is indeed a splendid conception, evincing that Mr. Taylor had attentively studied the essential characteristics of an effective popular leader—a leader who performs what Xenophon calls "the divine work of ruling over willing men,"[†] without any pre-established associations of rank or superstition, by the simple union of distinguished virtue and force of character. Assuredly this is a most interesting topic of contemplation, for every one who concerns himself at all about the larger interests of mankind, and Mr. Taylor has evidently bestowed upon it much deeper reflection than is common in the foundation of a modern poem. Both the text and the notes evince that the traits which form the striking character of his hero are not caught up at a hazard, merely as suitable

[*Henry Taylor, *Philip van Artevelde; a dramatic romance in two parts* (London: Moxon, 1834).]

[†See *Oeconomicus*, 21.5 and 12.]

themes for poetry, but that they are collected from an attentive perusal of history and its philosophical commentators.

A work, therefore, from the pen of Mr. Taylor, bearing the title of *The Statesman*, was calculated to raise considerable expectation. One might have imagined that it would be a delineation, in prose, and with reference to the circumstances of the present day, of the same *idéal* which the author had already exhibited in his political drama.

Such are the anticipations which the title of the present volume is calculated to suggest. But its contents will not fulfil these anticipations. Its merits are of another kind, and fall very short of the name bestowed upon it by the author.

A work fully corresponding, or even partially corresponding, to the full exigencies of so lofty a title as *The Statesman*, would indeed be among the most valuable contributions to modern politics and philosophy. To trace the greater lineaments of such a character, as it ought to exist, or must exist, in a state of society so complicated as that of England—to mark out the ends at which the statesman must aim, and the means whereby he must seek to accomplish them, if he would earn for himself any substantive name or lasting esteem—to shew how the powers of government may be most effectively employed to develope all the good tendencies of the age, and to subdue or mitigate its many corruptions—this, we say, would have been a task worthy of the highest intellect which our nation can afford; a statesman, such as Plato or Xenophon would have conceived, had they lived in the present time with the advantage of enlarged recorded experience, and with political phenomena open to their view, transcending both in extent and variety all which the ancient world could furnish. To execute this undertaking properly—of course it must have reference to some one given country and society—the highest powers of philosophical observation would indeed be required; that rare combination of accurate knowledge of fact, with comprehensive reasoning, which alone can enable an author to trace the virtues and the defects, the comforts and the miseries, of any given people, to their genuine sources and principles. M. de Tocqueville's work on the Democracy of America, though there is much of it in which we do not concur, furnishes a valuable specimen of enquiries undertaken in this spirit: and the picture of a statesman, such as he ought to be in this country, would be the deduction from a similar analysis, applied to the social and political phenomena of England. We are well aware indeed that such contemplations are usually stigmatised as visionary and Utopian: but they seem to us indispensably necessary, if it were only to keep alive in the mind of a statesman—that which official details have so great a tendency to obliterate—the obligation of acting with a view to results distant as well as results immediate, and of following out some coherent system of operations. Above all, they are necessary, if we are impressed with a due conviction of that important fact, without which moral and political science would be little better than a dreary void—the progressiveness of human nature; and the vast influence of good or bad government, as an accelerating or retarding cause of it. The goal which a wise statesman will seek to attain is a distant one, and his voyage of unknown length: he may often be driven out of his course, or altogether stopped, by temporary obstacles: but if the entire chart of the ocean in which he is sailing be open before him, both the deviations and the delay will be understood for what they are, and submitted to only so far as the iron hand of necessity may require: the exigencies of every day will be carefully provided for, even to their minutest details, yet with that constant reference towards the ultimate scope of the voyage, for which the captain of the vessel is especially responsible.

Certain it is, that if any future author shall sit down to compose a work called *The Statesman*, in the spirit which we have described, he will not be able to borrow much from the character of any minister whom England has produced for the last two centuries. Perhaps there are some who will consider this as a compliment to the English character, as well as to the English government: we need not say that, in our opinion, it is among the heaviest of all reproaches both to the one and to the other. To lay down any large principles of political action—to have any pre-conceived ends, with a scheme of means for attaining them—has been a proceeding either repudiated with scorn by English statesmen, or at least foreign to all their intellectual habits. Starting as they do, and as they always have done, from the hypothesis of absolute perfection in existing institutions, it is enough for them if they leave things *in statu quo*—if they provide for the pressing exigency of the day, with little or no thought for the morrow. Hence, during the last half century prior to 1830, while the individual energy of Englishmen has effected such miracles in the arts, in civilization, and in the acquisition of wealth, the proceedings of the government present only the spectacle of inglorious nullity, without the smallest evidence of superior wisdom or reach of thought—without any one lasting bequest to fix the eye and esteem of posterity. Yet during this same period there have been memorable evidences of statesmanlike activity in the countries around us: the Code Napoleon in France; the Federal Constitution in the United States of North America, deliberately planned and systematically reasoned out by its authors, freely accepted and faithfully obeyed by the people; while in Prussia, the condition of the entire population has been changed, by the abolition of glebe-servitude, the creation of municipal communities, and the universal diffusion of education,—all emanating from the direct scheme and unwearied interference of the government. What is there in the conduct of the English government, during the same interval, to attest either comprehensive design or forward beneficence?

If there be one quality more than another for the possession of which the mass of English citizens are distinguished, it is commercial activity, expertness in money-getting, and in turning their capital to account. It might reasonably be expected, therefore, that the public finances of such a nation would be administered with peculiar skill: yet when we look back upon the proceedings of the last war, in which financial affairs were not only of pressing importance, but conducted on the largest scale, how slender are the proofs of penetration and foresight on the part of the managing statesmen! Are we not now suffering under an unnatural increase of the national debt, arising out of the delusive trick of keeping up a sinking fund without any real surplus revenue? Have we not been deprived of the greatest of all facilities for diminishing the charge of the national debt during time of peace, by the practice of borrowing loans in stock at a low denomination of interest, and thus swelling the nominal amount of the capital funded? Look at the suspension of cash-payments by the Bank of England in 1797; did not the government of the day mainly contribute to bring on that calamitous event (the seeds of all the subsequent perilous disputes respecting currency), by the immense loans borrowed from the Bank Directors, and not repaid, in spite of the urgent remonstrances of the latter, who were thus stript of their principal means of controlling the amount of circulation? If such has been the improvidence of English statesmen, on their own ground of finance, in sacrificing future consequences to the convenience of the moment, can we wonder that they have left no monuments behind them in the shape of legislative amendment or improved institutions?

We are ready indeed to admit, that since the passing of the Reform Act, this utter apathy respecting legislative measures of permanent result has ceased to be in so great a degree the characteristic of English statesmen. Such is the first fruit of the newly acquired power of the people. Nor is it practicable under the prevailing keenness and activity of public discussion, that any minister can safely avoid attempting the settlement of important national grievances, from time to time, on some principles or other.

It is a considerable step thus to have roused the English statesman from absolute lethargy: nor ought we to forget that the great provocative cause of it—popular demand—in spite of all the obstructions and diversions which can be thrown in its way, is likely to increase rather than diminish for the future. But still this is not all. Public opinion may compel the minister to propose some measure or other; but it can hardly compel him, against his own inclination, to propose either a large measure or a wise one. He may think it sufficient just to stave off the loudest objectors, without concerning himself in any way about the substance or principle of the mischief: and whether he does so or not, will depend partly upon the reach of his own understanding, partly upon the idea which he has formed to himself of the obligations attached to his post. Hence the immense importance of keeping up the standard of duty in the mind of the statesman—of impressing on him the conviction that nothing except what is founded on large, sound, and comprehensive principles, can possibly either deserve or obtain lasting fame. There is so much in the daily life of an English minister which tends to extinguish all ideas of improvement, and to keep him buried under a load of routine, (not to mention the sinister interests under which he still lives and moves)—that if any sense of distant obligation, or any relish for lasting and critical esteem, is to be preserved in his mind, inspiring and instructive books are among the few aids to be reckoned upon for the purpose.

For the reasons which we have assigned, we think that a work really corresponding to the title of the *Statesman*, and applied to the present social and political state of England, would have been of signal utility; and we may be permitted to regret that, so far as regards the volume before us, the task still remains unperformed.

Mr. Taylor's book does not fulfil, and does not even attempt to fulfil, the promise of its title; which title in fact has no connexion with the design of the work, and must have been a very infelicitous *after-thought*. A more proper name would have been "Thoughts on Public Life," or "Reflections, Moral and Prudential, on a Political Career;" and the chapters should not have been called chapters, that is, parts of a whole, but essay first, essay second, and so on.

Mr. Taylor had a specific object, which he partially explains to us in his preface. He complains that writers on government and society have in general attended too much to scientific analysis, and too little to things in combined existence—that "while the structure of communities, and the nature of political powers and institutions have been extensively investigated, the art of *exercising* political functions, which might seem to be no unimportant part of political science, has occupied hardly any place in their speculations." (P. vi.) He remarks that those who have been practised in political affairs have written upon politics much better than philosophers, and he quotes Bacon, Burke, Machiavel, and Tacitus, as illustrations of this superiority. But these writers, he says, "still leave unattempted the formation of any coherent body of administrative doctrine." (P. x.) This deficiency, Mr. Taylor tells us, it would have been the height of his wish to supply, if he could have commanded leisure for the enterprise. Unfortunately he has not had leisure for any thing more than a few desultory disquisitions, tending towards the same point.

In the conclusion—which is in reality a second part of the preface—we find the reasons why the author thinks it peculiarly important at the present season to draw the attention of the public to questions of administrative government.

Of the two classes of political questions—those concerning forms of government, and those concerning its administration—there are seasons for both. I would sedulously guard myself against the error of undervaluing that class of questions of which I know least. I admit that under very many aspects of political society, questions concerning forms of government exceed all others in importance. I am far indeed from subscribing to that couplet of Mr. Pope's, which has obtained such singular celebrity,

> For forms of government let fools contest,
> Whiche'er is best administered is best.[*]

No rational man did ever dispute that a good administration of government is the *summum bonum* of political science: but neither can it be reasonably denied that good forms of government are essential to its good administration: they are contested on this ground; and to dismiss the contending parties with the epithet applied to them by Mr. Pope appears to be hardly worthy of an instructed writer.

But with all due respect for questions of form, and for an exclusive attention to them in their paramount season, what I would suggest is, that a time may come in which these questions should be degraded to a secondary rank, and questions of administration should take their place. I would observe that the contest concerning forms may be so engrossing and so long continued, as to defeat its own end. It may do so, not only for the time, but in its ultimate result.

Whilst all men's minds are agitated by these contests, whilst, owing to this agitation, administrative efficiency is suspended, and administrations are fugitive and precarious, it is clear that the end in view is sacrificed for the time being. And though it be not equally clear, it may yet be reasonably offered for consideration, that after constitutional reforms have been carried far enough to make it the interest of the government to engage in administrative reforms, the further progress of the former will be rather retarded than accelerated by the suspension of the latter. (Pp. 263–5.)

The foregoing extracts exhibit the general scope and origin of Mr. Taylor's work. We are very far from concurring in the estimate which he forms of the value of analytical writers on politics; though, as we also fully admit the importance of studying Machiavel and Tacitus, we are not curious in measuring whether one class of authors be a little above or a little below the other in the scale of utility. It is one thing to be master of general principles, and to be able to reason from them under assumed hypothetical circumstances: it is another thing to possess the talent of justly appreciating actual circumstances, so as to regulate the application of principles to any given

[*Alexander Pope, *An Essay on Man*, in *Works*, ed. Joseph Warton, *et al.*, 10 vols. (London: Priestley [Vol. X, Hearne], 1822, 1825), Vol. III, p. 115 (Epistle III, ll. 303–4).]

case. A man may possess the former who is totally destitute of the latter; but there cannot well be a first-rate statesman or administrator who does not combine the two, any more than there can be a first-rate physician who does not unite a comprehensive acquaintance with the principles of physiology and pathology, to enlarged experience and an expert eye for observation. "A coherent body of administrative doctrine," as we understand the meaning of the words, is not to be deduced from the authors whom Mr. Taylor extols. A statesman's skill in the contentious part of his business, the gaining of adherents and the struggling with rivals, may be improved by the insight which their writings afford into the passions and dispositions of men both individually and in masses—but not his knowledge of the business of administration properly so called, as we see it exemplified in the admirable life of a statesman like Turgot. Take the Poor-Law Commissioners, to whom so important a branch of the national administration is confided: suppose them seeking to prepare for themselves a stock of administrative doctrine, we doubt whether they would derive any special aid either from Bacon or Burke; but we are sure that they would find many parts of Mr. Bentham's works eminently conducive to their purpose—who comes, nevertheless, under the class set aside by Mr. Taylor as "analytical."

Nor do we concur in the opinion expressed by Mr. Taylor, that the progress of administrative reforms is retarded by the popular demand for constitutional reforms. We know that there are other countries in which much has been done in the former and little or nothing in the latter: but it is our clear opinion that in England increased responsibility to the people is the most effective way of creating in the minds of our administrators such dispositions as will insure the advance of administrative reforms. There might indeed be some force in Mr. Taylor's argument, if the fact were as he thinks, that "constitutional reforms have been carried far enough to make it the interest of a government to engage in administrative reforms." But is this so? Suppose those popular feelings, in which the demand for farther constitutional reform originates, to be extinguished among the constituencies, what would be the result? We should have the Tories restored to power without delay; and how many grains of administrative reform should we obtain from them? We doubt not that they would meditate attentively on the subjects of some of Mr. Taylor's chapters—On the Arts of Rising—On the Getting and Keeping of Adherents—Concerning Rank as a Qualification for High Office—On the Administration of Patronage—Concerning the Amusements of a Statesman; but they would adjourn to the Greek Calends his "Reform of the Executive," and they would skip over altogether his chapter "On the Conscience of a Statesman."

Mr. Taylor conceives that "the greatest want of the people, though the *least felt*, is that of moral, religious, and intellectual instruction." [P. 265.]

Let us ask, by whom this want is most felt, and by whom least? Much, by the people themselves; most of all, by the most popular-minded public men, whose influence would be increased by the increase of popular control, and who would thus be better enabled to provide for the supply of the want than they are now; least of all by the aristocratical classes in this country, whose passive instruments English statesmen have hitherto been, and from whose paralyzing grasp the executive government is yet but half extricated. If this first and greatest of all popular wants is ever destined to be supplied, it will be by a government emanating from keener popular control, and more deeply impressed with the necessity of rendering the people worthy to exercise control, than any which England has yet seen.

Although, however, we do not participate in Mr. Taylor's wish to draw away the attention of the public *from* constitutional reform, we are well pleased to see it invited *towards* administrative reform; and to this end, the first of all requisites is an improvement in the character, the abilities, and, most of all, the purposes, of administrators. Mr. Taylor's first chapter treats of the education of youth for a civil career, for which, as he complains, no special provision is now made, nor any definite course marked out. After remarking that historical studies, in this point of view, have been rated above their comparative value, he says,

A general knowledge of the laws of the land, and of international law, of foreign systems of jurisprudence, and especially a knowledge of the prominent defects of the system at home, should be diligently inculcated; and political economy should be taught with equal care, not less for the indispensable knowledge which it conveys, than as a wholesome exercise for the reasoning faculty—employed in this science less loosely than in ethics or history, less abstractedly than in mathematics. (P. 5.)

These are just recommendations; but if the study of political economy be useful, as most assuredly it is in a very high degree, surely the philosophy of the human mind and the philosophy of politics are no less so. Why should Mr. Taylor depreciate analysis in the latter, and extol it in the former? If the exceptions which he takes in his Preface against the analytical writers on government be of any avail, are they not equally applicable against political economy?—nay, have they not been actually advanced against it, almost in the precise terms employed by Mr. Taylor, a thousand and a thousand times over? The scheme of science is one and the same in every department of human thought and action to which analysis can be applied: deny its utility in any one, and you virtually disallow it in all.

It is somewhat surprising to us also that Mr. Taylor takes no notice whatever of classical studies. If there be any one vocation of active life to which classical studies belong with the most exact pertinence and speciality, it is that of a statesman; not merely from the consummate perfection of the ancient compositions in themselves, and the exquisite sense of what is appropriate and beautiful which they are thus calculated to create; though this too is of signal value, even if we consider statesmanship as a mere craft for individual advancement. But if it be true that the statesman exists not for himself merely, but for the public whom he serves—if the interests of that public require that the sense of obligation should in his case be peculiarly exalted, seeing that the circumstances around him tend for the most part to deaden and debase it—then, the study of the best works of classical antiquity comes recommended by still higher considerations; for the public obligations stood in the foreground of all the ancient morality; the idea of the commonwealth, as the supreme object of his duty and solicitude, attracted to itself the strongest emotions in the bosom of every virtuous man.

Now this tone of thought, when caught up and idealized by poets, orators, and philosophers, goes far to kindle and sustain that sense of enlarged patriotism which the details of a statesman's life are perpetually tending to supplant; at least it does as much as books can do towards that end, and much more in our opinion than modern books are at all calculated to do: for although the fulfilment of duties between man and man, and the forbearance from individual injury are carried now to a higher pitch than they were in antiquity, yet the ties which bind each individual to the community at large are comparatively far less seen and felt: they are neither recognizable in modern literature, nor in modern actual life; and hence the statesman comes to look upon himself as engaged only in one out of a variety of profit-seeking occupations, subject to no higher laws than those prescribed by the etiquette of the profession which he has chosen.

We shall now quote some of the most important of our author's counsels to statesmen, beginning with a chapter of which the title is the marrow of a whole treatise. "*A Statesman's most pregnant function lies in the choice and use of instruments.*" [Chap. ii, p. 13.]

The most important qualification of one who is high in the service of the state is his fitness for acting *through others*; since the importance of his operations vicariously effected ought, if he knows how to make use of his power, to predominate greatly over the importance which can attach to any man's direct and individual activity. The discovery and use of instruments implies indeed activity as well as judgment, because it implies that judgment which only activity in affairs can give. But it is a snare into which active statesmen are apt to fall, to lose, in the importance which they attach to the immediate and direct effects of their activity, the sense of that much greater importance which they might impart to it, if they applied themselves to make their powers operate through the most effective and the widest instrumentality. The vanity of a statesman is more flattered in the contemplation of what he does, than of what he causes to be done; although any man whose civil station is high ought to know that his causative *might* be, beyond all calculation, wider than his active sphere, and more important.

Therefore, no man who contemplates a public career should fail to begin early, and persist always in cultivating the society of able men, of whatsoever classes or opinions they may be, provided only they be honest. In every walk of life it were well that such men should associate themselves together, in order that combination may give increased effect to their lives; and in some of the middle walks of life the association does to a certain degree take place; but amongst those who are destined for a civil career, or are born to such a station in life as is likely to lead them into that career, the paramount importance of the object appears to be overlooked. Men in early life, seeking for enjoyment in society and for agreeable qualities only in their associates, their appetite for power yet unawakened, or their juvenile ambition anticipating the pleasures of power without foreseeing its wants, get themselves surrounded by companions who, though not perhaps unadorned with talents, are yet fit for no purposes in life but that of pleasing. At the entrance upon a public career, and in the first stages of it, the aspirant is not seasonably apprised by circumstances that this is against him, and that in his ascent and advancement, as he comes to have more and more scope for instruments, hardly any thing would be of so much moment to him as the number and serviceable quality of his associates, or of those with whom he has such intermediate connexion as may serve for requisite knowledge. (Pp. 13–16.)

No easy opportunity should be omitted of trying and proving men, and of recording the result. But so little is this somewhat obvious truth recognized, or such is the indifference of some statesmen to every thing but what is forced upon their attention, that men have been at the head of departments of the state, who might have had Bacon and Hooker in their service without knowing it. (P. 17.)

On this indifference of English public men to the value of intellectual ability, in comparison with some slight atom of trouble to themselves, hear our author in another place:

Yet such is the prevalent insensibility to that which constitutes the real treasure and resources of the country—its serviceable and statesmanlike minds—and so far are men in power from searching the country through for such minds, or men in parliament from promoting or permitting the search, that I hardly know if that minister has existed in the present generation who, if such a mind were casually presented to him, would not forego the use of it rather than hazard a debate in the House of Commons upon an additional item in his estimates. (Pp. 162–3.)

Well does Mr. Taylor continue:

Till the government of the country shall become a nucleus at which the best wisdom in the country contained shall be perpetually forming itself in deposit, it will be, except as regards the shuffling of power from hand to hand and class to class, little better than a government of fetches, shifts, and hand-to-mouth expedients.

Till a wise and constant instrumentality at work upon administrative measures (distinguished as they might be from measures of political parties) shall be understood to be essential to the government of a country, that country can be considered to enjoy nothing more than the embryo of a government,—a means towards producing, through changes in its own structure and constitution, and in the political elements acting upon it, something worthy to be called a government at some future time. For governing a country is a very different thing from upholding a government. *Alia res sceptrum, alia plectrum.* [Pp. 163–4.]

There being no sufficient amount of ability in the executive, and no sufficient desire to supply this want on the part of those on whom the task of supplying it would devolve, the following is the mode in which, according to our author, the ability which is neither had nor wished for, is done without. We do not think the tricks of mediocrity in high place were ever so pungently characterized in so few words. Mark how it is hit off to the life:

The far greater proportion of the duties which are performed in the office of a minister are, and must be, performed under no effective responsibility. Where politics and parties are not affected by the matter in question, and so long as there is no flagrant neglect or glaring injustice to individuals which a party can take hold of, the responsibility to parliament is merely nominal, or falls otherwise only through casualty, caprice, and a misemployment of the time due from parliament to legislative affairs. Thus the business of the office may be reduced within a very manageable compass, without creating public scandal. *By evading decisions wherever they can be evaded; by shifting them on other departments or authorities, where by any possibility they can be shifted; by giving decisions upon superficial examinations—categorically, so as not to expose the superficiality in propounding the reasons; by deferring questions till, as Lord Bacon says, "they resolve of themselves;" by undertaking nothing for the public good which the public voice does not call for; by conciliating loud and energetic individuals at the expense of such public interests as are dumb, or do not attract attention; by sacrificing every where what is feeble and obscure, to what is influential and cognizable*: by such means and shifts as these, the single functionary granted by the theory may reduce his business within his powers, and perhaps obtain for himself the most valuable of all reputations in this line of life, that of "a safe man;" and if his business, even thus reduced, strains, as it well may, his powers and his industry to the utmost, then (whatever may be said of the theory) the man may be without reproach—without other reproach at least than that which belongs to men placing themselves in a way to have their understandings abused and debased, their sense of justice corrupted, their public spirit and appreciation of public objects undermined. (Pp. 151–3.)

Far other is our author's conception of what is due to a nation from those who voluntarily undertake the sacred trust of guarding those of its interests on which all others are dependent.

Turning (I would almost say revolting) from this to another view of what these duties are, and of the manner in which they ought to be performed, I would, in the first place, earnestly insist upon this: that in all cases concerning points of conduct and quarrels of subordinate officers; in all cases of individual claims upon the public, and public claims upon individuals; in short, in all cases (and such commonly constitute the bulk of a minister's unpolitical business) wherein the minister is called upon to deliver a quasi-judicial decision, he should, on no consideration, permit himself to pronounce such decision unaccompanied by a detailed statement of all the material facts and reasons upon which his judgment proceeds. I know well the inconveniencies of this course; I know that authority is most imposing without reason alleged; I know that the reasons will rarely satisfy, and will sometimes tend to irritate the losing party, who would be better content to think himself overborne than convicted. I am aware that the minister may be sometimes, by this course, inevitably drawn into protracted argumentation with parties whose whole time and understanding is devoted to getting advantages over him; and, with a full appreciation of these difficulties, I am still of opinion, that, for the sake of justice, they ought to be encountered and dealt with. One who delivers awards from which there is no appeal, for which no one can call him to account (and such, as has been said, is practically a minister's exemption), if he do not subject himself to this discipline,—if he do not render himself amenable to confutation, will inevitably contract careless and precipitate habits of judgment; and the case which is not to be openly expounded will seldom be searchingly investigated. In various cases also which concern public measures, as well as those which are questions of justice, ample written and recorded discussion is desirable. Few questions are well considered till they are largely written about; and the minds and judgments of great functionaries transacting business *inter mœnia*, labour under a deficiency of bold checks from oppugnant minds. (Pp. 153–5.)

The truth and wisdom of these remarks must strike every one who has been largely conversant with public business, and whose conscience has not been seared by the exercise of irresponsible power, nor his intellect enslaved to habits of routine. A security against bad measures worth all others put together, and essential to the complete efficacy of every other, is the obligation of writing down the reasons of whatever is done. Our vast empire in India is governed upon this system. There is not an act of that government, from the greatest to the most trivial, the grounds of which are not extant upon the face of recorded documents, communicated generally to the parties interested, and always to the controlling authorities in England. The same system is largely acted upon by the home authorities in their own proceedings; and the result is a degree both of purity and wisdom in the conduct of Indian affairs, far enough from perfect, though progressively and constantly improving, but such as, we will venture to say, never were exemplified in circumstances of similar difficulty by any government upon earth, and such as no earthly expedient could have rendered possible, except that of compelling the grounds of every proceeding to be registered "upon the face," as our author says, "of producible documents." [P. 51.]

Mr. Taylor next animadverts upon that quality of our public men, which, most of all, deprives them of all title to the name of statesmen; their never thinking it any business of theirs to originate improvements, nor to bestir themselves for any purpose whatever, except what is forced upon them by "pressure from without:"[*]

[*See, e.g., Robert Peel, "Speech delivered at the Mansion House" (23 Dec., 1834), in *Speeches by the Right Honourable Sir Robert Peel, Bart., during his Administration, 1834–1835*, 2nd ed. (London: Roake and Varty, 1835), p. 11.]

Further, it is one business to do what must be done, another to devise what ought to be done. It is in the spirit of the British government, as hitherto existing, to transact only the former business; and the reform which it requires is to enlarge that spirit, so as to include the other. Of and from amongst those measures which are forced upon him, to choose that which will bring him the most credit with the least trouble, has hitherto been the sole care of a statesman in office; and as a statesman's official establishment has been heretofore constituted, it is care enough for any man. Every day, every hour, has its exigencies, its intermediate demands; and he who has hardly time to eat his meals cannot be expected to occupy himself in devising good for mankind. "I am," says Mr. Landor's statesman, "a waiter at a tavern, where every hour is dinner-time, and pick a bone on a silver dish."[*] The current compulsory business he gets through as he may; some is undone, some is ill done; but at least to get it done is an object which he proposes to himself. But as to the inventive and suggestive portions of a statesman's functions, he would think himself an Utopian dreamer if he undertook them: and such he would be if he undertook them in any other way than through a re-constitution and reform of his establishment.

And what then is the field for these inventive and self-suggested operations; and if practicable, would they be less important than those which are called for by the obstreperous voices of to-day and to-morrow?

I am aware that under popular institutions there are many measures of exceeding advantage to the people, which it would be in vain for a minister to project, until the people, or an influential portion of the people, should become apprized of the advantage, and ask for it; many which can only be carried by overcoming resistance; much resistance only to be overcome with the support of popular opinion and general solicitude for the object. And looking no further, it might seem that what is not immediately called for by the public voice was not within the sphere of practical dealing. But I am also aware that in the incalculable extent and multifarious nature of the public interests which lie open to the operations of a statesman in this country, one whose faculties should be adequate would find (in every month that he should devote to the search) measures of great value and magnitude, which time and thought only were wanting to render practicable. (Pp. 156–9.)

The sequel of the passage is truly admirable:

He would find them—not certainly by shutting himself up in his closet, and inventing what had not been thought of before—but by holding himself on the alert; by listening with all his ears (and he should have many ears abroad in the world) for the suggestions of circumstance; by catching the first moment of public complaint against real evil, encouraging it and turning it to account; *by devising how to throw valuable measures that do not excite popular interest into one boat with those that do*; by knowing (as a statesman who is competent to operations on a large scale may know) *how to carry a measure by enlargement such as shall merge specific objections that would be insurmountable in general ones that can be met*; in short, by a thousand means and projects lying in the region between absolute spontaneous invention on the one hand, and mere slavish adoption on the other; such means and projects as will suggest themselves to one who meditates the good of mankind, "sagacious of his quarry from

[*Walter Savage Landor, *Imaginary Conversations of Literary Men and Statesmen*, 5 vols. (London: Taylor and Hessey, 1824–29), Vol. I, p. 26.]

afar,"[*] but not to a minister whose whole soul is and must be in the "notices of motions" and the order book of the House of Commons, and who has no one behind to prompt him to other enterprize, no closet or office statesman for him to fall back upon, as upon an inner mind. This then is the great evil and want; that there is not within the pale of our government any adequately numerous body of efficient statesmen, some to be more externally active, and answer the demands of the day, others to be somewhat more retired and meditative, in order that they may take thought for the morrow. How great the evil of this want is, it may require peculiar opportunities of observation fully to understand and feel: but one who with competent knowledge should consider well the number and magnitude of those measures which are postponed for years, or totally pre-termitted, not for want of practicability, but for want of time and thought; one who should proceed with such knowledge to consider the great means and ap-pliances of wisdom which lie scattered through this intellectual country, squan-dered upon individual purposes, not for want of applicability to national ones, but for want of being brought together and directed; one who, surveying these things with a heart capable of a people's joys and sorrows, their happy virtue or miserable guilt on these things dependent, should duly estimate the abundant means unemployed, the exalted ends unaccomplished, could not choose, I think, but say within himself, that there must be something fatally amiss in the very idea of statesmanship on which our system of administration is based; or that there must be some moral apathy at what should be the very centre and seat of life in a country—that the golden bowl must be broken at the fountain, and the wheel broken at the cistern.[†]

Mr. Taylor's suggestions for remedying these evils, or rather, for render-ing it possible that they should be remedied, are contained in his chapter "On the Reform of the Executive."

He begins by describing what the constitution of a government office is, and the number as well as description of the persons who fill it. First, the minister: next, one or more political and parliamentary subordinates (under-secretaries of state, lords of the Treasury and Admiralty, &c.): thirdly, an officer of similar rank, not in Parliament, and permanent in the office, without reference to changes of ministry: fourthly, a private secre-tary, who comes and goes with his principal: fifthly, about twenty clerks, divided into three or four degrees of subordination.

Mr. Taylor delivers a strong opinion that this establishment is altogether insufficient for the public purposes which it ought to answer, and which it might, if enlarged, be made to answer.

The duties of councillor and legislator, he thinks, are quite sufficient to occupy all the time and energies of the minister himself, who ought to be relieved from all the office-business, in so far as regards the actual trans-action and superintendence of it; retaining only that general familiarity

[*John Milton, *Paradise Lost*, in *The Poetical Works* (London: Tonson, 1695), p. 166 (X, 281).]

[†Pp. 159–61. For the closing image, see Ecclesiastes, 12:6.]

with what is done, which may render him competent to explain or defend it in the House of Commons or in the Cabinet. The parliamentary assistant ought also to enjoy a similar exemption during the session of Parliament. Further, he thinks, that

> Whatever other things be necessary (and *they are many*)—it is indispensable that every minister of state charged with public business should be provided with four or six permanent under-secretaries, instead of one—that all of these should be efficient closet-statesmen, and two of them at the least be endowed, in addition to their practical abilities, with some gifts of philosophy and speculation, well cultivated, disciplined, and prepared for use. (P. 162.)

We fear that Mr. Taylor's suggestions of enlargement in the official establishment will be only of partial efficacy in rectifying that which is "fatally amiss" in the idea of English statesmanship and in the working of English administration.

We should indeed entertain greater hopes from his proposal, if we could believe that it was only the absorption of the minister's time which had hitherto stood in the way of administrative improvement. But is this the fact? The hindrance, we fear, is far more deeply seated, and more difficult to be removed.

Were we indeed to assume that the new persons introduced into the office would be of the superior character and dispositions which Mr. Taylor contemplates, and that their influence would be predominant in determining its proceedings, we should anticipate considerable improvement in matters of administration. But neither of these two essential conditions appears to us likely to be realized; for who are the persons in whose hands the appointment of the new under-secretaries would naturally be vested? The reader has seen the opinion Mr. Taylor himself entertains of their indifference to the value of pre-eminent mental endowments. They are not surely persons who would be disposed—we speak with no particular reference to the present cabinet—to seek out distinguished capacities such as Mr. Taylor's description prefigures; scarcely even to sustain or countenance such men, when pointed out to them either by public celebrity or by accidental causes.

Again, admitting that perfectly appropriate individuals were discovered and appointed, would they be allowed to exercise any predominant influence over official proceedings? Would they not be more likely to sink down to the pre-existing official level, than to elevate others to their own? The head of the office, who represents it both in the Cabinet and in Parliament would still remain as he is now, in possession of supreme and undiminished ascendancy. There is nothing in the scheme to render him more favourable to improvement than he is now: nor is it conceivable that improvement should ever be realized to any conspicuous extent, if he continued averse, or even backward in it.

For these and other reasons, we are far from expecting that the mere enlargement of the official establishment, in the way that Mr. Taylor recommends, would produce any considerable effects in the way of amended administration. It may be very true, as he contends, that the establishment as at present constituted is inadequate, and that if we assume ever so great a regeneration in the characters of the men composing it, they would still be too much loaded with the drudgery of details to discharge the higher functions effectively. Still, the change of spirit and purpose, in the bosoms of official leaders, would be the great victory to be achieved, and the main cause on which all the good to be done by the office, whether fully or sparingly mounted, must depend.

Mr. Taylor seems to think that it would be easy to distinguish administrative measures from the measures of political parties. However practicable it may be in the abstract to frame a classification in which the two shall stand pointedly apart, we doubt the possibility of causing such a distinction to be practically adhered to in England. If there be any one object which might reasonably have been expected to unite the favourable wishes of contending parties, it is the education of the people, and the cares of government for its universal diffusion: the more so, as we know that both Prussia and the United States of America, though differing as much as possible in respect of political constitution, have yet been alike distinguished for the solicitude of both governments to render education universal among the people. If we look at the manner in which this important question has been dealt with by the aristocracy and the Tories in England, we shall find that they have uniformly set themselves, as a party, in opposition to popular education; and that they have never been induced to acquiesce in it even partially, except as a means of rendering the people subservient to their own political church. To draw a measure within the sphere of political conflict, it is sufficient if one powerful party in the state choose so to deal with it: and when we remark the sectarian acrimony which has been displayed in opposition to such a cause as the education of the people, what hope can we indulge that administrative improvements of any kind will be discussed and opposed simply on their own specific merits?

However the case may be in other countries, it seems to us that in England political improvement and administrative improvement must emanate from the same hands and the same impulses. The friends of the former may not always be equally zealous friends of the latter; but the opponents of the former will always be the most vehement opponents of the latter, if it be undertaken on any considerable scale. Nothing but strong popular sympathy, which can only be earned in the present day by statesmen who are at least believed to be friendly to political reforms, will impart either boldness for projecting large administrative reforms, or power for accomplishing them. In truth, we think that the secret of the general degeneracy of English administration is, to a great degree, the working out in detail of the sinister political purposes which have animated English statesmen in the gross. Are not the vices, the prejudices, and the negligence, of our colonial management deducible chiefly from the corrupt use which our aristocracy has always proposed to make of the colonies for their own patronage and emolument? Suppose the additional under-secretaries proposed by Mr. Taylor to be attached to the Colonial Office—would it be possible for them to accomplish any perceptible improvement in that branch of administration, if they were tied down still to extract from the colonies the same amount of jobs and appointments as heretofore for the benefit of the aristocracy? It is only by political improvement that the general spirit and purposes of English administrators can be amended: when this is done, we are sensible that much remains for administrative ability to accomplish; but we think it chimerical to expect that those who are by the supposition averse or indifferent to the larger ends involved in political improvement, will be earnest in accomplishing the comparatively smaller objects included in administrative details.*

We do full justice to the spirit in which this chapter of Mr. Taylor's

*In confirmation of this opinion we may refer to one of Mr. Taylor's chapters, which treats of Special Commissions, and Committees of either House of Parliament, as aids to the statesman in his work. Mr. Taylor gives, most justly, the preference to the former. There cannot be the smallest comparison between the two in point of efficiency. The facts collected in evidence before a committee of parliament are often extremely valuable: the report is generally meagre and nugatory. The special commission, if composed of persons properly selected, furnishes a full and exhaustive view of the whole subject: evils together with their remedies—facts with the inferences deducible from them. In truth, it seems to us that as matters now stand in England, there is no other way of exposing all the facts of the case methodically to view, in sequence and coherence with each other, and with satisfactory assurance that nothing material is omitted: there is scarcely any other way of laying a broad and firm foundation for large administrative measures. Now it may not be amiss to remark, in reference to Mr. Taylor's ideas of disconnecting administrative reform from political reform, that there is hardly any subject on which the Tories in the House of Commons are more vehement, than in their denunciation of special commissions, as useless jobs and waste of the public money. Sir Robert Peel has more than once condemned them, as indefensible contrivances for saving the time and trouble of indolent members of parliament, and for accomplishing objects which might be easily attained by a committee of ordinary diligence upstairs. It will be found that the champions of political abuses are in the main constrained to take their stand on the *status quo*, entire as it exists; occasionally perhaps venturing to meddle with some small and isolated evil, but dreading the contagion of any large and systematic improvement, even in matters of simple administration.

volume is conceived, nor do we express any opinion unfavourable to such an extension of the executive as he recommends; but we are bound to state our belief that it will not change the spirit of official proceedings to the extent that he anticipates; and we must again repeat that the prosecution of administrative reforms apart from political reforms, seems to us, as a general rule, altogether hopeless in England.

In another place (p. 210) Mr. Taylor says:

With the narrow limits which opinion, as it exists, assigns to the duties of the executive government and its servants (to which narrowness of duty the government and its servants naturally confine themselves), responsibility for *defect of law* falls nowhere; or if it be held to fall upon the legislature, it is so diffused over that numerous body, as to be of no force or effect. When evil manifests itself, in however cognizable a shape, there is no member of the government, whether or not he be also a member of the legislature, or any servant of the public, who does not think that his case for non-interference is complete so soon as he makes out that the evil is owing to a fault in the law. The question, whose fault is it that the law is faulty, is asked of no man, and naturally no man asks it of himself. But that must needs be regarded as an imperfect system of administrative government which does not lay these faults at the door of some individual functionary, in the numerous cases in which it would be perfectly practicable to do so. Did C observe the evil and report it to B? if not, let him answer for it: did B consider of it, and suggest a remedy to A? if not, let B's neglect be denounced: did A adopt B's suggestion, or devise something better, and go to parliament for a remedial law? if not, let the charge lie against A. (Pp. 210–11.)

This is a just and forcible paragraph. But we think that the excuse here offered on behalf of "the Government and its servants," as if their spontaneous activity was chilled by a prevalent "opinion," is something more creditable than history has proved them to deserve. Has it not been the fashion for "the Government and its servants," up to the last year or two at the least, to denounce in unmeasured language every one who was forward in pointing out imperfections in the law, and to put forth all their ingenuity for the purpose of screening or denying the reality of abuse, instead of preventing or redressing it? Let the inestimable labours of Mr. Hume, and the incessant repulses which he has experienced, serve as a reply.

If then it be true that opinion tends to circumscribe unduly the functions of the executive, it is at least equally true that this boundary, how narrow and miserable soever, has been fully coextensive with the wishes and ideas of official persons themselves. We admit, however, with Mr. Taylor, that such an opinion has prevailed. The class from whom statesmen are usually taken have been but too well disposed to encourage the idea that the business of the executive was to be assimilated as much as possible to that of a private counting-house, in respect of the duties to be performed—that regularity in answering letters and applications, and plausibility in eluding parliamentary inquiry was the highest excellence attainable in their craft: above all, that anything which touched, however remotely, on the verge of theory was alike insane and pernicious. Popular-minded men, on the other hand, having observed—what has been uniformly the fact up to the last few years—that the efforts and purposes of English statesmen have been directed to exalt the aristocracy and keep down the people, have thought themselves fortunate if they could only restrict the sphere of such pernicious agency. Not being able to render the executive beneficent, they have been content to see it inert and languid. Thus the opinion has gained ground, among persons of opposite political sentiments, that it is a virtue in the executive to do nothing, and to let things take their own course. Of late, since the passing of the Reform Act, the popular masses have begun to take an altered measure of what the dispositions of the executive ought to be, and to conceive new hopes from its wakefulness and its activity. And we think that if a statesman of the present day does not discharge with tolerable zeal the important duties which this chapter of Mr. Taylor's work points out, it will be much more owing to his own reluctance, than to any bridle put upon him by opinion from without.

Chapter the tenth, on the Conscience of a Statesman, is one of the best in the volume.

The conscience of a statesman should be rather a strong conscience than a tender conscience: for a conscience of more tenderness than strength will be liable in public life to be perverted in two ways;—1st. By reflecting responsibilities disproportionately to their magnitude, and missing of the large responsibilities whilst it is occupied with the small. 2nd. By losing in a too lively apprehension of the responsibilities of action the sense of responsibility for inaction.

No doubt the most perfect conscience would be that which should have all strength in its tenderness, all tenderness in its strength, and be equally adapted to public and private occasions. But I speak of the consciences of men as they exist with their imperfect capacities, bearing in mind the truth, "ut multæ virtutes in vitia degenerant, et quod magis est, sæpe videas eosdem affectus, pro temporum sorte, nunc virtutes esse, nunc vitia."* And these dilemmas of virtue duly considered, it will be found to be better for the public interests that a statesman should have some hardihood, than much weak sensibility of conscience. (Pp. 60–1.)

After illustrating "the *mismeasurements* of a conscience tender to weakness," our author proceeds:

2nd. As to the conscience becoming, from an exceeding tenderness as to acts and deeds, too insensible on the point of inaction or delay. It is very certain that there may be met with, in public life, a species of conscience which is all bridle and no spurs. A statesman whose conscience is of the finest texture as to everything which he does, will sometimes make no conscience of doing nothing. His conscience will be liable to become to him as a quagmire, in which the faculty of action shall stick fast at every step. And to this tendency of the conscience

*J. Barclaii Argenis. [John Barclay, *Argenis* (Paris: Buon, 1621).]

the worldly interests of a statesman will pander. *Conscience is, in most men, an anticipation of the opinions of others*; and whatever the moral responsibility may be, official responsibility is much less apt to be brought home to a statesman in cases of error by inaction, than in contrary cases. What men might have done is less known than what they have actually done, and the world thinks so much less of it, and with so much less definiteness and confidence of opinion, that the sins of omissions are sins on the safe side as to this world's responsibilities.

The concluding paragraph is excellent:

Above all, it is to be wished that the conscience of a statesman should be an intelligent and perspicacious conscience—not the conscience of the heart only, but the conscience of the understanding—that wheresoever the understanding should be enabled to foresee distant consequences, or comprehend wide ones, there the conscience should be enabled to follow, *not failing in quickness because the good or evil results in question are less palpable, and perhaps less certain than in private life, are not seen with the eyes and heard with the ears*, but only known through meditation and foresight. Many magnify in words the importance of public duties, but few appreciate them in feeling; and that, not so much for want of feeling, as *for want of carrying it out to whatever results the understanding reaches*. It is impossible that the feeling in regard to public objects should be *proportionate* to the feeling for private ones, because the human heart is not large enough; and it is too often found that when the conscience is not sustained by a sense of due proportion, it gets thrown out altogether. It sometimes happens that he who would not hurt a fly will hurt a nation. (Pp. 63–5.)

The mental quality here indicated is of the highest importance, and we maintain that the best and most effectual method of imparting it is that training in analytical philosophy which Mr. Taylor's preface tends so much to depreciate. If a man is to be qualified for "foreseeing distant consequences or comprehending wide ones," he must be taught to distinguish the constant from the accidental sequences in human affairs—he must be familiarised with those larger classifications which alone serve as a basis for propositions extensively true and applicable,—his mind must be imbued with principles in their pure and uncombined state, and initiated in the art of applying them to real life, by previously reasoning from them in hypothetical cases. Such lessons form the only discipline for guarding the statesman against the exclusive surrender of his mind to what is near and present, and for enabling him to look both backward to causes and forward to results. If by any inherent acuteness of his own he should fall naturally into the same track in which analysis would have placed him, this is a mere fortunate accident, forming an exception to the ordinary rules of probability.

The chapter on this subject might be much enlarged, and there is one topic in particular which might have been insisted on with advantage. The feeling of obligation as it now exists, towards different individuals and different classes in the same community, is lamentably unequal. The comfort and suffering of one man, on the foreknowledge of which all rational sense of obligation towards him is based, counts in general estimation for something infinitely more than that of another man in a different rank or position. The great mass of our labouring population have no representatives in Parliament, and cannot be said to have any political station whatever; while the distribution of what may be called social dignity is more unequal in England than in any other civilized country of Europe, and the feeling of communion and brotherhood between man and man more artificially graduated according to the niceties of the scale of wealth. Assuming perfect rectitude of intentions on the part of a statesman, it is hardly possible that his moral calculations should not be more or less vitiated by the impurities of such an atmosphere. In laying his grounds for public measures, or in establishing administrative regulations, he will be almost unconsciously led to under-estimate the interests of the poorer multitude, and to give undue preponderance to those of the few who are clustered around him— whose pains and pleasures he has been accustomed to identify with his own, and whose complaints he readily anticipates even before they actually assail him. Some taint of this kind seems to us almost unavoidable, in a statesman who presides over such a society as ours, even though he be well intentioned, and perfectly free from the grosser corruption of oligarchical immorality; and warnings against it would find an appropriate place in any work professing to guide or rectify his conscience.

We question much, however, whether a conscience, such as Mr. Taylor would wish to create in his Statesman, will ever be found in one who has practised the Arts of Rising as they are described in his fourteenth chapter. These arts, he remarks [p. 92], "have commonly some mixture of baseness;" and we cannot say that they are divested of that quality in his description of them.

We pass to chapter the sixteenth—On the Ethics of Politics; a very important subject, which is not very successfully handled. Mr. Taylor takes a distinction between private and public life, in regard to the observance of the rules of morality. He admits that the primary test of right and wrong is, the balance of all the consequences of an act; and he thinks that, judging by this test, exceptions to the ordinary rules of morality are occasionally admissible in public life, but never under any circumstances justifiable in private life. He says,

Morality can only be maintained by the submission of individual judgments to general rules. Let us take this principle, and see whether it be equally applicable to private and to political life. The law of truth stands first in the code of private morality. Suppose this law adopted absolutely by statesmen acting in this country and in this age as members of a government. Not one in ten of the measures taken by the cabinet can win the sincere assent of every member of that cabinet. The opinions of fifteen or twenty individuals can never be uniformly concurrent. The law of truth would require the dissentient members not to express assent. Under this law, when the Speaker of the House of Commons bids those that are of this opinion to say aye, and those who are of the contrary opinion to say no, the dissentient members of the cabinet must say "no" accordingly. But if every such diversity of opinion is to be publicly declared, it is manifestly not in the nature of things, as society is at present constituted, that a plural government should exist. To this the moralist answers,—Ask not whether it can exist or no, but maintain truth and the immutable principles of right and wrong, and trusting to them, dare all consequences. I reply, If they *be* immutable principles of right and wrong, trust to them of course; but that is itself the question at issue.

I recur, therefore, to the primary test of right and wrong, namely, the balance of all the consequences, near and distant, obvious and involved; and I estimate the consequences of relaxing the law of truth in private life to shew a vast balance of evil; and the consequence of relaxing that law in public life to shew a serious array of evil certainly, but I hesitate to say a balance, because I feel myself unable to calculate the magnitude of the moral evils, and the extent of the destruction of moral principles, which would ensue either by a dissolution of the general frame of society, or by the secession of scrupulous men from the government, and the consequent delivery of it into the hands of the unscrupulous. (Pp. 111–14.)

Mr. Taylor seems to be somewhat ashamed of having gone so far as to admit the possibility of exceptions to the ordinary rules of morality in public life, and he shelters himself by displaying an extremity of rigour in regard to private life. We think his doctrine altogether untenable, and inconsistent with itself. If a man believes that the rules of morality derive their entire authority from a certain simple feeling called the moral sense, he puts the consideration of the consequences of acts altogether out of the question, and no exception to a moral rule, arising out of such consequences, can ever find a place in his system. But if we once admit as the supreme test of right and wrong in an act, the balance of all its consequences, by what approach to omniscience can we pretend to predict that such balance must always be on one side, in every conceivable diversity of cases? How can we foreknow individual circumstances in such manner as to assure ourselves that in no imaginable incident of private life can the specific evil of telling truth outweigh the general evil of telling falsehood? To admit the balance of consequences as a test of right and wrong, necessarily implies the possibility of exceptions to any derivative rule of morality which may be deduced from that test. If evil will arise in any specific case from our telling truth, we are forbidden by a law of morality from doing that evil: we are forbidden by another law of morality from telling falsehood. Here then are two laws of morality in conflict, and we cannot satisfy both of them. What is to be done but to resort to the primary test of all right and wrong, and to make a specific calculation of the good or evil consequences, as fully and impartially as we can? The evil of departing from a well-known and salutary rule is indeed one momentous item on that side of the account; but to treat it as equal to infinity, and as necessarily superseding the measurement of any finite quantities of evil on the opposite side, appears to us to be the most fatal of all mistakes in ethical theory.

When, after reading these remarks of Mr. Taylor on the morality of private life, we pass to what he says on that of public life, we are forcibly struck by the contrast. Considering that he thinks the law of truth-telling so inexorable, that the maximum of private evil can never in any case justify a deviation from it, we are surprised to find him speaking without disapprobation of the very questionable practice of forensic advocacy as now conducted, involving, as it does, not merely simulation on the part of the advocate himself, but the greatest exertions of ingenuity on his part to entrap the honest witness into falsehood, as well as to bolster up the deception of the mendacious witness. Then again Mr. Taylor seems to treat the manifestation of any dissent among the members of a plural cabinet as an evil sufficient to overbalance at once the obligations of veracity in public life. Even admitting, which we by no means do, that there is on the whole a balance of advantage in favour of this simulated unanimity, the contrary system is surely, to say the least of it, exceedingly practicable; and we shall find no difficulty in producing abundant cases of private life, wherein the specific evil to be weighed against the general obligation of veracity is infinitely greater than the inconvenience of a cabinet being known and avowed to be partially and occasionally dissentient.

It seems to us that all the reasons by which Mr. Taylor establishes the necessity of recognising exceptional cases to general rules of morality in public life are no less applicable to prove the like necessity in private life. There is no generic distinction between the two departments; though it may happen that the cases requiring specific calculation of good and evil are more numerous in public life, because the acts of the statesman are liable to affect directly large masses of men, while those of a private individual seldom directly reach any one beyond his own circle. The real difficulty is, in both cases, that which Mr. Taylor states it to be in regard to public life only —"in discriminating the cases of exemption: in the delimitation of those bounds within which a statesman's dispensation should be confined." (P. 116.) We must remark, however, that the use of such words as *exemption*, or *dispensation*, leads to a most erroneous conception of the case; for the necessity of weighing specific mischief against the evil of departure from a general rule, is in reality the heaviest of all obligations which can possibly be imposed either upon a statesman or upon a private individual; and moral acting would be rendered easier, instead of more difficult, if it could be reduced in every case to a blindfold obedience to some one pre-established

rule. Unfortunately this cannot be done, because the moral rules are perpetually liable to clash with one another, and actually do so clash in all those
exceptional cases now under consideration, so as to leave us no resource
except in a direct appeal to the supreme authority from whence all moral
rules are derived.

We know that those who hold this doctrine are accused of licensing immorality, and we admit that the process not only carries with it a serious
responsibility, but will be ill performed if there enter into it either bad faith
or want of intelligence. But is not the same thing true of the difficult conjunctures in every man's daily walk or profession—in trade, in navigation,
in medical practice? And do we really assist a virtuous man in these moral
emergencies, by enjoining him to shut his eyes to all the evil on one side of
the question? It is rather curious to remark, that the charge against the
philosophical moralists, who maintain the necessity of resorting to specific
calculation in certain exceptional cases, is the direct reverse of the reproach
which is addressed to philosophers in other departments of science. In other
sciences, philosophers are censured for attending exclusively to classes, and
despising individuals—for looking only to essential qualities, and neglecting
altogether what is accidental or particular to the case before them—for a
barbarous readiness to inflict any amount of specific evil, if it be necessary
in the carrying out of their theories. In moral philosophy, the analytical
writers incur the opposite imputation. Because they maintain the necessity
of specific calculation in certain exceptional cases, they are treated as if they
annihilated all moral rules—as if the individual action was everything, and
the class of actions nothing, in their estimation—as if they suffered themselves to be absorbed by that which is accidental and special to the case
before them, and were incapable of fully appreciating the more comprehensive considerations on the other side. Philosophy commands that in dealing
with any particular case, the whole of the circumstances, without exception,
should be taken into view, essential as well as accidental: and if a man
wilfully overlooks the latter, when they are pregnant with mischievous consequences, he cannot discharge himself from moral responsibility by pleading that he had the general rule in his favour. What should we say to a
physician, who communicated an agonising piece of family intelligence, in
reply to the inquiry of our sick friend, at a moment when the slightest
aggravation of malady threatened to place him beyond all hope of recovery?
In a case like this, surely there is no man of common sense or virtue, who
would think for a moment of sheltering himself under the inexorable law of
veracity, and refusing to entertain any thought of the irreparable specific
mischief on the other side.

We have gone to considerable length in pointing out the fallacy of that
distinction which Mr. Taylor takes between public life and private life, in

regard to the moral rules, because we think that such a distinction is not favourable to the genuine morality of either. Much more remains to be said on the subject: but we have already reached the utmost limit which we can allow it to occupy.

In Chapter the nineteenth, On Ambition, it is remarked, "that where there are large powers with little ambition, nature has given the machinery without the *vis motrix*. Hardly anything will call a man's mind into full activity, if ambition be wanting: where it is least forthcoming as a substantive and waking passion, there are various indirect adjuncts of other passions whereby it may be quickened—such as love, philanthropy, timidity, friendship in particular cases." (Pp. 132–3.) We doubt much whether ambition be so necessary as Mr. Taylor imagines to develope the maximum of mental powers, though it may be necessary to induce a man to undergo the fatigue, disgust, and anxiety inseparable from a training for high office in this country. Those statesmen in modern history, who have done the greatest honour to the character, such men as Turgot, Washington, Jefferson, have been, for the most part, men but moderately animated by ambitious feelings. And we may add, that Plato lays it down as a part of his idea of a perfect ruler,* that the unwillingness to exercise power is a necessary concomitant of those dispositions and capacities which enable a ruler to exercise it with the full measure of benefit to the governed. He considered that an eagerness to possess power was a strong presumptive proof of the absence of any superior fitness for exercising it. Ambition alone may be able to call forth the efforts necessary for crushing a man's rivals, and defending his power against assaults from without; but we question whether any high degree of it will ever co-exist, except by accident, with the nobler purposes of a statesman.

We dissent equally from the distinction which Mr. Taylor draws in the following passage between the state of mind suitable for the statesman, and that appropriate to the philosopher:

The independent thinking of persons who have trained and habituated themselves to philosophic freedom of opinion is unfavourable to statesmanship; because the business of a statesman is less with truth at large, than with truths commonly received. The philosopher should have a leaning *from* prescription, in order to counterbalance early prepossessions, and place the mind *in equilibrio*: the statesman, on the contrary, should have a leaning towards it. Having to act always with others, through others, and upon others, and those others for the most part *vulgus hominum*, his presumptions should be in favour of such opin-

*Plato, *Republic* [Vol. II, p. 142 (520^d)], vii. 5. Ἐν πόλει ᾗ ἥκιστα πρόθυμοι ἄρχειν οἱ μέλλοντες ἄρξειν, ταύτην ἄριστα καὶ ἀστασιαστότατα ἀνάγκη οἰκεῖσθαι, τὴν δὲ ἐναντίους ἄρχοντας σχοῦσαν, ἐναντίως. The motive on which Plato relies for inducing the best men to accept of power, is the fear of its being exercised by worse men.

ions as are likely to be shared by others; and the arguments should be cogent and easily understood, which shall induce him to quit the beaten track of doctrine. His object should be, first to go with the world as far as it will carry him; and from that point taking his start, to go farther if he can, but always as much as may be in the same direction, that is, guided by a reference to common ways of thinking. (Pp. 36–7.)

This, without much further explanation, appears to us both unsound and dangerous doctrine.

We are at a loss to conceive why, in describing the ideal perfection of a character like the statesman, we should enjoin either a leaning to, or a leaning from, prescription. Both the one and the other are defects, greater or less as the case may be: the grand and paramount interest is that of truth, which suffers by both of them. It is not the business of a philosopher to appear as standing counsel against received opinions; nor to strike out ingenious paradoxes: his task is to expose error, though it may happen to be accredited—to elicit and sustain truth, known or unknown, neglected or obnoxious. Sir Richard Phillips is the only physical philosopher of the present day who has called in question the Newtonian theory: we do not know that this leaning from prescription has ever obtained for him any peculiar compliment. On the other hand, it seems to us still more mischievous to number the leaning *to* prescription as among the virtues of a statesman; to treat him as the last man who ought to seek escape from the prejudices of his age. Surely this is not the light in which historical criticism views the statesmen of past times. A statesman of the fifteenth or sixteenth century, who had actively discountenanced the burning of heretics, would appear in the eyes of the present day a person deserving of superior admiration, precisely on account of his having dared to set a bad prescription aside. We cannot even concede so much to Mr. Taylor as to admit, that the leaning from prescription is a greater defect in a statesman than the leaning to it— if we are compelled to take our choice between the two, and if we compare them with reference to the supreme end, the public good—not with reference to the subordinate end, the personal ease and popularity of the individual. It is indeed necessary that he should take due account of the opinions and feelings prevalent around him, and that he should undertake nothing without having calculated beforehand this important element: but the accuracy of the calculation will not be assisted by any pre-existing bias in his own mind.

In chapter the ninth, Mr. Taylor examines how far the practice of granting personal interviews is convenient or useful to a statesman. He thinks that interviews seldom conduce to any good result, and are often the means of giving unjust preponderance to one side of a disputed case. We concur in most of his remarks on this head: but the most curious part of the chapter is the description which he gives, authenticated as it is by his own personal observation, of the incredible want of preparation in suitors or claimants, when they approach the minister at the appointed hour of interview:

It may be supposed that the interests which they have, or conceive themselves to have, at stake—the importance to themselves of the objects which they have in view—would infallibly induce such parties as these at least to take the utmost pains beforehand to make the interviews which they seek available to them. Yet most men who have been in office will have observed with how little preparation of their own minds even this class of persons do commonly present themselves to profit by the audience which they have solicited. One man is humble and ignorant of the world, has never set eyes on a minister before, and acts as if the mere admission to the presence of such a personage was all that was needful; which being accomplished, he must naturally flourish ever after. Another is romantic and sanguine; his imagination is excited, and he has thought he can do everything by some happy phrase or lively appeal, which, in the embarrassment of the critical moment, escapes his memory, or finds no place, or the wrong place, in the conversation. A third brings a letter of introduction from some person who is great in *his* eyes, but possibly inconsiderable in those of the minister; he puts his trust in the recommendation, and appears to expect that the minister should suggest to him, rather than he to the minister, what is the particular object to be accomplished for him; he "lacks advancement," and that, he thinks, is enough said. A fourth has not made up his mind how high he shall pitch his demands; he is afraid on the one hand to offend by presumption, on the other to lose by diffidence; he proposes, therefore, to feel his way, and be governed by what the minister shall say to him; but the minister naturally has nothing to say to him— never having considered the matter, and taking no interest in it. Thus it is that, through various misconceptions, the instances will be found in practice to be a minority, in which a claimant or suitor, who obtains an interview, has distinctly made up his mind as to the specific thing which he will ask, propose, or state. Still less does he forecast the several means and resources, objections and diffi- culties, conditions and stipulations, which may happen to be topics essential to a full development and consideration of his case.

In short, it may be affirmed as a truth well founded in observation, though per- haps hardly to be credited upon assertion, that even in matters personally and seriously affecting themselves, most men will put off thinking definitively till they have to act, to write, or to speak. There is no reason why the time of a minister should be employed in listening to the extempore crudities of men who are thus trusting themselves to the fortune of the moment. (Pp. 53–6.)

We doubt whether an American citizen, who goes to submit a case for the consideration of the executive functionaries at Washington is at all beset by the flutter of indefinite expectation which is alleged thus to unman an ordinary English applicant in Downing-street. We suspect that the American knows better both what his government can do for him, and what it ought to do for him; a species of knowledge which Mr. Taylor's testimony proves to be deplorably deficient amongst a class of the English community neither very poor nor very uneducated.

There are in Mr. Taylor's volume several other matters on which we differ from him, and several on which to show how far we agree with him or not, would involve us in too long a discussion. We prefer to cite (it need not be at great length) some few miscellaneous remarks which present themselves in turning over the pages of the volume.

The following remark is original, and shows much knowledge of the world:

> The arts of plausibility would not be practised with so much assurance and so little skill and caution, if plausible men were not more deceived than deceiving: but what they pretend to be, other men pretend to take them for. For men of the world, knowing that there are few things so unpopular as penetration, take care to wear the appearance of being imposed upon; and thus the man of plausibilities practises his art under the disadvantage of not knowing when he is detected, and what shallows to keep clear of for the future. (Pp. 21–2.)

In the following, a fact often noticed, is, perhaps for the first time in print, philosophically explained.

> If there be in the character not only sense and soundness, but virtue of a high order, then, however little appearance there may be of *talent*, a certain portion of *wisdom* may be relied upon almost implicitly; for the correspondencies of wisdom and goodness are manifold; and that they will accompany each other is to be inferred, not only because men's wisdom makes them good, but also because their goodness makes them wise. Questions of right and wrong are a perpetual exercise of the faculties of those who are solicitous as to the right and wrong of what they do and see; and a deep interest of the heart in these questions carries with it a deeper cultivation of the understanding than can be easily effected by any other excitement to intellectual activity. Although, therefore, simple goodness does not imply every sort of wisdom, it unerringly implies some essential conditions of wisdom; it implies a negative on folly, and an exercised judgment within such limits as nature shall have prescribed to the capacity. And where virtue and extent of capacity are combined, there is implied the highest wisdom, being that which includes the worldly wisdom with the spiritual. (Pp. 30–1.)

That "universal mediocrity of mankind" by which Madame Roland was so much astonished when she first mixed in the world, and became an observer of its most admired characters,[*] is, in truth, owing to nothing so much as to the fact, that not one man in a thousand feels any real interest in anything which he hears or sees, unless it somehow affects his own miserable vanities and worldlinesses. Let a person, of the most ordinary capacity, once acquire a sincere and lasting interest in anything, capable of affording exercise to the understanding, and see how that interest will call forth faculties never previously observed in him. This is one reason why periods

[*Jeanne-Marie Roland, "Notice historique sur la Revolution," in *Mémoires de Madame Roland*, ed. St. A. Berville and J. F. Barrière, 2 vols. (Paris: Baudoin, 1820), Vol. I, p. 389.]

of scepticism, though they may produce extraordinary individuals, are seldom rich, compared with other periods, in the general stock of persons of talent. For in an age of strong convictions, the second and third-rate talents, being combined with earnestness, grow up and attain full development, and fructify: but in an age of uncertainty, none but the very first order of intellects are able to lay for themselves so firm and solid a foundation of what they believe to be truth, as they can build upon afterwards in full self-reliance, and stake the repose of their consciences upon without anxiety. The people of second-rate talent feel sure of nothing, and therefore care for nothing, and by an inevitable chain of consequences, accomplish nothing.

In the following passage, the uses of imaginative culture to the perfection even of the thinking faculty, are strikingly sketched, though cursorily, and in a manner which will be intelligible only to those who already have the ideas intended to be conveyed:

The imaginative faculty is essential to the seeing of many things from one point of view, and to the bringing of many things to one conclusion. It is necessary to that fluency of the mind's operations which mainly contributes to its clearness. And finally, it is necessary to bring about those manifold sympathies with various kinds of men in various conjunctures of circumstance, through which alone an active observation and living knowledge of mankind can be generated. (Pp. 37–8.)

On indecisiveness:

The pretext for indecisiveness is commonly mature deliberation; but in reality indecisive men occupy themselves less in deliberation than others; for to him who fears to decide, deliberation (which has a foretaste of that fear) soon becomes intolerably irksome, and the mind escapes from the anxiety of it into alien themes. Or if that seems too open a dereliction of its task, it gives itself to inventing reasons of postponement; and the man who has confirmed habits of indecisiveness will come in time to look upon postponement as the first object in all cases, and wherever it seems to be practicable will bend all his faculties to accomplish it. With the same eagerness with which others seize opportunities of action, will these men seize upon pretexts for foregoing them; not having before their eyes the censure pronounced by the philosopher of Malmesbury, who says, "After men have been in deliberation till the time of action approach, if it be not then manifest what is best to be done, 'tis a sign the difference of motives the one way and the other is not great: therefore not to resolve then, is to lose the occasion by weighing trifles; which is pusillanimity." [*] (Pp. 144–5.)

On another very common and very fatal weakness:

A minister should adopt it as a rule, subject to few exceptions, that he is to make small account of testimonials and recommendations, unless subjected to severe scrutiny, and supported by proved facts. Men who are scrupulously con-

[*Thomas Hobbes, Leviathan, in The English Works of Thomas Hobbes, ed. William Molesworth (London: Bohn, 1839), Vol. III, p. 89.]

scientious in other things, will be often not at all so in their *kindnesses*. Such men, from motives of compassion, charity, good-will, have sometimes given birth to results which the slightest exercise of common sense might have taught them to foresee, and which, if foreseen, might have alarmed the conscience of a buc-caneer. I have known acts of kindness done by excellent persons in the way of recommendation, to which a tissue of evil passions, sufferings, cruelty, and blood-shed have been directly traceable; and these consequences were no other than might have been distinctly anticipated. The charity of such persons might be said to be twice cursed; but that the curse which it is to others may be remitted to them (let us hope) as too heavy a visitation for the sin of thoughtlessness. (Pp. 220–1.)

With the following passage, on faults of manner, we shall conclude:

What is conventional and immaterial in manner may be taught: but in regard to what is important, there is only one precept by which a man can profit; and that is, that so often as he shall be visited with any consciousness of error in this kind (which will not be infrequently in the case of the young and susceptible), he should search out the fault of character from which the fault of manner flows; and disregarding the superficial indication except *as* an indication, endeavour to dry up that source. Any want of essential good-breeding must grow out of a want of liberality and benevolence; any want of essential good taste in manner, out of some moral defect or disproportion; and when a man stands self-accused as to the out-growth, he should lay his axe to the root. The sense of shame for faults of manner would not be so strong a thing in men as it is, if it came out of the mere shallows of their nature, and were not capable of being directed towards some higher purpose than that of gracing their intercourse with society. At the same time nothing will accomplish this lesser purpose more effectually than merging the trivial sensitiveness upon such matters in an earnestness of desire to be right upon them in their moral point of view; and if a man shall make habitual reference to the principle of never doing anything in society from an ungenerous, gratuitously unkind, or ignoble feeling, he will hardly fail to obtain the ease and indifference as to every thing else which is requisite for good man-ners; and he will lose in his considerateness for other persons, and for principles which he feels to be worthy of consideration, the mixture of pride and disguised timidity, which is in this country the most ordinary type of inferiority of manner. There is a dignity in the desire to be right, even in the smallest questions wherein the feelings of others are concerned, which will not fail to supersede what is ego-istical and frivolous in a man's personal feelings in society. (Pp. 233–5.)

What is here said of faults of manner, is true of all faults of taste. *De gustibus non est disputandum* is a maxim as faulty in its philosophy as in its Latinity. Tastes, indeed, where they are not positively noxious to other people, are not proper subjects of condemnation *in themselves*; but they may be indications of faults of character or of intellect, to any conceivable extent; for there is hardly anything which goes so far into the inmost depths of a man's nature as his tastes. Most *actions* are the result of some one quality or deficiency only; but in determining the things which a man habit-ually takes pleasure in, every quality of his mind and heart has a share; his tastes are the aggregate result of his entire character, and are that by which, more than by all other symptoms, it is made outwardly manifest.

One word respecting the style of the *Statesman*. Both the phrases and the sentences indicate that close familiarity with the authors of the first half of the seventeenth century which enabled Mr. Taylor to impart such peculiar beauty to the versification of *Philip van Artevelde*, but which is not of equally happy effect in a prose volume. The perhaps unconscious and unintentional imitation of these models leads him occasionally into both obscurity and affectation.

Appendix B

Appendix to *Dissertations and Discussions*, Vol. I (1859)

Dissertations and Discussions, I (2nd ed., 1867), where the title is footnoted: "*London Review*, July and October 1835." This brief essay combines portions of "Rationale of Representation" (22–4) and "De Tocqueville on Democracy in America [I]" (71–74n), neither of which was reprinted in *D&D*. The portions reprinted are so indicated in those two essays above, and the variants given; but, as the "Appendix" to *D&D* was more widely read, the text is here given in that version, again with the variants.

In the variants, "35¹" indicates "Rationale of Representation"; "35²" indicates "De Tocqueville on Democracy in America [I]"; "59" indicates *D&D*, 1st ed.; "67" indicates *D&D*, 2nd ed.

FROM ᵃTHEᵃ PRINCIPLE of the necessity of identifying the interest of the government with that of the people, most of the practical maxims of a representative government are corollaries. All popular institutions are means towards rendering the identity of interest more complete. We say *more* complete, because (and this it is important to remark) perfectly complete it can never be. An approximation is all that is, in the nature of things, possible. By pushing to its utmost extent the accountability of governments to the people, you indeed take away from them the power of prosecuting their own interests at the expense of the people by force, but you leave to them the whole range and compass of fraud. An attorney is accountable to his client, and removable at his client's pleasure; but we should scarcely say that his interest is identical with that of his client. When the accountability is perfect, the interest of rulers approximates more and more to identity with that of the people, in proportion as the people are more enlightened. The identity would be perfect, only if the people were so wise, that it should no longer be practicable to employ deceit as an instrument of government; a point of advancement only one stage below that at which they could do without government altogether; at least, without force, and penal sanctions, not (of course) without guidance and organized co-operation.

ᵃ⁻ᵃ35¹   this

Identification of interest between the rulers and the ruled, being therefore, in a literal sense, impossible to be realized, *ought not to* be spoken of as a condition which a government must absolutely fulfil; but as an end to be incessantly aimed at, and approximated to as nearly as circumstances render possible, and as is compatible with the regard due to other ends. For *this* identity of interest, even if it were wholly attainable, not being the sole requisite of good government, expediency may require that we should sacrifice some portion of it, or (to speak more precisely) content ourselves with a somewhat less approximation to it than might possibly be attainable, for the sake of some other end.

The only end, liable occasionally to conflict with that which we have been insisting on, and at all comparable to it in importance—the only other condition essential to good government—is this: That it be government by a select body, not by the *public* collectively: That political questions be not decided by an appeal, either direct or indirect, to the judgment or will of an uninstructed mass, whether of gentlemen or of clowns; but by the deliberately formed opinions of a comparatively few, specially educated for the task. This is an element of good government which has existed, in a greater or less degree, in some aristocracies, though unhappily not in our own; and has been the cause of whatever reputation for prudent and skilful administration those governments have enjoyed. It has seldom been found in any aristocracies but those which were avowedly such. Aristocracies in the guise of monarchies (such as those of England and France) have very generally been aristocracies of idlers; while the others (such as Rome, Venice, and Holland) might partially be considered as aristocracies of experienced and laborious men. *Of all modern governments, however*, the one by which this excellence is possessed in the most eminent degree is the government of Prussia—a *f* powerfully and *g*strongly organized aristocracy of*g* the most highly-educated men in the kingdom. The British government in India partakes (with considerable modifications) of the same character.

When this principle has been combined with other fortunate circumstances, and particularly (as in Prussia) with circumstances rendering the popularity of the government almost a necessary condition of its security, a very considerable degree of good government has occasionally been produced, *i* without any express accountability to the people. Such

b–b351   must not
c–c351   the
d–d351   people
e–e351   But of all governments, ancient or modern
f351, 59   most
g–g351   skilfully organized aristocracy of all
h–h351   Where
i351   even

fortunate circumstances, however, are seldom to be reckoned upon. But though the principle of government by persons specially brought up to it will not suffice to produce good government, good government cannot be had without it; and the grand difficulty in politics will for a long time be, how best to conciliate the two great elements on which good government depends; to combine the greatest amount of the advantage derived from the independent judgment of a specially instructed *j*few, with the greatest degree of the security for rectitude of purpose derived from rendering those few responsible to the many.

What is necessary, however, to make the two ends perfectly reconcilable, is a smaller matter than might at first sight be supposed. It is not necessary that the many*j* should themselves be perfectly wise; it is sufficient if they be duly sensible of the value of superior wisdom. It is sufficient if they be aware, that the majority of political questions turn upon considerations of which they, and all persons not trained for the purpose, must necessarily be very imperfect judges; and that their judgment must in general be exercised rather upon the characters and talents of the persons whom they appoint to decide these questions for them, than upon the questions themselves. They would then select as their representatives those whom the general voice of the instructed pointed out as the *most* instructed; and would retain them, so long as no symptom was manifested in their conduct, of being under the influence of interests or of feelings at variance with the public welfare. This implies no greater wisdom in the people than the very ordinary wisdom, of knowing what things they are and are not sufficient judges of. If the bulk of any nation possess a fair share of this wisdom, the argument for universal suffrage, so far as respects that people, is irresistible; for the experience of ages, and especially of all great national emergencies, bears out the assertion, that whenever the multitude are really alive to the necessity of superior intellect, they rarely fail to distinguish those who possess it.

. . . .

The idea of a rational democracy is, not that the people themselves govern, but that they have *k*security*k* for good government. This security they cannot have by any other means than by retaining in their own hands the ultimate control. If they renounce this, they give themselves up to tyranny. A governing class not accountable to the people are sure, in the main, to sacrifice the people to the pursuit of separate interests and inclinations of their own. Even their feelings of morality, even their ideas of excellence, have reference, not to the good of the people, but to their own good: their very virtues are class virtues—their noblest acts of patriotism and self-devotion are but the sacrifice of their private interests to the

*j–j*351   Few . . . Few . . . Many . . . Many
*k–k*352   *security*

interests of their class. The heroic public virtue of a Leonidas was quite compatible with the existence of Helots. In no government will the interests of the people be the object, except where the people are able to dismiss their rulers as soon as the devotion of those rulers to the interests of the people becomes questionable. But this is the only *l*fit use to be made of popular power*l*. Provided good intentions can be secured, the best government (need it be said?) must be the government of the wisest, and these must always be a few. The people ought to be the masters, but they are masters who must employ servants more skilful than themselves: like a ministry when they employ a military commander, or the military commander when he employs an army surgeon. When the minister ceases to confide in the commander, he dismisses him and appoints another; but he does not *m*, if he is wise,*m* send him instructions when and where to fight. He holds him responsible only for *n*intentions and for*n* results. The people must do the same. This does not render the control of the people nugatory. The control of a government over the commander of *o*an*o* army is not nugatory. A man's control over his physician is not nugatory, *p*though*p* he does not direct his physician what medicine to administer. *q*

But in government, as in everything else, the danger is, lest those who can do whatever they will, may will to do more than is for their ultimate interest. The interest of the people is, to choose for their rulers the most instructed and the ablest persons who can be found; and having done so, to allow them to exercise their knowledge and ability for the good of the people *r*, under the check of the freest discussion and the most unreserved censure, but with the least possible direct interference of their constituents*r* —as long as it *is* the good of the people, and not some private end, that they are aiming at. A democracy thus administered would unite all the good qualities ever possessed by any government. Not only would its ends be good, but its means would be as well chosen as the wisdom of the age would allow; and the omnipotence of the majority would be exercised through the agency and *s*according to the judgment*s* of an enlightened minority, accountable to the majority in the last resort.

But it is not possible that the constitution of the democracy itself should provide adequate security for its being understood and administered in this

*l–l*352   purpose for which it is good to intrust power to the people
m–m+67
n–n+59, 67
*o–o*352   its
*p–p*352   although
*q*352   He either obeys the prescription of his physician, or, if dissatisfied with him, takes another. In that consists his security. In that consists also the people's security; and with that it is their wisdom to be satisfied.
*r–r*352   freely, or with the least possible control
*s–s*352   at the discretion

spirit *t* . This rests with the good sense of the people themselves. If the people can remove their rulers for one thing, they can for another. That ultimate control, without which they cannot have security for good government, may, if they please, be made the means of themselves interfering in the government, and making their legislators mere delegates for carrying into execution the preconceived judgment of the majority. If the people do this, they mistake their interest; and such a government, though better than most aristocracies, is not the kind of democracy which wise men desire.

*u*Some persons, and persons too whose desire for enlightened government cannot be *v*questioned*v*, do not take so serious a view of this perversion of the true idea of *w*an enlightened democracy*w*. They say, it is well that the many should evoke all political questions to their own tribunal, and decide them according to their own judgment, because then philosophers will be compelled to enlighten the multitude, and render them capable of appreciating their more profound views. *x* No one can attach greater value than we do to this consequence of popular government, *y* so far as we believe it capable of being realized; and the argument would be irresistible, if, in order to instruct the people, all that is requisite were to will it; if it were only the *discovery* of political truths which required study and wisdom, and the *z*evidences*z* of them when discovered could be made apparent at once to any person of common sense, as well educated as every individual in the community might and ought to be. But the fact is not so. Many of the truths of politics (in political economy, for instance) are the result of a concatenation of propositions, the very first steps of which no one who has not gone through a course of study is prepared to concede; there are others, to have a complete perception of which requires much meditation, and experience of human nature. How will philosophers bring these home to the perceptions of the multitude? Can they enable common sense to judge of science, or inexperience of experience? Every one who has even crossed the threshold of political philosophy knows, that on many of its questions the false view is greatly the most plausible; and a large portion of its truths are, and must always remain, to all but those who have specially studied them, paradoxes; as contrary, in appearance, to common sense, as the proposition that the earth moves round the sun. The multitude will never believe *a*those*a* truths, until tendered to them from an authority

---

*t*352   , and not according to the erroneous notion of democracy
*u–u*352   [*in footnote, which continues for five further sentences*]
*v–v*352   doubted
*w–w*352   democracy as we do
*x*352   [*paragraph*]
*y*352   in
*z–z*352   evidence
*a–a*352   these

in which they have as unlimited confidence as they have in the unanimous voice of astronomers on a question of astronomy. *b* That they should have no such confidence at present is no discredit to them; for *c*where are the persons who are entitled to it?*c* But we are well satisfied that it will be given, as soon as knowledge shall have made sufficient progress among the instructed classes themselves, to produce something like a general agreement in their opinions *d*on the leading points of moral and political doctrine*d*. Even now, on those points on which the instructed classes are agreed, the uninstructed have generally adopted their opinions.*u*

*b*352 [paragraph]
*c–c*352 show us the men who . . . it!
d–d+59, 67

Appendix C

Jowett on Civil Service Examinations (1854)

Extract from "Letter from the Rev. B. Jowett, Fellow and Tutor of Balliol College, Oxford, to Sir Charles Trevelyan," in "Report on the Organisation of the Permanent Civil Service," *Parliamentary Papers*, 1854, XXVII, 24–5 (this extract contains the remarks JSM criticizes in his comments [see 210 above]; the rest of Jowett's letter, which concerns the mode of examination, is irrelevant to JSM's discussion); and the footnote containing Jowett's response to JSM's criticism, in "Papers relating to the Re-organisation of the Civil Service," *Parliamentary Papers*, 1854–55, XX, 96n–97n.
See the Textual Introduction, lxxviii above, for comment.

DEAR SIR,

I think two objections are likely to be made to the report you were so good as to show me on the "Organisation of the Permanent Civil Service." First, that it is impossible to be assured of the moral character of persons elected by examination into the public service; secondly, that it is impossible to carry on an examination in so great a variety of subjects as would be required, and with such numberless candidates; in other words that the scheme, however excellent, is not practicable.

I am convinced that neither of these objections has any real foundation.

I. For the moral character of the candidates I should trust partly to the examination itself. University experience abundantly shows that in more than nineteen cases out of twenty, men of attainments are also men of character. The perseverance and self-discipline necessary for the acquirement of any considerable amount of knowledge are a great security that a young man has not led a dissolute life.

But in addition I would suggest that there should be a system of inquiries and testimonials, which might be made considerably more efficient than testimonials for orders are at present. The analogy of insurance offices would afford the best model for carrying out such a system. I would propose:

1. That the candidate should give notice (as in the case of orders) of his intention to offer himself at least three months before the examination.

2. That he should at the same time send papers comprising a certificate

of birth and baptism, with a precise statement of all the places of his education, whether at school or college, together with testimonials of his conduct for two years previously from the head of the school or college in which he was last a pupil, and also a statement of his present occupation and residence.

  3. That he should give references—

    1. To a medical man;

    2. To a magistrate; or, in case of inferior situations, to two respectable householders;

    3. To a clergyman or dissenting minister;

to all of whom carefully-drawn questions respecting the candidate in the form of an insurance office paper should be submitted; the answers to be confidential. To prevent the possible forgery of a character, an independent letter might be sent to a clergyman or magistrate in the district, with the view of his certifying to the existence and respectability of the references.

  The scrutiny of the character and testimonials of the candidates ought to be quite separate from the examination. The rejection should be absolute and without reasons; whether it took place on medical or moral grounds would remain uncertain. In case of Parliamentary inquiry, however, a register of the reasons might be privately kept in the office.

  With such or even a less amount of precaution the standard of character among public servants would surely be maintained as high as at present, or higher; as high certainly as the standard of character which can be ensured in persons admitted to holy orders.

· · · · · · ·

Yours, very truly,
B. Jowett.
Balliol College, January 1854.

· · · · · · ·

[Footnote to Mill's "Reform of the Civil Service"[*]]

Mr. Mill has misunderstood the intention of Mr. Jowett's recommendations, as will be seen from the following explanation which Mr. Jowett was invited to furnish. "I should object as strongly as Mr. Mill to the proposals contained in the paper relating to the examinations, if I understood them as he does.

  "1. The certificate of baptism was not required as a religious test, but as affording the readiest means of identifying the candidate, and verifying his age. If, from whatever cause, it could not have been obtained, it must have been dispensed with.

  "2. The reference to a clergyman or dissenting minister was equally

[*See p. 210 above.]

without any religious or party object. They were supposed to be friends of the candidate, chosen by himself. They would not, therefore, have refused testimonials to moral character because they differed from him in religious opinions.

"3. Neither for the same reason would they have brought secret accusations against him. It was not proposed that any inquiries should be made of persons not indicated by the candidate himself. He could surely trust his own references. If he were a man of decent character, he would easily find friends willing to act in that capacity. If he were of bad character, the manner in which the proposal would work would be, by his being unable to find them. But it seemed hardly fair to subject them against their will to an altercation with him about the mode of their answers.

"If, however, such suspicions as Mr. Mill suggests were engendered by any degree of secrecy or confidence, it would be far better that the inquiries should be entirely public. But there would then arise the fresh difficulty of casting a public stigma on the character of a young man for offences of which there would be no legal proof.

"The only reason for fixing on magistrates and ministers of religion, rather than any other known persons as the referees, was the necessity of adopting some general rule in a scheme so large as that proposed by the Report, instead of having to ascertain the respectability of each person who offered his testimony in favour of a candidate. Magistrates and ministers of religion appeared to be the most responsible class which could be selected, and sufficiently numerous not to be exclusive. The form of inquiries rather than testimonials was suggested, not with the view of instituting a minute investigation into the life and habits of the candidate, but only of avoiding the evasive and ambiguous use of language which has made testimonials a byword.

"I have made these remarks in justice to myself, though unwilling to obtrude the subjects discussed in the paper on examinations again on the attention of the public, and still more so to claim any authority for its suggestions as a part of the Report.

"My aim was to meet an objection at one time very strongly felt and strongly urged against the plan of Sir C. Trevelyan and Sir S. Northcote, that 'it would fill the Public Offices with clever scamps.' The various precautions enumerated are intended rather to show how completely such objections might be obviated than as necessary regulations to be precisely observed. Securities of this kind would be useful or mischievous according to the spirit in which they were enforced. In my own judgment a much less amount of precaution would be quite sufficient. The real and great precaution is the examination itself. Experience would probably show that hardly any other was required. I quite agree with Mr. Mill in thinking that any limitation not absolutely necessary would be in the highest degree injurious."

Appendix D

Substantive Variants between the People's Edition and
the final Library Edition of *On Liberty*

THE PEOPLE'S EDITION OF *On Liberty* (first published in 1865, with stereotyped reissues thereafter) agrees substantively with the 3rd Library Edition
(1864), except in the readings given below, none of which appears in the
4th Library Edition (1869), the copy-text for the present edition. (In the
two cases, 234*b–b* and 243*d–d*, where 1864 and 1869 differ, the People's Edition agrees with 1864.) In the following list (which, as throughout this
volume, includes changes in italicization as substantives), after the page
and line references, the first reading is that of 1869; the second, after a
bracket, is that of the People's Edition, with the page and column reference
to the latter in parentheses.

220.13   compel] compels (3b)
224.37   of man] of a man (6b)
239.38   and for attainments] and attainments (17b)
245.5   not with still] not still (21b)
251.19   to attain] to obtain (26a)
256.29–30   from the value of the moral] from the moral (29b)
260.33   is it] it is (33a)
265.25   conditions] condition (36a)
267.27   existed] exist (37b)
267.39   *more*] more (38a)
269.35–6   courage which it] courage it (39b)
272.12   is change] is a change (41b)
275.1–2   Improvements . . . promote] Improvement . . . promotes (43a)
276.21   going the] going to the (44a)
287.22   any number] a number (52a)
289.26   never can] can never (53b)
302.18   *require*] require (62b)
302.19   *providing*] providing (62b)

Appendix E

Substantive Variants between the People's Edition
and the final Library Edition of *Considerations on
Representative Government*

THE PEOPLE'S EDITION OF *Considerations on Representative Government*
(first published in 1865, with stereotyped reissues thereafter) agrees substantively with the 3rd Library Edition (also 1865), except in the readings
given below. The number of unique accidental readings (there are only
two cases where the punctuation agrees uniquely with the 2nd Library Edition, and one where it agrees with the 1st) suggests that the People's Edition was prepared from the 3rd edition (rather than from the 2nd), and not
vice versa; therefore the following readings have some claim to authority,
although in the present edition we have followed the policy of using the final
Library Edition in Mill's lifetime as copy-text. In the list below (which, as
throughout this volume, includes changes in capitalization and italicization
as substantives), after the page and line references, the first reading is that
of the Library Edition of 1865; the second, after a bracket, is that of the
People's Edition, with the page and column reference to the latter in parentheses.

> 380.8   *are*] are (5a)
> 380.22   *outside*] outside (5b)
> 405.30   to truth] to the truth (23a)
> 411.13   into the consultation] into consultation (27a)
> 419.40   and its] and by its (33a)
> 430.1   Bills] bills (40b)
> 430.17   Legislation] legislation (40b)
> 437.14   a hereditary] an hereditary (45a)
> 450.14–15   a majority] the majority (54b)
> 472.27   uncertificated] uncertified (69b)
> 477.14   me, more] me, a chance of more (73a)
> 494.24–5   takes interest] takes an interest (85a)
> 513.2   have] has (97a)
> 526.26   provoke] promote (106a)
> 529.36   the examiner] an examiner (108b)
> 530.29   a minister] the minister (109a)
> 536.5   State] state (111a)
> 561.17   of government] of the government (130a)
> 572.32   duties] duty (138b)

Appendix F

Bibliographic Index of Persons and Works Cited in the *Essays*, with Variants and Notes

Mill, like most nineteenth-century authors, is cavalier in his approach to sources, seldom identifying them with sufficient care, and frequently quoting them inaccurately. This Appendix is intended to help correct these deficiencies, and to serve as an index of names and titles (which are consequently omitted in the Index proper). Included also, at the end of the Appendix, are references to parliamentary reports and evidence, which are entered in order of date under the heading "Parliamentary Papers," and references to British statute law, which are entered in order of date under the heading "Statutes." The material otherwise is arranged in alphabetical order, with an entry for each person or work quoted or referred to in the text proper and in Appendices A and B (those in the Appendices are given in italic type). In cases of simple reference only surnames are given.

The entries take the following form:
1. Identification: author, title, etc., in the usual bibliographic form.
2. Notes (if required) giving information about JSM's use of the source, indication if the work is in his library, and any other relevant information.
3. A list of the places where the author or work is quoted, and a separate list of the places where there is reference only. Those works that are reviewed are so noted.
4. A list of substantive variants between JSM's text and his source, in this form: Page and line reference to the present text. Reading in the present text] Reading in the source (page reference in the source).

The list of substantive variants also attempts to place quoted passages in their contexts by giving the beginnings and endings of sentences. Omissions of two sentences or less are given in full; only the length of other omissions is given. Translated material from the French is given in the original. When the style has been altered, the original form is retained in the entries.

ABDY, EDWARD STRUTT. *Journal of a Residence and Tour in the United States of North America, from April, 1833, to October, 1834.* 3 vols. London: Murray, 1835.

REVIEWED: 93–115

QUOTED: 103, 111
103.19 'has been] has, in the latter country, been (II,130)
111.25 world, than among ourselves, while] world, while (I,13)

ABERDEEN. See Gordon.

ACTS. See Statutes.

ADAMS, JOHN. Referred to: 109

NOTE: the reference is in a quotation from E. Everett.

ADAMS, JOHN QUINCY. Referred to: 109

NOTE: the reference is in a quotation from E. Everett.

ADE, GEORGE. Referred to: 496n. See Parliamentary Papers, "Report from the Select Committee on the Corrupt Practices Prevention Act" (1860).

AKBAR (MOGHUL EMPEROR). Referred to: 224

ALCIBIADES. Referred to: 266, 460

ALEXANDER THE GREAT. Referred to: 532

ANDRÆ. Referred to: 466n

ANON. *Essays on Government.* London: Wilson, 1839.

REVIEWED: 151–2
QUOTED: 151, 152
151.7 "in] Assuming this as a recognised truth,—an established axiom, and that the progressive state of man is the result of a special decree of the creator, throughout these essays, it is taken for granted to be a fixed principle in nature, that the successive changes which take place, are no more left to chance in (2)
151.10 laws as] laws established by providence as (2)
151.10 seasons."] seasons; and setting out upon this principle, it is here intended to investigate what must be the necessary effect upon government, of an ignorant and barbarous people becoming generally educated and civilized. (2)
152.7 "Democracy] This, however, is an error; democracy (169)

ANON. *Thoughts on the Ladies of the Aristocracy.* See "Tomkins, Lydia."

ANON. "Tours in America, by Latrobe, Abdy, &c.," *Quarterly Review,* LIV (Sept., 1835), 392–413.

NOTE: the *Wellesley Index,* II, says the article is possibly by John Wilson Croker.
REFERRED TO: 115

ANTONINUS, MARCUS AURELIUS. Referred to: 236–7

ARANDA (Don Pedro Pablo Abarca de Boleo). Referred to: 382

ARISTIDES (the Just).   Referred to: 336, 494

NOTE: the references are identical, the second being in a passage in which Mill quotes himself.

ARISTOPHANES.   *The Knights*, in *Comediae cum commentariis et scholiis.* 9 vols. Leipzig: Weidmann, 1794–1822.

NOTE: in JSM's library, Somerville College.
REFERRED TO: 499

ARISTOTLE.   Referred to: 179, 235, 353

———— *Nicomachean Ethics.*

NOTE: as the reference is general, no edition is cited.
REFERRED TO: 143n

———— *Politics.*

NOTE: as the reference is general, no edition is cited.
REFERRED TO: 143n

———— *Rhetoric.*

NOTE: as the reference is general, no edition is cited.
REFERRED TO: 143n

ARNOLD OF BRESCIA.   Referred to: 238

AUGUSTUS.   See Caesar, Augustus.

AURELIUS.   See Antoninus.

AUSTIN, JOHN.   Referred to: 5n, 145n

———— *A Plea for the Constitution.* 2nd ed. London: Murray, 1859.

REVIEWED: 343–70
QUOTED: 344, 345, 346, 346–7, 349–50, 350, 350–1, 352
344.27   "All] In short, all (6)
345.6   government . . . . The long] government. The harmonious action of the three branches of the Parliament, and the long (7)
345.7   work . . . has] work, is perhaps the most wonderful of all the phenomena presented by the history of political institutions. It has (7)
345.12   Parliamentary] parliamentary (7)
345.19   "talent for compromise."] [*see text*, 345.3]
345.31–2   "the . . . House,"] [*see text*, 345.12–13]
346.13   "governed] With regard to the form of the sovereignty, the British Govern-

ment is decidedly more democratical than any other assignable government which has governed (9)

346.15–16 "has . . . time."] It must be remembered, however, that the solidity of the federal government, and the actual states' governments has . . . time; whilst the singular natural advantages, economical and other, with which these states have hitherto been favoured, have enabled them to live and prosper with little government of any kind, and, therefore, to bear the evils of extreme democracy. (10)

346.17–19 "in spirit and effect," . . . "the most democratical of . . . present."] But if, in respect of its form, the British Government ranks with democracies, it is the most democratical in spirit and effect of . . . present. (10)

346.24 Governments] governments (10)

347.4–5 public business] public interests (13)

347.10 parliamentary] Parliamentary (13) [*cf.* 347*a–a*]

347.10 country. From] country. [*paragraph*] From (13)

347.17 means . . . they] means, they are naturally superior to political adventurers in point of political morality: a natural superiority which they would continue to possess, although such adventures (as in the United States) are paid by the public for their Parliamentary services. As their incomes and social positions are independent of office, and are not dependent on seats in Parliament, they (13)

347.23 "gentlemanly honour"] [*see text*, 347.12]

349.34 'Would] A House of Commons representing the prejudices of the non-proprietory class, would not attempt the impossible task of governing the nation as a joint stock company; but they would (19)

349.39 commercial] economical (19)

350.4 minimum . . . maximum] *minimum . . . maximum* (19)

350.35–6 "insanity," . . . "atrocious outbreak,"] We believe that they [English men of no property] are not infected with the theoretical and insane socialism which in 1848 played so disastrous a part in France and Germany: inciting to unprovoked and wanton revolution, depraving the minds and hearts of large portions of the population, striking the remainder with a despair of political improvement, and stopping the peaceful and hopeful progress which those countries were making previously to the atrocious outbreak. (18)

350.38–9 "give . . . Commons,"] From the probable evils of the introduction of universal suffrage, we proceed to those of any reform of Parliament which would give . . . Commons. (22)

350.42 these] those (23)

350.43–4 would probably] would be far inferior in character to the majority of the present House. It would probably (23)

351.14 dislike . . . . According] dislike. Unless they were skilled in election tactics, or were masters of popular eloquence and popular histrionic faculties, they would have but a poor chance of sitting in the House of Commons; and to men endowed with superior reason and knowledge, the acquisition of those arts and faculties would be next to impossible, though they were not withheld from acquiring them by self-respect and taste. [*paragraph*] According (23)

351.19 practice . . . the] practice, the Parliament would become incapable of corporate action. From being the organ and the collective wisdom of the entire electoral body, the (23–4)

351.23 action . . . . Now] action, and incapable of acting in unison with the other branches of the Parliament. Now, (24)

351.29–30 instructions. There] instructions. [*paragraph*] There (24)

351.31 Government . . . . The] Government. This tendency, so far as it takes effect, defeats the important and wise purposes for which the sovereign Parliament commits those functions to the Crown. The (24)

351.33 while] whilst (24)

351.42 ministers] Ministers (24)

351.48 "unchecked ascendancy"] [*see text*, 350.39]

352.17   "vestrymen."] [*see text*, 351.38]
352.28–30   "The . . . views."] But the only opinion or sentiment favourable to the constitution, which the great majority of a people can generally hold in common, is the sentiment of constitutionality; for the . . . views. (37)
352.29   Sovereign Government] sovereign government (37)
352.31   "in . . . itself,"] To a people in whom this feeling is deep and general, the constitution of their sovereign government, *in . . . itself*, is an object of love and veneration. (37)

———   *The Province of Jurisprudence determined.* London: Murray, 1832.

REFERRED TO: 343

AYRTON.   Referred to: 352

BACON, FRANCIS.   Quoted: *627*.   Referred to: 17, *621, 623, 626*

NOTE: the quotation, which is in a quotation from Taylor, has not been located. The reference at 626 is in a quotation from Taylor.

———   *Of the Dignity and Advancement of Learning.* In *The Works of Francis Bacon.* 14 vols. Ed. James Spedding, Robert Leslie Ellis, and Douglas Denon Heath. London: Longman, *et al.*, 1857–74, IV, 273–V, 119.

NOTE: for ease of reference this ed., which is in JSM's library, Somerville College, is used.

QUOTED: 194
194.2   "sabbathless pursuit of wealth"] Moreover, although men should refrain themselves from injury and evil arts, yet this incessant, restless, and as it were sabbathless pursuit of fortune leaves not the tribute which we owe to God of our time; who we see demands and separates for himself a tenth part of our substance, but a seventh of our time. (V, 77)

BADEN, GRAND DUKE OF.   See Frederick I of Baden.

BAGEHOT, WALTER.   *Parliamentary Reform.* London: Chapman and Hall, [1859].

NOTE: reprinted, with additions, from *The National Review*, VIII (Jan., 1859), 228–73.

REFERRED TO: 364

BAILEY, SAMUEL.   *The Rationale of Political Representation.* London: Hunter, 1835.

REVIEWED: 17–46

QUOTED: 19, 20–1, 21–2, 25–6, 28n–29n, 30, 33–4, 34, 34–5, 35–6, 36, 37, 37n, 38, 38–9, 39, 39–40, 41

REFERRED TO: 55n, 481

19.4–5 'That . . . interest] It is a principle of human nature, that . . . interests (68)

19.20–4 'it . . . rest; since, from . . . interest;'] But it . . . rest. [*six-sentence omission*] Now, as from . . . interest, it [*as* 19.25] (69, 70–1)

19.25 'It] it (71) [*runs on from previous quotation*]

19.25–6 *to . . . identified.*][*no italics*] (71)

19.26–7 which meets] which effects (71)

19.30–2 *rendering . . . theirs.*] [*no italics*] (71)

19.35 of a representative,] of representative, (71)

19.38–40 *he . . . office.*'] [*no italics*] (71)

20.19 'Nothing] As to the first, nothing (16)

21.30 'Far'] Burke, who delighted to penetrate to the principles of every question, who was continually sounding the depth of his own argument as he went along, far (30)

21.32 he considers] considers (30)

25.6 'the] It is impossible to determine the point with exactness without reference to actual experience; and the experience of our own country, in combination with the preceding considerations, if well weighed, will probably lead the mind to fix three years as the (203)

25.44 body. Here] body. [*paragraph*] Here (298)

30.21 all. It] all. [*paragraph*] It (231)

30.24 1000*l*.] one thousand. (231)

34.11 'Large] The supreme legislative assembly is essentially, as already explained, a deliberative body; and it is acknowledged that large (160–1)

34.12 deliberation;'] deliberation. (161)

34.32 'This] In truth, this (193)

37.16 'maturity of years,'] But there is a qualification of even still greater importance than maturity of years; and that is, freedom from all other serious or momentous occupation—a qualification hitherto completely neglected. (181)

38.4 'in] In (180)

BARCLAY, JOHN. *Argenis*. Paris: Buon, 1621.

NOTE: the quotation is in a quotation from Taylor.

QUOTED: *635*

BARROT, CAMILLE HYACINTHE ODILON. *De la Centralisation et de ses Effets*. Paris: Dumineray, 1861.

REVIEWED: 581–613

QUOTED: 586

586.7–39 We . . . effects.] [*translated from:*] Nous ne voulons toucher en rien à cette belle unité française qu'un pouvoir fortement concentré a pu contribuer à constituer, mais que la liberté seule peut conserver et cimenter. Nous ne rejetons de la centralisation que son excès; or, à nos yeux, cet excès est dans toute centralisation qui, soit par la confusion des deux pouvoirs, soit par leur solidarité, dans un intérêt religieux ou dans un intérêt politique, porte une atteinte directe ou indirecte à la liberté des consciences et des cultes. Nous regardons également comme exagérée une centralisation qui, tantôt à titre de tutelle, tantôt à titre de police, soumettrait à son action préventive les droits collectifs ou même individuels des citoyens; qui, par exemple, sous le prétexte que les communes seraient incapables de faire leurs affaires, se chargerait de les faire elle-même par ses agents, désignerait leurs maires, leurs percepteurs, leurs maîtres d'école, leurs curés et bientôt leurs gardes-champêtres; ne permettrait à leurs conseils de s'assembler qu'avec sa permission; se réserverait de faire annuellement leurs budgets, et qui, même après la dépense votée et autorisée, prétendrait encore en régler l'exécution, en imposant à ces malheureuses communes qui paient, en définitive, ses plans, ses ingénieurs, ses architectes. Je tiens pour excessive une centralisation qui enlacerait presque tous les actes des citoyens dans la nécessité d'autorisations préalables, au point de ne leur permettre ni de prier Dieu, ni même de se mouvoir d'un lieu à un autre que sous son bon plaisir. Je n'hésite pas à déclarer abusive une centralisation qui, après avoir ainsi donné tout pouvoir aux agents de l'autorité sur les citoyens, refuserait à ceux-ci tout recours contre ces mêmes agents déclarés inviolables sous la protection d'un conseil d'État choisi par elle; une centralisation qui, à l'aide de conflits qu'elle élèverait et résoudrait selon sa volonté, dessaisirait la justice ordinaire et évoquerait la décision de toute cause dans laquelle elle se dirait intéressée. Je rejette enfin une centralisation dont les appétits toujours irrités et jamais satisfaits, menaceraient incessamment ce qui pourrait encore rester dans la société d'existences indépendantes; étendrait la main, tantôt sur les biens des hospices, tantôt sur ceux des communes, tantôt sur les grandes compagnies des chemins de fer et d'assurances. C'est cette centralisation qui finirait par réduire l'individu à l'état d'automate, que j'attaque et dont je vais essayer de décrire les funestes effets. (63–6)

BEAUMARCHAIS, PIERRE-AUGUSTINE CARON DE. *La Folle Journée, ou Le Mariage de Figaro*, in *Œuvres complètes*. 7 vols. Paris: Collin, 1809, II.

NOTE: a two-volume *Œuvres complètes* was formerly in JSM's library, Somerville College.

QUOTED: 427
427.15–16 *Il fallait . . . obtint,*] Le désespoir m'allait saisir; on pense à moi pour une place, mais par malheur j'y étais propre; il fallait . . . obtint. (II,276–7; Act V, Scene iii)

BEAUMONT, GUSTAVE AUGUSTE DE LA BONNIÈRE DE. *Marie; ou, l'Esclavage aux États-Unis, tableau de mœurs américaines*. 2 vols. 2nd ed. Paris: Gosselin, 1835.

REVIEWED: 93–115
QUOTED: 76, 102–3, 104n–105n, 111–12
102.33–103.13 'A . . . so.' . . . 'Because . . . faith.'] [*translated from:*] Peu de temps après mon arrivée en Amérique, comme j'entrais dans un salon où se trouvait réunie l'élite de la société de l'une des plus grandes villes de l'Union, un Français, fixé depuis long-temps dans ce pays, me dit; "Surtout n'allez pas mal parler des banqueroutiers." Je suivis son avis et fis bien; car, parmi tous les riches personnages auxquels je fus présenté, il n'en était pas un seul qui n'eût failli une ou deux fois dans sa vie avant de faire fortune. [*paragraph*] Tous les Américains faisant le commerce, et tous ayant failli plus ou moins souvent, il suit de là qu'aux États-Unis ce n'est rien que de faire banqueroute. Dans une société où tout le monde commet le même délit, ce délit n'en est plus un. L'indulgence pour les banqueroutiers vient d'abord de ce que c'est le malheur commun; mais elle a surtout pour cause l'extrême facilité que trouve le failli à se relever. Si le failli était perdu à jamais, ou [*sic*] l'abandonnerait à sa misère; on est bien plus indulgent pour celui qui est malheureux quand on sait qu'il ne le sera pas toujours. [*1-paragraph omission*] [*paragraph*] De ce que les Américains sont indulgens pour la banqueroute, il ne s'ensuit pas qu'ils l'approuvent: "l'intérêt est le grand vice des Musul-

mans, et la libéralité est cependant la vertu qu'ils estiment davantage[1]. [*footnote*: [1]Chateaubriand, *Itinéraire*, t.2, p. 38.] De même ces marchands, qui violent sans cesse leurs engagemens, vantent et honorent la bonne foi. (I, 284–6)

104.n7–105.n11 'The . . . existence.'] [*translated from*:] L'Américain, dès l'âge le plus tendre, est livré aux affaires; à peine sait-il lire et écrire qu'il devient commerçant; le premier son qui frappe son oreille est celui de l'argent; la première voix qu'il entend, c'est celle de l'intérêt; il respire en naissant une atmosphère industrielle, et toutes ses premières impressions lui persuadent que la vie des affaires est la seule qui convienne à l'homme. [*paragraph*] Le sort de la jeune fille n'est point le même; son éducation morale dure jusqu'au jour où elle se marie. Elle acquiert des connaissances en histoire, en littérature; elle apprend, en général, une langue étrangère (ordinairement le français); elle sait un peu de musique. Sa vie est intellectuelle. [*paragraph*] Ce jeune homme et cette jeune fille si dissemblables s'unissent un jour par le mariage. Le premier, suivant le cours de ses habitudes, passe son temps à la banque ou dans son magasin; la seconde, qui tombe dans l'isolement le jour où elle prend un époux, compare la vie réelle qui lui est échue à l'existence qu'elle avait rêvée. Comme rien dans ce monde nouveau qui s'offre à elle ne parle à son cœur, elle se nourrit de chimères, et lit des romans. Ayant peu de bonheur, elle est très religieuse, et lit des sermons. Quand elle a des enfans, elle vit près d'eux, les soigne et les caresse. Ainsi se passent ses jours. Le soir, l'Américain rentre chez lui: soucieux, inquiet, accablé de fatigue; il apporte à sa femme le fruit de son travail, et rêve déjà aux spéculations du lendemain. Il demande le dîner, et ne profère plus une seule parole; sa femme ne sait rien des affaires qui le préoccupent; en présence de son mari, elle ne cesse pas d'être isolée. L'aspect de sa femme et de ses enfans n'arrache point l'Américain au monde positif, et il est si rare qu'il leur donne une marque de tendresse et d'affection, qu'on donne un *sobriquet* aux ménages dans lesquels le mari, après une absence, embrasse sa femme et ses enfans; on les appelle *the kissing families*. Aux yeux de l'Américain, la femme n'est pas une compagne, c'est une associée qui l'aide à dépenser, pour son bien-être et son *comfort*, l'argent gagné par lui dans le commerce. [*paragraph*] La vie sédentaire et retirée des femmes, aux États-Unis, explique, avec les rigueurs du climat, la faiblesse de leur complexion; elles ne sortent point du logis, ne prennent aucun exercice, vivent d'une nourriture légère; presque toutes ont un grand nombre d'enfans; il ne faut pas s'étonner si elles vieillissent si vite et meurent si jeunes. [*paragraph*] Telle est cette vie de contrastes, agitée, aventureuse, presque fébrile pour l'homme, triste et monotone pour la femme; elle s'écoule ainsi uniforme jusqu'au jour où le mari annonce à sa femme qu'ils ont fait banqueroute; alors il faut partir, et l'on va recommencer ailleurs la même existence. (I,268–9)

111.26–112.9 'The . . . answerable.'] [*translated from*:] L'instruction donnée aux enfans est purement utile: elle n'a point en vue le développement des hautes facultés de l'âme et de l'esprit: elle forme des hommes propres aux affaires de la vie sociale. [*3-sentence omission*] Tout le monde écrit et parle, non sans prétention, mais sans talent. [*ellipsis indicates 8-page omission*] Personne ne connaît, en Amérique, cette vie tout intellectuelle qui s'établit en dehors du monde positif, et se nourrit de rêveries, de spéculations, d'idéalités; cette existence immatérielle qui a horreur des affaires, pour laquelle la méditation est un besoin, la science un devoir, la création littéraire une jouissance délicieuse, et qui s'emparant à la fois des richesses antiques et des trésors modernes, prenant une feuille au laurier de Milton, comme à celui de Virgile, fait servir à sa fortune les gloires et les génies de tous les âges. [*paragraph*] On ignore dans ce pays l'existence du savant modeste qui, étranger aux mouvemens du monde politique et au trouble des passions cupides, se donne tout entier à l'étude, l'aime pour elle-même, et jouit dans le mystère de ses nobles loisirs. [*1-paragraph omission*] [*paragraph*] L'Europe qui admire Cooper croit que l'Amérique lui dresse des autels; il n'en est point ainsi. Le Walter Scott américain ne trouve dans son pays ni fortune, ni renommée. Il gagne moins avec ses livres qu'un marchand d'étoffes; donc celui-ci est au-dessus du marchand d'idées. Le raisonnment est sans réplique. (I,252–3, 261–3)

BENEDICT XIV (Pope).   Referred to: 382

BENTHAM, JEREMY.   Referred to: 7, 11–12, 36, 481, 527, *623*

NOTE: the reference at 623 is generally to "Bentham's works" (before Bowring's edition). For ease of reference, all citations below are to *The Works of Jeremy Bentham*. Ed. John Bowring. 11 vols. Edinburgh: Tait, 1843. The reference at 36 is actually to an (unlocated) indirect quotation which is in a quotation from Bailey.

———— *An Introductory View of the Rationale of Evidence*, in *Works*, VI, 1–218.

QUOTED: 294
294.40   "preappointed evidence"] By the term preappointed evidence, may be understood any evidence whatsoever, considered in so far as provision is made for the creation or preservation of it, antecedently to the existence of any right or obligation for the support of which it may happen tó serve, or to the manifestation of any individual occasion for the production of it.(60) [See also Chap. xiv, and *Rationale of Judicial Evidence*, in *Works*, VI, 219–20, 508–85.]

———— *Leading Principles of the Constitutional Code*, in *Works*, II, 267–74.

REFERRED TO: 390

———— *Letters to Lord Grenville on the Proposed Reform in the Administration of Civil Justice in Scotland*, in *Works*, V, 1–53.

QUOTED: 521
521.20–1   "Boards" . . . "are screens."] A *board*, my Lord, is a *screen*.(17)

———— *Rationale of Judicial Evidence*, in *Works*, VI and VII.

NOTE: the quotation is indirect.
QUOTED: 441
441.6   sinister interests] [*a very common phrase in Bentham; see, e.g.,* VII, 385.]

BIBLE.   Referred to: 397, 570

————   New Testament.   Referred to: 248, 254, 255, 397

————   Old Testament.   Referred to: 254, 397

————   Acts.

NOTE: the reference at 236 is to 7:57—8:4
QUOTED: 381
REFERRED TO: 236
381.34–5   "consenting . . . death,"] And Saul was consenting . . . death. (8:1)

———— Colossians.

NOTE: the reference is inferential.
REFERRED TO: 255

———— Deuteronomy.

QUOTED: 441
441.34–5 "wax fat, and kick;"] But Jeshurun waxed fat, and kicked: thou art waxen
    fat, thou art grown thick, thou art covered with fatness; then he forsook God
    which made him, and lightly esteemed the Rock of his salvation. (32:15)

———— Ecclesiastes.

QUOTED: *630*

NOTE: the quotation is in a quotation from Taylor.
630.23–4 the golden bowl must be broken at the fountain, and the wheel broken at
    the cistern.] Or ever the silver cord be loosed, or the golden bowl be broken, or
    the pitcher be broken at the fountain, or the wheel broken at the cistern. (12:6)

———— James.   Referred to: 248

NOTE: the reference is to 5:12.

———— Luke.   Referred to: 248

NOTE: the reference is to 6:20–3.

———— Matthew.   Referred to: 236, 248–9

NOTE: the reference at 236 is to 26:65, those at 248–9 to 19:24, 7:1, 5:34, 19:19,
    5:40, 6:34, and 19:21.

———— Psalms.

QUOTED: 58
58.21   have eyes and see not, ears and hear not,] They have mouths, but they speak
    not; eyes have they, but they see not;/They have ears, but they hear not; neither
    is there any breath in their mouths. (135:16–17; *cf. ibid.,* 115:5–7)

BLACKSTONE, WILLIAM. *Commentaries on the Laws of England.* 4 vols.
    Oxford: Clarendon Press, 1765–69.

NOTE: the 5th ed. (Oxford: Clarendon, 1773) is in JSM's library, Somerville College.
REFERRED TO: 575

BLANC.   Referred to: 466n

BOCKH. See Boeckh.

BOECKH, AUGUST. *The Public Economy of Athens.* Trans. George Cornewall Lewis. 2 vols. London: Murray, 1828.

REFERRED TO: 3

BONAPARTE. See Napoleon I.

BOOTT.   Referred to: 109

NOTE: the reference, to "a gentleman of this city" who erected a marble tablet on the grave of Henry Kirke White, is in a quotation from Everett.

BORGIA.   Referred to: 598

NOTE: the reference is in a quotation from Dupont-White.

BOSWELL, JAMES. *Life of Johnson.* Ed. George Birkbeck Hill and L.F. Powell. 6 vols. Oxford: Clarendon Press, 1934–50.

NOTE: this edition used for ease of reference; in JSM's library, Somerville College, is the 2nd ed., 3 vols. (London: Dilly, 1793), where the quoted passage appears on II, 112 (cf. III, 258). The quotation is taken from Lewis.

QUOTED: 8

REFERRED TO: 237–8

8.19–20 "because he . . . justly,"] He has not a moral right [to think as he pleases]; for he . . . justly. (II,249; 7/5/73)

BRECKENRIDGE.   Referred to: 484

BRIGHT.   Referred to: 488, 511

BROUGHAM.   Referred to: 108

NOTE: the reference is in a quotation from E. Everett.

BULLER.   Referred to: 563

NOTE: the reference is to Buller as a "joint author," with Wakefield, of the Durham Report.

BULWER (later Bulwer-Lytton), EDWARD GEORGE EARLE LYTTON. *England and the English.* 2 vols. London: Bentley, 1833.

NOTE: see also under Mill, John Stuart, "Remarks on Bentham's Philosophy."

REFERRED TO: 34

BURKE, EDMUND.   Referred to: 351, *621, 623*

NOTE: the reference at 351 is in a quotation from Austin.

——— *Mr. Burke's Speech on presenting to the House of Commons (on the eleventh of February, 1780) a plan for the better security of the independence of Parliament, and the oeconomical reformation of the Civil and other establishments*, in *The Works of the Right Honourable Edmund Burke*. 8 vols. London: Dodsley (Vols. I–III), Rivington (Vols. IV–VIII), 1792–1827, II, 175–267.

NOTE: Vols. III, IV, and V were in JSM's library, Somerville College. The quotation is in a quotation from Bailey.

QUOTED: 21–2

21.37 "I] To avoid, therefore, this minute care which produces the consequences of the most extensive neglect, and to oblige members of parliament to attend to public cares, and not to the servile offices of domestic management, I (217)

21.38 economize by] [*in italics*] (217)

22.1 *nature of things*] [*no italics*] (217)

22.2 *the constitution of the human mind.*"] [*no italics*] (217)

——— *A letter from Mr. Burke to John Farr and John Harris, Esqs. Sheriffs of the City of Bristol, on the Affairs of America* (1777), in *The Works of the Right Honourable Edmund Burke*. 8 vols. London: Dodsley (Vols. I–III), Rivington (Vols. IV–VIII), 1792–1827, II, 101–55.

NOTE: Vols. III, IV, and V were in JSM's library, Somerville College. The quotation is in a quotation from Bailey.

QUOTED: 21

21.35 *on . . . man,*] [*no italics*] (145)

21.37 end."] end, as long as it was thought proper to adhere to it. (145)

BURNS. Referred to: 101

BUSSY. Referred to: 603

CAESAR, AUGUSTUS. Referred to: 403, 443

CAESAR, JULIUS. Referred to: 532

CAESAR, TIBERIUS. Referred to: 403

CAIAPHAS. Referred to: 236

CALHOUN, JOHN CALDWELL. "A Discourse on the Constitution and Government of the United States," in *The Works of John C. Calhoun*. 6 vols. Ed. Richard K. Cralle. Columbia, S.C.: General Assembly of the State of South Carolina, 1851–56, I, 109–406.

NOTE: Vol. I is in JSM's library, Somerville College, with a tipped-in printed sheet presenting the volume to JSM.

REFERRED TO: 558

CALIGULA.   Referred to: 600

CALVIN.   Referred to: 249

CAPET, HUGH.   Referred to: 416

CAPODISTRIAS, AUGUSTINE.   Referred to: 567[i]

CAPODISTRIAS, JOHN.   Referred to: 567[i]

CARACALLA.   Referred to: 597

CAREY, HENRY CHARLES.   *Principles of Social Science.* 3 vols. London: Trübner, 1858.

NOTE: the reference, from Carey, to the Report of the English Commissioners to the New York Exhibition is presumably to "New York Industrial Exhibition: General Report of the British Commissioners," *Parliamentary Papers,* 1854, XXXVI, 1–467; however, the passage has not been located.
QUOTED: 468n

CARLYLE, THOMAS.   "Boswell's Life of Johnson," *Fraser's Magazine,* V (May, 1832), 359–413.

NOTE: on 396–7 (just before the reference to the dying out of the age of booksellers), Carlyle notes that it had succeeded to the age of patronage, but does not attribute the comment on the death of patronage to Johnson.
REFERRED TO: 138. See also Johnson.

——— "Memoirs of the Life of Scott," *London and Westminster Review,* VI & XXVIII (Jan., 1838), 293–345.

NOTE: republished by Carlyle as "Sir Walter Scott."
QUOTED: 233
233.11–12 "destitute of faith, but terrified at scepticism"] The Genius of a rather singular age,—an age at once destitute of faith and terrified at scepticism, with little knowledge of its whereabout, with many sorrows to bear or front, and on the whole with a life to lead in these new circumstances,—had said to himself: What man shall be the temporary comforter, or were it but the spiritual comfit-maker, of this my poor singular age, to solace its dead tedium and manifold sorrows a little? (315)

——— *On Heroes, Hero-Worship, and the Heroic in History.* London: Fraser, 1841.

NOTE: in JSM's library, Somerville College.
REFERRED TO: 269

CATHERINE II (of Russia).   Referred to: 382

CAVENDISH.   Referred to: 164n

CECIL, ROBERT ARTHUR TALBOT GASCOYNE.   "The Theories of Parliamentary Reform," in *Oxford Essays*. 4 vols. London: Parker, 1855–58, IV, 52–79.

REFERRED TO: 353–5

CHARLEMAGNE.   Referred to: 224, 419

CHARLES II (of England).   Referred to: 283

CHARLES V (Holy Roman Emperor).   Referred to: 381

CHARLES X (of France).   Referred to: 608

CHÂTEAUBRIAND, FRANÇOIS RENÉ DE.   Referred to: 582

NOTE: the reference is in a quotation from Odilon Barrot.

———   *Itinéraire de Paris à Jerusalem et de Jerusalem à Paris*. 3 vols. Paris: Le Normand, 1811.

NOTE: the quotation, which is indirect, is in a quotation from de Beaumont.
QUOTED: 103
103.10–11   Self-interest . . . esteem.] [*translated from:*] L'intérêt est le grand vice des Musulmans; et la libéralité est la vertu qu'ils estiment davantage. (II,44)

CHATHAM. See Pitt (the elder).

CHEVALIER, MICHEL.   *Lettres sur l'Amérique du Nord*. 2 vols. Paris: Gosselin, 1836.

REFERRED TO: 177

CHRIST. See Jesus.

CICERO (Marcus Tullius).   Referred to: 245

———   *Letters to Atticus* (Latin and English). Trans. E. O. Winstedt. 3 vols. London: Heinemann; New York: Macmillan, 1912.

NOTE: this edition used for ease of reference. The Elzevir edition of 1642 is in JSM's library, Somerville College.
QUOTED: 251
251.28   "Socratici viri"] O Socrates et Socratici viri! numquam vobis gratiam referam. (III,230; xiv. 9)

————— *The Letters to his Friends* (Latin and English). Trans. W. Glynn Williams. 3 vols. London: Heinemann; New York: Putnam's Sons, 1927–29.

NOTE: this edition used for ease of reference.
QUOTED: 164
164.14   *novi homines*] Plus tibi virtus tua dedit, quam fortuna abstulit, propterea quod adeptus es, quod non multi homines, novi, amisisti, quae plurimi homines nobilissimi. (I,403; V.18.i)

————— *De Senectute*, in *De Senectute, De Amicitia, De Divinatione* (Latin and English). Trans. William Armistead Falconer. London: Heinemann; New York: Putnam's Sons, 1922.

NOTE: this edition cited for ease of reference. This reference is merely illustrative; other classical authors, of course, use this phrase.
QUOTED: 577
577.31   *Dî meliora*] Bene Sophocles, cum ex eo quidam iam affecto aetate quaereret, utereturne rebus veneriis, "di meliora!" inquit; "ego vero istinc sicut a domino agresti ac furioso profugi." (58; xiv.47)

CLABON, JOHN MOXON.   Referred to: 496n; see Parliamentary Papers, "Report from the Select Committee on the Corrupt Practices Prevention Act" (1860)

CLAY, HENRY.   Referred to: 109

NOTE: the reference is in a quotation from E. Everett.

CLAY, WILLIAM.   Referred to: 352

CLEON.   Referred to: 460

CLÉRON, JOSEPH OTHENIN BERNARD DE (Comte d'Haussonville). *Lettre au Sénat*. Paris: Dumineray, 1860.

REFERRED TO: 584

CLINTON, DEWITT.   Referred to: 111

NOTE: the reference is in a quotation from E. Everett.

CLINTON, HENRY PELHAM FIENNES PELHAM.   Referred to: 127

CLIVE.   Referred to: 532

COBDEN.   Referred to: 511

COCHRANE, BAILLIE.   Speech on Civil Service Examinations. *Parliamentary Debates*, 3rd ser., Vol. 158, cols. 2061–6 (5 June, 1860).

NOTE: the reference is presumably to Cochrane (see esp. cols. 2063–5), but Bentinck adduced other relevant questions (*ibid.*, cols. 2075–6).

REFERRED TO: 531n

COLBERT.   Referred to: 410, 438, 602

COLERIDGE, SAMUEL TAYLOR.   *First Lay Sermon* [*The Statesman's Manual*]. 2nd ed., in *On the Constitution of Church and State, and Lay Sermons*. London: Pickering, 1839.

NOTE: this edition, which is in JSM's library, Somerville College, contains the 3rd edition of *On Church and State* and the 2nd edition of *Lay Sermons*.

QUOTED: 444

444.7–8   the man makes the motive, not the motive the man] Strange as this position [that the knowledge taught in the Scriptures produces the motives] will appear to such as forget that motives can be causes only in a secondary and improper sense, inasmuch as the man makes the motive, not the motives the man; yet all history bears evidence to its truth. (220)

————   *On the Constitution of Church and State According to the Ideas of Each, and Lay Sermons: I. The Statesman's Manual. II. "Blessed are ye that sow beside all waters."* Ed. Henry Nelson Coleridge. London: Pickering, 1839.

NOTE: this edition, in JSM's library, Somerville College, is the one to which his references in "Coleridge" correspond (see *Collected Works*, X); it includes the 3rd edition of *Church and State*, and the 2nd edition of *Lay Sermons*. Also in JSM's library is the 2nd edition of *Church and State* (London: Hurst, Chance, 1830). The entries for the *Lay Sermons* are given under *First Lay Sermon* and *Second Lay Sermon*.

QUOTED: 384

384.13   Permanence and Progression] Now, in every country of civilized men, acknowledging the rights of property, and by means of determined boundaries and common laws united into one people or nation, the two antagonist powers or opposite interests of the State, under which all other State interests are comprised, are those of permanence and of progression.* [*2-paragraph footnote*] (24)

————   "Pitt," in James Gillman, *The Life of Samuel Taylor Coleridge*. London: Pickering, 1838, pp. 195–223.

NOTE: reprinted from the *Morning Post*, 19 March, 1800; also appears in Coleridge's *Essays on His Own Times, A Second Series of the Friend* (London: Pickering, 1850), II, 319–29. The indirect quotation occurs in a quotation from Bailey.

QUOTED: 30

30.26–7   shelter and weather-fend him from the elements of experience.] The influencer of his country and of his species was a young man, the creature of another's predetermination, sheltered and weather-fended from all the elements of experience; a young man, whose feet had never wandered; whose very eye had never turned to the right or to the left; whose whole track had been as curveless as the motion of a fascinated reptile! (199)

——— *Second Lay Sermon* [*"Blessed are ye that sow beside all waters"*]. 2nd ed., in *On the Constitution of Church and State, and Lay Sermons.* London: Pickering, 1839.

NOTE: the same passage is used in both quotations, which are indirect. This edition, which is in JSM's library, Somerville College, contains the 3rd edition of *On Church and State* and the 2nd edition of *Lay Sermons.*

QUOTED: 458, 572

458.11–12 votes were weighed as well as counted] Men, I still think, ought to be weighed not counted. Their worth ought to be the final estimate of their value. (409)

572.36–7 opinions may be weighed as well as counted] [*as above*]

COMTE, AUGUSTE. *Système de politique positive, ou Traité de sociologie, instituant la Religion de l'humanité.* 4 vols. Paris: Mathias, 1851–54.

NOTE: in JSM's library, Somerville College. At 227ᶜ⁻ᶜ Mill mistakenly refers to it as *Traité de Politique Positive,* another work by Comte.

REFERRED TO: 227

CONSTANT. Referred to: 582

NOTE: the reference is in an indirect quotation from Odilon Barrot.

CONSTANTINE. Referred to: 237

COOPER. Referred to: 112

NOTE: the reference is in a quotation from de Beaumont.

CORRUPT PRACTICES PREVENTION ACT. See under Statutes, 17 & 18 Victoria, c. 102 (1854).

COSENS, FREDERICK. Referred to: 496n; see Parliamentary Papers, "Report from the Select Committee on the Corrupt Practices Prevention Act" (1860).

CRAWFORD, WILLIAM. See under Parliamentary Papers, "Report of *William Crawford*" (1834).

Cyril Thornton. See Hamilton, Thomas.

DANTE ALIGHIERI. *Inferno.*

NOTE: JSM is citing from memory, so no edition is given; the line quoted (Canto IV, 1.131) refers to Aristotle as "il maestro di color che sanno." A copy of the translation of *The Divine Comedy* (London, 1849) by John A. Carlyle (Thomas's brother) is in JSM's library, Somerville College.

QUOTED: 235

DE CORBIÈRE. Referred to: 582

NOTE: the reference is in an indirect quotation from Odilon Barrot.

D'HAUSSONVILLE. See Cléron.

DEMOSTHENES. Referred to: 245, 458

NOTE: at 245 JSM refers to Cicero as the "greatest orator, save one [Demosthenes], of antiquity."

———— "Against Timocrates," in *Demosthenes against Meidias, Androtin, Aristocrates, Timocrates, Aristogeiton* (Greek and English). Trans. J. H. Vince. London: Heinemann; Cambridge, Mass.: Harvard University Press, 1935.

NOTE: the reference (to 463; xxiv, 139) is inferential. This edition used for ease of reference.

REFERRED TO: 238

DE PRESSENSÉ. Referred to: 584n, 611

DERBY, 15TH EARL OF. See Stanley, Edward Henry.

DE TOCQUEVILLE. See Tocqueville.

DE VILLÈLE. See Villèle.

DISRAELI, BENJAMIN. Speech on the Representation of the People Bill (1860). *Parliamentary Debates*, 3rd ser., Vol. 157, cols. 839–58 (19 March, 1860).

NOTE: the reference is to col. 854. The allusion to one of Russell's Reform Bills is to that introduced 16 Feb., 1854.

REFERRED TO: 452

DODDINGTON. Referred to: 78

DOLCINO, FRA (of Novario). Referred to: 238

DUNOYER. Referred to: 583

DUPLEIX. Referred to: 603

Du Plessis, Armand Jean, Cardinal Duc de Richelieu.   Referred to: 167, 416

―――― *Maximes d'état ou Testament politique.* 2 vols. Paris: Le Breton, 1764.

NOTE: the quotation is from Deuteronomy, 32:15; the reference given (I,225) is merely to a comparable statement.

QUOTED: 441

Dupont-White, Charles Brook.   *La Centralisation: suite à L'Individu et L'État.* Paris: Guillaumin, 1860.

REVIEWED: 581–613

QUOTED: 598, 599, 611, 612, 613

598.30–6   Suppose . . . out.] [*translated from:*] Supposez, il y a douze ou quinze ans, alors qu'il y avait une chambre de quatre cent cinquante députés, quarante-cinq députés parisiens au lieu de douze—supposez-les (et l'hypothèse n'est pas violente), pensant et votant avec l'opposition comme ces douze députés étaient dans l'habitude de le faire—voici, selon toute apparence, ce qui serait advenu: Certaine majorité ne se serait pas faite, certain cabinet n'eût pas duré huit ans, certaine révolution n'eût pas éclaté avec toutes ses suites. (277–8)

599.37–8   *de . . . pédagogie*] Ce n'est plus de la tutelle, c'est de la pédagogie: et encore voit-on tous les jours des enfants de seize ans plus libres sous la main de leur tuteur que le maire de Bordeaux régenté et couronné du préfet de la Gironde. (86)

611.31–4   The laws . . . own.] [*translated from:*] Mais elle leur demande, en retour de ces largesses, qu'ils veuillent bien se tenir en paix, ne pas s'inquiéter les uns les autres, s'abstenir de propagande, et ne pas réveiller les passions d'autrefois dans un temps qui a les siennes et qui n'en demande pas davantage. (291)

612.28–37   The feudal . . . period.] [*translated from:*] Reculez de quelques siècles et regardez vivre le seigneur féodal: Ce petit souverain peut prendre une très haute idée de lui-même et s'élever à l'orgueil, qui est le commencement de toute vertu. Sur un territoire où il abonde, il composera une classe; et cette classe créera pour l'éducation du pays un grand type capable de tout élever à sa suite. Il y aura toujours loin des sentiments aux conduites, des devises aux prouesses: Qu'importe? C'est déjà beaucoup de tel l'idéal dans une société. Il n'y survient plus une grande âme qui ne grandisse encore à l'escalade de ce modèle: d'un masque héroïque, il reste, il passe quelque chose dans les traits d'un peuple. Une lacune parmi les Russes est d'avoir été sans chevalerie. N'oublions pas que le sentiment de l'honneur est né du régime féodal; le duel est le plus beau titre de la société moderne. (15–16)

612.37   period. . . . Society] [*the ellipsis indicates the break between the two passages*]

612.37–9   Society . . . *espèce.*] [*translated from:*] Mais une société a beau eu être là, elle ne doit rien licencier de ce qui peut guinder notre indigente espèce. (112)

613.2–3   "Unity . . . intolerance"] [*translated from:*] L'unité, c'est l'intolérance, par autre chose. (188)

―――― *L'Individu et l'État.* 2me éd. Paris: Guillaumin, 1858.

REVIEWED: 581–613

QUOTED: 590–1, 593, 594, 596, 596–7, 597, 598, 607, 610, 611, 612

590.39–591.8   When . . . advantages. . . . Merely . . . attributions?] [*translated from:*] Quand l'État a fait justice de l'oppression légale il lui reste à prévenir l'exploitation naturelle. [*paragraph*] On s'est avisé de nos jours qu'il y a quelque chose de commun entre tous les hommes: le sens moral chez le plus stupide, la faillibilité chez le plus sage. D'où l'on a conclu que la loi ne doit pas subordonner et sacrifier les uns comme s'ils étaient de race inférieure aux autres, mais les traiter tous comme égaux en fait de justice de peines, d'impôts et d'admissibilité aux fonctions publiques: c'est ce qui s'appelle *l'Égalité devant la loi*. Mais ce ne peut être le dernier mot de la Civilisation, si grand qu'il soit. Comment oublier quelles différences laisse subsister d'un homme à l'autre ce fond de ressemblance qu'il y a entre tous les hommes? Comment perdre de vue que ces différences abandonées à elles-mêmes, livreraient toute faiblesse et toute ineptie à l'ascendant du plus fort, du plus habile, du plus persévérant; et que cette domination, de par la nature, serait aussi oppressive que celle qui s'exerçait jadis de par la loi. Or, qui corrigera l'abus des suprématies naturelles, si ce n'est l'État? Et comment l'État y parviendra-t-il, si ce n'est avec un surcroît de force et d'attributions? (54–5)

593.13–14 "Association . . . shareholders."] [*translated from*:] L'association tourne aisément au monopole envers le public, à la dictature envers les associés. (350)

594.10–20 The . . . crises.] [*translated from*:] L'État peut défrayer certains besoins de l'Individu, culte, éducation, routes, justice; érigeant en services publics ceux du prêtre, de l'instituteur, du juge, de l'ingénieur. C'est un bienfait pour le pauvre; car il profite de ces services publics au prorata de ses besoins qui sont quasi les mêmes chez tout homme, et il ne contribue à leur dépense que selon ses facultés. [*paragraph*] L'État peut être bienfaisant comme mandataire gratuit, par exemple quand il reçoit les petites épargnes, en sert l'intérêt, et en restitue le montant à toute heure. On put juger, il y a quelques années, de l'éminence de ce service par les embarras où il jeta les finances publiques. [*paragraph*] Enfin, la bienfaisance de l'État est quelquefois le don même, la charité. Tel est le cas de certaines mesures permanentes, comme la subvention aux hospices, les secours divers à défaut de pensions, l'école primaire gratuite, etc., et de certaines mesures accidentelles qui ne font guère défaut dans les pays civilisés aux temps de disette, d'épidémie, d'inondation, de crises commerciales. (86)

596.10–22 It . . . part.] [*translated from*:] Ainsi, et ce point est capital, c'est principalement le caractère collectif d'un intérêt, qui en détourne les hommes. Ils ne font les choses qui les intéressent le plus, que si elles peuvent être menées à bien par leurs seuls efforts, et si le profit leur en appartient tout entier. Vous pouvez compter sur la puissance de l'egoïsme pour l'agriculture, car ici le succès relève uniquement de l'individu: tout est de lui seul et pour lui seul: telle culture, telle moisson. Quant à l'éclairage et au pavage d'une ville, si importantes que soient ces choses pour l'individu, comme il ne peut les faire à lui seul, comme il n'est pas assuré que chacun en fera autant que lui, comme son propre effort équivaut à zéro s'il n'est encadré dans l'effort de tous il n'en fera rien. Ainsi l'intérêt collectif est négligé par les hommes, encore qu'il comprenne le leur. La règle est ceci: L'Individu s'abstient des choses qui lui sont les plus avantageuses, quand ne pouvant les faire à lui seul, il ne peut contraindre les autres à en faire autant que lui. [*footnote omitted*] (267–8)

596.26–597.3 Love . . . necessity.] [*translated from*:] Ce n'est pas un mobile à l'usage de tous les hommes que l'amour du bien-être et l'impatience des privations. Ce sentiment ne peut naître dans certaines conditions tellement misérables, qu'elles aspirent à s'oublier seulement et non à s'améliorer. Il ne faut pas s'abuser sur les services que rend au Progrès cette loi de la nécessité. Elle ne développe que ce qui existe. Otez-la, et peut-être que les grandes qualités enfouies chez les êtres privilégiés ne verront pas le jour. Elle est favorable à la fécondation et à l'épanouissement de ces dons; mais c'est là toute sa vertu: ailleurs elle est sans force. Ne croyez pas qu'elle enseigne au commun des hommes l'audace at la prévoyance; loin de là, elle les jette ou les entretient dans l'incurie et l'abandon d'eux-mêmes. L'aiguillon des forts n'est pour le vulgaire qu'un principe de désespoir. On ne dira pas que l'éducation de la nécessité ait manqué au peuple d'Irlande ni aux sauvages de l'Amérique du Nord; nul besoin n'est plus âpre que le leur: vivre est pour eux un problème de chaque jour. Cependant à cette dure école, ni l'Irlandais, ni l'Iroquois n'ont appris la prévoyance. [*ellipsis indicates a 5-sentence omission*] [*paragraph*] Les Gouvernements, plus sages que les sectes, ont compris qu'ils devaient, non pas se charger du bien-être de l'Individu, mais lui en offrir certains moyens, en éveiller chez lui l'espérance, et le rapprocher du but, si ce n'est l'y mener. [*paragraph*] Seriez-vous en peine des effets produits par cette assistance sur les caractères vigoureux qui peuvent s'en passer? Craignez-vous par hasard qu'ils n'en soient énervés au grand dommage de la société? mais on peut imaginer tel degré de tutelle qui serait profitable au plus grand nombre sans être nuisible aux natures privilégiées. Il s'agit de trouver cette limite et de s'y tenir. C'est un point de législation et de gouvernement assez délicat; mais enfin la voie des compromis est celle de la vérité faite pour les hommes. Vous plairait-il d'user d'un principe seulement au lieu de concilier des principes divers? Concluez donc, si vous l'osez, à la suppression des hôpitaux, dernière et surtout légitime conséquence du principe Individualiste et des doctrines de la nécessité. (298–9)

597.10–11 "This . . . society."] [*translated from:*] Ceci est la définition d'un caravansérail, de quelque chose comme Bade ou Hombourg, et non d'une société. (168)

597.34–6 "For . . . slavery."] [*translated from:*] Qu'un maître affranchisse son esclave, c'est l'effet d'une certaine grandeur d'âme; mais il suffit à l'État du moindre sens moral pour abolir l'esclavage. (346)

598.2–3 "Even . . . himself."] [*translated from:*] César Borgia ne souffrait dans ses États d'autre empoisonneur que lui-même. (308)

607.5 *le véto et l'initiative.*] Il faut s'arrêter dans cette voie, et peut-être au point que voici: déni de souveraineté, mais création de pouvoir parmi les communes, c'est-a-dire de *veto* et d'initiative. (81)

610.11–16 Consider . . . liberty?] [*translated from:*] Qu'on y songe un instant: Si la liberté est un principe d'élévation morale, c'est qu'elle signifie Pouvoir. L'homme libre trouve deux choses dans le pouvoir qu'il a sur lui-même, un espace nécessaire à ses facultés, et un sentiment qui le grandit à ses propres yeux. Mais alors, comment le pouvoir suprême, avec tout ce qu'il ouvre d'horizons et de carrières, avec tout ce qu'il éveille de sentiments, ne serait-il pas un principe d'exaltation analogue et supérieur à la liberté? (xxi–xxii)

611.3–8 The . . . world.] [*translated from:*] Or, qui a fait à la Grande-Bretagne tant de puissance et de prospérité [*4-sentence omission*] Cette fortune a deux causes entre autres, qui sont deux institutions, l'acte de navigation et la loi des pauvres—l'une en faveur de la marine britannique, et qui la protége contre la concurrence des marines étrangères, en fermant à celles-ci les ports de la Grande-Bretagne—l'autre, qui se résout en paix publique et en bas prix de la main d'œuvre, assurés à l'industrie anglaise. [*ellipsis indicates an 8-paragraph omission*] Il est donc vrai de le dire, l'industrie anglaise doit à la *loi des pauvres* la sécurité dont elle jouit, et surtout un taux des salaires qui lui permet de produire et de vendre à des prix inaccessibles pour ses concurrents, et victorieux sur presque tous les marchés du monde. (126, 129)

611.16–19 Why . . . intelligence?] [*translated from:*] D'où vient que la loi pénale est appliquée même au malfaiteur le plus ignare et le plus stupide? Parce qu'il est réputé la connaître. Et comment la connaîtrait-il, si ce n'est par ce rayon divin qui est le patrimoine de toute intelligence? (226)

612.8–13 In . . . perfection.] [*translated from:*] En général, les peuples qui arrivent les premiers à quelque grandeur religieuse ou politique, sont sujets à s'y éterniser; soit que les influences de race, de climat, de géographie capables de précipiter leur développement aient aussi bien la force de l'arrêter; soit que supérieurs d'abord à ce qui les entoure, ils y prennent l'illusion d'une excellence absolue, d'une perfection atteinte. (xxx)

612.16–18 The . . . Vedas.] [*translated from:*] La grande découverte occidentale ce n'est pas l'imprimerie, c'est la division du spirituel et du temporel: l'imprimerie toute seule n'eût servi qu'à multiplier des Coran et des Védas (xxix–xxx)

612.21–6 Whatever . . . progress.] [*translated from:*] Tout ce qui peut s'accumuler, se capitaliser, ne cesse de croître parmi les hommes, la richesse, la science et même la moralité. Mais la poésie, l'éloquence, la sculpture, sont-elles supérieures aujourd'hui à l'Illiade au Parthénon, à la tribune d'Athènes? [*ellipsis indicates a 3-paragraph omission*] En résumé, les éléments constitutifs ne changent pas plus dans l'espèce humaine que dans les autres espèces; mais certaines facultés de l'homme ont des produits susceptibles d'accumulation et de transmission: de là le Progrès, il vaudrait mieux dire de la société que de l'humanité, et le rôle toujours nécessaire des gouvernements. (360–1)

DURHAM. See Lambton, John George.

DURHAM REPORT. See under Parliamentary Papers, "Report on the Affairs of British North America" (1839).

DUVEYRIER, CHARLES. *Lettres Politiques.* 2 vols. Paris: Beck, 1843.

REFERRED TO: 200

———— *La Pairie dans ses rapports avec la situation politique; son principe, ses ressources, son avenir.* Paris: Guyot, 1842.

QUOTED: 201

REFERRED TO: 202

201.4–19 "Every . . . services."] [*translated from:*] En réalité, chaque peuple renferme et renfermera toujours probablement une administration et un public, c'est-à-dire deux sociétés: l'une dont l'intérêt commun est la loi suprême, où le principe de l'hérédité ne distribue pas les positions, qui classe les travailleurs d'après leur mérite, et les rétribue d'après leurs œuvres, et qui compense la modicité des salaires par leur fixité et surtout par l'honneur et la considération; l'autre, composée de propriétaires, de capitalistes, de maîtres et d'ouvriers, dont la loi suprême est celle de l'héritage, dont la règle principale de conduite est l'intérêt personnel, dont la concurrence et la lutte sont les élémens favoris.

Ces deux sociétés se servent mutuellement de contre-poids; elles agissent et réagissent continuellement l'une sur l'autre. La tendance du public est d'introduire dans l'administration le principe d'émulation qui lui manque; le penchant de l'administration, conforme à sa mission, est d'introduire de plus en plus dans la grande masse du public des élémens d'ordre et de prévoyance. Dans cette double direction, l'administration et le public se sont rendus et se rendent journellement des services réciproques. (12)

Edinburgh Review. Referred to: 20, 113

NOTE: the reference at 20 (which is generally to articles on political economy in the *Edinburgh Review*) is in a quotation from Bailey; that at 113 is in a quotation from E. Everett.

"THE EDUCATIONAL FRANCHISE," *The Times*, 19 Dec., 1857, 8.

NOTE: the reference is to a memorial to Lord Palmerston, the gist of which, with a long list of signators, appears in *The Times*.

REFERRED TO: 325n–326n

EDWARD II (of England).   Referred to: 437

ELIZABETH I (of England).   Referred to: 29n, 238, 437, 481

EPICTETUS.   *Discourses*, in *The Discourses as reported by Arrian, The Manual, and Fragments* (Greek and English). Trans. W. A. Oldfather. 2 vols. London: Heinemann; New York: Putnam's Sons, 1926, 1928.

NOTE: this edition used for ease of reference. As a single word is quoted, no collation is given; the term appears at I,8 (I.i.10) and II,180 (III.xxiii.32).
QUOTED: 355

Essays on Government.   See under Anon.

EULER.   Referred to: 143

EVERETT, ALEXANDER HILL.   "Men and Manners in America," *North American Review*, XXXVIII (Jan., 1834), 210–70.

NOTE: JSM was using a reprint of this article (published London: Miller, 1834) which has not been found.
REVIEWED: 93–115
QUOTED: 108–9, 109–10
110.23   chance.'] chance.'* [*footnote:* *Spirit of Laws, Book 2. Chap. 2.]

EVERETT, EDWARD.   "Prince Pückler Muscau and Mrs. Trollope," *North American Review*, XXXVI (Jan., 1833), 1–48.

QUOTED: 107–8, 112–13
107.42   "We] But we (47)
113.1–2   responsible authority] responsible English authority (42)

FAWCETT, HENRY.   *Mr. Hare's Reform Bill simplified and explained.* Westminster: Printed by T. Brettnell, 1860.

REFERRED TO: 454

Federalist.   See Hamilton, Alexander.

FIÉVÉE.   Referred to: 582

NOTE: the reference is in an indirect quotation from Odilon Barrot.

FOX, HENRY RICHARD VASSALL.   Referred to: 41

FOX, WILLIAM JOHNSON.   "*The London Review*. No II," *Monthly Repository*, n.s. IX (Sept., 1835), 627–8.

NOTE: in the passage referred to below, JSM identifies the author of the unsigned notice as the editor of the *Monthly Repository*. The reference to "Lydia Tomkins," *Thoughts on the Ladies of the Aristocracy* (*s.v.*), in that passage probably derives from Fox's mention of it in this notice.

REFERRED TO: 56n

FRANKLIN.   Referred to: 101, 468n

NOTE: the reference at 468n is in a quotation from Carey.

FREDERICK I (Grand Duke of Baden).   Referred to: 466n

FREDERICK II (of Prussia).   Referred to: 42, 382

FREEMAN, EDWARD AUGUSTUS.   *History of Federal Government, from the foundation of the Achaian League to the disruption of the United States.* Vol. I. Cambridge: Macmillan, 1863.

NOTE: JSM mistakenly refers to the work as *History of Federal Governments*. No more volumes appeared.

REFERRED TO: 555n

GALLATIN.   Referred to: 111

GANGANELLI.   Referred to: 382

George Barnwell.   See Lillo, George.

GLEICHEN.   Referred to: 239

GORDON.   Referred to: 318, 330

NOTE: both references are to the Reform Bill introduced by Lord Aberdeen's government; see under Parliamentary Papers, "A Bill further to amend the Laws relating to the Representation of the People" (1854).

GRESSET, JEAN BAPTISTE LOUIS.   *Le Méchant.* 2nd ed. Paris: Jorry, 1748.

NOTE: this edition was the earliest available to the editor.

QUOTED: 349

349.5   "les absents ont toujours tort"] Valere: Mais assez, ce me semble: / Nous étions élevés, accoûtumés ensemble, / Je la trouvois gentille, elle me plaisoit fort, / Mais Paris quérit tout, & les absens ont tort; / On m'a mandé souvent qu'elle étoit embellie; / Comment la trouvez-vous? (59; Act II, Scene vii)

GROTE, GEORGE.   *A History of Greece.* 12 vols. London: Murray, 1846–56.

NOTE: in JSM's library, Somerville College; each volume or set inscribed as a presentation copy.
REFERRED TO: 411

GUIZOT, FRANÇOIS PIERRE GUILLAUME.   Referred to: 608

——— *Cours d'histoire moderne*: *Histoire générale de la civilisation en Europe, depuis la chute de l'empire romain jusqu'à la révolution française*. Paris: Pichon and Didier, 1828.

NOTE: in Somerville College, without bookplate, but probably JSM's, with "I" on spine; see the next entry, which has the same general title. JSM refers to the same passage as that cited at 197 in his "Guizot's Essays and Lectures on History," *Edinburgh Review*, LXXXII (Oct., 1845), 390–3. The *leçons* are separately paged.
REFERRED TO: 94, 197

——— *Cours d'histoire moderne*: *Histoire de la civilisation en France, depuis la chute de l'empire romain jusqu'en 1789*. 5 vols. Paris: Pichon and Didier, 1829–32.

NOTE: in JSM's library, Somerville College, with "I" to "V" on spines: cf. the previous entry, which has the same general title.
REFERRED TO: 94

GUSTAVUS ADOLPHUS (of Sweden).   Referred to: 437

HACKET.   Referred to: 112

NOTE: the reference is in a quotation from E. Everett.

HAMILTON, ALEXANDER, with JOHN JAY, and JAMES MADISON.   *The Federalist*. Philadelphia: Lippincott, 1864.

NOTE: in JSM's library, Somerville College. The first complete edition appeared in 1788. The references are to "the authors of *The Federalist*."
REFERRED TO: 555, 558

HAMILTON, CHARLES.   *The Hedàya or Guide; A Commentary on the Mussulman Laws*. 4 vols. London: Bensley, 1791.

NOTE: JSM mistakenly attributes the quotation cited below to the *Koran*. It seems likely that he got the passage from Hamilton's work, which is in his library, Somerville College.
QUOTED: 255–6
255.40–256.1 "A ruler who appoints any man to an office, when there is in his dominions another man better qualified for it, sins against God and against the State."] It is incumbent on the Sultan to select for the office of *Kàzee* a person who is capable of discharging the duties of it, and passing decrees; and who is also in a superlative degree just and virtuous; for the prophet has said, "*Whoever appoints*

a person to the discharge of any office, whilst there is another amongst his subjects more qualified for the same than the person so appointed, does surely commit an injury with respect to the rights of GOD, *the* PROPHET, *and the* MUSSULMANS." (II,615)

HAMILTON, THOMAS.   *Men and Manners in America.* 2 vols. Edinburgh: Blackwood, 1833.

NOTE: the quotation is from E. Everett.

QUOTED: 110

REFERRED TO: 97, 108, 110
110.6   "retired] On the whole, I retired (II, 42)
110.6–7   interview he had with General Jackson, with] interview with (II, 42)
110.7   respect for] respect both for (II, 42)

————   *The Youth and Manhood of Cyril Thornton.* 3 vols. Edinburgh: Blackwood, 1827.

NOTE: the reference at 110 is in a quotation from A. H. Everett.

REFERRED TO: 97, 110

HAMILTON, WILLIAM.   "Study of Mathematics—University of Cambridge," *Edinburgh Review,* LXII (Jan., 1836), 409–55.

REFERRED TO: 142n

HARE, THOMAS.   *A Treatise on the Election of Representatives, Parliamentary and Municipal.* London: Longman, Brown, Green, Longmans, & Roberts, 1859.

NOTE: the reference at 454n is to the second edition, 1861. The third edition, 1865, inscribed "From the Author," is in JSM's library, Somerville College.

REVIEWED: 343–70

QUOTED: 367, 368, 369, 369–70

REFERRED TO: 339n, 452–66, 477, 481, 495–6, 518
367.23   "by . . . polling-place;"] It is proposed that the vote shall be given in the shape of a document, to be deliberately prepared and signed, and (except in some special cases, which will be the subject of a distinct chapter) personally delivered by . . . polling-place. (144–5)
369.8   "to] The charges, which it is absolutely necessary that a candidate should incur, ought not to exceed a sum sufficient to (126)
369.13   Exonerate] For this it is proposed to provide, by requiring a preliminary payment to the Registrar,* [*footnote:* *Clause VII., p. 113, *ante.* The sum there suggested is £50.] which shall exonerate (126)
369.30   One] The test of capacity should be one (309)
369.38   career. . . . The] career. He does not at that time of life require it from any regard to liberty or security, for the possession of the franchise by his seniors of the same class, having similar interests for themselves and their children, is a sufficient guard, and every day brings him nearer to the time when he may himself attain it. The (309)
369.9   the line of occupation] the fixed occupation (309)
370.3–5   "so . . . lot,"] There is nothing exclusive in such a rule when the standard

is so . . . lot that cannot be provided for in a subject having so extensive a bearing as the suffrage. (313)

370.6–8   "it . . . apply" . . . "to . . . multitude"] It . . . apply an educational test to . . . multitude. (310)

370.9–14   "it may exclude . . . sense" . . . "it would operate . . . suitable."] Any such test which might be applied may, moreover, exclude . . . sense; and it would especially operate . . . suited. (310–11)

HARRIS, JAMES HOWARD.   Letter to the Civil Service Commissioners (22/9/58), in Foreign Office Correspondence, in Appendix II of "Fourth Report of Her Majesty's Civil Service Commissioners," *Parliamentary Papers*, 1859, VIII, 203–4.

NOTE: the whole correspondence (198–210) is relevant to Malmesbury's ruling against a spelling examination for Foreign Office aspirants. In the Report of the Inquiry into the Civil Service Examinations (*Parliamentary Papers*, 1860, IX), some of the others who wished to denigrate a spelling test may be identified (e.g., Monckton Milnes, 28, and Clay, 36–7).

REFERRED TO: 531

HAWES.   Referred to: 352

HELPS, ARTHUR.   *The Spanish Conquest in America, and its relation to the history of slavery and to the government of the Colonies.* 4 vols. London: Parker and Son, 1855–61.

REFERRED TO: 571

HENRY III (of England).   Referred to: 437

HENRY IV (of France).   Referred to: 437

HILL.   Referred to: 439

HINCKES.   Referred to: 567

HOBBES, THOMAS.   Referred to: 17

———   *Leviathan, or the Matter, Form, and Power of a Commonwealth, Ecclesiastical and Civil*, in *The English Works of Thomas Hobbes*. Ed. William Molesworth. London: Bohn, 1839, III.

NOTE: the quotation is in a quotation from Taylor. This edition, which is in JSM's library, Somerville College, is used for consistency of reference, though the quotation antedates the edition.

QUOTED: *645*

645.34   "After] For after (89)

645.35   'tis] it is (89)

645.36   other is] other, are (89)

HOLLAND. See Fox, Henry Richard Vassall.

HOLYOAKE. Referred to: 239

HOMER. *Iliad.*

NOTE: the reference is in a quotation from Dupont-White. As specific wording is not involved, no edition is cited. A two-volume edition in Greek of *The Iliad* and *The Odyssey* (Oxford, 1800) is in JSM's library, Somerville College.

REFERRED TO: 612

HOOKER. Referred to: *626*

NOTE: the reference is in a quotation from Taylor.

HORACE (Quintus Horatius Flaccus). *Ars poetica,* in *Satires, Epistles and Ars Poetica* (Latin and English). Trans. H. Rushton Fairclough. London: Heinemann; New York: Putnam's Sons, 1926.

NOTE: the reference is in a quotation from Bailey; this edition used for ease of reference. JSM's library, Somerville College, contains *Opera* (Glasgow: Mundell, 1796), in which the passage occurs on p. 538.

QUOTED: 33
33.24–5 *Nec . . . nodus,*] nec . . . nodus / inciderit, nec quarta loqui persona laboret. (466; 11.191–2)

——— "Carmina Liber III, xxx," in *The Odes and Epodes* (Latin and English). Trans. C. E. Bennett. London: Heinemann; New York: Macmillan, 1914.

NOTE: this edition is used for ease of reference. *Opera* (Glasgow: Mundell, 1796) is in JSM's library, Somerville College.

QUOTED: 42
42.3–4 *monumentum ære perennius*] Exegi monumentum aere perennius / regalique situ pyramidum altius, / quod non imber edax, non Aquilo impotens / possit diruere aut innumerabilis / anorum series et fuga temporum. (278; 11.1–5)

——— *Epistles,* in *Satires, Epistles and Ars Poetica* (Latin and English). Trans. H. Rushton Fairclough. London: Heinemann; New York: Putnam's Sons, 1926.

NOTE: this edition used for ease of reference. JSM's library, Somerville College, contains *Opera* (Glasgow: Mundell, 1796).

QUOTED: 157
157.28–30 *candidus imperti . . . his utere mecum.*] Vive, vale! si quid novisti rectius istis, / candidus imperti; si nil, his utere mecum. (290; Epistle I,vi,67–8)

HORSLEY, SAMUEL. *The Speeches in Parliament of Samuel Horsley.* Ed. H. Horsley. Dundee: Chalmers, 1813.

NOTE: the comment was made by Bishop Horsley in Committee of the House of Lords on the Treason Bill introduced by Lord Grenville on 6 November, 1795. On the third reading, 13 November, the remark was attacked by Lord Lauderdale, and defended by Horsley.

QUOTED: 469

469.29 "has no business with the laws except to obey them,"] all that the people had to do with the laws of the country was to obey them (167–8)

HUMBOLDT, CARL WILHELM VON. *The Sphere and Duties of Government.* Trans. Joseph Coulthard. London: Chapman, 1854.

NOTE: the quotation at 300 is indirect. This edition is in JSM's library, Somerville College.

QUOTED: 215, 261, 300

REFERRED TO: 261–2, 274, 300–1, 304

215.2   argument unfolded] argument hitherto unfolded (65)

215.4   diversity.] diversity; but national education, since at least it presupposes the selection and appointment of some one instructor, must always promote a definite form of developement, however careful to avoid such an error. (65)

261.29   "the end of man] The true end of Man (11)

261.30   or] and (11)

261.32-6   whole;" . . . "towards . . . individuality of power and developement;"] whole. [*2-page omission*] This individual vigour, then, and manifold diversity, combine themselves in *originality*; and hence, that on which the consummate grandeur of our nature ultimately depends,—that towards . . . *Individuality of Power and Developement.* (11, 13)

261.36-7   "freedom . . . situations;"] Now, it is clear (to apply these conclusions to the respective conditions for culture,—freedom, . . . situations), that, on the one hand, individual energy is essential to the perceived and perceiver, into which social unions may be resolved; and, on the other, a difference between them, neither so great as to prevent the one from comprehending the other, nor so inconsiderable as to exclude admiration for that which the other possesses, and the desire of assimilating it into the perceiver's character. (13)

261.37-8   "individual . . . diversity," . . . "originality."] [*see above*, 261.32–6]

HUME, JOSEPH.   Referred to: *634*

HUME, DAVID.   "Of Commerce," in *Essays and Treatises on Several Subjects.* 2 vols. London: Cadell, 1793.

NOTE: in JSM's library, Somerville College. The quotation is in a quotation from Bailey.

QUOTED: 21

21.14–17   "Tis certain," . . . "that . . . prevail] But however intricate they may seem, it is certain, that general principles, if just and sound, must always prevail (I,251)

HYPERBOLUS.   Referred to: 460

An Introduction to the Latin Tongue, for the Use of Youth. A New Edition revised. Eton: Pote and Williams, 1806.

NOTE: the text chosen is merely illustrative. The quoted phrase traditionally (from the sixteenth century) was used in Latin grammars as a rubric for the section on masculine nouns. (For the origins of these grammars, see C. G. Allen, "The Sources of 'Lily's Latin Grammar,'" *The Library*, 5th ser., IX [June, 1954], 85–100, where it is argued that "The Royal Grammar" is a better general title than "Lily's.")

QUOTED: 31

31.22 *Propria quae maribus.*] *Propria quæ maribus tribuuntur, mascula dicas; / Ut sunt Divorum;* Mars, Bacchus, Apollo: *Virorum; / Ut,* Cato, Virigilius: *Fluviorum; ut,* Tibris, Orontes: / *Mensium; ut,* October: *Ventorum; ut,* Libs, Notus, Austen. (63)

IRVING, WASHINGTON.   Referred to: 109

NOTE: the reference is in a quotation from E. Everett.

———— *History of New York from the beginning of the world to the end of the Dutch Dynasty, by Diedrich Knickerbocker.* London: Sharpe, 1821.

NOTE: in JSM's library, Somerville College. The reference is in a quotation from E. Everett.

REFERRED TO: 112

JACKSON, ANDREW.   Referred to: 110

NOTE: the reference is in a quotation from A. H. Everett.

———— *Proclamation by the President of the United States* [10 Dec., 1832, relative to an ordinance passed in the State Convention of South Carolina, refusing to be bound by the revenue laws of the Congress of the United States]. London: Miller, 1833.

REFERRED TO: 77

JAMES, EDWIN.   Referred to: 496n; see under Parliamentary Papers, "Report from the Select Committee on the Corrupt Practices Prevention Act" (1860).

JAY.   Referred to: 110

NOTE: the reference is in a quotation from A. H. Everett. See also under Hamilton, Alexander, *The Federalist.*

JEFFERSON.   Referred to: 100, 109–11, 438, *641*

NOTE: the references at 109–10 are in a quotation from E. Everett.

JESUS.   Referred to: 235, 236, 249, 255, 256

JOHN (of England).   Referred to: 437

JOHNSON, SAMUEL.   See also Boswell, *Life of Johnson*; and Carlyle, "Boswell's Life of Johnson."

QUOTED: 8   REFERRED TO: 138, 237–8

JOHNSTON.   Referred to: 40

NOTE: the reference is to the "honorable member for St. Andrew's."

JOSEPH II (Holy Roman Emperor).   Referred to: 382

JOWETT, BENJAMIN.   Letter in "Report on the Organisation of the Permanent Civil Service," in *Parliamentary Papers*, 1854, XXVII, 24–31.

NOTE: reprinted above as Appendix C.

QUOTED: 210

210.10   "school or college"] 2. That he [the candidate] should at the same time send papers comprising a certificate of birth and baptism, with a precise statement of all the places of his education, whether at school or college, together with testimonials of his conduct for two years previously from the head of the school or college in which he was last a pupil, and also a statement of his present occupation and residence. (24)

210.16   "confidential"] 3. That he should give references—1. To a medical man; 2. To a magistrate; or, in case of inferior situations, to two respectable householders; 3. To a clergyman or dissenting minister; to all of whom carefully-drawn questions respecting the candidate in the form of an insurance office paper should be submitted; the answers to be confidential. (25)

210.17   "absolute and without reasons."] The rejection should be absolute and without reasons; whether it took place on medical or moral grounds would remain uncertain.

JUVENAL.   *Satires*, in *Juvenal and Persius* (Latin and English). Trans. G. G. Ramsay. London: Heinemann; New York: Putnam's Sons, 1918.

NOTE: this edition used for ease of reference. Two editions (London, 1744 and 1835) formerly in JSM's library, Somerville College.

QUOTED: 426

426.23   *quis custodiet custodes?*] sed quis custodiet ipsos / custodes? (110; VI. 347–8: *cf.* 114; VI. O31–2)

KANT.   Referred to: 304

KENYON.   Referred to: 127

KING.   Referred to: 319. See also, under Parliamentary Papers, "A Bill to Extend the franchise," 21 Victoria (27 April, 1858).

"KNICKERBOCKER, DIEDRICH."   See Irving.

KNOX.   Referred to: 249, 266

Koran. Referred to: 612. See also Charles Hamilton, *The Hedàya or Guide.*

NOTE: the reference, from Dupont-White, being general, no edition is cited. At 255–6 JSM attributes, mistakenly, a quotation to the *Koran*; see the entry under Hamilton cited above.

LABOULAYE. Referred to: 466n, 584n

LA BRUYÈRE, JEAN DE. *Les Caractères ou les mœurs de ce siècle.*

NOTE: the reference, which is in a quotation from Tocqueville, is to Chap. xi, "Des grands." As the reference is general, and the work is not in JSM's library, no edition is cited; the work was first published (with La Bruyère's *Caractères de Théophraste*) in Paris in 1688.

REFERRED TO: 81–2

LAMBTON, JOHN GEORGE. See under Parliamentary Papers, "Report on the Affairs of British North America" (1839).

LANDOR, WALTER SAVAGE. *Imaginary Conversations of Literary Men and Statesmen.* 5 vols. London: Taylor and Hessey, 1824–29.

NOTE: the quotation is in a quotation from Taylor. The conversation is between Lord Brooke and Sir Philip Sidney, the latter being the speaker.

QUOTED: *629*

629.10–11 "I am," . . . "a waiter at] I have known several such, and when I have inno-
cently smiled at them, their countenances seemed to say, "*I wish I could despise you: but alas! I am a runaway slave, and from the best of mistresses to the worst of masters; I serve at* [*rest of sentence also in italics*] (I,26)

629.12 on] *upon* (I,26)

LANFREY. Referred to: 584n

LAGRANGE. Referred to: 143

LAPLACE. Referred to: 143

LATROBE, CHARLES JOSEPH. *The Rambler in North America: 1832–1833.* 2 vols. London: Seeley and Burnside, 1835.

REVIEWED: 93–115

QUOTED: 114–15

114.25–6 *Having . . . points*] [*no italics*] (I,68)
115.5 unjust.—Hence] unjust. [*paragraph*] Hence (I,70)

LAVERGNE, LOUIS GABRIEL LÉONCE GUILHAUD DE. "Royer-Collard, orateur et politique," *Revue des Deux Mondes,* XXXV (1 Oct., 1861), 566–97.

NOTE: Lavergne is quoting Royer-Collard.

QUOTED: 608

608.4–18 Who . . . force.] [*translated from*:] "Qui vote dans les collèges? Les électeurs sans doute? Non, c'est pour un très grand nombre le ministère. Le ministère vote par l'universalité des emplois et des salaires que l'état distribue, et qui, tous ou presque tous, directement ou indirectement, sont le prix de la docilité prouvée; il vote par l'universalité des affaires et des intérêts que la centralité lui soumet; il vote par tous ces établissemens, religieux, civils, militaires, scientifiques, que les localités ont à perdre ou qu'elles sollicitent; il vote par les routes, les ponts, les canaux, les hôtels de ville, car les besoins publics satisfaits sont des faveurs de l'administration, et pour les obtenir, les peuples, nouveaux courtisans, doivent plaire. En un mot, le ministère vote de tout le poids du gouvernement qu'il fait peser en entier sur chaque département, chaque commune, chaque profession, chaque particulier. Et quel est ce gouvernement? C'est le gouvernement impérial, qui n'a pas perdu un seul de ses cent mille bras, qui a puisé au contraire une nouvelle vigueur dans la lutte qu'il lui a fallu soutenir contre quelques formes de liberté, et qui retrouve toujours au besoin les instincts de son berceau, la force et la ruse. (586–7)

LEONIDAS. Referred to: 71, *651*

LEOPOLD II (Holy Roman Emperor). Referred to: 382

LEWIS, GEORGE CORNEWALL. Referred to: 497n; see Parliamentary Papers, "Report from the Select Committee on the Corrupt Practices Prevention Act" (1860). See also Boeckh; and Mueller.

———— *An Examination of Some Passages in Dr. Whately's Elements of Logic.* Oxford: Parker; London: Murray, 1829.

REFERRED TO: 3

———— *Remarks on the Use and Abuse of some Political Terms.* London: Fellowes, 1832.

REVIEWED: 3–13

QUOTED: 4–5, 8, 9, 11, 12

8.25 "mischievous,] But if it were argued, that *justice*, not *law*, ought to be administered in courts of *justice*; that no man can have a *right* to do that which is *wrong*; that in a *kingdom* the institutions ought to be *monarchical*, &c.; then the ambiguity is mischievous, (xv)

9.3 "claims] Sometimes, however, it is used to mean a claim recommended by the practice, analogy, or doctrines of the constitution, *i.e.* a *constitutional* right; and, sometimes, a claim (8)

9.3 policy;"] policy, *i.e.* a *moral* right. (8)

11.40 "seems] In this case, *natural* seems (182–3)

12.23 "that . . . laws;] This opinion is supported by the often quoted sentence of Tacitus, "that . . . laws;" (205)

LEWIS, THOMAS FRANKLAND. Referred to: 3

LIEBER, FRANCIS. *Reminiscences of an Intercourse with George Berthold Niebuhr, the historian of Rome.* London: Bentley, 1835.

REFERRED TO: 97

———— *The Stranger in America.* 2 vols. London: Bentley, 1835.

REVIEWED: 93–115

QUOTED: 101n, 103n, 106n, 113
106.n8 'regulators,'] regulators (I,16)
106.n9–10 justice. Of] justice; of (I,17)
113.9 Americans] American (II,77)
113.28 experience.*" Which] experience," which (II,78)

LILLO, GEORGE. *The London Merchant: or the History of George Barnwell.* London: Gray, 1731.

REFERRED TO: 281

LINCOLN. Referred to: 484

LIVINGSTON, EDWARD. *A System of Penal Law for the United States of America: consisting of a code of crimes and punishments; a Code of procedure in criminal cases, a Code of prison discipline; and a Book of definitions.* Prepared and presented to the House of Representatives of the United States, . . . Printed by order of the House of Representatives. Washington, printed by Gales & Seaton, 1828.

REFERRED TO: 77

LOCKE, JOHN. Referred to: 7, 143, 304

———— *Some Thoughts Concerning Education,* in *Works.* New Ed. 10 vols. London: Tegg, Sharpe, Offor, Robinson, Evans, 1823, IX, 1–205.

NOTE: this edition is in JSM's library, Somerville College. It is unlikely that JSM had a specific passage in mind when citing "principling" from Locke; the two passages referred to in the note on 141 (i.e., 29 and 148) show Locke's use of "principle" as a verb in relevant contexts. (The passage in Locke on 90–1, where the word is not used, expresses the notion more fully, and may have significance for JSM's own education.) A similar usage is in Locke's *Essay Concerning Human Understanding,* Bk. I, Chap. iii.

QUOTED: 141

———— *Two Treatises on Government,* in *Works.* New Ed. 10 vols. London: Tegg, Sharpe, Offor, Robinson, Evans, 1823, V, 209–485.

NOTE: this edition is in JSM's library, Somerville College. The passage referred to (Bk. II, Chap. ii, §14) actually is cited by Lewis.

REFERRED TO: 10

LORIMER, JAMES. *Political Progress not Necessarily Democratic: Or Relative Equality the True Foundation of Liberty*. London and Edinburgh: Williams and Norgate, 1857.

NOTE: the quotation at 499n is indirect.

REVIEWED: 343–70

QUOTED: 353, 355–6, 357, 368, 499n

353.7–8 "final . . . governments;"] Whatever may be the variations in the earlier stages of the sequence, if the final result to which it points be trustworthy, it conveys to us this very pregnant fact, that the rule of the numerical majority is the degenerate form to which not only popular governments are prone, but that it is the final . . . governments whatsoever. (130–1)

353.16 "removing] If on the present occasion I have succeeded [*sic*] in removing (vii)

353.17–18 and showing] and thus by shewing (vii)

353.18 recognition," to "pave the] recognition, have paved the (vii)

353.20 tread."] tread, a good work will have been accomplished. (vii)

353.22 "The sum of *influences* should] On the contrary it is quite consistent with their views, and is indeed contemplated by both, that the sum of *influences*,* [**three-sentence footnote*] instead of coinciding with, should (17)

355.23 and the] and still that the (17)

355.23 State] state (17)

355.24 individual, whatever] individual, we shall afterwards see that whatever (17)

355.30 utterance. But] utterance. [*paragraph*] But (18)

355.30 State] state (18)

355.31–2 indispensable,'] indispensable, and Savigny recognises it expressly, "Above all, individuals must be understood to constitute the state, not as such, but in their constitutional divisions." (18)

355.33 The] It thus appears that the (49)

355.36 deals.] deals; and that the problem of reconciling liberty with order, without infringing on either, will be solved by such a development of the latter, as to enable it, in each particular case, to take complete and accurate cognisance of the claims of the former. (49)

355.37 The] It having been thus determined that the (226)

355.38 community.] community, the questions which fall next to be answered have reference to the form or forms of suffrage by which this may be adequately and *permanently* accomplished. (226)

356.8 acquired.] *acquired*. (227)

368.24 "inducement] By paying representatives you create an inducement (169)

368.25 affairs, the] affairs, and the (169)

368.25 would be] is (169)

LOUIS XI (of France). Referred to: 167

LOUIS XIV (of France). Referred to: 82, 83, 167, 416, 443

NOTE: the references at 82 and 83 are in quotations from Tocqueville.

LOUIS XVIII (of France). Referred to: 582

LOUIS NAPOLEON. See Napoleon III.

LOUIS-PHILLIPE (of France). Referred to: 587, 599, 608

NOTE: the reference at 599 is in an indirect quotation from Dupont-White.

LUTHER.   Referred to: 238, 381

LYCURGUS.   Referred to: 42

NOTE: the reference is to the laws of Lycurgus.

LYTTON, EDWARD BULWER.   See Bulwer.

LYTTON, ROBERT.   See under Parliamentary Papers, "Report by Mr. Lytton" (1864).

MACAULAY, THOMAS BABINGTON.   "Mill's Essay on Government," *Edinburgh Review*, XLIX (March, 1829), 159–89.

NOTE: the second reference at 20 is in a quotation from Bailey.
QUOTED: ˙20
REFERRED TO: 22
20.9–10 'beyond maxims] beyond those maxims (186)
20.12   it is not possible] we do not believe that it is possible (187)
20.24   "general rules] general rule (187)

MACHIAVELLI.   Referred to: *621, 622*

NOTE: "Machiavel" is the form used.

MACKINTOSH, SIR JAMES.   *The History of England*. 10 vols. London: Longman, Rees, Orme, Brown, & Green, 1830–40.

NOTE: the same passage is cited in all three cases (and also in the *Logic*; see *Collected Works*, VII, 151–2). The exact quotation does not appear in this work, but the sense is given at I, 72 (and also in Mackintosh's "Speech on the Annexation of Genoa," in *Miscellaneous Works*, 3 vols. [London: Longman, Brown, Green, & Longmans, 1854], III, 351–2). JSM probably took it from Samuel Bailey, *Rationale of Political Representation*, 381–5, 428 (Note F), who discusses Mackintosh's use of this image, and gives both the above references.
QUOTED: 41–2, 374, 380

MADISON.   Referred to: 100, 109, 111

NOTE: the reference at 109 is in a quotation from A. H. Everett. See also under Hamilton, Alexander, *The Federalist*.

MAHOMET.   Referred to: 41, 416

NOTE: the reference at 41 is to the laws of Mahomet.

MALMESBURY (3rd Earl of).   See Harris, James Howard.

MARCUS AURELIUS.   See Antoninus.

MARSHALL, JAMES GARTH.   *Minorities and Majorities; their relative rights. A letter to the Lord John Russell, M.P. on Parliamentary Reform.* London: Ridgway, 1853.

REFERRED TO: 330, 452

MARVELL.   Referred to: 500

NOTE: JSM's spelling is Marvel.

MARY (of England).   Referred to: 238

MASSEY, WILLIAM NATHANIEL.   Speech at Manchester, reported in "Mr. Massey, M.P., Upon the Indian Mutinies. (From the *Manchester Examiner* of yesterday.)" *The Times*, 14 Nov., 1857, p.4.

QUOTED: 240n–241n
240.n10   'Toleration] He was going to make a proposition which would perhaps startle them: he believed that toleration (4)
240.n12   Government, had] Government had been in a main degree instrumental—had (4)
240.n13–14   Christianity. . . . Toleration] Christianity. But they must not misunderstand him. Toleration (4)
241.n2–3   *among . . . foundation*] [*no italics*] (4)
241.n4   *Christians . . . mediation.*'] [*no italics*] (4)
241.n4   *mediation.*'] mediation; but to apply the word toleration to a people who worshipped miserable and bloodstained idols, whose religion was founded on principles shocking to humanity and disgraceful to human nature—to say that toleration was to be extended to such superstitions was, in his opinion, a gross abuse of the term. (4)

MAURICE, JOHN FREDERICK DENISON.   *Eustace Conway: or, The Brother and Sister.* 3 vols. London: Bentley, 1834.

QUOTED: 139–40
139.32   Treasury] treasury (II, 80)
140.1   whom] which (II, 80)
140.9   "we] "We (II, 81)

MEDICI.   Referred to: 443

MELETUS.   Referred to: 235

NOTE: the accuser (*inter alia*) of Socrates.

Men and Manners in America.   See Hamilton, Thomas.

MILL, HARRIET HARDY TAYLOR.   Referred to: 216

MILL, JAMES.   "Aristocracy," *London Review*, II (Jan., 1836), 283–306.

NOTE: the reference is to "the first article of our present Number."
REFERRED TO: 99

———— "The Ballot—A Dialogue," *London Review*, I (April, 1835), 201–53.

REFERRED TO: 25

———— *Elements of Political Economy*. 3rd ed. London: Baldwin, Cradock, and Joy, 1826.

NOTE: the reference is general, so the final edition is cited.
REFERRED TO: 12

———— *A Fragment on Mackintosh: being strictures on some passages in the dissertation by Sir James Mackintosh, prefixed to the Encyclopædia Britannica*. London: Baldwin and Cradock, 1835.

NOTE: the 2nd ed. (London: Longmans, Green, Reader and Dyer, 1870) is in JSM's library, Somerville College.
QUOTED: 22
22.22–4 'It . . .ages' . . . 'pitiful objections.'] It . . . ages, from the pitiful objections of a man who, finding it stated in some quarter which he disliked, that identity of interests with the community is the best security the community can have for the good conduct of its rulers; gives out a proposition which has no bearing on the matter, and cries out, *"There!* I have demolished your best security: men sometimes mistake their true interest: therefore, the identity of the interests of the rulers with the interests of the community is not the best security for care of the interests of the community." (288–9)

———— ("F.F.") *The Article Government, reprinted from The Supplement to the Encyclopædia Britannica*. London: Traveller Office, 1821.

NOTE: the words in italic are taken from Lewis, who quotes the full sentence given in the collation, adding the italics.
QUOTED: 12
12.11   *corruptive operation*] Prudence is a more general characteristic of the people, without the advantages of fortune, than of the people who have been thoroughly subject to their corruptive operation. (31)

———— *The History of British India*. 3rd ed. 6 vols. London: Baldwin, Cradock, and Joy, 1826.

NOTE: this edition is in JSM's library, Somerville College.
QUOTED: 331n–332n, 332
331.n4   advantageous: there] advantageous. There (III, 451)
331.n13   acted on] acted upon (III, 451)
332.n9–10   security. . . . There] security. [*4-sentence omission*] There (III, 451–2)
332.11   "base . . . vote"] [*see text*, 332.n8]

MILL, JOHN STUART.   "Austin's Lectures on Jurisprudence," *Tait's Edinburgh Magazine*, IX (Dec., 1832), 343–8.

QUOTED: 134
134.26   food, and] food of all qualities, and (343)
134.33   What wonder] Who wonders (343) [*cf*. 134*i–i*]
134.34   hardly a] no (343) [*cf*. 134*k–k*]

——— *Autobiography*. Ed. Jack Stillinger. Boston: Houghton Mifflin, 1969.

NOTE: this ed., which gives the corrected text, is used for ease of reference. The reference is to JSM's use of a phrase, "the astonishing pliability of our nature," in "Civilization," that closely parallels one, "the 'extraordinary pliability of human nature' ", that he says, in the *Autobiography* (107), he "somewhere borrowed" from John Austin.
REFERRED TO: 145n

——— "De Tocqueville on Democracy in America [I]."

NOTE: i.e., the essay printed at 47–90 above. The changes are given as variants to the essays.
QUOTED: 174–5
REFERRED TO: 18n, 94, 99, 106, 108

——— "De Tocqueville on Democracy in America [II]."

NOTE: i.e., the essay printed at 153–204 above. The quotation is indirect, merely reproducing an illustrative image.
QUOTED: 380

——— "Duveyrier's Political Views of French Affairs," *Edinburgh Review*, LXXXIII (Apr., 1846), 453–74.

NOTE: the changes in the quotation are given as variants to the second article on Tocqueville. JSM says (200) that the article is a review of Duveyrier's *Lettres politiques*; however, it also deals with Duveyrier's *La Pairie*.
QUOTED: 201–4

——— *On Liberty*.

NOTE: i.e., the essay printed at 213–310 above.
REFERRED TO: 534n

——— "Pledges," *Examiner* (1 July, 1832), 417–18.

QUOTED: 41n

——— "Pledges," *Examiner* (15 July, 1832), 449–51.

REFERRED TO: 41n

———— *Principles of Political Economy*. London: Parker, 1848. *Collected Works*, Vols. II and III. Toronto: University of Toronto Press, 1965.

REFERRED TO: 534n

———— "Rationale of Representation."

NOTE: i.e., the essay printed at 15–46 above.

QUOTED: 54n

REFERRED TO: 71

54.n34 'which,] Into the reasons of any other kind, which may be given for the exclusion of women, we shall not enter; not because we think any of them valid, but because the subject (though in a philosophical treatise on representation it could not have been passed over in silence) is not one which, (29n *above*)

———— "Recent Writers on Reform."

NOTE: i.e., the essay printed at 341–70 above. The concluding quotation from this essay in *Thoughts on Parliamentary Reform* (see 339^k) is not there reproduced, as it appeared only in the pamphlet version of the latter; in *Dissertations and Discussions*, III, the two essays appeared one after the other, and so the quotation was unnecessary. The different readings of the quotation at 449n–500n and its original are given as variants to "Recent Writers on Reform" and *Considerations on Representative Government*.

QUOTED: 339n, 449n–500n

REFERRED TO: 339n

———— "Reform of the Civil Service."

NOTE: i.e., the essay printed at 205–11 above.

REFERRED TO: 306

———— "Remarks on Bentham's Philosophy," App. B in Edward Bulwer Lytton, *England and the English*. London: Bentley, 1833, II, 321–44. In *Collected Works*, Vol. X. Toronto: University of Toronto Press, 1969, 3–18.

NOTE: the changes (mainly deletions of references to Bentham) are recorded as variants to the essay. Bulwer's work is in JSM's library, Somerville College.

QUOTED: 42–3

42.29 'How] He was not, I am persuaded, aware, how (II, 342; *CW*, X,17) [cf. 42^{l-l}]

42.36 one. The] one [*3-sentence omission*] The (II, 343; *CW*, X,17) [cf. 42^m]

———— Speech "On the British Constitution," printed in *Autobiography*. Ed. Harold J. Laski. London: Oxford University Press, 1924, 275–87.

NOTE: the MS from which Laski printed his version has not been located, but a typescript of it has survived (in the possession of the Fabian Society). The passage has been collated against the typescript (indicated below by "T") as well as against Laski's printed version (indicated below by "L"); in the one place in the collation where the accidentals differ within a substantive change, the typescript is followed.

———   "State of Society in America."

———   *Thoughts on Parliamentary Reform.* 2nd ed. London: Parker, 1859.

————, with Joseph Blanco White. "Guizot's Lectures on European Civilization," *London Review*, II (Jan., 1836), 306–36.

REFERRED TO: 94

MILTON, JOHN.   *Artis Logicæ Plenior Institutio, ad Petri Rami Methodum concinnata.* London: Printed by Spencer Hickman, 1672.

REFERRED TO: 4

NOTE: JSM's library, Somerville College, has (minus Vol. II) *The Prose Works of John Milton*, ed. Charles Symmons. 7 vols. (London: Johnson *et al.*, 1806), which includes the *Artis Logicæ* in VI, 195–349.

———— *Paradise Lost*, in *The Poetical Works of Mr. John Milton*. London: Tonson, 1695.

NOTE: the quotation is in a quotation from Taylor.

QUOTED: *629–30*

629.47–630.1 'sagacious of his quarry from afar,'] So scented the grim Feature, and upturn'd/His Nostril wide into the murky Air,/Sagacious of his Quarry from so far. (166; X,279–81)

MOHL.   Referred to: 466n

MOLESWORTH.   Referred to: 352, 566

MOLIÈRE.   Referred to: 82

NOTE: the reference is in a quotation from Tocqueville.

MONROE.   Referred to: 109, 111

NOTE: the reference at 109 is in a quotation from E. Everett.

MONTEAGLE.   See Spring-Rice.

MONTESQUIEU, CHARLES DE SECONDAT, BARON DE.   Referred to: 57

———— *De l'esprit des lois.* 2 vols. Geneva: Barillot, 1748.

NOTE: the quotation is in a quotation from E. Everett.

QUOTED: 110

110.19–23 'the . . . chance.'] [*translated from*:] Le Peuple est admirable pour choisir ceux à qui il doit confier quelque partie de son Autorité. [*remainder of paragraph omitted*] Si l'on pouvait douter de la capacité naturelle qu'a le Peuple pour discerner le mérite, il n'y auroit qu'à jetter les yeux sur cette suite continuelle de choix etonnans que firent les *Athéniens* & les *Romains*; ce qu'on attribuera pas sans doute au hasard. (I,14–15)

MOREAU.   Referred to: 103n

NOTE: the reference is in a quotation from Lieber.

MOSES.   Referred to: 41

NOTE: the reference is to the laws of Moses.

MUELLER, CARL OTFRIED.   *The History and Antiquities of the Doric Race.* Trans. by H. Tufnell and G. C. Lewis. 2 vols. Oxford: Murray, 1830.

REFERRED TO: 3

MULLER.   See Mueller.

NAPIER, WILLIAM FRANCIS PATRICK.   *History of the War in the Peninsula and in the South of France, from the year 1807 to the year 1814.* 6 vols. London: Murray, 1828–40.

REFERRED TO: 123

NAPOLEON I (of France).   Referred to: 42, 123, 196, 601

NAPOLEON III (of France).   Referred to: 228n, 327, 583, 601

NOTE: the reference at 228n is by implication.

NELSON.   Referred to: 209

NEWCASTLE.   See Clinton, Henry Pelham.

NEWTON.   Referred to: 143

NICHOLAS II (of Russia).   Referred to: 307

NICIAS.   Referred to: 460

NIEBUHR.   Referred to: 97

NORTHCOTE, STAFFORD HENRY.   See under Parliamentary Papers, "Report on the Organisation of the Permanent Civil Service" (1854).

ODILON BARROT.   See Barrot.

PAKINGTON, JOHN.   Speech on the Representation of the People Bill

(1860). *Parliamentary Debates*, 3rd ser., Vol. 157, cols. 1034–47 (22 March, 1860).

NOTE: the reference is to col. 1043; Pakington does not mention Disraeli in this passage, but expresses a contrary view to that expressed by Disraeli, *ibid.*, col. 854 (19 March, 1860). The allusion to one of Russell's Reform Bills is to that introduced 16 Feb., 1854.

REFERRED TO: 452n

PALEY. Referred to: 143

PALMERSTON (3rd Viscount). See Temple; and "The Educational Franchise."

PARSONS. Referred to: 164n

PEEL, ROBERT. Referred to: 438, *633*

———— Speech at Glasgow, 12 Jan., 1837, in *The Times*, 16 Jan., 1837, 4. (Quoted in the advertisement pages of Reeve's translation of Tocqueville's *Democracy in America*.)

NOTE: JSM refers, apparently in error, to Peel's "Tamworth Oration." There are substantive variants between the version in *The Times* and that in the advertisement pages of Reeve's translation, but not in the words JSM quotes.

QUOTED: 156
156.15 "earnestly requested the perusal"] Let me earnestly advise your perusal, if you have not yet read the work [*Democracy in America*], of a most able and intelligent native of France, who has made the institutions of the United States the peculiar object of his consideration. (4)

———— "Speech delivered at the Mansion House" (23 Dec., 1834), in *Speeches by the Right Honourable Sir Robert Peel, Bart., during his Administration, 1834–1835*. 2nd ed. London: Roake and Varty, 1835, 9–15.

NOTE: the citation is merely illustrative of the current use of the phrase.

QUOTED: *628*
628.43 "pressure from without:"] We hate the pressure from without—[loud and protracted cheering drowned the conclusion of the sentence.] (11)

———— Speech at Tamworth, 4 Sept., 1835, in *The Times*, 5 Sept., 1835, p.4, cols. 1–3.

REFERRED TO: 105–6

PERICLES. Referred to: 266, 438, 460

PERIER, CASIMIR.   Quoted: 4

NOTE: the quotation has not been located.

PETER I (of Russia).   Referred to: 419

PETER LEOPOLD.   See Leopold II.

PHILLIPS.   Referred to: *642*

PHINN, THOMAS.   Referred to: 496n; see Parliamentary Papers, "Report from the Select Committee on the Corrupt Practices Prevention Act" (1860).

PIGOTT, GILLERY.   Quoted: 497n; see under Parliamentary Papers, "Report from the Select Committee on the Corrupt Practices Prevention Act" (1860).

PITT (the elder).   Referred to: 438

PITTACUS.   Referred to: 403

PLATO.   Referred to: 7, 235, *618*

———— *Dialogues.*   Referred to: 251

NOTE: the reference being general, no edition is cited. *Opera omnia*, ed. Immanuel Bekker, 11 vols. (London: Priestley, 1826) is in JSM's library, Somerville College.

———— *Apology*, in *Euthyphro, Apology, Crito, Phaedo, Phaedrus* (Greek and English). Trans. H. N. Fowler. London: Heinemann; New York: Macmillan, 1914.

NOTE: this edition used for ease of reference. The reference is to 24b–c. *Opera omnia*, ed. Immanuel Bekker, 11 vols. (London: Priestley, 1826) is in JSM's library, Somerville College. JSM translated the *Apology* for the *Monthly Repository*, IX (1835), 112–21, 169–78.
REFERRED TO: 235

———— *Gorgias*, in *Lysis, Symposium, Gorgias* (Greek and English). Trans. W. R. M. Lamb. London: Heinemann; New York: Putnam's Sons, 1925.

NOTE: this edition used for ease of reference. The reference is to 513a–c. *Opera omnia*, ed. Immanuel Bekker, 11 vols. (London: Priestley, 1826) is in JSM's library,

Somerville College. JSM translated the *Gorgias* for the *Monthly Repository*, VIII (1834), 691–710, 802–15, 829–42.

REFERRED TO: 508

——— *Phaedrus.* See Plato, *Theaetetus.*

NOTE: JSM's reference is erroneous.

——— *Republic* (Greek and English). Trans. Paul Shorey. 2 vols. London: Heinemann; New York: Putnam's Sons, 1930, 1935.

NOTE: this edition used for ease of reference. The first quotation is inferentially attributed; Plato (II, 352; ix.2 [576ª]) uses the singular form (τυραννικὴ φύσις The references at 484 and 498, as well as the quotation at *641n*, are to the same matter (also referred to, without mention of Plato, at 400), touched on by Plato at II, 142 (520ᵈ), 144 (521ª), I, 74 (346ª), 80 (347ᶜ⁻ᵈ). *Opera omnia*, ed. Immanuel Bekker, 11 vols. (London: Priestley, 1826) is in JSM's library, Somerville College.

QUOTED: 610, *641n*

REFERRED TO: 484, 498

——— *Theaetetus*, in *Theaetetus and Sophist* (Greek and English). Trans. H. N. Fowler. London: Heinemann; New York: Putnam's Sons, 1921.

NOTE: JSM erroneously attributes the passage to the *Phaedrus*. This edition used for ease of reference. The reference is to 149ª⁻ᵇ (cf. 161ᵉ). *Opera omnia*, ed. Immanuel Bekker, 11 vols. (London: Priestley, 1826) is in JSM's library, Somerville College.

REFERRED TO: 6

POLIGNAC. Referred to: 608

NOTE: the reference is to the Polignac government.

POLYBIUS. Referred to: 353

POMBAL. Referred to: 382

POOLEY. Referred to: 239

POOR LAWS. See under Statutes, 4 & 5 William IV, c. 76.

POPE, ALEXANDER. *An Essay on Man*, in *Works*. New ed. Ed. Joseph Warton, *et al.* 9 vols. and Supplementary Vol. London: Priestley, 1822 (Supp. Vol., London: Hearne, 1825), III, 1–160.

NOTE: in JSM's library, Somerville College. The quotation is in a quotation from Taylor.

QUOTED: *622*

622.12–3   For forms of government let fools contest,/Whiche'er is best administered is best.] For Forms of Government let fools contest;/Whate'er is best administer'd is best:/For Modes of Faith let graceless zealots fight;/His can't be wrong whose life is in the right:/In Faith and Hope the world will disagree,/But all Mankind's concern is Charity:/All must be false that thwart this one great End;/And all of God, that bless Mankind or mend. (III,115–18; Epistle III, ll. 303–10)

POPE, SAMUEL.   Letter to Lord Stanley (26 Sept., 1856), in "Lord Stanley, M.P. and the United Kingdom Alliance," *The Times*, 2 Oct., 1856, 8–9.

NOTE: the full title of the Association, established in 1853, was The United Kingdom Alliance for the Legislative Suppression of the Sale of Intoxicating Liquors.

QUOTED: 288

288.2–5   'deeply . . . persecution,' . . . 'broad . . . barrier'. . . . 'All] In common with your Lordship, I should deeply . . . persecution, and a broad . . . barrier presents itself to my mind as a natural limit. All (9, col.2)

288.16   'I claim,] I do not claim the right to legislate for moral evil; I do claim, (9, col.3)

PRÉVOST-PARADOL, LUCIEN ANATOLE ["Lucien Sorel"].   *Les Anciens Partis*. Paris: Dumineray, 1860.

REFERRED TO: 584–5

Quarterly Review.   Referred to: 112. See also Anon. "Tours in America."

NOTE: the reference is in a quotation from E. Everett.

REFORM ACT (Bill) of 1832.   See under Statutes, 2 & 3 William IV, c. 45.

REFORM BILL OF 1852.   See under Parliamentary Papers, "A Bill to Extend the Right of voting" (1852).

REFORM BILL OF 1854.   See under Parliamentary Papers, "A Bill further to amend the Laws relating to the Representation of the People" (1854).

REFORM BILL OF 1859. See under Parliamentary Papers, "A Bill to Amend the Laws relating to the Representation of the People" (1859).

RÉMUSAT, CHARLES FRANÇOIS MARIE DE.   *Politique libérale, ou Fragments pour servir à la défense de la révolution française*. Paris: Lévy frères, 1860.

NOTE: the passage cited (423–4) does not exactly correspond to JSM's indirect quotation.

QUOTED: 545

Revue des Deux Mondes.   Referred to: 584. See also Lavergne.

Revue Nationale.   Referred to: 584

RICHARD II (of England).   Referred to: 437

RICHELIEU.   See Du Plessis.

ROEBUCK.   Referred to: 563n

ROLAND DE LA PLATIÈRE, MARIE-JEANNE (née Phlipon). "Notices historiques sur la Révolution," in *Mémoires de Madame Roland; avec une notice sur sa vie, des notes et des éclaircissemens historiques.* Ed. St. A. Berville and J. F. Barrière. 2 vols. Paris: Baudoin, 1820.

QUOTED: *644*
644.33   "universal mediocrity of mankind"] [*translated from:*] La chose qui m'ait le plus surprise depuis que l'élévation de mon mari m'eut donné la faculté de connaître beaucoup de personnes, et particulièrement celles employées dans les grandes affaires, c'est l'universelle médiocrité; elle passe tout ce que l'imagination peut se représenter, et cela dans tous les degrés, depuis le commis qui n'a besoin que d'un esprit juste pour bien saisir une question, de méthode pour la traiter, d'un peu de style pour rédiger des lettres, jusqu'au ministre chargé du gouvernement, au militaire qui doit commander les armées, et à l'ambassadeur fait pour négocier. (I,389)

"ROSCOMMON, FRANCIS". *Letters for the Press; on the Feelings, Passions, Manners and Pursuits of Men.* London: Wilson, 1832.

NOTE: the quotation is taken by JSM from Bailey.
QUOTED: 41
41.4   When] Hence, when (82)

ROSSE.   See Parsons.

ROUSSEAU.   Referred to: 7, 10, 155, 253

ROYER-COLLARD, ALBERT PAUL.   Referred to: 582

NOTE: the reference is in an indirect quotation from Odilon Barrot.

————   Speech in the French National Assembly. See Lavergne.

NOTE: JSM quotes Royer-Collard's speech from Lavergne, "Royer-Collard, orateur et politique."
QUOTED: 608

RUSSELL.   Referred to: 316–17, 318, 347, 352, 452

NOTE: the reference at 347 is to "two noblemen advanced in years" (i.e., Russell and Palmerston); that at 452 is to Russell's Reform Bill of 1854, *q.v.* under Parliamentary Papers, "A Bill further to amend the Laws relating to the Representation of the People" (1854).

ST. ETIENNE, RABAUT.   Quoted: 613

NOTE: the quotation is taken from Scott's *Life of Napoleon, q.v.*

ST. PAUL.   Referred to: 236, 255, 381

NOTE: the reference at 381 is to "the Apostle of the Gentiles."

ST. STEPHEN.   Referred to: 381

NOTE: the reference is to "the proto-martyr."

SALVADOR, JOSEPH.   *Histoire des institutions de Moïse et du peuple hébreu.* 3 vols. Paris: Ponthieu, 1828.

REFERRED TO: 397

SAUL.   See St. Paul.

SAVONAROLA.   Referred to: 238

SCOTT, WALTER.   Referred to: 108, 112

NOTE: the reference at 108 is in a quotation from A. H. Everett; that at 112 is in a quotation from de Beaumont.

———   *The Heart of Midlothian,* in *Tales of my Landlord, 2nd series, collected and arranged by Jedediah Cleishbotham, Schoolmaster and Parish-clerk of Gandercleugh.* 4 vols. Edinburgh: Constable, 1818.

QUOTED: 375
375.38   "are aye growing" while men "are sleeping."] Jock, when ye hae naething else to do, ye may be aye sticking in a tree; it will be growing, Jock, when ye're sleeping. (I,194)

———   *The Life of Napoleon Buonaparte, Emperor of the French, with a preliminary view of the French Revolution.* 9 vols. Edinburgh: Cadell; London: Longman, Rees, Orme, Brown, & Green, 1827.

QUOTED: 613
613.8–11   "One God, one France, one King, one Chamber," was . . . commentary, "one mouth, one nose, one ear, and one eye."] "One God," exclaimed Rabaut St. Etienne, "one Nation, one King, and one Chamber." This advocate for unity at once and uniformity, would scarce have been listened to if he had added, "one nose, one tongue, one arm, and one eye"; but his first concatenation of unities

formed a phrase; and an imposing phrase, which sounds well, and can easily be repeated, has immense force in a revolution. (I,178)

SÉVIGNÉ, MARIE DE RABUTIN-CHANTAL, MARQUISE DE. *Lettres.* Ed. Gérard-Gailly. 3 vols. Paris: Gallimard, 1953–57.

NOTE: the reference is to a citation by Tocqueville; this edition used for ease of reference.
REFERRED TO: 181

SHAKESPEARE, WILLIAM.   *Hamlet.*

NOTE: the comparative passage is taken from the Variorum Edition of Horace H. Furness.
QUOTED: 103n
103.n3–4   "germane to the matter"] The phrase would be more germane to the matter if we could carry cannon by our sides; I would it might be hangers till then. (V,ii,152–4)

SHIRREFF, PATRICK. *A Tour through North America, together with a comprehensive view of the Canadas and United States, as adapted for agricultural emigration.* Edinburgh: Oliver and Boyd, 1835.

REFERRED TO: 113n

SMITH.   Referred to: 290

NOTE: the reference is to Mormonism's "prophet and founder."

SOCRATES.   Referred to: 6, 235, 241, 251

SOLON.   Referred to: 42, 403

NOTE: the reference at 42 is to the laws of Solon.

"SOREL, LUCIEN."   See Prévost-Paradol.

SPRING-RICE, THOMAS.   Speech in the House of Lords. *Parliamentary Debates*, 3rd ser., Vol. 131, col. 650 (13 March, 1854).

NOTE: the quotation is indirect.
QUOTED: 208

STANLEY, EDWARD HENRY. Letters to the Secretary of the United Kingdom Alliance, in "Lord Stanley, M.P., and The United Kingdom Alliance," *The Times*, 2 Oct., 1856, 9–10.

NOTE: see also Pope, Samuel.
REFERRED TO: 287

STEPHENSON.   Referred to: 468n

NOTE: the reference is in a quotation from Carey.

STERLING, JOHN.   "Simonides," in *Essays and Tales*. Ed. Julius Charles Hare. 2 vols. London: Parker, 1848, I, 188–251. (First published in *London and Westminster Review*, XXXII [Dec., 1838], 99–136.)

NOTE: in JSM's library, Somerville College, with "Mrs. Taylor" on the flyleaf of Vol. I.
QUOTED: 266
266.1–2 "Pagan self-assertion" . . . "Christian self-denial."] This assertion is only limited, and not overthrown, by the consideration that, when, after many centuries of dark struggle, faith had at last grown into harmony with life,—or, in other words, when, by a process long and painful in proportion to the value of the result. Christian self-denial and Pagan self-assertion had attained an equipoise, strengthening and elevating each other,—then was realized, in being and action, in men and their works, in Raffaelle and Shakspere, in De Sales and Melanchthon, a still higher and sublimer ideal than had been divined by Phidias, Sophocles, and Plato. (I,190)

SULLA.   Referred to: 191

NOTE: the identification is inferential, the reference being to the first Roman military dictator.

SULLY.   Referred to: 438

SWIFT, JONATHAN.   *Gulliver's Travels*, in *Works*, XII. Ed. Walter Scott. Edinburgh: Constable, 1814.

NOTE: this ed. in JSM's library, Somerville College. The quotation, which is indirect, and partly disguised by 473ᵍ⁻ᵍ, is from Voyage IV ("A Voyage to the Country of the Houyhnhnms"), Chap. iii. (As the phrase recurs in Swift, no page reference is given.) In Swift, saying "the thing which was not" is equivalent to lying or expressing falsehood.
QUOTED: 473
473.26 a thing which is not] *the thing which was not* [cf. 473ᵍ⁻ᵍ]

TACITUS.   Referred to: *621, 622*

——— *The Annals*, in *The Histories and The Annals* (Latin and English). Trans. Clifford Moore and John Jackson. 4 vols. London: Heinemann; New York: Putnam's Sons, 1925–37.

NOTE: this edition used for ease of reference. Two editions (Leyden: Elzevir, 1640; and Amsterdam: Elzevir, 1672–73) formerly in JSM's library, Somerville College. The quotation at 12 is in a quotation from Lewis.
QUOTED: 12, 289
12.24 *in corruptissima . . . leges*;] Iamque non modo in commune, sed in singulos homines latæ quæstiones, et corruptissima . . . leges. (II,566; III,xxviii)
289.27 "Deorum injuriæ Diis curæ."] Ius iurandum perinde æstimandum quam si Iovem fefellisset: deorum iniurias diis curæ. (II,368; I,lxxiii)

TAYLOR, HENRY. *Philip van Artevelde; a dramatic romance in two parts.*
London: Moxon, 1834.

REFERRED TO: *617, 647*

———— *The Statesman.* London: Longman, Rees, Orme, Brown, Green,
& Longman, 1836.

NOTE: in JSM's library, Somerville College, inscribed "From the author." Many of the
passages quoted in the review are marked in the Somerville copy by vertical lines
in the margin and/or slash marks in the text; also JSM indicates added italics (see
the collation below).

REVIEWED: *617–47*

QUOTED: *621, 622, 623, 624, 625, 626, 626–7, 627, 627–8, 628, 629, 629–30, 631,
634, 635, 635–6, 636, 637, 637–8, 639, 641, 641–2, 643, 644, 645, 645–6, 646*
621.30 "while] And whilst (vi)
621.31 institutions have been] institutions were thus (vi)
621.33–4 in their speculations."] in the speculations of its professors. (vi)
621.37 "still leave unattempted] But although the works of these three politicians, to
whose names that of Tacitus is, as far as I know, the only one which could be
properly associated, contain numerous civil precepts applicable to the administration as well as to the constitution of governments, they leave still unattempted
(ix–x)
622.31 the government] a government (265)
623.41–2 "the greatest want of the people, though the *least felt*, is . . . instruction."]
Suppose, for example, the case of a people who felt the want of good laws in
general, but whose greatest want, though the least felt, was . . . instruction: and
suppose them living under a form of government so imperfect as not to make it
the interest of their rulers to supply their wants. (265)
626.21 No] In short, no (17)
627.18–27 *By . . . cognizable:*] [*no italics*] [*in the margin of his copy, JSM has
written* all in Italics] (152)
628.38 "upon the face," . . . "of producible documents."] Every step of his procedure,
and every ground upon which he rests every step, should appear upon the face of
producible documents. (51)
629.12 bone on] bone upon [*as in* Source] (157)
629.35 "He] [*follows directly on* 629.33] (158)
629.39–41 *by . . . do;*] [*no italics*] [*in the margin of his copy, JSM has written* Ital] (159)
629.42–4 *how . . . met;*] [*no italics*] [*in the margin of his copy, JSM has written* Ital]
(159)
630.4 mind. This] mind. [*paragraph*] This (160)
630.22 moral] mortal (161)
631.5 Whatever] But to a free and balanced understanding I would freely say, that
whatever (162)
631.5 *they are many*] [*no italics*] (162)
631.5–6 is indispensable that] is in the first place indispensable to a reform of the
executive government of this country, that (162)
631.6 with public] with a particular department of public (162)
631.7–8 these should] these four or six should (162)
634.8 "With] But with (210)
634.9–10 government . . . government] Government . . . Government (210)
634.10-11 *defect of law*] [*no italics*] [*underlined by JSM in his copy*] (210)
634.13 government] Government (210).
634.26 "the . . . servants,"] [*see text above,* 634.9–10]

634.27 "opinion"] [*see text above*, 634.8]
635.21 conscience: for] conscience. For (60)
635.n1 T. Barclaii] J. Barclaii (61) [*treated as typographical error*]
636.1–2 *Conscience . . . others;*] [*no italics*] [*underlined by JSM in his copy*] (63)
636.4 in contrary] in the contrary (63)
636.13–15 *not . . . ears,*] [*no italics*] [*underlined by JSM in his copy*] (64)
636.18–19 *for . . . reaches.*] [*no italics*] [*underlined by JSM in his copy*] (65)
637.26 "have . . . baseness;"] The arts of rising, properly so called, have . . . baseness—
more or less according as the aid from natural endowments is less or more. (92)
637.38 rules. Let] rules. The evil consequences *involved* in a departure from any such
rule in any case, will always overbalance the *ostensible* good consequences; so that
on the whole it is truly an act of evil consequence, or a doing of evil. The maxim
means then, "Do not for the sake of certain good consequences, though they be
perhaps the only ones directly perceivable, an act which, as being a departure
from a general rule of morality, must be evil upon the balance of consequences."
[*paragraph*] Let (111–12)
637.38 principle, and] principle thus understood, and (112)
637.39 life. The] life. [*paragraph*] The (112)
638.4–5 aye . . . no,] "Aye" . . . "No," (112)
638.5 "no"] "No" (112)
639.34 "in] The real difficulty lies (as I conceive) in (116)
641.5 "that where] Where (132)
641.6 ambition, nature has] ambition (which will happen sometimes, though seldom)
nature may be said to have fallen short of her purposes; for she has (132)
641.8 wanting: where] wanting; but where (132)
641.10–11 quickened—such as love, philanthropy, timidity, friendship in particular
cases."] quickened. Love may be a provocative, if advancement in life be a facility
to the courtship. Philanthropy leads to it; for who can do good to mankind
without power? Timidity is driven to it; for, as Mucianus said, "Confugiendum est
ad imperium."* [*footnote:* *Tacitus, Hist., ii.76.] Friendship suggests it; for a man
gratifies his friends when he advances himself. (132–3)
641.31 "The] And the (36)
641.32 is unfavourable] is also unfavourable (36)
643.14 thought he] thought that he (54)
644.17 "If] But if (30)
644.19 implicitly; for] implicitly. For (30)
644.29 nature] Nature (31)
645.37 pusillanimity."] pusillanimity."*[*footnote:* *Leviathan, part i. chap.ii] (145)

TEMPLE. Referred to: 326n, 347

NOTE: the reference at 347 is to "two noblemen advanced in years" (i.e., Palmerston
and Russell).

TERTULLIAN. *Apology* (Latin and English), in *Apology and De Spectaculis* (trans. T. R. Glover) and *Minucius Felix* (trans. G. H. Rendall).
London: Heinemann; New York: Putnam's Sons, 1931.

NOTE: this edition cited for ease of reference.
QUOTED: 249
249.21–2 "See how these Christians love one another"] "Look," they say, "how they
love one another" (for themselves hate one another); "and how they are ready
to die for each other" (for themselves will be readier to kill each other). (177;
xxxix.7)

THEMISTOCLES. Referred to: 419, 438, 458

THERAMENES. Referred to: 460

THIERS. Referred to: 584

NOTE: the reference is to "writers of M. Thiers' school."

THIRLWALL, CONNOP. *A Letter to the Rev. Thomas Turton, D.D., Regius Professor of Divinity in the University of Cambridge, and Dean of Peterborough, on the Admission of Dissenters to Academical Degrees.* Cambridge: Deighton; London: Rivington, 1834.

REFERRED TO: 142

Thoughts on the Ladies of the Aristocracy. See "Tomkins, Lydia."

TIBERIUS. See Caesar, Tiberius.

TOCQUEVILLE, ALEXIS CLÉREL DE. *L'Ancien régime et la révolution.* Paris: Lévy, 1856.

NOTE: autograph copy in JSM's library, Somerville College. The quotation is indirect.
QUOTED: 274

——— *De la Démocratie en Amérique.* 2 vols. 2nd ed. Paris: Gosselin, 1835. Seconde Partie. 2 vols. Paris: Gosselin, 1840.

——— *Democracy in America.* Trans. Henry Reeve. Vols. I and II. London: Saunders and Otley, 1835. Vols. III and IV. London: Saunders and Otley, 1840.

NOTE: autograph copies of the French edition in JSM's library, Somerville College. In the references, the two volumes of the Seconde Partie are given as III and IV to avoid confusion and to correspond to the Reeve edition. Where JSM used Reeve (see 49n and 162*q* above), his version as well as the original has been collated (evidently only the first volume of the Reeve translation was available to JSM when he wrote his first review).

REVIEWED: 49–90 (the first two volumes, and Reeve's translation of Vol. I), 153–204 (all four volumes, with Reeve's translation of them)

QUOTED: 49, 51–2, 52–3, 54, 58–60, 60–1, 61–3, 64–5, 67, 67–8, 68–70, 74, 74–5, 76, 77, 81–2, 82–3, 84, 87–8, 88–9, 89–90, 111, 126, 156, 159–62, 170–1, 172–3, 175, 179, 180, 181, 183–4, 185, 186–7, 187–8, 189–90, 193, 200, 219

REFERRED TO: 18n, 94, 96, 97, 102, 106, 108, 109, 112, 113, 468, 557, 582–3, *618*
49.6   it gives] by giving (I,xiii)
49.6   character] tenour (I,xiii)
49.7   it imparts] by imparting (I,xiii)
49.8   governed. I] governed. [*paragraph*] I (I,xiii)

49.10   private] civil (I,xiii)
49.10   government] Government (I,xiii)
49.14   conditions was] conditions is (I,xiv)
49.16   and imagined] where I imagined (I,xiv)
49.17   discerned there also] discerned (I,xiv)
49.18–20   conditions, though . . . them; and] conditions, is daily progressing towards those extreme limits which it seems to have reached in the United States; and (I,xiv)
49.21   From that moment I conceived] [*paragraph*] I hence conceived (I,xiv)
49.3–22   Amongst . . . reader.] [*translated from:*] Parmi les objets nouveaux qui, pendant mon séjour aux États-Unis, ont attiré mon attention, aucun n'a plus vivement frappé mes regards que l'égalité des conditions. Je découvris, sans peine, l'influence prodigieuse qu'exerce ce premier fait sur la marche de la société; il donne à l'esprit public une certaine direction, un certain tour aux lois; aux gouvernans des maximes nouvelles, et des habitudes particulières aux gouvernés. [*paragraph*] Bientôt je reconnus que ce même fait étend son influence fort au-delà des mœurs politiques et des lois, et qu'il n'obtient pas moins d'empire sur la société civile que sur le gouvernement : il crée des opinions, fait naître des sentimens, suggère des usages, et modifie tout ce qu'il ne produit pas. [*paragraph*] Ainsi donc, à mesure que j'étudiais la société américaine, je voyais de plus en plus, dans l'égalité des conditions, le fait générateur dont chaque fait particulier semblait descendre, et je le retrouvais sans cesse devant moi comme un point central où toutes mes observations venaient aboutir. [*paragraph*] Alors je reportais ma pensée vers notre hémisphère, et il me sembla que j'y distinguais quelque chose d'analogue au spectacle que m'offrait le Nouveau-Monde. Je vis l'égalité des conditions qui, sans y avoir atteint comme aux États-Unis ses limites extrêmes, s'en rapprochait chaque jour davantage, et cette même démocratie, qui régnait sur les sociétés américaines, me parut en Europe s'avancer rapidement vers le pouvoir. [*paragraph*] De ce moment j'ai conçu l'idée du livre qu'on va lire. (I,3–4)
51.26   fearful] most alarming (I, xxii)
51.27   forward] along (I,xxii)
51.31   reanimate] warm (I,xxii)
51.32   regulate] direct (I,xxii)
51.32–3   for its inexperience a knowledge of business] a knowledge of business for its inexperience (I,xxii)
51.33   and for its blind instincts an . . . interests;] and an . . . interests for its blind propensities; (I,xxii)
51.35   with circumstances and characters.] with the occurrences and the actors of the age. (I,xxii)
51.39–40   us toward an unseen abyss.] us backwards toward the gulf. (I,xxii)
51.43–4   thought of making any preparation for it,] had any forethought for its exigencies, (I,xxiii)
51.44   in spite of their resistance,] without their consent (I,xxiii)
52.2   Democracy] The people (I,xxiii)
52.2–3   untutored instincts] wild propensities (I,xxiii)
52.4–5   aught of society but its vices and its miseries] aught but the vices and wretchedness of society (I,xxiii)
52.6–7   then servilely] was then (I,xxiii)
52.7   smallest wish] caprices (I,xxiii)
52.9   annihilating it] annihilating its power (I,xxiii)
52.9–10   bad tendencies. No] vices; no (I,xxiii)
52.10   the sole thought was of excluding] but all were bent on excluding (I,xxiii)
52.11   government] Government (I,xxiii)
52.13   *material*] [*no italics*] (I,xxiii)
52.14   habits] customs (I, xxiii)
52.15   severed from whatever would lessen] but without the conditions which lessen (I,xxiv)

52.17   are yet] are (I,xxiv)
52.17   might] may (I,xxiv)
51.26–52.18   The . . . confer.] [*translated from:*] Les peuples chrétiens me paraissent
   offrir de nos jours un effrayant spectacle; le mouvement qui les emporte est déjà
   assez fort, pour qu'on ne puisse le suspendre, et il n'est pas encore assez rapide
   pour qu'on désespère de le diriger : leur sort est entre leurs mains; mais bientôt il
   leur échappe. [*paragraph*] Instruire la démocratie, ranimer, s'il se peut, ses
   croyances, purifier ses mœurs, régler ses mouvemens; substituer peu à peu la
   science des affaires à son inexpérience, la connaissance de ses vrais intérêts à ses
   aveugles instincts; adapter son gouvernement aux temps et aux lieux, le modifier
   suivant les circonstances et les hommes : tel est le premier des devoirs imposés
   de nos jours à ceux qui dirigent la société. [*paragraph*] Il faut une science politique
   nouvelle à un monde tout nouveau. [*paragraph*] Mais c'est à quoi nous ne
   songeons guère : placés au milieu d'un fleuve rapide, nous fixons obstinément les
   yeux vers quelques débris qu'on aperçoit encore sur le rivage, tandis que le
   courant nous entraîne et nous pousse à reculons vers des abîmes. [*paragraph*] Il
   n'y a pas de peuples de l'Europe chez lesquels la grande révolution sociale que je
   viens de décrire ait fait de plus rapides progrès que parmi nous; mais elle y a
   toujours marché au hasard. [*paragraph*] Jamais les chefs de l'État n'ont pensé à
   rien préparer d'avance pour elle; elle s'est faite malgré eux ou à leur insu. Les
   classes les plus puissantes, les plus intelligentes et les plus morales de la nation
   n'ont point cherché à s'emparer d'elle, afin de la diriger. La démocratie a donc
   été abandonnée à ses instincts sauvages; elle a grandi comme ces enfans privés
   des soins paternels, qui s'élèvent d'eux-mêmes dans les rues de nos villes et qui ne
   connaissent de la société que ses vices et ses misères. On semblait encore ignorer
   son existence, quand elle s'est emparée à l'improviste du pouvoir. Chacun alors
   s'est soumis avec servilité à ses moindres désirs; on l'a adorée comme l'image de
   la force; quand ensuite elle se fut affaiblie par ses propres excès, les législateurs
   conçurent le projet imprudent de la détruire au lieu de chercher à l'instruire et à
   la corriger, et, sans vouloir lui apprendre à gouverner, ils ne songèrent qu'à la
   repousser du gouvernement. [*paragraph*] Il en est résulté que la révolution
   démocratique s'est opérée dans le matériel de la société, sans qu'il se fît dans les
   lois, les idées, les habitudes et les mœurs, le changement qui eût été nécessaire
   pour rendre cette révolution utile. Ainsi nous avons la démocratie, moins ce qui
   doit atténuer ses vices et faire ressortir ses avantages naturels; et voyant déjà
   les maux qu'elle entraîne, nous ignorons encores les biens qu'elle peut donner.
   (I,10–12)
52.26   several] several different (I,xxiv)
52.26–7   which cannot easily be appreciated or conceived in our times.] which can
   now scarcely be appreciated or conceived. (I,xxiv)
52.28   set insurmountable barriers] was an insurmountable barrier (I,xxiv)
52.30–1   from . . . inspired, a . . . power.] a . . . power from . . . inspired. (I,xxiv)
52.32   Although lifted so high] High as they were placed (I, xxiv)
52.32   nevertheless, took] could not but take (I,xxiv)
52.33   kindly] benevolent (I,xxiv)
52.34   poor man . . . equal] poor . . . equals (I,xxiv)
52.34–5   over his destiny as a trust which Providence had confided to their care.]
   over the destiny of those whose welfare Providence had entrusted to their care.
   (I,xxiv)
52.36   state of society] social condition (I,xxiv)
52.37   their own] its own (I,xxiv)
52.37–8   ever becoming the rivals of their chiefs] ever ranking with its chiefs (I,xxv)
52.38   accepted their benefits] received benefits from them (I,xxv)
52.38   They felt] It grew (I,xxv)
52.39   and submitted] and it submitted (I,xxv)
52.40   oppressions,] exactions (I,xxv)

52.40   as to] as to the (I,xxv)

52.40–1   Usages and manners had] Custom, and the manners of the time, had (I,xxv)

52.43   him of] him of the (I,xxv)

52.46   a sort of mutual good-will might arise between] a mutual exchange of good-will took place between (I,xxv)

52.47   favoured] gifted (I,xxv)

52.49–53.1   It is not by . . . power or by . . . obedience that men are debased; it is] Men are not corrupted by . . . power or debased by . . . obedience; but (I,xxv)

53.1   illegitimate] illegal (I,xxv)

53.2   unjust] oppressive (I,xxv)

53.3   were] was **(I,xxv)**

53.4   elegances] elegance (I,xxvi)

53.4   intellect] wit (I,xxvi)

53.4   culture] religion (I,xxvi)

53.5   were] was (I,xxvi)

53.5   rudeness, and ignorance] and a rude ignorance (I,xxvi)

53.7   wild] independent (I,xxvi)

53.7   Society] The body of a State (I,xxvi)

53.8   possess stability, power, and, above all, glory] boast of its stability, its power, and, above all, of its glory (I,xxvi)

53.9   barriers] divisions (I,xxvi)

53.10   properties are broken down] property is divided (I,xxvi)

53.11   subdivided] held in common (I,xxvi)

53.12   more equally] equally (I,xxvi)

53.12   state of society] State (I,xxvi)

53.13–14   institutions and manners] the institutions and the manners of the nation (I,xxvi)

53.15   can now] can (I,xxvi)

53.15–16   all, regarding the law as emanating from themselves, would give it their attachment and their ready submission;] all men would profess an equal attachment and respect for the laws of which they are the common authors; (I,xxvi)

53.20   and feeling secure of retaining them,] which he is sure to retain, (I,xxvi)

53.22   their] its (I,xxvii)

53.23–4   to its burthens.] to satisfy its demands. (I,xxvii)

53.25   supply the place of] supply (I,xxvii)

53.27   state] State (I,xxvii)

53.28   be duly] be (I,xxvii)

53.29   towards improvement. If] forwards; if (I,xxvii)

53.30–1   enjoyments may be less intense, but comfort] the pleasures of enjoyment may be less excessive, but those of comfort (I,xxvii)

53.31   highly] perfectly (I,xxvii)

53.36   experience. Each] experience: each (I,xxviii)

53.36–7   individual, being equally weak, will feel an equal] individual will feel the same (I,xxviii)

53.37   fellow-citizens;] fellow-citizens to protect his own weakness; (I,xxviii)

53.37–8   that he can obtain their good offices only by giving his,] that if they are to assist, he must cooperate, (I,xxviii)

53.42   powerful] strong (I,xxviii)

53.43–4   they despair of being better,] it despairs of amelioration, (I,xxviii)

53.44   because they know that they are well.] because it is conscious of the advantages of its condition. (I,xxviii)

53.46   such of them as were so;] such as were useful and good; (I,xxviii)

52.24–53.48   While . . . afford.] [*translated from*:] Quand le pouvoir royal, appuyé sur l'aristocratie, gouvernait paisiblement les peuples de l'Europe, la société, au milieu de ses misères, jouissait de plusieurs genres de bonheur qu'on peut difficilement concevoir et apprécier de nos jours. [*paragraph*] La puissance de quelques sujets élevait des barrières insurmontables à la tyrannie du prince; et les rois se sentant d'ailleurs revêtus aux yeux de la foule d'un caractère presque divin, puisaient, dans le respect même qu'ils faisaient naître, la volonté de ne point abuser de leur pouvoir. [*paragraph*] Je conçois alors une société où tous, regardant la loi comme leur ouvrage, l'aimeraient et s'y soumettraient sans peine; où l'autorité du gouvernement étant respectée comme nécessaire et non comme divine, l'amour qu'on porterait au chef de l'État ne serait point une passion, mais un sentiment raisonné et tranquille. Chacun ayant des droits et étant assuré de conserver ces droits, il s'établirait entre toutes les classes une mâle confiance et une sorte de condescendance réciproque aussi éloignée de l'orgueil que de la bassesse. [*paragraph*] Instruit de ses vrais intérêts, le peuple comprendrait que, pour profiter des biens de la société, il faut se soumettre à ses charges. L'association libre des citoyens pourrait remplacer alors la puissance individuelle des nobles, et l'État serait à l'abri de la tyrannie et de la licence. [*paragraph*] Je comprends que, dans un État démocratique constitué de cette manière, la société ne sera point immobile; mais les mouvemens du corps social pourront y être réglés et progressifs. Si l'on y rencontre moins d'éclat qu'au sein d'une aristocratie, on y trouvera moins de misères; les jouissances y seront moins extrêmes et le bien-être plus général; les sciences moins grandes et l'ignorance plus rare; les sentimens moins énergiques et les habitudes plus douces; on y remarquera plus de vices et moins de crimes. [*paragraph*] A défaut de l'enthousiasme et de l'ardeur des croyances, les lumières et l'expérience obtiendront quelquefois des citoyens de grands sacrifices; chaque homme étant également faible sentira un égal besoin de ses semblables; et connaissant qu'il ne peut obtenir leur appui qu'à la condition de leur prêter son concours, il découvrira sans peine que pour lui l'intérêt particulier se confond avec l'intérêt général. [*paragraph*] La nation prise en corps sera moins brillante, moins glorieuse, moins forte peut-être; mais la majorité des citoyens y jouira d'un sort plus prospère, et le peuple s'y montrera paisible, non qu'il désespère d'être mieux, mais parce qu'il sait être bien. [*paragraph*] Si tout n'était pas bon et utile dans un semblable ordre de choses, la société du moins se serait approprié tout ce qu'il peut présenter d'utile et de bon, et les hommes, en abandonnant pour toujours les avantages sociaux que peut fournir l'aristocratie, auraient pris à la démocratie tous les biens que celle-ci peut leur offrir. (I,12–15)

54.6   But we—what have we] But here it may be asked what we have (I,xxviii)
54.7   abandoned? The] abandoned. [*paragraph*] The (I,xxviii)
54.9   have] has (I,xxix)
54.11   existences] beings (I,xxix)
54.12   the government has alone] it is the Government that has (I,xxix)
54.14–15   to the strength, sometimes oppressive, but often conservative, of a few, has succeeded the weakness of all.] the weakness of the whole community has therefore succeeded that influence of a small body of citizens, which, if it was sometimes oppressive, was often conservative. (I,xxix)
54.17   but the] but it would seem that the (I,xxix)
54.17   seems] is (I,xxix)
54.19   right] Right (I,xxix)
54.19   a stranger] insensible (I,xxix)
54.20   force is, in the eyes of both] Force affords to both (I,xxix)
54.21   resource] guarantee (I,xxix)
54.24–5   without having acquired the knowledge which enlightens it] without understanding the science which controls it (I,xxix)
54.25   selfishness] egotism (I,xxx)
54.26   is conscious of] relies upon (I,xxx)
54.27   and of its] and its (I,xxx)
54.27–8   but, on the contrary, because it believes itself weak and infirm, and fears that a] but because it knows its weakness and its infirmities; a (I,xxx)
54.28   life. Everybody] life; everybody (I,xxx)

54.29   regrets] regret (I,xxx)
54.30   no visible or permanent fruits.] nothing that is visible or permanent, like the passions of old men which terminate in impotence. (I,xxx)
54.32   the compensations naturally belonging to] any compensation from (I,xxx)
54.33   an aristocratic society,] an aristocracy, (I,xxx)
54.6–35   But we . . . them.] [*translated from*:] Mais nous, en quittant l'état social de nos aïeux, en jetant pêle-mêle derrière nous leurs institutions, leurs idées et leurs mœurs, qu'avons-nous pris à la place? [*paragraph*] Le prestige du pouvoir royal s'est évanoui, sans être remplacé par la majesté des lois; de nos jours, le peuple méprise l'autorité, mais il la craint, et la peur arrache de lui plus que ne donnaient jadis le respect et l'amour. [*paragraph*] J'aperçois que nous avons détruit les existences individuelles qui pouvaient lutter séparément contre la tyrannie; mais je vois le gouvernement qui hérite seul de toutes les prérogatives arrachées à des familles, à des corporations ou à des hommes; à la force quelquefois oppressive, mais souvent conservatrice, d'un petit nombre de citoyens, a donc succédé la faiblesse de tous. [*paragraph*] La division des fortunes a diminué la distance qui séparait le pauvre et le riche; mais en se rapprochant, ils semblent avoir trouvé des raisons nouvelles de se haïr, et jetant l'un sur l'autre des regards pleins de terreur et d'envie, ils se repoussent mutuellement du pouvoir; pour l'un comme pour l'autre, l'idée des droits n'existe point, et la force leur apparaît, à tous les deux, comme la seule raison du présent et l'unique garantie de l'avenir. [*paragraph*] Le pauvre a gardé la plupart des préjugés de ses pères, sans leurs croyances; leur ignorance, sans leurs vertus; il a admis, pour règle de ses actions, la doctrine de l'intérêt, sans en connaître la science, et son égoïsme est aussi dépourvu de lumières que l'était jadis son dévouement. [*paragraph*] La société est tranquille, non point parce qu'elle a la conscience de sa force et de son bien-être, mais au contraire parce qu'elle se croit faible et infirme; elle craint de mourir en faisant un effort; chacun sent le mal, mais nul n'a le courage et l'énergie nécessaire pour chercher le mieux; on a des désirs, des regrets, des chagrins et des joies qui ne produisent rien de visible ni de durable, semblables à des passions de vieillards qui n'aboutissent qu'à l'impuissance. [*paragraph*] Ainsi nous avons abandonné ce que l'état ancien pouvait présenter de bon, sans acquérir ce que l'état actuel pourrait offrir d'utile; nous avons détruit une société aristocratique, et, nous arrêtant complaisamment au milieu des débris de l'ancien édifice, nous semblons vouloir nous y fixer pour toujours. (I,15–17)
58.38   state] State (I,75)
59.1   governed] subject (I,75)
59.2   town-council;] corporation; but (I,75)
59.3   appointed] designated (I,75)
59.4   the mere execution of the laws.] the simple and ordinary executive business of the State. [*footnote omitted*] (I,75)
59.5   opposed to our habits,] different from our customs, (I,76)
59.7   functions] duties (I,76)
59.8–9   portion of the business of administration] proportion of administrative power (I,76)
59.10   the selectmen.] "the Selectmen." [*footnote omitted*] (I,76)
59.11   state] State (I,76)
59.13   and which if they neglect they are personally responsible.] but which they can only neglect on their own responsibility. (I,76)
59.14   state] State (I,76)
59.16–17   left to be determined by the local authorities,] determined by the town-meeting, (I,76)
59.24   they state the exigency] they explain the urgency (I,77)
59.27   determines] marks out (I,77)
59.27   leaves] confides (I,77)
59.29   summoning] calling (I,77)

59.30   called upon] requested (I,77)
59.30   landed proprietors] citizens (I,77)
59.32   and retain] but they have (I,77)
59.33   meeting.] meeting. [*footnote omitted*] (I,77)
59.35   officers] magistrates (I,77)
59.38   to lend his personal aid to] to forward (I,78)
59.40–1   records the proceedings of the town-meetings, and keeps the register of births]
          records all the town votes, orders, grants, births (I,78)
59.42   administration] action (I,78)
59.43–4   for the superintendence of the schools and public] to attend to the schools
          and to public (I,78)
59.43   inspectors of roads,] road surveyors, (I,78)
59.45   There . . . subdivisions:] They . . . subdivided; and (I,78)
59.48   direct the efforts of the citizens] direct the citizens (I,78)
59.50   inspectors] sealers (I,78)
59.50   measures.] measures. [*footnote omitted*] (I,78)
60.2   under a pecuniary penalty,] on pain of being fined, (I,78)
60.5   public] its (I,78)
58.37–60.7   In . . . done.] [*translated from*:] Dans la Nouvelle-Angleterre, la majorité
agit par représentant lorsqu'il faut traiter les affaires générales de l'État. Il était
nécessaire qu'il en fût ainsi; mais dans la commune où l'action législative et gou-
vernementale est plus rapprochée des gouvernés, la loi de la représentation n'est
point admise. Il n'y a point de conseil municipal; le corps des électeurs, après avoir
nommé ses magistrats, les dirige lui-même dans tout ce qui n'est pas l'exécution
pure et simple des lois de l'État. [*footnote omitted*] [*paragraph*] Cet ordre de
choses est si contraire à nos idées, et tellement opposé à nos habitudes, qu'il est
nécessaire de fournir ici quelques exemples pour qu'il soit possible de le bien
comprendre. [*paragraph*] Les fonctions publiques sont extrêmement nombreuses
et fort divisées dans la commune, comme nous le verrons plus bas; cependant la
plus grande partie des pouvoirs administratifs est concentrée dans les mains d'un
petit nombre d'individus élus chaque année et qu'on nomme les select-men [*footnote omitted*] [*paragraph*] Les lois générales de l'État ont imposé aux select-men
un certain nombre d'obligations. Ils n'ont pas besoin de l'autorisation de leurs
administrés pour les remplir, et ils ne peuvent s'y soustraire sans engager leur
responsabilité personnelle. La loi de l'État les charge, par exemple, de former,
dans leur commune, les listes électorales; s'ils omettent de le faire, ils se rendent
coupables d'un délit. Mais, dans toutes les choses qui sont abandonnées à la
direction du pouvoir communal, les select-men sont les exécuteurs des volontés
populaires, comme parmi nous le maire est l'exécuteur des délibérations du conseil
municipal. Le plus souvent ils agissent sous leur responsabilité privée, et ne font
que suivre, dans la pratique, la conséquence des principes que la majorité a pré-
cédemment posés. Mais veulent-ils introduire un changement quelconque dans
l'ordre établi; désirent-ils se livrer à une entreprise nouvelle, il leur faut remonter
à la source de leur pouvoir. Je suppose qu'il s'agisse d'établir une école: les select-
men convoquent à certain jour, dans un lieu indiqué d'avance, la totalité des électeurs; là, ils exposent le besoin qui se fait sentir; ils font connaître les moyens d'y
satisfaire, l'argent qu'il faut dépenser, le lieu qu'il convient de choisir. L'assemblée, consultée sur tous ces points, adopte le principe, fixe le lieu, vote l'impôt,
et remet l'exécution de ses volontés dans les mains des select-men. [*paragraph*] Les
select-men ont seuls le droit de convoquer la réunion communale (town-meeting),
mais on peut les provoquer à le faire. Si dix propriétaires conçoivent un projet
nouveau et veulent le soumettre à l'assentiment de la commune, ils réclament une
convocation générale des habitans; les select-men sont obligés d'y souscrire, et ne
conservent que le droit de présider l'assemblée [*footnote omitted*] [*paragraph*]
Ces mœurs politiques, ces usages sociaux sont sans doute bien loin de nous. Je n'ai
pas en ce moment la volonté de les juger ni de faire connaître les causes cachées qui

les produisent et les vivifient; je me borne à les exposer. [*paragraph*] Les select-men sont élus tous les ans au mois d'avril ou de mai. L'assemblée communale choisit en même temps une foule d'autres magistrats municipaux [*footnote omitted*], préposés à certains détails administratifs importans. Les uns, sous le nom d'assesseurs, doivent établir l'impôt; les autres, sous celui de collecteurs, doivent le lever. Un officier, appelé constable, est chargé de faire la police, de veiller sur les lieux publics, et de tenir la main à l'exécution matérielle des lois. Un autre nommé le greffier de la commune, enregistre toutes les délibérations; il tient note des actes de l'état civil. Un caissier garde les fonds communaux. Ajoutez à ces fonctionnaires un surveillant des pauvres dont le devoir, fort difficile à remplir, est de faire exécuter la législation relative aux indigens; des commissaires des écoles, qui dirigent l'instruction publique; des inspecteurs des routes, qui se chargent de tous les détails de la grande et petite voirie, et vous aurez la liste des principaux agens de l'administration communale; mais la division des fonctions ne s'arrête point là: on trouve encore, parmi les officiers municipaux [*footnote omitted*], des commissaires de paroisses qui doivent régler les dépenses du culte; des inspecteurs de plusieurs genres, chargés, les uns, de diriger les efforts des citoyens en cas d'incendie; les autres, de veiller aux récoltes; ceux-ci, de lever provisoirement les difficultés qui peuvent naître relativement aux clôtures; ceux-là, de surveiller le mesurage du bois, ou d'inspecter les poids et mesures. [*paragraph*] On compte en tout dix-neuf fonctions principales dans la commune. Chaque habitant est contraint, sous peine d'amende, d'accepter ces différentes fonctions; mais aussi la plupart d'entre elles sont rétribuées, afin que les citoyens pauvres puissent y consacrer leur temps sans en souffrir de préjudice. Du reste, le système américain n'est point de donner un traitement fixe aux fonctionnaires. En général, chaque acte de leur ministère a un prix, et ils ne sont rémunérés qu'en proportion de ce qu'ils ont fait. (I,99–103)

60.24–61.19   The . . . surface.] [*translated from:*] La commune est la seule association qui soit si bien dans la nature, que partout où il y a des hommes réunis il se forme de soi-même une commune. [*paragraph*] La société communale existe donc chez tous les peuples, quels que soient leurs usages et leurs lois; c'est l'homme qui fait les royaumes et crée les républiques; la commune paraît sortir directement des mains de Dieu. Mais si la commune existe depuis qu'il y a des hommes, la liberté communale est chose rare et fragile. Un peuple peut toujours établir de grandes assemblées politiques, parce qu'il se trouve habituellement dans son sein un certain nombre d'hommes chez lesquels les lumières remplacent, jusqu'à un certain point, l'usage des affaires. La commune est composée d'élémens grossiers qui se refusent souvent à l'action du législateur. La difficulté de fonder l'indépendance des communes, au lieu de diminuer à mesure que les nations s'éclairent, augmente avec leur lumière. Une société très civilisée ne tolère qu'avec peine les essais de la liberté communale; elle se révolte à la vue de ses nombreux écarts, et désespère du succès avant d'avoir atteint le résultat final de l'expérience. [*paragraph*] Parmi toutes les libertés, celles des communes, qui s'établit si difficilement, est aussi la plus exposée aux invasions du pouvoir. Livrées à elle-mêmes, les institutions communales ne sauraient guère lutter contre un gouvernement entreprenant et fort; pour se défendre avec succès, il faut qu'elles aient pris tous leurs développemens et qu'elles se soient mêlées aux idées et aux habitudes nationales. Ainsi tant que la liberté communale n'est pas entrée dans les mœurs, il est facile de la détruire et elle ne peut entrer dans les mœurs qu'après avoir long-temps subsisté dans les lois. [*paragraph*] La liberté communale échappe donc, pour ainsi dire, à l'effort de l'homme. Aussi arrive-t-il rarement qu'elle soit créée; elle naît en quelque sorte d'elle-même. Elle se développe presque en secret au sein d'une société demi-barbre [*sic*]. C'est l'action continue des lois et des mœurs, les circonstances et surtout le temps qui parviennent à la consolider. De toutes les nations du continent de l'Europe, on peut dire qu'il n'y en a pas une seule qui la connaisse. [*paragraph*] C'est pourtant dans la commune que réside la force des peuples libres. Les institutions communales sont à la liberté ce que les écoles primaires sont à la science; elles la mettent à la portée du peuple; elles lui en font goûter l'usage paisible et l'habituent à s'en servir. Sans institutions communales une nation peut se donner un gouvernement libre, mais elle n'a pas l'esprit de la liberté. Des passions passagères, des intérêts d'un moment, le hasard des circonstances, peuvent lui donner les formes extérieures de l'indépendance; mais le despotisme refoulé dans l'intérieur du corps social reparaît tôt ou tard à la surface. (I,95–7; cf. Reeve, I,71–3.)

61.26   power.] authority. (I,82)

61.29   would not] may not (I,82)

61.30–1   seldom attach themselves but where there is power.] generally lie on the side of authority. (I,82)

61.32   so much] only (I,82)

61.33   a free and powerful corporation] a social body (I,83)

61.34–6   and of which to influence the government is an object worth exerting himself for. [paragraph] In] and whose government claims and deserves the exercise of his sagacity. In (I,83)

61.36–7   regret even to governments themselves; for every] regret to those who are in power; every (I,83)

61.38   but nobody knows how to create it.] and yet nothing is more difficult to create. (I,83)

61.38–9   They fear that if the localities] If the municipal bodies (I,83)

61.40   and the state exposed to anarchy.] and the peace of the country endangered. (I,83)

61.40–1   deprive the locality of] without (I,83)

61.41–3   it may contain subjects, but it will have no citizens. [paragraph] Another] a town may contain good subjects, but it can have no active citizens. Another (I,83)

61.44   arousing strongly] arousing (I,83)

61.45   elective] elected (I,83)

62.1   state] State (I,83)

62.2–3   inducement to most men, sufficient to draw them away] inducement sufficient to draw men away (I,83)

62.3   centre of their private interests] circle of their interests (I,83)

62.5   these] these individuals (I,83)

62.7–8   federal offices of a high order are generally attained, as it were accidentally, by persons who have already distinguished themselves in] federal functionaries are generally men who have been favoured by fortune, or distinguished in (I,83)

62.9   Their attainment] Such (I,83)

62.9   of an ambitious life.] of the ambitious. (I,84)

62.9–12   In the township, therefore, in the centre of the ordinary relations of life, become concentrated the desire of public esteem, the thirst for the exercise of influence, and the taste . . . popularity;] But the township serves as a centre for the desire of public esteem, the want of exciting interests, and the taste . . . popularity, in the midst of the ordinary relations of life; (I,84)

62.17–18   to take a direct share in the government, there are innumerable functionaries] into action, the body politic is divided into innumerable functionaries and officers, (I,84)

62.22   while it] which (I,84)

62.23–4   obligations imposed by the township upon its members.] functions of the town officers. (I,84)

62.25–6   observance. [paragraph] In] observance. In (I,84)

62.26–7   every person is continually reminded that he belongs to the community; his connexion with it] the activity of the township is continually perceptible; it (I,84)

62.30–1   the state for the same reason which makes the mountaineer cling] his home, as the mountaineer clings (I,85)

62.31–3   because he finds in his country more marked features, a more decided physiognomy than elsewhere. [*paragraph*] The] because the characteristic features of his country are there more distinctly marked than elsewhere. The (I,85)

62.37   Besides, the] The (I,85)

62.39   the distinction of ranks does not exist even in memory;] no tradition exists of a distinction of ranks; (I,85)

62.40   community, therefore, is] community is (I,85)

62.40–1   and acts of injustice which injure] and the abuses which may injure (I,85)

62.43   yet so long as it contrives to go on, the fact] the fact (I,85)

62.44   governs, casts] governs, and that it acts, either ill or well, casts (I,85)

62.45–8   Besides, they have nothing to compare it with. England formerly ruled over the aggregation of . . . people always managed their own local affairs. The sovereignty of the people is, in the commune, not] No term of comparison disturbs the satisfaction of the citizen: England formerly governed the mass of . . . people was always sovereign in the township, where its rule is not (I,85)

62.50–63.2   powerful: he feels interested in it, because he takes part in its management: the prosperity he enjoys in it makes it an object of his attention: he centres in it his ambition and his hopes. He] free: his cooperation in its affairs ensures his attachment to its interest; the well-being it affords him secures his affection; and its welfare is the aim of his ambition and of his future exertions: he (I,85–6)

63.4–5   without which liberty can only take the shape of revolution;] which can alone ensure the steady progress of liberty; (I,86)

63.6   mutual play of concurrent authorities,] union or the balance of powers, (I,86)

61.25–63.8   The . . . rights.] [*translated from*:] En Amérique, non seulement il existe des institutions communales, mais encore un esprit communal qui les soutient et qui les vivifie. [*paragraph*] La commune de la Nouvelle-Angleterre réunit deux avantages qui, partout où ils se trouvent, excitent vivement l'intérêt des hommes, savoir: l'indépendance et la puissance. Elle agit, il est vrai, dans un cercle dont elle ne peut sortir; mais ses mouvemens y sont libres. Cette indépendance seule lui donnerait déjà une importance réelle, quand sa population et son étendue ne la lui assureraient pas. [*paragraph*] Il faut bien se persuader que les affections des hommes ne se portent en général que là ou il y a de la force. On ne voit pas l'amour de la patrie régner long-temps dans un pays conquis. L'habitant de la Nouvelle-Angleterre s'attache à sa commune, non pas tant parce qu'il y est né, que parce qu'il y voit dans cette commune une corporation libre et forte dont il fait partie et qui mérite la peine qu'on cherche à la diriger. [*paragraph*] Il arrive souvent, en Europe, que les gouvernans eux-mêmes regrettent l'absence de l'esprit communal; car tout le monde convient que l'esprit communal est un grand élément d'ordre et de tranquillité publique; mais ils ne savent comment le produire. En rendant la commune forte et indépendante, ils craignent de partager la puissance sociale et d'exposer l'État à l'anarchie. Or, ôtez la force et l'indépendance de la commune, vous n'y trouverez jamais que des administrés et point de citoyens. [*paragraph*] Remarquez d'ailleurs un fait important: la commune de la Nouvelle-Angleterre est ainsi constituée qu'elle put servir de foyer à de vives affections, et en même temps il ne se trouve rien à côté d'elle qui attire fortement les passions ambitieuses du cœur humain. [*paragraph*] Les fonctionnaires du comté ne sont point élus et leur autorité est restreinte. L'État lui-même n'a qu'une importance secondaire, son existence est obscure et tranquille. Il y a peu d'hommes qui, pour obtenir le droit de l'administrer, consentent à s'éloigner du centre de leurs intérêts et à troubler leur existence. [*paragraph*] Le gouvernement fédéral confère de la puissance et de la gloire à ceux qui le dirigent; mais les hommes auxquels il est donné d'influer sur ses destinées sont en très petit nombre. La présidence est une haute magistrature à laquelle on ne parvient guère que dans un âge avancé; et quand on arrive aux autres fonctions fédérales d'un ordre élevé, c'est en quelque sorte par hasard et après qu'on s'est déjà rendu célèbre en suivant une autre carrière. L'ambition ne peut pas les prendre pour le but permanent de ses efforts. C'est dans la commune, au centre des relations ordi-

naires de la vie, que viennent se concentrer le désir de l'estime, le besoin d'intérêts réels, le goût du pouvoir et du bruit; ces passions qui troublent si souvent la
société, changent de caractère lorsqu'elles peuvent s'exercer ainsi près du foyer
domestique et en quelque sorte au sein de la famille. [*paragraph*] Voyez avec quel
art, dans la commune américaine, on a eu soin, si je puis m'exprimer ainsi, d'*épar-
piller* la puissance, afin d'intéresser plus de monde à la chose publique. Indépendam-
ment des électeurs appelés de temps en temps à faire des actes de gouvernement,
que de fonctions diverses, que de magistrats différens, qui tous, dans le cercle de
leurs attributions, représentent la corporation puissante au nom de laquelle ils
agissent! Combien d'hommes exploitent ainsi à leur profit la puissance communale et s'y intéressent pour eux-mêmes! [*paragraph*] Le système américain, en
même temps qu'il partage le pouvoir municipal entre un grand nombre de citoyens, ne craint pas non plus de multiplier les devoirs communaux. Aux États-
Unis on pense avec raison que l'amour de la patrie est une espèce de culte auquel
les hommes s'attachent par les pratiques. [*paragraph*] De cette manière, la vie
communale se fait en quelque sorte sentir à chaque instant; elle se manifeste
chaque jour par l'accomplissement d'un devoir ou par l'exercice d'un droit. Cette
existence politique imprime à la société un mouvement continuel, mais en même
temps paisible, qui l'agite sans la troubler. [*paragraph*] Les Américains s'attachent à la cité par une raison analogue à celle qui fait aimer leur pays aux habitans des montagnes. Chez eux la patrie a des traits marqués et caractéristiques;
elle a plus de physionomie qu'ailleurs. [*paragraph*] Les communes de la Nouvelle-
Angleterre ont en général une existence heureuse. Leur gouvernement est de leur
goût aussi bien que de leur choix. Au sein de la paix profonde et de la prospérité
matérielle qui règnent en Amérique, les orages de la vie municipale sont peu
nombreux. La direction des intérêts communaux est aisée. De plus, il y a long-
temps que l'éducation politique du peuple est faite; ou plutôt il est arrivé tout
instruit sur le sol qu'il occupe. Dans la Nouvelle-Angleterre, la division des rangs
n'existe pas même en souvenir; il n'y a donc point de portion de la commune qui
soit tentée d'opprimer l'autre, et les injustices, qui ne frappent que des individus
isolés, se perdent dans le contentement général. Le gouvernement présentât-il
des défauts, et certes il est facile d'en signaler, ils ne frappent point les regards,
parce que le gouvernement émane réellement des gouvernés, et qu'il lui suffit de
marcher, tant bien que mal, pour qu'une sorte d'orgueil paternel le protège. Ils
n'ont rien d'ailleurs à quoi le comparer. L'Angleterre a jadis regné sur l'ensemble
des colonies, mais le peuple a toujours dirigé les affaires communales. La souveraineté du peuple dans la commune est donc non seulement un état ancien, mais
un état primitif. [*paragraph*]. L'habitant de la Nouvelle-Angleterre s'attache à sa
commune, parce qu'elle est forte et indépendante; il s'y intéresse, parce qu'il con-
court à la diriger; il l'aime, parce qu'il n'a pas à s'y plaindre de son sort: il place
en elle son ambition et son avenir; il se mêle à chacun des incidens de la vie communale: dans cette sphère restreinte qui est à sa portée, il s'essaie à gouverner la
société; il s'habitue aux formes sans lesquelles la liberté ne procède que par révolution, se pénètre de leur esprit, prend goût à l'ordre, comprend l'harmonie des
pouvoirs, et rassemble enfin des idées claires et pratiques sur la nature de ses devoirs ainsi que sur l'étendue de ses droits. (I,107–11)

64.23–4   of the government in any country:] of authority in a nation: (I,89)
64.28   to establish political freedom] to lay the foundations of freedom (I,89)
64.29   the government] authority (I,89)
64.31   among] in (I,89)
64.32–3   all the power is intrusted which is necessary for the performance of the
task specially imposed upon him.] the degree of power necessary for him to perform his duty is entrusted. (I,89)
64.35–6   power of government, thus divided, is indeed rendered] action of authority is
indeed thus rendered (I,89)
64.36   destroyed.] totally suppressed. (I,89)

64.37–8   calm and considerate love] mature and dignified taste for (I,89)
64.38   and indefinite] or ill-defined (I,89)
64.39   its] but its (I,89)
64.40   to order and legality.] to whatever was lawful and orderly. (I,89)
64.43   else. No idea was] else; no idea was (I,90)
64.44   calling in question or limiting the rights or powers of society] attacking the principles, or of contesting the rights of society (I,90)
65.1   of those powers was divided among many hands,] of its authority was divided, (I,90)
64.23–65.4   There . . . free.] [*translated from*:] Il y a deux moyens de diminuer la force de l'autorité chez une nation: [*paragraph*] Le premier est d'affaiblir le pouvoir dans son principe même, en ôtant à la société le droit ou la faculté de se défendre en certains cas: affaiblir l'autorité de cette manière, c'est en général ce qu'on appelle en Europe fonder la liberté. [*paragraph*] Il est un second moyen de diminuer l'action de l'autorité: celui-ci ne consiste pas à dépouiller la société de quelques-uns de ses droits, ou à paralyser ses efforts, mais à diviser l'usage de ses forces entre plusieurs mains; à multiplier les fonctionnaires en attribuant à chacun d'eux tout le pouvoir dont il a besoin pour faire ce qu'on le destine à éxécuter. Il se rencontre des peuples que cette division des pouvoirs sociaux peut encore mener à l'anarchie; par elle-même, cependant, elle n'est point anarchique. En partageant ainsi l'autorité, on rend, il est vrai, son action moins irrésistible et moins dangereuse; mais on ne la détruit point. [*paragraph*] La révolution, aux États-Unis, a été produite par un goût mûr et réfléchi pour la liberté, et non par un instinct vague et indéfini d'indépendance. Elle ne s'est point appuyée sur des passions de désordre; mais, au contraire, elle a marché avec l'amour de l'ordre et de la légalité. [*paragraph*] Aux États-Unis donc on n'a point prétendu que l'homme dans un pays libre eût le droit de tout faire; on lui a au contraire imposé des obligations sociales plus variées qu'ailleurs; on n'a point en l'idée d'attaquer le pouvoir de la société dans son principe, et de lui contester ses droits; on s'est borné à le diviser dans son exercice. On a voulu arriver de cette manière à ce que l'autorité fût grande et le fonctionnaire petit, afin que la société continuât à être bien réglée et restât libre. (I,115–16)
67.6–7   is, that its function is that of an arbitrator.] is the duty of arbitration. (I,136)
67.7–8   To warrant the interference of a tribunal, there must be a dispute: before there can be a judgment, somebody must bring an action.] But rights must be contested in order to warrant the interference of a tribunal; and an action must be brought to obtain the decision of a judge. (I,136)
67.9   an enactment gives rise to no lawsuit,] a law is uncontested, (I,136)
67.17   case] point (I,137)
67.18–19   by showing that every other consequence of the principle will be annulled in a similar manner,] by passing a judgment which tends to reject all the inferences from that principle, and consequently to annul it, (I,137)
67.20–1   principle, and sets it aside, without] principle without (I,137)
67.21   quits] leaves (I,137)
67.23   part] influence (I,137)
67.25–6   until it is appealed to—until . . . it.] unless it is appealed to or until it has taken cognizance of an affair. (I,137)
67.26   universal] general (I,137)
67.28   is in its own] is by its (I,137)
67.28–9   it cannot act without an impulse from without.] it must be put in motion in order to produce a result. (I,137)
67.29–30   When a criminal is brought before it to be tried, it will convict and punish him; when called upon to redress a wrong,] When it is called upon to repress a crime, it punishes the criminal; when a wrong is to be redressed, (I,137)
67.32   inquire into facts,] examine its evidence (I,138)

67.33–4   take the initiative, and erect himself into a censor of] open proceedings, and usurp the censureship of (I,138)

67.34   to this] to the (I,138)

67.37   power. An] power; an (I,138)

67.38   he can only pronounce upon an individual case,] he is only conversant with special cases, (I,138)

67.3–40   The . . . court.] [*translated from:*] Les Américains ont conservé au pouvoir judiciaire tous les caractères auxquels on a coutume de le reconnaître. Ils l'ont exactement renfermé dans le cercle où il a l'habitude de se mouvoir. [*paragraph*] Le premier caractère de la puissance judiciaire, chez tous les peuples, est de servir d'arbitre. Pour qu'il y ait lieu à action, de la part des tribunaux, il faut qu'il y ait contestation. Pour qu'il y ait juge, il faut qu'il y ait procès. Tant qu'une loi ne donne pas lieu a une contestation, le pouvoir judiciaire n'a donc point occasion de s'en occuper. Elle existe, mais il ne la voit pas. Lorsqu'un juge, à propos d'un procès, attaque une loi relative à ce procès, il étend le cercle de ses attributions, mais il n'en sort pas, puisqu'il lui a fallu, en quelque sorte, juger la loi pour arriver à juger le procès. Lorsqu'il prononce sur une loi, sans partir d'un procès, il sort complètement de sa sphère et il pénètre dans celles du pouvoir législatif. [*paragraph*] Le second caractère de la puissance judiciaire est de prononcer sur des cas particuliers et non sur des principes généraux. Qu'un juge, en tranchant une question particulière, détruise un principe général, par la certitude où l'on est que, chacune des conséquences de ce même principe étant frappée de la même manière, le principe devient stérile, il reste dans le cercle naturel de son action. Mais que le juge attaque directement le principe général, et le détruise sans avoir en vue un cas particulier, il sort, du cercle où tous les peuples se sont accordés à l'enfermer. Il devient quelque chose de plus important, de plus utile peut-être qu'un magistrat; mais il cesse de représenter le pouvoir judiciaire. [*paragraph*] Le troisième caractère de la puissance judiciaire est de ne pouvoir agir que quand on l'appelle, ou, suivant l'expression légale, quand elle est saisie. Ce caractère ne se rencontre point aussi généralement que les deux autres. Je crois cependant que, malgré les exceptions, on peut le considérer comme essentiel. De sa nature, le pouvoir judiciaire est sans action; il faut le mettre en mouvement pour qu'il se remue. On lui dénonce un crime, et il punit le coupable; on l'appelle à redresser une injustice, et il la redresse; on lui soumet un acte, et il l'interprète; mais il ne va pas de lui-même poursuivre les criminels, rechercher l'injustice et examiner les faits. Le pouvoir judiciaire ferait en quelque sorte violence à cette nature passive, s'il prenait de lui-même l'initiative et s'établissait en censeur des lois. [*paragraph*] Les Américains ont conservé au pouvoir judiciaire ces trois caractères distinctifs. Le juge américain ne peut prononcer que lorsqu'il y a litige. Il ne s'occupe jamais que d'un cas particulier; et, pour agir, il doit toujours attendre qu'on l'ait saisi. (I,164–6)

67.42   dangers] evils (I, 142)

67.43   by debarring them from the use of any except strictly judicial means.] by the obligation which has been imposed of attacking the laws through the courts of justice alone. (I,142)

67.44–5   in a sweeping and general way;] on the ground of theoretical generalities; (I,142)

67.45   to take the initiative, and to] to open an attack or to (I,142)

67.48–68.1   law, in an obscure proceeding, and in some particular application,] law, applied to some particular case in (I,142)

68.2   is partly] is (I,142)

68.2–3   is aimed directly only at] bears upon (I,142)

68.3–4   wounded, it is only as it were by accident.] slighted, it is only collaterally. (I,142)

68.6   the tribunals.] judicial functionaries. (I,142)

68.7–9   moreover, be readily understood that by leaving it to private interests to call the *veto* of the tribunals into action, and by closely uniting the attack upon the law with a suit against an individual, the laws are] readily be understood that by connecting the censureship of the laws with the private interests of members of the community, and by intimately uniting the prosecution of the law with the prosecution of an individual, the legislation is (I,142–3)

68.11 only in obedience to an exigency which is actually felt; it] whenever their evil consequences are most felt; and it (I,143)

68.13 be the] be at once the (I,143)

68.14–15 order. [*paragraph*] If] order. If (I,143)

68.25 being guilty of a denial of justice.] abdicating the duties of his post. (I,143)

68.27 censorship] censureship (I,144)

68.28 acts of the legislature] legislation (I,144)

68.29 indefinitely] indistinctly (I,144)

68.30 formal] exact (I,144)

68.31 is inclined to carry it into] cares to bring it before (I,144)

68.32–3 justice. [*paragraph*] The] justice. The (I,144)

68.35–6 dangerous. [*paragraph*] Even within] dangerous. Within (I,144)

67.41–68.39 The political . . . assemblies.] [*translated from:*] Les Américains ont donc confié à leurs tribunaux un immense pouvoir politique. Mais en les obligeant à n'attaquer les lois que par des moyens judiciaires, ils ont beaucoup diminué les dangers de ce pouvoir. [*paragraph*] Si le juge avait pu attaquer les lois d'une façon théorique et générale; s'il avait pu prendre l'initiative et censurer le législateur, il fût entré avec éclat sur la scène politique; devenu le champion ou l'adversaire d'un parti, il eût appelé toutes les passions qui divisent le pays à prendre part à la lutte. Mais quand le juge attaque une loi dans un débat obscur et sur une application particulière, il dérobe en partie l'importance de l'attaque aux regards du public. Son arrêt n'a pour but que de frapper un intérêt individuel; la loi ne se trouve blessée que par hasard. [*paragraph*] D'ailleurs, la loi ainsi censurée n'est pas détruite: sa force morale est diminuée, mais son effet matériel n'est point suspendu. Ce n'est que peu à peu, et sous les coups répétés de la jurisprudence, qu'enfin elle succombe. [*paragraph*] De plus on comprend sans peine qu'en chargeant l'intérêt particulier de provoquer la censure des lois, en liant intimement le procès fait à la loi au procès fait à un homme, on s'assure que la législation ne sera pas légèrement attaquée. Dans ce système, elle n'est plus exposée aux agressions journalières des partis. En signalant les fautes du législateur, on obéit à un besoin réel: on part d'un fait positif et appréciable, puisqu'il doit servir de base à un procès. [*paragraph*] Je ne sais si cette manière d'agir des tribunaux américains, en même temps qu'elle est la plus favorable à l'ordre public, n'est pas aussi la plus favorable à la liberté. [*paragraph*] Si le juge ne pouvait attaquer les législateurs que de front, il y a des temps où il craindrait de le faire; il en est d'autres où l'esprit de parti le pousserait chaque jour à l'oser. Ainsi il arriverait que les lois seraient attaquées quand le pouvoir dont elles émanent serait faible, et qu'on s'y soumettrait sans murmurer quand il serait fort. C'est-à-dire que souvent on attaquerait les lois lorsqu'il serait le plus utile de les respecter, et qu'on les respecterait quand il deviendrait facile d'opprimer en leur nom. [*paragraph*] Mais le juge américain est amené malgré lui sur le terrain de la politique. Il ne juge la loi que parce qu'il a à juger un procès, et il ne peut s'empêcher de juger le procès. La question politique qu'il doit résoudre se rattache à l'intérêt des plaideurs, et il ne saurait refuser de la trancher sans faire un déni de justice. C'est en remplissant les devoirs étroits imposés à la profession du magistrat, qu'il fait l'acte du citoyen. Il est vrai que, de cette manière, la censure judiciaire, exercée par les tribunaux sur la législation, ne peut s'étendre sans distinction à toutes les lois, car il en est qui ne peuvent jamais donner lieu à cette sorte de contestation nettement formulée qu'on nomme un procès. Et lorsqu'une pareille contestation est possible, on peut encore concevoir qu'il ne se rencontre personne qui veuille en saisir les tribunaux.

[*paragraph*] Les Américains ont souvent senti cet inconvénient, mais ils ont laissé le remède incomplet, de peur de lui donner, dans tous les cas, une efficacité dangereuse. [*paragraph*] Resserré dans ces limites, le pouvoir accordé aux tribunaux américains, de prononcer sur l'inconstitutionnalité des lois, forme encore une des plus puissantes barrières qu'on ait jamais élevées contre la tyrannie des assemblées polititiques. (I,170–2)

68.46–70.43 We . . . it.] [*translated from*:] On doit distinguer soigneusement, dans les lois, le but qu'elles poursuivent, de la manière dont elles marchent vers ce but; leur bonté absolue, de celle qui n'est que relative. [*paragraph*] Je suppose que l'objet du législateur soit de favoriser les intérêts du petit nombre aux dépens de ceux du grand; ses dispositions sont combinées de façon à obtenir le résultat qu'il se propose dans le moins de temps et avec le moins d'efforts possibles. La loi sera bien faite, et son but mauvais; elle sera dangereuse en proportion de son efficacité même. [*paragraph*] Les lois de la démocratie tendent en général au bien du plus grand nombre; car elles émanent de la majorité de tous les citoyens, laquelle peut se tromper, mais ne saurait avoir un intérêt contraire à elle-même. [*paragraph*] Celles de l'aristocratie tendent, au contraire, à monopoliser, dans les mains du petit nombre, la richesse et le pouvoir; parce que l'aristocratie forme toujours de sa nature une minorité. [*paragraph*] On peut donc dire, d'une manière générale, que l'objet de la démocratie, dans sa législation, est plus utile à l'humanité que l'objet de l'aristocratie dans la sienne. [*paragraph*] Mais là finissent ses avantages. [*paragraph*] L'aristocratie est infiniment plus habile dans la science du législateur, que ne saurait l'être la démocratie. Maîtresse d'elle-même, elle n'est point sujette à des entraînemens passagers; elle a de longs desseins qu'elle sait mûrir jusqu'à ce que l'occasion favorable se présente. L'aristocratie procède savamment; elle connaît l'art de faire converger en même temps, vers un même point, la force collective de toutes ses lois. [*paragraph*] Il n'en est pas ainsi de la démocratie: ses lois sont presque toujours défectueuses ou intempestives. [*paragraph*] Les moyens de la démocratie sont donc plus imparfaits que ceux de l'aristocratie: souvent elle travaille, sans le vouloir, contre elle-même; mais son but est plus utile. [*paragraph*] Imaginez une société que la nature, ou sa constitution, ait organisée de manière à supporter l'action passagère de mauvaises lois, et qui puisse attendre, sans périr, le résultat de la *tendance générale* des lois, et vous concevrez que le gouvernement de la démocratie, malgré ses défauts, soit encore de tous le plus propre à faire prospérer cette société. [*paragraph*] C'est précisément là ce qui arrive aux États-Unis; je répète ici ce que j'ai déjà exprimé ailleurs: le grand privilège des Américains est de pouvoir faire des fautes réparables. [*paragraph*] Je dirai quelque chose d'analogue sur les fonctionnaires publics. [*paragraph*] Il est facile de voir que la démocratie américaine se trompe souvent dans le choix des hommes auxquels elle confie le pouvoir; mais il n'est pas aussi aisé de dire pourquoi l'État prospère en leurs mains. [*paragraph*] Remarquez d'abord que, si dans un État démocratique, les gouvernans sont moins honnêtes ou moins capables, les gouvernés sont plus éclairés et plus attentifs. [*paragraph*] Le peuple, dans les démocraties, occupé comme il l'est sans cesse de ses affaires, et jaloux de ses droits, empêche ses représentans de s'écarter d'une certaine ligne générale que son intérêt lui trace. [*paragraph*] Remarquez encore que, si le magistrat démocratique use plus mal qu'un autre du pouvoir, il le possède en général moins long-temps. [*paragraph*] Mais il y a une raison plus générale que celle-là, et plus satisfaisante. [*paragraph*] Il importe sans doute au bien des nations que les gouvernans aient des vertus ou des talens; mais ce qui, peut-être, leur importe encore davantage, c'est que les gouvernans n'aient pas d'intérêts contraires à la masse des gouvernés. Car, dans ces cas, les vertus pourraient devenir presques inutiles, et les talens funestes. [*ellipsis indicates 2-paragraph omission*] Ceux qu'on charge, aux États-Unis, de diriger les affaires du public, sont souvent inférieurs en capacité et en moralité aux hommes que l'aristocratie porterait au pouvoir. Mais leur intérêt se confond et s'identifie avec celui de la majorité de leurs concitoyens. Ils peuvent donc commettre de fréquentes infidélités et de graves erreurs; mais ils ne suivront jamais systématiquement une tendance hostile à cette majorité; et il ne saurait leur arriver d'imprimer au gouvernement une allure exclusive et dangereuse. [*paragraph*] La mauvaise administration d'un magistrat, sous la démocratie, est d'ailleurs un fait isolé qui n'a d'influence que pendant la courte durée de cette administration. La corruption et l'incapacité ne sont pas des intérêts communs, qui puissent lier entre eux les hommes d'une manière permanente. [*paragraph*] Un magistrat corrompu, ou incapable, ne combinera pas ses efforts avec un autre magistrat, par la seule raison que ce dernier est incapable et corrompu comme lui, et ces deux hommes ne travailleront jamais de concert à faire fleurir la corruption et l'incapacité chez leurs arrière-neveux. L'ambition et les manœuvres de l'un serviront, au contraire, a démasquer l'autre. Les vices du magistrat, dans les démocraties, lui sont en général tout personnels. [*paragraph*] Mais les hommes publics, sous le gouvernement de l'aristocratie, ont un intérêt de classe qui, s'il se confond quelquefois avec celui de la majorité, en reste souvent distinct. Cet intérêt forme entre eux un lien commun et durable; il les invite à unir et à combiner leurs efforts vers un but qui n'est pas toujours le bonheur du plus grand nombre: il ne lie pas seulement les gouvernans les uns aux autres, il les unit encore à une portion considérable de gouvernés; car beaucoup de citoyens, sans être revêtus d'aucun emploi, font partie de l'aristocratie. [*paragraph*] Le magistrat aristocratique rencontre donc un appui constant dans la société, en même temps qu'il en trouve un dans le gouvernement. [*paragraph*] Cet objet commun, qui dans les aristocraties unit les magistrats à l'intérêt d'une partie de leurs contemporains, les identifie encore et les soumet pour ainsi dire à celui des races futures. Ils travaillent pour l'avenir aussi bien que pour le présent. Le magistrat aristocratique est donc poussé tout à la fois vers un même point, par les passions des gouvernés, par les siennes propres, et je pourrais presque dire par les passions de sa postérité. [*paragraph*] Comment s'étonner, s'il ne résiste point? Aussi voit-on souvent, dans les aristocraties, l'esprit de classe entraîner ceux même qu'il ne corrompt pas, et faire qu'à leur insu ils accommodent peu à peu la société à leur usage, et la préparent pour leurs descendans. [*ellipsis indicates 2-paragraph omission*] Aux États-Unis, où les fonctionnaires publics n'ont point d'intérêts de classe à faire prévaloir, la marche générale et continue du gouvernement est bienfaisante, quoique les gouvernans soient souvent inhabiles, et quelquefois méprisables. [*paragraph*] Il y a donc, au fond des institutions démocratiques, une tendance cachée qui fait souvent concourir les hommes à la prospérité générale, malgré leurs vices ou leurs erreurs; tandis que dans les institutions aristocratiques, il se découvre quelquefois une pente secrète qui, en dépit des talens et des vertus, les entraîne à contribuer aux misères de leurs semblables. C'est ainsi qu'il peut arriver que, dans les gouvernemens aristocratiques, les hommes publics fassent le mal sans le vouloir, et que dans les démocraties ils produisent le bien sans en avoir la pensée. (II,108–14; cf. Reeve, II,114–20.)

74.4–10 A custom . . . meeting.] [*translated from:*] Il se répand de plus en plus, aux États-Unis, une coutume qui finira par rendre vaines les garanties du gouvernement représentatif: il arrive très fréquemment que les électeurs, en nommant un député, lui tracent un plan de conduite et lui imposent un certain nombre d'obligations positives dont il ne saurait nullement s'écarter. Au tumulte près, c'est comme si la majorité elle-même délibérait sur la place publique. (II,135–6; cf. Reeve, II,144–5).

74.14–75.42 Many . . . that.] [*translated from:*] Bien des gens, en Europe, croient sans le dire, ou disent sans le croire, qu'un des grands avantages du vote universel est d'appeler à la direction des affaires des hommes dignes de la confiance publique. Le peuple ne saurait gouverner lui-même, dit-on, mais il veut toujours sincèrement le bien de l'État, et son instinct ne manque guère de lui désigner ceux qu'un même désir anime et qui sont les plus capables de tenir en main le pouvoir. [*paragraph*] Pour moi, je dois le dire, ce que j'ai vu en Amérique ne m'autorise point à penser qu'il en soit ainsi. A mon arrivée aux États-Unis, je fus frappé de surprise en découvrant à quel point le mérite était commun parmi les gouvernés et combien il l'était peu chez les gouvernans. C'est un fait constant que, de nos jours, aux États-Unis, les hommes les plus remarquables sont rarement appelés aux fonctions publiques, et l'on est obligé de reconnaître qu'il en a été ainsi à mesure que la démocratie a dépassé toutes ses anciennes limites. Il est évident que la race des hommes d'État américains s'est singulièrement rapetissée depuis un demi-siècle. [*paragraph*] On peut indiquer plusieurs causes de ce phénomène. [*paragraph*] Il est impossible, quoi qu'on fasse, d'élever les lumières du peuple au dessus d'un certain niveau. On aura beau faciliter les abords des connaissances humaines, améliorer les méthodes d'enseignement et mettre la science à bon marché, on ne fera jamais que les hommes s'instruisent et développent leur intelligence sans y consacrer du temps. [*paragraph*] Le plus ou moins de facilité que rencontre le peuple à vivre sans travailler, forme donc la limite nécessaire de ses progrès intellectuels. Cette limite est placée plus loin dans certains pays, moins loin dans certains autres; mais pour qu'elle n'existât point, il faudrait que le peuple n'eût plus à s'occuper des soins matériels de la vie; c'est-à-dire qu'il ne fût plus le peuple. Il est donc aussi difficile de concevoir une société où tous les hommes soient très éclairés, qu'un État où tous les citoyens soient riches; ce sont là deux difficultés corrélatives. J'admettrai sans peine que la masse des citoyens veut très sincèrement le bien du pays; je vais même plus loin, et je dis que les classes inférieures de la société me semblent mêler, en général, à ce désir moins de combinaisons d'intérêt personnel que les classes élevées; mais ce qui leur manque toujours, plus ou moins, c'est l'art de juger des moyens tout en voulant sincèrement la fin. Quelle longue étude, que de notions diverses sont nécessaires pour se faire une idée exacte du caractère d'un seul homme! Les plus grands génies s'y égarent et la multitude y réussirait! Le peuple ne trouve jamais le temps et les moyens de se livrer à ce travail. Il lui faut toujours juger à la hâte et s'attacher au plus saillant des objets. De là vient que les charlatans de tout genre savent si bien le secret de lui plaire; tandis que, le plus souvent, ses véritables amis y échouent. [*paragraph*] Du reste, ce n'est pas toujours la capacité qui manque à la démocratie pour choisir les hommes de mérite, mais le désir et le goût. [*paragraph*] Il ne ne faut pas se dissimuler que les institutions démocratiques développent à un très haut degré le sentiment de l'envie dans le cœur humain. Ce n'est point tant parce qu'elles offrent à chacun des moyens de s'égaler aux autres, mais parce que ces moyens défaillent sans cesse à ceux qui les emploient. Les institutions démocratiques réveillent et flattent la passion de l'égalité sans pouvoir jamais la satisfaire entièrement. [*3-sentence omission*] Beaucoup de gens s'imaginent que cet instinct secret, qui porte chez nous les classes inférieures à écarter autant qu'elles le peuvent les supérieures de la direction des affaires, ne se découvre qu'en France. C'est une erreur. L'instinct dont je parle n'est point français, il est démocratique; les circonstances politiques ont pu lui donner un caractère particulier d'amertume, mais elles ne l'ont pas fait naître. [*paragraph*] Aux États-Unis, le peuple n'a point de haine pour les classes élevées de la société; mais il se sent peu de bienveillance pour elles, et les tient avec soin en dehors du pouvoir; il ne craint pas les grands talens, mais il les goûte peu. En général, on remarque que tout ce qui s'élève sans son appui obtient difficilement sa faveur. [*ellipsis indicates 1-paragraph omission*] Il m'est démontré que ceux qui regardent le vote universel comme une garantie de la bonté des choix se font une illusion complète. Le vote universel a d'autres avantages, mais non celui-là. (II,43–47; cf. Reeve, II,47–51)

76.3–13   Hence . . . it.] [*translated from:*] Il en résulte que, dans les temps de calme, les fonctions publiques offrent peu d'appât à l'ambition. Aux États-Unis, ce sont les gens modérés dans leurs désirs, qui s'engagent au milieu des détours de la politique. Les grands talens et les grandes passions s'écartent en général du pouvoir, afin de poursuivre la richesse; et il arrive souvent qu'on ne se charge de diriger la fortune de l'État que quand on se sent peu capable de conduire ses propres affaires. [*paragraph*] C'est à ces causes, autant qu'aux mauvais choix de la démocratie, qu'il faut attribuer le grand nombre d'hommes vulgaires qui occupent les fonctions publiques. Aux États-Unis, je ne sais si le peuple choisirait les hommes supérieurs qui brigueraient ses suffrages; mais il est certain que ceux-ci ne les briguent pas. (II,58–9; cf. Reeve, II,62–3)

77.10–27   In . . . prosper.] [*translated from:*] Dans la Nouvelle-Angleterre, où l'éducation et la liberté sont filles de la morale et de la religion; où la société, déjà ancienne et depuis long-temps assise, a pu se former des maximes et des habitudes, le peuple, en même temps qu'il échappe à toutes les supériorités que la richesse et la naissance ont jamais créées parmi les hommes, s'est habitué à respecter les supériorités intellectuelles et morales, et à s'y soumettre sans déplaisir. Aussi voit-on que la démocratie dans la Nouvelle-Angleterre fait de meilleurs choix que partout ailleurs. [*paragraph*] A mesure au contraire qu'on descend vers le midi, dans les États où le lien social est moins ancien et moins fort, où l'instruction s'est moins répandue et où les principes de la morale, de la religion et de la liberté se sont combinés d'une manière moins heureuse, on aperçoit que les talens et les vertus deviennent de plus en plus rares parmi les gouvernans. [*paragraph*] Lorsqu'on pénètre enfin dans les nouveaux États du sud-ouest, où le corps social, formé d'hier, ne présente encore qu'une agglomération d'aventuriers ou de spéculateurs, on est confondu de voir en quelles mains la puissance publique est remise, et l'on se demande par quelle force indépendante de la législation et des hommes l'État peut y croître et la société y prospérer. (II,49–50; cf. Reeve, II,53–4)

81.7–82.12   When . . . America.] [*translated from:*] Lorsqu'on vient à examiner quel est aux États-Unis l'exercice de la pensée, c'est alors qu'on aperçoit bien clairement à quel point la puissance de la majorité surpasse toutes les puissances que nous connaissons en Europe. [*paragraph*] La pensée est un pouvoir invisible et presque insaisissable, qui se joue de toutes les tyrannies. De nos jours, les souverains les plus absolus de l'Europe ne sauraient empêcher certaines pensées hostiles à leur autorité, de circuler sourdement dans leurs États et jusqu'au sein de leurs cours. Il n'en est pas de même en Amérique: tant que la majorité est douteuse, on parle; mais dès quelle s'est irrévocablement prononcée, chacun se tait; et amis comme ennemis semblent alors s'attacher de concert à son char. La raison en est simple; il n'y a pas de monarque si absolu qui puisse réunir dans sa main toutes les forces de la société, et vaincre les résistances comme peut le faire une majorité revêtue du droit de faire les lois et de les exécuter. [*paragraph*] Un roi d'ailleurs n'a qu'une puissance matérielle qui agit sur les actions et ne saurait atteindre les volontés; mais la majorité est revêtue d'une force tout à la fois matérielle et morale, qui agit sur la volonté autant que sur les actions, et qui empêche en même temps le fait et le désir de faire. [*paragraph*] Je ne connais pas de pays où il règne en général moins d'indépendance d'esprit et de véritable liberté de discussion qu'en Amérique. [*paragraph*] Il n'y a pas de théorie religieuse ou politique qu'on ne puisse prêcher librement dans les États constitutionnels de l'Europe, et qui ne pénètre dans les autres; car il n'est pas de pays en Europe tellement soumis à un seul pouvoir, que celui qui veut y dire la vérité n'y trouve un appui capable de le rassurer contre les résultats de son indépendance. S'il a le malheur de vivre sous un gouvernement absolu, il a souvent pour lui le peuple; s'il habite un pays libre; il peut au besoin s'abriter derrière l'autorité royale. La fraction aristocratique de la société le soutient dans les contrées démocratiques, et la démocratie dans les autres. Mais au sein d'une démocratie, organisée ainsi que celle des États-Unis, on ne rencontre qu'un seul pouvoir, un seul élément de force et de succès, et rien en dehors de lui. [*paragraph*] En Amérique, la majorité trace un cercle formidable autour de la pensée. Au dedans de ces limites, l'écrivain est libre, mais malheur à lui s'il ose en sortir. Ce n'est pas qu'il ait à craindre un auto-da-fé; mais il est en butte à des dégoûts de tous genres et à des persécu-tions de tous les jours. La carrière politique lui est fermée; il a offensé la seule puis-sance qui ait la faculté de l'ouvrir. On lui refuse tout, jusqu'à la gloire. Avant de publier ses opinions il croyait avoir des partisans; il lui semble qu'il n'en a plus, maintenant qu'il s'est découvert à tous; car ceux qui le blâment s'expriment haute-ment, et ceux qui pensent comme lui, sans avoir son courage, se taisent et s'éloignent. Il cède, il plie enfin sous l'effort de chaque jour, et rentre dans le silence, comme s'il éprouvait des remords d'avoir dit vrai. [*ellipsis indicates 3-paragraph omission*] Chez les nations les plus fières de l'ancien monde, on a publié des ouvrages destinés à peindre fidèlement les vices et les ridicules des contemporains; La Bruyère habitait le palais de Louis XIV quand il composa son chapitre sur les grands, et Molière critiquait la cour dans des pièces qu'il faisait représenter devant les courtisans. Mais la puissance qui domine aux États-Unis n'entend point ainsi qu'on la joue. Le plus léger reproche la blesse, la moindre vérité piquante l'effarouche; et il faut qu'on loue depuis les formes de son langage jusqu'à ses plus solides vertus. Aucun écrivain, quelle que soit sa renommée, ne peut échapper à cette obligation d'encenser ses concitoyens. La majorité vit donc dans une perpétuelle adoration d'elle-même; il n'y a que les étrangers ou l'expérience qui puissent faire arriver certaines vérités jusqu'aux oreilles des Américains. [*para-graph*] Si l'Amérique n'a pas encore eu de grands écrivains, nous ne devons pas en chercher ailleurs les raisons: il n'existe pas de génie littéraire sans liberté d'esprit, et il n'y a pas liberté d'esprit en Amérique. (II,149–53; cf. Reeve, II,158–63)

82.17–83.25 In . . . more?] [*translated from*:] Dans les pays libres, où chacun est plus ou moins appelé à donner son opinion sur les affaires de l'État; dans les ré-publiques démocratiques, où la vie publique est incessamment mêlée à la vie pri-vée, où le souverain est abordable de toutes parts, et où il ne s'agit que d'élever la voix pour arriver jusqu'à son oreille, on rencontre beaucoup plus de gens qui cherchent à spéculer sur ses faiblesses, et à vivre aux dépens de ses passions, que dans les monarchies absolues. Ce n'est pas que les hommes y soient naturellement pires qu'ailleurs, mais la tentation y est plus forte, et s'offre à plus de monde en même temps. Il en résulte un abaissement bien plus général dans les âmes. [*para-graph*] Les républiques démocratiques mettent l'esprit de cour à la portée du grand nombre, et le font pénétrer dans toutes les classes à la fois. C'est un des principaux reproches qu'on peut leur faire. [*paragraph*] Cela est surtout vrai dans les États démocratiques, organisés comme les républiques américaines, où la ma-jorité possède un empire si absolu et si irrésistible, qu'il faut en quelque sorte renoncer à ses droits de citoyen, et pour ainsi dire à sa qualité d'homme, quand on veut s'écarter du chemin qu'elle a tracé. [*paragraph*] Parmi la foule immense qui, aux États-Unis, se presse dans la carrière politique, j'ai vu bien peu d'hom-mes qui montrassent cette virile candeur, cette mâle indépendance de la pensée, qui a souvent distingué les Américains dans les temps antérieurs, et qui, partout où on la trouve, forme comme le trait saillant des grands caractères. On dirait, au premier abord, qu'en Amérique les esprits ont tous été formés sur le même mo-dèle, tant ils suivent exactement les mêmes voies. L'étranger rencontre, il est vrai, quelquefois des Américains qui s'écartent de la rigueur des formules; il arrive à ceux-là de déplorer le vice des lois, la versatilité de la démocratie, et son manque de lumières; ils vont même souvent jusqu'à remarquer les défauts qui altèrent le caractère national, et ils indiquent les moyens qu'on pourrait prendre pour les corriger; mais nul, excepté vous, ne les écoute, et vous, à qui ils confient ces pensées secrètes, vous n'êtes qu'un étranger, et vous passez. Ils vous livrent volon-tiers des vérités qui vous sont inutiles, et, descendus sur la place publique, ils tien-nent un autre langage. [*paragraph*] Si ces lignes parviennent jamais en Amérique, je suis assuré de deux choses: la première, que les lecteurs élèveront tous la voix pour me condamner; la seconde que beaucoup d'entre eux m'absoudront au fond de leur conscience. [*paragraph*] J'ai entendu parler de la patrie aux États-Unis.

J'ai rencontré du patriotisme véritable dans le peuple; j'en ai souvent cherché en vain dans ceux qui le dirigent. Ceci se comprend facilement par analogie: le despotisme déprave bien plus celui qui s'y soumet, que celui qui l'impose. Dans les monarchies absolues, le roi a souvent de grandes vertus; mais les courtisans sont toujours vils. [paragraph] Il est vrai que les courtisans, en Amérique, ne disent point Sire, et Votre Majesté, grande et capitale différence! Mais ils parlent sans cesse des lumières naturelles de leur maître; ils ne mettent point au concours la question de savoir quelle est celle des vertus du prince qui mérite le plus qu'on l'admire; car ils assurent qu'il possède toutes les vertus, sans les avoir acquises, et pour ainsi dire sans le vouloir; ils ne lui donnent pas leurs femmes et leurs filles pour qu'il daigne les élever au rang de ses maîtresses; mais en lui sacrifiant leurs opinions, ils se prostituent eux-mêmes. [paragraph] Les moralistes et les philosophes, en Amérique, ne sont pas obligés d'envelopper leurs opinions dans les voiles de l'allégorie; mais, avant de hasarder une vérité fâcheuse, ils disent: Nous savons que nous parlons à un peuple trop au-dessus des faiblesses humaines, pour ne pas toujours rester maître de lui-même. Nous ne tiendrions pas un semblable langage, si nous ne nous adressions à des hommes que leurs vertus et leurs lumières rendent seuls, parmi tous les autres, dignes de rester libres. [paragraph] Comment les flatteurs de Louis XIV pouvaient-ils mieux faire? (II,155–8; cf. Reeve, II,165–8)

84.11–44   The . . . government.] [translated from:] Mais ce ne sont pas seulement les fortunes qui sont égales en Amérique, l'égalité s'étend jusqu'à un certain point sur les intelligences elles-mêmes. [paragraph] Je ne pense pas qu'il y ait de pays dans le monde où, proportion gardée avec la population, il se trouve aussi peu d'ignorans et moins de savans qu'en Amérique. [paragraph] L'instruction primaire y est à la portée de chacun; l'instruction supérieure n'y est presque à la portée de personne. [paragraph] Ceci se comprend sans peine, et est pour ainsi dire le résultat nécessaire de ce que nous avons avancé plus haut. [paragraph] Presque tous les Américains ont de l'aisance; ils peuvent donc facilement se procurer les premiers élémens des connaissances humaines. [paragraph] En Amérique il y a peu de riches; presque tous les Américains ont donc besoin d'exercer une profession. Or, toute profession exige un apprentissage. Les Américains ne peuvent donc donner à la culture générale de l'intelligence que les premières années de la vie; à quinze ans, ils entrent dans une carrière; ainsi leur éducation finit le plus souvent à l'époque où la nôtre commence. Si elle se poursuit au-delà, elle ne se dirige plus que vers une matière spéciale et lucrative; on étudie une science comme on prend un métier, et l'on n'en saisit que les applications dont l'utilité présente est reconnue. [paragraph] En Amérique, la plupart des riches ont commencé par être pauvres; presque tous les oisifs ont été, dans leur jeunesse, des gens occupés; d'où il résulte que, quand on pourrait avoir le goût de l'étude, on n'a pas le temps de s'y livrer; et que quand on a acquis le temps de s'y livrer, on n'en a plus le goût. [paragraph] Il n'existe donc point en Amérique de classe dans laquelle le penchant des plaisirs intellectuels se transmette avec une aisance et des loisirs héréditaires, et qui tiennent en honneur les travaux de l'intelligence. Aussi la volonté de se livrer à ces trauvaux manque-t-elle aussi bien que le pouvoir. [paragraph] Il s'est établi en Amérique, dans les connaissances humaines, un certain niveau mitoyen. Tous les esprits s'en sont rapprochés, les uns en s'élevant, les autres en s'abaissant. [paragraph] Il se rencontre donc une multitude immense d'individus qui ont le même nombre de notions à peu près en matière de religion, d'histoire, de sciences, d'économie politique, de législation, de gouvernement. (I,84–5; cf. Reeve, I,59–60)

87.4–88.27   There . . . cupidity.] [translated from:] Il existe un amour de la patrie qui a principalement sa source dans ce sentiment irréfléchi, désintéressé et indéfinissable qui lie le cœur de l'homme aux lieux où l'homme a pris naissance. Cet amour instinctif se confond avec le goût des coutumes anciennes, avec le respect des aïeux et la mémoire du passé; ceux qui l'éprouvent chérissent leur pays comme on aime la maison paternelle. Ils aiment la tranquillité dont ils y jouissent; ils tiennent aux paisibles habitudes qu'ils y ont contractées; ils s'attachent aux souvenirs qu'elle leur présente, et trouvent même quelque douceur à y vivre dans l'obéissance. Souvent cet amour de la patrie est encore exalté par le zèle religieux, et alors on lui voit faire des prodiges. Lui-même est une sorte de religion; il ne raisonne point, il croit, il sent, il agit. Des peuples se sont rencontrés qui ont, en quelque façon, personnifié la patrie, et qui l'ont entrevue dans le prince. Ils ont donc transporté en lui une partie des sentimens dont le patriotisme se compose; ils se sont enorgueillis de ses triomphes, et ont été fiers de sa puissance. Il fut un temps, sous l'ancienne monarchie, où les Français éprouvaient une sorte de joie en se sentant livrés sans recours à l'arbitraire du monarque, et disaient avec orgueil: "Nous vivons sous le plus puissant roi du monde." [paragraph] Comme toutes les passions irréfléchies, cet amour du pays pousse à de grands efforts passagers plutôt qu'à la continuité des efforts. Après avoir sauvé l'État en temps de crise, il le laisse souvent dépérir au sein de la paix. [paragraph] Lorsque les peuples sont encore simples dans leurs mœurs et fermes dans leur croyance; quand la société repose doucement sur un ordre de choses ancien, dont la légitimité n'est point contestée, on voit régner cet amour instinctif de la patrie. [paragraph] Il en est un autre plus rationnel que celui-là; moins généreux, moins ardent, peut-être, mais plus fécond et plus durable; celui-ci naît des lumières; il se développe à l'aide des lois, il croît avec l'exercice des droits, et il finit, en quelque sorte, par se confondre avec l'intérêt personnel. Un homme comprend l'influence qu'a le bien-être du pays sur le sien propre; il sait que la loi lui permet de contribuer à produire ce bien-être, et il s'intéresse à la prospérité de son pays, d'abord comme à une chose qui lui est utile, et ensuite comme à son ouvrage. Mais il arrive quelquefois, dans la vie des peuples, un moment où les coutumes anciennes sont changées, les mœurs détruites, les croyances ébranlées, le prestige des souvenirs évanoui, et où, cependant, les lumières sont restées incomplètes, et les droits politiques mal assurés ou restreints. Les hommes alors n'aperçoivent plus la patrie que sous un jour faible et douteux, ils ne la placent plus ni dans le sol, qui est devenu à leurs yeux une terre inanimée; ni dans les usages de leurs aïeux, qu'on leur a appris à regarder comme un joug; ni dans la religion dont ils doutent; ni dans les lois qu'ils ne font pas, ni dans le législateur qu'ils craignent et méprisent. Ils ne la voient donc nulle part, pas plus sous ses propres traits que sous aucun autre, et ils se retirent dans un égoïsme étroit et sans lumière. Ces hommes échappent aux préjugés sans reconnaître l'empire de la raison; ils n'ont ni le patriotisme instinctif de la monarchie, ni le patriotisme réfléchi de la république; mais ils se sont arrêtés entre les deux, au milieu de la confusion et des misères. [paragraph] Que faire en un pareil état? Reculer; mais les peuples ne reviennent pas plus aux sentimens de leur jeunesse, que les hommes aux goûts innocens de leur premier âge; ils peuvent les regretter, mais non les faire renaître. Il faut donc marcher en avant, et se hâter d'unir aux yeux du peuple l'intérêt individuel à à l'intérêt du pays: car l'amour désintéressé de la patrie fuit sans retour. [paragraph] Je suis assurément loin de prétendre que, pour arriver à ce résultat, on doive accorder tout-à-coup l'exercice des droits politiques à tous les hommes. Mais je dis que le plus puissant moyen, et peut-être le seul qui nous reste d'intéresser les hommes au sort de leur patrie, c'est de les faire participer à son gouvernement. De nos jours, l'esprit de cité me semble inséparable de l'exercice des droits politiques; et je pense que désormais on verra augmenter ou diminuer en Europe le nombre des citoyens, en proportion de l'extension de ces droits. [paragraph] D'où vient qu'aux États-Unis, où les habitans sont arrivés d'hier sur le sol qu'ils occupent, où ils n'y ont apporté ni usages, ni souvenirs; où ils s'y rencontrent pour la première fois sans se connaître; où, pour le dire en un mot, l'instinct de la patrie peut à peine exister; d'où vient que chacun s'intéresse aux affairs de sa commune, de son canton et de l'État tout entier comme aux siennes mêmes? c'est que chacun, dans sa sphère, prend une part active au gouvernement de la société. [paragraph] L'homme du peuple, aux-États-Unis, a compris l'influence qu'exerce la prosperité générale sur son bonheur, idée si simple et cependant si peu connue du peuple. De plus, il s'est accoutumé à regarder cette prospérité comme son ouvrage. Il voit donc dans la fortune publique la sienne propre, et il travaille au bien de l'État non seulement par devoir ou par orgueil, mais j'oserais presque dire par cupidité. (II,114–17; cf. Reeve, II, 121–5)

88.30–89.12 It . . . affection.] [*translated from*:] Il n'est pas toujours loisible d'appeler le peuple entier, soit directement, soit indirectement, à la confection de la loi; mais on ne saurait nier que, quand cela est praticable, la loi n'en acquière une grande autorité. Cette origine populaire, qui nuit souvent à la bonté et à la sagesse de la législation, contribue singulièrement à sa puissance. [*paragraph*] Il y a dans l'expression des volontés de tout un peuple une force prodigieuse. Quand elle se découvre au grand jour, l'imagination même de ceux qui voudraient lutter contre elle en est comme accablée. [*paragraph*] La vérité de ceci est bien connue des partis. [*paragraph*] Aussi les voit-on contester la majorité partout où ils le peuvent. Quant elle leur manque parmi ceux qui ont voté, ils la placent parmi ceux qui se sont abstenus de voter; et, lorsque là encore elle vient à leur échapper, ils la retrouvent au sein de ceux qui n'avaient pas le droit de voter. [*paragraph*] Aux États-Unis, excepté les esclaves, les domestiques et les indigens nourris par les communes, il n'est personne qui ne soit électeur et qui à ce titre ne concoure indirectement à la loi. Ceux qui veulent attaquer les lois sont donc réduits à faire ostensiblement l'une de ces deux choses; ils doivent ou changer l'opinion de la nation, ou fouler aux pieds ses volontés. [*paragraph*] Ajoutez à cette première raison cette autre plus directe et plus puissante: qu'aux États-Unis, chacun trouve une sorte d'intérêt personnel à ce que tous obéissent aux lois; car celui qui aujourd'hui ne fait pas partie de la majorité, sera peut-être demain dans ses rangs; et ce respect qu'il professe maintenant pour les volontés du législateur, il aura bientôt occasion de l'exiger pour les siennes. Quelque fâcheuse que soit la loi, l'habitant des États-Unis s'y soumet donc sans peine, non-seulement comme à l'ouvrage du plus grand nombre, mais encore comme au sien propre; il la considère sous le point de vue d'un contrat, dans lequel il aurait été partie. [*paragraph*] On ne voit donc pas, aux États-Unis, une foule nombreuse et toujours turbulente, qui, regardant la loi comme un ennemi naturel, ne jette sur elle que des regards de crainte et de soupçons. Il est impossible, au contraire, de ne point apercevoir que toutes les classes montrent une grande confiance dans la législation qui régit le pays, et ressentent pour elle une sorte d'amour paternel. (II,123–5; cf. Reeve, II,131–2)

88.15–90.5 It . . . advantages.] [*translated from*:] Il est incontestable que le peuple dirige souvent fort mal les affaires publiques; mais le peuple ne saurait se mêler des affaires publiques sans que le cercle de ses idées ne vienne à s'étendre, et sans qu'on ne voie son esprit sortir de sa routine ordinaire. L'homme du peuple qui est appelé au gouvernement de la société conçoit une certaine estime de lui-même. Comme il est alors une puissance, des intelligences très eclairées se mettent au service de la sienne. On s'adresse sans cesse à lui pour s'en faire un appui; et en cherchant à le tromper de mille manières différentes, on l'éclaire. En politique, il prend part à des entreprises qu'il n'a pas conçues, mais qui lui donnent le goût général des entreprises. On lui indique tous les jours de nouvelles améliorations à faire à la propriété commune, et il sent naître le désir d'améliorer celle qui lui est personnelle. Il n'est ni plus vertueux ni plus heureux, peut-être, mais plus éclairé et plus actif que ses devanciers. Je ne doute pas que les institutions démocratiques, jointes à la nature physique du pays, ne soient la cause, non pas directe, comme tant de gens le disent, mais la cause indirecte du prodigieux mouvement d'industrie qu'on remarque aux États-Unis. Ce ne sont pas les lois qui le font naître, mais le peuple apprend à le produire en faisant la loi. [*paragraph*] Lorsque les ennemis de la démocratie prétendent qu'un seul fait mieux ce dont il se charge que le gouvernement de tous, il me semble qu'ils ont raison. Le gouvernement d'un seul, en supposant de part et d'autre égalité de lumières, met plus de suite dans ses entreprises que la multitude; il montre plus de persévérance, plus d'idée d'ensemble, plus de perfection de détail, un discernement plus juste dans le choix des hommes. Ceux qui nient ces choses n'ont jamais vu de république démocratique, ou n'ont jugé que sur un petit nombre d'exemples. La démocratie, lors même que les circonstances locales et les dispositions du peuple lui permettent de se maintenir, ne présente pas le coup d'œil de la régularité administrative et de l'ordre méthodique dans le gouvernement; cela est vrai. La liberté démocratique n'exécute pas chacune de ses entreprises avec la même perfection que le despotisme intelligent. Souvent elle les abandonne avant d'en avoir retiré le fruit, ou en hasarde de dangereuses; mais à la longue elle produit plus que lui; elle fait moins bien chaque chose, mais elle fait plus de choses. Sous son empire, ce n'est pas surtout ce qu'exécute l'administration publique qui est grand, c'est ce qu'on exécute sans elle et en dehors d'elle. La démocratie ne donne pas au peuple le gouvernement le plus habile, mais elle fait ce que le gouvernement le plus habile est souvent impuissant à créer; elle répand, dans tout le corps social, une inquiète activité, une force surabondante, une énergie qui n'existent jamais sans elle, et qui, pour peu que les circonstances soient favorables, peuvent enfanter des merveilles. Là sont ses vrais avantages. (II,130–2; cf. Reeve, II,138–40)

111.22 'niveau mitoyen'] [see above, 84]
126.26–7 "Il . . . nouveau."] [see above, 51–2]
160.4 extend] exert (I,xv)
160.5–6 government . . . church] Government . . . Church (I,xv)
160.12 their tribunals] the tribunals (I,xv) [cf. 160^{g-g}]
160.21 the arts] art (I,xvi)
160.21 knowledge] science (I,xvi)
160.22 became a] led to (I,xvi)
160.23 state] State (I,xvi)
160.28 through] by the (I,xvi)
160.30 crown] Crown (I,xvi)
160.32 inferior] lower (I,xvi)
160.33 lowering] repressing (I,xvii)
160.33–4 aristocracy. [paragraph] As] aristocracy. [paragraph omission] As (I,xvii)
160.39 fashion, the] fashion, and the (I,xvii)
160.42 a] the (I,xviii)
160.44 truth, every] truth, and every (I,xviii)
160.47 without respect of persons,] with an equal hand, (I,xviii)
160.47 of democracy] of the democracy (I,xviii) [cf.160^{k}]
161.2 bringing] throwing (I,xviii) [cf.161^{l-l}]
161.8 with] of (I,xviii)
161.9 corporate towns] communities (I,xviii)
161.12 established] organized (I,xix)
161.18 was happening] has happened (I,xix) [cf.161^{m-m}]
161.22 other.] other, and they will very shortly meet. (I,xix)
161.26 Everywhere the] The (I,xix)
161.26 have turned] have everywhere turned (I,xix)
161.34 and possesses] and it possesses (I,xx)
161.37 it be] it, then, be (I,xx)
161.40 bourgeois] citizen (I,xx) [cf.161^{p-p}]
161.41–2 weak? [paragraph] It] weak? [2-paragraph omission] It (I,xx–xxi)
161.44–5 events. [paragraph] The] events: I know, without a special revelation, that the planets move in the orbits traced by the Creator's finger. [1-paragraph omission] The (I,xxi–xxii)
159.38–162.2 Let . . . longer.] [translated from:] Je me reporte pour un moment à ce qu'était la France il y a sept cents ans: je la trouve partagée entre un petit nombre de familles qui possèdent la terre et gouvernent les habitans; le droit de commander descend alors de générations en générations avec les héritages; les hommes n'ont qu'un seul moyen d'agir les uns sur les autres: la force; on ne découvre

qu'une seule origine de la puissance, la propriété foncière. [*paragraph*] Mais voici le pouvoir politique du clergé qui vient à se fonder et bientôt à s'étendre. Le clergé ouvre ses rangs à tous, au pauvre et au riche, au roturier et au seigneur; l'égalité commence à pénétrer par l'Église au sein du gouvernement, et celui qui eût végété comme serf dans un éternel esclavage, se place comme prêtre au milieu des nobles et va souvent s'asseoir au-dessus des rois. [*paragraph*] La société devenant avec le temps plus civilisée et plus stable, les différens rapports entre les hommes deviennent plus compliqués et plus nombreux. Le besoin des lois civiles se fait vivement sentir. Alors naissent les légistes; ils sortent de l'enceinte obscure des tribunaux et du réduit poudreux des greffes, et ils vont siéger dans la cour du prince, à côté des barons féodaux couverts d'hermine et de fer. [*paragraph*] Les rois se ruinent dans les grandes entreprises; les nobles s'épuisent dans les guerres privées; les roturiers s'enrichissent dans le commerce. L'influence de l'argent commence à se faire sentir sur les affaires de l'État. Le négoce est une source nouvelle qui s'ouvre à la puissance, et les financiers deviennent un pouvoir politique qu'on méprise et qu'on flatte. [*paragraph*] Peu à peu, les lumières se répandent; on voit se réveiller le goût de la littérature et des arts; l'esprit devient alors un élément de succès; la science est un moyen de gouvernement; l'intelligence une force sociale; les lettrés arrivent aux affaires. [*paragraph*] A mesure cependant qu'il se découvre des routes nouvelles pour parvenir au pouvoir, on voit baisser la valeur de la naissance. Au XIᵉ siècle, la noblesse était d'un prix inestimable; on l'achète au XIIIᵉ; le premier anoblissement a lieu en 1270, et l'égalité s'introduit enfin dans le gouvernement par l'aristocratie elle-même. [*paragraph*] Durant les sept cents ans qui viennent de s'écouler, il est arrivé quelquefois que, pour lutter contre l'autorité royale ou pour enlever le pouvoir à leurs rivaux, les nobles ont donné une puissance politique au peuple. [*paragraph*] Plus souvent encore, on a vu les rois faire participer au gouvernement les classes inférieures de l'État, afin d'abaisser l'aristocratie. [*1-paragraph omission*] Dès que les citoyens commencèrent à posséder la terre autrement que suivant la tenure féodale, et que la richesse, mobilière, étant connue, put à son tour créer l'influence et donner le pouvoir, on ne fit point de découvertes dans les arts, on n'introduisit plus de perfectionnemens dans le commerce et l'industrie, sans créer comme autant de nouveaux élémens d'égalité parmi les hommes. A partir de ce moment, tous les procédés qui se découvrent, tous les besoins qui viennent à naître, tous les désirs qui demandent à se satisfaire, sont des progrès vers le nivellement universel. Le goût du luxe, l'amour de la guerre, l'empire de la mode, les passions les plus superficielles du cœur humain comme les plus profondes, semblent travailler de concert à apauvrir les riches et à enrichir les pauvres. [*paragraph*] Depuis que les trauvaux de l'intelligence furent devenus des sources de force et de richesses, on dut considérer chaque développement de la science, chaque connaissance nouvelle, chaque idée neuve, comme un germe de puissance mis à la portée du peuple. La poésie, l'éloquence, la mémoire, les grâces de l'esprit, les feux de l'imagination, la profondeur de la pensée, tous ces dons que le Ciel répartit au hasard, profitèrent à la démocratie, et lors même qu'ils se trouvèrent dans la possession de ses adversaires, ils servirent encore sa cause en mettant en relief la grandeur naturelle de l'homme; ses conquêtes s'étendirent donc avec celles de la civilisation et des lumières, et la littérature fut un arsenal ouvert à tous, où les faibles et les pauvres vinrent chaque jour chercher des armes. [*paragraph*] Lorsqu'on parcourt les pages de notre histoire, on ne rencontre pas pour ainsi dire de grands évènemens qui, depuis sept cents ans, n'aient tourné au profit de l'égalité. [*paragraph*] Les croisades et les guerres des Anglais déciment les nobles et divisent leurs terres ; l'institution des communes introduit la liberté démocratique au sein de la monarchie féodale; la découverte des armes à feu égalise le vilain et le noble sur le champ de bataille; l'imprimerie offre des ressources égales à leur intelligence; la poste vient déposer la lumière sur le seuil de la cabane du pauvre comme à la porte des palais; le protestantisme soutient que tous les hommes sont également en état de trouver le chemin du ciel.

L'Amérique, qui se découvre, présente à la fortune mille routes nouvelles, et délivre à d'obscurs aventuriers les richesses et le pouvoir. [*paragraph*] Si, à partir du xIᵉ siècle, vous examinez ce qui se passe en France de cinquante en cinquante années, au bout de chacune de ces périodes, vous ne manquerez point d'apercevoir qu'une double révolution s'est opérée dans l'état de la société. Le noble aura baissé dans l'échelle sociale, le roturier s'y sera élevé; l'un descend, l'autre monte. Chaque demi-siècle les rapproche, et bientôt ils vont se toucher. [*paragraph*] Et ceci n'est pas seulement particulier à la France. De quel côté que nous jetions nos regards, nous apercevons la même révolution qui se continue dans tout l'univers chrétien. [*paragraph*] Partout on a vu les divers incidens de la vie des peuples tourner au profit de la démocratie; tous les hommes l'ont aidée de leurs efforts : ceux qui avaient en vue de concourir à ses succès et ceux qui ne songeaient point à la servir; ceux qui ont combattu pour elle, et ceux mêmes qui se sont déclarés ses ennemis; tous ont été poussés pêle-mêle dans la même voie, et tous ont travaillé en commun, les uns malgré eux, les autres à leur insu, aveugles, instrumens dans les mains de Dieu. [*paragraph*] Le développement graduel de l'égalité des conditions est donc un fait providentiel, il en a les principaux caractères: il est universel, il est durable, il échappe chaque jour à la puissance humaine; tous les évènemens, comme tous les hommes, servent à son développement. [*paragraph*] Serait-il sage de croire qu'un mouvement social qui vient de si loin, pourra être suspendu par les efforts d'une génération? Pense-t-on qu'après avoir détruit la féodalité et vaincu les rois, la démocratie reculera devant les bourgeois et les riches? s'arrêtera-t-elle maintenant qu'elle est devenue si forte et ses adversaires si faibles? [*2-paragraph omission*] Il n'est pas nécessaire que Dieu parle lui-même pour que nous découvrions des signes certains de sa volonté; il suffit d'examiner quelle est la marche habituelle de la nature et la tendance continue des évènemens; je sais, sans que le Créateur élève la voix, que les astres suivent dans l'espace les courbes que son doigt a tracées. [*paragraph*] Si de longues observations et des méditations sincères amenaient les hommes de nos jours à reconnaître que le développement graduel et progressif de l'égalité est à la fois le passé et l'avenir de leur histoire, cette seule découverte donnerait à ce développement le caractère sacré de la volonté du souverain maître. Vouloir arrêter la démocratie paraîtrait alors lutter contre Dieu même, et il ne resterait aux nations qu'à s'accommoder à l'état social que leur impose la Providence. [*continued as above*, 51] (I,4–10)

170.32   people] lower orders (II,138)
170.34   occupations] acquirements (II,138) [cf.170ᵍ⁻ᵍ]
170.36–7   power, minds more . . . own offer him their services.] authority, he can command the services of minds much more . . . own. (II,138)
170.37   claimants] applicants (II,138)
170.37–171.1   who need his support; and who, seeking to . . . ways, instruct him during the process.] who seek to . . . ways, but who instruct him by their deceit. (II,138) [cf.170ʰ⁻ʰ]
171.2   a general taste for such undertakings.] a taste for undertakings of the kind. (II,138) [cf.171ⁱ⁻ⁱ]
171.3   suggested to him] pointed out (II,138)
171.5   peculiarly] more peculiarly (II,139)
171.10–11   but it proceeds from habits acquired through participation in making the laws.] but the people learn how to promote it by the experience derived from legislation. (II,139)
171.12   Democracy] democracy (II,139)
171.13   functions] duties (II,139)
171.13   better] much better (II,139)
171.14   people at large] community (II,139)
171.15   equal degree] equality (II,139)
171.15–16   has more constancy, more preserverance, than] is more consistent, more perservering, and more accurate than (II,139)

171.16–17   multitude; more combination in its plans, and more perfection in its details; and is better] multitude, and it is much better (II,139)
171.18   this,] what I advance, (II,139)
171.18   have] have certainly (II,139)
171.19–20   only upon a few instances. It must be conceded that] upon very partial evidence. It is true that (II,139)
171.23–4   intelligent] adroit (II,139) [cf. 171*j–j*]
171.26   greater results] more (II,140)
171.26–7   government. It . . . well, but it] government, and if it . . . well, it (II,140)
171.27–9   Not what is done by a democratic government, but what is done under a democratic government by private agency, is really great.] Under its sway, the transactions of the public administration are not nearly so important as what is done by private exertion. (II,140)
171.32   an] and an (II,140)
171.32   never seen elsewhere] inseparable from it (II,140)
170.31–171.34   It . . . democracy.] [cf. above, 88.15–90.5]
172.10   "support] Let us now imagine a community so organized by nature that it can support (II,115)
172.11   and can] and that it can (II,116)
172.11–12   the result of the general tendency of the laws,"] the general tendency of the legislation: we shall then be able to conceive that a democratic government, notwithstanding its defects, will be most fitted to conduce to the prosperity of this community. (II,116)
172.10–12   "support . . . laws,"] [translated from:] Imaginez une société que la nature, ou sa constitution, ait organisée de manière à supporter l'action passagère de mauvaises lois, et qui puisse attendre, sans périr, le résultat de la tendance générale des lois, et vous concevrez que le gouvernement de la démocratie, malgré ses défauts, soit encore de tous le plus propre à faire prospérer cette société. (II,109)
172.24   hostile to the] opposed to the will of the (II,118)
172.25   character] tendency (II,118)
172.26   is, moreover, a] is a (II,118)
172.27   the effects of which do not last beyond the] which only occurs during the (II,118)
172.28–9   which connect] which may connect (II,118) [cf.172*o*]
172.31   corrupt and incapable like] as corrupt and incapable as (II,118)
172.32   promote or screen] promote (II,118)
172.32   or inaptitude] and inaptitude (II,118)
172.34   the magistrate] a magistrate (II,118)
172.35   those of his individual character.] peculiar to his own person. (II,118)
172.37   blended] confounded (II,118)
172.38   frequently] very frequently (II,119)
172.38   is a] is the (II,119)
172.39   and combine] and to combine (II,119)
172.40   towards attaining] in order to attain (II,119)
172.40   is not always the happiness] does not always ensure the greatest happiness (II,119)
172.41   it not only connects] it serves not only to connect (II,119)
172.41–2   authority with each other, but links them also] authority, but to unite them (II,119)
172.42   governed] community (II,119)
173.2–3   therefore, finds himself supported in his own natural tendencies by a portion of society itself, as] is therefore constantly supported by a portion of the community, as (II,119)
173.3   government] Government (II,119)
173.5   object] purposes (II,119)

173.7   it also with] it with that of (II,119)

173.7–8   generations of their order. They labour for ages to come as well as for their own time.] generations; their influence belongs to the future as much as to the present. (II,119)

173.8   thus urged] urged at the same time (II,119)

173.9   those who surround him,] the community, (II,119)

173.9   might almost say] may almost add (II,119)

173.10   Is it] Is it, then, (II,119)

173.10   should not resist?] does not resist such repeated impulses? (II,119)

173.10–13   And hence it is that the class spirit often hurries along with it those whom it does not corrupt, and makes them unintentionally fashion . . . particular ends, and pre-fashion it] And indeed aristocracies are often carried away by the spirit of their order without being corrupted by it; and they unconsciously fashion . . . ends, and prepare it (II,119) [cf.173^{q-q}]

173.13   descendants] own descendants (II,119)

172.19–173.13   The . . . descendants.] [cf. above, entry for 68.46–70.43]

179.1–2   "a useful study for doing otherwise and better."] To evade the bondage of system and habit, of family-maxims, class-opinions, and, in some degree, of national prejudices; to accept tradition only as a means of information, and existing facts only as a lesson used in doing otherwise and doing better; to seek the reason of things for oneself, and in oneself alone; to tend to results without being bound to means, and to aim at the substance through the form; such are the principal characteristics of what I shall call the philosophical method of the Americans. (III,2)

179.1–2   "a . . . better."] [translated from:] Échapper à l'esprit de système, au joug des habitudes, aux maximes de familles, aux opinions de classe, et, jusqu'à un certain point, aux préjugés de nation; ne prendre la tradition que comme un renseignement et les faits présents que comme une utile étude pour faire autrement et mieux; chercher par soi-même et en soi seul la raison des choses; tendre au résultat sans se laisser enchaîner au moyen; et viser fond à travers la forme, tels sont les principaux traits qui caractérisent ce que j'appellerai la méthode philosophique des Américains. (III,2)

179.23   "Faith] The intellectual dominion of the greater number would probably be less absolute amongst a democratic people governed by a king than in the sphere of a pure democracy, but it will always be extremely absolute; and by whatever political laws men are governed in the ages of equality, it may be foreseen that faith (III,19)

179.24   "becomes in such countries a . . . religion,] will become a . . . religion there, (III,19)

179.25   prophet."] ministering prophet. (III,19)

179.23–5   "Faith . . . prophet."] [translated from:] Il est à croire que l'empire intellectuel du plus grand nombre serait moins absolu chez un peuple démocratique soumis à un roi qu'au sein d'une pure démocratie; mais il sera toujours très-absolu, et, quelles que soient les lois politiques qui régissent les hommes dans les siècles d'égalité, l'on peut prévoir que la foi dans l'opinion commune y deviendra une sorte de religion dont la majorité sera le prophète. (III,15)

180.11   infiniment plus nombreux] Ces riches ne seront point liés aussi étroitement entre eux que les membres de l'ancienne classe aristocratique; ils auront des instincts différents et ne posséderont presque jamais un loisir aussi assuré et aussi complet; mais ils seront infiniment plus nombreux que ne pouvaient l'être ceux qui composaient cette classe. (III,57–8; cf. Reeve, III,73)

180.23   "immense."] The number of those who cultivate science, letters, and the arts, becomes immense. (III,75) [translated from:] Le nombre de ceux qui cultivent les sciences, les lettres et les arts, devient immense. (III,59)

181.8   "Il] Mais il (III,64; cf. Reeve, III,81)

183.7   does not] dares not (III,212)

183.12   selfishness is afraid of itself.] egotism fears its own self. (III,212)
183.17   to be forgetful of self.] to forget themselves. (III,212)
183.20   opportunities of] opportunities for (III,212)
183.20   oftener] the oftener (III,213) [cf. 183z]
183.23   mutual] violent (III,213)
183.28   indifference. . . .] [*ellipsis indicates 1½-paragraph omission*] (III,213)
183.29–32   requires a . . . services and obscure good offices, a . . . disinterestedness.]
    a . . . services rendered and of obscure good deeds, a . . . disinterestedness, will
    be required. (III,215)
183.33   affections] affection (III,215)
183.34–6   and of those with whom they are in contact, perpetually draws men back
    to one another, in . . . them; and forces them to render each other mutual assis-
    tance.] and of their kindred, perpetually brings men together, and forces them to
    help one another, in . . . them. (III,215)
183.38–9   with them] with the lower classes (III,215)
183.40–1   democratic times a poor man's attachment depends more on manner than
    on] democratic ages you attach a poor man to you more by your manner than by
    (III,215)
183.42   very magnitude] magnitude (III,215)
183.42–3   by setting the difference of conditions in a strong light,] which sets off the
    difference of conditions, (III,215)
183.44   irresistible . . . . This] irresistible: their affability carries men away, and even
    their want of polish is not always displeasing. This (III,216)
183.45   penetrate at once into] take root at once in (III,216)
184.7   are incessantly using] constantly use (III,216)
184.8   means of augmenting] truths which may augment (III,216)
184.8   when] if (III,216)
184.10   people. . . .] [*ellipsis indicates 4-sentence omission*] (III,216–17)
184.11   I] I must say that I (III,217)
184.12–13   a hundred times remarked that, in case of need, they hardly ever fail] re-
    marked a hundred instances in which they hardly ever failed (III,217)
184.15–16   is a member of society] lives in society (III,217) [cf. 184a-a]
184.16   at every] every (III,217) [cf. 184b-b]
184.18   reason for disliking them] ground of animosity to them (III,217)
184.21   calculation] intentional (III,218)
183.7–184.28   When . . . freedom.] [*translated from:*] Quand le public gouverne, il
    n'y a pas d'homme qui ne sente le prix de la bienveillance publique et qui ne cher-
    che à la captiver en s'attirant l'estime et l'affection de ceux au milieu desquels il
    doit vivre. [*paragraph*] Plusieurs des passions qui glacent les cœurs et les divisent
    sont alors obligées de se retirer au fond de l'âme et de s'y cacher. L'orgueil se dis-
    simule; le mépris n'ose se faire jour. L'égoïsme a peur de lui-même. [*paragraph*]
    Sous un gouvernement libre, la plupart des fonctions publiques étant électives, les
    hommes que la hauteur de leur âme ou l'inquiétude de leurs désirs mettant à
    l'étroit dans la vie privée, sentent chaque jour qu'ils ne peuvent se passer de la
    population qui les environne. [*paragraph*] Il arrive alors que l'on songe à ses
    semblables par ambition, et que souvent on trouve en quelque sorte son intérêt à
    s'oublier soi-même. Je sais qu'on peut m'opposer ici toutes les intrigues qu'une
    élection fait naître; les moyens honteux dont les candidats se servent souvent et
    les calomnies que leurs ennemis répandent. Ce sont là des occasions de haine, et
    elles se représentent d'autant plus souvent que les élections deviennent plus fré-
    quentes. [*paragraph*] Les maux sont grands sans doute, mais il sont passagers,
    tandis que les biens qui naissent avec eux demeurent. [*paragraph*] L'envie d'être
    élus peut porter momentanément certains hommes à se faire la guerre; mais ce
    même désir porte à la longue tous les hommes à se prêter un mutuel appui; et s'il
    arrive qu'une élection divise accidentellement deux amis, le système électoral rap-
    proche d'une manière permanente une multitude de citoyens qui seraient toujours

restés étrangers les uns aux autres. La liberté crée des haines particulières; mais le despotisme fait naître l'indifférence générale. [*ellipsis indicates 5-paragraph omission*] On peut, par une action d'éclat, captiver tout-à-coup la faveur d'un peuple; mais, pour gagner l'amour et le respect de la population qui vous entoure, il faut une longue succession de petits services rendus, de bons offices obscurs, une habitude constante de bienveillance et une réputation bien établie de désintéressement. [*paragraph*] Les libertés locales qui font qu'un grand nombre de citoyens mettent du prix à l'affection de leurs voisins et de leurs proches, ramènent donc sans cesse les hommes les uns vers les autres, en dépit des instincts qui les séparent, et les forcent à s'entr'aider. [*paragraph*] Aux États-Unis, les plus opulents citoyens ont bien soin de ne point s'isoler du peuple; au contraire, ils s'en rapprochent sans cesse, ils l'écoutent volontiers, et lui parlent tous les jours. Ils savent que les riches des démocraties ont toujours besoin des pauvres, et que dans les temps démocratiques on s'attache le pauvre par les manières plus que par les bienfaits. La grandeur même des bienfaits, qui met en lumière la différence des conditions, cause une irritation secrète à ceux qui en profitent; mais la simplicité des manières a des charmes presque irrésistibles: leur familiarité entraîne, et leur grossièreté même ne deplaît pas toujours. [*paragraph*] Ce n'est pas du premier coup que cette vérité pénètre dans l'esprit des riches. Ils y résistent d'ordinaire tant que dure la révolution démocratique, et ils ne l'admettent même point aussitôt après que cette révolution est accomplie. Ils consentent volontiers à faire du bien au peuple; mais ils veulent continuer à le tenir soigneusement à distance. Ils croient que cela suffit; ils se trompent. Ils se ruineraient ainsi sans réchauffer le cœur de la population qui les environne. Ce n'est pas le sacrifice de leur argent qu'elle demande; c'est celui de leur orgueil. [*paragraph*] On dirait qu'aux États-Unis il n'y a pas d'imagination qui ne s'épuise à inventer des moyens d'accroître la richesse et de satisfaire les besoins du public. Les habitants les plus éclairés de chaque canton se servent sans cesse de leurs lumières pour découvrir des secrets nouveaux propres à accroître la prospérité commune; et, lorsqu'ils en ont trouvé quelques-uns, ils se hâtent de les livrer à la foule. [*ellipsis indicates 2-paragraph omission*] Je dois dire que j'ai souvent vu des Américains faire de grands et véritable sacrifices à la chose publique, et j'ai remarqué cent fois qu'au besoin ils ne manquaient presque jamais de se prêter fidèle appui les uns aux autres. [*paragraph*] Les institutions libres que possèdent les habitants des États-Unis, et les droits politiques dont ils font tant d'usage, rappellent sans cesse et de mille manières, à chaque citoyen qu'il vit en société. Elles ramènent à tous moments son esprit vers cette idée, que le devoir aussi bien que l'intérêt des hommes est de se rendre utiles à leurs semblables; et comme il ne voit aucun sujet particulier de les haïr, puisqu'il n'est jamais ni leur esclave ni leur maître, son cœur penche aisément du côté de la bienveillance. On s'occupe d'abord de l'intérêt général par nécessité, et puis par choix; ce qui était calcul devient instinct; et, à force de travailler au bien de ses concitoyens, on prend enfin l'habitude et le goût de les servir. [*paragraph*] Beaucoup de gens en France considèrent l'égalité des conditions comme un premier mal, et la liberté politique comme un second. Quand ils sont obligés de subir l'une ils s'efforcent du moins d'échapper à l'autre. Et moi je dis que, pour combattre les maux que l'égalité peut produire, il n'y a qu'un remède efficace: c'est la liberté politique. (III,165–70)

185.10   enlightened self-interest] interest rightly understood (III,253)

185.11–12   impracticable efforts] excessive exertion (III,253)

185.13   adaptation] admirable conformity (III,253)

185.14   is its] is that (III,253)

185.15   it employs self-interest itself to correct self-interest,] the principle checks one personal interest by another, (III,253)

185.16   very] very same (III,253)

185.17   The doctrine of enlightened self-interest] The principle of interest rightly understood (III,253)

185.19   virtuous man] man virtuous (III,253)

185.19   multitude] number (III,253)
185.21   at once lead men] lead men straight (III,254)
185.21   by their] by the (III,254)
185.21   draws them gradually] gradually draws them (III,254)
185.22   "interest rightly understood"] [no quotation marks] (III,254)
185.24   That principle] The principle of interest rightly understood (III,254)
185.26   others] other men (III,254)
185.26   below that level] far below it (III,254)
185.26   upheld] restrained (III,254)
185.28   enlightened self-interest] interest rightly understood (III,254)
185.32   judge it] judge it to be (III,254)
185.32–3   necessary. [paragraph] No] [1-paragraph omission] (III,254)
185.34   impelling] inclining (III,255)
185.34   inclining] leading (III,255)
185.35   concentrate his affections on himself] be wrapped up in himself (III,255)
185.38   interest.] interest. If the members of a community, as they become more equal,
    become more ignorant and coarse, it is difficult to foresee to what pitch of stupid
    excesses their egotism may lead them; and no one can foretell into what disgrace
    and wretchedness they would plunge themselves, lest they should have to sacrifice
    something of their own well-being to the prosperity of their fellow-creatures.
    (III,255–6)
185.39   doctrine of self-interest,] system of interest, (III,256)
185.40   is self-evident in . . . parts;] is, in . . . parts, self-evident; (III,256)
185.41   instructed] educated (III,256)
185.41–2   Instruct them, then, at all hazards;] Educate, then, at any rate; (III,256)
185.43   flying] flitting (III,256)
185.44   instruction] education (III,256)
185.10–44   The . . . instruction.] [translated from:] L'intérêt bien entendu est une
    doctrine peu haute, mais claire et sûre. Elle ne cherche pas a [sic] atteindre de
    grands objets; mais elle atteint sans trop d'efforts tous ceux auxquels elle vise.
    Comme elle est à la portée de toutes les intelligences, chacun la saisit aisément et
    la retient sans peine. S'accommodant merveilleusement aux faiblesses des hom-
    mes, elle obtient facilement un grand empire, et il ne lui est point difficile de le
    conserver, parce qu'elle retourne l'intérêt personnel contre lui même [sic], et se
    sert, pour diriger les passions, de l'aiguillon qui les excite. [paragraph] La doctrine
    de l'intérêt bien entendu ne produit pas de grands dévouements, mais elle suggère
    chaque jour de petits sacrifices; à elle seule, elle ne saurait faire un homme ver-
    tueux, mais elle forme une multitude de citoyens, réglés, tempérants, modérés,
    prévoyants, maîtres d'eux-mêmes; et, si elle ne conduit pas directement à la vertu,
    par la volonté, elle en rapproche insensiblement par les habitudes. [paragraph] Si
    la doctrine de l'intérêt bien entendu venait à dominer entièrement le monde moral,
    les vertus extraordinaires seraient sans doute plus rares, mais je pense aussi qu'a-
    lors les grossières dépravations seraient moins communes. La doctrine de l'inté-
    rêt bien entendu empêche peut-être quelques hommes de monter fort au-dessus
    du niveau ordinaire de l'humanité; mais un grand nombre d'autres qui tombaient
    au-dessous la recontrent et s'y retiennent. Considérez quelques individus, elle les
    abaisse. Envisagez l'espèce, elle l'élève. [paragraph] Je ne craindrai pas de dire que
    la doctrine de l'intérêt bien entendu me semble, de toutes les théories philosophi-
    ques, la mieux appropriée aux besoins des hommes de notre temps, et que j'y vois
    la plus puissante garantie qui leur reste contre eux-mêmes. C'est donc principale-
    ment vers elles que l'esprit des moralistes de nos jours doit se tourner. Alors même
    qu'ils la jugeraient imparfaite il faudrait encore l'adopter comme nécessaire. [2-
    paragraph omission] Il n'y pas de pouvoir sur la terre qui puisse empêcher que
    l'égalité croissante des conditions ne porte l'esprit humain vers la recherche de
    l'utile, et ne dispose chaque citoyen à se resserrer en lui-même. [paragraph] Il faut
    donc s'attendre que l'intérêt individuel deviendra plus que jamais le principal,

sinon l'unique mobile des actions des hommes; mais il reste à savoir comment chaque homme entendra son intérêt individuel. [*paragraph*] Si les citoyens en devenant égaux, restaient ignorants et grossiers il est difficile de prévoir jusqu'à quel stupide excès pourrait se porter leur égoïsme, et l'on ne saurait dire à l'avance dans quelles honteuses misères ils se plongeraient eux-mêmes, de peur de sacrifier quelque chose de leur bien-être à la prospérité de leurs semblables. [*paragraph*] Je ne crois point que la doctrine de l'intérêt, telle qu'on la prêche en Amérique, soit évidente dans toutes ses parties; mais elle renferme un grand nombre de vérités si évidentes, qu'il suffit d'éclairer les hommes pour qu'ils les voient. Eclairez-les donc à tout prix; car le siècle des dévouements aveugles et des vertus instinctives fuit déjà loin de nous, et je vois s'approcher le temps où la liberté, la paix publique et l'ordre social lui-même ne pourront se passer des lumières. (III,197–9)

186.21 The] When, on the contrary, the distinctions of rank are confounded together and privileges are destroyed,—when hereditary property is subdivided, and education and freedom widely diffused, the (III,265)

186.24 for those] for these (III,265)

186.27 precious, so incomplete, and so] delightful, so imperfect, so (III,265)

186.28 inquire] were to inquire (III,265)

186.28 are at once] are (III,265)

186.30 can] could (III,265)

186.30 to them] to their condition (III,265)

186.32–3 and along with them it becomes preponderant.] with them it preponderates. (III,265)

186.36 longing towards] envy on (III,266)

186.36–7 not indulge . . . in those] not possess . . . of those (III,266)

186.40 the indulgences of riches,] physical gratifications, (III,266)

186.42 the stimulus of privation,] the sting of want, (III,266)

186.43 have long struggled with adverse fortune;] were long a prey to adverse fortunes; (III,266)

187.2 petty] small (III,266)

187.6 these] these men (III,266)

187.7–8 physical comfort has] well-being is now (III,267) [cf. 187*i–i*]

186.21–187.9 The . . . course.] [*translated from:*] Lorsque, au contraire, les rangs sont confondus et les privilèges détruits, quand les patrimoines se divisent et que la lumière et la liberté se répandent, l'envie d'acquérir le bien-être se présente à l'imagination du pauvre, et la crainte de le perdre à l'esprit du riche. Il s'établit une multitude de fortunes médiocres. Ceux qui les possèdent ont assez de jouissances matérielles pour concevoir le goût de ces jouissances, et pas assez pour s'en contenter. Ils ne se les procurent jamais qu'avec effort et ne s'y livrent qu'en tremblant. [*paragraph*] Ils s'attachent donc sans cesse à poursuivre ou à retenir ces jouissances si précieuses, si incomplètes et si fugitives. [*paragraph*] Je cherche une passion qui soit naturelle à des hommes que l'obscurité de leur origine ou la médiocrité de leur fortune excitent et limitent, et je n'en trouve point de mieux appropriée que le goût du bien-être. La passion du bien-être matériel est essentiellement une passion de classe moyenne; elle grandit et s'étend avec cette classe; elle devient prépondérante avec elle. C'est de là qu'elle gagne les rangs supérieurs de la société et descend jusqu'au sein du peuple. [*paragraph*] Je n'ai pas rencontré, en Amérique, de si pauvre citoyen qui ne jetât un regard d'espérance et d'envie sur les jouissances des riches et dont l'imagination ne se saisît à l'avance des biens que le sort s'obstinait à lui refuser. [*paragraph*] D'un autre côté, je n'ai aperçu chez les riches des États-Unis ce superbe dédain pour le bien-être matériel qui se montre quelquefois jusque dans le sein des aristocraties les plus opulentes et les plus dissolues. [*paragraph*] La plupart de ces riches ont été pauvres, ils ont senti l'aiguillon du besoin, ils ont long-temps combattu une fortune ennemie, et, maintenant que la victoire est remportée, les passions qui ont accompagné la lutte lui survivent; ils restent comme enivrés au milieu de ces petites jouissances qu'ils ont poursuivies quarante ans. [*paragraph*] Ce n'est pas qu'aux États-Unis, comme ailleurs, il ne se rencontre un assez grand nombre de riches qui, tenant leurs biens par héritage; possèdent sans efforts une opulence qu'ils n'ont point acquise. Mais ceux-ci même ne se montrent pas moins attachés aux jouissances de la vie matérielle. L'amour du bien-être est devenu le goût national et dominant; le grand courant des passions humaines porte de ce côté, il entraîne tout dans son cours. (III,206–7)

187.13–14   "leading men away in search of forbidden enjoyments, but absorbing them in the pursuit of permitted ones.] The reproach I address to the principle of equality, is not that it leads men away in the pursuit of forbidden enjoyments, but that it absorbs them wholly in quest of those which are allowed. (III,272)

187.13–14   "leading . . . ones.] [*translated from*:] Ce que je reproche à l'égalité, ce n'est pas d'entraîner les hommes à la poursuite des jouissances défendues; c'est de les absorber entièrement dans la recherche des jouissances permises. (III,211)

187.15   This spirit is] It may even be (III,271)

187.15–17   This . . . another."] [*translated from*:] Souvent même il vient à se combiner avec une sorte de moralité religieuse; on veut être le mieux possible en ce monde, sans renoncer aux chances de l'autre. (III,210–11)

187.25–6   is so] he is so (III,278)

187.28–9   gratifications. . . . [*paragraph*] At] [*ellipsis indicates 1-paragraph omission*] (III,278–9)

187.30   uneasy] restless (III,279)

187.30   spectacle is] spectacle itself is (III,279)

187.31   example] exemplification (III,279)

187.31–2   it . . . . [*paragraph*] When] [*ellipsis indicates 3-paragraph omission*] (III, 279–80)

187.38   individually feeble. It] less able to realize them: it (III,281)

187.38   while] whilst (III,281)

187.39   restrained by their own weakness,] themselves powerless, (III,281)

188.1–2   they have now to encounter the competition of all. The] they have opened the door to universal competition: the (III,281) [cf. 188*m–m*]

188.2   place] position (III,282)

188.3–4   to get on fast] to walk quick (III,282)

188.4   homogeneous] dense (III,282)

188.5   upon him.] him. (III,282)

188.5   wishes] propensities (III,282)

187.22–188.7   It . . . mind.] [*translated from*:] C'est une chose étrange de voir avec quelle sorte d'ardeur fébrile les Américains poursuivent le bien-être, et comme ils se montrent tourmentés sans cesse par une crainte vague de n'avoir pas choisi la route la plus courte qui peut y conduire. [*paragraph*] L'habitant des États-Unis s'attache aux biens de ce monde, comme s'il était assuré de ne point mourir, et il met tant de précipitation à saisir ceux qui passent à sa portée, qu'on dirait qu'il craint à chaque instant de cesser de vivre avant d'en avoir joui. Il les saisit tous, mais sans les étreindre, et il les laisse bientôt échapper de ses mains pour courir après des jouissances nouvelles. [*ellipsis indicates 2-paragraph omission*] On s'étonne d'abord en contemplant cette agitation singulière que font paraître tant d'hommes heureux, au sein même de leur abondance. Ce spectacle est pourtant aussi vieux que le monde; ce qui est nouveau c'est de voir tout un peuple qui le donne. [*ellipsis indicates 5-paragraph omission*] Quand toutes les prérogatives de naissance et de fortune sont détruites, que toutes les professions sont ouvertes à tous, et qu'on peut parvenir de soi-même au sommet de chacune d'elles une carrière immense et aisée semble s'ouvrir devant l'ambition des hommes, et ils se figurent volontiers qu'ils sont appelés à de grandes destinées. Mais c'est là une vue erronée que l'expérience corrige tous les jours. Cette même égalité qui permet à chaque citoyen de concevoir de vastes espérances, rend tous les citoyens individuellement faibles. Elle limite de tous côtés leurs forces, en même temps qu'elle permet à leurs désirs de s'étendre. [*paragraph*] Non-seulement ils sont impuissants par eux-mêmes, mais ils trouvent à chaque pas d'immenses obstacles qu'ils n'avaient point aperçus d'abord. [*paragraph*] Ils ont détruit les privilèges gênants de quelques-uns de leurs semblables; ils rencontrent la concurrence de tous. La borne a changé de forme plutôt que de place. Lorsque les hommes sont à peu près semblables et suivent une même route, il est bien difficile qu'aucun d'entre eux marche vite et perce à travers la foule uniforme qui l'environne et le presse. [*paragraph*] Cette opposition constante qui règne entre les instincts que fait naître l'égalité, et les moyens qu'elle fournit pour les satisfaire, tourmente et fatigue les âmes. (III,216–19)

189.8–9   comes to have] has (II,153)

189.9   is, to be equally] is to say, when it is equally (II,153–4)

189.10   it is either falling into a revolutionary state or into dissolution."] it must either pass through a revolution, or fall into complete dissolution. (II,154)

189.8–10   "When . . . dissolution."] [*translated from*:] Quand une société en vient à avoir réellement un gouvernement mixte, c'est-à-dire également partagé entre des principes contraires, elle entre en révolution ou elle se dissout. (II,144–5)

189.14   "checked] I am therefore of opinion that some one social power must always be made to predominate over the others; but I think that liberty is endangered when this power is checked (II,154)

189.14–15   "checked . . . vehemence."] [*translated from*:] Je pense donc qu'il faut toujours placer quelque part un pouvoir social supérieur à tous les autres; mais je crois la liberté en péril lorsque ce pouvoir ne trouve devant lui aucun obstacle qui puisse retenir sa marche, et lui donner le temps de se modérer lui-même. (II,145)

189.22   democracy . . . is] democracy in Christendom, is (II,267)

189.22   our] the (II,267)

189.21–2   "The . . . time."] [*translated from*:] L'organisation et l'établissement de la démocratie parmi les chrétiens est le grand problème politique de notre temps. (II,254)

189.33–4   of. [*paragraph*] In] [*no paragraph*] (IV,341)

189.35   weakness. The] weakness. The outlined society itself was not easily discernible, and constantly confounded with the different powers by which the community was ruled. The (IV,342)

189.38   to public.] to the interests of the public. (IV.342) [cf. 189*q*]

190.4   The general character of old society was diversity;] In olden society everything was different: (IV,342) [cf. 190*r–r*]

190.5   all things threaten] everything threatens (IV,342)

190.6   will be] will soon be (IV,342)

190.7   in the uniformity of the general aspect.] in the general aspect of the world. (IV,342)

190.10   of an] of a private (IV,343)

190.10   ought] ought always (IV,343)

190.12   immovable] settled (IV,343)

190.13   the ruling power] the government (IV,343)

190.14   secure] to secure (IV,343)

190.14   of their] of those (IV,343)

190.15   originality] original power (IV,343)

190.17   for the legislator in the age] of legislators in the ages (IV,343)

190.20   effect great things] make things great (IV,343)

190.21   value upon] value on (IV,343)

190.25   of citizens personally feeble and pusillanimous.] pusillanimous and enfeebled citizens. (IV,344)

189.31–190.25   I . . . pusillanimous.] [*translated from*:] Je terminerai par une idée générale qui renferme dans son sein non seulement toutes les idées particulières qui ont été exprimées dans ce présent chapitre, mais encore la plupart de celles que ce livre a pour but d'exposer. [*paragraph*] Dans les siècles d'aristocratie qui ont précédé le nôtre, il y avait des particulièrs très-puissants et une autorité sociale fort débile. L'image même de la société était obscure, et se perdait sans cesse au milieu de tous les pouvoirs différents qui régissaient les citoyens. Le principal effort des hommes de ces temps-là dut se porter à grandir et à fortifier le pouvoir social, à accroître et à assurer ses prérogatives et, au contraire à resserrer l'indépendance individuelle dans des bornes plus étroites, et à subordonner l'intérêt particulier à l'intérêt général. [paragraph] D'autres périls et d'autres soins attendent les hommes de nos jours. [paragraph] Chez la plupart des nations modernes, le souverain, quels que soient son origine, sa constitution et son nom, est devenu presque tout-puissant, et les particuliers tombent, de plus en plus, dans le dernier degré de la faiblesse et de la dépendance. [paragraph] Tout était différent dans les anciennes sociétés. L'unité et l'uniformité ne s'y rencontraient nulle part. Tout menace de devenir si semblable dans les nôtres que la figure particulière de chaque individu se perdra bientôt entièrement dans la physionomie commune. Nos pères étaient toujours prêts à abuser de cette idée que les droits particuliers sont respectables, et nous sommes naturellement portés à exagérer cette autre que l'intérêt d'un individu doit toujours plier devant l'intérêt de plusieurs. [paragraph] Le monde politique change; il faut désormais chercher de nouveaux remèdes à des maux nouveaux. [paragraph] Fixer au pouvoir social des limites étendues, mais visibles et immobiles; donner aux particuliers de certains droits, et leur garantir la jouissance incontestée de ces droits; conserver à l'individu le peu d'indépendance, de force et d'originalité qui lui restent; le relever à côté de la société et le soutenir en face d'elle; tel me paraît être le premier objet du législateur, dans l'âge où nous entrons. [paragraph] On dirait que les souverains de notre temps ne cherchent qu'à faire avec les hommes des choses grandes. Je voudrais qu'ils songeassent un peu plus à faire de grands hommes; qu'ils attachassent moins de prix à l'œuvre et plus à l'ouvrier, et qu'ils se souvinssent sans cesse qu'une nation ne peut rester long-temps forte quand chaque homme y est individuellement faible, et qu'on n'a point encore trouvé de formes sociales ni de combinaisons politiques qui puissent faire un peuple énergique en le composant de citoyens pusillanimes et mous. (IV,271–2)

193.33 "The . . . luxury,"] To mimic virtue is of every age; but the . . . luxury belongs more particularly to the ages of democracy. (III,100)

193.33 "The . . . luxury,"] [*translated from*:] La démocratie ne fait pas naître ce sentiment qui n'est que trop naturel au cœur de l'homme; mais elle l'applique aux choses matérielles; l'hypocrisie de la vertu est de tous les temps; celle du luxe appartient plus particulièrement aux siècles démocratiques. (III,78)

200.13 "tyranny of the majority."] [*see text above*, 156]

219.35 "tyranny of the majority."] [*see previous entry*]

"Tomkins, Lydia." *Thoughts on the Ladies of the Aristocracy, by Lydia Tomkins.* London: Hodgsons, 1835.

NOTE: see the note under Fox, William Johnson, "*The London Review* No. II."
REFERRED TO: 56n

Trevelyan, Charles Edward. Referred to: 201; see also under Parliamentary Papers, "Report on the Organisation of the Permanent Civil Service" (1854).

Trollope, Frances. *Domestic Manners of the Americans.* 2 vols. London: Whittaker, Treacher, and Co., 1832.

NOTE: the reference at 113n is in an indirect quotation from Shirreff.
REFERRED TO: 112, 113n

TRUELOVE.   Referred to: 239

TUFNELL.   Referred to: 3

NOTE: see also Boeckh, and Mueller.

TURGOT.   Referred to: *623, 641*

TYLER.   Referred to: 166

VAUBAN.   Referred to: 532

NOTE: the reference is to "Vauban's rules."

Vedas.   Referred to: 407, 612

NOTE: the reference at 612 is in a quotation from Dupont-White.

VICTORIA (of England).   Referred to: 370, 481

NOTE: the reference (to her reign) at 370 is in a quotation from Hare.

VILLÈLE.   Referred to: 582, 608

NOTE: the reference at 582 is in an indirect quotation from Odilon Barrot; those at 608 are to the Villèle ministry and government.

VOLTAIRE.   Referred to: 155

WAKEFIELD, EDWARD GIBBON.   Referred to: 563

NOTE: the reference is to Wakefield as a "joint author," with Buller, of the Durham Report.

————   *England and America; a comparison of the Social and Political State of both Nations.* 2 vols. London: Bentley, 1833.

REFERRED TO: 100

WALPOLE.   Referred to: 78

WASHINGTON.   Referred to: 100, 109, 111, 438, *641*

NOTE: the reference at 109 is in a quotation from A. H. Everett.

WASON, RIGBY.   Referred to: 496n–7n; see under Parliamentary Papers, "Report from the Select Committee on the Corrupt Practices Prevention Act" (1860).

WATT.   Referred to: 468n

NOTE: the reference is in a quotation from Carey.

WEBSTER.   Referred to: 109, 111n

NOTE: the reference at 109 is in a quotation from E. Everett.

WELFORD, RICHARD GRIFFITHS.   Referred to: 496n–7n; see under Parliamentary Papers, "Report from the Select Committee on the Corrupt Practices Prevention Act" (1860).

WELLESLEY.   Referred to: 209, 532

WELLINGTON.   See Wellesley.

WHATELY.   Referred to: 3

WHEWELL, WILLIAM.   *Thoughts on the Study of Mathematics, as a Part of a Liberal Education.* Cambridge: Deighton, 1835.

REFERRED TO: 142

WHITE, HENRY KIRKE.   Referred to: 109

NOTE: the reference is in a quotation from A. H. Everett.

WHITE, JOSEPH BLANCO, with John Stuart Mill.   "Guizot's Lectures on European Civilization," *London Review*, II (Jan., 1836), 306–36.

REFERRED TO: 94

WILLIAM I (of Orange).   Referred to: 419

WILLIAM III (of England).   Referred to: 419

WILLIAM III (of Orange).   See William III (of England).

WORDSWORTH.   Referred to: 4n–5n

XENOPHON.   Referred to: *618*

——— *Oeconomicus.*

NOTE: as no edition is cited or now in JSM's library, none is here given; the quotation would appear to be a conflation of 21.5 and 21.12.

QUOTED: *617*

PARLIAMENTARY PAPERS

"Report of *William Crawford*, Esq., on the Penitentiaries of the *United States*, addressed to His Majesty's Principal Secretary of State for the Home Department," *Parliamentary Papers*, 1834, XLVI, 349–669.

REFERRED TO: 106

"Report on the Affairs of British North America, from the Earl of Durham," *Parliamentary Papers*, 1839, XVII.

REFERRED TO: 563. See also Lambton, Buller, and Wakefield.

"A Bill to Extend the Right of voting for Members of Parliament, and to amend the Laws relating to the Representation of the People in Parliament," 15 Victoria (12 February, 1852), *Parliamentary Papers*, 1852, III, 353–96.

NOTE: the Bill was not enacted. The reference is to Clause XVIII and Schedule B.
REFERRED TO: 316–17

"A Bill further to amend the Laws relating to the Representation of the People in England and Wales," 17 Victoria (16 February, 1854), *Parliamentary Papers*, 1854, V, 375–418.

NOTE: the references at 330 and 452 are to Clause XII (p. 377). The Bill was not enacted.
REFERRED TO: 313^a, 318, 330, 452

"Report on the Organisation of the Permanent Civil Service, together with a letter from the Rev. B. Jowett," *Parliamentary Papers*, 1854, XXVII, 1–31.

NOTE: the Report was prepared by Sir Stafford Northcote and Sir Charles Trevelyan, who date it 23 Nov., 1853. The quotations are from Jowett's letter, which appears on 24–31 of the "Report," and is reprinted above in Appendix C.
QUOTED: 210 (for the collation, see Jowett, Letter)
REFERRED TO: 201, 207–11

"New York Industrial Exhibition: General Report of the British Commissioners," *Parliamentary Papers*, 1854, XXXVI, 1–467. See Henry Carey, *Principles of Social Science*.

"A Bill to Extend the franchise in Counties in England and Wales, and to improve the Representation of the People in Respect of such franchise," 21 Victoria (27 April, 1858), *Parliamentary Papers*, 1857–58, I, 561–4.

NOTE: the Bill was not enacted. Locke King brought forward the proposal on several occasions in the 1850s; while approval of the specific clause was sometimes secured, none of the Bills in which it was incorporated was enacted. See, e.g., "A Bill to make the Franchise in Counties in England and Wales the same as that in Boroughs, by giving the right of voting to all Occupiers of Tenements of the annual Value of Ten Pounds," 14 Victoria (7 March, 1851), *Parliamentary Papers*, 1851, II, 211–14.

REFERRED TO: 319

"A Bill to Amend the Laws relating to the Representation of the People in England and Wales, and to facilitate the Registration and Voting of Electors," 22 Victoria (28 February, 1859), *Parliamentary Papers*, 1859 (Session 1), II, 649–715.

NOTE: the Bill was not enacted.

REFERRED TO: 313, 319, 328

"Fourth Report of Her Majesty's Civil Service Commissioners," *Parliamentary Papers*, 1859, VIII. See Harris, James Howard.

"Report from the Select Committee on the Corrupt Practices Prevention Act (1854), &c.; together with the Proceedings of the Committee, Minutes of Evidence, Appendix, and Index." *Parliamentary Papers*, 1860, X.

NOTE: the "several" witnesses mentioned in the first sentence of 496n were (with JSM's page references in parentheses): Thomas Phinn (46), Edwin James (54–7), Rigby Wason (67), Frederick Cosens (123), John Moxon Clabon (198–202), and George Ade (208). The Chief Commissioner of the Wakefield Inquiry, who is quoted, was Gillery Pigott. By the "distinguished member of the Committee" JSM probably means Sir George Cornewall Lewis (see, e.g., 8, 46, 95, 169–70), though Sir George Grey expressed similar sentiments (e.g., 97, 201), and both were members of the Cabinet. The references in the concluding sentence of the note are to Richard Griffiths Welford (20, 277), and Rigby Wason (65–70).

QUOTED: 497n

497.n9–10 "If they . . . work. . . .] That [disqualifying a person guilty of bribery from holding any office] would have great effect; the fact of that being enacted in an Act of Parliament would have a great moral effect; if they . . . work, and I do not think that it would be necessary to prosecute in many cases. (32) [Evidence of Gillery Pigott.]

497.n10–12. I . . . opinion."] Yes [one has to guard against the prospective payment of corrupt expenditure]; Mr. Hardy was suggesting when Mr. Vaughan was examined, that people do not look upon this as an offence against morality; I am quite of that opinion, though I think the feeling is growing that it is immoral; I . . . opinion. (26) [Evidence of Gillery Pigott.]

"Report of the Commissioners appointed to Inquire into the Existence of Corrupt Practices at Elections for the Borough of Wakefield; together with the Minutes of Evidence," *Parliamentary Papers*, 1860, XXVII, 1–460.

REFERRED TO: 497n

"Report by Mr. Lytton, Her Majesty's Secretary of Legation, on the Election of Representatives for the Rigsraad," in "Reports of Her Majesty's Secretaries of Embassy and Legation on the Manufactures, Commerce, &c., of the Countries in which they reside (No. 7). Denmark," *Parliamentary Papers*, 1864, LXI, 578–99.

NOTE: reprinted as an appendix to the pamphlet, *Personal Representation. Speech of John Stuart Mill, Esq., M.P., delivered in the House of Commons, May 29, 1867.* London: printed by Henderson, Rait, and Fenton, 1867.

REFERRED TO: 466n

STATUTES

BRITISH

43 Elizabeth, c. 2. An Act for the reliefe of the poore (1601).

REFERRED TO: 609

39 & 40 George III, c. 106. An Act to repeal an Act passed in the last Session of Parliament, intituled, *An Act to prevent unlawful Combinations of Workmen*; and to substitute other Provisions in lieu thereof (29 July, 1800).

NOTE: this was the most important Act to prevent combinations of workmen. It was repealed by 5 George IV, c. 95 (21 June, 1824), and certain of its provisions reintroduced by 6 George IV, c. 129 (6 July, 1825).

REFERRED TO: 29

5 George IV, c. 74. An Act for ascertaining and establishing Uniformity of Weights and Measures (17 June, 1824).

REFERRED TO: 602

9 George IV, c. 60. An Act to amend the Laws relating to the Importation of Corn (15 July, 1828).

REFERRED TO: 199

2 & 3 William IV, c. 45. An Act to amend the Representation of the People in *England* and *Wales* (7 June, 1832).

REFERRED TO: 34, 37, 125, 194, 313, 314, 315, 343, 361, *620, 635*

3 & 4 William IV, c. 96. An Act to apply the Sum of Six Millions out of the Consolidated Fund to the Service of the Year One thousand eight hundred and thirty-three, and to appropriate the Supplies granted in this Session of Parliament (29 August, 1833).

REFERRED TO: 609

3 & 4 William IV, c. 103. An Act to regulate the Labour of Children and young Persons in the Mills and Factories of the United Kingdom (29 August, 1833).

REFERRED TO: 592, 602

4 & 5 William IV, c. 76. An Act for the Amendment and better Administration of the Laws relating to the Poor in *England* and *Wales* (14 August, 1834).

NOTE: see also 43 Elizabeth, c. 2. The references at 594 (one of which is in a quotation from Dupont-White) and at 611 are generally to the Poor Laws.
REFERRED TO: 64, 169, 540, 542, 594, 599, 606, 609, 611

5 & 6 William IV, c. 53. An Act to repeal an Act of the Ninth Year of His late Majesty, for regulating the Carriage of Passengers in Merchant Vessels from the United Kingdom to the *British* Possessions on the Continent and Islands of *North America*; and to make further Provision for regulating the Carriage of Passengers from the United Kingdom (31 August, 1835).

REFERRED TO: 592, 602, 611

6 & 7 William IV, c. 76. An Act to reduce the Duties on Newspapers, and to amend the Laws relating to the Duties on Newspapers and Advertisements (13 August, 1836).

NOTE: JSM's reference is, of course, predictive.
REFERRED TO: 135

5 & 6 Victoria, c. 99. An Act to prohibit the Employment of Women and Girls in Mines and Collieries, to regulate the Employment of Boys, and to make other Provisions relating to Persons working therein (10 August, 1842).

REFERRED TO: 592

7 & 8 Victoria, c. 15. An Act to amend the Laws relating to Labour in Factories (6 June, 1844).

REFERRED TO: 592, 602

11 & 12 Victoria, c. 63. An Act for promoting the Public Health (31 August, 1848).

REFERRED TO: 592, 602

12 & 13 Victoria, c. 29. An Act to amend the Laws in force for the Encouragement of *British* Shipping and Navigation (26 June, 1849).

NOTE: the 1849 Act repealed those of 12 Charles II, c. 18 (1651), and 3 & 4 William IV, c. 54 (1833).

REFERRED TO: 611

13 & 14 Victoria, c. 23. An Act to repeal an Exception in an Act of the Twenty-Seventh Year of King Henry the Sixth concerning the Days whereon Fairs and Markets ought not to be kept (10 June, 1850).

NOTE: other relevant acts include 11 & 12 Victoria, c. 49 (An Act for regulating the Sale of Beer and other Liquors on the Lord's Day [14 August, 1848]); 17 & 18 Victoria, c. 79 (An Act for further regulating the Sale of Beer and other Liquors on the Lord's Day [7 August, 1854]); and 18 & 19 Victoria, c. 118 (An Act to repeal the Act of the Seventeenth and Eighteenth Years of the Reign of her present Majesty for further regulating the Sale of Beer and other Liquors on the Lord's Day, and to substitute other Provisions in lieu thereof [14 August, 1855]).

REFERRED TO: 288–9

13 & 14 Victoria, c. 93. An Act for improving the Condition of Masters, Mates, and Seamen, and maintaining Discipline, in the Merchant Service (14 August, 1850).

REFERRED TO: 592, 602

14 & 15 Victoria, c. 13. An Act to regulate the Sale of Arsenic (5 June, 1851).

REFERRED TO: 293–5

16 & 17 Victoria, c. 137. An Act for the better Administration of Charitable Trusts (20 August, 1853).

REFERRED TO: 599

17 & 18 Victoria, c. 81. An Act to make further Provision for the good Government and Extension of the University of *Oxford*, of the Colleges therein, and of the College of *Saint Mary Winchester* (7 August, 1854).

REFERRED TO: 143n

17 & 18 Victoria, c. 102. An Act to consolidate and amend the Laws relating to Bribery, Treating, and undue influence at Elections of Members of Parliament (10 August, 1854).

NOTE: usually referred to as the Corrupt Practices Prevention Act.

REFERRED TO: 316, 333, 496n

19 & 20 Victoria, c. 88. An Act to make further Provision for the good Government and Extension of the University of *Cambridge*, of the Colleges therein, and of the College of King *Henry* the Sixth at *Eton* (29 July, 1856).

REFERRED TO: 143n

FRENCH

D.P. 41.3.116. Loi relative au travail des enfants employés dans les manufactures, usines ou ateliers (22 March, 1841).

REFERRED TO: 601n

Index

Volume XVIII *contains pages 1–310, and Volume* XIX *pages 311–753.*
Page numbers in italic type refer to the Appendices.

undemocratic government, 167; advantages of despite deficiencies, 171; government serving general interest in, 171–3; influence of on intellect, 179–80; isolation of individuals in, 182; moral sentiment characteristic of, 184–5; dangers posed by, 188; correctives for political evils characteristic of, 188–90 See also England, France, Government, United States

Denmark, 465n–6n

Despotism: Tocqueville on, 51, 57, 82–3, 167, 171, 175–6, 183; and judiciary, 66; of majority not formidable evil within limits of civil life, 178; of Caesars, 191, 433–4; in France, 219, 408, 416, 561, 583–4; when legitimate or necessary, 224, 377, 394, 567; Comte's social system and, 227; eras of history when mental thrown off, 243; and individuality, 266; of custom, 272–3; state education and mental, 302; of bureaucracy, 308; and universal suffrage, 327; obedience under, 384; and slavery, 395; Chinese, 396; false idea of good, 399–403; superiority of free communities over despotisms, 406; limits on individuality in, 410; of executive, 414; of military leader over savage tribes, 415; and emancipation of Russian serfs, 417; mischiefs of, 436; of majority in America, 460; of majority in single-assembly legislature, 514; in countries made up of different nationalities, 547; and blending of nationalities, 551; German Bund as instrument for maintaining, 554; worse when ignorant, 568; transaction of business within, 581; Dupont-White on, 588, 589, 599; central preferable to local, 606. See also Tyranny

Diet of Worms, 381

Discussion, freedom of: Tocqueville on obstacles to in America, 81–2; need for, 231; assumption of infallibility in restriction of, 233; argument of enemies of, 246; consequences of absence of, 247; and evils of sectarianism, 257; and mental well-being, 257–8; and administration of justice, 391; despotism and, 402; political value of, 436; as security against executive, 587

Diversity: of opinion necessary for pursuit of truth, 252, 254, 257; and individuality, 270, 275; of character, culture, and progress of Europe, 274; need for in opinions, conduct, and education, 302; of modes of action, 306; as main determining principle of improvement, 613

EAST INDIA COMPANY, 523, 573, 575, 576, 577, 603

East Prussia, 549

Edinburgh, 100–1

Education: need for radical reform of aristocratic educational institutions, 27, 138–46; and franchise qualification, 30–1, 32, 325, 326–8, 355, 356, 370, 470–1, 475, 476–7, 508, 511; of women, 56n; Tocqueville on American, 62, 84; need for, 63; in well-constituted democracy, 80; character of in America, 102, 111n, 167; Abdy on American, 111–12; need for national institutions of, 136; and need for regeneration of opulent classes, 138–46; definition of, 168–9; Tocqueville on as corrective of democratic political evils, 188; and checking of commercial spirit, 198; and private morality, 256; and development of individuality, 261; eagerness for improvement in, 273; extension of promotes uniformity, 274; as promoter of self-regarding and social virtues, 277; and social control, 282; of labouring classes, 299; role of state in, 301–4, 545, 583, 609; activities promoting political, 305, 417–18, 535–6; political institutions as agencies of, 322, 348, 393, 411–12, 467–9; low standard of in England, 327, 530; and appetite for freedom, 403; propertied generally possess more, 474; and constitutional influence, 478–9; deference to persons of, 512; and Civil Service examinations, 529, 530; value of for public service, 531; and professional qualifications, 532; in India, 570; Dupont-White on need for doctrinal competition in, 595; English voluntary associations and, 603; universality of in Prussia, 619; Taylor on people's need for, 623; failure of aristocratic government to deliver, 624; prospective public

and 1832 Reform Bill, 194; attitude to strikes of members of, 405; reference of Bills to Select Committee in, 429; creation of Legislative Commission within, 431; state of society and efficacy of, 514; as centre of resistance to democracy, 515; ineffectual as check upon democracy, 516; representation in, 517–18; quality of membership of, 604; deficiencies of committees in, *633n*; mentioned, 66, 108

Human nature: Bailey on penal legislation and, 21; Bailey on Burke's view of, 21–2; as foundation of political principle, 22; Tocqueville's knowledge of, 57; and pursuit of private interests, 83; in various peoples, 94; and study of American democracy, 106, 157; philosophy of, 119; value of literature to, 137; content of university education and, 145, 146; Tocqueville on in classical literature, 195n; effect of preponderance of any variety in community, 196; and "law of progress," 197; fallibility of, 222, 229–30, 260; and disposition to impose opinions as rule of conduct on others, 227; requires growth and development, 263; and deficiency of personal impulses, 264; effects of conformity on, 265; and anti-Calvinist conception of excellence, 265–6; and public's ideal of character, 271–2; struggle to improve, 388; energy essential for perfecting of, 410; possession of power unleashes bad parts of, 445; love of power most evil passion of, 610; Dupont-White on elements of, 612; good government and progressiveness of, *619*

Hungary, 548, 549

IMAGINATION: Tocqueville on, 160, 184, 186, 195n; response of to changes in substance and form, 461; Taylor on, *645*

Improvement: factors promoting, 93–4, 99, 197, 224, 272, 386, 406, 407, 409, 459, 468–9, 475, 613; *North American Review* on in America, 107–8; civilization as, 119; of working classes, 166; spirit of in backward society, 224; obstacles to, 271, 272, 327, 410, 417–18; eagerness for, 273; regulation of vices hindering, 280–1;

parliamentary reform and spirit of, 314, 348; idea of, 384; struggle for, 388; influence of government on, 394, 396–8, 403, 412, 413, 416–18, 419, 420, 567, 601; Hare's scheme and awakened interest in, 461–2; tendencies of social, 479–80; and absorption of one nationality by another, 550; Dupont-White on, 588, 592–4; government ministers and ideas of, *621*; connection in England between political and administrative, *632–4. See also* Progress

India: British government in, 23 (*649*); English acquisition of, 123, 550, 603; Sepoy insurrection in, 240n; government councils in, 522–3; and Civil Service examinations, 530; distant prospect of representative government in, 562; government of, 568–77; mentioned, 285n, 517, *628*

Individual: Tocqueville on patriotism of in democracy, 87; impact of growth of civilization on power of, 126, 129–34, 227; need to define limits of society's power over, 217; and tyranny of society, 219; need to preserve independence of, 220; principle to govern society's dealings with, 223–4; indirect interest of society in some actions of, 225–6; Comte's social system and despotism of society over, 227; inclination to stretch unduly powers of society over, 227; liberty of in pagan morality, 255; limits to sovereignty of, 260, 276; censorship of society over, 264; and prevalent mediocrity, 268–9; public interference with self-regarding concerns of, 282, 285; encroachment on liberty of, 284; examples of illegitimate interference with liberty of, 287–91; accountability of for actions, 292–305; limits to government interference for benefit of, 305–10; Lorimer on political institutions and influence of, 355; open to demagogic appeals, 368; forms of government affect character of, 410–12; and freedom of choice, 479; defining limits to government's interference with, 581; Odilon-Barrot on effect of centralization on, 586; Dupont-White on limitations of as agent of social progress, 595–8; proper and improper state interference with, 601–2;

548; British bestowal of colonial, 562; provide check on executive, 587; Taylor on, *629*

local: argument for free, 305; form of English, 534n–5n; educational function of, 535; chief imperfection of, 538–9; Dupont-White on, 599

Intellect: masses benefit from victories of, 50; Tocqueville on, 84, 160, 178–81, 188; influence of democracy on, 107; *North American Review* on respect for in America, 108–9; university education and, 144–6; insularity of English national, 155; virtues of well cultivated, 209; and wisdom, 232; low average of, 252; need for, 267; constitutional organization and advancement of, 392; organization of under Hare's scheme, 463; obtaining for government benefits of superior, 506; impact of despotism on French, 583–4

Interest: Bailey on government and identification of, 19–20; government and identification of, 22–4 (*648–50*), 30, 71–2 (*650–1*), 218, 228, 573; of electors, 27, 332, 335–6, 486, 491, 493–4, 507, 511; of children and parents, 27n–8n; of women and men, 28n–9n; representation of, 43–6, 358, 465; political participation and public, 169, 412; lack of conflict of in America, 176; Duveyrier on French Chamber of Peers and general, 201; problem of class interests, 221, 334, 463, 467, 492, 507, 516, 519, 536–7, 573; rules of conduct and self-, 221; view of government as opposed to public, 223; of man as progressive being and concept of utility, 224; of individuals and society and authority of latter, 276–7; institutions may produce opposition of between individuals, 292; treatment of persons whose interest is opposed to public, 296–7; of public and need for publicity, 336, 494; problem of defining society's aggregate, 383; good government recognizes general, 390; despotism and collective, 400, 401; popular government as security for individual, 404; predominance of self-, 404–5; problem of sinister, 436, 441–7, *621*; exercise of suffrage broadens conception of, 469; distribution of political influence in man-

agement of joint, 473–4; voter should consider public, 490; payment of M.P.'s and private, 499n–500n; and distribution of local representation, 537; identity of and advisability of federation, 553; of delegated administration in India, 573–4; protection of collective against individual, 601; statesman's obligation to public, *625, 627*; Taylor on statesman and public, *627, 629, 635*; statesman's neglect of multitude's, *637*

Tocqueville on: government and identification of, 69–72 (*650–1*), 88, 172–3; public and private in France, 168; American regard for public, 168; of greatest number served by democracy, 171–3; dominance of self-interest in democratic community, 184–5; value of enlightened self-, 185; need to subject private to public in aristocratic ages, 189; modern threat to individual, 190

Dupont-White on: government as arbitrator of conflicting, 588, 600; state intervention and public, 592–3, 598–9; individual and collective, 595–8

Intolerance: mankind's, 222; public's of free expression of opinion, 229; English middle-classes', 240; results of social, 241–2; of individuality, 271; Puritans', 283; and religious persecution, 289

Ionian Islands, 567n

Ireland: peerage of, 518; English rule in, 550–1; Dupont-White on, 596; mentioned, 442, 565, 570, 600

Italy: achievements and decline of, 191; persecution in, 238; patriots in, 379–80; transformation of, 417n; national feeling in, 546–7; feasibility of unitary government in, 560; Dupont-White on destruction of cities of, 600; mentioned, 143, 406, 438, 548, 551

JAPAN, 571

Jesuits, 308, 396, 403, 439

Jews: and crucifixion of Christ, 236; institutions of, 397; mentioned, 289

Joint-stock companies, 125, 136, 354, 425, 601

Judges: selection of, 391; and hypothetical English Senate, 517; objections

770 INDEX

Legislature. *See* Parliament

Liberal Party: and plural voting, 354; and selection of borough members, 362–3; political creed of, 373; and limiting access to Parliament, 498; mentioned, 347, 452n, 464, 506

Liberalism: predominance of in Tocqueville's age, 56; and Civil Service reform, 207; in Europe, 218, 382; and centralization in France, 582

Liberation Society, 463

Liberty: in savage society, 129, 394–5, 401; of petition in England, 162; barbaric aspect of in America, 178; apparent extinction of in Greece by Macedonian invaders, 191; in Italy, 191, 379–80; definition of civil and social, 217; historical significance of term, 217–18; principle which should govern interference with individual, 223; when principle of applicable, 224; proper area of human, 225–6; need for expression of opinions favourable to, 253–4; of individual in pagan morality, 255; justifiable limitations on individual, 260, 280–2, 296–7, 299–301; undervaluing of, 261; atmosphere of necessary for thriving of genius, 267–8; attitude of vulgar to, 271n; despotism of custom opposed to, 272; in East, 273; unjustifiable interference with individual, 280, 282–91; and trade, 293, 558; invasion of for prevention of crime, 294–5; misapplications of, 301–4; transitory nature of in some countries, 305; centralization as threat to, 308, 600–1, 607–8; when people unfit for, 377; taxation and individual, 387; under despotism, 402; and progress in Spain, 408n; and obedience to distant monarch, 416; not cared for among people of place-hunters, 420; legislature needs power to secure nation's, 432; products of in ancient Rome, 443; blotting-out of minority not entailed by, 452; of choice, 479; in Athens, 490; popular suffrage essential to, 527; securities for, 535; armies composed of various nationalities as extinguishers of, 548; federation as preserver of, 553; British understanding of, 565; changed view of French thinkers on, 583–4; Odilon Barrot on excessive centralization as infringe-

ment on, 586; Royer-Collard on French government's struggle against, 608; meaning of love of, 610–11

Tocqueville on: municipal institutions and spirit of, 60–1; in America, 64–5, 68, 81–3, 159, 168; in France, 161, 168; danger in social democracy of insufficient spirit of, 167, 184; deficiencies and advantages of democratic, 171; effects of, 183; enlightened self-interest and future of, 185; as corrective for democratic political evils, 188; need in democracy to protect individual moral, 189

of thought: Tocqueville on lack of in America, 81–3; universities and, 142, 146; case for, 227–59; want of in Egypt and China, 396

Dupont-White on: providing newly emancipated classes with, 590; distinction between political and civil, 600; as power, 610

See also Discussion, Press, Religion

Literature: in America, 100; bad effects of modern civilization on, 134–5; place in university curriculum of ancient, 144–5; study of as part of modern history, 145; Tocqueville on, 160, 161, 179–81, 195n; of Roman Empire, 191; monetary rewards of in England derive from middle class, 195; and nationality, 546; ties binding individual to community not seen in modern, *625*

Liverpool, 100, 101, 461

Livonia, 549, 590

Locrians, legislation of, 238

Logic: study and neglect of, 3; applied to terms of political philosophy, 4; negative use of, 6, 7; infringement of rules of, 8; at English universities, 139, 146; disparagement of negative, 251

Lombardy, 417n

London: cultural significance of, 101, 180; electoral character of shopocracy in, 352; local government in, 538, 539; political capacity of middle and working classes of, 598–9; mentioned, 155, 230, 322, 352, 362, 456, 463, 485

London, University of, 5n, 102, 208

MACEDONIA, 191, 550

Maine Law, 293, 297, 463

and executive power of dissolution, 525; and selection of judges in America, 528n; constitutional questions and American, 557. *See also* Conservative Party, Liberal Party

Political philosophy, terms in, 4–13 *passim*

Political science: Bailey on, 36; Tocqueville on, 51, 126; JSM on breakthrough made by Tocqueville in, 156; and progressiveness of human nature, *619*; Taylor on administration of government and, *621, 622*

Poor Law (1834): and popular representation, 64; local self-government and agitation against, 169; near theoretical perfection of, 169–70; administrative character of, 309–10, 540, 599, 606; and election of Guardians, 338, 495n; and composition of Boards of Guardians, 536–7; Parliament and principles of, 544; Dupont-White on, 594, 611; conditions rendering creation of central Board feasible, 609; and wages, 611

Press: democratic influence of, 125, 162, 165, 501–2; as voice of public opinion, 135; liberty of, 228, 306, 397, 402, 415, 587, 595; persecution of Mormonism by, 290; effective public opinion requires, 378; and administration of justice, 391; interference of in local and national affairs, 542

Primogeniture, 99n

Progress: Tocqueville on democratic, 50, 158; principles of social, 151; law of and human nature, 197; and problem of liberty and authority, 217; obstacles to spontaneous, 224; substitutes one incomplete truth for another, 252; factors promoting, 253–4, 261, 273, 385–7, 435; and adoption of political constitution, 376; tendencies of different forms of government to promote, 378; problem of defining requisites of government in terms of order and, 384–8; role of legislature in revealing tendencies of, 432; and equality of influence, 478; individual agency and social, 594; Dupont-White on limited services necessity renders to, 596–7; Dupont-White on individual and state as instruments of, 595–8; and state intervention, 601, 605;

often requires new legislation, 602; and voluntary associations, 603; Dupont-White on foundation of, 612. *See also* Improvement

Property: Bailey on franchise and possession of, 30; franchise and possession of, 31–2, 316; security of, 51, 80, 120, 129, 176, 178, 355, 386, 442, 541; Tocqueville on division of, 54; inheritance of in America and France, 99; former concentration of in Europe, 121; diffusion of, 121–2, 124; representation of in government, 152; Tocqueville on in mediaeval France, 160; and rise of poor in England, 162; democratic advances and alarm of large possessors of, 162; relation of to political power in England, 163–4; and middle class, 166, 192; Tocqueville on in America, 171; principle of needs support, 253–4; and diffusion of socialist opinions, 286–7; attitude to universal suffrage of people of, 327; and position of women, 334, 479, 481, 492; Austin on working classes' attitude to, 350; Hare on suffrage qualification and, 369–70; and taxation, 446; and assigning of electoral influence, 474; Dupont-White on state and, 590, 595

Protestant Reformation: and government of public opinion in England, 162; suppressed many times before Luther, 238; and intellectual condition of Europe, 243; era of eminent monarchs, 437; mentioned, 143

Protestantism: Tocqueville on democratic progress in France and, 161; and persecution of Catholic schools in America, 177; persecution of, 238; and cultivation of intellect and judgment, 244; and individual responsibility for choice of religion, 246; and theological morality of Catholic Church, 255; and centralization in France, 584n

Prussia: governing ability in, 23, 24 (*649*); national education in, 31, *632*; breaking up of large properties in, 124, 125; and failure of German Bund, 554; beneficial interference of government in, *619–20*. *See also* Germany

Public opinion: Tocqueville on despotism of in America, 81–3, 178; near unanimity of in America, 85; su-